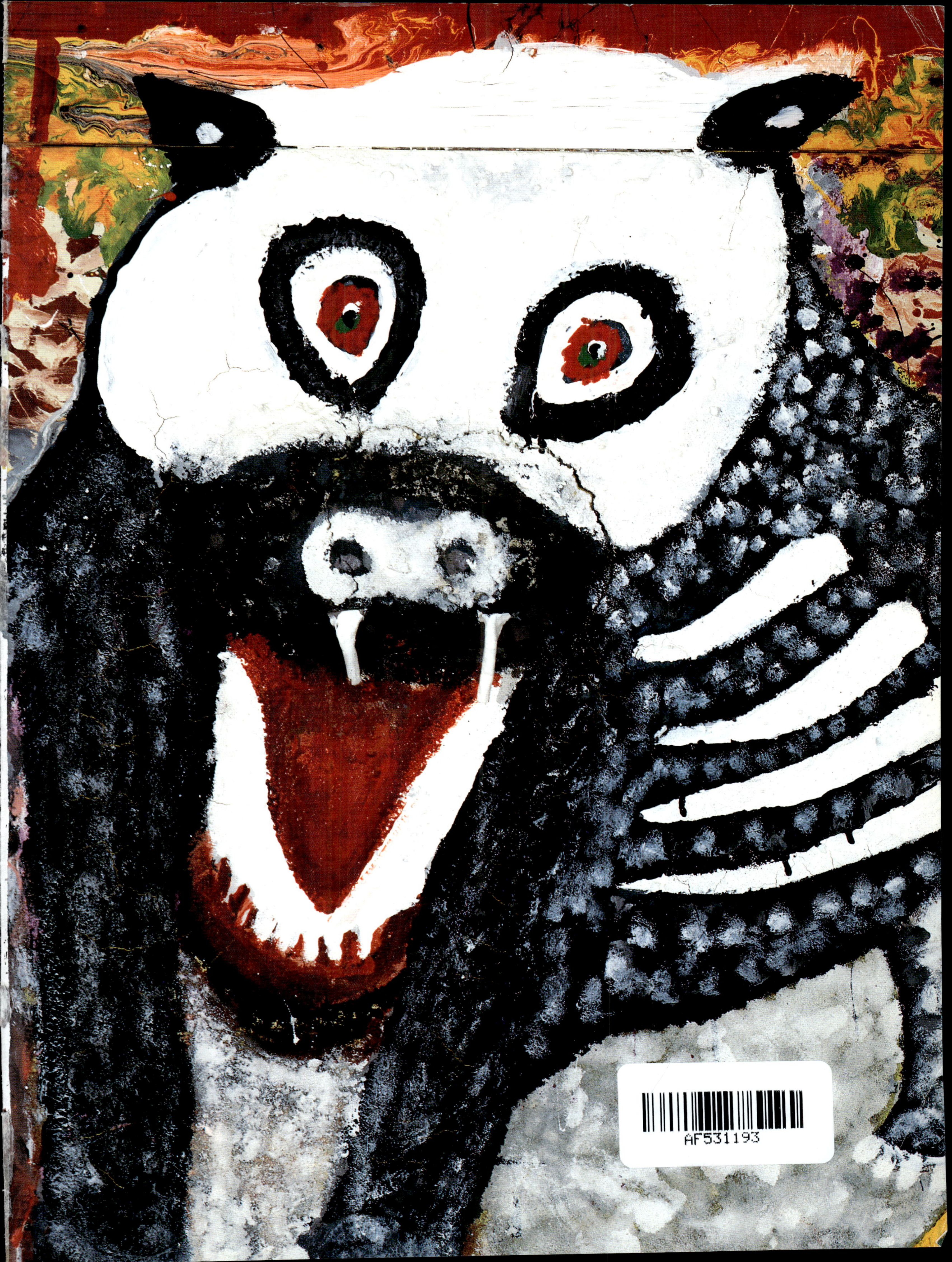

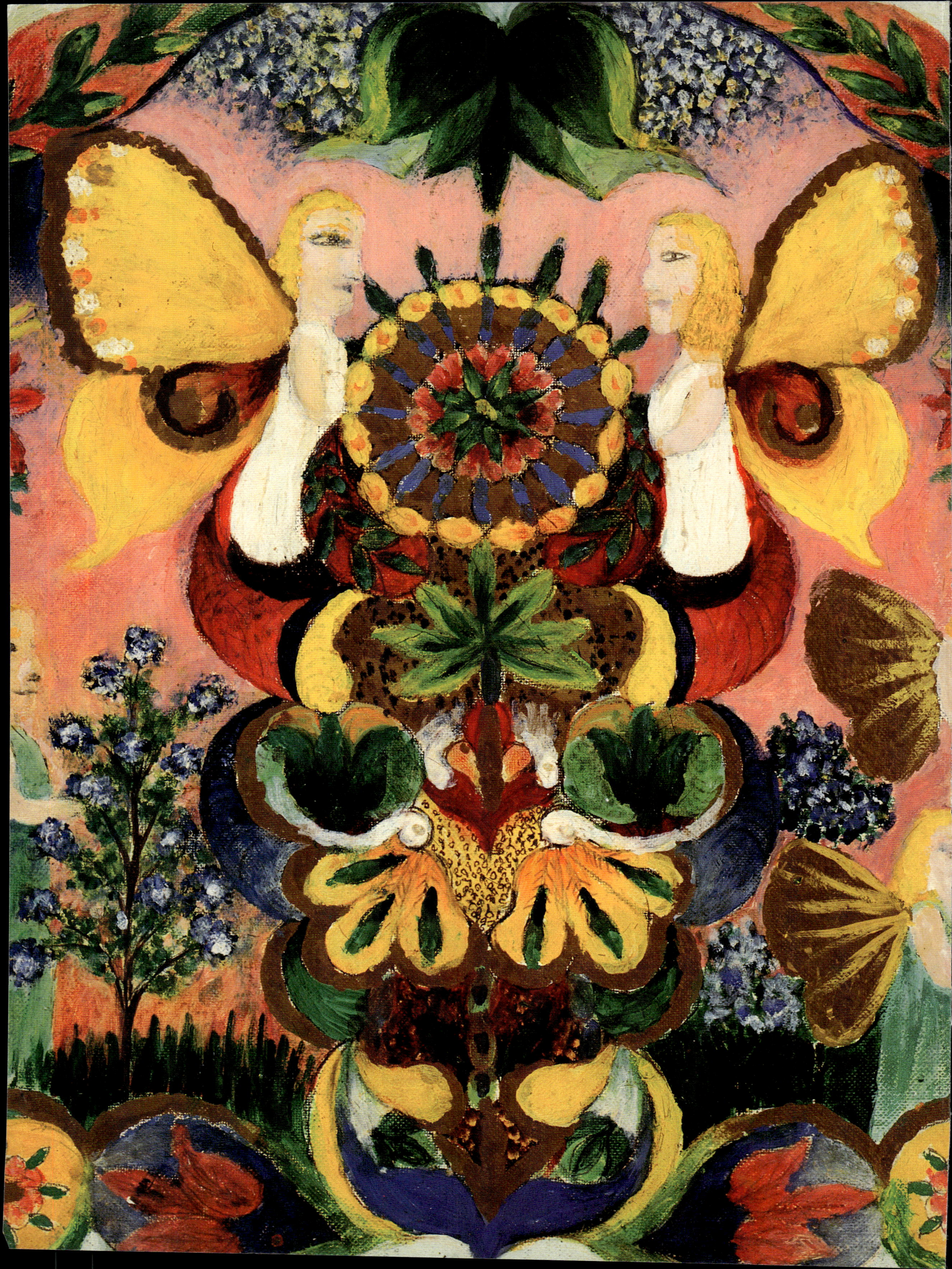

PASSIONATE VISIONS
OF THE AMERICAN SOUTH

Self-Taught Artists from 1940 to the Present

ALICE RAE YELEN

with essays by

William Ferris
Susan Larsen
Jane Livingston
Lowery Stokes Sims

This exhibition, its national tour, and catalogue are sponsored by
The Lila Wallace–Reader's Digest Fund

Additional generous support for the exhibition
and catalogue was provided by
The Henry Luce Foundation, Inc.

New Orleans Museum of Art

Distributed by

University Press of Mississippi

Dedicated to my husband, Kurt. A. Gitter, whose vision was integral to the shaping of this exhibition; to the memory of our friend Robert Bishop, whose leadership brought contemporary American folk art to public appreciation; and to the many artists included in this show who did not live to see it to fruition.

This volume is published in conjunction with *Passionate Visions of the American South: Self-Taught Artists from 1940 to the Present*, an exhibition organized and circulated by the New Orleans Museum of Art.

The exhibition, its national tour, catalogue, and public education and outreach programs were made possible by a generous grant from the Lila Wallace–Reader's Digest Fund.

Additional major support for the exhibition and catalogue was generously provided by the Henry Luce Foundation, Inc.

Exhibition Itinerary
New Orleans Museum of Art
October 23, 1993–January 30, 1994

University Art Museum and Pacific Film Archive,
University of California, Berkeley
March 2–July 10, 1994

San Diego Museum of Art
December 3, 1994–January 15, 1995

Corcoran Gallery of Art, Washington, D.C.
March 4–May 7, 1995

North Carolina Museum of Art, Raleigh
June 10–August 27, 1995

Library of Congress Cataloging-in-Publication Data
Yelen, Alice Rae.
Passionate visions of the American South : self-taught artists from 1940 to the present / Alice Rae Yelen : with essays by William Ferris, Susan Larsen, Jane Livingston, Lowery Stokes Sims.
p. cm.
Catalog of an exhibition held at the New Orleans Museum of Art, Oct. 1993–Jan. 1994, and at other museums.
Includes bibliographical references and index.
ISBN 0-87805-676-9 (cloth). — ISBN 0-87805-677-7 (paper)
1. Outsider art—Southern States—History—20th century—Exhibitions. I. New Orleans Museum of Art. II. Title.
N6520.Y45 1993
709'.75'07476335—dc20 93-29397

Notes to the Reader
Dimensions are given in inches followed by centimeters; height precedes width precedes depth.
Titles inscribed by artists have been transcribed with conventional spellings.
The following abbreviations are used throughout the notes:
ARY = Alice Rae Yelen
ESC = Wilson, Charles Reagan, and William Ferris, eds. *Encyclopedia of Southern Culture*. Chapel Hill, N.C.: University of North Carolina Press, 1989
KAG = Kurt A. Gitter

Produced by Marquand Books, Inc.
Edited by Suzanne Kotz
Editorial assistance by Patricia Draher
Designed by Ed Marquand with assistance by Tomarra LeRoy
Typeset by G & S Typesetters, Inc.
Printed and bound in Hong Kong

Cover: O. W. "Pappy" Kitchens, *Peace in the Valley* (detail), cat. no. 151
Back cover: Sister Gertrude Morgan, *Way in the Middle of the Air* (detail), cat. no. 178
Page 1: William Hawkins, *Tasmanian Tiger No. 2* (detail), cat. no. 117
Frontispiece: Minnie Evans, *Butterfly Design* (detail), cat. no. 80

Distributed by
University Press of Mississippi
3825 Ridgewood Road
Jackson, MS 39211-6492
1-800-737-7788

CONTENTS

FOREWORD

The New Orleans Museum of Art has been a forerunner in the exhibition and collection of the work of contemporary self-taught artists. Self-taught artists, frequently older citizens, many with blue-collar work experience, often come to art late in life, and their subject matter is generally derived from their personal surroundings, experiences, and inner visions. The museum has featured self-taught artists in its exhibition schedule since the 1950s, and it has actively collected their work since the 1960s. As early as 1952 the museum hosted an exhibition of the paintings of Grandma Moses and later organized exhibitions of the artwork of Clementine Hunter (1955); Charles Hutson (1965); Marion Souchon, Bruce Brice, Clementine Hunter, and Sister Gertrude Morgan (1973); David Butler (1976); Clementine Hunter (1985); and Sister Gertrude Morgan (1988).

In recent years, the artwork of the self-taught has gained increasing recognition in the mainstream art world, and it is fitting that the New Orleans Museum of Art continue its leadership in the field by organizing *Passionate Visions of the American South: Self-Taught Artists from 1940 to the Present.* This exhibition identifies and documents the superb aesthetic achievement of selected artists from thirteen southern states who, by definition, have not sought didactic art training, traditional diplomas, or association with other artists or with the established art world in general. This overview of painting and sculpture is the first large-scale effort to consider the work of self-taught southern artists according to intrinsic artistic merit and without regard to race, religion, or gender.

When Alice Rae Yelen, assistant to the director at the New Orleans Museum of Art, and her husband, Kurt A. Gitter, came to me in 1990 with the idea for *Passionate Visions*, I recognized the strength of their proposal and their combined talents. Alice is a seasoned museum curator and exhibition coordinator who also served as the museum's chief curator of education for a decade. Kurt is a long-time museum trustee, a passionate collector, connoisseur, and generous donor of Japanese art, and, more recently, a collector of self-taught American contemporary art. Together they have produced a well-researched exhibition, drawn from museum and private collections, conceived to appeal to both the general public and connoisseurs. Alice has worked with inexhaustible energy to meet tight deadlines, conceptualizing the show and writing the catalogue while overseeing the development of public programs, a task made doubly difficult by a museum undergoing a major building expansion. Kurt contributed untold hours as a project consultant, soliciting and selecting objects for the show, aiding in the editing of the catalogue, and providing innumerable research materials. Together they demonstrated an unflagging willingness to share their sophisticated insights and to solve the inevitable conundrums that accompany a complex project. A testament to their commitment to the project was their decision to gather the best examples of work in this field while excluding their own remarkable collection of contemporary self-taught American art.

The New Orleans Museum of Art is pleased to share this landmark exhibition with audiences throughout the nation as the show travels to the University Art Museum and Pacific Film Archive, University of California, Berkeley; the North Carolina Museum of Art; the San Diego Museum of Art; and the Corcoran Gallery of Art.

I would like to express our deep gratitude to the Lila Wallace–Reader's Digest Fund and the Henry Luce Foundation, Inc., for their extraordinarily generous funding. It is our hope that this exhibition and publication will bring further honor to our sponsors, as it contributes to scholarship in the field of contemporary self-taught art and stimulates its further study.

E. John Bullard
Director

PREFACE AND ACKNOWLEDGMENTS

It is fitting that the investigation of this personal art form was ignited by a personal quest. *Passionate Visions of the American South: Self-Taught Artists from 1940 to the Present* arose from my interest in and exploration of the creative expressions of contemporary self-taught American artists. Pursuing familiarity and an understanding of the work of these artists, in 1988 I began traveling, with my husband, Kurt A. Gitter, throughout the South and the nation, meeting artists in their own environments and seeking their works in private and public collections as well as in an increasing number of art galleries. We became entranced not only by the artworks but by the artists we met, and determined to undertake a comprehensive exhibition of their remarkable works.

While the Northeast has long been considered the cradle of nineteenth- and twentieth-century folk art, self-taught artists have clearly flourished in the southern United States during the past half-century. Through my travels, and a survey of prior exhibitions and publications, it became clear that the work of southern contemporary self-taught artists had emerged as a dominant force in the American folk art scene. This was confirmed by the disproportionately large number of southern self-taught artists represented in prior exhibitions and publications. For example, of twenty artists featured in *Black Folk Art in America, 1930–1980*, organized in 1982 at the Corcoran Gallery of Art, nineteen were southern. Approximately 40 percent of the artists recorded in the *Museum of American Folk Art Encyclopedia of Twentieth-Century Folk Art and Artists* (1990), whose scope is national, are from the South.

Exhibition plans for *Passionate Visions* formally began in 1990, with the unwavering support of John Bullard, director of the New Orleans Museum of Art. We received critical support and encouragement from Selwyn Garraway, program associate for the Lila Wallace–Reader's Digest Fund, and Mary Jane Crook, then program director for the arts for the Henry Luce Foundation, Inc. Generous funding by both agencies not only has made this important undertaking possible but has allowed us to treat the topic with an unprecedented comprehensiveness, seen in the scope of the exhibition, its catalogue, and its public programs.

Passionate Visions is the first exhibition to provide an overview of painting and sculpture by contemporary southern self-taught artists selected solely on the basis of artistic merit without regard to race, age, religion, or gender. Although other exhibitions of self-taught art have chosen a national, statewide, or Southern black perspective, none has approached southern folk art as a regional phenomenon based on aesthetic merit, regardless of the artist's background. Our goal was to be representative but not encyclopedic. *Passionate Visions* brings to public view 270 extraordinary works by eighty southern artists that reflect an indigenous artistic expression. Rather than relying on a handful of well-known private collections, the show was selected from 110 private and public collections in twenty-three states. The list of lenders is in itself a substantial record of the scope and breadth of collections of southern self-taught art.

The exhibition contains paintings and sculptures by recognized masters such as Bill Traylor, Hunter, Sam Doyle, Edgar Tolson, William Edmondson, Howard Finster, and John "J. B." Murry, as well as the works of outstanding but relatively unheralded artists such as J. P. Scott, Willie White, Willie Massey, and Ralph Griffin. Among other little or newly recognized artists, this volume introduces Eddie Kendrick, David Strickland, Rev. J. L. Hunter, Anderson Johnson, Homer Green, and Bernice Sims. The majority of artists have spent their lives in the South; some artists were raised in the region and then migrated elsewhere, but their early experiences produced lifelong artistic and creative tendencies that appear in their paintings and sculptures. A few artists were raised in the North but spent substantial parts of their adult life in the South. In all cases, their artwork bears the indelible mark of their southern experience.

To provide insight into the cultural and historical framework in which this imagery was created, works have been divided into thematic groups reflecting frequently seen subjects: autobiography, daily life, religious and visionary imagery, social commentary and popular culture, patriotism, and nature. The thematic divisions provide a context for understanding and interpreting the work, but they are neither rigid nor exclusive. Some works readily fit into more than one category, comfortably exemplifying multiple themes. This points up the inescapable observation that most imagery by self-taught artists reflects their daily world; even the religious focus of many works can be interpreted as an everyday phenomenon. Besides providing a framework by which to consider the artists' work, the categories reduce the tendency to explain it in terms of individual eccentricities or unusual lifestyles, a strategy too often employed as a method of engaging viewer interest.

Rapid changes in American society compel us to recognize, before it completely disappears, the particular environment that allowed the creation of the passionate, forthright, and raw expressions of self-taught southern artists. Since the 1982 Corcoran show first brought public attention to this material, we have witnessed the passing of an era—the different, more insular world that nurtured the pre–World War II generation of rural southern artists has virtually disappeared. Futhermore, thirty of the artists in this exhibition have died since 1980. The exhibition and catalogue seek to describe the distinctive milieu that shaped self-taught artists while suggesting that they will continue to rely on their immediate, albeit changed, environments for inspiration, impelled to create by their own internal visions.

Any project of this scope requires the shared knowledge and support of many colleagues. First and foremost, I am grateful to E. John Bullard and the Board of Trustees of the New Orleans Museum of Art for the open trust and authority granted me in the planning, coordinating, and implementing of this project. William A. Fagaly, assistant director for art, inspired this show through his previous work at the New Orleans Museum of Art. A recognized and productive proponent for the work of self-taught artists, Bill encouraged the initial exhibition idea and served as an enthusiastic consultant throughout the project. The late Robert Bishop, formerly director of the Museum of American Folk Art, New York, gave one of the first and most wholehearted endorsements of this effort.

I am indebted to the artists included in the exhibition, many of whom opened their special worlds to us and shared their thoughts on art. Their own words enliven the text while enriching our lives.

Initially I had no idea of the number of private collectors and institutions throughout the nation collecting the work of southern self-taught artists. The success of our efforts ultimately resides in their willingness to loan works of art, and I am indebted to each and every one of them.

This enterprise could not have been implemented without the daily assistance, for well over two-and-a-half years, of my husband, Kurt A. Gitter. Kurt's superb eye was integral in the selection of the entire show, and his informed input is evident in each page of this catalogue. His effective networking produced reams of visual material for our viewing; his keen sense of direction maneuvered us to the isolated homes of many artists; and his warm rapport no doubt accounted for the openness of our reception by many artists as well as the frankness with which they responded to our queries.

I am deeply indebted to Suzanne Kotz, editor of this volume, whose overall guidance, accessibility, and editorial assistance were superb, consistent, penetrating, and on a human level, compassionate in the face of stressful deadlines. No one could have been a better friend to this effort, sharpening my word while touching my heart.

Ed Marquand, the book's designer, was creative, attentive, resourceful, and a true pleasure to work with. His enthusiastic response to this material can be seen throughout this volume. Photographer Owen Murphy helped formulate a plan for commissioning photographs throughout the country and photographed local works.

A project of this magnitude required the efforts of many New Orleans Museum of Art staff members, whose professional efforts are seen throughout this catalogue and exhibition. I extend a special thank-you to Dannal Perry, curatorial assistant. Dannal ably acted as a liaison to other museum departments, catalogued the voluminous slides used in selection, collected photographs of the artists from across the nation, developed and maintained the checklist, compiled the bibliography, culled transparencies and research material, checked footnotes, wrote some artist biographies, and administered some public programs. I am grateful to Kimberly Nichols, a volunteer project intern who for more than eighteen months has assisted in varied research tasks. Kim wrote more than 90 percent of the artists' biographies, checked footnotes, helped prepare exhibition labels, and assisted in any effort asked of her with a thoroughly uplifting spirit.

Nilima Mwendo, outreach coordinator, enthusiastically and energetically developed outreach audiences and administered some public programs specifically for this show; Lee Morais, assistant director of education, creatively integrated this plan with the museum's public programs and contributed his filmmaking experience to the production of a related video. Ann Moore, associate curator for education, planned training for many groups. Elizabeth Sullivan, slide librarian, assisted in all audiovisual needs. Virginia Weaver enthusiastically secured press coverage for our efforts. Sharon Litwin, assistant director for development, aided in securing public program funding.

For secretarial assistance, I am grateful to Rebecca Smith, administrative assistant, and Joyce Armstrong. The registrar's office, under the guidance of Paul Tarver, assisted by Pat Pecoraro and Denise Klingman, communicated with lenders and oversaw the packing, shipping, and crating of artworks. Daniel Piersol, chief curator, arranged for the installation of this large show; Darrell Lee Brown processed the labels. Thom Herrington and his adept preparators produced a magnificent installation. Jacquelyn Sullivan, assistant director for administration, assisted in all financial and contractual matters. To the many other museum staff members who worked on varied aspects of this project, I express my gratitude.

Conversations with the catalogue's guest contributors added much to the formation of my concepts for the exhibition and the manuscript. From the project's inception, William Ferris was an accessible, knowledgeable consultant on many matters, particularly those related to southern culture. Susan Larsen influenced the development of my philosophical point of view. Jane Livingston was an effective, supportive consultant on all aspects of catalogue and exhibition planning. In addition, I am most grateful to the following readers of selected text: Bill C. Malone, professor of history, Tulane University, whose knowledge of southern folk culture was indispensable; Charles Reagan Wilson, professor of history, University of Mississippi, whose comments on southern religion were vitally appreciated; and William A. Fagaly, assistant director for art, New Orleans Museum of Art, and Gary Schwindler, professor of art history, Ohio State University, whose critical readings were invaluable.

Colleagues at other institutions generously shared their knowledge of individual artists as well as insights into overall concepts. Anna Cohn, director, Smithsonian Institution of Traveling Exhibitions, lent her astute input to the framework of this catalogue. Stephen Weil, deputy director, Hirshhorn Museum and Sculpture Garden, provided consistent philosophical and practical support. Marcella Brenner has been an inspiring mentor and encouraging friend since the early days of my museum career.

Many scholars, collectors, and dealers generously helped us to reach artists and supplied invaluable research and biographical materials. I especially wish to thank Aarne Anton, Barbara Archer, Jim Arient, Bill Arnett, Rick Berman, Jack Black, A. J. Boudreaux, Theresa Buchanan, Gertrude and Ben Caldwell, Jeffrey Camp, E. Jane Connell, Joanne Cubbs, Josh Feldstein, Estelle Friedman, Marilyn Gaber, Richard Gasperi, Deborah Gilman, Douglas Gitter, Andrew Glasgow, Baron and Ellin Gordon, Sally Griffiths, Anton Haardt, Robert Hicks, Lisa Howorth, Dr. and Mrs. Allen W. Huffman, Bert Hunecke, A. Everette James, Caroline Kerrigan, Louanne Laroche, Susan Lee, Tim Lee, Juan Lezcano, Warren and Sylvia Lowe, Steve Maklansky, Frank Maresca, Anne Miller, Joyce Miller, Leslie Muth, John Ollman, William and Ann Oppenhimer, Tom Patterson, Susan Purvis, Dorothy and Leo Rabkin, William Rose, Chuck and Jan Rosenak, Luise Ross, Sal Scalora, Betty-Carol Sellen, John and Stephanie Smither, Murray Smither, David Steel, Willem Steen, Tom Sternal, Adrian Swain, Cezar Trasobares, Robert Vogele, Willem Volkersz, Charles Watkins, Jay Wehnert, Tom Wells, and Lynn Adams Wilkins. Many others responded energetically to our queries.

Lastly, I am grateful to my sister, Susan Yelen, and my brother, Richard Yelen, for their unwavering belief in me. I have been blessed by the patient and loving spirit of my daughter, Manya Jean, as well as the unyielding faith, tolerance, and consistent encouragement of my husband, Kurt, in the face of months of long nights and weekends of research and writing.

Alice Rae Yelen
Assistant to the Director

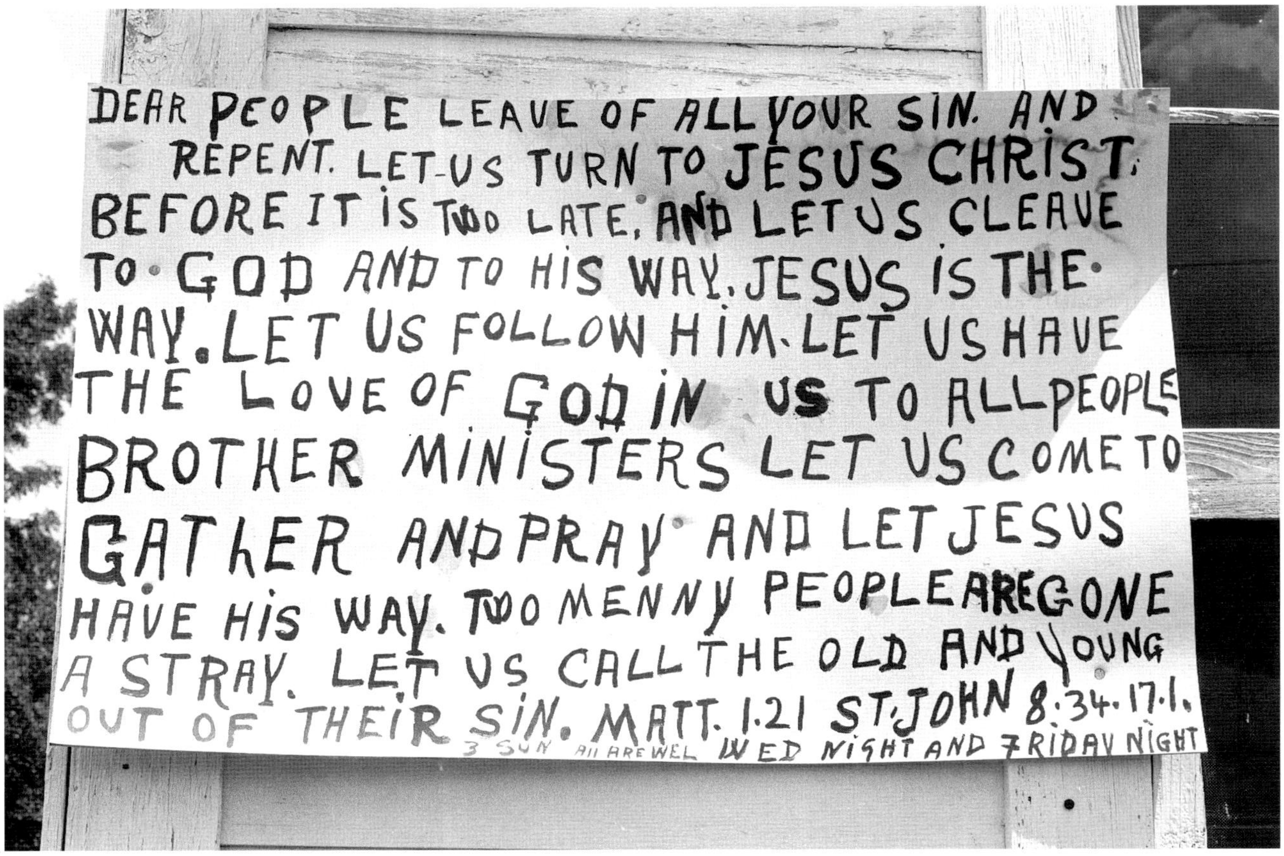

Fig. 1. Church of God in Christ, Clarksdale, Mississippi, 1960s. Photo William Ferris.

FOLK ART AND THE AMERICAN SOUTH

WILLIAM FERRIS

The American South has always stood as a world distinct from the rest of our nation. Long before the founding of our nation, Native American peoples well appreciated the region's special climate and geography. Its fertile soil and abundant wildlife sustained tribes such as the Choctaw, Chickasaw, and Natchez.

The distinctive designs on the pottery and baskets made by artists in these tribes reflect the diverse cultures that occupied the South long before the arrival of European and African peoples. The art forms and dramatic burial mounds of Native Americans in the Mississippi River Valley suggest the profound, enduring relationship they felt toward their homeland.

From these first Native American settlers to the present, the American South has shaped her people in complex ways. The land has exerted a distinctive power over each generation, and as Faulkner reminds us, in the South the past is a living force that molds contemporary life. This past and the land itself are brooding presences that shape southern worlds in unspoken but firm ways. Within these worlds a reverence for both past and place offers a foundation for an art that is at once inspired and haunted by the region.

Black and white southerners trace their heritage to Africa and Europe respectively, and their old world cultures have been transformed within the region over several centuries. African music provided the foundation for blues and jazz, while European ballads and dance tunes shaped country music. These traditions and the lives of those who perform and listen to them are rooted in southern worlds. Black bluesmen such as W. C. Handy celebrated small towns in the Mississippi Delta like Moorehead, "Where the Southern crosses the Dog" (the intersection of the Southern and Yazoo Delta railroads), just as white country music singer Hank Williams longed for a simpler farm life:

> I'm gonner pack my troubles underneath my arm.
> Going back to my Momma's farm,
> And lose these honky tonk blues.

Hank Williams first learned to play his guitar from a black musician named Tee Tot, suggesting how black and white peoples in the South share a common world in which historic memory and imagination are intertwined. While southern storms of civil war, Jim Crow segregation, and civil rights have raged on the surface of the region's culture, deep creative currents have evolved over time in a profound, purposeful manner.

During the twentieth century, southerners have produced written, oral, and visual art forms that are rich and distinctive. These arts reflect the diverse worlds of literary and folk traditions among white and black cultures, and together they define the cultural landscape of the region. They offer a unique window on southern people within which southern faces and voices are captured with a living, immediate presence. If the past is ever present in the South, then art is its embodiment. Southern characters summoned from the past appear greater than life in the fiction of William Faulkner, Alice Walker, and Richard Wright, just as southern homes, landscapes, and faces are preserved on the canvases of folk artists like Howard Finster, Gertrude Morgan, and James Henry "Son" Thomas.

If we view southern culture as a holistic world within which all of the arts are connected, we can see how oral, written, and visual artistic traditions inform and enrich each other. Southern writers borrow folktales from storytellers to use in their fiction, and studio painters are inspired by the design and color of quilts and folk art in painting their canvases.

While our region's writers and painters are internationally recognized for their work, our folk artists have only recently been discovered and seriously studied. Standing outside the academy, these artists create images that offer an important contrast with the classic portraiture and landscape often associated with the South. Folk images of everyday scenes, like parables, are familiar worlds that the artist shares with friends in their community. The southern folk artist draws us to a familiar message that we instinctively understand and return to for inspiration.

This catalogue of southern folk art is particularly exciting because it represents the work of black and white artists from all parts of the American South. As we look at their images, we might well ask, "Why the South?" What makes the region such a rich climate for creativity? How can we explain the apparent contradiction of a people whose feet are firmly planted on red clay soil while their art soars to imaginative heights? In a region where Protestants scorn graven images, we discover colorful, surreal religious worlds painted and sculpted in both black and white churches. Within this old and deep mix of African and European cultures overlaying the Native American, we find patterns that shape the southern folk imagination. Southerners create tales, music, and art that bridge past and present worlds and freeze time into images that evoke memory.

As this catalogue suggests, folk artists deserve the same careful study we have given our great southern writers and painters. Their art stands in dramatic contrast to literary and classical visual arts associated with the region. The latter are products of an educated black and white elite whose work graces the bookshelves and walls of the region's "big houses." Folk art, on the other hand, is associated with the smaller dogtrot and shotgun homes where the South's poor white and black families live. These families exist on the margin of southern society, and folk art reflects their struggle to survive.

This catalogue gathers images of religious scenes and rural worlds from throughout the South that describe a shared culture. White and black faces appear in the repertoire of artists of both races, as the artist leads the viewer beyond a rigid separation of white and black worlds. This theme of a shared culture bonds black and white folk artists and is significant in their work.

Race is the oldest and most complex southern tale. It hearkens back to the biblical story of Cain and Abel wrestling, back to Huck and Jim floating down the Mississippi River on their raft in Mark Twain's *Adventures of Huckleberry Finn*. The struggle of white and black peoples to live together in the South is the central theme of the region's history, and no aspect of the region's life, be it food, language, religion, or politics, can be understood apart from race.

Blacks were first brought to the South as slaves and were the foundation of the region's agricultural economy. Colonial figures like Thomas Jefferson measured their wealth by the acres of land and number of slaves they owned. Jefferson was part of a southern planter elite who based their empire on two commodities—slavery and cotton.

It is said that a people who resist change most strongly will be changed most dramatically, and such change is a familiar part of the South's history. The resistance of southern whites to equality of their black brothers and sisters is a theme that begins in slavery and continues today. Its major chapters are chronicled in slavery and the Civil War, a war followed by a reconstruction period that raised hopes that blacks might participate in the politics and economic development of the region. In the 1890s Jim Crow segregation signaled the return of white supremacy as public facilities such as drinking fountains, lunch counters, and schools were divided by race. As whites used violence and lynching to terrorize blacks, they firmly reestablished their control of the South.

During the first half of the twentieth century, blacks fled southern Jim Crow worlds through the military and enlisted during World War I and World War II. These wars, even more than the Civil War, transformed southern life. They laid the seeds of the civil rights movement and set the stage for the charismatic leadership of Reverend Martin Luther King, Jr., who mobilized black churches as the foundation of his civil rights effort. King inspired thousands in a movement that liberated both black and white southerners through the destruction of the old institutions of segregation.

The result of their courageous struggle is seen when we consider how a region known for its segregation and resistance to change has been transformed into a multiracial culture. Mississippi, a state torn by racial strife in the 1960s, has more black elected officials than any other state in the union. Mike Espy, the first black congressman elected in Mississippi since reconstruction, now serves as our nation's first black Secretary of Agriculture. His appointment by President Bill Clinton signals the distance black and white southerners have traveled in their race relations. Their journey is marked by both a conflict and an intimacy that is unique to the region. White and black families in southern communities have lived and known each other for generations. Their shared history is revealed ever so clearly in the work of southern black and white artists and writers who treat their common worlds with familiarity and compassion. Southern churches, schools, and homes provide a familiar setting for a history that now spans more than two centuries. This history both divides and binds its people and marks them with conflicting feelings of love and hatred for their world. Southern literature distills and restates this world for each generation through the ever-familiar sound of black and white southern voices.

Paralleling southern literature is the world of southern folk art, whose images capture black and white worlds with equal intimacy. As we view these images, we should imagine sounds of blues, country music, and gospel, for folk art and folk music are kindred spirits in the South. They emerge from a common world as they present themes such as love and religion. Sultan Rogers's *Male and Female Figure* (cat. no. 197), a sensuous image of the two sexes, is reminiscent of the blues, while Sister Gertrude Morgan's *Self-portrait with Jesus* (cat. no. 176) strikes a familiar theme in gospel music. Folk art is a visual counterpart of the lyrics and rhythms of southern folk music. James Henry "Son" Thomas's *Man in Coffin* (cat. no. 237) is a grim visual reminder of lyrics by Jimmie Rodgers, the father of country music, who sang:

> Gee but the graveyard is a lonesome place
> They put you on your back, throw that mud down
> in your face.

Texas bluesman Blind Lemon Jefferson struck a similar chord with his request that his friends "see that my grave is kept clean." A clean grave, a song, and a work of art that adorns a wall are all forms of immortality.

Folk art mediates between the two worlds of life and afterlife. While Bill Traylor presents a stark image of farm life in his *Man with Mule Plowing* (pl. 39), Gertrude Morgan explores the afterlife with her *New Jerusalem City* (cat. no. 174). Morgan merges these two worlds in *Way in the Middle of the Air* (pl. 18) just as southern folk preachers sometimes urge their congregations to "call up Jesus on the phone." Religion serves as a natural bridge between this world and the afterlife, and folk artists move us comfortably between the two.

Southern religion grew from an evangelical movement known as the Great Awakening at the end of the eighteenth century, when the region was the nation's western frontier and was known as the "Old Southwest." Itinerant ministers preaching at camp meetings converted thousands of white and black southerners at outdoor services. Communities then constructed "brush arbor" churches using tree limbs to construct primitive shelters for worship. Many rural southern churches stand on the same sites where these original shelters were built.

While white and black congregations worship the same god, their approach to scripture has taken predictably different courses. White congregations draw heavily from the New Testament and stress personal salvation in their sermons. Black believers, on the other hand, are more comfortable with the Old Testament and identify with the Children of Israel in their common struggle for equality. The messages of Martin Luther King and Billy Graham are clear examples of the different paths black and white believers have followed in the South.

Southern religion is the deepest and most enduring force in the lives of the region's folk artists. Virtually every child in the South has attended church services and heard sermons filled with biblical images. Both Old and New Testaments are familiar to folk artists, and we find biblical scenes captured in Gertrude Morgan's *Book of Revelation* (pls. 91, 92) and *Self-portrait with Jesus*. The crucifixion of Christ is a powerful New Testament image in southern folk art, and three striking examples are Edgar Tolson's *Crucifixion* (pl. 95), Jesse Aaron's *Crucifixion* (pl. 93), and George Williams's *Crucifixion* (pl. 94). Each of these images is starkly haunting, and together they focus on the crucifixion of Christ as a central image in southern Protestant belief. The body of Christ hanging from the cross, at times with two thieves beside him, suggests that death can be both frightening and attractive.

From its inception, southern religion has been a frontier experience carried by itinerant ministers to small rural communities within the region. The frontier experience and its strongly evangelical religion are still alive in the American South, and folk artists capture both past and present religious worlds through their images.

Southerners have always felt a special reverence toward the written word. In a region where both mule traders and preachers sway their audiences with biblical texts, southern schools developed an emphasis on the fundamental "three r's"—reading, writing, and arithmetic. It is not surprising to find that southerners Robert Penn Warren and Cleanth Brooks stressed a close reading of the text as the focus of their literary criticism. Known as the New Critics, they adapted a familiar southern emphasis on the text in their study of poetry, fiction, and drama.

Brooks and Warren's emphasis on text was influenced by a love of classicism that has long been associated with southern education, where the study of Latin and Greek was a familiar requirement. Cleanth Brooks once remarked that in the South more people could read Latin and Greek, and fewer could read at all, than in any other region. Brooks aptly pointed to the old, enduring division between the South's educated black and white elite and her often-illiterate working-class population. Many of the latter group of southerners, who appear throughout the pages of the region's great literature, painfully signed their names by making a cross with a scrawled X.

Within their working-class world, southern folk art makes its home. Plagued by illiteracy, folk artists viewed the printed word with special reverence, as the blind might view eyesight. These artists often display text as art and set it within a religious world. Many rural churches display handwritten signs that feature biblical scripture and religious messages. These stark texts, which often appear at a church entrance and on interior walls, have artistic as well as religious significance. A literal transcription of one such sign (fig. 1), at the entrance of the Church of God in Christ in Clarksdale, Mississippi, in the 1960s, reads:

> Dear People leave of all your sin and
> repent. let us turn to Jesus Christ
> before it is two late. And let us cleave
> to God and to his way. Jesus is the
> way. Let us follow him. Let us have
> the love of God in us to all people
> Brother ministers let us come to
> gather and pray and let Jesus
> have his way. Two menny people are gone
> a stray. Let us call the old and young
> out of their sin. Matt. 1.21 St. John 8.34.17.1.
> 3 Sun all are wel Wed night and Friday night

This sign is similar to the style of Howard Finster, who frequently uses handwriting in his art and draws our eye both to the literal message of his script and to its artistic design. Script frequently shares the canvas with pictorial illustrations in paintings such as *The Discovery of Finster Art* (pl. 14). Mary T. Smith also juxtaposes text and image in *The Lord Is Head of the World* (pl. 99). And in his *St. Helena's First Black Midwife* (pl. 48), Sam Doyle paints a seated female figure with the title of his piece inscribed boldly beside her.

Benjamin F. Perkins uses religious text on a painted gourd that bears his inscription, "This is the Godhead of all the family of God in heaven and earth" (cat. no. 187). Gourds traditionally hang on poles as birdhouses, and we can imagine the gourd with its religious inscription nudged by breezes as it hangs from a pole profiled against the sky. The image lifts the eye of our imagination upward and offers a fascinating connection between art and religion that is literally rooted in place.

Folk artists like Perkins and Finster use text as a talisman to conjure and evoke the viewer's emotions. They animate their text with primary colors and bold lettering, and at times this text shares the canvas with visual images. Their work is clearly influenced by hand-painted signs found beside roads and on buildings throughout the South. These signs have important aesthetic qualities, and their use of color and design informs our understanding of folk art. As an evocative element of the region's landscape, they should be viewed as part of a continuum of hand-painted texts that range from signs posted along roadsides and on churches and storefronts to folk art hanging on walls inside homes.

Deeply rooted in their local community, folk artists transform their worlds into colorful, highly imaginative forms. Homes, landscapes, animals, and people inspire an art that has both real and dreamlike qualities. To look at influences such as family, religion, and community is to see only part of the force that shapes this art. These literal worlds are transformed into images that one artist described as "something never before seen." Their art presents the viewer with imaginative worlds, and the connection of each work to the literal subject described, be it religion, farm life, or a portrait, is oblique. It both is and is not about the captioned title. We come closer to understanding each image if we move beyond its title and embrace its churning color and dizzying forms. Through the image we can approach the concealed imaginative world of the artist, a sea that is largely uncharted.

When we speak with artists about their inspiration, they often describe dreams as the primary source for their work. They often awaken in the middle of the night, rise from their beds, and begin to draw. Possessed by an image, they release its spirit onto plywood, cardboard, and Masonite surfaces. Rarely does the artist have the luxury of working with canvas. As the painting is executed, the artist exorcises himself or herself of the dream.

The folk artist develops a comfortable relationship with the unconscious and moves freely between dream and waking reality. Their art is a filter, a lens through which we view interior worlds that are deeply personal. Through this lens we look into a creative womb of southern folk culture. We tap nerves that run deep into a people who, denied education, wealth, and social status, shape a profound and tender message about their world. Working in mobile homes and cabins along southern roads, they shape their images without thought of fame or even the idea that they might be "art," a word rarely used by the artists. Their work is organic to their lives. Like the birthing of children or the changing of seasons, the artist is bound to southern culture and produces his or her work as an artistic duty.

Whether or not folklorists and art historians discover these artists and exhibit their work, the tradition will continue. Shaped by the region's culture and its roots in Native American, African, and European traditions, this art is redefined by each new generation of artists. Like the South's great writers, folk artists draw from an imaginative well that is unquenched. Their art will always continue to flow, and, as we view it, we discover a new world and are transformed by it.

William Ferris is director of the Center for the Study of Southern Culture, University of Mississippi.

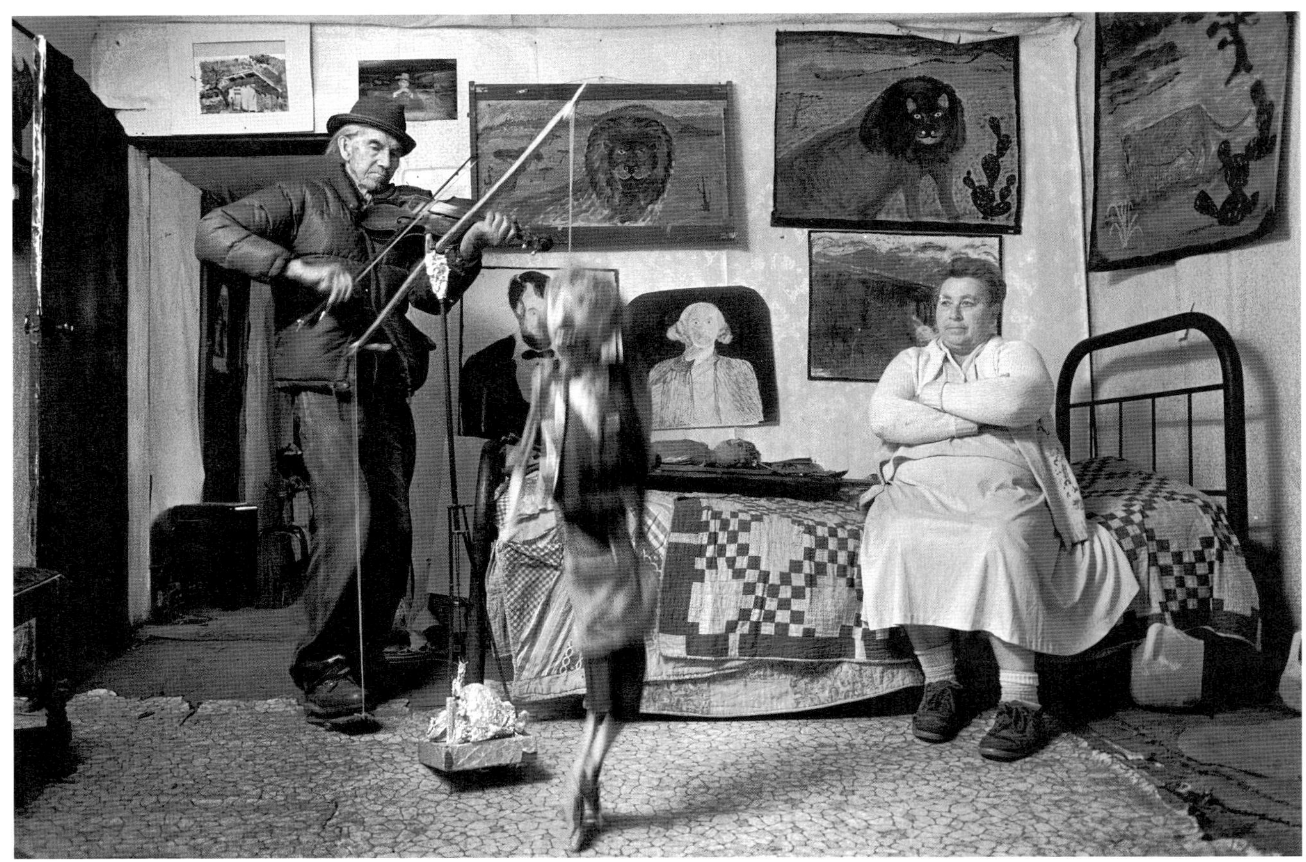

Fig. 1. Charles Kinney, Vanceburg, Kentucky. Kinney pursues a favorite pastime—playing his fiddle while making a homemade puppet dance to the music. His sister-in-law Hazel watches. Kinney's artworks cover the walls. Photo Talis Bergmanis.

SELF-TAUGHT ARTISTS: WHO THEY ARE

ALICE RAE YELEN

From 1940 until now, academically trained American and international artists, striving to achieve recognition in the mainstream art world, have sought to live and exhibit in urban areas. The American abstract expressionist painters of the 1950s relocated the focus of the international art world from Paris to New York, and Manhattan became the target community for American and international artists seeking an artistic life-style that was truly "genuine."

This move by artists to the cities was motivated by the mutually beneficial systems that developed between artists, collectors, dealers, curators, scholars, and cultural institutions. In the city, artists could experience the zeitgeist of the time and be a part of a thriving, metropolitan milieu. In the city, they could study with recognized masters, meet other artists, exhibit in group shows, associate with developing movements, and explore the art holdings of museums and galleries. In the city, they could also meet collectors as well as scholars and curators who might aid in securing museum exhibitions and attracting reputable galleries to represent and sell their work.

The exceptional work of southern self-taught artists impels one to rethink the validity of this concept of the city as sole cultural mecca. These self-taught artists are generally not part of an urban milieu; they are not even what the public construes to be artists. Southern self-taught artists born before World War II were primarily raised in rural environments, deeply rooted and often irrevocably connected to their land, communities, traditions, and families. When they begin making art (frequently later in life), it is without knowledge of the artistic mainstream; initially they do not seek its acceptance nor do they depend on it for their livelihood. These factors alone dramatically distinguish the self-taught artist from his or her trained counterparts.

Unlike individuals who deliberately strive to develop their artistic talents, the self-taught, at least at first, do not consider themselves artists nor do they typically intend to sell their work.[1] They create from an unbidden inner drive, often with a missionary zeal. Those self-taught artists who have relocated to urban centers did so not to promote and develop their careers within the artistic mainstream but to seek employment or more equitable social conditions.

Self-taught artists as a rule do not share in the dynamic synergy that occurs among dealers, collectors, and scholars. Even those who live in cities generally do not seek involvement with other artists or exposure through group shows, publications, museum exhibitions, or critical reviews. Many don't know other artists and have never been to a museum. Only in the past decade, and especially in the past five years, have a limited number of self-taught artists even seen their own works and that of others on public display at gallery or museum exhibitions.[2] Characteristically and most important, even if they become aware of the mainstream artistic milieu, self-taught artists are minimally affected, if at all, by exposure to the work of other artists.

Self-taught artists, by definition, have never formally studied painting or sculpture in art schools or at universities.[3] This lack of conventional training might actually be a liberating rather than hindering feature; unencumbered by preconceived ideas or outwardly imposed models of what art should be, they are free to create without external expectations or guidance. Nonetheless, like all artists, the self-taught are plainly individuals whose innate artistic impulses and internal ideation are expressed visually in varied materials to achieve aesthetic solutions. But unlike trained artists, they usually do so by intuition rather than with consciously acquired skills.

Self-taught artists characteristically express their unique visions in a spontaneous, direct, and raw fashion, unfiltered by any prescribed canon of what art should be and how it must look: direct, because their singular vision is the sole artistic lens though which they see; unfiltered, because their judgment is the sole artistic basis of their aesthetic decision making. The compounded impact of the work of others need not be sorted, assimilated, or digested for them to express their own conceptions. Thus, the commonality among self-taught artists springs from their untutored creativity and personal vision, not from a shared technique, style, or ideology. This factor differentiates their work from that of schooled artists.

Self-taught artists create in response to inner visions as well as to visual stimuli from all aspects of their daily lives. Their stylistic production is as broad as one finds today in mainstream contemporary American art. Self-taught art of the twentieth-century *is* contemporary art—so much so that a walk past New York's Madison Avenue galleries shows that some trained artists have adopted deliberately naive styles in an effort to appear self-taught.

The various styles of untutored artists range widely from figurative to nonrepresentational, from "primitive" or "naive" to sophisticated, from the recognizably realistic to the whimsically fantastic. The term "naive," coined in the early twentieth century to describe the work of untutored artists like Henri Rousseau, has come to indicate a simple, uncomplicated style that generally portrays a recognizable scene from daily life. These representative paintings are generally termed memory painting, as they depict landscape scenes remembered by artists from their own lives, such as Grandma Moses' renderings of farm life. But not all naive paintings are memory paintings, and not all visual recollections of past experience can be called memory painting.

Most works by self-taught artists do relate to personal experience, some present, some past, but they are executed in thoroughly individualistic styles. While the uncomplicated figures and simple landscapes of Clementine Hunter, Philo Levi "Chief" Willey, Bernice Sims, and John William "Uncle Jack" Dey can be associated with naive painting, the abstractions of Purvis Young and John "J. B." Murry, or the found-object assemblages of Charlie Lucas and David Strickland, are visually sophisticated statements. Even though their intent might be the translation of a figurative subject, these artists have a tendency toward visual nonrepresentation that is not easily distinguished from the work of mainstream master artists.

For formally tutored artists, evolution of style is a significant measure of artistic growth over time, to be analyzed in depth by the artist, friends, peers, critics, collectors, dealers, and museums. But the style of a self-taught artist may or may not substantially evolve. The work of Ed "Mr. Eddy" Mumma, "Uncle Jack" Dey, Benjamin F. Perkins, J. P. Scott, and George Williams, for example, has shown little stylistic development and change over time, whereas other artists such as Thornton Dial, Sr., William Hawkins, Howard Finster, and Jimmy Lee Sudduth demonstrate remarkable evolution. Regardless of growth, diversity, or similarity, stylistic development is not an issue of concern to the self-taught artist.

Self-taught artists as defined here typically receive little formal education, and there might be a link between artists working comfortably without connection to the art "system" and their level of schooling. Education, particularly higher education, encourages systematic learning and entices students to study accepted paradigms in their fields of interest. In so doing, the student learns to assimilate and synthesize verbal and visual information, and to selectively accept or reject data, thereby formulating his or her own point of view. Formal education thus motivates one to use the efforts of others as a point of departure in one's own development.

Therefore, if an educated person emerges as a self-taught artist, as many do after retirement or later in life, it is likely that he or she will instinctively apply this method of learning to his or her artistic endeavor, both seeking out and incorporating the concepts of other artists into his or her own work. Such individuals are likely to have encountered, learned from, or been influenced by the art of others, the arts community, art history classes, and museums or gallery exhibitions. They often begin with preconceived standards for what art should look like. In this regard, their situation is analogous to that of trained artists, who must often overcome studied and learned techniques to tap into the individual creativity of their own artistic voices.

In its emphasis on originality, formal art education encourages artists to continually evolve without repeating subject, design, or materials. In contrast, many untutored self-taught artists, such as Clementine Hunter, Anderson Johnson, Jimmie Lee Sudduth, and William Dawson, are not preoccupied with originality, which allows them to explore repetitive imagery without concern that their creativity is in question.

The definition of unschooled artists as well as the best single term to describe them has been debated for several decades. Folk artist, outsider, naive, primitive, visionary, art brut, and self-taught are among the many terms generally employed. This uncertain terminology indicates that the mainstream art world is still grappling with who these artists are and how they relate to prevailing concepts of what art is and who can be called an artist.

Terms, it must be noted, are conceptual tools that lend structure to our understanding of an issue. Like all art historical categories, those used to describe self-taught artists were devised by individuals on the basis of characteristic patterns they found in the artworks. In the case of self-taught artists, the feature typically used to link their work has been their untutored processes. Traditional categorization by stylistic similarity, such as impressionism or abstract expressionism, is not appropriate for self-taught artists, who, if they share biographical similarities, employ vastly different styles, techniques, and materials.

Although no one term accurately describes the work of all these artists, self-taught seems to be the most adequate. They have most commonly been known as folk artists, and are still referred to as such today, but they are not folk artists as traditionally defined: they do not work within a communally accepted style, ideology, or symbolism, nor do they create works for functional purposes. Such folk art, exemplified by the work of split-cane basket makers, decoy makers, or quilters, who create according to a prescribed style with communally conceived and understood formulas, patterns, and symbolism, has little relationship to the individualized, personally expressive styles of self-taught artists.

The term "outsider," however, is pertinent here in that self-taught artists, whether rural or urban, operate outside the established art world. Many self-taught artists are geographically isolated, living in distant rural areas connected by poor roads, or in impoverished, largely hermetic urban areas. Yet their lives are not isolated or self-contained; they are rooted within their immediate culture, often closely integrated with family, church, and community life. Their individual expression through art may, indeed, tag them as eccentric or different within their communities. In that, however, they are not unlike many other artists, who are commonly perceived as operating in solitude and on the fringes of society. Perhaps the only true outsider artists, as defined by MacGregor,[4] are those whose artwork is not seen by anyone while the artist is alive or those who are institutionalized on a long-term basis.

Although ranging in focus, each of the terms noted above attempts to describe self-taught artists. To paradoxically structure boundaries around who they are with strict definitions is to limit their creative process. In the future, hopefully, they perhaps will simply be referred to as artists and be permitted to create on their own terms.

So must the work of self-taught artists be legitimized? Certainly not by the artists themselves, who often have no sense of and little interest in the goals of the art world that increasingly courts them. The notion of being "in" or "out" of the artistic establishment is irrelevant, for these artists live within the mainstream they most value, that of their own culture. Self-taught artists have emerged into the artistic mainstream, but it has been trained artists, collectors, dealers, and scholars who have coaxed them out. They have not sought the art world; the art world has come to them.

Emergence into the artistic mainstream by no means has been synonymous with total acceptance. A select number of trained art historians with diverse backgrounds, from Renaissance painting to African sculpture and contemporary American art, have embraced this work,[5] but most have been slow to formally respond. A limited number of art museums collected contemporary self-taught art prior to 1980, and university art history departments have shown even less interest. Only a few university art history programs have even begun to consider self-taught art as a serious field of study.[6]

Why the hesitancy to accept this visually intriguing imagery? Simply put, the aesthetic influences of self-taught artists, their working methods, and their backgrounds, both artistic and socioeconomic, do not conform to the profile of an academically trained artist.

Stanford art historian Wanda Corn, in forecasting the future of scholarship in American art, has described the normative process critics have used to assess art and artists:

> The art we have traditionally studied is by people who call themselves artists. Using connoisseurship skills or those of stylistic analysis, we have determined changes in growth and development in their work and have decided which are their finest pieces.[7]

Self-taught artists challenge each aspect of this process. They typically do not call themselves artists; they do not operate within an established canon from which one can evaluate their work; and they do not seem to be concerned with stylistic growth. More often repetition of style, themes, and/or materials prevails.

But most important, questions of art historical influence are not applicable to the work of self-taught artists. Works by acknowledged masters have long provided natural models from which trained artists could learn and perhaps borrow as they developed individual styles, and art historians traditionally study the work of trained artists within this context. Self-taught artists, however, do not consciously seek or respond to inspiration from other artists; they do not separate the formal aspects of their work from its subject. This contrasts with those trained artists for whom technique often doubles as subject.

Trained artists, conscious of the art historical framework into which their work will fit, seek to be original and innovative. But because self-taught artists do not draw on the same construct, they are unaware of and unconcerned with the contribution or place of their work within the history of art. This, too, poses a challenge for art historians.

Even though issues of originality and art historical inspiration are of little use in the study of self-taught artists, the aesthetic features of their work often meet contemporary criteria for work by mainstream artists and cannot always be distinguished from it. Broadening the parameters of "art historical" influence to "visual" influence, however, does allow the work of self-taught artists to be assessed with art historical questions and tools by seeking culturally based visual sources for individual works or analyzing an artist's tendencies according to his or her environment or prevailing cultural assumptions. Considering the influence of *all* visual stimuli lends a fuller perspective to the study of any artist's work. Artists, trained or not, do not "see" only in the confines of a studio or when standing before a museum masterpiece. The sensibilities of looking, seeing, and perceiving take place in all waking hours for all creative artists, not only those who have had the benefit of sanctioned art school programs.

Self-taught artists experience an extraordinarily rich visual world despite their art historical "isolation." Their design sense is affected by their contemporary environment, which abounds with commercial art. This art has familiarized self-taught artists with twentieth-century design, composition, subject matter, style, scale, and sometimes materials, all of which have influenced their aesthetic principles and ideas. This exposure might explain why the work of many contemporary self-taught artists is so visually compatible with that of trained artists of the same period who, especially in recent decades, often have looked to the same commercial sources for subjects and suggestions of style. In this sense, the distinction between "high" and "low" art becomes moot, reinforcing the reasonableness of considering self-taught art as part of a horizontal rather than vertical artistic continuum. All artists—self-taught or trained—remain rooted in and subject to their times,[8] steeped in their shared visual culture.

NOTES

1. With increasing exposure to dealers, collectors, scholars, and the press, many do later come to consider themselves artists and rightfully expect financial compensation. Younger artists particularly, such as Charlie Lucas, Lonnie B. Holley, Purvis Young, Herbert Singleton, and others, have more fully felt the impact of the recent boom in the folk art market. They do consider themselves full-time artists, and their art is the primary source of their livelihoods.

2. Several artists attended the opening for the seminal exhibition *Black Folk Art in America,* held at the Corcoran Gallery of Art in 1982. In 1988 Mose Tolliver, Thornton Dial, Sr., Lonnie B. Holley, and Charlie Lucas, among other featured artists, attended the opening of *Outside the Mainstream: Folk Art in Our Time* at Atlanta's High Museum. For Dial and others this was a first visit to a museum.

3. A few self-taught artists (e.g., Purvis Young, Bernice Sims, Sybil Gibson, William Dawson, "Prophet" Royal Robertson) have enrolled briefly in informal adult education art classes, but their art remains largely uninfluenced by the experience.

4. John M. MacGregor, lecture, Los Angeles County Museum of Art, Oct. 1992. For a further analysis of institutionalized artists, see MacGregor's *The Discovery of the Art of the Insane* (Princeton: Princeton University Press, 1989).

5. David Steel, Renaissance specialist and curator of European art at the North Carolina Museum of Art, was responsible for the 1989 exhibition *Signs and Wonders: Outsider Art inside North Carolina*; William Fagaly, an Africanist and contemporary art curator at the New Orleans Museum of Art, organized the first museum exhibitions of the work of Sister Gertrude Morgan, David Butler, and Clementine Hunter; Russell Bowman, director of the Milwaukee Museum of Art and a specialist in contemporary art, organized *Common Ground/Uncommon Vision,* an exhibition of the Michael and Julie Hall folk art collection, in 1993.

6. The only U.S. university granting advanced degrees in the field is New York University, where, in conjunction with the Museum of American Folk Art, New York, a master of arts in folk art studies is offered. Selected universities are beginning to accept master's theses on the subject.

7. "Scholarship in American Art: Foresights—Problems and Triumphs of the 1990s," *Smithsonian American Art Network Newsletter,* suppl. vol. 4, no. 2 (Fall 1991), p. 2.

8. Stephen Weil, deputy directy, Hirshhorn Museum and Sculpture Garden, unpublished ms.

THE ART OF THE SELF-TAUGHT/ THE ART OF OUR TIME

JANE LIVINGSTON

THE INVISIBLE CULTURE

The flowering of American visual art in the post–World War II period has long been recognized as a signal of the artistic independence of our nation. From the late 1930s well into the 1960s, the clear ascendancy of the new painting and sculpture being made in New York, vis-à-vis European advanced art, was convincingly established. The torch was passed, as it were, across the ocean from Paris, London, and Berlin. Moreover, theorists and practitioners alike argued that this New World vanguardist art was the only high art in its deliberate rejection of kitsch and in its self-aware embracing of Western modernist culture and all that it implies.

Beginning in the 1940s with a number of influential articles by critics Clement Greenberg, Harold Rosenberg, and others, interacting with bodies of painting and sculpture by the likes of Arshile Gorky, Jackson Pollock, Willem de Kooning, and David Smith, a process of educating the American intelligentsia about the true importance of the new art of their time gained a momentum that persisted for decades. The perceived danger of the vulgarization of American culture by an engagement with the middle-class or lower-class culture of the newly prosperous masses seemed to have been warded off once and for all. Following the so-called first generation of artists, another, slightly younger group carried high art's banner—painters such as Joan Mitchell in Paris, Morris Louis in Washington, D.C., and Sam Francis in California. These artists were generally accepted by the original promoters of abstract expressionism. But other artists began to claim their place in the high art ranks of their time; even those outspoken heretics of the church of Clement Greenberg and Michael Fried, such as Donald Judd, Dan Flavin, and Robert Morris, managed in effect to extend its authority.

Then, after thirty years of development, it seemed all at once that the clear separation between rigorous modernism and popular culture threatened to dissolve. Vernacular imagery crept into ambitious art; much was made of a perceived dissolution of the boundaries between various art forms. In all the arts, for lack of a better term, people began to speak of either a "new pluralism" or a "new regionalism."

The heady and dramatic occurrence of abstract expressionism—that New York–based movement that established the United States firmly in the lead in terms of serious, inventive, sometimes genius-driven visual culture—gave way to a succession of styles. In an often predictable progression (thesis, antithesis, synthesis)—commencing in the late 1950s with two simultaneous and opposing styles, pop art and post-painterly abstraction—variants on tendencies such as op art or photo-realism succeeded one another. Beginning in the early 1970s, minimalist and conceptual bodies of work evolved as much out of the current art criticism as from the look or style of these late modernist movements, and marched straight through the decade. To a sophisticated artist, critic, or curator anywhere in America in the mid-1970s, it seemed that the inventiveness of mainstream avant-gardism would somehow go on, one pioneering idea or ism succeeding the last, in a never-ending effluence of intellectual and commercial fecundity. For many years, it didn't seem to register to the busy members of the artistic establishment that a few sensitive listeners were hearing a different drumbeat, that as early as the 1930s such sophisticated and influential artists as Elie Nadelman, John Graham, and Walker Evans were attuned to another reality in American culture.

What superseded the astonishingly coherent and universally adopted vanguard doctrines of the long postwar era in the United States, at least at the time it was happening, seemed at first a chaotic set of events, or perhaps a single development springing from several different impulses occurring at once. To some, it seemed as though a strangely *retardataire* reengagement of figuration or literalist representation was unpredictably gaining currency. Sometimes such expressions seemed to be academic in origin, connoting nostalgia for old-fashioned anatomical study, or, more often, a new fascination with photo-realist images. Sometimes, in contrast, the new representation shamelessly embraced a folksy sensibility that many critics interpreted as a descent into cynical mannerism or some other brand of cultural decadence. To others, an unpredicted new regionalism was being observed, an inexplicable fragmentation of style and iconography during a historical era supposed to be universalizing, replacing localisms with an ever more homogeneous global village. Emerging "schools" of young artists were located in Texas, in the Northwest, in Southern California, and in New England.

To many, these proliferations of localized artistic activity seemed mere wheel spinning, or the churning out of professional artists by art schools for the sake of market consumption, without allegiance to the truer, always gratuitous, artistic imperative. Whether hypothesizing decay or some new cultural provincialism, few establishment critics saw much redemption in the mysterious collapse of modernist vanguardism. Even the most agnostic critics seemed at a loss for labels to apply to these new tendencies; they resorted to the term pluralism to characterize the artistic insurgencies of the 1970s and 1980s.

"Pluralism" seemed to indicate that several sources were coming together to form a new style, or, perhaps, that any number of different and possibly unrelated sources were suddenly fair game for contemporary artists, and that the previous hierarchic imperative no longer reigned. But in fact one of the primal impetuses for this newly diverse style in American art sprang from a shared awareness of the roots of modern art. It should not be forgotten that Picasso's love affair with African masks, as well as Gauguin's and Brancusi's and Giacometti's affinities to the art of so-called primitive cultures, laid the groundwork for our later understanding of the relationships between modernism and "primitivism." Nor did any college course in modern art in the 1960s ignore the presence of Jean Dubuffet and art brut. But Picasso and Dubuffet's open acknowledgment of sources in "primitive" art were most often introduced as relatively isolated cases. Even as late as 1984, with the Museum of Modern Art's ambitious exhibition *"Primitivism" in 20th Century Art*, the contemporary art community seemed unable to accept, or at least to credit, the argument for a thoroughgoing impact of the art brut aesthetic on modern artists.

It is difficult to exaggerate the force of influence exerted by the established critical emphasis on "high culture" in postwar America. But it didn't entirely preclude either the ongoing existence of other traditions or the interest in alternative cultural forms among a few of the intelligentsia. As has been well documented by folklorists and American folk art experts, the current wide interest in so-called contemporary self-taught or visionary artists working in various parts of the United States began to be institutionalized as early as the 1930s. Before that time, some attention, if not a great deal, had been paid to late eighteenth- and nineteenth-century crafts and folk art. But events in the 1930s such as the Museum of Modern Art's exhibition of the sculpture of Tennessee stone carver William Edmondson (discovered, actually, not by one of the museum's curators but by the photographer Louise Dahl Wolf) marked the beginning of an appreciation of current folk artists by the sophisticated modernist sensibilities of curators and artists. A few other events built on this one during the 1940s, 1950s, and 1960s, notably the founding of the Abby Aldrich Rockefeller Folk Art Center in Williamsburg, Virginia, dedicated to American folk art and crafts, but these decades were remarkably barren of any truly influential recognition of the self-taught artistic traditions that continued to thrive and grow despite nearly universal neglect.

RECOLLECTIONS OF A CONVERT

It happens that during the mid-1970s I was witnessing firsthand much of this shift in the dynamic of American art, since I was traveling frequently to various parts of the United States to jury exhibitions. This was owing to my role as an establishment figure in the domain of contemporary painting, sculpture, and photography, via my position as a museum curator and writer on art, first at the Los Angeles County Museum of Art and, after 1975, at the Corcoran Gallery of Art in Washington, D.C. What I began increasingly to see, whether in Des Moines, Buffalo, or La Grange, Georgia, was not just a great deal of stylistic and imaginative diversity coming from the studios of local artists, but a plethora of imagery seemingly based on so-called self-taught or visionary art. Everywhere artists seemed to be flattening the field of their paintings or drawings and depicting figures or landscapes or interiors, or all of these at once, in a strangely compressed and spatially ambiguous arena. Often a strong narrative was expressed, sometimes transparently, sometimes with an apparently surreal lack of coherency or logic. A great upsurge of both playful and satirical content in visual art was occurring in many regions simultaneously.

It was difficult to know just what to make of this phenomenon: there was something salutary in much of this ironical and whimsical work, yet I began increasingly to be visited by a suspicion that much of it was a borrowing from, or transposition of, something better or more authentic than itself. I could see some of its sources in various popular illustrative forms, such as the comic strip. But, like nearly everyone else, I assumed its roots were primarily in other high art.

By about 1975, one particularly ubiquitous strain of this new, cartoonlike but "serious" figuration began to be identified largely with the influence of a single artist, Philip Guston, who had taken a lonely road out of the acceptable abstraction of his day and had begun to paint in an idiosyncratic, intentionally crude, illustrative yet mythic manner that seemed at once distantly ironic and ruefully humorous, and was often autobiographical. Guston's example was emulated to a greater or lesser degree not only by such recognized painters as Nicholas Africano, Jonathon Borofsky, Richard Artschwager, and Lois Lane but by artists operating farther out of the mainstream, both geographically and spiritually.

If a new passion for narrative imagery appeared to be springing up in virtually every region of the country, its most energetic and original embodiments were coming out of the southern states, including Texas. In fact, I realized, there were precedents for this seemingly new funky-narrational art other than in such mass popular imagery as comic strips. It had been present in mainstream American art emerging as early as the late 1960s. Probably the earliest manifestation of this new kind of irreverent, iconoclastic painting and object making had arisen in Chicago, where a group of artists including H. C. Westermann, Ed Paschke, Jim Nutt, and Roger Brown had been either taking inspiration from or collecting the work of self-taught American artists. At about the same time, a few artists in California, among them Ed Kienholz, William T. Wiley, and Roy De Forest, began to gain recognition, joined by the Texan-turned-New Yorker Red Grooms, and by such consummately sophisticated New York artists as Neil Jenney, Robert Moskowitz, and Joe Zucker. Later, more and more artists moved into some variant of a figural, often spatially flat mode; several important sculptors, prime among them Martin Puryear and Joel Shapiro, seemed to embrace an aesthetic informed by folk sculpture, or at least by some of the movingly elemental forms adopted directly from folk objects a generation earlier by Elie Nadelman.[1]

It took some time to recognize the true sources for much of what was happening in this kind of "sophisticated" American art. Coming to Washington, D.C., from Los Angeles in early 1975, I had been inclined to equate current "folk art" with crafts: I had had bouts of infatuation with Southwest Indian rugs, with Mission-style and Shaker furniture, and with Mexican masks. Like most of my colleagues in California, my knowledge of recent American folk art was due primarily to the electrifying discovery of and struggle to preserve Simon Rodia's Watts Towers, that amazing, environmentally scaled monument to one man's obsession.

Once transplanted to the East Coast, I abruptly turned my attention in a southerly direction. I soon realized that the Corcoran Gallery, besides being the art museum in Washington most responsive to local artists, also had an unofficial status as headquarters for contemporary artists from the southeast United States. In North and South Carolina, in Georgia and Alabama, the Corcoran represented the hopes of at least two generations of artists aspiring for inclusion in the gallery's venerable biennial exhibition of contemporary art, or, better still, a one-person show.

In the process of familiarizing myself with not just artists from Washington, D.C., Maryland, and Virginia, but those farther south, I was led to a revelation. It dawned on me that the apparently mysterious or unexplained impetus behind so much of the pluralist phenomenon in contemporary American culture had in truth a quite visible primary source: other art, the art of individuals who seemed to be physically isolated, unrelated to each other, whose own sources were mysterious—an art that had long been with us, nearly invisible and yet pervasively sensed. This other art seemed to be found mostly in the South. As I began to understand this, and to exert the will of the new convert, I also began to observe a distinct unwillingness or resistance on the part of many curators and critics to acknowledge the importance of this "outsider art," even when its existence was known.

Rarely did establishment curators or critics or even dealers lead me to the artists whose work began to explain much of the new tendencies in the mainstream art of the 1970s and 1980s. I was educated mainly by artist friends such as Ed McGowin, Scott Burton, William Christenberry, William Dunlap, and the Texans James Surls, John Alexander, and James Hill.[2] All these artists had been exposed to folk art in various ways, and, if they didn't directly use its inspiration, they were fascinated by its energy, amazing formal inventiveness, and immediacy. Through them the world of self-taught art, recent and contemporary, opened up.

Three unforgettable discoveries in 1975 and 1976 were to lay the groundwork for my growing interest and work in the field of current American folk or outsider art. The first was catalyzed by artist friends in Houston and Dallas, who led me to the dealer Murray Smither, and thus to the work of the late George White. The second, thanks to James Harithas, then director of the Contemporary Arts Museum, Houston, and New Orleans jazz and blues impresario Alan Jaffe, was the discovery of Sister Gertrude Morgan. Harithas took me to her small white house, in New Orleans's Saint Bernard Parish, filled with white furniture (even the black keys on her piano were painted white), where Sister Gertrude showed us some of her extraordinary paintings, bestowed upon us one of her powerful blessings, and made sure we noticed her unique front yard, covered with a blanket of four-leaf clovers. Finally, thanks to my colleague William Fagaly of the New Orleans Museum of Art, I was treated to the unforgettable experience of a visit to the home of David Butler in Patterson, Louisiana. We arrived at Butler's house at a particularly propitious moment, a time when his garden was richly planted with the snipped metal, brightly painted sculptures that he continually produced and that were continually given to or taken away by neighbors, acquaintances, and sometimes strangers.

It would be five years before these experiences would coalesce into a project, one that eventually gathered in an additional seventeen black folk artists, nearly all from the South. *Black Folk Art in America, 1930–1980*, an exhibition organized for the Corcoran Gallery of Art by myself and my colleague John Beardsley, became a focal point for the longstanding, but somehow inchoate, or at least unarticulated, feeling for this aesthetic on the part of many. We were generously assisted in our research for this show by many who knew far more than we about the world of the self-taught artist in America: Michael and Julie Hall, Herbert W. Hemphill, William Ferris, Jr., Maude Wahlman, Gregg Blasdel, Jeff Camp, and Phyllis Kind all opened doors, and worlds, to us in our odyssey of 1980 and 1981.

To recapitulate my own experience in the discovery of American self-taught artists is not to suggest that it was in any way unique, or that it occurred at a particularly early moment in the history of the discovery of twentieth-century American folk art. Many went before. By 1980, a number of devoted and prescient collectors, dealers, and curators had paved the way for the preservation and appreciation of this phenomenon. The work of New York museum professionals Holger Cahill, Jean Lipman, Bert Hemphill, Mary Black, and others was carried on simultaneously to, and often ignored by, the mainstream vanguard art activity of the 1960s and 1970s. And these folk art devotees weren't the only ones to whom we later enthusiasts were indebted: the occasional "mainstream" curatorial venture into the realm of the folk-art-inspired trends in high art, such as Robert Doty's 1969 exhibition at the Whitney Museum of American Art, *Human Concern/Personal Torment: The Grotesque in American Art*, were pioneering yet successfully ignored by the establishment.

For the most part the artists, not the authorities on them, have paved the way to a greater awareness and appreciation of self-taught artists. This is true no matter what the artist's medium might be: the photographer Walker Evans, for example, was one of the earliest discoverers of the kind of art being explored here. Artists, unlike most writers on them, quickly perceive artistic objects not just on the basis of style or "artfulness" but on a level of physical process. The act of making the object and the inventiveness of the decisions made in the course of its creation are perhaps more directly evident to the artist than to the aesthetician. And it is perhaps on this level—the domain in which one grasps the creative process itself and reimagines the moves made in its enactment—that we have the most to learn from these artists. Artists often understand before the rest of us what resistances need to be overcome in order to open ourselves to a new aesthetic experience or a "changed seeing."

THE CONTROVERSIES

At least since the 1930s, when American folk art began to be institutionalized in the museum and academic communities, a certain conflict has simmered between those "conservative" folk art proponents focused primarily on objects from the eighteenth and nineteenth centuries, and those who ventured ever further into art being produced in the twentieth century. The Museum of American Folk Art in New York became an arena for the playing out of this battle; when its increasingly audacious curator, Bert Hemphill, dared to exhibit objects under rubrics such as "Occult" or "Tattoo" in the early 1970s, many who wanted the museum to limit its activities to "authenticated" early American art and craft were outraged. To this day, many folk art dealers and collectors remain unconvinced that the increasing number of contemporary artists gaining recognition in projects such as the present one have legitimacy. It continues to be an act of courage to put forth such claims as are being made here for the importance of this large group of twentieth-century artists.

Art that is removed from one's own reality simply by its chronological distance is easier to accept and understand than contemporary art, and this odd mechanism works intensely in the acceptance of self-taught artists. The work of the early nineteenth-century portraitists, such as Ammi Phillips or Erastus Salisbury Field, or the so-called American limners, such as the gifted black painter Joshua Johnston, despite its characteristic lack of modeling or illusionistic verisimilitude, has for a generation been accepted as a part of the mainstream legacy of American art. And the genre paintings of Edward Hicks or Susan Whitcomb are firmly embedded in the Americanist's canon. The more recent the vintage, the slower the academy has been to embrace the self-taught artist: the twentieth-century artist Horace Pippin has now been admitted to the fold, and Morris Hirshfield is on the verge of admission, but many of their contemporaries are not. It may take another decade or more for many of the artists included in the present exhibition to be adopted by the academicians.

FOLK ART AND HIGH ART: HOW THEY DIVERGE

Even at enough historic remove so that a subject takes on the patina of age, the more quaintly appealing or decorative the art of the naive, the more readily it is accepted. For example, in portraiture, the more obdurate, perhaps the more honest and penetrating, the portrayals of eighteenth- and nineteenth-century limners, the harder they are to sell than their prettier sisters; this is true whether or not the homely picture is actually better than the ingratiating one.[3] This may seem paradoxical in an aesthetic era that has tended to prefer toughness and to abhor sentimentality in its contemporary vanguard artists. This may, however, be an unconsciously bourgeois reaction, reflecting the threat felt by many in the presence of a complex achievement apparently won without the benefit of the classical education that we Americans undertake as the irreplaceable path to success. Yet the often-present quality of a kind of stubborn nondecorativeness in folk art of virtually any vintage seems to intimidate even the most astute and uncompromising art historians.

In terms of the so-called folk art aesthetic, the present group of artists cannot be reduced to any single style or even a coherent cultural ethos. Though many of the themes in their work, and many of the outlines of their biographies, might resemble one another—with striking frequency, for example, their artistic production began late in life—significant differences exist among them. One primary distinction discernible even on a cursory viewing of this large body of work can be characterized only as "picturesqueness," in contrast to a quality one might call "the aesthetic of ugliness."

Many of those whose notion of folk art remains fixated in the look of nineteenth-century quilts and samplers, or in the thematically nostalgic work of an artist like Grandma Moses, will have some difficulty accepting the work of Sam Doyle, Mose Tolliver, Steven Ashby, or Jimmy Lee Sudduth. A seemingly intentional crudeness of composition, combined with the humbleness of the materials these artists use, imparts a sense of coarseness that literally can be felt to defy any notion of "fine art." It takes a second reading to perceive the underlying subtlety and sophistication these painters and sculptors bring to their use of color and shape; eventually, these artists' toughness of vision and their compositional audacity work to their advantage. Moreover, their psychological acuity occasionally defies analysis. Many devotees of contemporary visionary art come to prefer this ruder and less obviously decorative approach to that of other self-taught artists, whose primary concern may seem to be either refined craftsmanship for its own sake or a formulaic use of rhythmic pattern.

Gradually these more recalcitrant figures, such as William Hawkins, Thornton Dial, Sr., Mary T. Smith, and James Henry "Son" Thomas, are gaining an ever stronger foothold in the ranks of accepted folk art. This is not to say that the process of winning respectability in American museum and academic circles has been without contentiousness. Indeed, heated debate continues among and between folklorists and collector-curators about the very nature and value of contemporary folk art. Folklorists trained in cultural anthropology persist in their deeply ingrained abhorrence of the notion that objects created in the name of what they conceptualize as either communal, ritual, or didactic purposefulness should be decontextualized and treated as gratuitous aesthetic icons. This resistance continues to divide the experts whose background or bias comes from social science and those trained and inclined toward art and aesthetics. And even though the debate is couched in new terms, as was attempted, for example, in the Smithsonian Institution's 1991 symposium and book titled *Exhibiting Cultures*,[4] it remains fundamentally the same debate that has raged for decades.

So a seemingly unresolvable conflict between the anthropologists and the art historians continues to exist on the subject of "visionary" artists (one whose nature reminds us of the abstract painter Barnett Newman's observation that aesthetics is to artists as ornithology is to birds). And there are other controversies within the community of the aestheticians. Virtually everyone who has tried to distinguish between the characteristics of contemporary folk art, that is, work made after the 1920s or 1930s, and earlier folk art has struggled to find the concepts and terms to do this. Most people comparing, for example, the work of Horace Pippin and that of Elijah Pierce find that a clear affinity exists between them: a generation apart, they seem to belong to a single tradition. And yet they are profoundly different. To describe these differences, however, seems more problematic than to describe the similarities.

One of the distinguishing features of modernism is its connection to an idea of development. The notion of linear relationships among "inventions" in modernist art—i.e., from impressionism to fauvism to cubism to surrealism to abstraction—gives it the character of being somehow progressive. This developmental idea is perhaps a metaphor for the concept of industrial progress so integral to Western thought throughout the nineteenth and twentieth centuries: we have long been wedded to the illusion that technology can bring both universal freedom from brute labor and improvement in our level of civilization.

A distinguishing feature of the art of the self-taught is its paradoxical timelessness. Visionary art doesn't participate in a dialectical unfolding of style; rather, it reflects an immediacy in the life and consciousness of its creator. One of the central contradictions of folk art is its simultaneous embedment in its own exact time and place, and its discontinuity of relationship to other art. The folk art object is concrete in a way that a sophisticated abstract painting can never be, and yet it takes on a kind of universal accessibility of meaning that most high art lacks. The last thing most of the artists in this exhibition are interested in is hidden meaning or abstruse symbolism; their symbols tend to be familiar. Certain signs or images that refer to history and culture recur among these artists, such as the American flag, the sailor uniform, the familiar visage of Abraham Lincoln, the Statue of Liberty. Biblical references—Noah's ark, Adam and Eve, the Madonna and Child appear again and again. And some images seem to have a flexible interpretability, such as the snake, which can refer to Christian original sin or to its centuries-old presence in African lore; or the monkey, whose significance in the vocabulary of southern black artists seems both ancient and contemporary; the skull, whose referent is as cross cultural as any symbol can be; the eagle, referring to the freedom of the soul, or more mundanely, American patriotism.

Rather than carrying on a dialectical progression, in which a given painting or sculpture is influenced by and in turn influences other art, a folk art object engages in a conversation with its own maker and with its audience. Unlike the audience for high art, the viewer of folk art is tacitly assumed to be a participant in the artist's own universe and to share in the artist's stock of signs and symbols. No specialized knowledge or education are posited within which the artist addresses his or her aesthetic message; no advancing line of endeavor, no narrow or iconoclastic tradition, limits the folk artist's field of play. The circle is opened, the object released from its trajectory.

Certainly many facts about the folk artist—his or her relative isolation from other art; the peculiarly high incidence of late-in-life beginnings as artists; the frequency with which the folk artist seems to let materials, whether tree branches or quarry stone, dictate form—would seem to separate these individuals from their schooled or professional confreres. Yet to suggest that folk artists, unlike other artists, are somehow outside the world of mainstream culture is to misunderstand the nature of visual art itself. To some degree, all art expresses a shared communal mythology; all good art, in any event, on some level needs to be intelligible to others besides the maker. And it is important to remember that, in most cases, those we call folk artists view themselves simply as artists.

Some confusion continues to exist as to whether certain so-called folk arts, anonymously or communally practiced, deserve the same status as the painting and sculpture in the present exhibition. For example, some would claim that the artifacts of various populist subcultures in our society merit the same attention as any other folk art. The costumes of the Hell's Angels, for instance, or their tattoos, or even their customized bikes, may have as much claim to artistic definition as any other objects. These objects can indeed take on an undeniable character of beauty and originality of conception. Similarly, it is hard to disagree with those who see in some early or recent American quilts, furniture, or rugs an artistic quality that makes them "equal" to any other aesthetic object. But there is a difference between such objects and the works of the artists in this exhibition. It is a difference of intentionality. When an artist like Nellie Mae Rowe states that she may enjoy seeing the paintings and sculptures in the Metropolitan Museum of Art but still prefers "to look at my own art,"[5] it is a statement to be taken at no less face value than if it were made by Willem de Kooning.

Moreover, the gaining of mastery—the gradual sharpening and refining of an artist's medium and imaginative powers—is no less important to the self-taught artist than to the schooled one. Even when the tools and materials of relatively poor or isolated artists limit the degree of physical permanence or technical perfection of their work, we sense in the best visionary art a commitment to and a striving for mastery.

Nevertheless, several important distinctions remain to be drawn between the individual artistic development of the visionary or self-taught painter and sculptor, and the academic or avant-garde artist, and it is these differences that perhaps account for the relative slowness of many critics and historians to understand, or take seriously, the former. First, many, perhaps most, folk artists maintain a striking evenness of quality in their work over years or decades. While they may improve as craftsmen, the fundamental attributes of their stylistic energy and of their continued or repeated adherence to related subjects might not change significantly.[6] Folk art's essential nature as a form of communication that engages myth and parable as its subject, and seeks to be transparent rather than obscure or abstract, seems to account in part for its strangely nondevelopmental character. And its transparency may also relate to the question of its fundamental presentness, its apparent immediacy and spontaneity of impulse, even when clearly a part of a repetitive and occasionally formulaic body of work.

It is tempting to explain the possibility that we are dealing with a truly dying cultural form by a simple idea—namely, that the artists practicing it have tended to live in rural parts of the nation, primarily the South. (In fact, these artists may embody the strongest visual culture the South has produced.) Thus the conditions allowing them to remain both connected to the stories and legends that are so often their subjects, and to live in relative isolation from middle-class, commodity-oriented American culture, are endangered by the factors with which we are all too familiar in our increasingly urbanized and homogenized nation. This can't, however, be the whole story. These artists have certainly not escaped the presence of television, and indeed they use contemporary mass icons just as they used earlier ones. Surely the fading of many craft traditions, such as basket making, pottery such as the face jug, and the production of musical instruments such as the cane fife, takes its toll on the "higher" folk art tradition. But perhaps most important is the life of the culture as a whole. The art in this exhibition has flourished in a climate of optimism. One of its underlying characteristics is a shared feeling of redemption or rebirth, even when its subject is secular. It often takes as its subject themes reflecting the history of the nation, from slavery and its abolition, to the fading of an agricultural way of life and its replacement by other forms of work and recreation. This art assumes generational continuity in terms of family and community. In an era defined by uneasiness, when the future presents only the unknown, when traditional resolutions to familiar dilemmas have failed, an art of people's struggle, celebrating a society's triumphs and aspirations, will founder.

During the early 1980s, when John Beardsley and I were intensely involved in the task of organizing *Black Folk Art in America*, I remember feeling increasingly concerned about the future of the art form we were discovering and interpreting. Of the artists in our exhibition who were still living, the youngest, James Henry "Son" Thomas, was born in 1926. Though we visited a few younger artists, such as the Alabama sculptor Lonnie B. Holley, who was born in 1950 and began his career making tombstones, it seemed that perhaps we were seeing the last generation in a vital, yet fragile tradition. The growing suspicion of the transience of our subject—a sense that it might be confined to three generations, beginning in the 1890s and ending in the 1990s—lent an urgency to that project that I admit I continue to feel, if less acutely, in relation to the present exhibition.

In the years since the presentation of *Black Folk Art in America*, my knowledge of the subject has been enriched by the discovery of artists unknown to us then, including one or two, such as Josephus Farmer and Mary T. Smith, who might well have been included. But the sense remains that the end of a precious tradition is drawing near. At the same time, we have reached the end of another unique and inestimably valuable tradition in American culture—the high art efflorescence that has been with us for so many decades has now virtually dissipated. Visual art will have to take inspiration from other sources than the ones dictated by the long battle against kitsch, against sentimentality and the facile adoption of popular imagery in the name of commercial aesthetic products. If we are confronting a period in which various layers or realms of vital creativity are ending or changing, we are also faced with a welcome area for new appreciation. Recent high art in America has long been the subject of self-examination and objective analysis. The same cannot be said for twentieth-century folk art. Exhibitions such as this one are excavating new ground in our immediate past; they are opening the way for more understanding and more inspiration. The continued exploration of recent folk art, this rich field of formal invention and allegorical continuity, is perhaps one of the last frontiers in twentieth-century American art.

Jane Livingston is former associate director and chief curator of the Corcoran Gallery of Art, Washington, D.C. She is presently an author and president of Jane Livingston and Associates, Washington, D.C.

NOTES

1. In the early stages of my repeated exposure to this avalanche of quirky narrative art, whatever predilection I developed for a few of these artists stemmed from my earlier close familiarity with the extraordinarily independent and tough-minded, if magically seductive, sculptures of Cliff Westermann: I had installed a retrospective exhibition of his work at the Los Angeles County Museum of Art in 1971. Westermann was, and remains, perhaps the greatest artist of his eccentric genre to emerge in the 1960s; until Philip Guston's late period, few could match his conceptual inventiveness and formal authority. But it had become ever clearer to me that sources other than the handful of Chicago or California artists working against the grain of abstraction and minimalism had to be at work in creating the conditions for the efflorescence of this kind of art in the 1970s—and soon I was to find them for myself.

2. In the 1977 Corcoran biennial, a show that featured artists from all parts of the United States, I included a single folk artist, O. W. "Pappy" Kitchens, with his ambitious cycle of paintings, *Redeye the Rooster*. To my surprise, no one remarked on its anomalousness.

3. I know this from experience as a purchasing museum curator. The same principle applies much less predictably when dealing with such highly tutored artists as William Copley or Ralph Earl; here a more "difficult" picture may win out over an immediately seductive one, in the name of psychological veracity or compositional superiority. With the untrained artist, formal attributes seem to apply less reliably: many errors of judgment are thus allowed to remain unchallenged.

4. *Exhibiting Cultures: The Poetics and Politics of Museum Display* (Washington, D.C.: Smithsonian Institution Press, 1991).

5. Jane Livingston and John Beardsley, *Black Folk Art in America, 1930–1980* (Jackson: University Press of Mississippi; Washington, D.C.: Corcoran Gallery of Art, 1982), p. 20.

6. The often-observed practice among folk artists of passing on their craft to children, or others, whose imitative efforts generally produce works inferior to those of the elder artist, is a separate, if in its own way intriguing, matter.

ARTISTS, FOLK AND TRAINED: AN AFRICAN-AMERICAN PERSPECTIVE

LOWERY STOKES SIMS

In the Fall 1991 issue of *American Art* magazine, Kinshasha Conwill, director of the Studio Museum in Harlem, made the following observations about the favor currently enjoyed by African-Americans in the folk art field:

> In the past two decades, the art of self-taught African-American artists has been increasingly in demand. What is it about this art that is so engaging that curators, collectors, dealers, critics, and trained artists have devoted major exhibitions, publications, hours of discussion, and passion to its study and acquisition? Is it mere coincidence that so many of the artists are southern, poor, black and without formal training, and that those who collect their work are often white, educated, and affluent? Why are some of these same individual collectors and institutions apparently less interested in the work of trained black artists, such as Maren Hassinger, Melvin Edwards, or Howardena Pindell? Is the incorporation of formalist strategies by these artists a liability? Is the work of self-taught artists somehow more "authentic" . . . ?[1]

These sentiments echo the quandary in which I found myself a few years ago while jurying an exhibition of emergent African-American artists for the Southeastern Center for Contemporary Art in Winston-Salem, North Carolina. Among the nominees for inclusion in the exhibition, *Next Generation: Southern Black Aesthetic*,[2] were a number of well-known African-American folk artists. Given the long and continuous struggle of African-American artists for recognition in the art world, I was concerned that the inclusion of works by self-taught artists might skew the message sent to the art world. After all, many so-called trained African-American artists continue to struggle against glib presumptions about politically correct African-American art. Those who do abstract art are still dismissed as imitators of their white counterparts (in spite of the pervasive tradition of abstraction in African art and design) and are thus effectively denied wider recognition and acceptance in the art world.

In the winter of 1989–90, as I reviewed the slide trays over and over, the incipient competition I had in mind between "black stream" (i.e., politically correct, figurative, "ethnic") versus "mainstream" (assimilationist, abstract, universal) African-American artists carried over to folk artists and professional artists. In the final tally I did include several self-taught artists—Hawkins Bolden, Lonnie B. Holley, Jesse Lott—but this decision was predicated on the innate strength of their work, which was compatible with that of the other artists chosen. It also made sense in view of the fact that several of the trained artists, in turn, used folk characteristics or elements as part of their style (Terry Adkins, Joyce Scott, Gregory A. Henry) or subject matter (Thomas Miller, Beverly Buchanan). This work was indicative of the cultural reclamation made by African-American artists during the 1980s, in which they introduced a myriad of African-American folklore elements into their work and sparked a renewed interest in and integration of various "outsider" artistic populations—including folk art—into the artistic mainstream. These phenomena and the historical background that informs them will be the basis for this discussion.

Despite Kinshasha Conwill's concern, the relationship between African-American "high" art and "folk" art has always been tantalizingly close. Particular events in the history of modernism in European and American art as a whole encouraged this. Folk art was only one source for the modernist aesthetic that revolutionized and radicalized academic painting. In Paris and New York, Euro-American artists also looked to traditional African, Pre-Columbian, Native American, and Oceanic arts (and sometimes Asian and Near Eastern art, especially Islamic art) and to the art of children and the mentally challenged (from deficiency to insanity). These art manifestations were celebrated, observed, and even copied in an attempt to reach the source of spontaneous, "authentic" artistic expression.

As played out in the social climate of the Western cultural world, the interjection of African-Americans into this aesthetic fray resulted in peculiar and particular intersections and juxtapositions. For example, the interest in African tribal art coincided with a vogue in popular culture for other nonacademic (then, anyway) forms of expression that sprang from the creative wellspring of African-Americans, most notably the blues, jazz, popular dances from the Caribbean (e.g., the beguine), and models of elegant and nubile sensuality, exemplified in the persona of a Josephine Baker.

During the Harlem Renaissance, while many of the stereotypical postures that catered to white fantasies often resulted in the kitschier forms of black expression, African-Americans themselves critiqued assimilationist postures within their more bourgeois ranks and searched for ways to unite incipient Afrocentric aspirations[3] with the "essentialist" aesthetic of art deco and its stylistic offspring, the so-called moderne style. An example of this phenomenon was Aaron Douglas's mural, *Aspects of Negro Life* (1934), installed at the Countee Cullen branch of the New York Public Library. These four panels display allegorical representations of various historical periods and cultural manifestations of the African-American in the United States. Douglas created densely populated compositions, painted in delicate purples, mauves, yellows, and greens, in a style that artist and art historian David Driskell has characterized as a combination of "modernism and Africanism in an astonishing synthesis, creating compositions that were spatially flat, formally abstracted."[4]

In adapting a "geometric symbolism instead of concrete realism,"[5] Douglas directed African-American artists to a modernist idiom that could accommodate an ethnocentric perspective. He conceived a style in which forms were reduced to flat, silhouetted shapes in elegant positions that directly served the organizational needs of the composition and allowed a more "ethnic" look to his work. In his murals Douglas avoided the caricature that similar stylistic means led to in the work of other contemporary artists—be they white (Paul Colin), Mexican (Miguel Covarrubias), or African-American (Palmer Hayden)—by eliminating specific articulation of the features of each figure, presenting instead more anonymous entities.

Jacob Lawrence later confirmed the success of this approach to figuration as an ethnically useful modernist statement. In gouache paintings of episodes from African-American life and history that appeared in the late 1930s and early 1940s, Lawrence employed similar flat, simplified areas of color and a direct expressiveness, manifested in exaggerated body proportions and gestures, to depict the sagas of heroes and heroines such as Toussaint L'Ouverture, Frederick Douglass, and Harriet Tubman as well as the daily lives of African-Americans. His work has continued to straddle the designations of illustration and image making, narrative realism and abstraction, and for this reason has been subject to divergent critical assessment—one being to place him among folk artists, despite his formal art training. In his 1943 publication *Modern Negro Art*, James Porter included Lawrence in his chapter on "Naive and Popular Sculpture and Painting." Porter interpreted Lawrence's deliberate modernisms—the cultivation of simplified, flat areas of color, emphasis on design, eschewing of pictorial conventions such as one-point perspective—as evidence of the artist's alleged "innocence" and "unspoiled" quality.[6] Porter's perspective on Lawrence might be explained by a bias for more "academically" accomplished work as the desirable route for African-American artists attempting to gain wider acceptance in the arts. But his attitude contrasts with that of other writers—both white and African-American—who thought that African-American artists should pursue styles that expressed their unique racial heritage. As explored during the period between the two world wars, these debates were the latest in a prolonged process of defining the role and position of African-Americans within American art.

During the eighteenth and nineteenth centuries, discussions about African-American creativity mainly concerned whether African-Americans were capable—both intellectually and spiritually—of embarking on careers in the "fine" arts. Through the efforts and achievements of artists such as Robert Duncanson, Edmonia Lewis, Edmund Bannister, and Henry Tanner—to name only a few—this question was laid to rest. By the 1920s African-Americans could boast of a solid history of achievement within the stylistic currents of the art establishments of America and Europe, and now they were faced with decisions about what and how they should paint. While nineteenth-century artists had produced work that spoke only occasionally to the black condition, and then only in the most appropriate of high art mannerisms, African-American artists in the twentieth century were asked to consider why they had forsaken their African roots to produce copies of the work of their white counterparts. At first haunted by doubts of their ability to assimilate, they were now being urged to return to the very cultural roots that white society had previously reviled and defiled—all because European and Euro-American art circles had finally recognized the art of Africa!

The Harmon Foundation launched one of the first volleys in this discussion. In the late 1920s the foundation encouraged African-American recipients of its visual art awards to cultivate a style predicated on African art, and to strive to "develop an art devoid of academic or Caucasian influence, and to promote the African-American theme as a vital phase in the artist's expression of African-American life."[7] In this context we might look at the work of Palmer Hayden, who in 1926 received the first Harmon Foundation Gold Award for painting. Hayden's figural style shows the stereotypical imagery that was then popular in advertising and decorative arts in the United States and Europe. Although the figures in Aaron Douglas's murals are comparable to those in Hayden's watercolors, Hayden's work has always been suspect in certain African-American contexts because his delineation of facial features—emphasizing a stark contrast between skin color and exaggerated lips, and large, staring eyes—flaunted similarities with popular black stereotypes. But in fact Hayden was drawing on sources from popular art, and the modernist simplification that characterized the permutations of cubism found in 1920s modernist design—a convention also seen in the work of Jacob Lawrence—led some to confuse Hayden's work with folk art and its philosophical base. In Hayden's case the confusion was amplified by the fact that he had spent some time in the early 1920s with a circus troupe for which he did show advertisements in a direct, simplified, "folk" style.[8]

But it was not only white agencies such as the Harmon Foundation that called for the development of an African-American art style. Indeed, writing in 1931, no less an individual than Alain Locke, the quintessential African-American man of letters, also came to the conclusion that African-American artists "must evolve a racial style gradually and naturally."[9] Locke's comments were published in tandem with reviews of exhibitions of African-American art by white critics, such as Cyril Kay Scott,[10] who complained about the "imitative and derivative character" of the work of African-American artists. Scott wrote that "African sculpture . . . has been pronounced by some of our greatest living art critics as comparable in importance to that of the Greeks."[11] African-American art students evidently were not interested, however, as "they want to paint and sculpt like everyone else. What they get from Africa comes in tenth-rate dilution when the fountain head is at their feet."[12] Scott's antidote to this "white washing" was the "simplicity and directness of folk art" and African primitive art, which had already "so profoundly affected the great European modernists."[13] Locke enjoined his own support of "the constructive lesson of African art," whose "art creed is beauty in use . . . an art vitally rooted in the crafts, uncontaminated with the blight of the machine and soundly integrated with life."[14]

This celebration of manual work and crafts as a remedy for mechanization is a familiar strain in writings on American folk art. Holger Cahill and Sidney Janis, who curated exhibitions of folk art in the 1930s and 1940s, lauded this aspect of folk art—both in the appreciation of historical examples and in the work of contemporary individuals. But while such nostalgia could easily be indulged by Euro-American artists in search of spiritual revival, its adoption by African-American artists seemed to hamper any gains toward the professionalization of their work (which was at least accessible to Euro-American artists). The utilitarian emphasis of these principles closely paralleled the focus on tradesmanship that formed the cornerstone of Booker T. Washington's educational philosophy, which stood in stark contrast to the more philosophical and academic approach favored by W. E. B. du Bois.

There was one African-American artist who willingly accepted the conventions of folk art and primitivism: William Henry Johnson. His work has garnered attention for its forthright adoption of stylistic conventions that have been characterized as "folk" but are more precisely related to European primitivism as seen in German and Scandinavian expressionism in the first two decades of this century. As art historian Richard J. Powell has observed, however, Johnson's lifelong exploration of "primitivism" is distinctive in that he turned the exploration in on himself rather than outward to the appropriation of other cultural forms. Powell writes:

> Johnson believed his work stood apart from the then-prevalent European preoccupation with "the primitive." . . . He observed in a 1932 interview for a Danish newspaper, "I have still been able to preserve the primitive in me. . . . My aim is to express in a natural way what I feel, what is in me, both rhythmically and spiritually, all that which in time has been saved up in my family of primitiveness and tradition, and which is now concentrated in me."[15]

While his fellow artist Romare Bearden—writing three years later—would concur with the Harmon Foundation line in only the most general terms (encouraging African-American artists to develop "a social philosophy and definite ideology" distinct from their white contemporaries),[16] Johnson "attributed his artistic talents to his background's racial and cultural blend" of African and Native American cultures.[17] As Powell notes:

> For Johnson . . . the primitive impulse presented itself not only in works that resembled so-called tribal arts but in all works that took a life-and-death, heartfelt and intuitive cue from their non-Western counterparts. . . . Johnson's primitivism turned inward, focusing on a self defined by racial difference, cultural distinctiveness, a marginal status in society, and an identification with black, fundamentalist spirituality.[18]

Johnson's attitude is contrasted with George S. Schuyler's insistent denial of distinct African-American racial characteristics in the arts. In a 1926 article, "The Negro Art Hokum," Schuyler stated bluntly:

> Negro art "made in America" is as non-existent as the widely advertised profundity of Cal Coolidge, the "seven years of progress" of Mayor Hylan, or the reported sophistication of New Yorkers. Negro art there has been, is, and will be among the numerous black nations of Africa; but to suggest the possibility of any such development among the ten million colored people in this republic is self-evident foolishness. . . . Aside from his color . . . your American Negro is just plain American. Negroes and white from the same localities in this country talk, think, and act about the same. Because a few writers . . . have seized upon imbecilities of the Negro rustics and clowns and palmed them off as authentic and characteristic Aframerican behavior, the common notion that the black American is so "different" from his white neighbor has gained wide currency.[19]

Schuyler's brusque dismissal of a unique black aesthetic cuts to the quick of the problematic nature of claiming a racial basis in the arts. Although traces of African culture can be found in a multitude of customs, habits, beliefs, and speech, for the most part the black bourgeoisie by the twentieth century was well assimilated into American life. The postulation of a genetic propensity toward certain behaviors and attitudes took on a particularly problematic nuance in the 1930s with the ascendancy of the racialist ideologies of Nazism.[20]

If the art establishment and certain African-American spokesmen were stymied by intimations of racial determinism, or by mere careerist ambitions on the part of African-American artists in their search for an "essential" artistic African-American self, they were able to find the desired qualities of authenticity and ethnic individuation in the work of African-American folk artists. And it was in the person of Horace Pippin that the American avant-garde would find its first "authentic" folk artist. Pippin's rise exemplifies the peculiar relationships that informed a folk artist's career in the era of twentieth-century art. Born in 1888, Pippin began painting after World War I, when he returned to West Chester, Pennsylvania, disabled by a wounded right arm and hand. He began to paint, probably to expiate painful memories of the war, and was discovered by Christian Brinton, of the West Chester Art Center, and N. C. Wyeth. Philadelphia art dealer Robert Carlin soon began to represent his work, and ultimately the collector Albert C. Barnes became a patron. Pippin's work was soon included in exhibitions of popular and folk art organized by Holger Cahill and Sidney Janis at the Museum of Modern Art, among other institutions.

Barnes's interest in Pippin's work was informed by his own engagement with the potentialities of African-American creativity. This, in turn, was a logical outgrowth of his interest in modern art. The innovators in twentieth-century Western art sought the wellspring of nonacademic, non-Western peoples to revitalize and renovate their own art. Barnes lent his voice to those debating whether a uniquely black art could be developed in the United States. If the Harmon Foundation tended to support more professional artists, a folk artist like Pippin undoubtedly whetted Barnes's interest because of the presumption of "authenticity."[21] A notice in *Art Digest* in 1941 hailed the emergence of Pippin and noted the recent acquisition of his work by the Barnes Foundation and the Philadelphia Museum of Art. But this blurb goes on to note the importance of Pippin's work because of the absence of the "sophisticated primitivism seen so often among school-trained pretenders."[22] This comment seems to indicate that seekers of authenticity were attuned to its genuine manifestations. After all, Pippin's formal approach to painting is quite distinct from that of Johnson, Lawrence, and Douglas, and none of their work is particularly "authentic" as an African art.

Horace Pippin's work was included in several important exhibitions of "self-taught" or "naive" artists during the 1930s and 1940s. Holger Cahill's *Masters of Popular Art* opened in 1938, and Sidney Janis's *They Taught Themselves: American Primitive Painting of the 20th Century* appeared in 1942 with an accompanying publication. These exhibitions occurred alongside but distinct from exhibitions of American "folk" art which marked the resurgence of interest in America's artistic heritage of the eighteenth and nineteenth centuries. These latter exhibitions—debuting with Juliana Force's 1924 exhibition at the Whitney Studio Club—were part of a wider American folk art activity at commercial galleries such as the Downtown Gallery, whose founder, Edith Halpert, was an early supporter of American modernist artists Stuart Davis, Charles Sheeler, and others. They also coincided with the founding of the Abby A. Rockefeller Folk Art Center in Virginia, whose principal patron was also one of the founding members of the Museum of Modern Art. As noted earlier, this revival occurred within the embrace of modernism because, as Holger Cahill noted, "primitive and naive art . . . had a quality which gave them a certain kinship with modern art."[23]

But for the most part African-Americans in general and twentieth-century self-taught artists in particular were not included in this folk art revival. This was the result of the peculiar ways in which the two fields were defined as well as some rather pointed historical biases and perhaps, more or less explicitly, some class ones. In his introduction to the catalogue for the 1932 exhibition *American Folk Art: The Art of the Common Man in America, 1750–1900*, Holger Cahill noted that the exhibition included "pictures and sculptures . . . [by] . . . craftsmen and amateurs of the eighteenth and nineteenth centuries who . . . [were] house painters, sign painters, portrait limners, carpenters, cabinet makers, shipwrights, wood carvers, stone cutters, metal workers, black smiths, sailors, farmers, businessmen, housewives and girls in boarding school. . . . This work gives a living quality to the story of American beginnings in the arts, and is a chapter, intimate and quaint, in the social history of this country."[24] African-Americans certainly figured in that social history. Their absence could be explained by their anonymity, although Euro-American folk artists were not immune to such a fate.

The peculiar dynamic in the case of African-Americans, of course, was that in the eighteenth and nineteenth centuries most artists from that community—folk or otherwise—were slaves. But certainly free African-Americans were working, as testified by the career of Joshua Johnston in Baltimore. His absence from Cahill's exhibition might be explained by the fact that his career wasn't fully explicated until the publication in 1942 of a monograph by Dr. J. Hall Pleasants.[25] The issue of genre might also explain this lacuna in the 1932 exhibition. Cahill explicitly concentrated on painting and sculpture even within his definition of folk art—a decision that inadvertently expressed the often-encountered prejudice of "high" or "fine" art as opposed to "low" or "popular" art.[26] As revealed in the research undertaken by scholars such as Judith Wragg Chase, Regenia Perry, and John M. Vlach over the last two decades, African-Americans as slave tradesmen and artisans tended to be involved in more decorative or utilitarian object making.[27]

But such painstaking explanations are rendered unnecessary by Cahill's comment that "most of the early craftsmen were English."[28] He acknowledged the presence of Scotch, Welsh, Irish, Dutch, German, Swedish, and French populations and noted their influence, but made no mention of African-Americans. That he was aware of ethnic traditions other than those of northern Europe is clear from his nod to the folk art of the southwestern United States, which, he observed, had "Spanish influence" and a "religious character related to Mexican colonial art."[29] But, he noted, this work was not included in the exhibition. Cahill's use of the word "folk," then, presumed specific biases of historical precedent and Eurocentricism that affected the American folk art field.

Sidney Janis responded to this situation ten years later in his publication *They Taught Themselves: American Primitive Painters of 20th Century Art*. Janis made explicit the role of American folk art in defining an American ethos, one which presumably could not include African-Americans, recent immigrants, Latinos, or contemporary, living individuals, since folk art collecting is "based on historical interest and national sentiment, as well as esthetic evaluation."[30] For that reason, Janis noted, the "primitives of the late 19th century and today do not share this recognition."[31] Janis undertook an examination of terminology to illuminate the distinctions that informed the field at the time. It is interesting that he ultimately rejected "folk artists," "instinctives," "naives," and even "primitives" as designations for self-taught artists and settled on "self-taught," because this term could also accommodate trained artists who consciously adapted the mannerisms of the self-taught.[32] This didn't much help the situation of African-American artists. Inevitably reviews of group exhibitions of African-American artists in the 1930s and 1940s made note of the occupations of the artists[33]—in much the same way self-taught artists were written about—as if this rendered their efforts any less serious or professional than those of their white counterparts.

The turning point for contemporary black folk art was clearly the exhibition *Black Folk Art in America, 1930–1980*, organized in 1982 by Jane

Livingston and John Beardsley at the Corcoran Gallery of Art, Washington, D.C. Their work, along with that of the African-American art historian Regenia Perry, redefined the approach to this art. In the catalogue of the Corcoran exhibition, Livingston declared a new standard for looking at African-American folk art:

> The style I am characterizing has to do not with crafts or traditional utilitarian artisanship, but with full-fledged gratuitous art objects, paintings and drawings and sculptures. The artists working in this esthetic territory are generally untutored yet masterfully adept, displaying a grasp of formal issues so consistent and so formidable that it can be neither unselfconscious nor accidentally achieved.[34]

Gone were the gratuitous references to "day" jobs and implications of a lack of serious, sustained commitment on the part of these artists. Livingston cleared the smog of utilitarianism from the purview of the African-American folk artist. The persistent infatuation of the 1980s art world with authenticity was now to be seen against a revival of "primitivist" postures, which paradoxically made certain kinds of art by trained African-American artists more acceptable. That art invariably was not purely abstract; it was suffused with content specific to African-American culture, and in many cases, it aped the conventions of folk art. And, again, as in the case of William Henry Johnson, the comparison was not unwelcome but actually cultivated. After years of worrying about assimilation, African-American artists found reinforcement for their work, acknowledgment of their authenticity within primitivist postures, and forthrightly declared their experience as the focus of their subject matter.

This was explicitly noted in the published report for "The Arts of Black Folk," a conference on African-American folk arts sponsored in 1988 by the Schomburg Center for Research in Black Culture (New York Public Library) and the Folk Art Program of the New York State Council on the Arts. Diana N'Diaye, folk cultural specialist in the Office of Folk Life Programs at the Smithsonian Institution, declared a new relationship between folk and trained artists:

> The folk arts are a source of inspiration for much of our contemporary music, dance literature and visual arts. African-American art is replete with references and inspirations from traditions. . . . Beyond the richness and delight that the folk arts bring to our lives, they are also important adaptive mechanisms. The folk artists give us a sense of being rooted in time as they reflect and reinforce our connection to other communities of African Descent. They honor our elders on their own terms, and celebrate our creativity as a people. Properly interpreted, they promote a sense of continuity and self-esteem for us and our children. They present us to the world with dignity, often countering negative stereotypical, superficial and shallow images.[35]

What intervened to assuage the contentiousness of the African-American art world before World War II was black liberation, whose forces gained momentum during the late 1950s and 1960s. As part of this attempt to define a new assertive African-American identity, artists began to ally themselves with their communities. They experimented incessantly with ways to make the visual arts more relevant to African-Americans as a whole and to reinsert themselves into a community from which they had long estranged themselves due to specific notions of career advancement. From the communal collage that Romare Bearden suggested to the artist group Spiral in the early 1960s, to the community murals and collaborative projects embarked on by the Smokehouse group (spearheaded by artists William T. Williams and Mel Edwards), to Benny Andrews and Cliff Joseph's Black Emergency Cultural Coalition, African-American artists were at the forefront of redefining the conceptual nature of "community" among African-Americans. It was, therefore, no wonder that a good number of them would return to African-American folk art.

Diana N'Diaye specifically mentioned Romare Bearden and Faith Ringgold as visual artists who were influenced and inspired by black folk art traditions.[36] Both artists moved away from abstraction to figuration, from expounding "universalist" themes to finding the universal in the African-American experience. Bearden adapted a collage technique grounded in cubism to celebrate the lush sensuality, raw economic challenge, and creativity of life in rural North Carolina and urban Pittsburgh and New York, where he divided his time in childhood. In myriad works created between the mid-1960s and his death in 1988, Bearden featured two aspects of African-American folk expression: the blues musician and the quilt created by women. They function as creative surrogates for masses of African-Americans, and at the same time, these two folk arts ground Bearden's own endeavors in a historical context, imbuing it with a validity established according to African-American criteria.

Besides utilizing subject matter from folk art, some artists also adapted folk idioms to their work. This can be seen in the work of Faith Ringgold. Ringgold brought quilt making into the realm of the fine arts by combining sewing and appliqué work with painting on canvas. She developed this technique in collaboration with her mother, Willie Posey, who was a seamstress and dress designer. Ringgold's work is also contextualized within feminist art concerns that seek to validate and celebrate the private and often anonymous creativity of women, so often ignored in the official art historical records. The quilt seems to be the most obvious genre for that statement. Since the late 1960s Ringgold has adopted a straightforward figural style to illustrate her narrative or group compositions which further links her work to the private obsessions and eye for detail that informs so much folk art.

Baltimore-based Joyce Scott also has worked collaboratively with her mother, Elizabeth Scott, an inventive and expressionistic quilter. Scott brings to her beaded sculpture and related jewelry, or "art wear," craft skills honed in residencies and travels all over the world. Scott enjoys political commentary, which is most directly conveyed in her performance work but can be accommodated even in her jewelry making, where her complex narratives in three dimensions seem to belie the decorative function of her work.

This sense of generational continuity in the arts and the close association between what would be considered "fine" and "folk" art are surprisingly prevalent among the community of African-American artists. Even sculptor Mel Edwards attributes his artistic interests to his father's attempts at self-taught Sunday painting, and Beverly Buchanan traces her sculptural impulses to observing her father tinker in his workshop. In the case of Betye Saar and Alison Saar, two generations have found a wellspring for their work in mediating the boundaries between folk art and high art, starting with Betye Saar's pioneering use of flea market finds and popular imagery of blacks to reconstitute an assertive African-American identity. The elder Saar has sustained her creative skill in manipulating found objects for more than thirty years. The box assemblages that first brought her notice in the 1960s and 1970s are replete with manufactured folk nuances, recalling our natural predilection for heirlooms and remembrances. They incorporate snapshots and greeting cards with stereotypical images in a way that suggests the personal creative gestures by which we claim our own lives. Alison, the daughter, has played off the ethereal legacy evoked by her mother to create sculptural works that more forthrightly proclaim their folk inspiration, both in subject matter and in technique. Although Saar notes that she is not interested in imitating folk art, she does respect the fact that self-taught artists continue to work "even though no one is out there saying, 'So go ahead, make art and you can be a famous artist.' They're just doing it for reasons that are internal and they really have a message."[37] In the Saars' work, a syncretic blend of African-American, Caribbean, and Latin American elements finds new meaning and context.

Stylistic and technical parallels can be seen between the work of self-taught artists and that of other African-American artists who received critical notice in the 1980s. Terry Adkins's sculpture from existing industrial detritus approaches the assemblages made from found elements by folk artist Lonnie B. Holley. Painter Gregory A. Henry's use of flat simplified shapes to depict everyday objects finds a kinship with the drawings of folk artist Bill Traylor. Beverly Buchanan's shack sculpture and Tyree Guyton's architectural reclamations in the Detroit Heidenburg Project defy the distinction between vernacular and "professional" architecture and recall the environmental aspects of James Hampton's *The Throne of the Third Heaven of the Nation's Millennium General Assembly*. In her site-specific installations, Martha Jackson Jarvis mimics the practice of placing broken crockery on African-American graves to symbolize the break with this world as one enters the next. Jarvis recycles bits of broken clay tiles and forms as she installs the wall pieces that have become her hallmark. As she has observed, her works are "reconstructed vehicles of communication, conduits through which forces flow," and these forces emanate from the "powers that affect life in its broadest aspects in the society."[38] And finally, Tom Miller's reappropriation of black stereotypes and tropical decorative motifs in his painted, constructed furniture prove the richness of source material in popular culture for artists.

These are but a few examples of contemporary artists working within folk idioms. Robert Farris Thompson has inferred that it is through the appreciation of African-American folk art that the art world was at last able to grapple with the unique aspects of the work of trained African-American artists in its midst.[39] The careers of African-American folk artists, in the meanwhile, have continued to build on the momentum established by the Corcoran exhibition and consequently have assumed a more "professional" cast. Indicative of the reclamation of traditional folk culture within the ranks of professional African-American artists, a number of self-taught artists are regularly included in historical surveys of African-American art, including William Edmondson, Bill Traylor, Minnie Evans, and Clementine Hunter, as well as Horace Pippin. More recent "discoveries" such as Bessie Harvey, Nellie Mae Rowe, Mose Tolliver, and members of the Dial family have also found currency within the discussion of African-American art as a whole. The aforementioned search for authenticity certainly engendered the explosion of interest in this work, and in the context of the 1980s indicated a particular urge to counteract the perception of widespread social, political, and economic excesses of the time.

This renewed interest in folk art comes as the southern United States experiences a resurgence, perhaps most pointedly indicated by the Democratic ticket elected into office just as this essay was being written. That African-American folk artists would be bolstered in this context is almost a foregone conclusion. As Jane Livingston noted in her catalogue essay for the 1982 Corcoran exhibition: "Perhaps fully half of the truly great artists in the recent American folk genre from the early 1920s to the present are black, and predominantly southern black."[40] This fact poses interesting questions about the influence of an African-American ethos in not only the southern aesthetic but also folk art as a whole. In the catalogue for the 1990 exhibition *Another Face of the Diamond: Pathways through the Black Atlantic South*, Judith McWillie and Robert Farris Thompson convincingly argued for the direct expression of African symbologies that have survived in this hemisphere, particularly in the work of African-American folk artists.[41] Of the eleven artists in that exhibition, nine are also included here: Hawkins Bolden, Thornton Dial, Sr., Minnie Evans, Ralph Griffin, Lonnie B. Holley, Joe Louis Light, Charlie Lucas, John "J. B." Murry, and Mary T. Smith. With the integration of these artists into this exhibition, the success of color-blind evaluation of art becomes clear. Their inclusion affirms the commonality of experience and vision that George Schuyler so vociferously proclaimed back in 1926 and begs the question of the marginal status of African-American artists. This project breaks some long-standing, unspoken taboos and conspires against claims of exclusivity or cultural hegemony on the part of any group. In that case, these artists, who work for the joy of the work itself, may succeed where others have not in affirming the equality of all cultural expressions which has been the goal of a multicultural coalition of American artists during the 1980s and 1990s.

Lowery Sims is associate curator of twentieth-century art, Metropolitan Museum of Art, New York.

1. Kinshasha Conwill, "In Search of an 'Authentic Vision': Decoding the Appeal of the Self-Taught African-American Artist," *American Art* 5, no. 4 (Fall 1991), pp. 2, 4.

2. Lowery S. Sims and Adrian Piper, *Next Generation: Southern Black Aesthetic* (Winston-Salem, N.C.: Southeastern Center for Contemporary Art, 1990).

3. The most prominent of these was Marcus Garvey's drive for repatriation to Africa. Others included pre–World War II conceptions of black cultural reclamation which coalesced in Africa, the Caribbean, and the United States in a worldwide liberation movement in the 1950s and 1960s.

4. David C. Driskell, *Two Centuries of Black American Art* (Los Angeles: Los Angeles County Museum of Art; New York: Alfred A. Knopf, 1976), p. 62.

5. Elsa Fine Honig, *The Afro-American Artist: A Search for Identity* (New York: Holt, Rinehart and Winston, 1971), p. 86.

6. James Porter, *Modern Negro Art* (New York: Dryden Press, 1943), p. 152.

7. Honig, *The Afro-American Artist*, p. 88.

8. See Lowery S. Sims, *The Many Facets of Palmer Hayden* (New York: Just Above Midtown Gallery, 1977), unpaginated.

9. Alain Locke, "The American Negro as Artist," *Magazine of Art* 22, no. 3 (Sept. 1931), p. 220.

10. "The Negro Annual," *Art Digest* 8 (May 15, 1934), p. 18.

11. Ibid.

12. Ibid.

13. Quoted in Locke, "The American Negro as Artist," p. 218.

14. Ibid., p. 220.

15. Richard J. Powell, "'In My Family of Primitiveness and Tradition': William H. Johnson's *Jesus and the Three Marys*," *American Art* 5, no. 4 (Fall 1991), p. 21.

16. Romare Bearden, "The Negro Artist and Modern Art," *Opportunity* 13 (Dec. 1934), pp. 371–72.

17. Powell, "'In My Family,'" p. 21. Powell also notes that Johnson's parentage was more likely white and African-American (p. 22).

18. Ibid., p. 26.

19. George Schuyler, "The Negro Art Hokum," *The Nation* (June 16, 1926), reprinted in Nathan Huggins, *Voices from the Harlem Renaissance* (New York: Oxford University Press, 1976), pp. 309–12.

20. Both James Porter and art historian Meyer Shapiro tackled the issue of race in relationship to art; see James A. Porter, "Negro Art and Racial Bias," *Art Front* 4 (June–July 1937), pp. 8–9, and Meyer Shapiro, "Race, Nationality and Art," *Art Front* 3 (March 1936), pp. 10–12.

21. See Albert C. Barnes, "Negro Art, Past and Present," *Opportunity* 4 (May 1926), pp. 148–49, 168–69.

22. "Museums Buy Pippin," *Art Digest* 43 (March 1, 1944), p. 13.

23. Holger Cahill, *American Folk Art: The Art of the Common Man in America, 1750–1900* (New York: Museum of Modern Art, 1932), pp. 26–27.

24. Ibid., pp. 3, 5.

25. J. Hall Pleasants, *Joshua Johnston, the First American Negro Portrait Painter* (Baltimore: Maryland Historical Society, 1942).

26. Michael D. Hall makes note of Kenneth Ames's provocative supposition that the category commonly known as "folk" art may be a "cultural fabrication," which "tells us about ourselves and about the worlds we invent to support the social-cultural myths we live by"; see Michael D. Hall, "The Mythic Outsider, Handmaiden to the Modern Muse," *New Art Examiner*, Sept. 1991, p. 16.

27. See Judith Wragg Chase, *Afro-American Art and Craft* (New York: Van Nostrand Reinhold, 1971); Regenia Perry, "Black American Folk Art: Origins and Early Manifestations," in Jane Livingston and John Beardsley, *Black Folk Art in America, 1930–1980* (Jackson: University Press of Mississippi; Washington, D.C.: Corcoran Gallery of Art, 1982), pp. 25–37; John M. Vlach, *The Afro-American Tradition in Decorative Arts* (Cleveland: Cleveland Museum of Art, 1978; reprint, Athens: University of Georgia Press, 1990).

28. Cahill, *American Folk Art*, p. 4.

29. Ibid., p. 8.

30. Sidney Janis, *They Taught Themselves: American Primitive Painters of the 20th Century* (New York: The Dial Press, 1942), p. 4.

31. Ibid.

32. Ibid., pp. 11–13.

33. See, for example, "Negro Artists in Fifth Harmon Foundation Exhibit," *Art Digest* 7 (March 1, 1933), p. 23; "Harmon Foundation Exhibition of Paintings and Sculpture," *Art Digest* 5 (Feb. 15, 1931), p. 7; and "Harlem Library Shows Negro Art" *Art News* 31 (May 20, 1933), p. 14.

34. Livingston and Beardsley, *Black Folk Art in America*, p. 11.

35. Deirdre L. Bibby and Diana Baird N'Diaye, eds., *The Arts of Black Folk* (New York: Schomburg Center for Research in Black Culture, New York Public Library), p. 7.

36. Ibid.

37. Dinah Berland, "Artist Finds Magic in the Everyday Object, Individual," *Los Angeles Herald Examiner*, Feb. 21, 1987, sec. B, p. 2.

38. Artist's statement, in Leslie King Hammond and Lowery Stokes Sims, *Art As a Verb* (Baltimore: Maryland Institute College of Art, 1988), unpaginated.

39. Robert Farris Thompson, John Mason, and Judith McWillie, *Another Face of the Diamond: Pathways through the Black Atlantic South*, exh. cat. (New York: INTAR Hispanic Arts Center, 1989), p. 36

40. Livingston and Beardsley, *Black Folk Art in America*, p. 11.

41. Thompson, Mason, and McWillie, *Another Face of the Diamond*, pp. 5–11, 23–53.

A VIEW OF PARADISE FROM A DISTANT SHORE

SUSAN LARSEN

"The friendly and flowing savage, who is he?
Is he waiting for civilization, or past it and mastering it?"
—Walt Whitman, "Song of Myself," 1855[1]

A friendly regard for the art of the self-taught seems an innocent and egalitarian instinct in our age of widespread promotion and dissemination of every aspect of contemporary art. The art of the self-taught in America is boundless and seemingly ubiquitous, emerging as it has from every age group, race, gender, region, and social class. Precarious and premature hierarchies of value and expectation for this art in academic discourse are challenged each time a powerful spirit emerges from an unlikely corner of some rural county or just across town from one of our great urban museums. Among the special attractions of self-taught art is this volatility. Its story is never completely told, as compelling images and vast bodies of work emerge long after their making, thus upsetting our chronologies and requiring us to revise our texts.

We respect but are also confused by the personal unresponsiveness of the self-taught to the very precepts of style and concept we try to suggest for their art. Canons of style and contemporary theory, if encountered by them at all, are generally greeted as something created to circumscribe freedom of expression. Appreciation and support from the professional art world is often seen by these artists as just another form of admiration for their work, no more important or valuable than that of a friend or neighbor. The typical gifted artist working outside academic and contemporary norms, if indeed there is such a typical person, listens to a private inner voice quite apart from the verbal discourse by which the professional art world sets its goals and limits. The direction of the self-taught artist's work preexists his or her relationship with an art world audience and is trusted and followed despite favorable or unfavorable commentary. As we discover, evaluate, and discuss these artists, we must be aware that our point of view originates from a distant shore. Ours is an outsider's view of a private experience seen through the clouded lens of our own cultural expectations.

If the evolution of styles and concomitant conceptual shifts of emphasis in contemporary art are unknown to the self-taught, it is often the case that a rich and complete alternative cosmology and set of stylistic goals and norms have evolved within an individual's own artistic life and work. It is a mistake to assume that such artists have merely misunderstood the conventions of art making, that, ignorant of perspective and anatomy and unlearned in the theoretical constructs of recent art, they thus constitute a category of artistically retarded if inspired brethren whose value exists in the naive charm of their work or its unwitting revelations of mental pathology. Many, indeed most, of the self-taught who interest us deeply command our attention because the visual language they have fashioned is capable of an original and emotionally compelling artistic expression. We would be well-advised to study the presence and nature of these languages rather than merely their deviance from stereotypical conventions of contour modeling, perspective, and optical proportion, indexes of value long out of use in any other domain of contemporary art.

Much of the confusion, and also the vitality, of this field has arisen because the art of the self-taught has, for the most part, found its home within or alongside collections of American folk art. Eyes accustomed to the rough contours of historical folk art and its direct form of address encompassing a wide realm of religious, social, and political subject matter feel comfortable with the directly described personal experiences re-created in the art of the self-taught. It is tempting to view some self-taught contemporaries as counterparts to admired historical American painters and sculptors such as Henry Church, S. P. Dinsmoor, Edward Hicks, Morris Hirshfield, Olaf Krans, and Horace Pippin. Similarities of style and striking parallels in the biographies of older folk artists and contemporary self-taught artists have led to an inevitable bringing together of two perhaps quite dissimilar artistic worlds.

The term "outsider" is frequently used to designate the art of the self-taught, particularly those who have experienced some mental, economic, or social disability that has isolated them from the mainstream of American life. This is an evocative term, which seems to fit the circumstances of individuals who dedicate themselves to their art while functioning outside of any artistic community and often outside the norms of middle-class American experience. Outsider artists as studied and discovered in Europe in the early twentieth century were most often individuals suffering from known mental disabilities, as in the cases of the vastly gifted but deeply disturbed autodidacts Heinrich Mebes and Adolph Wolffli. Their lives as social isolates were ones of probable misfortune, filled with pain and deprivation. Studies on European outsiders are useful models when we are confronted by visionary American artists of similar tragic personal circumstances, such as Henry Darger and Martin Ramirez.

Misunderstanding arises, however, when the term outsider with its more narrow European construction is applied broadly and generally to American self-taught artists who may eschew the blandishments of galleries, critics, and appreciative viewers but are sane and functioning members of their own communities, people whose lives are typical of the vast majority of Americans, save for an unbroken commitment to the solitary path of their self-designated artistic adventure. Life outside the professional world of art, as most of our citizens can attest, is not one of tragically disabling isolation. Considering these very different forms of outsiderness as related or concomitant conditions has caused a good deal of confusion in the worlds of American folk art and contemporary art. That art historians, critics, and collectors have engendered this confusion is perhaps a reflection of their myopic focus on the narrow world of art. That we finally acknowledge it as untenable is an index of our urgent need to finally study the real creative lives of the gifted individuals whose art we profess to admire.

As we struggle to find appropriate contemporary models and acceptable terminology for the art of the self-taught in America, many who are primarily involved in mainstream art ask a pertinent and simple question. If the work of a disorganized and numberless group of self-taught Americans is so difficult to evaluate, obeys none of the norms of polite artistic society, is of modest market value, and represents wildly varying styles and marginal voices in society, then why spend the effort of will and mind to address it at all?

The many attractions of this work speak to several important value systems in twentieth-century art and also to the historical core of American artistic and political life. The attraction begins, of course, with the works of art themselves and the qualities of direct expression, innovative form, and uncensored content they present to the open-minded viewer. The boldly colorful style, dense yet accessible iconography, and wonderful speaking power of an artist like Sister Gertrude Morgan transcend the usual conceptual and chronological evaluations made by art critics. What does it matter if her art seems unrelated to the achievements of the New York School, her chronological contemporaries in American art? Indeed, an argument can be made that her religious and epistemological quest is part of a larger search among her generation for enduring spiritual values in an age of marked stress and doubt. To the extent that Sister Gertrude Morgan is acknowledged as a fully functioning and articulate American artist and not as a notable exponent of some disabled but persevering outsider class, her work and its iconography can be measured in the broader context of American art.

The self-taught artist and his autodidact contemporaries in other fields enjoyed a high level of esteem in eighteenth- and nineteenth-century America. Profound distrust of academic doctrines coupled with egalitarian support for self-definition helped to shape our national taste in the arts. Admonitions to aspiring artists abound in early American popular literature. Poor Richard, the well-known chronicler of colonial mores, offered this recipe in 1756 to aspirants in all walks of life, especially the arts, "Simplicity, Innocence, Industry, Temperance are Arts that lead to Tranquility." He went on to underscore the importance of simplicity as "pure and upright Nature, free from Artifice, Craft or deceitful ornament."[2] Clearly an overly decorative style was seen to have the potential to corrupt one's morals, but the noble and the chaste, in life and art, could lead one to self-expression and fidelity to nature.

Early American writing on the arts also commonly stressed the surpassing significance of the essential idea motivating a work of art rather than any merely meretricious grace in its execution. In the debate over style and concept, the conceptual insight of the artist earned the highest praise. An inelegant but revealing tract appearing in the *New*

York Magazine of August 13, 1796, was titled, "Rules for Judging the Beauties of Painting, Music and Poetry; Founded on a New Examination of the Word 'Thought' As Applied to the Fine Arts." It concluded, "A work of art should be judged by the thought behind it, whether in music, painting or architecture."[3]

These early homespun recipes and admonitions, while not qualifying as systematic art theory, document a consistent and deeply lodged suspicion of academic art and of professional artisans and artists who based their canons of form and content on ancient Greco-Roman or more recent European models. Simplicity and modesty rather than virtuosity and sophistication have long been trusted in American life as indicators of sincerity and honesty. The spare and elegantly crafted forms of Shaker architecture and furniture epitomize the American desire to achieve beauty through diligence and modesty. The cult of plainness has a vast literature in American art, architecture, design, literature, and philosophy. Artistic and social values engendered in the realm of folk craft and religious thought found their way into American painting as it evolved in its early years. As John M. Vlach observed in *Plain Painters* (1988): "Early New England paintings thus were works of fine art adapted to the expression of Puritan values, not works of folk art imbued with traditional values."[4]

An assumed connection between traditional craft forms of American folk art and the work of self-taught contemporaries in our midst has offered us little encouragement to study the work of gifted self-taught contemporaries in a manner this work often requires and deserves. Vlach is cool, stern, but mostly accurate when he concludes: "Given the terms with which it is usually described, twentieth-century folk art is really modern art created by artists who happen to lack a studio pedigree and who have no connection to folk culture, and it is consumed by collectors more interested in the art of the contemporary scene than in the art of traditional societies."[5] Vlach's primary interest lies in historically documented, traditional expressions of American cultural life such as utilitarian craft objects, commemorative forms of painting, and works of regional community architecture which repeat and reinforce ideals and themes created to bind together a group, a region, and a national identity.

Folk culture with its emphasis on group and community is threatened with disruption historically and in our own time by the individualistic art of the self-taught. Paradoxically, the right of the individual to self-expression is also a primary American myth taught universally in our homes, schools, and even our churches. The permission to create one's own mythology and iconography exists broadly in American life. It should be regarded as no particular surprise, and certainly as no aberration or misfortune, that we find self-taught artists who dare to make a world of their own out of paint, canvas, concrete, wood, plastic, stone, glass, and virtually any other material the twentieth century has evolved and disseminated.

In so doing they recall the artistic adventures of previous American visionaries such as Washington Allston, Erastus Salisbury Field, Albert Pinkham Ryder, John Quidor, and Elihu Vedder. In his landmark study, the art historian Abraham Davidson described their role: "The visionary painter adds to the world he depicts; he makes of it something poetic, sometimes frightening; he finds myths where in reality myths are simply inventions."[6] Davidson also concluded that the visionary impulse in American art had virtually died in the late 1950s, supplanted by the art of Jasper Johns, Andy Warhol, and others eager to demythologize American culture and its system of visual signifiers. Extending Davidson's remarks, made some fifteen years ago, one can speculate upon the great appeal of self-taught visionary artists in our own time. They may be filling a perennial role in American artistic life abandoned by the professional art world but beloved by a national audience at all levels of sophistication.

Today when we embrace the visionary and highly personal art of the self-taught it is for its unique ability to fuse concrete experiences in daily life with the imaginative play of the mind and spirit. Our interest is not merely that of the idly curious, nor do we offer our interest out of purely political or charitable motives. The ambivalence of our scholarship is oddly joined to a persistent emotional and intellectual need for the art of the self-taught. Art historians, critics, and collectors return to it again and again, each time with different models and new questions to ask of it and of ourselves.

One recalls with respect and longing the careful treatment this work enjoyed in the 1930s and early 1940s, the very years when the artists of the New York School were being discovered. Sidney Janis's landmark exhibition and book *They Taught Themselves* (1942) treated the art of gifted Americans such as John Kane, Horace Pippin, Mary Robertson Moses, and many others as the signal achievements of individuals who had lived the adventure of the artist in circumstances set apart from the professional world of art.[7] No attempt was made to connect these individuals to the long-standing literature on American folk art, and their life histories as written by Janis stand in all their normalcy and complexity as corollaries to the lives of millions of Americans, save for their focused commitment to their art.

In 1943 Alfred Barr opened the doors of the Museum of Modern Art to the work of Morris Hirshfield, a retired manufacturer of women's clothing whose abstractly stylized environments and doll-like female nudes found an appreciative audience in the circle of surrealist artists then living in New York. Barr's support of the Hirshfield exhibition, curated by art dealer and critic Sidney Janis, earned him the wrath of many MOMA trustees and supporters. The exhibition catalogue's assessment of Hirshfield is admiring, as it addresses the plain facts of his artistic background as it is relevant to the work and inspiring as an interesting tale. It may be that in the 1950s, as a robust market emerged for historical folk art, and as the art of the self-taught made its irregular and wayward course through the art system in the midst of American pride in post-war cultural achievements, the temptation to link contemporary work to older folk art became economically irresistible. A natural stylistic affinity and the ease with which folk art collectors assimilated the art of the self-taught must have encouraged this connection and helped to legitimize it. By now an established adjunct to the world of historical folk art, the art of the self-taught continues this uneasy symbiosis into the present day.

It is time to propose a more normative and accurate position for the art of the gifted self-taught in our country. No longer passing for latter-day folk art, nor qualifying for outsider status by virtue of a sensationalized artistic biography, the best of this work deserves the kind of calm and measured regard it received at the hands of pioneers like Barr and Janis. It is time for the work of the gifted self-taught to be presented in museums of art alongside that of their trained brethren, or in exhibitions devoted to the art of the self-taught as a special class of endeavor. It is time to see in-depth, seriously considered one-person exhibitions building upon the familiarity and critical judgments made possible by recent thematic or geographic surveys. If we doubt whether self-taught artists can sustain such scrutiny, we deserve the opportunity to test these limits and see if our interest is warranted and if we might indeed break through to other levels of understanding by looking more deeply. It is time to use biography fairly and calmly to merely tell us about these artists and their work rather than to use it as a vehicle to maneuver them into one category or another. It is time to lose our self-consciousness and sentimentality over this work and to treat it as art, nothing more, nothing less.

With the issue of the artist's training put aside, we might see striking parallels in the aspirations and achievements of the self-taught with those of beloved and respected figures in American art history. For example, does the spiritual fervor and communicative ability of J. B. Murry compare to the spirituality elicited in other graphic abstracted images created in our time? Is the urgency of his communication a form of expressionism or has his transcendental goal erased the self in the service of the message? Does his art have anything in common with the enterprise of reductive abstract artists who seek a state of expressive anonymity? How much did Murry invest of his consciousness in the pursuit of form? The extant literature on contemporary art may offer a great deal to the serious analysis of the art of the self-taught if we merely credit these untutored but accomplished individuals with having learned and achieved a great deal through self-teaching. By respecting their very genuine achievements, we create a common ground for them with other contemporary artists and broaden our own perspectives for analysis and understanding.

It is in our national spirit and in our hearts to honor the autodidact as our forebears did in every generation since the founding of this country. Professionals in one realm are often autodidacts in another; among the outstanding self-taught innovators in American history are such individuals as John Singleton Copley, Thomas Edison, Benjamin Franklin, Thomas Jefferson, Samuel F. B. Morse, Charles Willson Peale, and Walt Whitman. Accomplished and well-trained in some areas of life, each gave himself permission to change the artistic and scientific and political rules of his day, and some of these individuals distinguished themselves in multiple areas of endeavor entirely through their own self-directed inquiry. Most living artists will admit, indeed proudly, that the crucial developmental periods in their lives occurred outside the classroom, hence the emphasis upon gradual evolution and independent development in most artists' biographies.

We are all, to one degree or another, self-taught. The complexities of life require all of us to teach ourselves as we solve practical problems every day and master new tasks and information. The term "amateur" has a variety of meanings in common American speech. An amateur is literally one who loves a particular pursuit for itself alone and apart from any thought of remuneration or professional status. We also know that amateur can connote a degree of ineptitude or the absence of serious study of the intricacies of a given task. We often witness timidity in the performance and in the aspirations of the amateur together with an eagerness to copy accepted models such as clichés or even kitsch expressions in art, literature, music, craft, or fashion. We are perhaps rightly suspicious of the artistic products of the amateur even when his or her efforts arise from a love of a favorite endeavor. In the realm of the amateur as in the professional world of art, intentions matter little in the face of evident results.

Amateurism of the latter sort casts a dark shadow over the worthy efforts of the gifted self-taught. This is true even if we factor in a native American sentiment for the underdog and a mistrust of elitist professionalism. The gifted self-taught artist in America faces countless obstacles to recognition. It is indeed fortunate that most of these artists do not think of professional recognition as their primary goal, and that they do not place much emphasis upon the efforts of historians and critics to explicate their work. Few would be pleased to be cast into the role of the outsider as it is defined in Europe. Few self-taught artists live in the type of secluded communities where authentic folk culture can thrive undisturbed. The strong and authentic artistic voices of the self-taught are those of fellow citizens living in our own time. They are among our most capable spirits. The evidence of their art will refute any attempt to present them otherwise.

As the twenty-first century is about to begin, we have finally recognized that the folklorists' rejection of twentieth-century self-taught art was perhaps a reasoned response to a perceived end of historical folk culture. A self-taught art unabashedly individualistic, participating in late twentieth-century life, aware of technology and alive to the imagery of mass media, sometimes rootless, always dynamic, does not fit the slow, even static patterns of traditional folk art. It is instead a unique and vital ongoing complement of American cultural life, difficult to contain or chronicle, ubiquitous and unlicensed, a wilder, more perilous domain of artistic freedom.

As we mature in our consideration of the art of the self-taught, one suspects a more generous continuum will emerge. Artistic achievement among the self-taught will weigh more heavily than outward evidence of easy charm or naivete. A broader consensus is already emerging as important artists and significant bodies of self-taught art set standards by which other work is measured. The entire field will lose its novelty and acquire a more normative and productive place within the world of scholarship, museums, galleries, collectors, and the art press. Exhibitions such as the present landmark survey of southern self-taught art do a great service to the growth of this field as they deepen our understanding and acquaintance with major figures and set their work within the social, geographical, and religious worlds in which the artists lived. In the end we will have regained a valuable segment of American cultural life, which flourished during the birth of this country and has existed persistently and patiently despite many attempts to caricature or dismiss it. The art of the self-taught will not replace that of professionals nor will it supply a latter-day traditional folk culture. It has withstood our admiration and our scorn. It is perennial as the grass and will endure.

We should also look for parallel developments in other areas of American cultural life, in literature, music, horticulture, indeed across the spectrum of human endeavor. Self-taught philosopher Eric Hofer remarked, "Elitist intellectuals hug the conviction that talent and genius are rare exceptions. They are inhospitable to any suggestion that the mass of people are lumpy with unrealized potentialities. Yet there is evidence that the masses are a mine rich in all conceivable talents. We have as yet no expertise of talent mining but must wait for a chance to wash nuggets out of hidden veins."[8]

The art of the self-taught is as deeply attractive for our generation as the tribal art of Africa was for early twentieth-century European modernists or the sculpture of the Northwest Coast was for early abstract expressionists in New York City. This art sings a siren's song of freedom and as such is a seductive influence to an art world grown overripe, increasingly uncertain of its direction and hungry for an infusion of energy from some source at once alien and yet accessible. As yet we have merely identified that it exists and that its expressive power and authenticity strikes us as something legitimately a part of American art, reflecting its broadest historical and most generous identity.

Perhaps we shall reaffirm a chorus of independent voices making up our national art and recognize that it is a hearty and expansive one. Walt Whitman heard that warm and generous voice of his countrymen and knew it as his own:

> You will hardly know who I am or what I mean,
> But I shall be good health to you nevertheless,
> And filter and fibre your blood.
>
> Failing to fetch me at first keep encouraged,
> Missing me one place search another,
> I stop somewhere waiting for you.
>
> —Walt Whitman, "Song of Myself," 1855[9]

Susan Larsen is professor of art history at the University of Southern California, Los Angeles.

1. Walt Whitman, "Song of Myself," in *Leaves of Grass*, privately printed, 1855, stanza 39.

2. *Poor Richard's Almanac*, 1756, quoted in J. Meredith Neil, *Toward a National Taste: America's Quest for Aesthetic Independence* (Honolulu: University of Hawaii Press, 1975), p. 4.

3. "Rules for Judging the Beauties of Painting, Music and Poetry," *New York Magazine*, August 13, 1796, p. 65.

4. John M. Vlach, *Plain Painters: Making Sense of American Folk Art* (Washington, D.C.: Smithsonian Institution Press, 1988), p. 103.

5. Ibid., p. 175.

6. Abraham A. Davidson, *The Eccentrics and Other American Visionaries* (New York: E. P. Dutton, 1978), p. 188.

7. Sidney Janis, *They Taught Themselves* (New York: The Dial Press, 1942).

8. Eric Hofer, "Innovation and Intellectuals," in *Between the Devil and the Dragon* (New York: Harper and Row, 1982), p. 72.

9. Whitman, "Song of Myself," stanza 52.

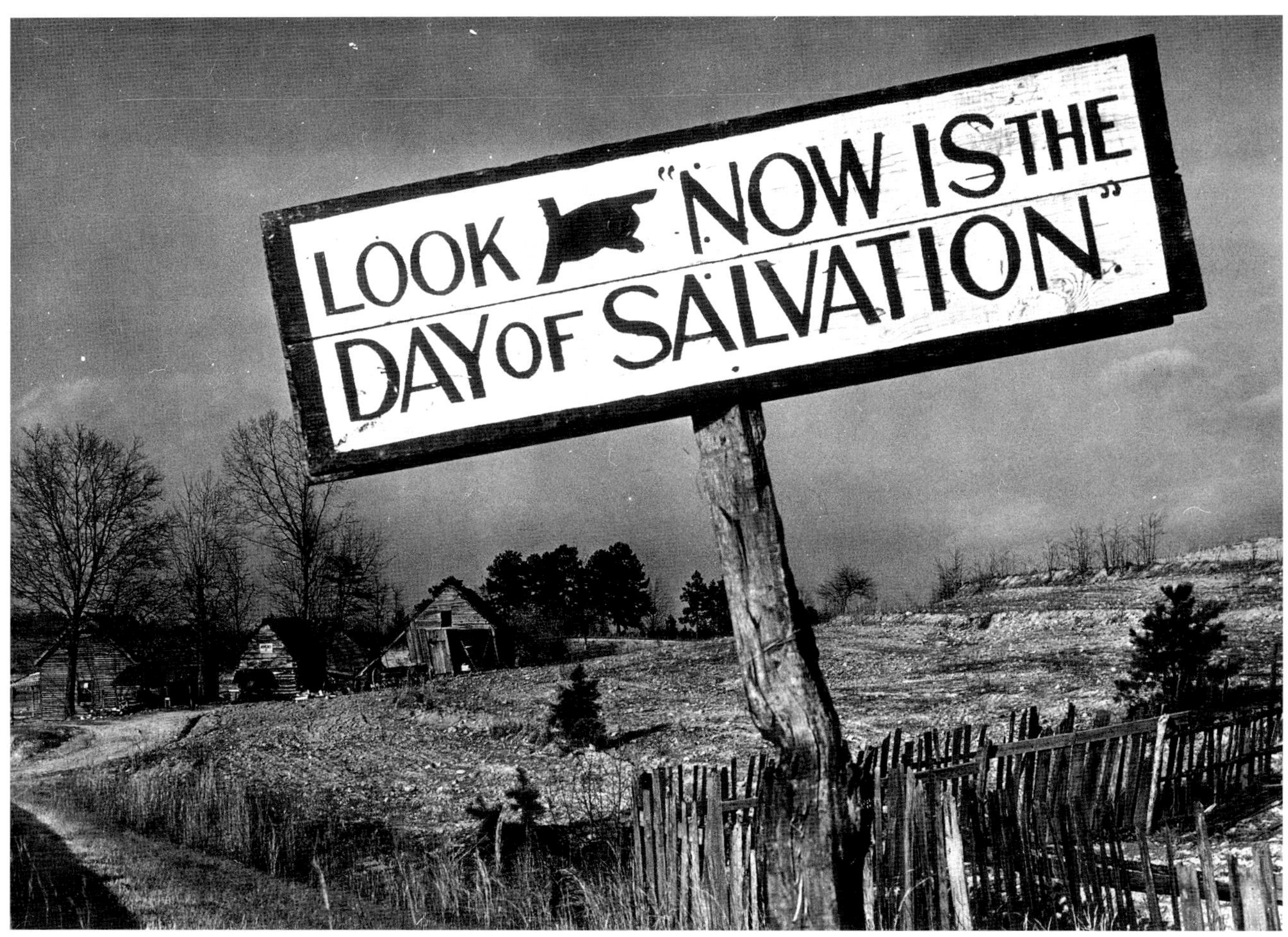

Fig. 1. "Look Now Is the Day of Salvation," Hull, Georgia, 1936. Photo Margaret Bourke-White, Margaret Bourke-White Papers, Syracuse University Library, Special Collections Department.

THE SETTING: THE SOUTH

ALICE RAE YELEN

Self-taught artists know no geographic boundaries: they exist regionally, nationally, and internationally. Since they live in communities rather than as isolated individuals, their work is informed by their cultural context. As is true of all great art, the images of the self-taught aesthetically stand on their own as powerful visual statements, revealing the individual artistic vocabulary of each maker. Yet appreciation deepens with an understanding of their context, the rich cultural environment in which the artists created and from which they emerged.

The South has long felt a sense of distinctiveness from the rest of the nation. Theories on the source of this singularity take into account the impact of slavery on the South, and the region's defeat and subsequent slow economic recovery from the Civil War, its predominately agrarian life-style, and the pervasiveness of evangelical Protestant religion.[1] This milieu contrasts with the North, for example, which experienced both military and economic success, early urban industrialization, and a far less homogeneous cultural and religious environment. In the South, people retained a sense of connection to the land, and their culture remained personalized even after urbanization and industrialization occurred.[2]

Regardless of the arguable causes, southern history has clearly stood alone within the context of American history, and southerners today still take pride in their special regional identity. Since the primary influence on most self-taught artists has been their daily environment, it is helpful to have a fuller perspective of the historical and cultural matrices that have shaped them and that inform their artwork. Among the factors that affected the region, three are paramount: the South's history of slavery and subsequent racial relations, its prolonged rural nature, and the pervasive impact of religion.

Africans were brought as slaves to the South in the middle of the seventeenth century. Although less than 5 percent of whites in the fifteen slave states were slave owners in 1850,[3] any white person, regardless of economic class, educational level, or personal morality, was viewed as superior to a black. This attitude of entitlement has been a central component of the struggle between blacks and whites. But even while complex, often virulent racial hatreds engulfed southern life, strong human relationships often formed between individual whites and blacks, who encountered one another as employer and employee after the Civil War.

When slaves were freed after the Civil War, they had no cash, no land, and no work.[4] Emerging from an unequal and often paradoxical relationship with their "masters," blacks now had to provide themselves and their families with food, clothing, and shelter. Free, but not equal, blacks experienced widespread prejudice and segregation, conditions that were formally perpetuated by Jim Crow laws. In place throughout the South by 1896, these laws were created by whites to ensure that racial segregation was strictly enforced after Emancipation. The laws mandated separate facilities for all African-Americans and effectively made them second-class citizens.

The inequities of the Jim Crow laws were closely allied to those of sharecropping. Yet tenant farming, which took hold in the reconstruction period following the Civil War, profoundly affected the lives of both black and white farmers. A landlord supplied capital, acreage, and shelter; the tenant and his family supplied their labor. The sharecropper, on the lowest rung of the tenancy farming system, seldom made any money at the end of the year and was lucky just to break even.[5] To start his next crop, the sharecropper would once again have to borrow capital, thereby re-entering a repetitive cycle with little hope of escape.

When World War II began, higher-paying factory jobs beckoned at the same time that the mechanization of farm equipment was pushing people off the land. But until then, sharecropping remained entrenched in the South. In the late 1930s, most southerners still lived in rural areas.[6] Most of the artists in this exhibition were born on farms, or their parents were raised on farms, and all but six were born by 1938. Thus an examination of the South in the 1930s and 1940s speaks of the agrarian milieu that formed most of the artists' early life experiences and attitudes.

Farm families were scattered across the countryside. Towns were predominantly small, and few and far between. (Urban centers like New Orleans, Memphis, Charleston, and Atlanta were the exceptions.) The geographic isolation of farm families was intensified by poorly developed roads. Inferior roads prolonged the provincial life-style of the rural South into the 1960s, long after good transportation had opened up other areas of the country.[7]

But isolation mandated self-reliance. With limited economic resources and neighbors too far away for easy assistance, rural citizens learned "to do" and "to make" as a function of daily life. This self-reliance often resulted in an individualism that, in those people with natural artistic impulses, translated into creative and innovative expressions. Seasonal, labor-intensive work centered on spring planting and the fall harvest, which left plenty of time for doing and making during bad weather and slow periods. This sense of reprieve helped to create a generally positive attitude in the South toward the notion of "passing the time," and many self-taught artists availed themselves of free time either throughout their lives or in retirement to pursue their creative activities. Shields Landon "S. L." Jones confirmed this sentiment: "Whittling was something I was pretty good at. Something I did to pass the time."[8]

Not only did circumstances sow the seeds of the self-taught artist's individual creativity, but the uncanny openness of southern communities to unusual behavior permitted these artists to thrive. A long-prevailing cultural attitude within the South has been a remarkable acceptance of unthreatening differences. Thus eccentrics, the poor, needy, mentally disturbed, and disabled were often countenanced and cared for by the community. This tolerance has extended to the unique, although seemingly eccentric, expressions of self-taught artists. Notwithstanding this acceptance, except for rare instances self-taught artists were not nurtured in the first half of the century. Even today, neighbors and members of their own communities, unless financially motivated, rarely encourage, understand, or place value upon their work.

Although the South demonstrated exceptional internal anomalies, it rejected challenges to its community standards, whether internal or external (such as from the North). This attitude most clearly manifested itself in racial intolerance. Not until 1954, when the Supreme Court, in its landmark decision *Brown v. Board of Education of Topeka*, declared segregation in all U.S. public schools to be unconstitutional, did the South's separate-but-equal racial barriers begin to break down. The artists in this show, all born by 1955, witnessed the significant economic, political, and social changes of the civil rights movement of the late 1950s and 1960s, the black power movement of the 1960s, and the subsequent development of African-American consciousness and the continued struggle for racial equality.

The harshness of the southern sharecropping system, combined with economic opportunities and perceived racial equality in the North, encouraged blacks to leave the South in huge numbers in the post–World War I era in what became known as the Great Migration. Whites also began relocating during the Great Depression, a movement that became a groundswell during World War II. Displaced by the mechanization of farming in the late 1930s, they too sought factory wages, particularly during World War II, in the cities of the South and North, or the promise of steady farm work in California.[9] This shift greatly affected the distribution of the South's population. Southern cities grew more than three times faster than similar American cities at a time when rapid urbanization was a nationwide phenomenon. Predominantly rural in the 1930s, with 5.5 million agricultural workers, the South by 1950 had only 3.2 million farm workers.[10] A parallel statistic describes the change in the southern black population. In 1910 (almost half the artists in this exhibition were born by this date), approximately 90 percent of the nation's blacks lived in the rural South.[11] By 1960 only one of every two remained, and of those, only one of four lived in rural areas.[12]

The shared experiences of their rural lives have bound together southern blacks and whites, despite their differences, creating a unique culture that incorporates characteristics of each. This synthesis of black and white cultural attributes might seem unlikely given the intense segregation that persisted in the South until well into the twentieth century. Yet southern blacks and whites clearly have had more general interaction with one another in daily life than their northern counterparts.

The interaction of white and black cultures has created an interesting fusion that is the dominant basis of southern culture. Among the several significant cultures that have made their imprint on the South, the special synthesis of two—Euro-American and African-American—is well confirmed by the study of folktales. The folk narratives of each group have ultimately been borrowed and changed by one another,[13] and eventually integrated into the shared southern trait of storytelling. This cultural affinity for storytelling is evident in the work of many black and white self-taught artists, including Charles Kinney, O. W. "Pappy" Kitchens, Johnnie Swearingen, Charlie Lucas, Lonnie B. Holley, Herbert Singleton, Philo Levi "Chief" Willey, and Jimmy Lee Sudduth.

Likewise, aesthetic characteristics frequently attributed to one group or another have been assimilated cross-culturally. A wonderfully rough and imperfect aesthetic incorporating natural and man-made found objects is characteristic of the imagery of many African-American artists, including J. P. Scott, Charlie Lucas, Steven Ashby, Hawkins Bolden, Thornton Dial, Sr., Ralph Griffin, Willie Massey, Mary T. Smith, and Purvis Young. Black aesthetic values have been defined by folklorist John Michael Vlach as emphasizing experimentation and improvisation,[14] resulting in unbalanced compositions that combine familiar motifs in novel ways. Scholars such as Robert Farris Thompson have documented the link between the use of found and recycled materials by black self-taught artists and their African heritage.[15] But as prevalent as such aesthetic traits are in the work of black artists, they are not unique to them. These characteristics can also be seen, albeit to a somewhat lesser degree, in the work of white folk artists such as Howard Finster, Sybil Gibson, R. A. Miller, Glassman, David Strickland, Minnie Black, and Benjamin F. Perkins, each of whom uses found or recycled objects available in his or her environment.

Religiously inspired creations, too, are aptly attributed to black artists such as Sister Gertrude Morgan, William Edmondson, Minnie Evans, Elijah Pierce, and John "J. B." Murry. Yet religiously inspired art is clearly noted among white artists like Howard Finster, R. A. Miller, Ronald Cooper, Benjamin F. Perkins, and Raymond Coins. The religious fervor of the South is not limited by racial barriers. Although blacks and whites tend to worship separately even today, they share a common foundation of evangelical Protestant beliefs that rely on the authority of the Bible, the availability of personal conversion through divine revelation, an individualistic morality, and informal worship.[16] Nonetheless they retain distinctive features in their religious practices. For whites, evangelicalism and the conversion of souls is a primary focus, whereas for blacks, worship and attending church in themselves provide religious fulfillment.[17]

The individual conversion process and the literal belief of southern religion in biblical miracles readily translate to contemporary visions. This phenomenon in turn is compatible with African tradition and its allowance for the presence of spirits in one's daily life.[18] Both belief systems were conducive and receptive to the acceptance of visions, which in testimony to their shared cultural ground, are frequently expressed in religiously inspired images made by both black and white southern self-taught artists.

In fact, there are no hard and fast rules regarding the aesthetic characteristics of black or white self-taught American artists. The work of a southern black cannot always be visually distinguished from that of a southern white. One cannot always easily ascertain the race of the artist by looking at the black faces of Shields Landon "S. L." Jones, the irregular images of Charles Kinney, the symmetrical frontal portraits of Anderson Johnson, the bold color of Ed "Mr. Eddy" Mumma, the rough aesthetic of Glassman's broken glass assemblages, the refined painting of Joe Louis Light, the symmetrical fine carving of William Edmondson, the colorful contemporary abstractions of John "J. B." Murry, or the joyful, impressionistic colors of Ezekiel Gibbs.

The South's particular culture has exerted a powerful, holistic influence on the themes, content, and forms of all its twentieth-century self-taught artists. The artists' visions were shaped by their shared cultural concepts, the people with whom they interacted, the materials readily available to them, and the visual world they saw around them.

WHAT THEY SAW

Most of the artists considered in this volume grew up in the agrarian South; the impoverished life-style they knew had prevailed for at least six decades. The pervasiveness of the natural environment drew them close to the land and its animals, as it does today. Man-made additions to the landscape were few and simple, usually essential structures such as homes, barns, and general stores.

From the conclusion of the Civil War in 1865, which virtually ravaged the region, through the Great Depression and after World War II, the rural South remained largely destitute. In this century, dust storms stripped the earth of its rich topsoil, the boll weevil devastated cotton crops, and the mechanization of farm equipment robbed laborers of their jobs. By 1938 a presidential commission established

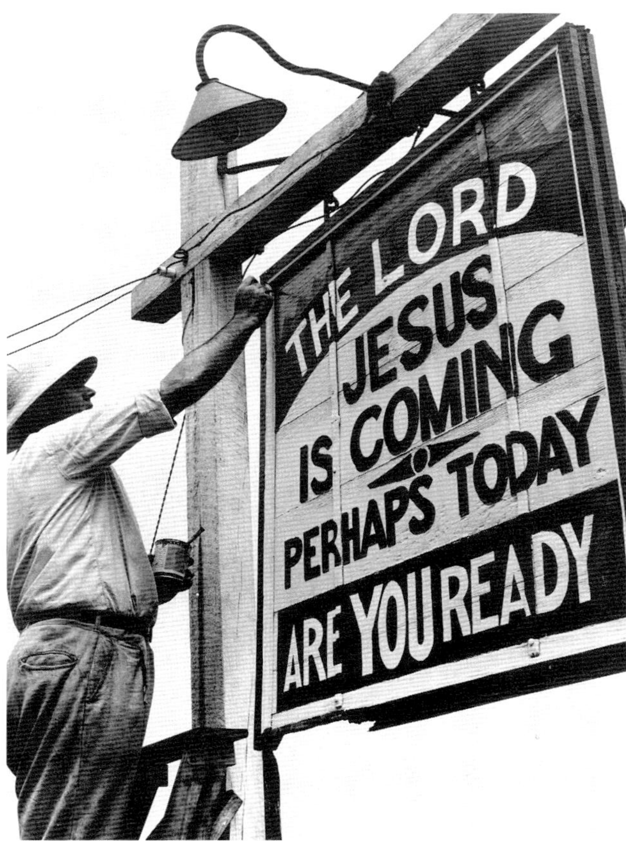

Fig. 2. "The Lord Jesus Is Coming," Augusta, Georgia, 1936. Evangelical signs similar to this still dot the southern landscape. Photo Margaret Bourke-White, Margaret Bourke-White Papers, Syracuse University Library, Special Collections Department.

by Franklin Roosevelt referred to the South as "the Nation's number one economic problem."[19] As part of the New Deal, Roosevelt formulated the Farm Security Administration (FSA), which offered loans to farmers, undertook the renewal of land, and set up camps for migrant workers.[20]

To gain public support for its social programs, the FSA employed accomplished photographers, such as Walker Evans, Dorothea Lange, and Russell Lee, to document the calamitous events occurring in the South. The imagery of these powerful photographs would have been familiar to each of the seventy-four artists in this show who were born by 1938, for this was the setting in which most of them were raised. Many came from farm families and had lived in or visited rural homes like those depicted by the FSA photographers. Other artists, whose families had moved to towns and cities, learned about rural culture from their parents.

While the FSA photographs consistently portray human dignity in conditions of hardship, and resignation to a difficult life, the images of self-taught artists often transmit a richly positive and joyous spirit, an uplifting view clearly displayed through subject matter, style, color, and technique. This is true even in paintings based on memories of farm life, which was portrayed as richly colorful even in the South's most destitute times: Clementine Hunter's *Sugar Plantation* (pl. 22), Bernice Sims's *Spring Cleaning* (pl. 28), and Bill Traylor's *Man with Mule Plowing* (pl. 39).

The visual environment surrounding the artists had a cumulative and generally unrecognized effect on their design sensibilities and creative expression. Like other members of their communities, the artists saw and were constantly exposed to handmade road signs, commercial posters and billboards, illustrated calendars, magazines, newspapers, church art, and larger-than-life public sculptures. Because this commercial art was often designed and produced in accordance with the trends of the contemporary mainstream art world, it provided inadvertent access to twentieth-century design, scale, style, and content well beyond the artists' immediate experience.[21] This subtle influence was often reflected in the artists' work.

A particularly pervasive visual model was the road sign. Painted, often on wood, and placed throughout the countryside, these signs exhorted the traveler with religious truisms, such as "The Lord Jesus is coming. Perhaps today. Are you ready" (fig. 2). Such hand-painted signs soared above the southern landscape in the 1930s, and they are found even today in sparsely populated rural areas like Carthage, Mississippi, where a sign asks, "Or what shall a man give in exchange for his soul?," or in northern Alabama, where the words "Get right with God today" fill the surface of a tin cross. Such signs are recalled when one confronts the probing question of Howard Finster's *What Is the Soul of Man* (pl. 73) or the tin cutout by R. A. Miller, *Lord Love You* (cat. no. 167). Hand-painted business signs, too, were copious, alerting buyers to the availability of basics like cider or bait (fig. 3) or, in church signs, to a particularly relevant biblical passage. Such signs were attached to gates, fences, doors, and walls or stuck in the ground with no formal sense of placement. Religion was a pervasive element in secular daily life, and the line between it and business was not always distinct, as in a small-town grocery store whose hand-printed sign states: "Jesus Christ owns this store. We work for him. . . . God loves you read John 3:16" (fig. 4).

These signs were visual models in their often haphazard style of presentation and unusual combinations of materials or imagery. The juxtaposition of word and image in hand-painted signs and commercial art provided a significant visual cue that probably prompted self-taught artists to in-

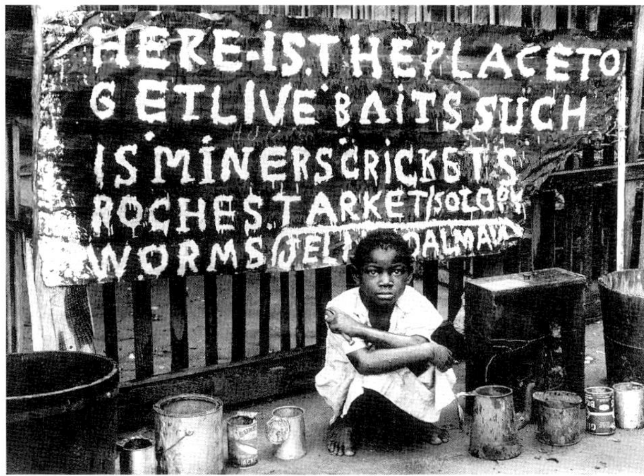

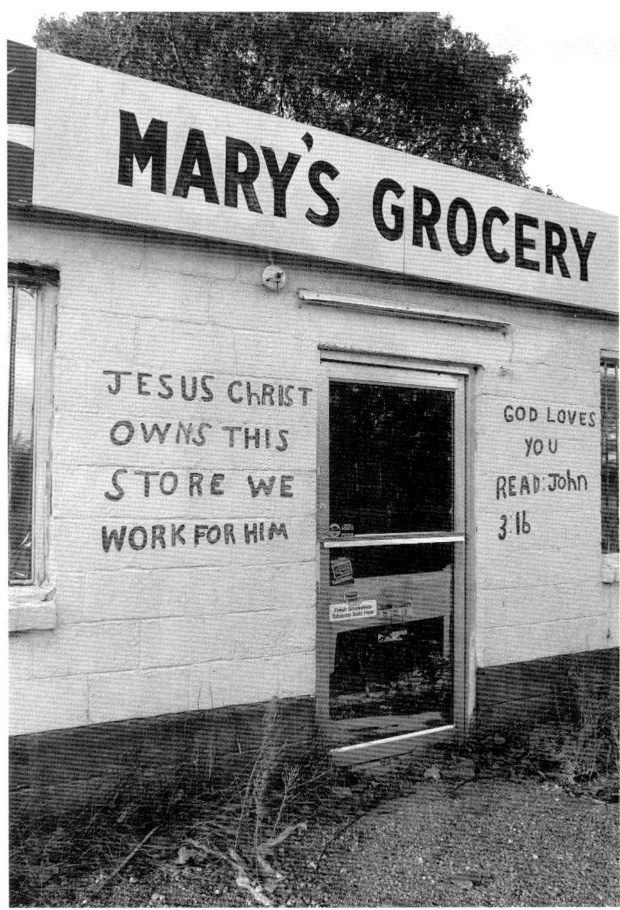

Fig. 3 *(above)*. Augusta, Georgia, 1936. Photo Margaret Bourke-White, Margaret Bourke-White Papers, Syracuse University Library, Special Collections Department. Fig. 4 *(right)*. Mary's Grocery, Simpson County, Mississippi, 1990. The hand-painted inscription reflects the powerful role of religious doctrine in daily southern life. Photo Susan B. Lee.

clude calligraphy in their imagery. From design to narrative, from the secular to the religious, words are a well-integrated component of their work. In a religious sense the word of God was the ultimate biblical authority; in a secular sense, words pervaded the imagery of popular culture.

Sister Gertrude Morgan consistently used calligraphic writing as an essential element of her art. Although intended purely to inspire and proselytize, the calligraphy in her work, balanced with painting, is exciting and provocative, much like a calligraphic inscription on a Japanese painting, for which an artist would create a poem to commemorate the scene or event depicted in the work. In some of Morgan's works, the calligraphy even occupies more space than the picture.

Like Sister Gertrude, Howard Finster utilized the word of God, the ultimate authority, in his missionary zeal. In *What Is the Soul of Man*, the arrangement of words is the primary design element as well as the subject of the work. Calligraphy as an expression of divine inspiration fills the picture plane of *Untitled* (pl. 120) by "J. B." Murry, an illiterate artist who made pictures in "spirit script" when impelled by God. Other visionary artists, such as Eddie Kendrick in *This Plane Is Heaven Bound* (pl. 80) or R. A. Miller in *Lord Love You* (cat. no. 167), used only a few words to clarify the spiritual message of some works.

Self-taught artists freely use calligraphy as a vehicle of narrative storytelling. "Prophet" Royal Robertson's writing on *Cute City Region* (pl. 114) alludes to misdeeds and adultery on the part of his ex-wife. In some cases writing simply clarifies the scene depicted, as in Charles Kinney's *George Washington* (pl. 156), on which the artist wrote "George cutting tree." Simple words identify characters, as in Sam Doyle's *Rae* (Ray Charles) (cat. no. 68), or provide directions to viewing, such as "top" and "bottom," in Zebedee "Z. B." Armstrong's *1986 Weekly/Monthly Calendar* (pl. 118). Occasionally, unrelated words previously imprinted on found objects become part of the visual composition, as in Bill Traylor's *Radio* (pl. 38).

Another prevalent graphic device in the self-taught artist's landscape was the colorful, commercially produced, billboard-size poster. Advertisements for national products such as Coca-Cola and Camel cigarettes, movie posters, Barnum and Bailey Circus signs, and picture ads for minstrel shows decorated general stores, post offices, and roadside barns. Such ads, in unexpected juxtapositions, sometimes engulfed country storefronts and created the impression of larger-than-life collages (fig. 5). In other instances, a single, stylized ad would be placed with a near-minimalist sensibility (fig. 6). Hand-painted, temporary signs advertised daily store specials.

Evidence of the impact of commercially produced graphics can be seen in the work of many self-taught artists. Howard Finster's *Coca-Cola #1123*

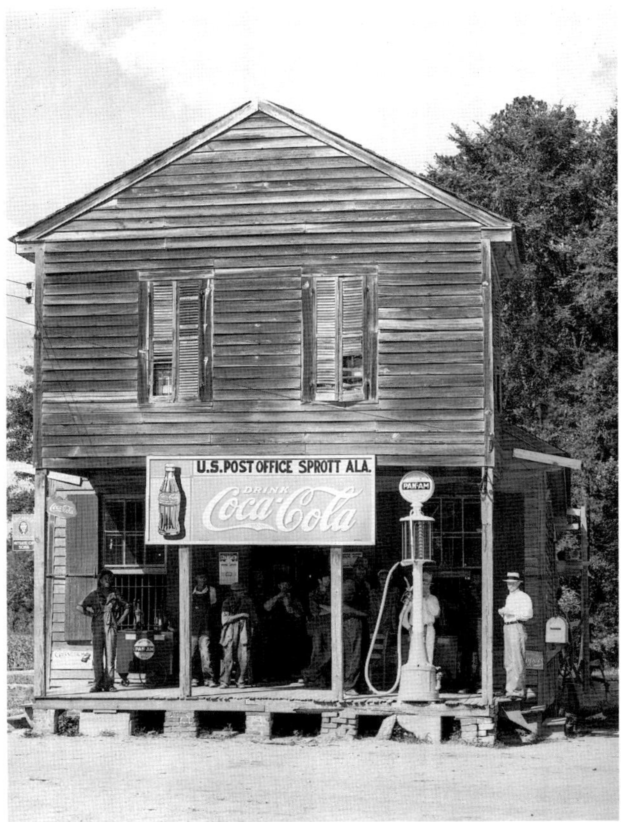

Fig. 5. U.S. post office, Sprott, Alabama, 1936. Commercially designed Coca-Cola signs were an everyday part of the rural and small town landscape. Howard Finster created a series of cutout works based on the classic Coke bottle shape. Photo Walker Evans, U.S. Farm Security Administration, Prints and Photographs Division, Library of Congress.

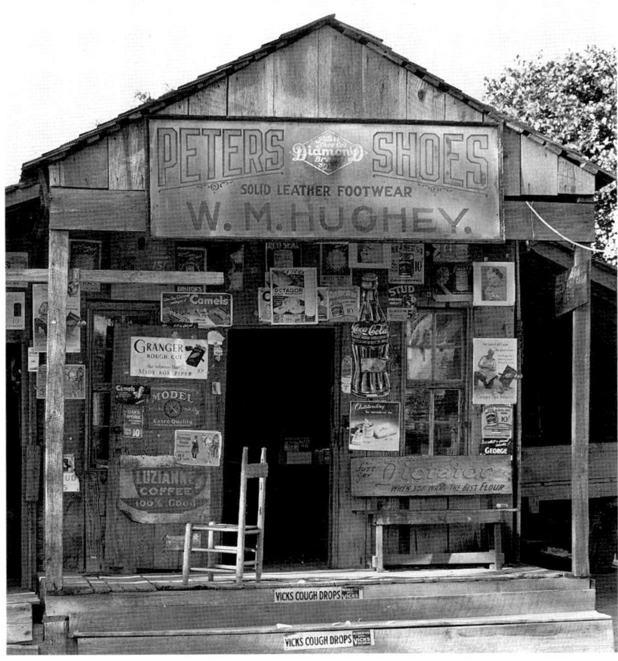

Fig. 6. Country store, near Moundville, Alabama, 1936. The collagelike combination of ads, pictures, and text that commonly covered southern storefronts may have helped to shape the visual aesthetic of self-taught artists. Photo Walker Evans, U.S. Farm Security Administration, Prints and Photographs Division, Library of Congress.

(pl. 148) reflects the widespread appeal of this product, considered "the holy water of the American South"[22] and invented in the artist's native Georgia. The runaway popularity of the soft drink and the pervasiveness of its advertising is implied in one of his numerous Coca-Cola cutouts, which is inscribed, "Coke would sell without any advertisement" (private collection). Some ad signage from the 1930s simulated a three-dimensional Coke bottle; other signs, made of tin in slight relief, held thermometers and still exist in rusted form on old rural barns. Finster most likely saw some or all of these sources, particularly as he traveled on the religious revival-meeting circuit.

Bill Traylor made a drawing of a camel from a Camel cigarette package and drew animals from circus posters he had seen.[23] Throughout southern communities, prominently featured in store windows or affixed to exterior building walls, posters portraying exotic animals advertised the circus. William Hawkins, too, attended the circus and most likely saw animals in two-dimensional circus posters. He recalled seeing a Ringling Brothers and Barnum and Bailey circus parade and noted having seen Jumbo the elephant. This episode probably influenced the appearance of elephants in works rendered by Hawkins in his last years: *Elephant* (1985), *Mastodon* (1986), and *Jumbo Elephant* (1988).[24] Philo Levi "Chief" Willey worked as a teamster for the Barnum and Bailey Circus, which most likely influenced his painting *The One-Room Circus* (1975).[25]

The often poorly constructed homes of the rural poor, usually struggling sharecroppers, typically had simple plank walls, and to stop the wind from whistling through, inhabitants sometimes applied newspaper over the cracks with a flour and water mixture.[26] This "wallpaper," a combination of image and word, was as varied as the daily news itself and often included graphically bold ads for cars or movies (fig. 7). By virtue of having newspapers line their walls, inadvertent exposure to advertisement took place even in those homes whose inhabitants were illiterate. Illustrated wall calendars, widely distributed by advertisers free of charge, were prominently displayed in bedrooms or living rooms. Images incorporated above the calendar grid ranged from the religious to the secular.

The church was a religious and social center for southerners. While biblical illustrations were available, the most distinctive and widely circulated form of church art was the fan. Designed to cool

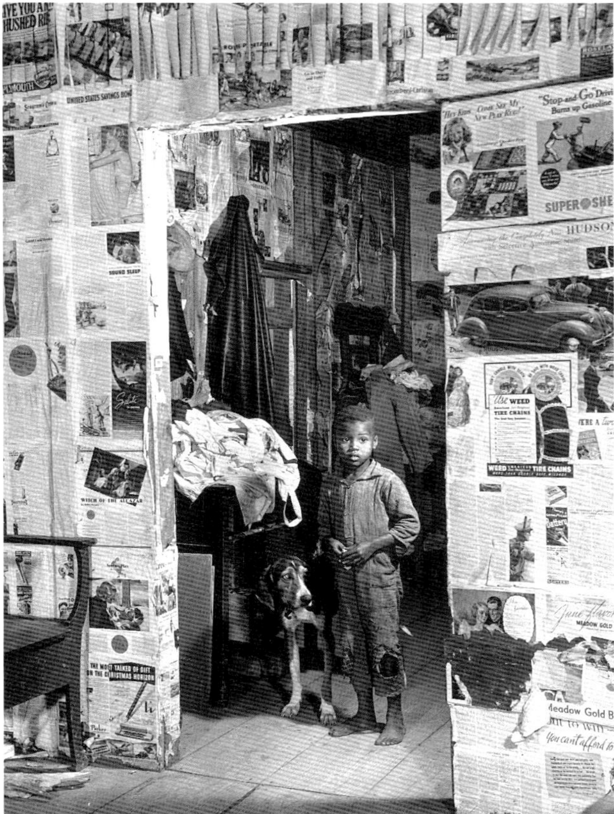

Fig. 7. East Feliciana Parish, Louisiana, 1936. Newspaper "wallpaper," used in impoverished southern homes for its nominal insulating value, had the coincidental effect of exposing inhabitants to a kaleidoscopic array of words and text. Photo Margaret Bourke-White, Margaret Bourke-White Papers, Syracuse University Library, Special Collections Department.

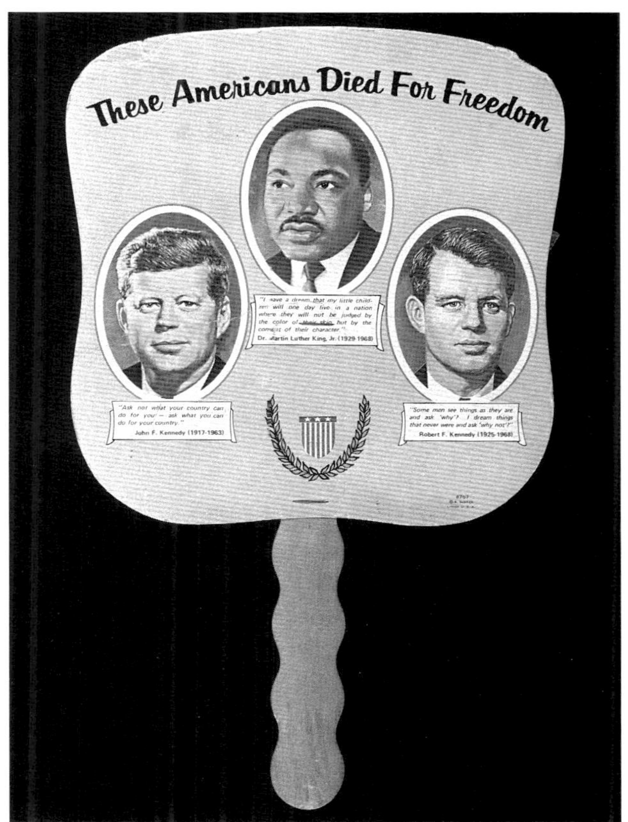

Fig. 8. Fans that combined commercial advertising on one side with biblical imagery or commemorative portraits on the other were widely used in church services to combat the heat. Collection Charles Reagan Wilson, University of Mississippi, photo courtesy University of Mississippi Special Collections.

parishioners in the days before air conditioning, these fans were used indoors during church services, weddings, or funerals, and outdoors in the heat of the sun for baptisms. Made of paper and attached to wooden Popsicle-style sticks, they were decorated on both sides. Images on the front might show Christ or a Bible scene, or a civil rights figure such as Martin Luther King, John F. Kennedy, or Robert F. Kennedy (fig. 8). The fan's back displayed an advertisement from a sponsoring company, usually a funeral home. Such imagery may have served as an inspiration for the religious or patriotic works of artists, and the fan format itself probably provided a conceptual prototype for Sister Gertrude Morgan's two-sided fan, *Charity Hospital 523-2311* (pl. 19), which she most likely used in her evangelical mission.

Other important sources for visual imagery were popular magazines and mail-order catalogues. The Sears, Roebuck catalogue had particular importance in the rural South. One southerner reminisced about its impact:

> Without that catalog, our childhood would have been radically different. . . . The Federal government ought to strike a medal for Sears, Roebuck Company for sending all those catalogs to farming families for bringing all that color and all that mystery and all that beauty into the lives of the country people.[27]

While the local country store supplied staples, the Sears catalogue sold almost everything, from furniture, clothes, and musical instruments to ice and wood boxes. Its offerings were so extensive that when Sears announced that its mail-order operations would fold in January 1993, the Associated Press referred to the catalogue as "perhaps our best record of American material culture from the turn of the century to the present."[28] Designed for leisurely reading and browsing, the catalogue's pages joined attractive illustrations and photography with descriptive text. While it gave rural Americans a continuing view of a distant urban life and the latest word on modern styles and taste, it provided self-taught artists with copious designs uniting word

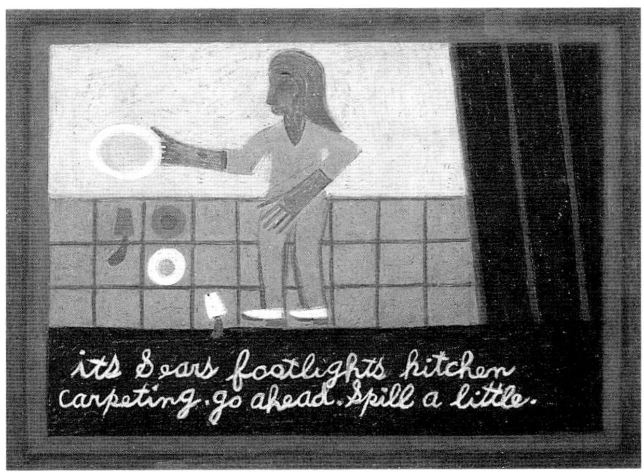

Fig. 9. Eddie Arning, *Sears Kitchen* (cat. no. 5). Arning's work, often inspired by ads or illustrations, reflects the far-reaching impact of commercial art on self-taught artists.

and image. Eddie Arning, who utilized graphic ads and article illustrations as inspiration for his work, could have borrowed his inscription on *Sears Kitchen* (fig. 9) right from the ad copy: "It's Sears footlights kitchen carpeting. Go ahead. Spill a little."

Life magazine, introduced in late 1936, was also a favorite for perusal, if not purchase, as soon as it became available. Known for its high-quality images by photographers such as Walker Evans, Dorothea Lange, André Kertész, Brassaï, Henri Cartier-Bresson, Alfred Eisenstaedt, and Margaret Bourke-White, *Life* featured aesthetically superb visuals with stories on political and cultural events as well as the most fashionable commercial ads. The true circulation of *Life* cannot really be known, as it, like other magazines, often was passed from house to house and was usually shared and read in shops where people congregated and familiarized themselves with the finest visual and written material of the day.

After World War II, the most potent visual stimulus for self-taught artists was television, the ever-present equalizer of society. Reaching most American households by the mid-1950s, television brought greater exposure to contemporary visual imagery and to popular cultural figures like Elvis (pls. 147, 149), Red Skelton (pl. 151), Jackie Robinson (cat. no. 65), and Cher (cat. no. 219). Many artists viewed television regularly as their primary contact with the world of news and popular culture beyond their immediate environment. For Juanita Rogers, for example, a relative recluse in her later years, it was a vital visual source and a primary link to the outside world.

Although often geographically isolated, rural southern self-taught artists have long responded to the vast omnipresent body of twentieth-century design and imagery around them. But only now is the indigenous cultural richness of the visual arts in the South beginning to be recognized. The region has long been maligned as a cultural backwater or, worse, a wasteland. In 1920, journalist and critic H. L. Mencken wrote that "[the South] is almost as sterile, artistically, intellectually, culturally, as the Sahara Desert." He concluded, "Obviously it is impossible for intelligence to flourish in such an atmosphere."[29] Even administrators of the FSA, who had closely observed the region, referred to the South in the 1930s as "barren of artistic talent."[30] Yet it was precisely in this time and setting that the creative self-taught artists seen in this volume were formed and nourished.

The South's pre–World War II agrarian culture no longer exists. Southern life has evolved into a more urban and small town society, in keeping with the ongoing move toward urbanization throughout America. Now, printed and electronic materials abound, and combined with accessible car, train, and air transportation, they provide easy availability to a wide array of information, ideas, and products. Particularly for younger artists whose perceptions were formed in this new age, as well as for some older artists, this means that recent work is more likely to confront issues of contemporary life-styles: urban living, racial conflict, homelessness. These issues are as much a part of their lives as anyone's, and the inclusion of them in their work only shows the consistency with which self-taught artists have looked to their immediate experience for sources and inspiration.

1. For a general overview of the distinctive aspects of southern culture, see C. Vann Woodward, "The Search for Southern Identity," in *The Burden of Southern History* (Baton Rouge: Louisiana State University Press, 1968).

2. David M. Potter, "The Enigma of the South," in *The South and the Sectional Conflict* (Baton Rouge: Louisiana State University Press), pp. 15–16.

3. Jack Temple Kirby, "Plantations," *ESC,* p. 27.

4. Sam Doyle's grandparents received fifteen acres at the end of the Civil War when the land on St. Helena Island was divided among the slaves who had worked there (Chuck and Jan Rosenak, *Museum of American Folk Art Encyclopedia of Twentieth-Century American Folk Art and Artists* [New York: Abbeville Press, 1990], p. 108), but this was an exceptional case. Despite widespread and persistent rumors after the war that each freed man would receive forty acres and a mule with which to start a new life, most former slaves were left landless.

5. Thomas C. Holt, "Black Life," *ESC,* p. 136.

6. Woodward, "The Search for Southern Identity," p. 6.

7. Howard L. Preston, "Good Roads Movement," *ESC,* p. 23.

8. Ramona Lampell and Millard Lampell with David Larkin, *O, Appalachia: Artists of the Southern Mountains* (New York: Stewart, Tabori, and Chang, 1989), p. 21.

9. Self-taught artists such as William Hawkins, William Dawson, Josephus Farmer, and Sultan Rogers participated in this migration, bringing their southern rural culture with them.

10. Woodward, "The Search for Southern Identity," p. 6.

11. Marsha Jean Darling, "Landownership, Black," *ESC,* p. 169.

12. Holt, "Black Life," p. 136.

13. Charles Joyner, "Folktales," *ESC,* p. 477.

14. John M. Vlach, *The Afro-American Tradition in Decorative Arts* (Athens, Ga.: Brown Thrasher Books, University of Georgia Press, 1990), p. 3. Vlach suggests that for blacks these novel compositions arise from cultural rather than personal norms.

15. See Robert Farris Thompson, *Flash of the Spirit: African and Afro-American Philosophy* (New York: Random House), 1983.

16. Samuel S. Hill, "Religion," *ESC,* p. 1269.

17. Ibid., p. 1272.

18. Lynne Adele, *Black History/Black Vision: The Visionary Image in Texas* (Austin: Archer M. Huntington Art Gallery, College of Fine Arts, University of Texas, 1989), p. 16.

19. Woodward, "The Search for Southern Identity," p. 17.

20. Arthur Rothstein, *The Depression Years as Photographed by Arthur Rothstein* (New York: Dover Publications, 1978), unpaginated.

21. For one perspective on the relationship between modern art and popular imagery, see Kirk Varnedoe and Adam Gopnik, *High and Low: Modern Art and Popular Culture* (New York: Museum of Modern Art, 1990), p. 19.

22. E. J. Kahn, Jr., "Coca-Cola," *ESC,* p. 737.

23. Frank Maresca and Roger Ricco, *Bill Traylor: His Art, His Life* (New York: Alfred A. Knopf, 1991), p. 29.

24. Gary Schwindler, "William L. Hawkins: A Biography," unpublished ms., p. 349.

25. Barbara Wahl Kaufman and Didi Barrett, *A Time to Reap* (New York: Museum of American Folk Art, n.d.), p. 41.

26. James Agee movingly described the sorry state of poor southern homes in James Agee and Walker Evans, *Let Us Now Praise Famous Men* (Boston: Houghton Mifflin, 1941), pp. 152–53.

27. Elizabeth M. Makowski, "Sears, Roebuck Catalog," *ESC,* p. 46.

28. Michelle Landbert, "Sears Catalog Is One for the History Book," *The Times-Picayune,* Jan. 26, 1993, sec. C, p. 1.

29. H. L. Mencken, "The Sahara of the Bozart," in *Prejudices: Second Series* (New York: Alfred A. Knopf, 1920), pp. 136, 154.

30. Richard D. McKinzie, *The New Deal for Artists* (Princeton University Press, 1973), p. 31.

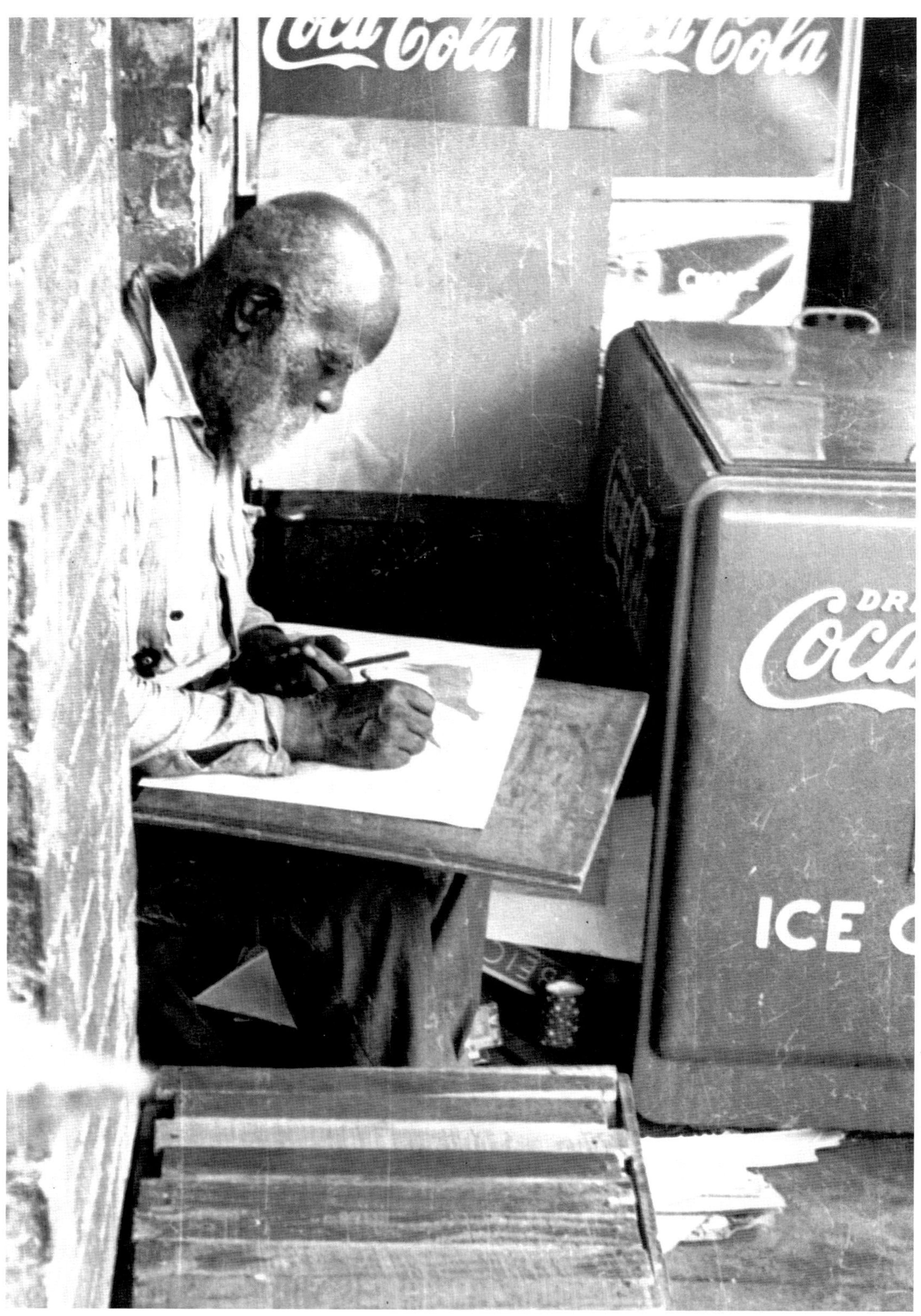

Fig. 1. Bill Traylor, Montgomery, Alabama, 1939–40. Traylor painted and drew on timeworn materials on a downtown Montgomery street. Photo Charles Shannon.

MATERIALS AND ENVIRONMENTS

ALICE RAE YELEN

Since the Renaissance, Western art history has considered the standard format for two-dimensional work to be oil paint on a rectangular canvas. Three-dimensional sculpture, too, has had its favored materials, classically bronze and marble. But self-taught artists, who do not develop within this art tradition, are essentially unfamiliar with these expectations and often without access to such standard materials. Unlike this century's contemporary artists, their liberation from the restrictions of symmetrically shaped canvas and evenly applied paint, or the constraints of stable sculpture materials, has been unknowing. They experiment with irregular formats and unconventional media as natural innovators who, frequently without conscious consideration, use those items that are readily available and appealing to their eye and hand.

With no sense of the fine art tradition and its media, self-taught artists develop independent preferences based on what they see and find around them in their immediate daily environments. Knowing how to "make do" might relate to a rural self-reliance associated with their usually low economic status, and, in some cases, their geographic distance from sources of specialized commercial materials.

Farm Security Administration photographs of the South in the 1930s document the effects of time and the elements on the articles—often hand-me-down items—that decorated rural homes: magazine and newspaper illustrations and posters peel from the walls of homes and from the exteriors of buildings, barns, stores, and fences (fig. 2). Casual wear and tear soon transformed graphics from regular to random, asymmetrical shapes. Hand-painted and commercial signs became chipped, ripped, faded, or soiled and developed unusual patinas that appeared unfinished, imperfect, rough, or just plain worn.

Many self-taught artists, both rural and urban, seem to have acquired a visual comfort with the look of used or worn artifacts, which in turn has influenced their aesthetic judgments. Salvaging materials from a junkyard or trash pile is not an uncommon or self-conscious venture for a self-taught artist (as it would be for a suburban college student or an established artist). Self-taught artists generally are not concerned with the future life of their art, and they rarely consider issues of preservation or conservation in the selection of medium. Thus their materials range from the natural to the man-made, from the fragile to the sturdy. For many of them, an effortless use of found and used materials—roofing tin, window shades, paper bags, manila envelopes, and dried gourds, to name a few—results in unconventional, asymmetrical artworks, often with textured surfaces and layers of patinaed color.

The exterior and interior environments of the usually modest homes inhabited by self-taught artists often serve as both work and display spaces. The warm southern climate allows artists to work outdoors for a good portion of the year, and, because rural land is plentiful, artists often have room in their backyards to create, store, or show their art, which might be large-scale sculptural works or paintings. The words "display" or "show" are used here in their simplest sense and do not imply a formal viewing area meant for visitors. Most of these makers never conceived that enthusiastic art lovers would one day admire, photograph, purchase, and write about their creations.

The work space of a self-taught artist does not have the same connotation as a trained artist's studio. Work spaces usually are well-integrated into daily living spaces, if not comprising the entire area itself, and a specific studio or an easel is rarely

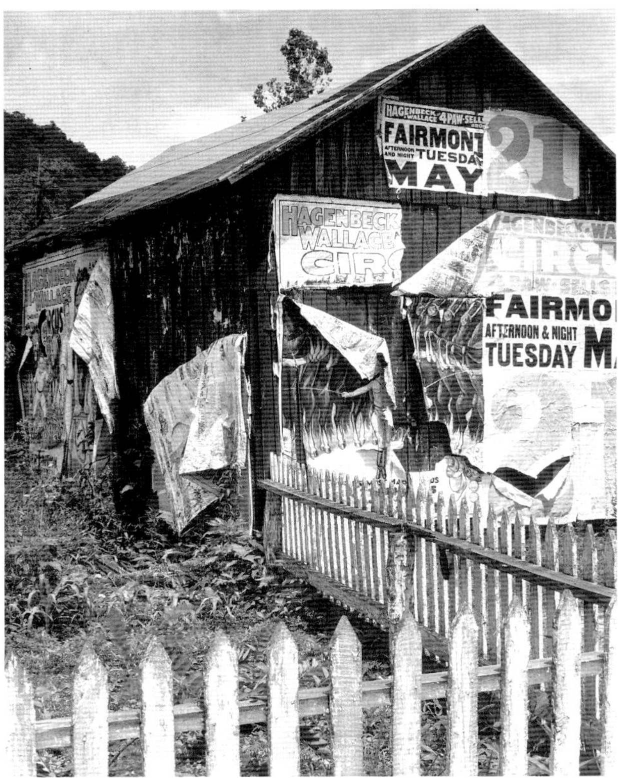

Fig. 2. Roadside barn, Monongalia County, West Virginia, 1935. Photo Walker Evans, U.S. Farm Security Administration, Prints and Photographs Division, Library of Congress.

noted. "Standard" tools for the self-taught range from brushes to fingers and from pocketknives to chain saws. But even when self-taught artists use conventional art supplies, their application of them tends to challenge our preconceived notions about art making.

Sometimes the distinction between home and work environment is completely obscured or tied to a greater agenda. Howard Finster's famed Paradise Garden surrounds his home in northwestern Georgia. Intended to be a place of spiritual encounter, it includes his World's Folk Art Church, outdoor sculpture and paintings, and artistically designed, intricately paved pathways. Benjamin F. Perkins fashioned his Fayette County, Alabama, church and home in patriotic red, white, and blue (p. 234, fig. 1). His painted images and calligraphy interact to convey his messages of religious worship, love of church, salvation, and patriotism.

James Harold Jennings divides his living quarters and art workshop in Pinnacle, North Carolina, between several old school buses. His property is densely populated with his fanciful wooden constructions (p. 66, fig. 3). Clyde Jones's unassuming Bynum, North Carolina, home is surrounded by a diverse menagerie of painted wooden animals fashioned from tree limbs with a chain saw. He has extended his personal environment by placing the

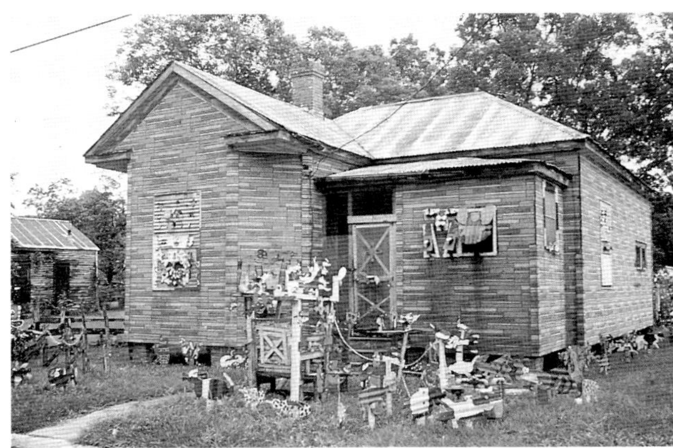

Fig. 3. David Butler's home, Patterson, Louisiana, 1980. Butler's yard, house, windows, and doors all display his fanciful work. His window coverings are designed to let patterned light filter in while still affording privacy. Photo John Geldersma.

sculptures not only throughout his yard but in adjacent neighborhoods, public places, and parks. Even the local post office, which doubles as Bynum's only general store, has two Jones works at its front door.

Mary T. Smith decorated her creative, well-manicured garden and fence in Hazelhurst, Mississippi, with painted roofing tin and wooden boards (fig. 5). She used a small, colorful outdoor shed near her house as a work and display area. Similarly, R. A. Miller's yard on a hill above a highway in Cumberland, Georgia, is adorned with whirligigs of animals and other figures as well as plaques.

Charlie Lucas's rural environment is replete with large-scale sculptures fashioned from welded, rusted auto parts (fig. 6). When asked about a piece in his yard, Lucas replied, "It's not ready yet."[1] He wanted the piece to rust and age even more. Lonnie B. Holley lives amid a dense jungle of innovative assemblages so closely packed that it can be difficult to find a path. Holley says, "My environment is always changing and evolving, like a garden that needs tending."[2]

Once "discovered" by collectors and dealers, self-taught artists are often offered supplies, yet some continue to employ used or found objects. J. P. Scott, for example, likes to scavenge for materials. "People try to give me stuff to build with, but they can't do that, 'cause I gotta do it myself."[3] For Charlie Lucas, the search for material is part of his creative process: "I get parts anywhere I can find them. I think the metal talks to me more when I'm scrounging around looking for it, rather than when I'm looking for a specific piece. . . . If I look . . . in the junkyard, the piece will tell me exactly what it is, what I want. When I get home with it, it will fit perfectly into what I'm working on and I don't have to grind it or shape it."[4] Bill Traylor, too, must have

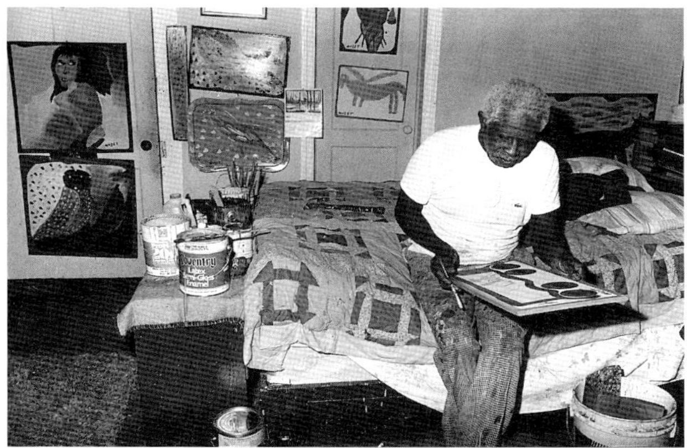

Fig. 4. Mose Tolliver, Montgomery, Alabama, 1989. Tolliver paints while sitting on his bed, using his lap as an easel. The bedroom serves as studio, display space, and reception area. Photo Guy Mendes.

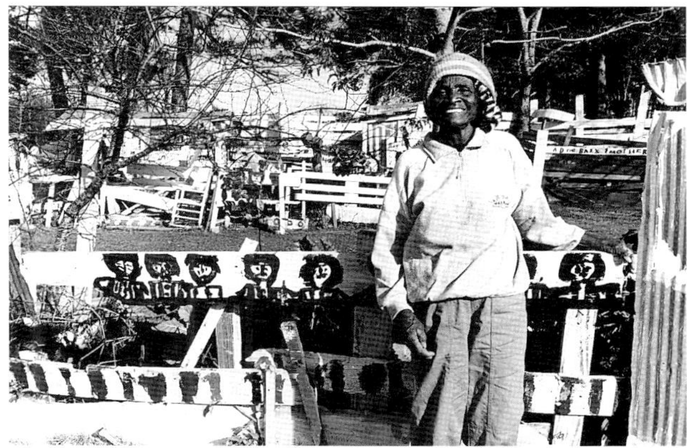

Fig. 5. Mary T. Smith, Hazelhurst, Mississippi, 1989. Smith embellished her yard with her paintings on board and tin. Photo Guy Mendes.

preferred the irregular character of ragged used materials for drawings and paintings. When he was given poster board, he put it away until it acquired the worn look of pieces he had found.[5]

Some artists go so far as to purchase used material for their work. Benjamin F. Perkins, for example, bought flea market furniture—tables, chairs, a child's toilet (pl. 163), suitcases—to be transformed into his distinctive imagery. Ronald and Jessie Cooper recycle old desks, oil heaters (pl. 101), and antique trunks (pl. 78) in their artistic endeavors. David Strickland purchases antique farm equipment for his assemblages (pl. 126).

These artists use readily accessible material with a discerning, aesthetically attuned eye but without a greater conceptual intent. In general, they would not use the term "recycled" to refer to the re-use of an object for another purpose, no matter how ecologically chic this might be in the 1990s. Nor would they refer to the contemporary art concept of the "found object," as did Marcel Duchamp in 1917 when he first transformed quotidian objects into artworks. But the self-taught artist does respect the intrinsic value of re-used materials. Lonnie B. Holley, for example, a consummate assemblage artist, has commented, "Art is everything we have used, waiting to be used again."[6] Benjamin F. Perkins inscribed his *All American Potty* (pl. 163) with these telling words: "This all American baby pottie served its purpose with honor and was not recycled but became folk art antique to adorn some place in art society."

Thornton Dial, Sr., whose work incorporates diverse recycled materials (sponges, nets, tin, carpet, rope, cement, beer cans), has a sense of revitalizing old materials into new forms, an attitude linked to his philosophy of life: "Anything you pick up, somebody know about. You picking up the spirit of somebody. . . . Leaves fall off a tree got a spirit in them. Cows, dirt, rocks, the whole world, all that stuff carry on life. A old house got old, tin fall off . . . but it done did many people some good before it fall. It can still do somebody some good. Old life just makes new life. That's what recycle is all about. When God died, he rose again."[7]

Sam Doyle's preferred material was corrugated tin, the primary roofing material on his home on St. Helena Island, South Carolina, and popular for siding and roofing on many lower-income southern homes (fig. 7). Doyle skillfully incorporated the vertical rippled lines of the tin into compositions such as *Slave* (pl. 130) and *Adlade* (pl. 8), where the central ripple bisects the standing figures. The width of Doyle's pieces, generally twenty-six inches, is determined by the ready-made measurement of the tin.[8] Some works are multiples of the measure, as Doyle occasionally splices tin pieces together.

Mary T. Smith also prefers roofing tin, rough-edged and irregularly shaped, which she often hand-cuts and paints (pl. 99). Occasionally she pieces together several panels to create an unusual shape, such as the image of Christ in *I Was in a Wreck* (pl. 98).

David Butler cut old, rusted roofing tin by hand and painted it to create whirligig animals and cut-outs of unusual forms and bold colors. R. A. Miller uses discarded gutters, which he flattens with a hammer and then cuts and paints as animals and figures.[9]

Standard-size window shades serve as backing for Sam Doyle's *Lincoln at Frogmore* (pl. 159), Clementine Hunter's *Panorama of Baptism on Cane River* (pl. 79), Charles Kinney's *"Cheter Cat"* (pl. 173), and Sister Gertrude Morgan's *Book of Revela-*

tion (pl. 91). Paint thinly applied to the lightly embossed plastic surface gives a sheen to the works; close observation, particularly of Morgan's piece, reveals the zigzag pattern of the shade. In addition to working on standard paper, poster board, found wooden placards, and cardboard, Morgan painted on white styrofoam meat trays from the grocery store.

Herbert Singleton, Joe Louis Light, and, on occasion, Purvis Young have all used doors as a support medium. Masonite is a frequently seen backing for two-dimensional work, as are found board and cardboard, whose varying sizes and shapes contribute to the rough-edged, unfinished aesthetic of self-taught artworks.

Sybil Gibson regularly uses brown paper shopping bags as a ground for painting. She first soaks and washes a bag to unhinge its glued edges. The washing process often results in a rich, rippled texture that contrasts magnificently with her pale, wispy pastel imagery (pl. 210).

Henry Ray Clark once worked on a manila envelope, designing even the interior of the gummed label (pl. 115). He incorporated the envelope's mustard color as the background of geometric compositions drawn in ballpoint and felt-tip pens. Producing most of his work in prison, he is a prime example of an artist who is able to create with very limited supplies.

Found objects—natural gourds, wood, stone, old car and farm equipment parts—also provide the structure for three-dimensional items created by self-taught artists. Benjamin F. Perkins purchased and dried gourds before painting them with patriotic images. Minnie Black assembles pieces of cut gourd with glue to create animal forms that she then paints (pls. 170, 195).

Ralph Griffin coaxed emerging figures from found river driftwood. The figures betray a striking emotional range, from alarm to despair to peacefulness. Yet Griffin never sculpted his materials—he just interpreted what he saw in the shape and texture of the natural wood, which he highlighted with paint. Bessie Harvey, too, achieves stunning results from found wood, to which she adds paint and sometimes sequins, shells, or raffia.

William Edmondson used limestone from demolished buildings and curbs as the medium for his symmetrically carved sculptures.[10] Raymond Coins searches out local river rock, which he etches and carves.

Charlie Lucas, once a car mechanic, incorporates old car parts in his welded metal assemblages, exemplified by his use of a car hood in *Bondo* (pl. 191), whereas David Strickland, a former welder who spent summers on his grandmother's farm, purchases antique farm equipment and parts from which to fashion his sculpture. Lonnie B. Holley creates figurative and abstract assemblages, often of large size, from wood, clothing, and other found materials.

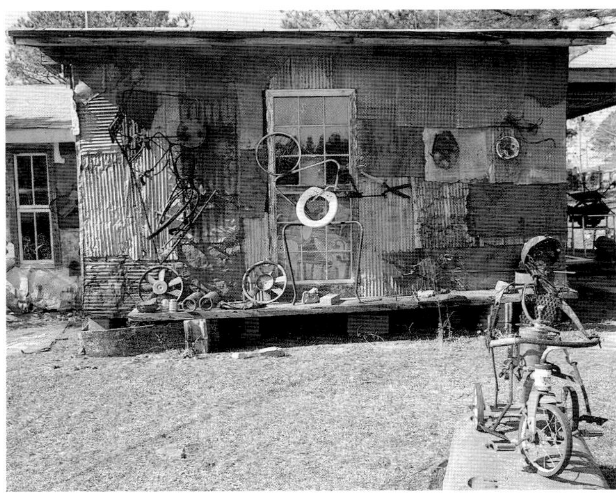

Fig. 6. Charlie Lucas's yard, Prattville, Alabama, 1993. Photo Robert Fouts.

J. P. Scott is among the most inventive makers of three-dimensional artwork from found objects. He carefully selects his materials in nearby junkyards, trash piles, and along the road (but often purchases paint). His wooden boats, buildings, and oil rigs are carefully constructed and decorated with found tin, Mardi Gras beads, linoleum, small American flags, rope, and used cans. Windows are made from plastic 7-Up bottles (pl. 1).

Some artists alter the texture of their painted surfaces by adding grainy substances such as mud, cornmeal, or sawdust. Archie Byron, in *Despair* (pl. 140), mixed sawdust, glue, and paint. William Hawkins built up the surfaces of otherwise two-dimensional works with cornmeal and paint, and by occasionally adding a wooden armature, as in the protruding mouth of *Tasmanian Tiger No. 2* (pl. 193).

Artists frequently add other miscellaneous items that provide a textured, dimensional quality to their work. Mose Tolliver placed clippings of his own hair on the head of his self-portrait (pl. 15), and James Henry "Son" Thomas used unginned Delta cotton to simulate the hair of an aging George Washington (pl. 169). J. L. Hunter applies screw tops for eyes and plastic beads for buttons on his painted carved figures; Elijah Pierce used rhinestones for the eyes of a leopard (pl. 177); Clyde Jones fashions 35mm film canisters and plastic flowers into eyes and textile spools into the quills of a porcupine (pl. 208). Glassman, who has a preser-

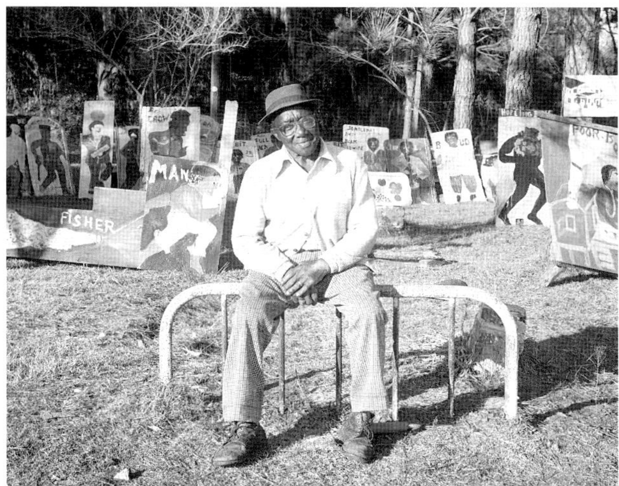

Fig. 7. Sam Doyle, St. Helena Island, South Carolina, 1983. Photo © Roger Manley.

vationist's aesthetic, makes silhouettes from shattered glass on found board, but he will not break an object to obtain his material (pl. 168).[11]

Jimmy Lee Sudduth finds most of his materials within walking distance of his home. He paints with hues of mud ranging from yellows to browns, applying extra color by rubbing in leaves, vines, or flowers. He mixes the mud with sugar, using flour to lighten and coffee or coal to darken the color, and applies it with his fingers: "Brushes don't work well. . . . I paint with my finger 'cause that's why I got it and that brush don't wear out. When I die, the brush dies."[12] He usually works on found board, commercial plywood, or occasionally tin. Sudduth's use of natural, local materials perhaps best exemplifies the inventive, self-reliant attitude of the self-taught artist.

A significant number of self-taught artists do work in more conventional art materials, such as poster board, plywood, canvas, pencils, crayons, and frequently house paint. Often folk art enthusiasts provide these materials to artists. William Dawson, for example, was happy to receive pieces of basswood from supporters rather than to continue scavenging for wooden furniture legs. In the 1980s dealers began to request works from Jimmy Lee Sudduth in conventional paint instead of his preferred mud.[13] Sudduth complied by using paint with mud, creating a unique textural surface while demonstrating the incorruptibility of his own vision. Many artists who use conventional materials similarly imbue them with their own aesthetic imprimaturs.

The self-taught artist ingeniously incorporates flaws of color, texture, or shape as an integral part of a composition, skillfully designing a work to conform to the nonuniform surface or unusual shape of a material. Bill Traylor, for example, incorporated as a design element a gray horizontal line in the paper on which *Man with Mule Plowing* (pl. 39) is drawn; he constructed an aesthetic arrangement of men, dog, bird, and a building within the unusual rounded shape of *Radio* (pl. 38). Purvis Young integrated a diamond window in the door on which *The Boat People* (pl. 143) is painted; and Herbert Singleton utilized a hole in the base of a carved relief, *Behind the Eight Ball* (pl. 132), as a natural space between a man's beard and his chest.

Some self-taught artists do not limit themselves to one side of a surface. For Ed "Mr. Eddy" Mumma, this was a given: "But a painting has to be painted on both sides—to be complete."[14] His *Three Men and House* (pl. 49) has a single figure drawn on the opposite side. Bill Traylor's *Red Dog* (pl. 187) has a man leading a mule drawn on the reverse. Henry Ray Clark's *Magnificent Pretty Boy* (pl. 115) displays an equally dense and articulate geometric image with three faces on its opposite side. Artists working in three dimensions, such as Ralph Griffin and Bessie Harvey, sometimes create two or three different images in one piece depending on the formation of their found wood. In these instances, there is no primary image, no front or back.

Many self-taught artists create frames for their imagery. Like their paintings, their frames are often irregular in shape and unconventional in decoration, as well as in their relationship to their paintings. Jimmy Lee Sudduth said, "I like to finish my paintings." A frame, he believes, does just that.[15] Sudduth's frames are often simple paint or mud lines that surround the edge of a work's surface (pls. 6, 7); others reiterate patterning found on a central figure (pl. 176).

William Hawkins created frames, both painted and three-dimensional, because he believed they made it easier to sell works.[16] *Handing the Keys to St. Peter* (pl. 84) has a black edge with white X's to simulate a frame. The colors beautifully integrate and visually complete the painting's palette and composition. In *Tasmanian Tiger No. 2* (pl. 193), the main image actually overlaps from the picture plane into the frame.

Howard Finster made frames for selected works, sometimes burning designs into the wood (pl. 157). John William "Uncle Jack" Dey often bought frames and painted them at the time he made his paintings. Charlie Lucas is known to have framed a painting in pieces of green rubber hose. Willie Massey worked on the backside of stretched canvas, incorporating the wooden stretcher as part of his imagery and creating a frame-in-shadow-box effect (pl. 174).

Perhaps the epitome of integration of frame with work is demonstrated by Purvis Young, whose distinctively assembled frames are in themselves interesting constructions. Young adds to the irregular shape of his work by applying assorted pieces of wood. In *Angels Over the City* (pl. 144), thirteen different rectangular pieces are nailed or glued onto the painted canvas surface, rather than to its edge. This combination of diverse pieces of wood—some painted white or brown, some varnished or natural, some of Masonite—creates its own irregular construction, which does not consistently hug the painting's border. Clearly Young's frames are made to enhance his works, not necessarily to frame them in a traditional sense. Of his unusual frames, Young says, "Sometimes I look at a Roman movie and see how a picture frame is made a thousand years ago. . . . I want to make it look old fashioned. . . . To me that's beautiful art."[17]

Whether these southern self-taught artists use conventional or unconventional materials, their unique visions shine through in their distinctively independent and individual expressions. Whether using found materials, standard art supplies from collectors and dealers, or purchased materials, they do so with a discerning eye and personal vision, skillfully responding to the inherent characteristics of their media. If one defines artistic achievement or creativity by doing the most with what one has, self-taught artists clearly qualify. They truly "make something from nothing" in their creative transformation of the commonplace into extraordinary, expressive artworks.

NOTES

1. Charlie Lucas, interview, ARY, Nov. 1991.
2. *In/Outsiders from the American South* (Montgomery, Ala.: Montgomery Museum of Fine Arts, 1992), unpaginated.
3. J. P. Scott, quoted in Deborah Ann Gilman, "A Study of Four Contemporary Untrained Artists from Southern Louisiana," M.A. thesis, Louisiana State University, 1989, p. 81.
4. Charlie Lucas, interview, ARY, March 1993.
5. Charles Shannon, "Remembering Bill Traylor: An Interview with Charles Shannon," in Frank Maresca and Roger Ricco, *Bill Traylor: His Art, His Life* (New York: Alfred A. Knopf, 1991), p. 11.
6. *In/Outsiders from the American South.*
7. *Thornton Dial: Strategy of the World* (Jamaica, N.Y.: Southern Queens Park Association, 1990), p. 4.
8. Louanne LaRoche, ed., *Sam Doyle* (Kyoto: Shoin International, 1989), unpaginated.
9. R. A. Miller, interview, ARY, Aug. 1992.
10. Georganne Fletcher, ed., *William Edmondson: A Retrospective* (Nashville: Tennessee Arts Commission, 1981), p. 12.
11. Frances M. Chmielewski, "Baltimore Glassman: A Folk Art Punster," *Folk Art Finder* (Spring 1993), pp. 14, 15.
12. Jimmy Lee Sudduth, interview, ARY, Aug. 1992.
13. Ibid.
14. Chuck Rosenak and Jan Rosenak, *Museum of American Folk Art Encyclopedia of Twentieth-Century American Folk Art and Artists* (New York: Abbeville Press, 1990), p. 221.
15. Jimmy Lee Sudduth, interview, ARY, Aug. 1991.
16. Gary Schwindler, interview, ARY, Dec. 1992.
17. Purvis Young, interview, ARY, May 1992.

COLOR PLATES AND COMMENTARY

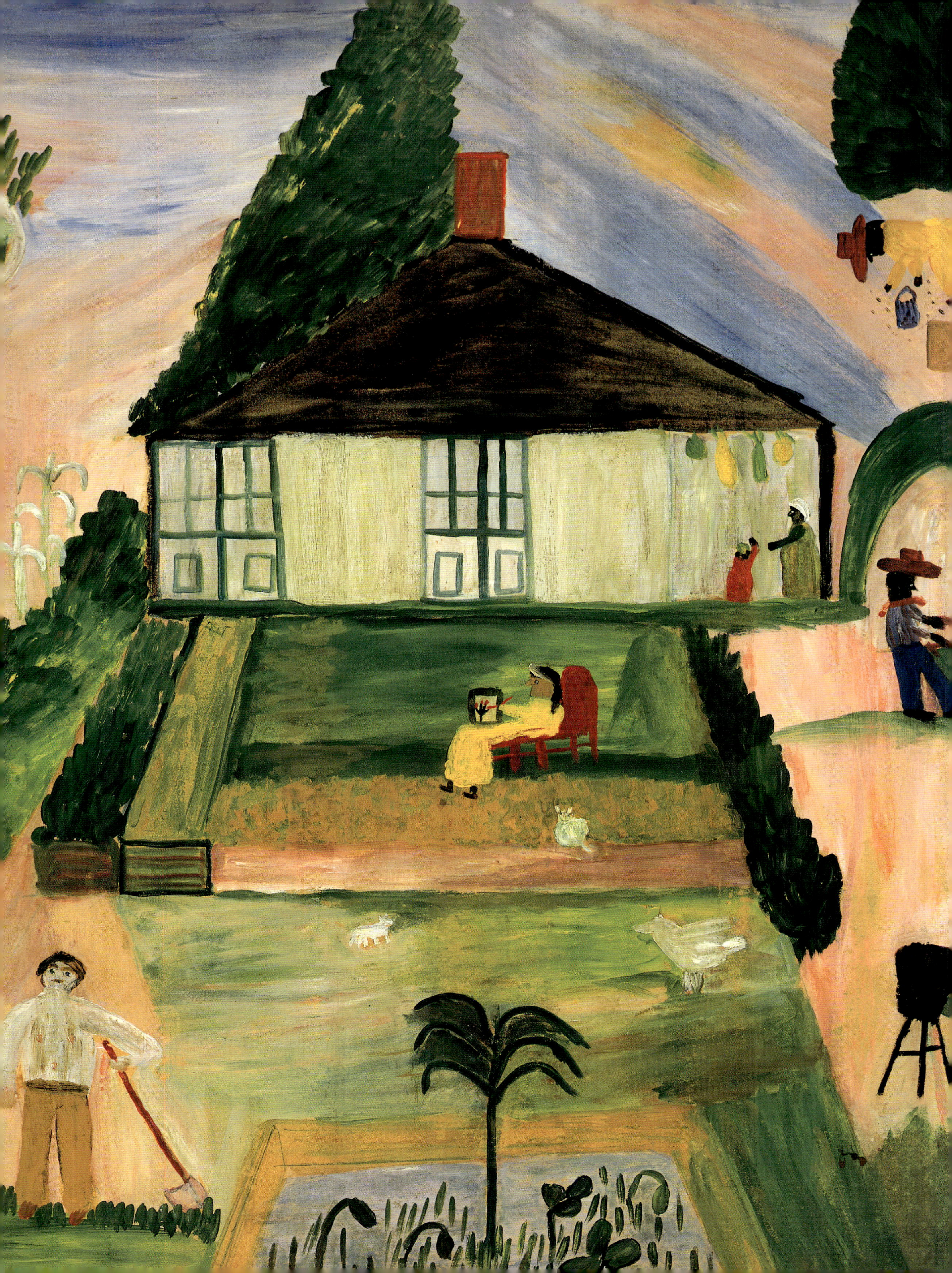

AUTOBIOGRAPHY

Works by southern self-taught artists are implicitly autobiographical. Artists record and respond to both secular and religious issues in their daily lives, often capturing their most personal views of themselves while reflecting their signature styles, media, and formats.

No underlying common aesthetic unites these "portraits," personal creative expressions that characteristically do not subscribe to a specific art canon. Whether or not a depiction is true to the original subject, it retains its spirit, if only by the inclusion of relevant contextual references. Many artists, such as Jimmy Lee Sudduth, Raymond Coins, Sam Doyle, Edgar Tolson, Joe Louis Light, and Steven Ashby, paint themselves in nearly conventional single-figure pictures that disclose insights into their self-concepts. Other artists depict themselves set in recurring themes of their lives and work, such as Clementine Hunter at the plantation on which she worked, Sister Gertrude Morgan amid a host of angels with her groom, Jesus Christ, and Ezekiel Gibbs with his family in a farm scene.

Artists also commemorate loved ones in works such as Sam Doyle's depiction of his great-aunt in *Adlade* (pl. 8) and Jimmy Lee Sudduth's portrayal of his beloved dog in *Toto with Ball* (pl. 7). Others focus on objects of personal meaning, as David Butler's marvelously expressive *David's Bike* (pl. 2) or Anderson Johnson's *Portable Pulpit* (pl. 65), from which he preached. Some recollect significant life events: Philo Levi "Chief" Willey reminisced about his honeymoon voyage in *Three Day Wedding Trip up the Mississippi* (pl. 17), and Howard Finster celebrated his own history as an artist in *The Discovery of Finster Art* (pl. 14).

Jimmy Lee Sudduth created his *Self-portrait* (pl. 6) from earth-toned muds and a chalky white substance on a plywood base painted a flat, solid blue. With short, energetic, vibrant strokes, Sudduth portrayed himself in overalls, his usual daily attire, with stooped shoulders and undefined hands and shoes. The shading and modeling of the face create form while showing Sudduth's adept use of natural, local muds as an unconventional art material. Sudduth applied isolated dabs of black paint with his forefingers to highlight the eyes, nostrils, and overall buttons. The artist signed the work "Jim Sudduth" on the figure's cap, which resembles one Sudduth often wears (fig. 1).

Sudduth's portrayal of his dog Toto is poignant (pl. 7). Although frontal and direct like the self-portrait, here the use of mud, with some paint, and the chalky white clay is reversed. Toto and his ball, their silhouettes shadowed, emerge from a mud background. The dog's form is in varying intensities of white, his features in mud, paint, and shoe polish, which Sudduth often used as a source for black.

Edgar Tolson portrayed himself as a whittler holding a pocketknife and a piece of wood in a rare self-portrait (pl. 10). From Appalachia, where carving was a popular pastime, Tolson whittled toys as a child but devoted himself to carving only after an accident in 1957 paralyzed one side of his body. His prior experience as a carpenter and chair maker, as well as his knowledge of local crafts, familiarized him with the sort of refined carving seen in *Self-portrait with Whittling Knife*. His art, "a God-given job"[1] according to the artist, is simple and understated. His unadorned style articulates the essentials through minimal form carved in slight relief. The only applied color, black, covers the figure's glasses. Like his minimalist design, Tolson's tool was simple: a pocketknife.

Tolson drew a distinction between whittling and carving: "Well there are differences in it. When you're carving something you've got your mind

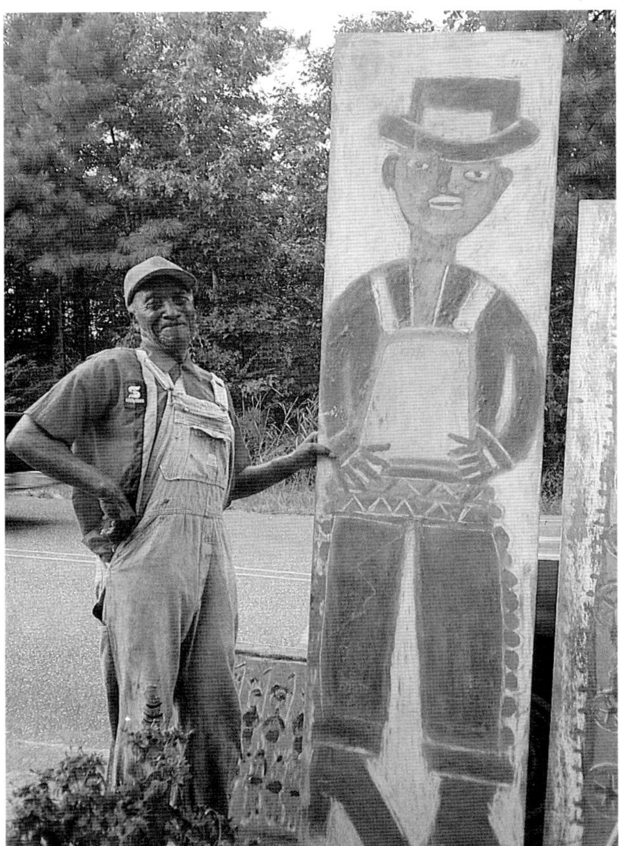

Fig. 1. Jimmy Lee Sudduth, Fayette, Alabama, 1988. The artist stands beside a self-portrait much like cat. no. 225 (pl. 6). Photo Kurt A. Gitter.

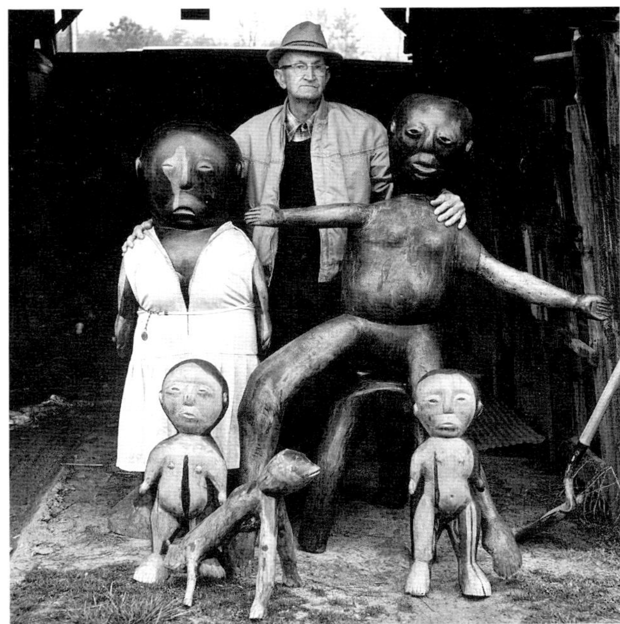

Fig. 2. Raymond Coins, Westfield, North Carolina, 1983. The artist is flanked by his nearly life-size carvings, *Raymond* and *Ruby* (pl. 11), representing himself and his wife. Photo © Roger Manley.

with it. You have your whole being in it. You have to. But just sitting there whittling on a stick, you ain't got nothing in it but just a little time."[2] According to his own definition, Tolson was a carver: "You don't make it with your hands. You *form* it with your hands. . . . You make it with your mind."[3]

Raymond Coins portrayed himself and his wife of more than fifty years, Ruby, in carved, standing life-size sculptures (pl. 11, fig. 2). Ruby Coins insisted that the female figure wear one of her own dresses because she objected to its exposed breasts.[4] The pedestal upon which Raymond rests shows that, like Coins's small stone sculptures, these works are not self-supporting. Carved from cedar and sycamore limbs, the irregular figures are determined in part by the shape of the tree limbs and represent their subjects mostly in body type.

Another Coins work, *Mailbox Man* (cat. no. 35), is of partially painted, carved wood with a metal mailbox attached. Coins actually used this sculpture to receive mail in front of his home in Pilot Mountain, North Carolina.[5]

Angel (pl. 90) is a memorial to Coins's dog, who died in 1984. Carved from soft blue river stone, a powerful angel emerges from a horizontal slab. Incised and carved on the angel's surface are houses, plants, birds, and the deceased dog himself.

The many nieces and nephews with whom Sam Doyle lived called him "Unk Sam," and the artist so titled approximately twelve self-portraits[6] (sometimes spelled "Onk"), of which *Onk Sam* is one (pl. 9). Painted on laminated board, once probably a tabletop, this image may have been reworked several times before reaching this final stage.[7] "Unk" is a word from the Gullah language, which mixes English with aspects of African languages. Used by slaves like Doyle's ancestors, Gullah is still spoken on isolated islands off the coast of Georgia and South Carolina, including Doyle's St. Helena.[8] Doyle was expressing himself in his native language, just as his works often reflect his indigenous culture.

Doyle also chronicled the lives of family members, friends, and historical figures on St. Helena Island. *Adlade* (pl. 8) is an image of his great-aunt Adelaide Washington, a freed slave, shown setting off for her day's work in the cotton fields. She totes a basket on her head, puffs on a pipe, and carries a hoe and hat in her hand. She worked until dark, according to Doyle, taking with her a supper basket of potatoes and peas.[9] In Doyle's preferred material, enamel paint on corrugated roof tin (commonly used on the island), the work both commemorates a loved one and remembers a rural life-style.

While incarcerated for burglary, Joe Louis Light first heard the Lord's voice speak to him about the Old Testament.[10] The bird, said Light, "is the spirit of God,"[11] and to indicate that he is in touch with the Lord, in *Bird* (pl. 5), the artist depicted himself with a blue and red bird firmly planted on his head. Broad, flat planes of bold color outlined in black typify Light's powerful, compelling work.

Steven Ashby's self-portrait, *Man with Scythe* (cat. no. 8), is fashioned from wood, paint, cloth, metal, and attached collage elements. Ashby, who lived most of his life as a farmhand in Virginia, declares in this powerful masterwork his affinity for the land and nature, a sentiment he expressed in simple terms: "I like to work the land."[12] The life-size figure, made from a tree trunk, stands erect, wearing the artist's own cloth pants. Attached tree limbs represent arms and the scythe used for cutting hay and grass. A commercial bow tie graces his neck; wooden collage items define his face and nose; and tacks mark his eyes.

Ashby often attached hair, clothes, photos, and other found objects to his assemblages. He was proud of the sexual completeness of his figures, which are often anatomically explicit. His kinetic figures and animals sometimes resemble unsophisticated versions of the work of Jean Tinguely, the twentieth-century Swiss sculptor.

When asked how many self-portraits he had done, Mose Tolliver replied, "Bales of them. . . . Sometimes I make them to resemble me, sometimes not."[13] The first time Tolliver deemed himself the subject of his work, it was after the fact. In the mid-1970s, the late Robert Bishop, then director of the Museum of American Folk Art, New York, asked Tolliver who was depicted in a work Bishop had just purchased. "I drew it," responded Tolliver, "And I didn't want to name it for no one else,"[14] and so he said it was himself.

In *Mose, Willie Mae, Moose Lady Going Over to Paradise for Anniversary* (pl. 15),[15] Tolliver stands between his recently deceased wife of fifty years, Willie Mae, and a woman on an exercise bar. Snakes and birds surround them. The artist leans on two hand-held canes, representing the metal walker he has used since the late 1960s, after a loading dock accident left him partially crippled. His graying, curly hair is painted in this work; in others the artist glues clippings of his own hair to the painting's surface.

The woman on the exercise rack or "scooter," as Tolliver calls it, balances on her hands, her legs spread above her head. A phallic shape attached to the rack points to her graphically depicted genitalia, a recurring fantasy expressed in Tolliver's paintings. The idea for the image came to Tolliver when a female friend told him she could not "keep up with her fling, and he suggested that with such a gadget she could give herself [sexual] pleasures."[16]

Although the visual elements of this work typify Tolliver's brush and style, the format is unusually large for the artist, who, because of his disability, works seated with a board on his lap. To achieve this scale, he had to rest part of the work on other chairs and seek assistance to rotate the board to paint the remaining sections. Tolliver typically paints flat, frontal figures on a colored background with little other adornment. A lack of individual modeling contributes to the uniform appearance of the faces: their shape is round or oval; noses are long brushstrokes extending from the hairline to the tip of the nose; and eyes are almond-shaped. A supreme colorist, Tolliver selects from myriad house paint colors to create exciting combinations. Race is not indicated by paint color—Mose is depicted in gray hues, his wife, also African-American, is shown as white. Although most brushstrokes are flat, Tolliver often employs energetic, painterly dabs of paint, as seen in the birds and snakes in this work.

Lonnie B. Holley's *Yielding to the Ancestors While Controlling the Hands of Time* (pl. 12) is a self-portrait in the sense of bearing tribute to the artist's African-American forebears. "I try to make art from the heart that honors something or someone. . . . I'm trying to make people see deeper to where the mind takes over," Holley says.[17] In his ten-foot-tall construction, the artist created a powerful totem from wood planks, foundry molds, and industrial parts, asserting himself as a consummate master of assemblage. Two faces, one on top of the other, are stacked above a simulated clock whose hands symbolize the passage of time, the conduit between the artist and his ancestral figures. Of the work, Holley has said, "The person controlled by his inner self, his spiritual part, is controlling the hands of time. If he doesn't yield to the ways of the ancestors, he destroys time."[18]

Harold Crowell often paints or draws portraits, and sometimes self-portraits, with relative likeness. In *Two Sailors* (pl. 4), in acrylic on cardboard, he depicted his father, a Methodist minister, in his navy captain's uniform standing with a friend against a bright expanse of aqua sea, blue sky, and golden beach.[19] The painting typifies Crowell's vibrant, dramatic color sense and his upbeat, realistic imagery.

Mentally handicapped since birth, Crowell was first encouraged to draw by his mother to keep him from getting restless during church services and to occupy him at home.[20] Institutionalized at age twenty-three, Crowell has been encouraged in his creative endeavors for their therapeutic value. Unlike the obsessively patterned work created by many other institutionalized artists, Crowell's images

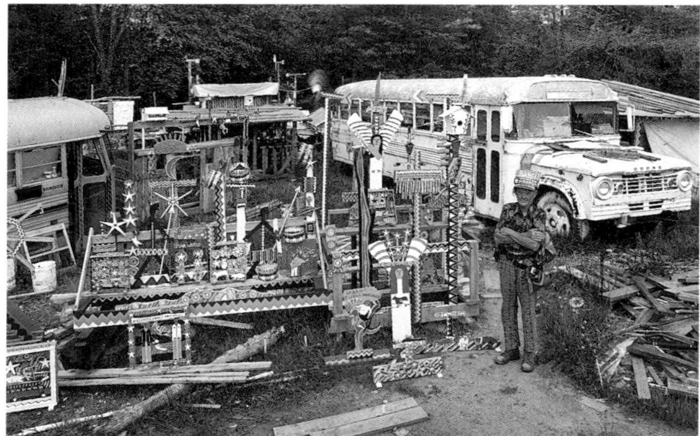

Fig. 3. James Harold Jennings, Pinnacle, North Carolina, 1988. The artist, who lives and works in the buses on his land, often represents the crown he wears in his large assemblages. Photo Marcus Schubert.

tend to reflect realistically the people he has met and the places he has seen.

James Harold Jennings, in the energetic conglomerate of diverse symbols and visual elements that make up *Arts* (pl. 3), made a self-portrait without literally depicting himself. The crown that tops a star-studded tepee is a rendering of the painted metal crown that the artist himself wears on special occasions (fig. 3); Jennings has referred to himself as the "sun, moon, and star artist."[21] These symbols, liberally strewn throughout his work, reflect his astrological beliefs: "Everything we have on the earth and all of our powers comes from the sun, the moon, and the stars. If it wasn't for them, we wouldn't be here."[22] An orange, half-circle sun rests on the letter M of his bold signature at the assemblage's base. Stars adorn the Ferris wheel, vertical posts, and the blue base. Color and movement predominate in this intricate, busy construction. The Ferris wheel and decorated small hanging panels around the totem on the right all move in the wind. The many small animals, Indians, and patterned circles and zigzags were all painstakingly cut by hand with a saber saw.

Jennings's recent work exemplifies his fascination with painted design, an interest evident in the many detailed abstracted panels in *Arts,* an early work. This eight-foot construction became a prototype for smaller works, like *Art* (cat. no. 128), which often incorporated full-figure self-portraits of the artist wearing a crown. The exuberance of Jennings's work belies his fairly reclusive life-style: "I wake up with the sun, take a ride on my bike, come home, and work right through till it's too dark to see."[23] His art is a clear result of his internal vision: "Just about everything I make in my art comes to me through my dreams."[24] Jennings would sometimes press his fingers to his closed eyes and find imagery in the colored blotches that would appear.[25]

In *Secret Garden, Melrose Plantation* (pl. 21) Clementine Hunter portrayed herself as an artist, seated, painting in front of the main house of Melrose Plantation, where she was employed for most of her life, first in the fields and later as a domestic. Various scenes of plantation life surround the artist: corn fields, a gourd harvest, pecan picking. Figures at the lower left, reportedly François Mignon and his secretary, hold garden tools. Mignon, who from 1938 to 1970 lived on the plantation as curator of the estate and its library and collections, was the most important figure in Hunter's artistic development. He encouraged her to paint by providing materials, purchasing her works, arranging exhibitions, informing critics and dealers, and writing about her paintings.[26]

Ezekiel Gibbs began to draw in 1972 at the age of eighty-three after Josephine, his wife of sixty-two years, died. In *Untitled* (pl. 16), a multicolored watercolor, Gibbs depicted himself and a neighbor in the lower left. Using multiple color dots and small dabs of paint, Gibbs characteristically filled the entire surface. The two brown caskets at the upper left possibly represent those of two children whom he outlived. His wife is shown lying in her gray coffin, with their two surviving sons, Lloyd and Boyd, depicted beside her. The rooster and the beet in the foreground speak of the importance of rural experience to this Texas artist, a lifelong farmer.

As an expression of religious fervor and evangelical mission, Sister Gertrude Morgan's *Charity Hospital—523-2311* (pl. 19) is a self-portrait that intricately interweaves the religious themes of her daily life. Like her painted guitar case (cat. no. 176) carried for street preaching, this decorative fan was a tool of her religious zeal. The fan is divided into longitudinal cardboard sections which record her recurring visual imagery: a portrait of Morgan standing, dressed in white; seated with her savior and spiritual spouse, Jesus Christ, in an airplane on her salvation journey to the New Jerusalem; and looking up at an angel, an emissary from the Lord. A boat surrounded by allusions to verses from Luke 5:1–11 is bordered by an inscription, "Drop your net," which suggests Christ's command to the Apostles, who would become fishermen for souls.

One panel of the fan reads, "Charity Hospital 523-2311 [the hospital's phone number during Morgan's lifetime]. Now do you believe in Jesus. He's the greatest doctor I no. Just put your trust in Jesus and call him and every deamon in you hafter come on out and go." Charity Hospital has cared for New Orleans's indigent sick since its founding in 1736. Sister Gertrude might have preached at the hospital, and she most likely received medical attention there.

Gillespie City (cat. no. 51) typifies the autobiographical paintings of John William "Uncle Jack" Dey. Usually done in model-airplane paint on Masonite, his paintings are personal reflections of his life experiences and memories. Dey often affixed a letter to the back of a work to explain its story. In a letter attached to the reverse of *Gillespie City*, Dey wrote: "I bought one of Mr. Russell Gillespie's cabins. He is a wood carver of considerable talent in the estimation of Uncle Jack. Now for the picture, their are seven ducks in the picture, 6 drake's and one hen. Mr. Russell Gillespie has had considerable luck fishing, he even fish up a boot according to picture. Crows who delovep [develop] a taste for fish are a pest, and known as fish crows. . . . Now if you don't like this picture, think it's too high, don't in tend to take care of it, leave it hang. I don't care whether you buy it or not and that's a fact, by an old coot known as Uncle Jack."[27] The letter provides a glimpse into the determined character of this artist, who worked as a trapper and lumberjack as a young man, and later as a barber and a policeman. His meticulous, charming paintings display vibrant blues, blacks, greens, reds, oranges, yellows, and browns, often creating a dramatic dynamism (pls. 52, 97).

David Butler's symbolic self-portrait is his bicycle, a most personal object that he used daily for transportation (pl. 2). The decoration of *David's Bike* echoes the works with which the artist adorned and enlivened his home and yard after the death of his wife and a debilitating head injury that occurred while working for a lumber company.[28] Attached to the bike, fashioned from flattened, corrugated roofing tin, hand-cut with shears into whimsical shapes, and painted with colorful house paint, are decorative whirligigs, flat figures of birds, beasts, and stars, and cutout designs and figures, the varied formats seen throughout his work.

Butler had already decorated the bicycle—a truly kinetic work—by 1974, when his work was "discovered,"[29] but the current version bears components changed through the years, probably due to wear and whim. Reflectors attached to tin designs on the wheels and elsewhere are both decorative and functional. A rubber bulb horn and tassels hang from the handlebars. Cut tin flowers on the wheels, stars at the center spokes, and colored paint on the tire rims add to the bike's joyous humor and playfulness. Imagine the sight of Butler riding through his small community of Patterson, Louisiana, with whirligig churning, reflectors flashing, and the carnival-like colors of the rotating wheels creating optical illusions!

C. J. P. Scott (pl. 1), short for Captain J. P. Scott, is a model shrimp boat constructed of found objects. Scott, who grew up surrounded by boats in the small waterways of Louisiana's bayou country, had a strong personal relationship to all kinds of watercraft. He worked on boats his entire life. During his breaks he sometimes recorded their details in sketches, which he eventually constructed as remarkably crafted images.[30] Scott collects his materials from trash heaps near his home in Lafitte, Louisiana: wood and metal for the hull, string for the rigging, plastic for the horn, empty plastic tape rolls for the hanging buoys. The precisely fashioned green plastic windows, usually made from large 7-Up bottles, are cut and shaped to fit. The boat is fully equipped with a metal rudder, a painted, articulated steering wheel, and a hefty anchor and chain. Although Scott attaches wooden elements of his boats with nails, he patiently inserts window panes, linoleum tile, and other plastic pieces, only occasionally using the smallest amount of Elmer's glue. Despite his exacting methods, Scott's boats have an imperfect, appealing aesthetic. He is known to work and rework his boats for many weeks and months before he will exhibit them in his yard or sell them. "If it isn't just right, Cap, I take it down and start it up again until it's right."[31]

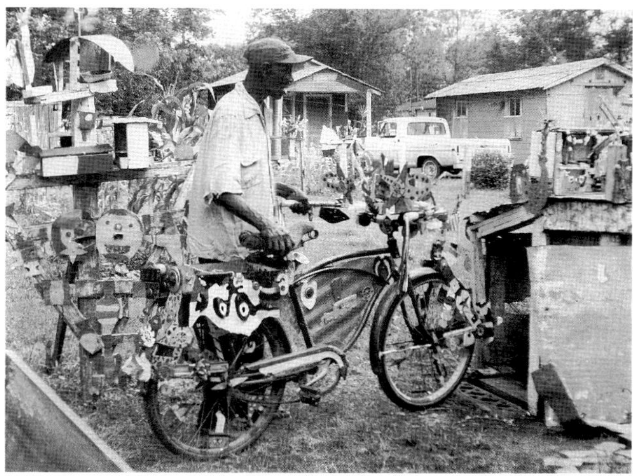

Fig. 4. David Butler, Patterson, Louisiana, 1975. Butler stands amid his whirligig-filled yard with his whimsically decorated bicycle (pl. 2). Photo Charles Kimball, courtesy John Geldersma.

Philo Levi "Chief" Willey, a superb colorist, commemorated his own honeymoon in a triptych, *Three Day Wedding Trip up the Mississippi* (pl. 17).[32] The *Bayou Bell*, a paddleboat typical of the Delta waterways, plies the Mississippi River, which runs through each panel. In two panels the boat progresses through characteristic Willey landscapes. The third depicts a spatially rearranged New Orleans waterfront and Jackson Square, where Willey painted. Despite the license Willey took, distinguishing features of the area can be noted: the Café du Monde, the historic twenty-four-hour spot for café au lait and beignets, the warehouse district, which houses supplies transported on the river, horses and buggies lined up day and night for tourist rides on Decatur Street, and a large white church, probably St. Louis Cathedral, the oldest cathedral in the South. Willey's highly organized spatial arrangement, brimming with whimsical birds and trees, is delineated in his colorful signature style, which often depicts a forest green background under a deep royal blue sky with red-yellow or orange accents of buildings and animals.

In *The Discovery of Finster Art* (pl. 14), Howard Finster recorded the course of the public's familiarity with his work, from friend Edith Wilson's report of it to an Atlanta television station in the early 1960s[33] to subsequent newspaper and magazine accounts and ongoing notice by museums, collectors, and filmmakers. Finster acknowledged the impact of his developing fame in an inscription on the painting's horizon: "What a great fire Edith Wilson started with her little match."

Similar occurrences have dramatically changed the lives of many other contemporary self-taught artists, who began by making imagery of their personal experiences with no sense of becoming recognized artists. From these intimate, self-referential works emerge not only an appreciation of the individuality of southern self-taught artists but an awareness of the interconnectedness of their lives to their major themes: autobiography, daily life, religion, social commentary, patriotism, and nature.

1. *Edgar Tolson: Kentucky Gothic* (Lexington: University of Kentucky Art Museum, 1981), p. 10.

2. Michael T. Hall, "You Make It with Your Mind: The Art of Edgar Tolson," *The Clarion* 12, no. 2/3 (Spring/Summer 1991), p. 37.

3.Ibid., p. 43.

4. Allen and Barry Huffman, interview, ARY, July 1991. The Huffmans bought the piece from Coins in 1982.

5. Coins made several versions of these mailboxes, which bear a resemblance to him. At least two are known to be in private collections.

6. Louanne Laroche, collector and dealer of Doyle's works, interview, ARY, March 1992.

7. A photograph of Doyle's front yard portrays a similar work, even worn in the same upper left corner, see Jane Livingston and John Beardsley; *Black Folk Art in America* (Jackson: University Press of Mississippi; Washington, D.C.: Corcoran Gallery of Art, 1982), p. 53.

8. Confirmation of "unk" as a Gullah word was provided by Emory Cambell, director, the Penn Center, St. Helena Island, South Carolina, April 1993. For further information on Gullah, see Frederic G. Cassidy, "Gullah," *ESC*, pp. 772–73.

9. Sam Doyle, interview, Paul Figuero, director, Gibbs Art Gallery, Charleston, South Carolina, and curator of *The Art of Sam Doyle* (Nov. 19, 1982–Jan. 2, 1983), Oct. 1982.

10. Joe Light, interview, KAG, Feb. 1992. Light added that when he later converted to Judaism, a new legal opinion rendered him as criminally insane and added years to his prison term.

11. Ibid.

12. Steven Ashby as told to Chuck Rosenak, interview, KAG, Dec. 1992. When Rosenak purchased the piece, the artist acknowledged it as a self-portrait.

13. Mose Tolliver, interview, ARY, Nov. 1991.

14. Ibid.

15. The title *Mose, Willie Mae, Moose Lady Going Over to Pair Dyke for Anniversary* is recorded on the back of the painting in the hand of someone other than Tolliver, who is illiterate. "Pair Dyke" was a misunderstanding of Tolliver's pronunciation for "paradise," a place "beyond heaven," which Tolliver obviously associates with sexual pleasures; Mose Tolliver, interview, ARY, Feb. 1993.

16. Mose Tolliver, interview, ARY, Nov. 1991.

17. Bruce Lineker, *In/Outsiders from the American South* (Montgomery, Ala.: Montgomery Museum of Fine Arts, 1992), unpaginated.

18. Lonnie B. Holley, as told to William Arnett, collector and dealer, interview, ARY, April 1993.

19. Chesley Sigmon, Crowell's art therapist and director of creative therapy, Western Carolina Center, Morganton, North Carolina, identified Crowell's father as one of the subjects of this painting; interview, KAG, July 1992.

20. Roger Manley, *Signs and Wonders: Outsider Art inside North Carolina* (Raleigh: North Carolina Museum of Art, 1989), p. 98.

21. *Baking in the Sun: Visionary Images from the South* (Lafayette: University Art Museum, University of Southwestern Louisiana, 1987), p. 92.

22. Tom Patterson, "Roadside Art: Beating a Path to the Homemade World of James Harold Jennings," *Art Papers* 11, no. 6 (Nov./Dec. 1987), p. 31.

23. Ramona Lampell and Millard Lampell with David Larkin, *O, Appalachia: Artists of the Southern Mountains* (New York: Stewart, Tabori, and Chang, 1989), p. 174.

24. Patterson, "Roadside Art," p. 30.

25. *Baking in the Sun*, p. 92.

26. Two sources for further information on the relationship between Hunter and Mignon are James L. Wilson, *Clementine Hunter: American Folk Artist* (Gretna, La.: Pelican Publishing, 1988), and François Mignon, *Plantation Memo: Plantation Life in Louisiana, 1750–1970, and Other Matters* (Baton Rouge, La.: Claitor's Publishing Division, 1972).

27. Chuck Rosenak provided a photocopy of the original letter, dated Jan. 14, 1975, affixed to *Gillespie City*.

28. William A. Fagaly, assistant director for art, New Orleans Museum of Art, interview, ARY, April 1993.

29. William A. Fagaly referred to the bike as a kinetic work in progress; interview, ARY, April 1993. Fagaly organized the first one-man show of Butler's work at the New Orleans Museum of Art in 1976.

30. J. P. Scott, interview, ARY, Sept. 1991.

31. J. P. Scott, interview, KAG, Oct. 1991.

32. Willey told this to Dr. Robert Bishop when he purchased the work. Dr. Bishop related the personal nature of the triptych to KAG, Jan. 1990.

33. Howard Finster, interview, ARY, Feb. 1993. Edith Wilson was the wife of the choir director in Finster's church.

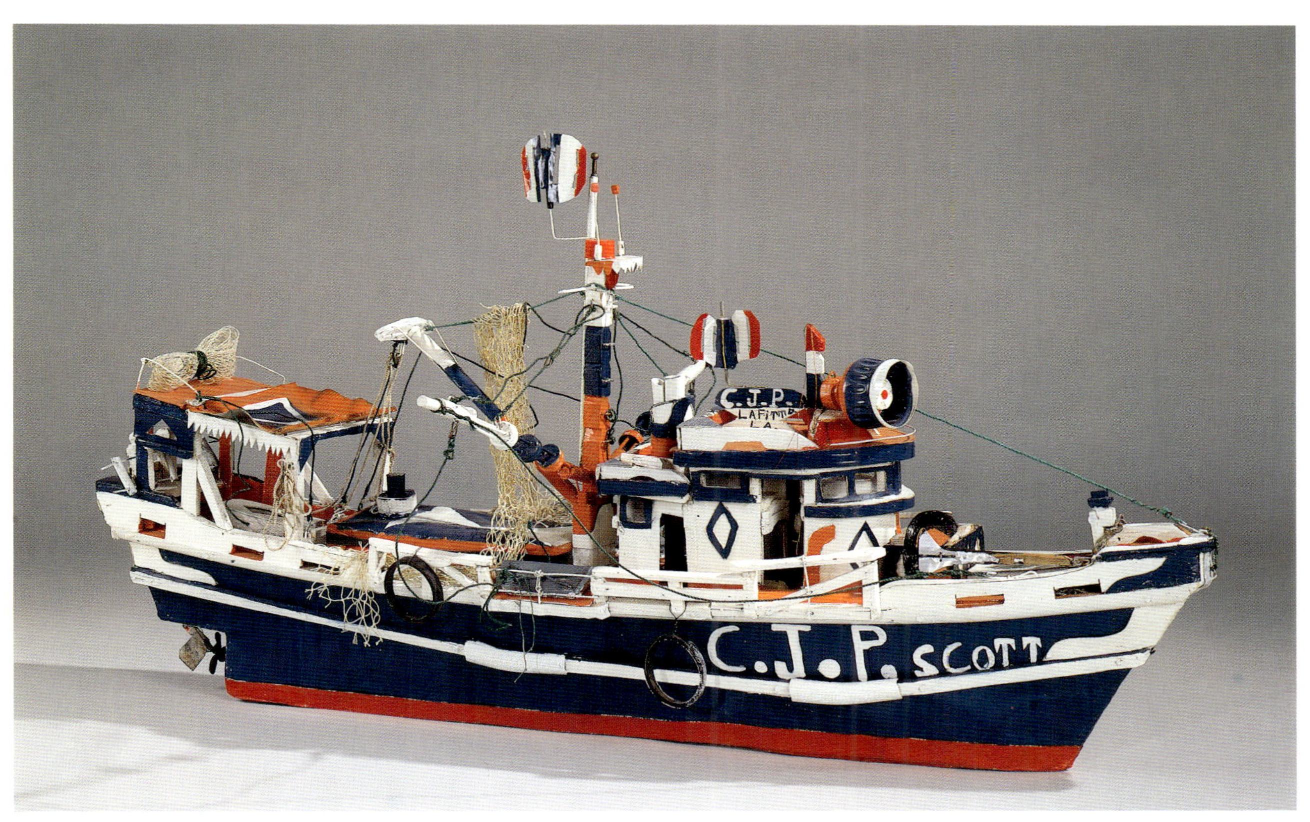

1

J. P. SCOTT

C. J. P. Scott, n.d.

(cat. no. 201)

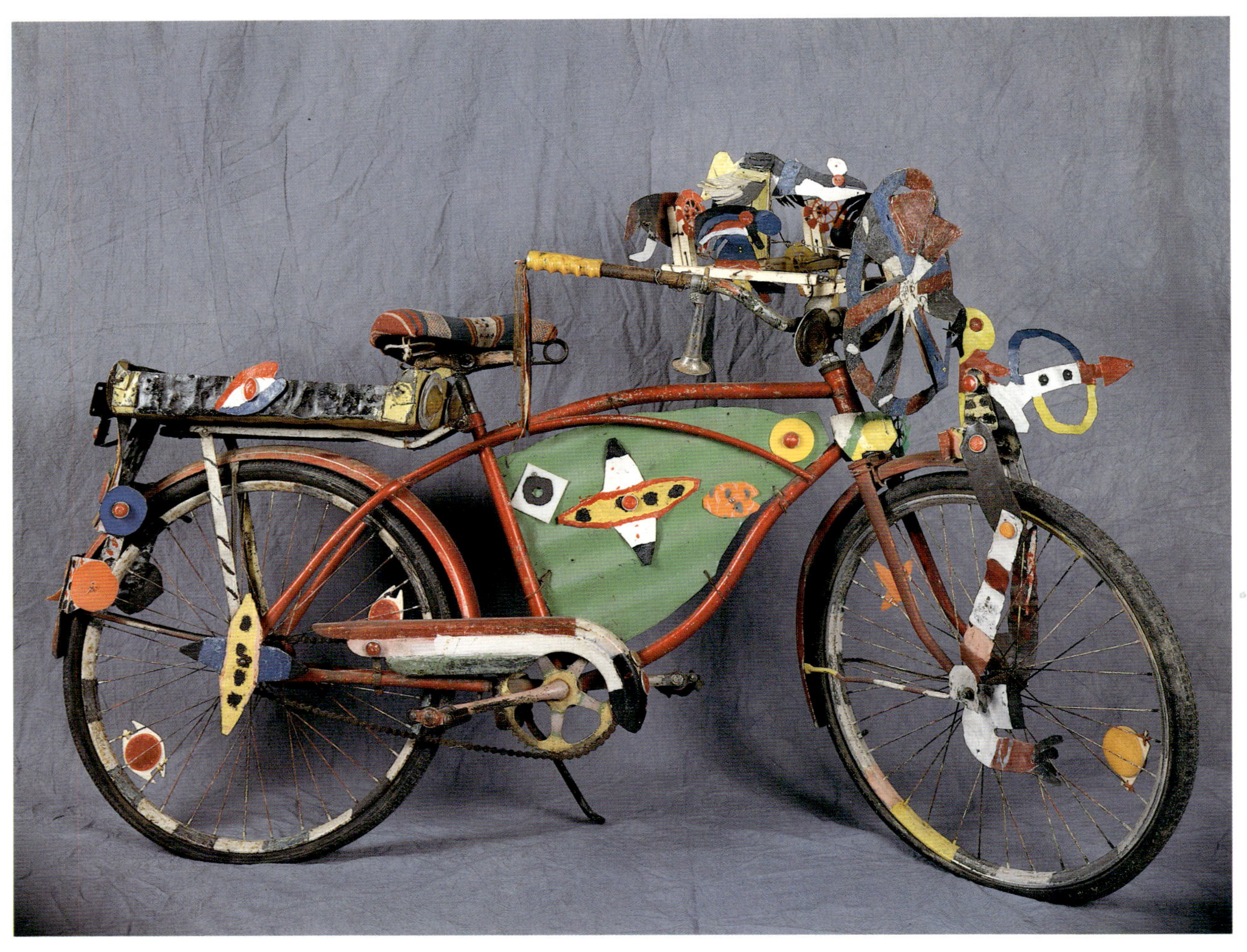

2

DAVID BUTLER
David's Bike, 1976
(cat. no. 17)

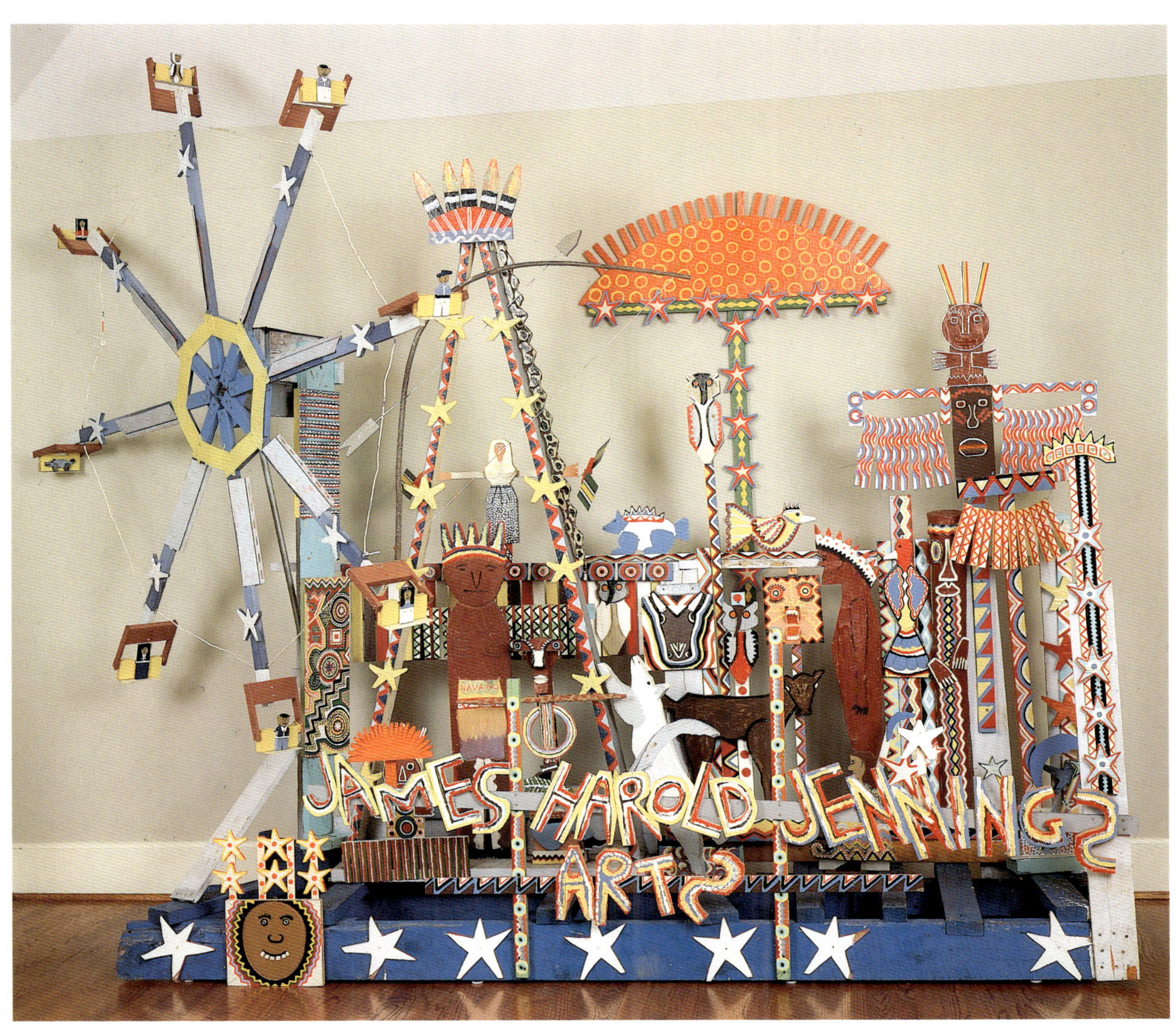

3

JAMES HAROLD JENNINGS
Arts, 1986
(cat. no. 129)

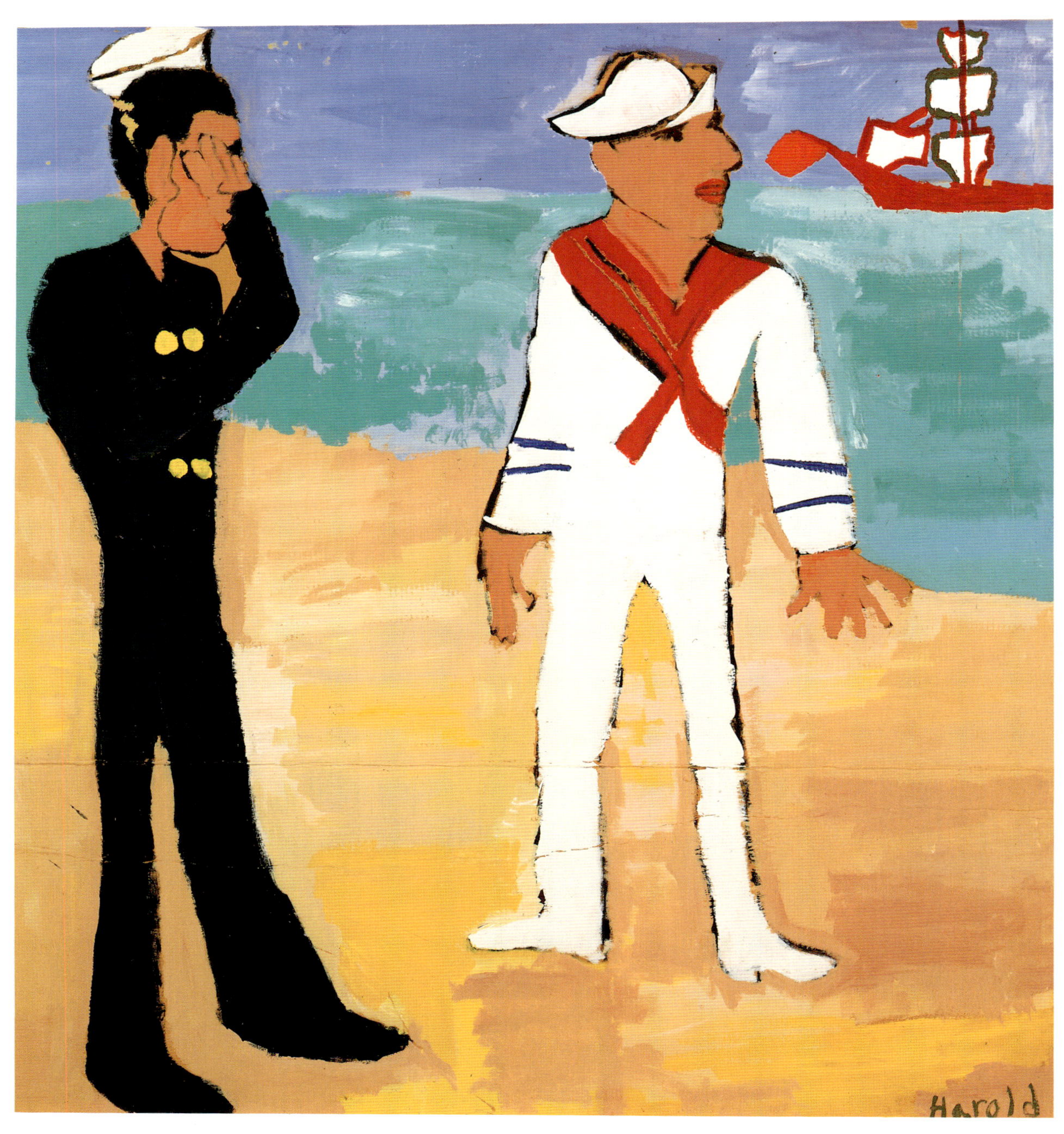

4

HAROLD CROWELL
Two Sailors, 1982
(cat. no. 41)

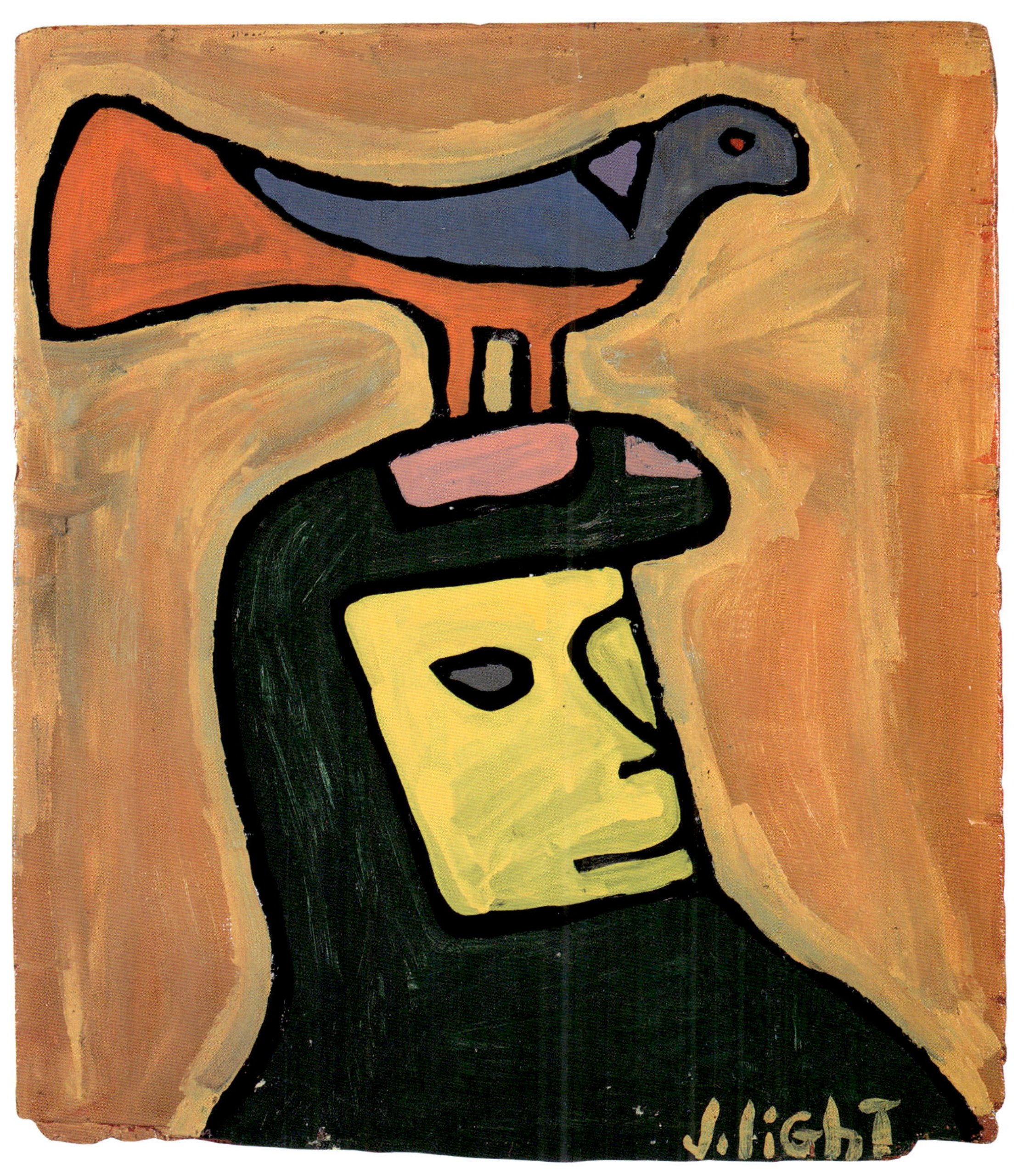

5

JOE LOUIS LIGHT

Bird, 1987

(cat. no. 152)

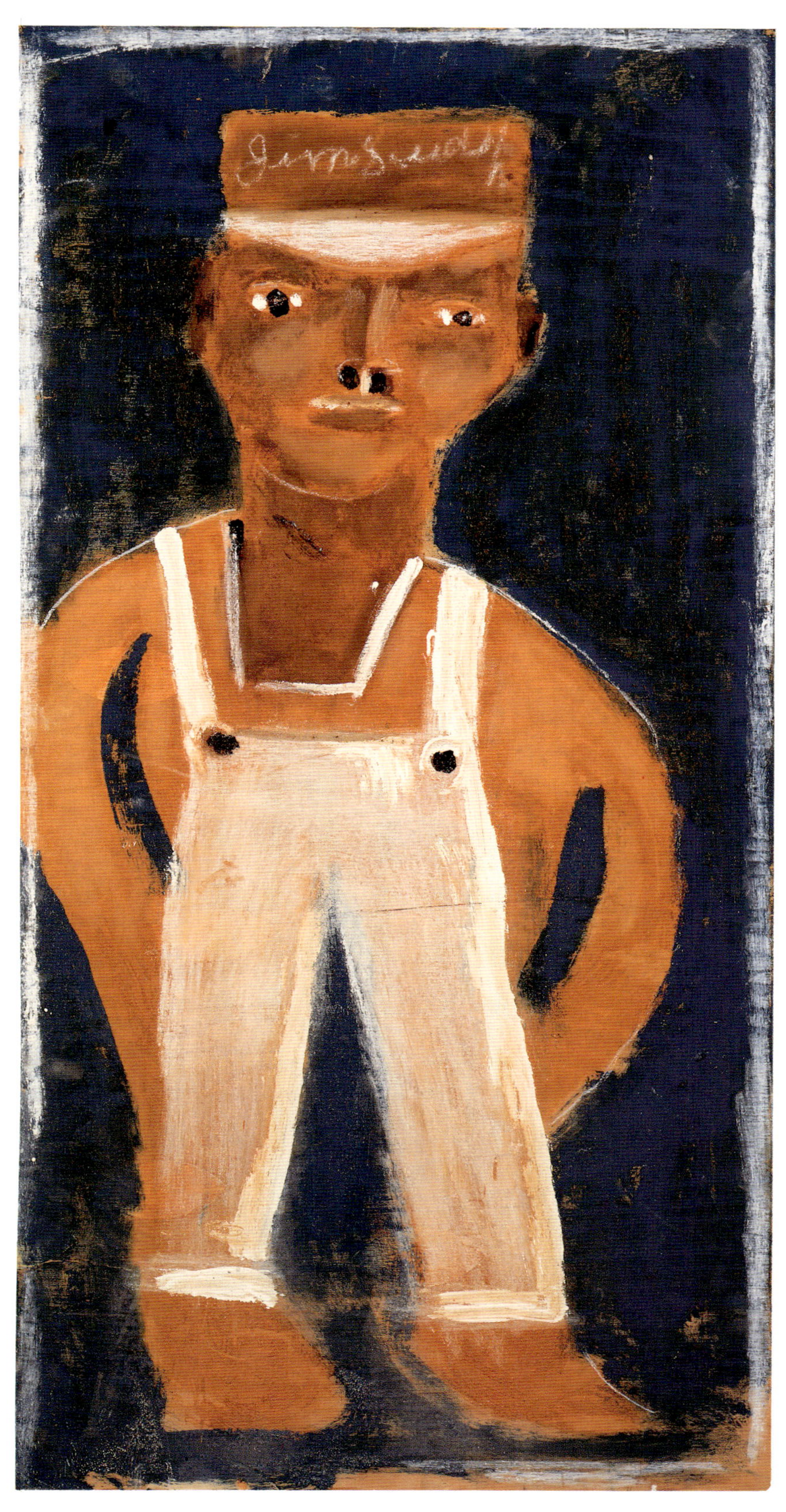

6

JIMMY LEE SUDDUTH

Self-portrait, n.d.

(cat. no. 225)

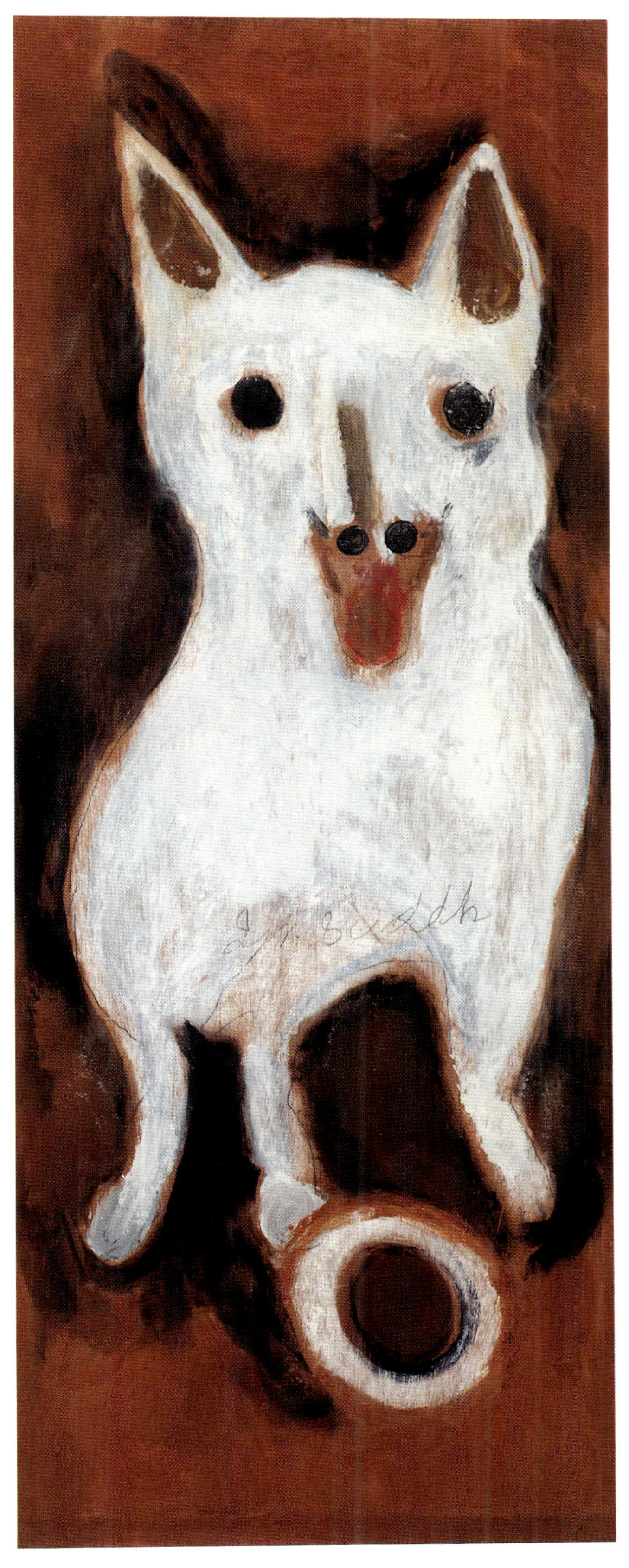

7

JIMMY LEE SUDDUTH

Toto with Ball, n.d.

(cat. no. 227)

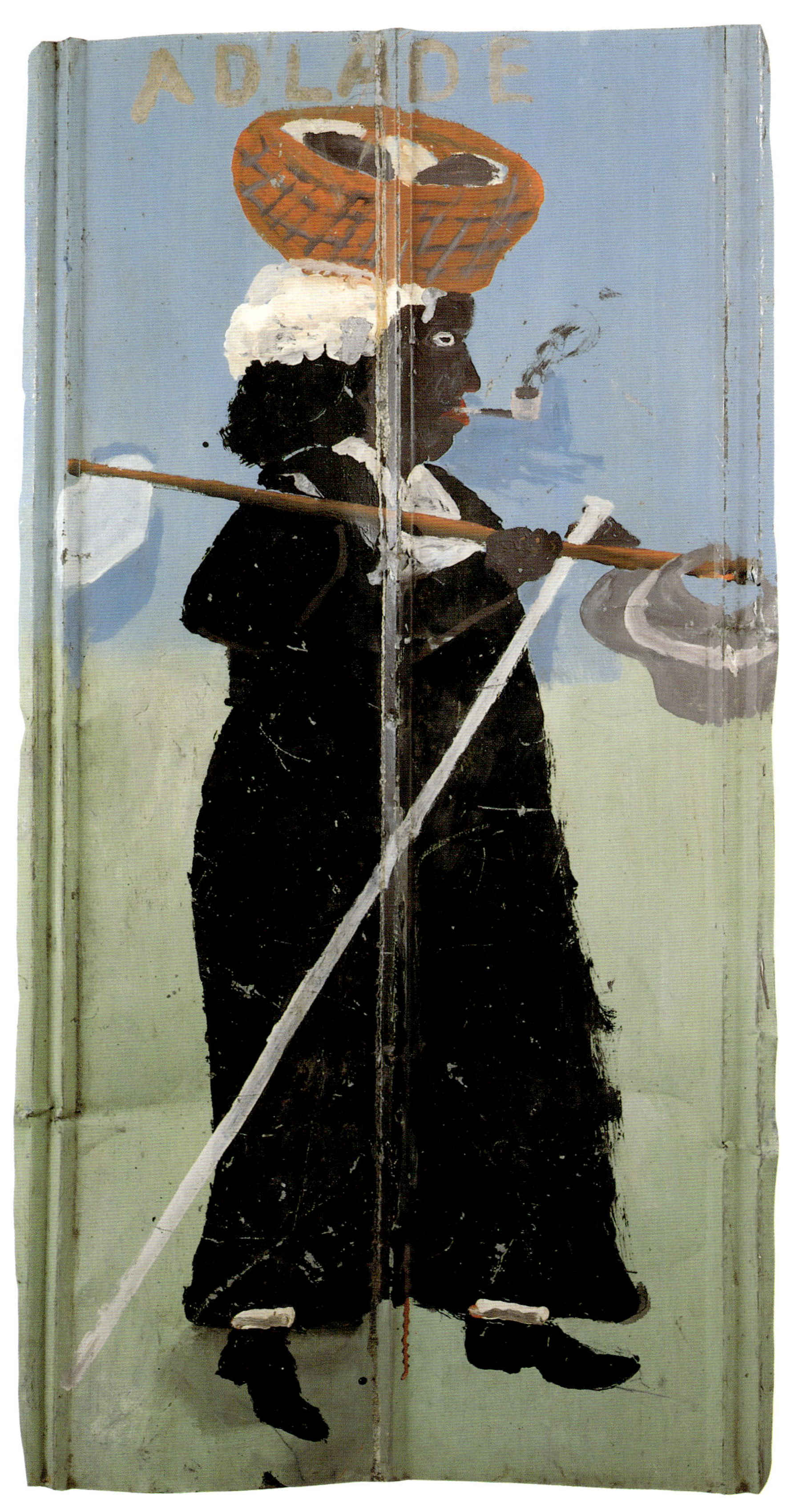

8

SAM DOYLE

Adlade, n.d.

(cat. no. 60)

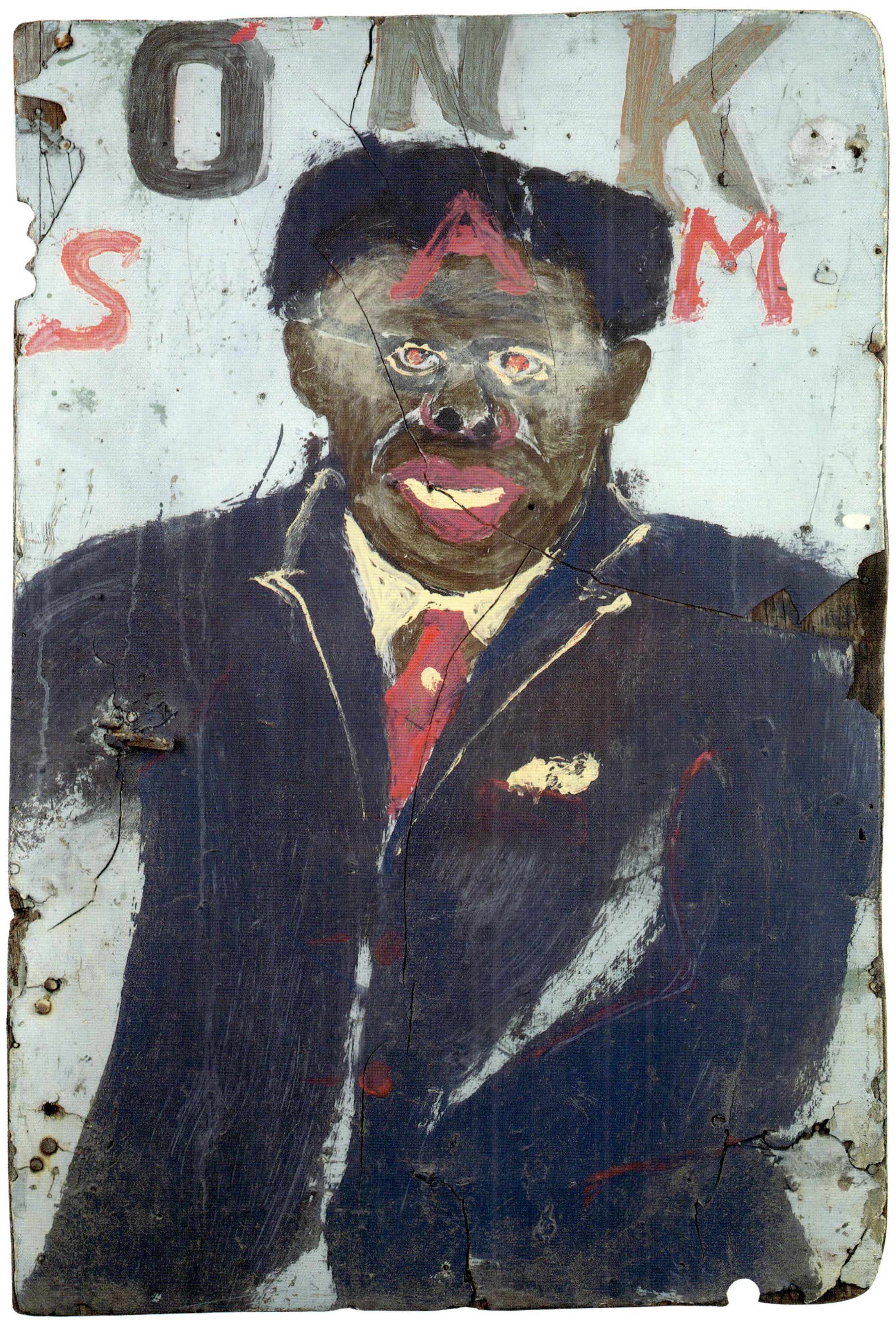

9

SAM DOYLE

Onk Sam, 1978

(cat. no. 71)

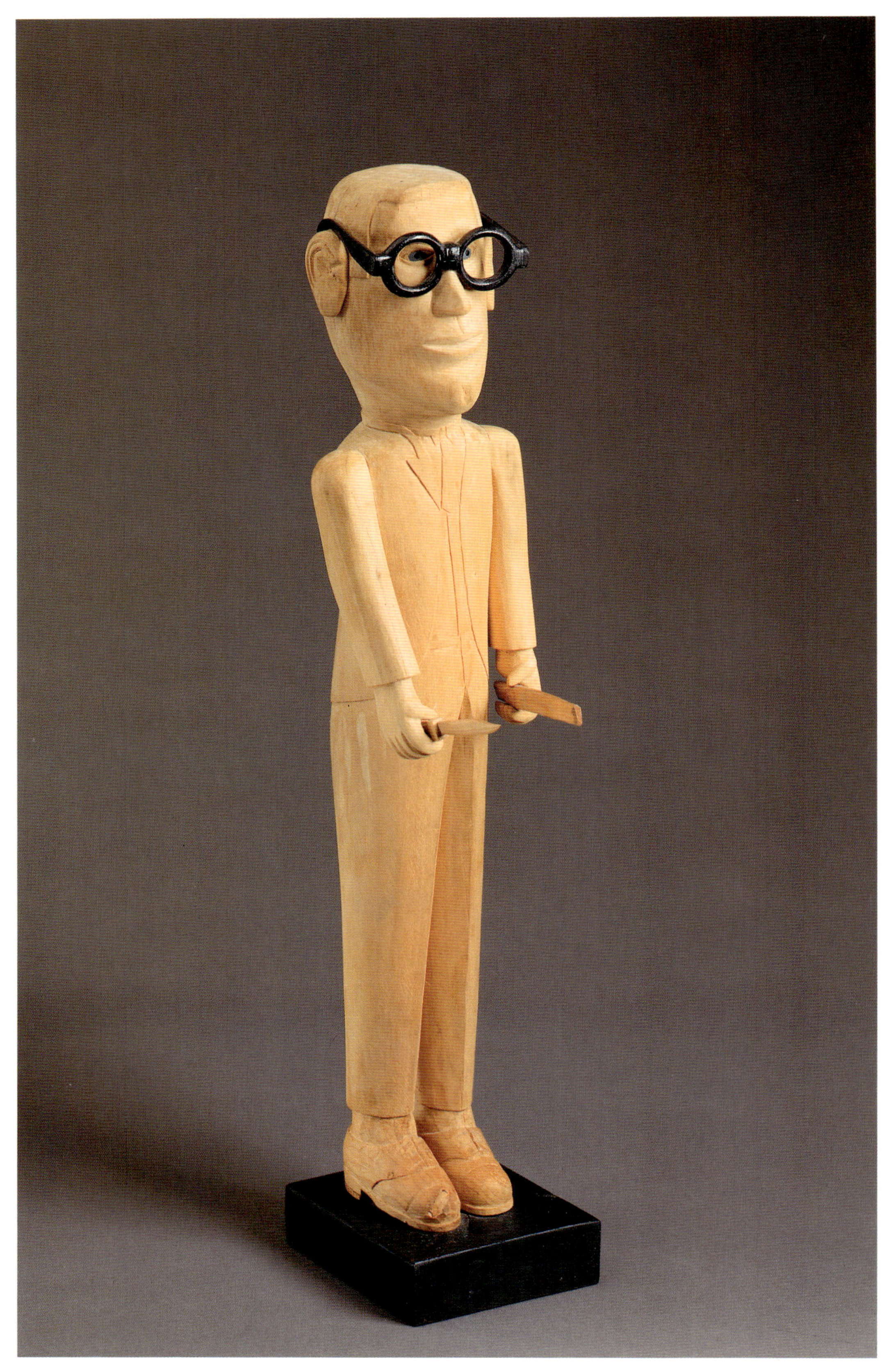

10

EDGAR TOLSON

Self-portrait with Whittling Knife, 1971

(cat. no. 244)

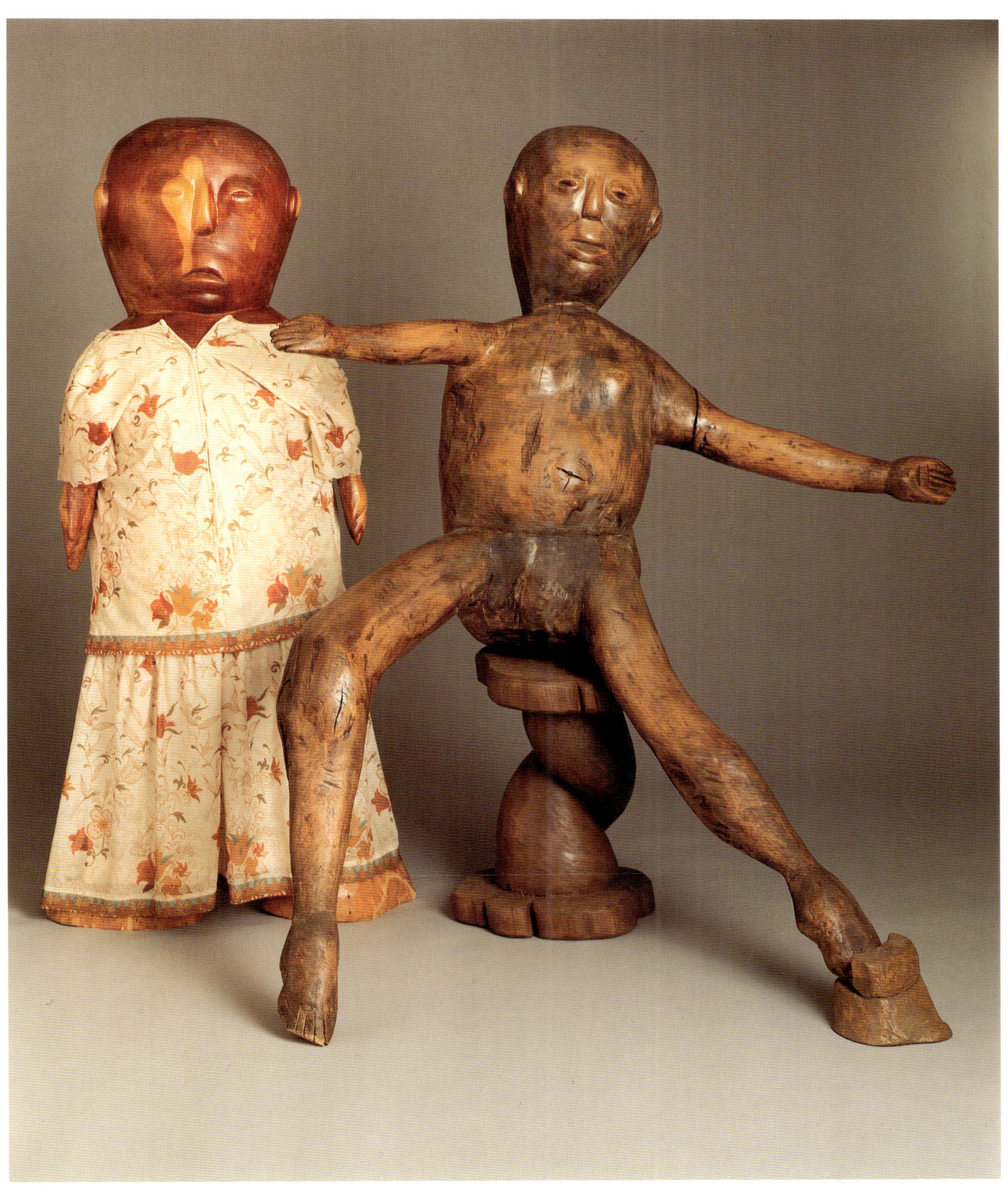

11

RAYMOND COINS

Raymond and Ruby, 1982

(cat. no. 36)

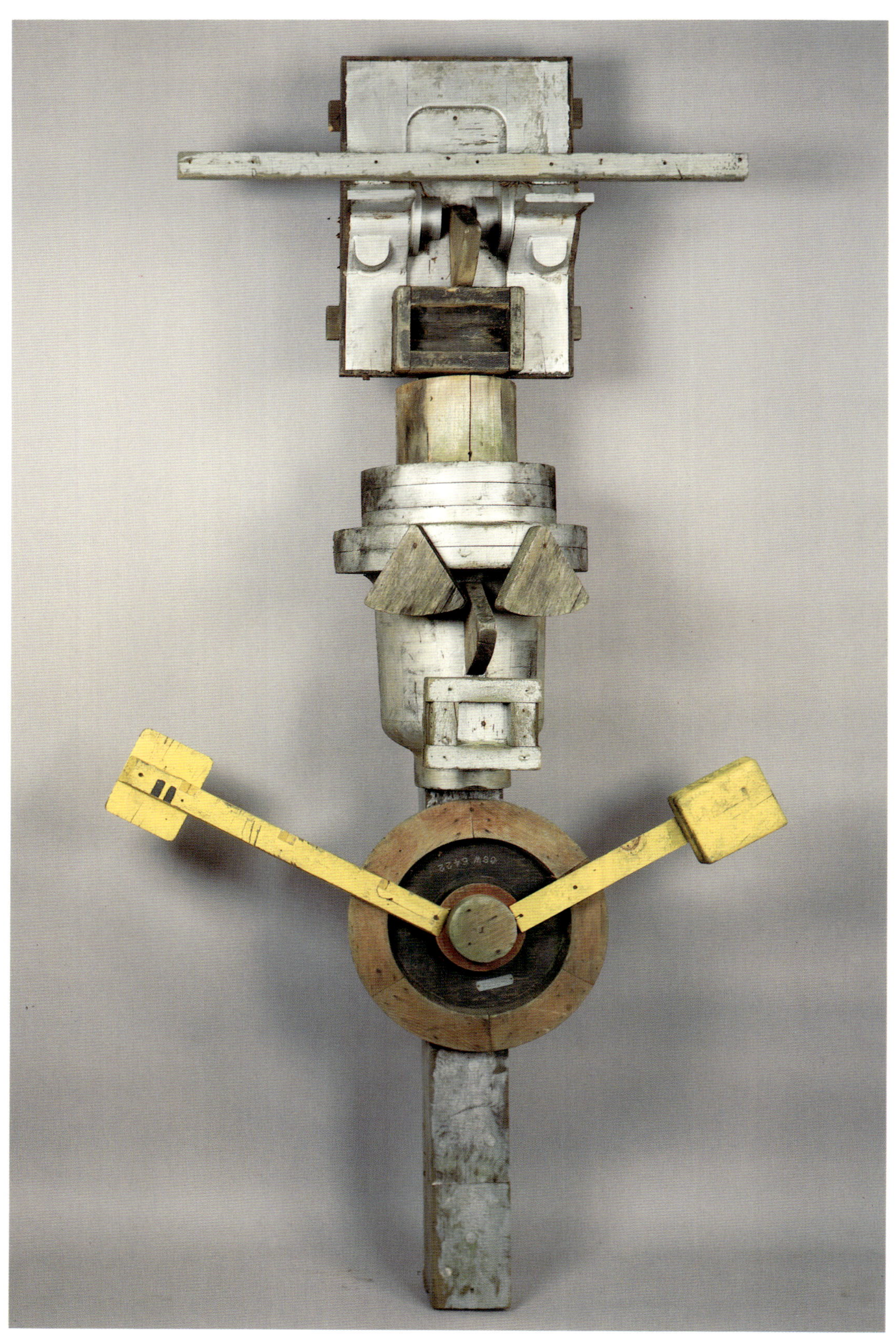

12

LONNIE B. HOLLEY

Yielding to the Ancestors While Controlling the Hands of Time, 1992

(cat. no. 121)

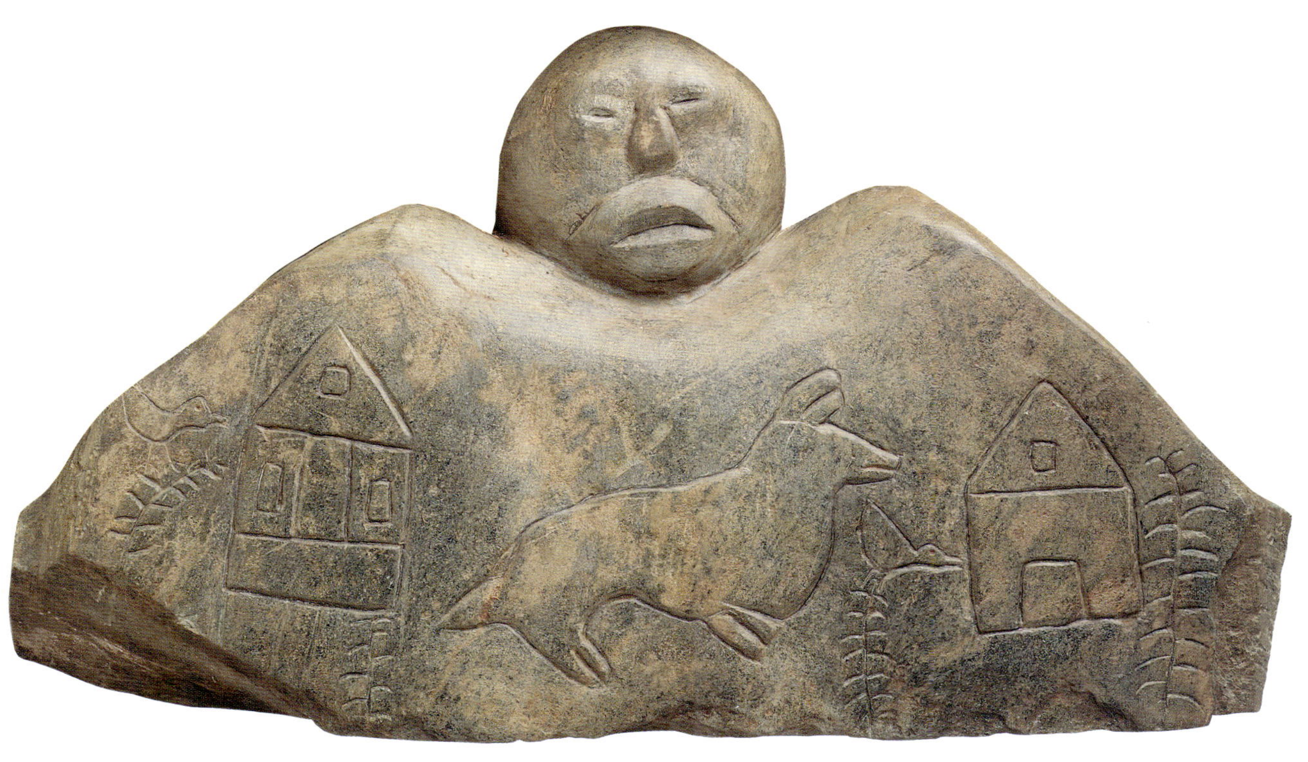

13

RAYMOND COINS
Angel, ca. 1979
(cat. no. 29)

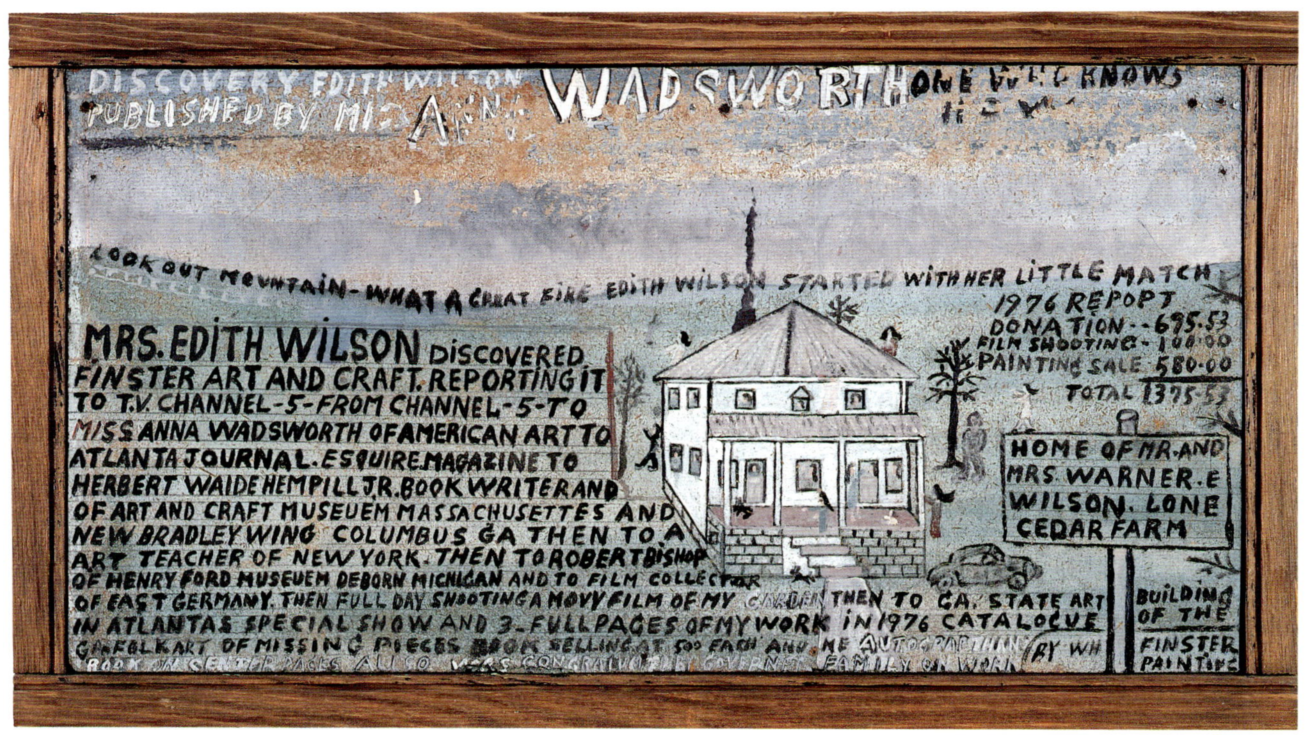

14

HOWARD FINSTER

The Discovery of Finster Art, 1976

(cat. no. 86)

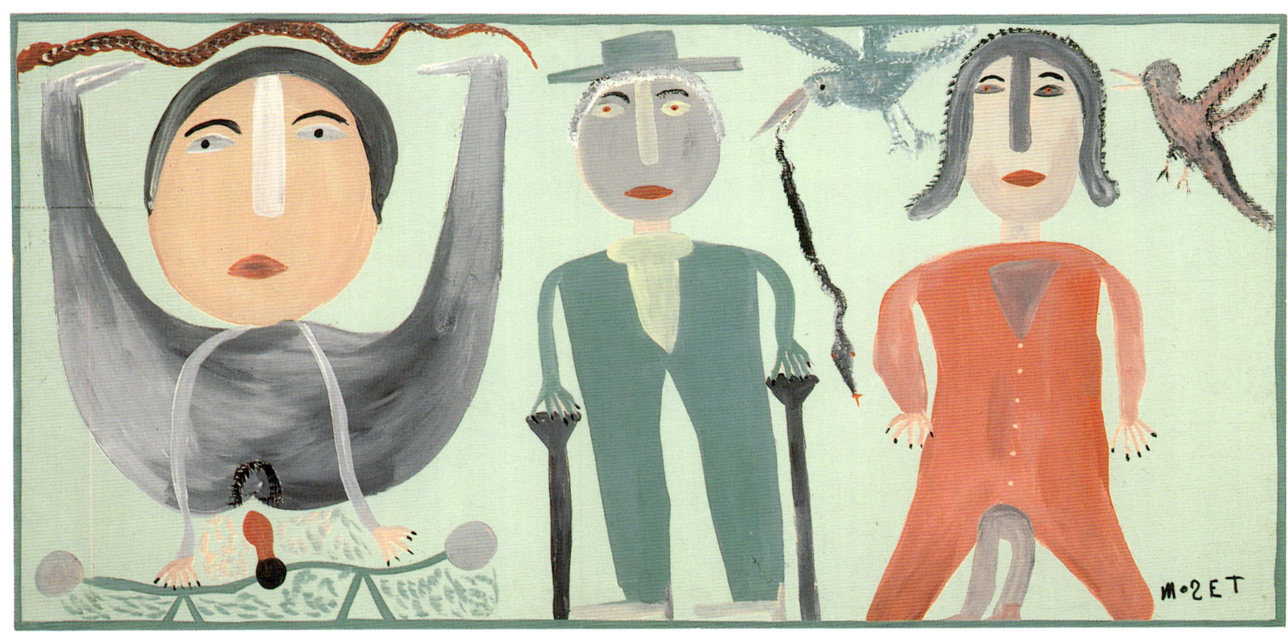

15

MOSE TOLLIVER

Mose, Willie Mae, Moose Lady Going Over to Paradise for Anniversary, 1990

(cat. no. 240)

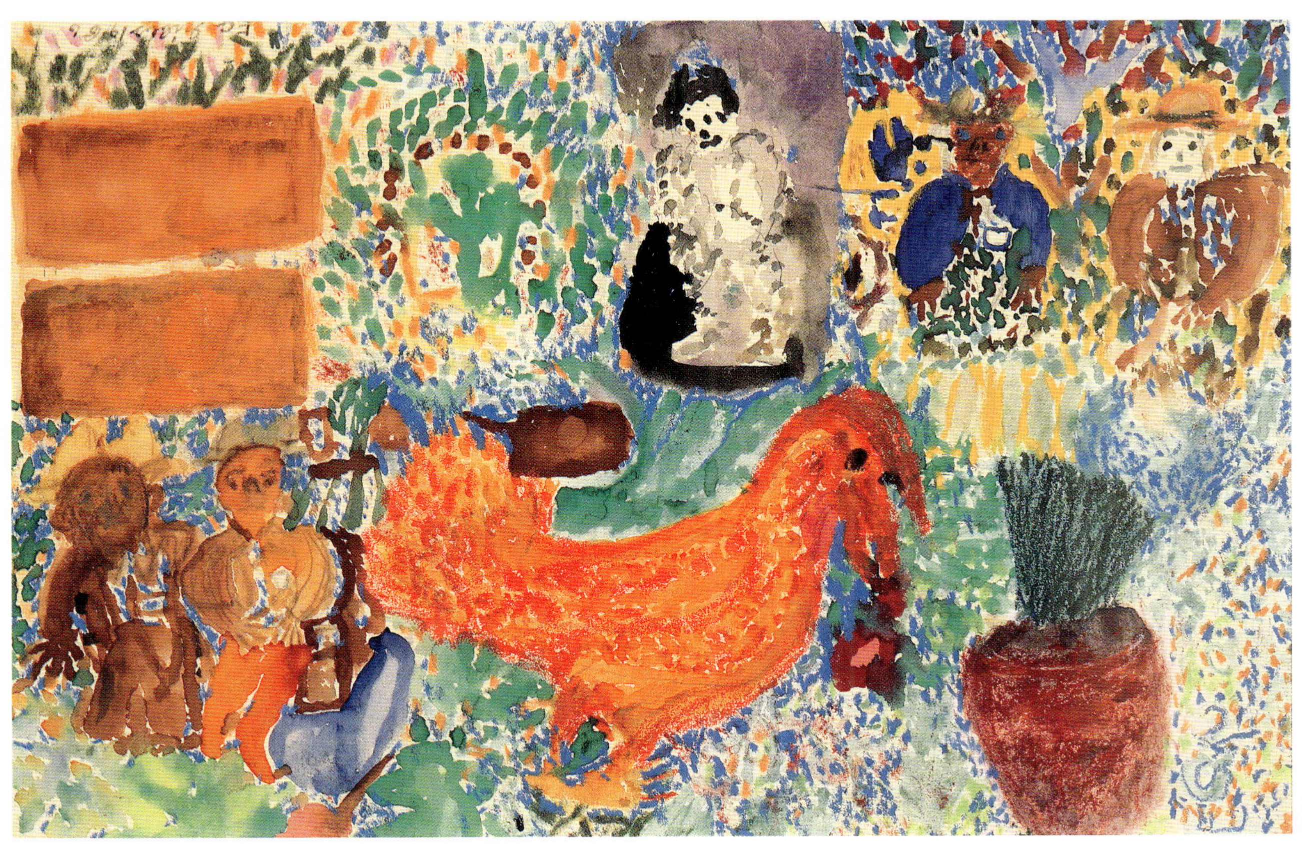

16

EZEKIEL GIBBS

Untitled, 1986

(cat. no. 96)

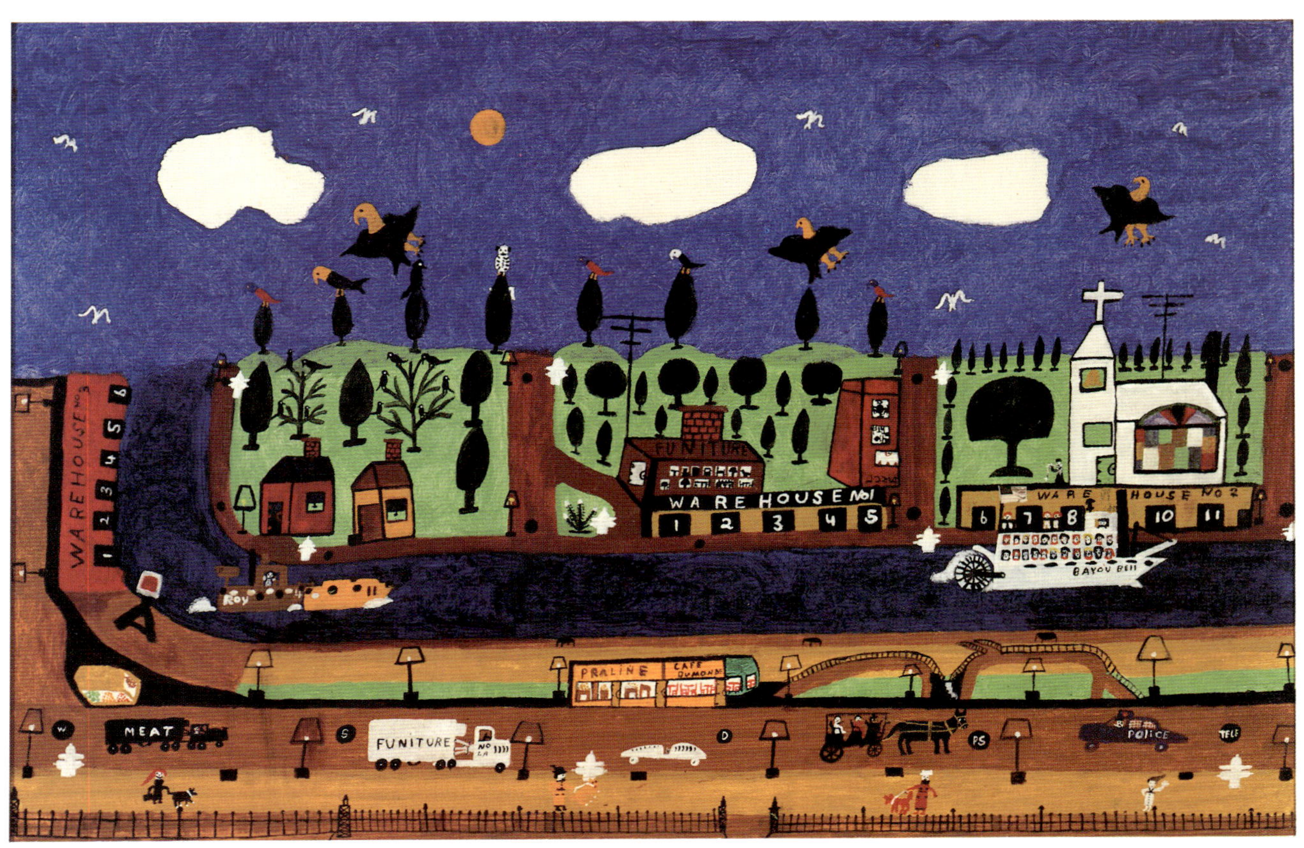

17

PHILO LEVI "CHIEF" WILLEY

Three Day Wedding Trip up the Mississippi

(triptych), 1976

(cat. no. 261)

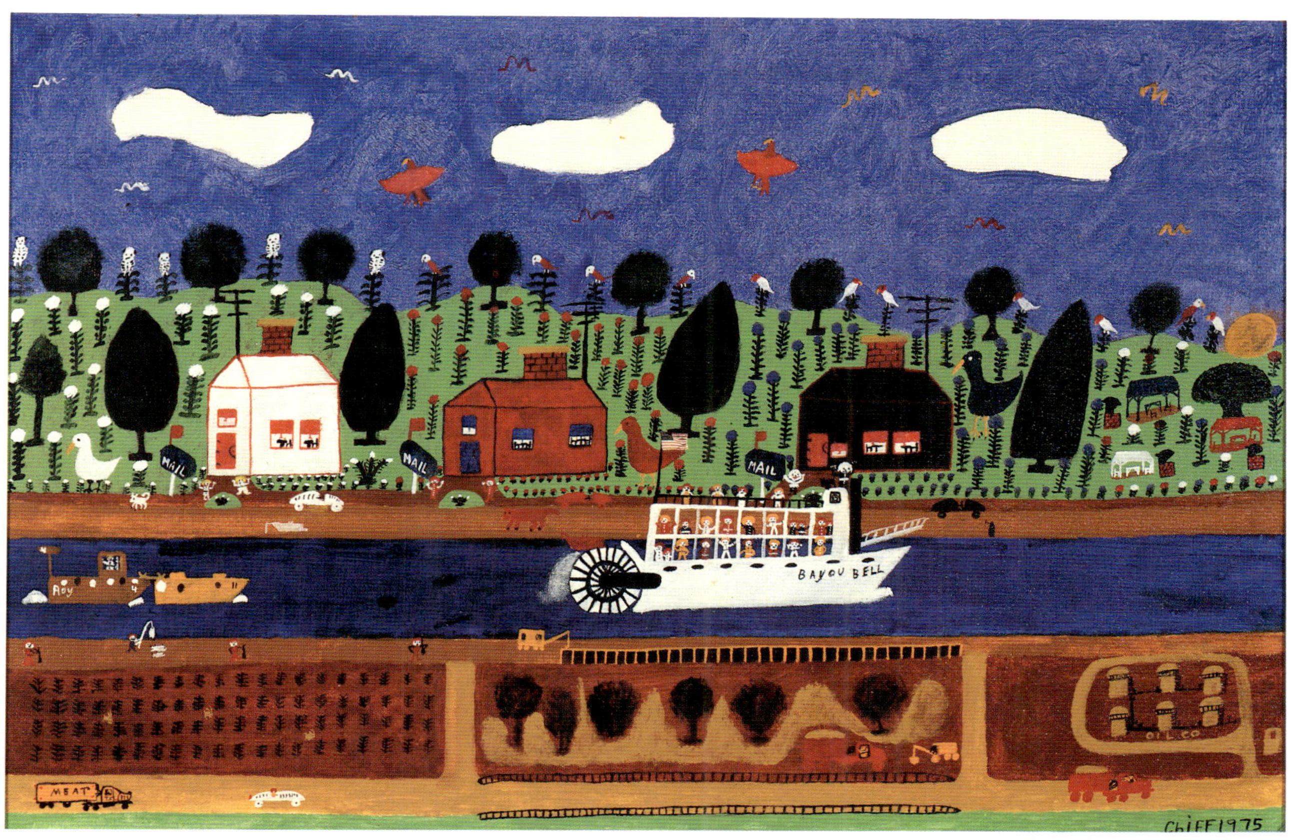
MAIL
MAIL
MAIL
BAYOU BELL
Roy
MEAT
ChIEF 1975

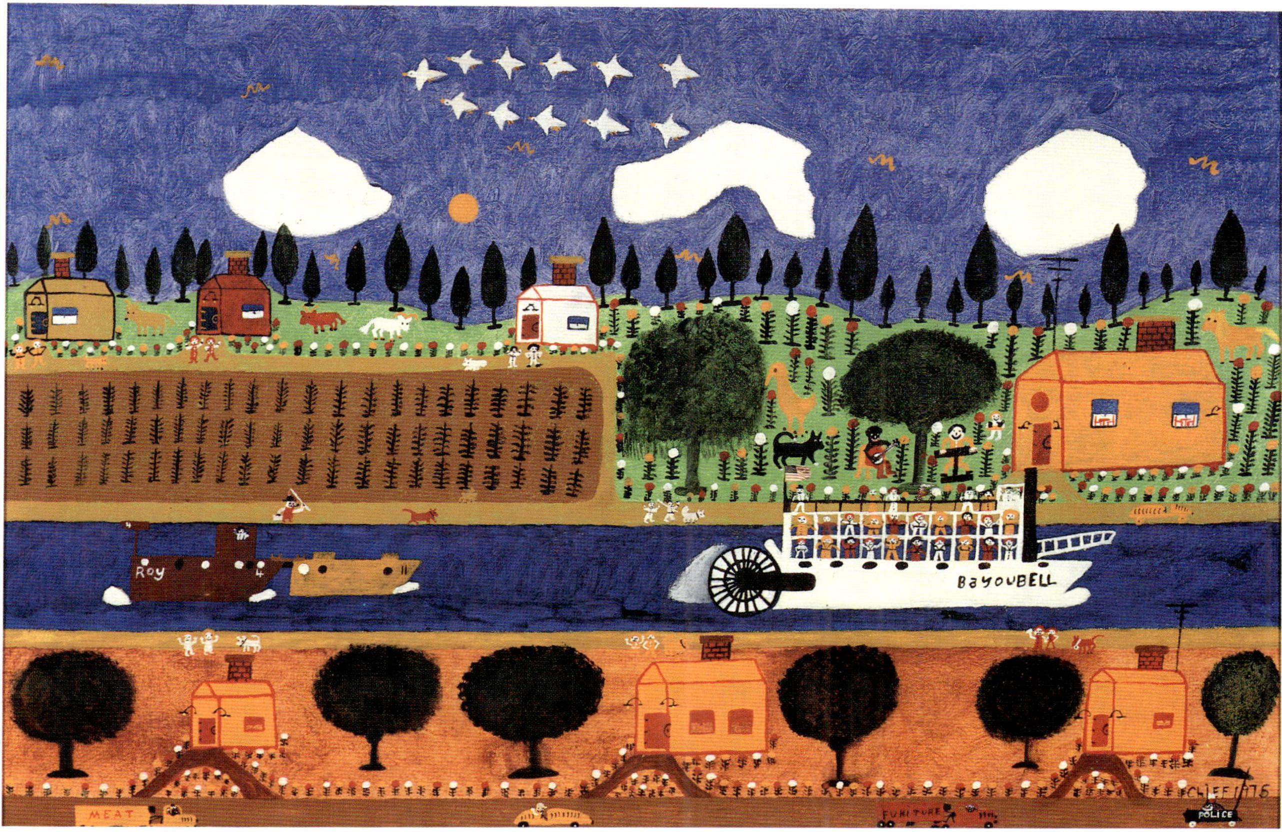
Roy
BayouBELL
MEAT
FURNITURE
POLICE
CHIEF 1976

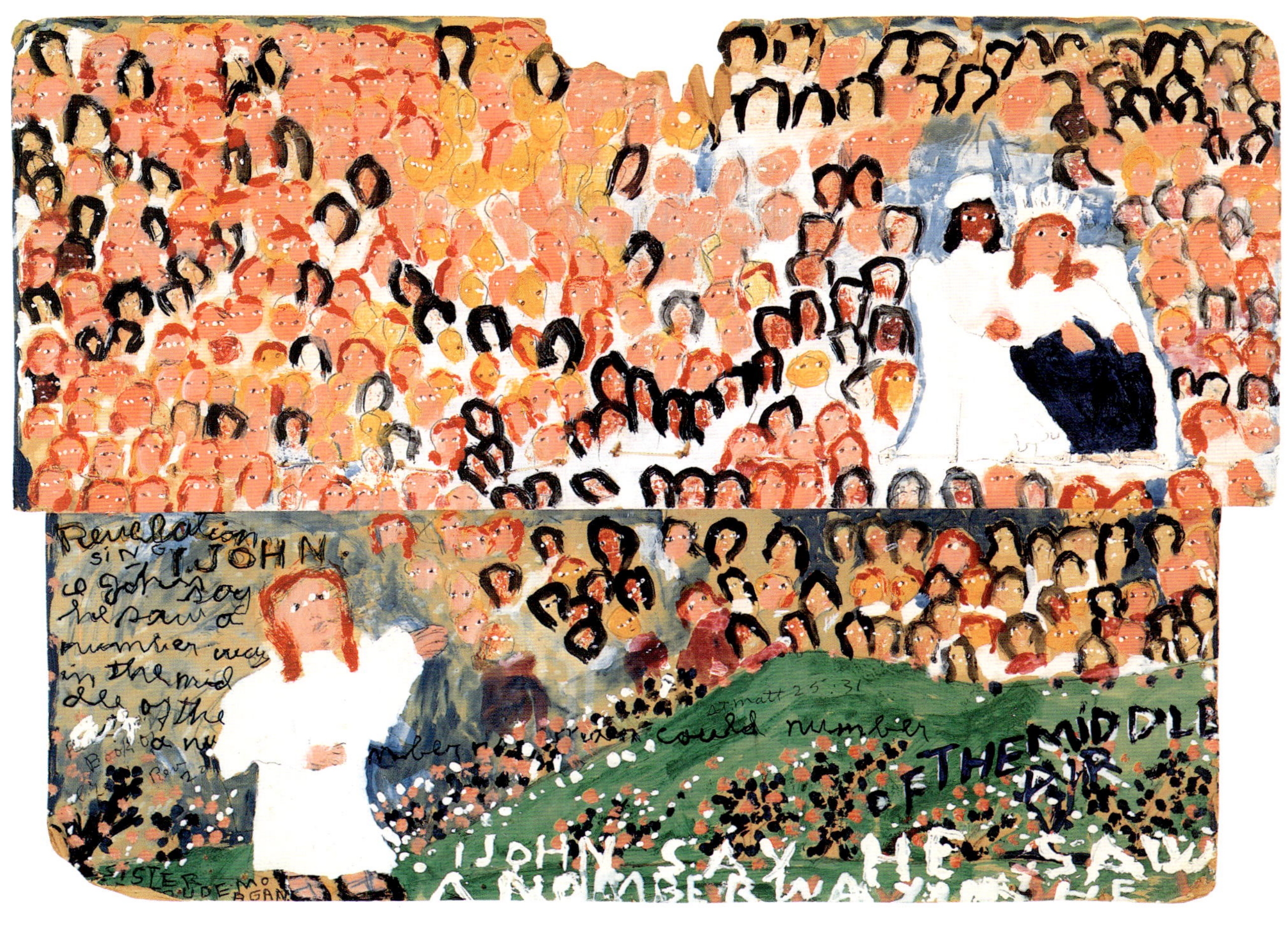

18

SISTER GERTRUDE MORGAN

Way in the Middle of the Air, n.d.

(cat. no. 178)

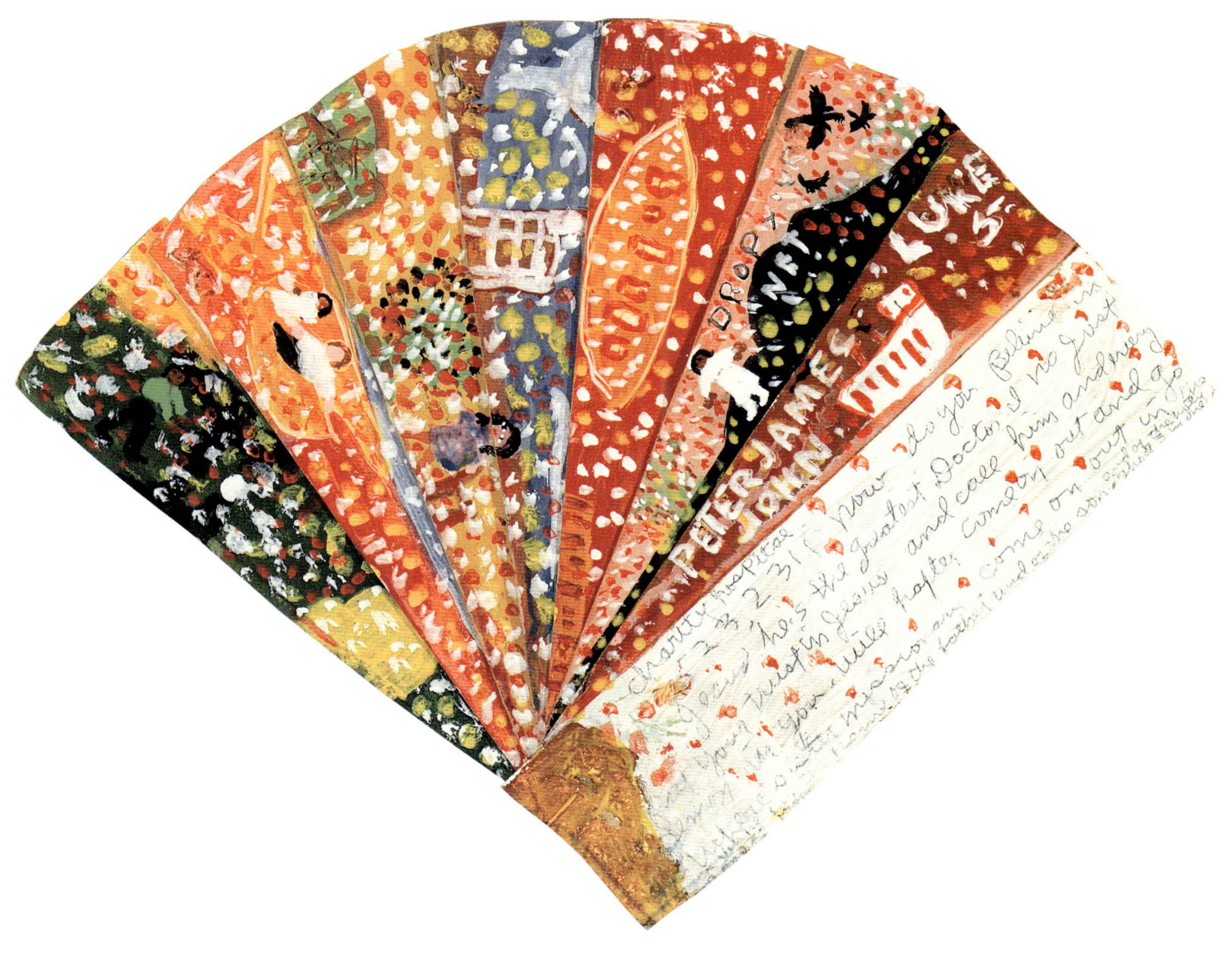

19

SISTER GERTRUDE MORGAN

Charity Hospital—523-2311, ca. 1970s

(cat. no. 170)

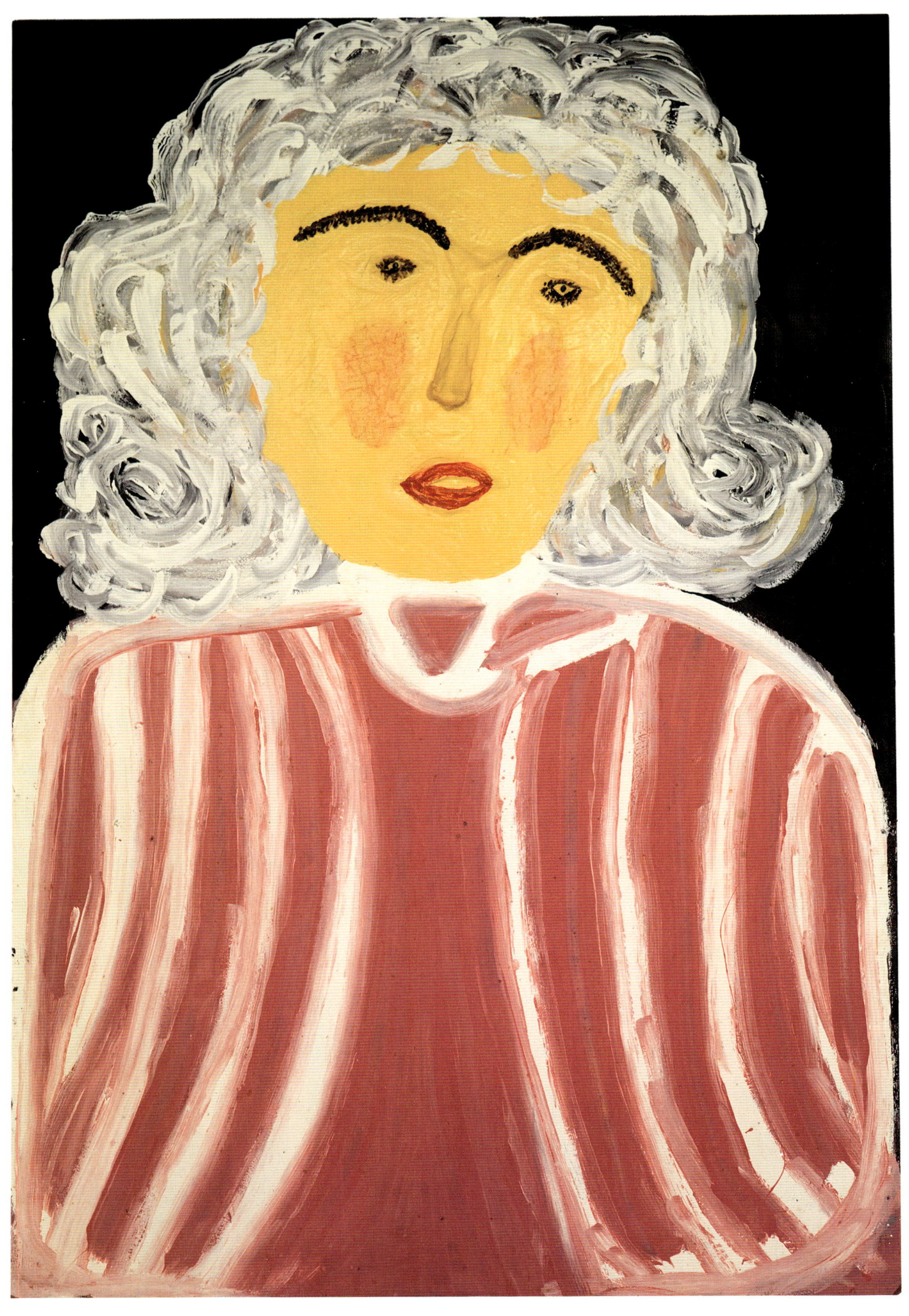

20

THORNTON DIAL, SR.

My Teacher, 1990

(cat. no. 57)

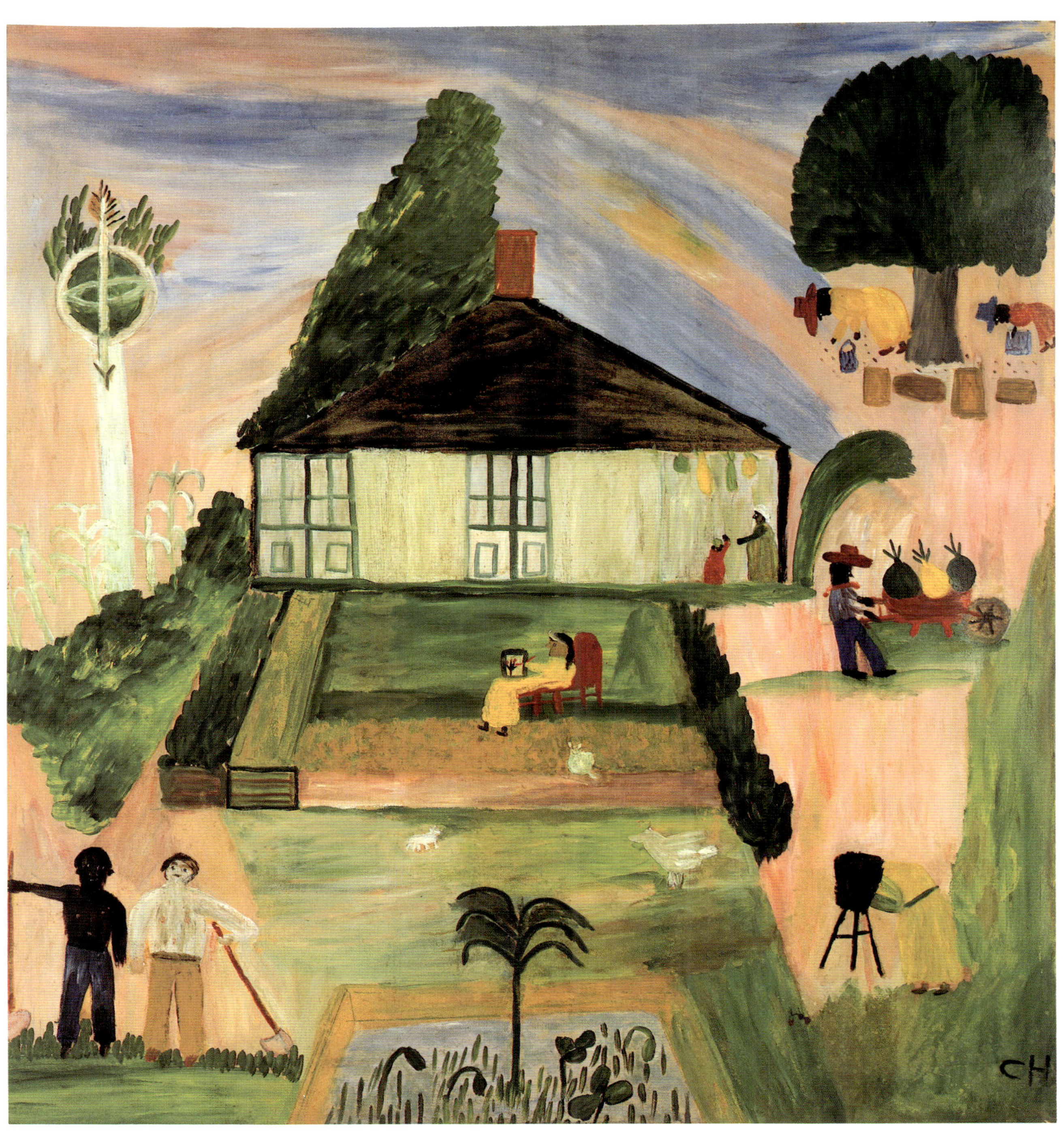

21

CLEMENTINE HUNTER

Secret Garden, Melrose Plantation, 1955

(cat. no. 125)

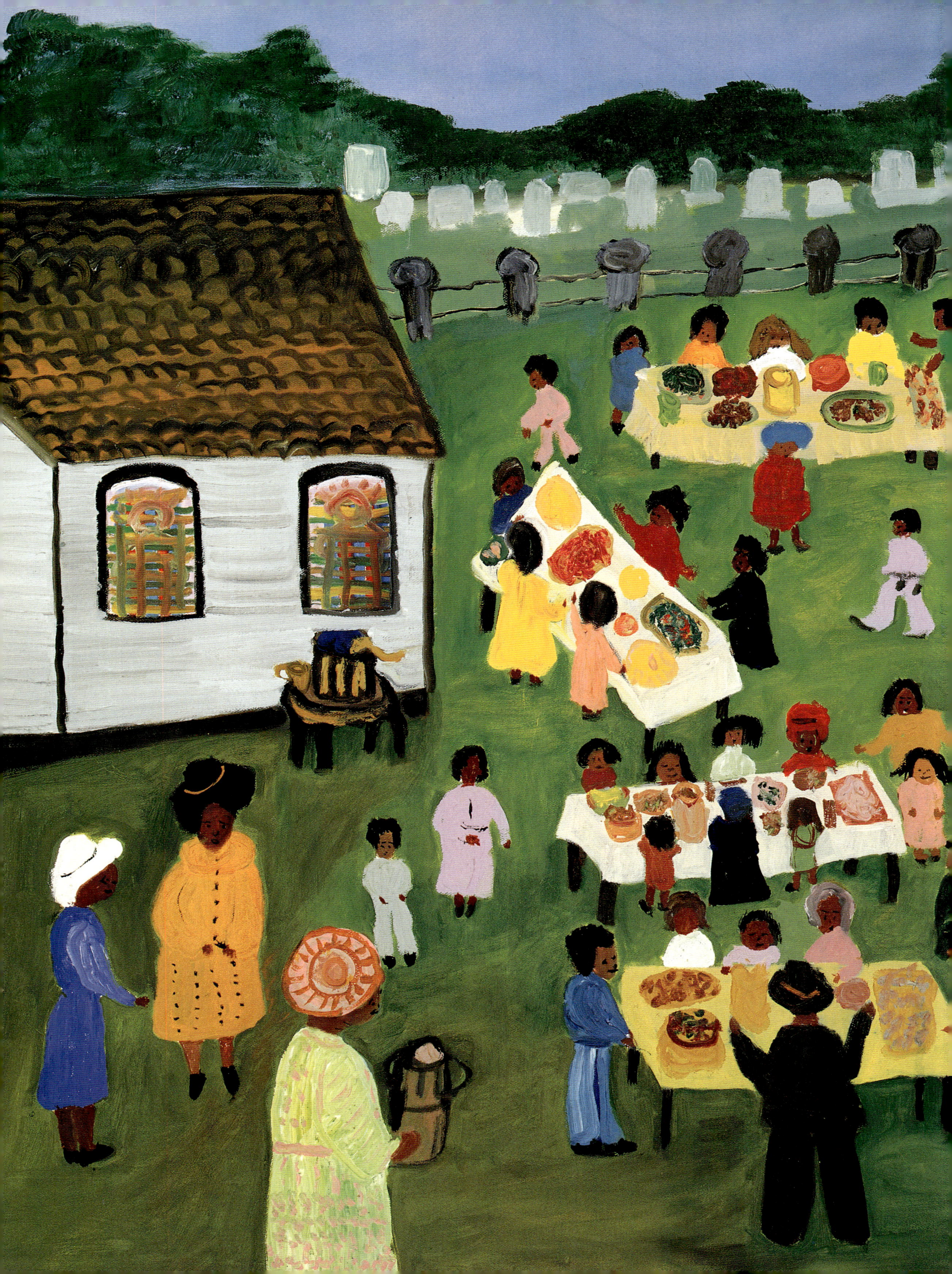

DAILY LIFE

Daily life and its experiences are the primary visual source and inspiration for southern self-taught artists. Their imagery narrates the essential elements of their secular daily lives: their means of livelihood and sustenance, milestones from pregnancy to death, the secular aspects of religion, their environments and vehicles, and friends or individuals they have observed.

In contrast to the heavily industrialized and urbanized North, the South retained its largely rural character into the 1950s, when the mechanization of farm equipment eliminated most manual jobs and forced laborers off the land. The majority of the artists in this exhibition were teenagers or older by that time, and their early experiences and perceptions were formed in this predominantly agrarian milieu.

In the cooler and hillier upper South, tobacco was the primary cash crop; in the warmer and flatter Deep South, cotton was king. Louisiana, the most tropical southern U.S. state, was also the home of sugar plantations. A significant number of self-taught artists had experience working on farms. The majority were sharecroppers, who rented small, often inadequate plots where they raised crops and paid their landlord with a percentage of their harvest. Others worked on a salary basis as farmhands; a few owned and worked their own land. Regardless of the arrangement, they were poor and barely survived economically.

The centrality of farming is shown by the individualistic renditions of plowing scenes by two artists: Charles Kinney, a tobacco farmer in Kentucky, and Bill Traylor, who worked on a cotton plantation in Alabama.

Charles Kinney was a self-employed tobacco farmer and jack-of-all-trades in eastern Kentucky. Kinney painted as a hobby from the first grade, but since the mid-1960s he devoted more time and energy to his art[1] when his farm was "let go wild."[2] Kinney's pencil and tempera drawing *Farmer* (pl. 26) depicts a scene from the tobacco farm he inherited from his father and where he and his brother, the sculptor Noah Kinney, spent their entire lives. This landscape is recognizable as the area of his farm at the time of his death in 1991, although by then the region's simple log cabins and tobacco barns symbolized a bygone era. Access to the Kinney farm was exceedingly difficult. The brothers lived in a hidden valley whose main access was a steep, precipitous dirt road, which cars could traverse only with caution. As elsewhere in Appalachian Kentucky, this treacherous geography slowed and in some cases prohibited ordinary forms of modern communication, even more so than in other parts of the South.

In the drawing, the hilly Kentucky terrain is shown by a blue-gray mound in the central middle ground, flanked and balanced by pencil drawings of tobacco barns. The mild ascension of hills behind them attests to Kinney's dabbling in perspective, a technique not often pursued by academically untutored artists. In the foreground, which is indicated by a light green plot of grass, two mules pull an antique red plow. The man pushing the plow resembles the artist, tall and lean, with his shirt hanging out.

Similar imagery is seen in Bill Traylor's *Man with Mule Plowing* (pl. 39). Born a slave, Traylor farmed cotton on an Alabama plantation twelve miles from Selma until the last nine years of his life. In 1938, at the age of eighty-four, he moved to Montgomery when in his own words, "my white folks had died and my children scattered."[3] Homeless, Traylor slept first on the floor of a funeral home and later in a shoe repair shop. He spent his days seated

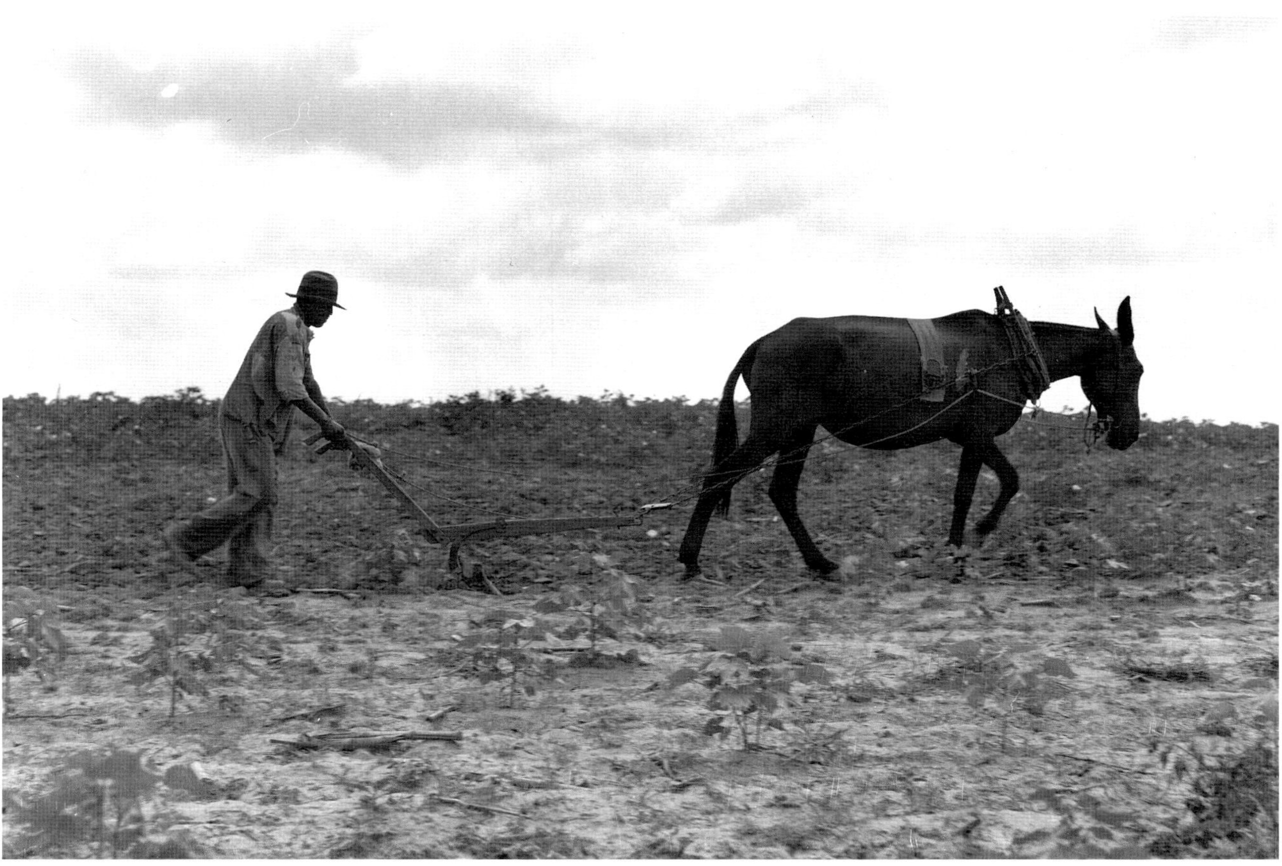

Fig. 1. Green Country, Georgia, July 1937. This plowing scene typifies the rural southern life experienced by self-taught artists such as Bill Traylor and Charles Kinney. Photo Dorothea Lange, U.S. Farm Security Administration, Prints and Photographs Division, Library of Congress.

on a box in the same location on a busy downtown street, and there he drew. First in pencil and later in paint, he portrayed animals and human figures on used cardboard and other available paper materials.

Man with Mule Plowing is typical of Traylor's work in its simplified visual elements, centralized subject, empty background, and restricted palette. Positioned solidly on unpainted cardboard, a mule-drawn plow is pushed by a man designated by solid areas of blue and black paint. Placed diagonally from top left to bottom right, the figures fill the picture plane of the irregularly cut board in a most pleasing fashion. A thin gray streak, an irregularity in the cardboard, crosses the plow from top right to bottom left, subtly creating an X shape that adds visual interest to the piece. Traylor, who possessed a keen sense of design, often magnificently integrated such flaws into his compositions.

Devoid of background details of crops or outbuildings, Traylor's composition clearly focuses on the central figure. Although he drew on an active city street, Traylor had an intuitive sense for editing out the superfluous. His images are isolated and absolutely clear; the setting is declared unimportant.

The authenticity of *Man with Mule Plowing* is supported by a 1930s Farm Security Administration photograph of a lone man, mule, and plow in a field, which captures a comparable calm isolation (fig. 1). Although plantation farm life was grueling, it was clearly central to Traylor's experience. Once, as he drew a plowing scene from a Montgomery city street, he reportedly said, "I wanted to be plowing so bad today, I draw'd me a man plowing."[4]

Cotton was the primary crop of the South. Artists such as Clementine Hunter and Johnnie Swearingen frequently depicted the activities of cotton cultivation, picking, and processing. In Swearingen's *Picking Cotton* (pl. 23), fourteen parallel rows of cotton sweep diagonally across the canvas to the horizon, where they are stopped by a row of trees. Eleven figures with cotton sacks strapped over their shoulders pick gloriously ripe cotton, approximated by small daubs of white paint. The cloth cotton sacks, approximately twelve feet long and with reinforced bottoms that allowed them to withstand dragging on the ground, became harder to lift the fuller they got. Pickers were paid by the pound; good pickers could get a couple of hundred pounds a day. The long black and brown wagon in the picture's center probably contained a scale to weigh the bales before the harvest was hauled to the cotton gin and processed. The linear, detailed organization and subdued oil palette of *Picking Cotton* identify it as an early Swearingen work. His later compositions are generally larger, bolder, and more curvilinear, painted in brightly colored oil paints and often outlined in black.

In *Sugar Plantation* (pl. 22),[5] Clementine Hunter portrayed an annual event on the Melrose plantation in Louisiana where she lived and worked from about the age of fifteen until about ten years before her death in 1988 at approximately 102 years old. Using representative shades of soft pinks and green, Hunter employed a serial technique to represent the events surrounding the sugar harvest. Her depiction of a story through sequential imagery is a visual reflection of the oral storytelling tradition so prevalent in the South. Sugar cane is cut (top right), carried to a wagon to be processed (center), and pressed (bottom right). At bottom left, the sugar is boiled in huge cast iron pots (now collector's items themselves). Hunter wryly placed a figure in one of the boiling sugar pots. At the top left the white-skinned plantation owner and patron of the artist, Miss Cammie Henry, arranges flowers in front of a large white mansion.

Whereas the cash crops of cotton, tobacco, and sugar cane occupied most of their land, sharecroppers fed their families with the harvest from the small plots they allocated to sustenance farming. Food and related substances are an occasional but not frequent subject of southern self-taught artists. Tomatoes and vegetables can be seen in Ezekiel Gibbs's colorful, whimsical *Farm Scene* (pl. 16), while abundant watermelons and local creole tomatoes are frequently featured in Willie White's whimsical drawings (pls. 212, 213).

Domestic scenes of farm and rural life are common in the work of self-taught artists. Bernice Sims's oil painting *Spring Cleaning*, done on commercially primed canvas, features a colorful scene of beautifully designed quilts airing outside a small rural home with dirt roads and chickens scattered about. The naive figures lack anatomical delineation; their sex is distinguishable only by their dress. Perhaps the anonymity of the figures demonstrates the importance of community over the individual in Sims's work, where scenes of daily life consistently prevail over individual portraiture.

Sims consciously uses her visual art to describe her memories of life in rural Alabama: "People don't have these things anymore. I want our children to know what things were like. . . . We had no electricity, no indoor plumbing. We had different toys. . . . Kids these days see those things . . . and they don't believe them."[6]

The church played an important role in the secular and religious daily life of southerners, particularly in rural areas. The church as a social center is shown in Bernice Sims's *Church Scene* (pl. 27), and Ezekiel Gibbs's *Church Meeting* (pl. 50) depicts a delightful congregation in oil, pastel, and pencil on the back of a brown envelope. *The Preacher and Wife* (pl. 56) by Shields Landon "S. L." Jones, carved and painted in the late 1970s, is one of his largest and finest works.[7] A well-dressed, life-sized standing couple smiles as though they are greeting congregants or passersby. The preacher's stance, with a Bible raised in one hand, suggests a social rather than a sermonizing mood. His attire, a simple white shirt and bow tie, without a jacket, perhaps reflects an interest in staying on an equal footing with his working class congregants. The couple appears as though frozen by a camera's flash, their expressions like mannequins. The woman particularly projects a 1950s image, with accentuated breasts and a low V-neck sweater. The welcoming figures bring to mind nineteenth-century cigar-store Indians.

Jones, who knows the nature of his wood, located and hauled his own heavy logs until recent years, when the strenuousness of the task made him rely on others to provide materials. When he feels a log is properly aged, he approximates its sculpted form with a chain saw and then refines its smallest details with chisels and a knife.[8]

Artists occasionally depict the vital, human experiences of pregnancy and death. Pregnancy is shown in the work of Steven Ashby, a rural farmer (cat. no. 9), and Purvis Young, an urban ghetto artist. Young's fascination with the pregnant women who populate his Miami ghetto has been a feature of his artistic expression since the early 1970s. In *Love Dance* (pl. 46), his sinuous calligraphic renderings of figures appear like swimming sperm around a copulating couple. The painting's Mylar surface retains an unusual reflective, textured effect.

Southern death customs are significant social and ritualistic events, and black funerary rites in particular tend to be extravagant happenings, often following meticulous plans made during the deceased's life.[9] Zebedee "Z. B." Armstrong, for example, began paying burial dues in the 1950s to the Solomon Hodges Pauper's Burial Society in Thompson, Georgia, to assure his own proper burial (which took place in 1993).[10] In the slave era, true freedom for African-Americans was thought to come after death, either through salvation for Christians or, for those who had maintained African beliefs, a reunion with ancestors. Although loved ones mourned, they also celebrated the deceased's liberation.[11]

In *New Orleans Jazz Funeral* (pl. 45), Herbert Singleton depicts a unique local burial tradition for musicians. A jazz band playing a slow-paced, lamenting melody accompanies mourners to the cemetery. A trumpeter and saxophonist precede pallbearers and a drummer, followed by a woman with an opened umbrella. Following the burial, the mourners will pick up the pace and dance in the traditional "second line," a sinuous procession that celebrates the deceased's new heavenly state. The arrangement of colors—dark-skinned men wearing black suits and white hats, and black and white shoes against a blue background—echoes the rhythm of the music and the movement of the mourners' feet.

In *Funeral Day Procession* (pl. 44) Purvis Young rendered an array of attenuated figures in gray, black, and purple carrying a casket in a long procession along a horizontal ground. James Henry "Son" Thomas, who worked as a grave digger, paid homage to a deceased individual. A clay male figure lies in an open coffin of Mississippi Delta clay (cat. no. 237), imagery typical of Thomas's work.

When the horse and buggy or one's feet were the only methods of transportation, travel was time consuming and difficult. The greater mobility afforded by train, bus, and eventually car travel radically changed life in the rural South, as it did throughout the nation, by allowing a free exchange of goods and influences.

The train has long appealed to artists as a subject. When railroads revolutionized transportation in France in the late nineteenth century, the impressionists incorporated the train and its billowing smoke into their landscapes. The fascination that the train held for rural southerners is similarly reflected in the work of self-taught artists. Jimmy Lee Sudduth for many years lived alongside the tracks of the Southern Railroad, less than a mile from a train station. To entertain passengers passing his home, Sudduth in the early 1970s painted a cow on the tin siding of his shed, which faced the tracks. Sudduth has depicted both passenger trains (pl. 34) and freight cars, perhaps hauling logs for the Brown lumber mill in Brownville, Alabama, for which he once worked.[12]

Other self-taught artists who paid homage to the train are Charles Kinney and David Butler. Kinney's *Kentucky Landscape with Train* (pl. 25) depicts a train passing through a starkly rural landscape, perhaps transporting tobacco or coal, both products of eastern Kentucky where the artist lived. Butler's whimsical painted tin cutout, *Locomotive Engine with Rooster* (pl. 60), is topped by a rooster and adorned with a tin bell attached with a plastic cord to the hand of the engineer.

Travel in the South was made even easier with the mass production of Henry Ford's Model-T in the early part of the twentieth century. Howard Finster celebrated the self-made inventor in *Henry Ford at 2 ½ Years Old #1849* (pl. 51). A rural Michigan boy, Ford in the 1920s became a cultural hero of particular appeal to rural southerners whose geographic isolation was reduced by the affordable automobile. Ford's praises were literally sung in southern folk tunes:

> Everybody know a Henry Ford car,
> Everybody knows they're the best they are
> You ought to take a ride
> Just get in a Ford
> Oh my Lord[13]

Finster was so attracted to inventors that he originally conceived his famed backyard environment, Paradise Garden, as a museum to represent the inventions of mankind, because, as the artist said, "Mankind is made in the image o' God, and that's why we keep creatin' and inventin' things."[14]

In waterway areas dependent on shipping and fishing, the boat is a popular subject. The flotilla of boats made of found objects by J. P. Scott reveals his infatuation with all kinds of watercraft, most of which he worked on in the bayou waterways of Lafitte, Louisiana: shrimp and oyster boats, pogy boats, trawlers, freighters, and tankers.

Hubert Walters's boat *Love and Time* (pl. 59) was based on the artist's own maritime experience. Prior to immigrating to the United States in 1971 from Jamaica, Walters built and worked on small boats for commercial fishing. He started fashioning miniature sailing vessels such as *Love and Time* in the mid-1980s because he "wanted to keep active making boats . . . as I did in Jamaica."[15] Walters made *Love and Time* with an interior armature and wooden frame, which he covered with Bondo and painted with a glossy car paint. The figure of a captain at the rear of the vessel might even represent Walters, who had himself been a captain.

At the age of twenty-one, in 1916, William Hawkins migrated from Union City, Kentucky, to Columbus, Ohio, to escape potential complications with a young pregnant sweetheart.[16] Recalling his good life on the farm, Hawkins said he never would have left Kentucky if he had not been forced.[17] That he never forgot his roots is manifested by his trademark signature in large capital letters, "WILLIAM

L. HAWKINS born KY July 27, 1895," always beautifully integrated into the designs of his compositions. Hawkins worked in vibrant colors, transforming often ordinary images into visual spectacles. At one time a construction worker, he was interested in and sensitive to architectural subjects. He recorded numerous Ohio cityscapes he knew as well as architectural scenes about which he had dreamed or seen in photographs.

In *Yaekle Building* (pl. 29) Hawkins represented a fine brick building in his Columbus neighborhood. The structure, an old inn, was condemned and torn down not long after Hawkins painted it. This was probably the first flat-surface painting to which Hawkins added three-dimensional materials, a technique he subsequently often employed.[18] Here he placed wooden sticks on the painting's surface around the windowsills on the far left and right, imaginatively altering his subject to achieve a heightened visual effect.

In the exceptional *Ohio Stadium No. 1* (pl. 32), Hawkins used pattern and contrasting colors to portray the interior of a Columbus sports stadium. A patterned arrangement of black and white delineates the seating, and green and white horizontal lines represent the football field. The striking flat design was probably developed from an aerial photograph of the site.[19] Although Hawkins demonstrated his ability to portray perspective in works such as *Broad and High Streets* (pl. 30), he tended to flatten perspective in an exaggerated fashion, simplify forms, and emphasize patterns to create powerful, direct works. J. P. Scott occasionally assembles architectural structures from found objects such as *Quarter House* (pl. 63), an interpretation of the typical homes found in the famed New Orleans historic district.[20] In actuality Scott's "house" looks more like a houseboat, a familiar sight on bayou waterways.

Street life in towns and urban areas became a natural subject for several self-taught artists. In addition to scenes drawn from his memories of plantation life, Bill Traylor sketched people he knew and unknown passersby from his sidewalk spot on a downtown Montgomery street.[21] His interpretations range from the richly colored, curvilinear single figure of *Blue Man with Pipe and Bottle* (pl. 43) and *Red Man* (pl. 42) to the more subdued palette and rigid stance of *Man in Blue with Small Dog* (pl. 40) and *Man with Two Canes* (pl. 41). *Kitchen Scene, Yellow House* (pl. 36) imaginatively narrates, in the upper work, a tranquil domestic scene and, below, a raucous outdoor environment. In the kitchen, a man and a woman quietly work amid stove, table, pots, and a gentle dog. But outside a fierce dog chases a man, and a chicken thief is about to be cudgeled by a man wielding a mallet.[22]

Hubert Walters's *Figures* (pl. 58) depicts a cluster of individuals whose features were inspired by "congregations of people" the artist saw "at church, in the marketplace, or on the street."[23] The painted figures are made of Bondo on wood or stucco poured in a handcrafted wooden mold. J. L. Hunter fashioned single-figure painted wood sculptures of individuals engaged in quotidian tasks such as waiting tables (cat. no. 127), hauling water buckets, and toting fishing poles.

Three Men and House (pl. 49) typifies Ed "Mr. Eddy" Mumma's painterly expressionistic style, distinguished by bold, often thickly textured colors and heavy black outlines. Three frontal Rouault-like figures with prominent eyes, dressed in costumes of olden days, stand against a backdrop of house and garden. Mumma often expresses his compulsive need to paint by working on both sides of a surface, as in this work, which bears a figure painted on the opposite side.

Jimmy Lee Sudduth portrays the buildings and people of the small town of Fayette, Alabama (pop. 4,909), where he has spent most of his adult years. Sudduth's reputation for clearly rendering local turn-of-the-century buildings is ably displayed in *Mud Architectural of State Capitol* (pl. 35). He boldly illustrated the seat of state government surrounded by citizens in his own remarkable medium: mud mixed with sugar and applied by finger to plywood. The thirty-six colors of rich local Alabama clay that Sudduth collects locally impart an obviously earthy dynamic to his work. Sudduth's original mud technique is unique; it is perhaps the most naturalistic of all processes, requiring only his fingers as tools and the surrounding earth as paint. In *Mud Architectural of State Capitol*, paint helps to define the capitol building, but in his earliest works Sudduth used only his natural mud colors ranging from blacks and browns to oranges, yellows, and reds. Yet as early as the 1970s, when *Fantastic Building* (pl. 33) was painted, the artist began to augment his mud works with paint, in this case, with a background of royal blue. Although he creates images with paint, it is typically augmented with mud. Sudduth continues today to produce works of all natural materials: "I'd rather paint with mud than paint," he said in 1992.[24]

An overwhelming reference to daily life experience is a hallmark of southern self-taught artists. Even as the South changes from predominantly rural to a small town and city milieu, these artists continue to find inspiration in their immediate environment.

1. Adrian Swain, curator, Folk Art Museum, Morehead State University, Morehead, Kentucky, interview, ARY, Dec. 1992.

2. Chuck and Jan Rosenak, *Museum of American Folk Art Encyclopedia of Twentieth-Century American Folk Art and Artists* (New York: Abbeville Press, 1990), p. 173.

3. Charles Shannon, "Remembering Bill Traylor: An Interview with Charles Shannon," in Frank Maresca and Roger Ricco, *Bill Traylor: His Art, His Life* (New York: Alfred A. Knopf, 1991), p. 8.

4. Ibid., p. 29.

5. This image is published in Herbert W. Hemphill, Jr., and Julia Weissman, *Twentieth-Century American Folk Art and Artists* (New York: E. P. Dutton, 1974), p. 63, under the title *Louisiana Syrup Makers*.

6. Michael Suchcicki, "Folk Artist Preserves Past So Future Generations Can Learn Lessons of History," *Pensacola News Journal*, Feb. 17, 1991, p. 1.

7. Jeff Camp, longtime dealer of S. L. Jones's work, dated this sculpture; interview, ARY, March 1993.

8. Ramona Lampell and Millard Lampell with David Larkin, *O, Appalachia: Artists of the Southern Mountains* (New York: Stewart, Tabori, and Chang, 1989), p. 20.

9. For an overview of the distinctive nature of black funerary customs, see John Vlach, "Funerary Customs, Black," *ESC*, pp. 161–62.

10. Zebedee "Z. B." Armstrong, as told to dealer Tom Wells, who discovered the artist and lived near him in Thompson, Georgia; interview, ARY, Dec. 1992.

11. Vlach, "Funerary Customs," pp. 161–62.

12. Jack Black, director, Fayette Civic Center, interview, ARY, Dec. 1992. Sudduth worked at the Fayette branch of the company, not far from Brownville.

13. The song, "On the Dixie Bee-line," by Dave Macon (1926), was cited in a lecture by Bill C. Malone, professor of history, Tulane University, March 1992.

14. Quoted in Tom Patterson, *Howard Finster: Stranger from Another World* (New York: Abbeville Press, 1989), p. 101.

15. Hubert Walters, interview, ARY, July 1991.

16. The Hawkins family feared that William's girlfriend could eventually make claim on the family farm and assets, so they sent Hawkins north to live with his uncle for a while; Gary Schwindler, "William L. Hawkins: A Biography," unpublished ms., pp. 79–82.

17. Gary Schwindler, interview, ARY, Dec. 1992.

18. Ibid.

19. Ibid.

20. J. P. Scott, interview, ARY, Sept. 1991.

21. Shannon, "Remembering Bill Traylor," p. 29.

22. Sabine Rewald, "Recent Acquisitions: A Selection, 1991–1992," *Metropolitan Museum of Art Bulletin* 50, no. 2 (Fall 1992), p. 65.

23. Hubert Walters, interview, ARY, July 1991.

24. Jimmy Lee Sudduth, interview, ARY, Aug. 1992.

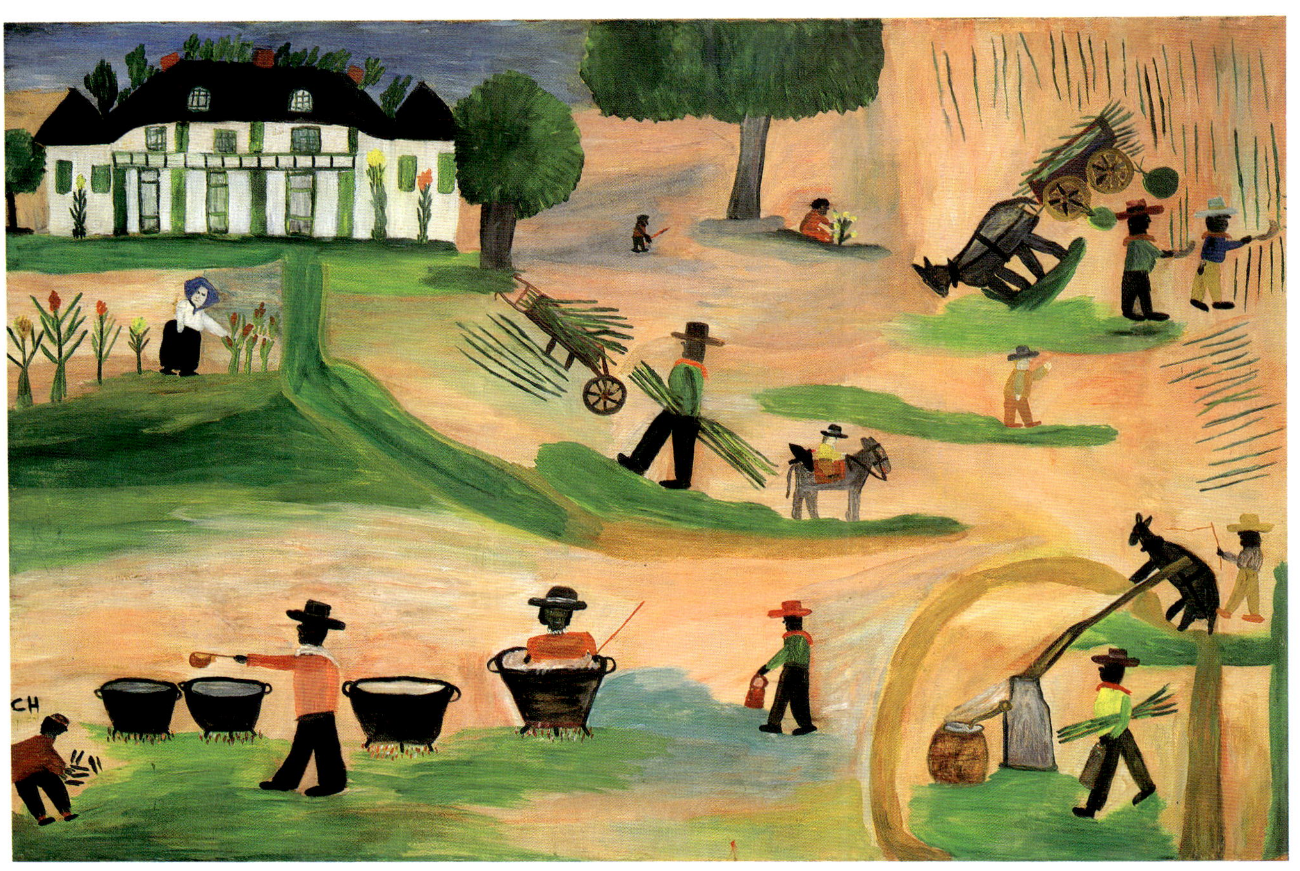

22

CLEMENTINE HUNTER

Sugar Plantation, n.d.

(cat. no. 126)

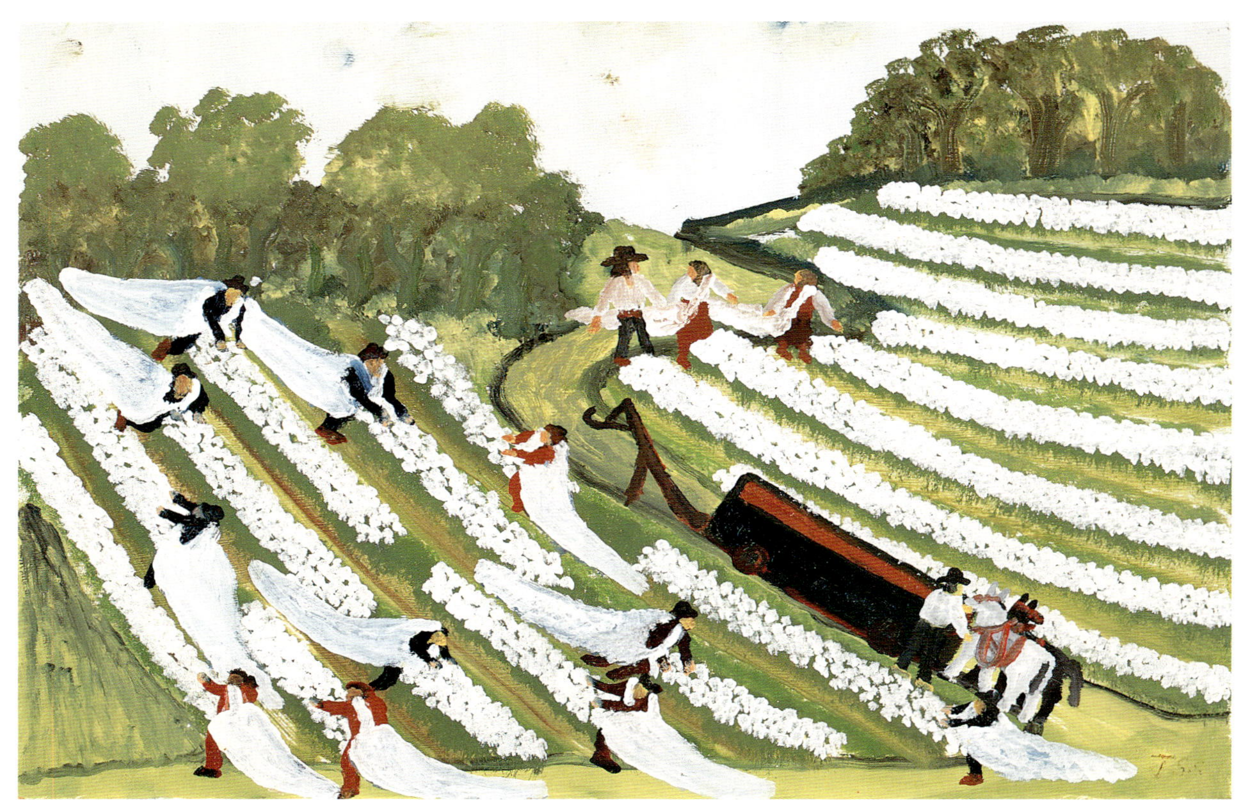

23

REV. JOHNNIE SWEARINGEN

Picking Cotton, 1978

(cat. no. 232)

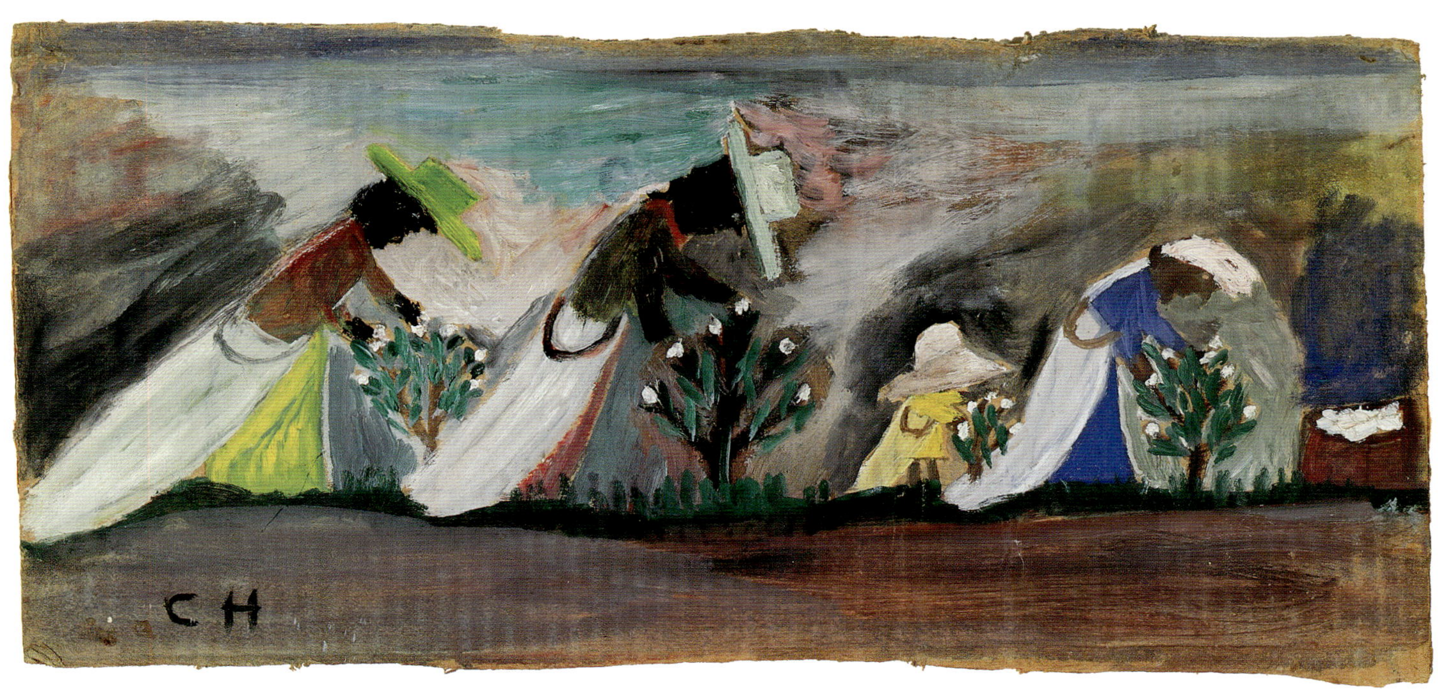

24

CLEMENTINE HUNTER

Cotton Picking, ca. 1955

(cat. no. 122)

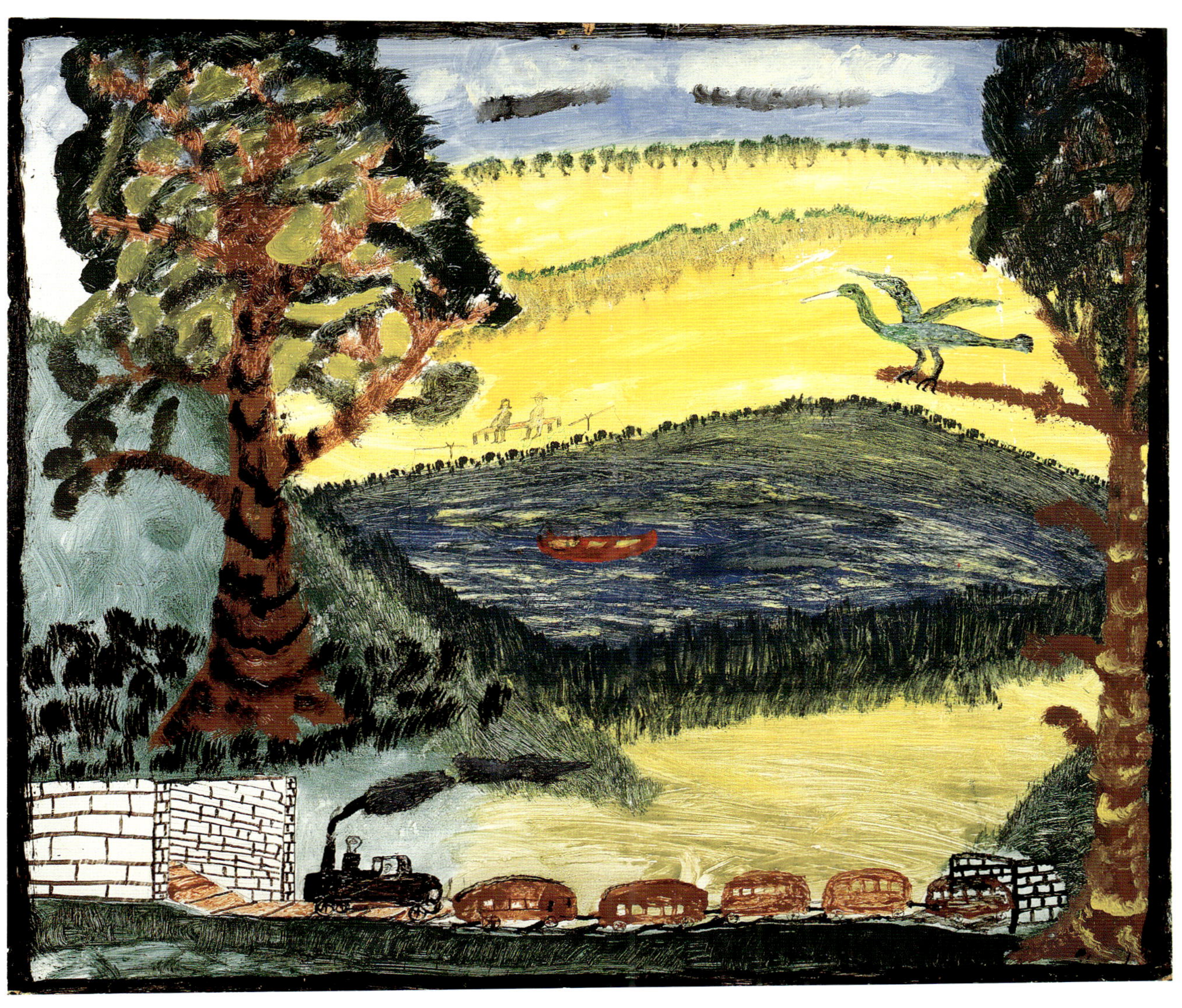

25

CHARLES KINNEY

Kentucky Landscape with Train, ca. 1970–71

(cat. no. 148)

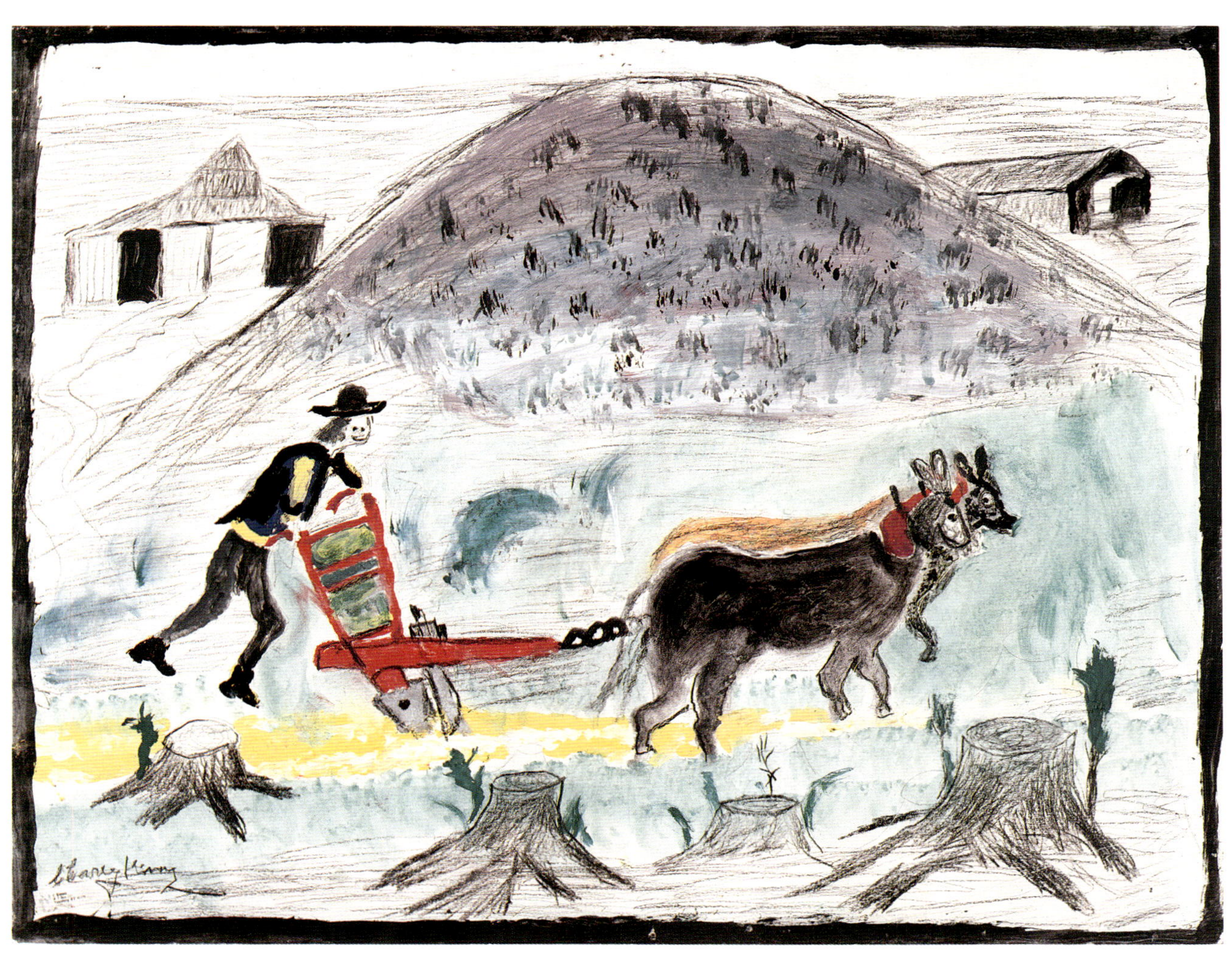

26

CHARLES KINNEY

Farmer, 1985

(cat. no. 146)

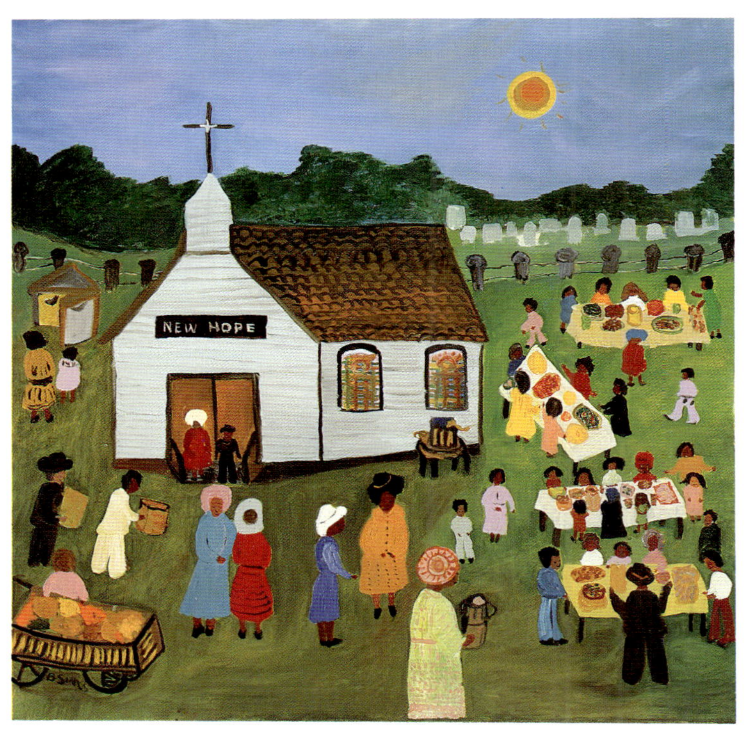

27

BERNICE SIMS

Church Scene, 1989

(cat. no. 206)

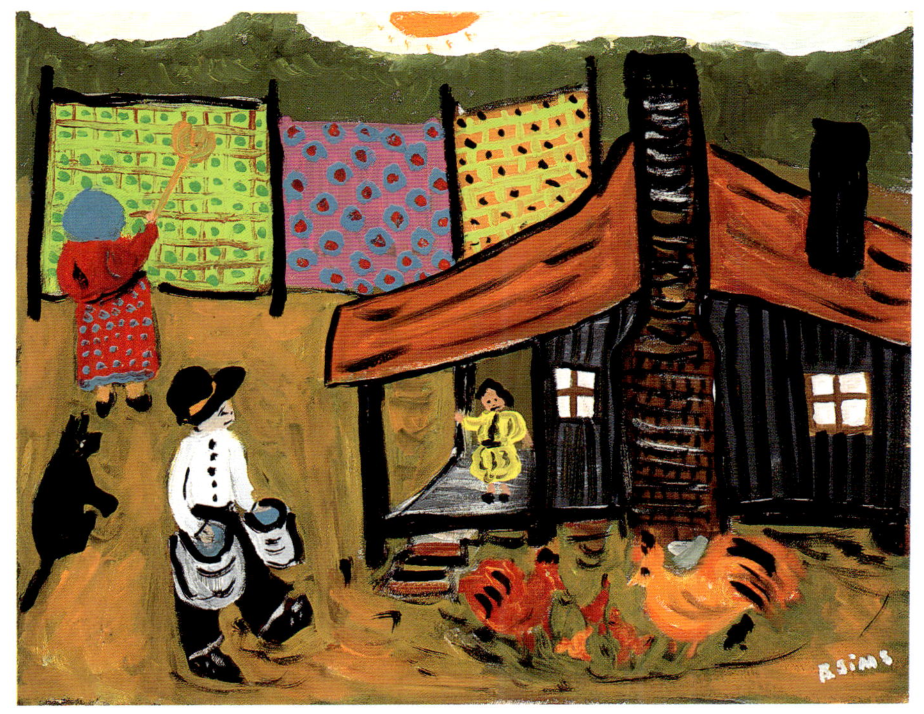

28

BERNICE SIMS

Spring Cleaning, 1990

(cat. no. 207)

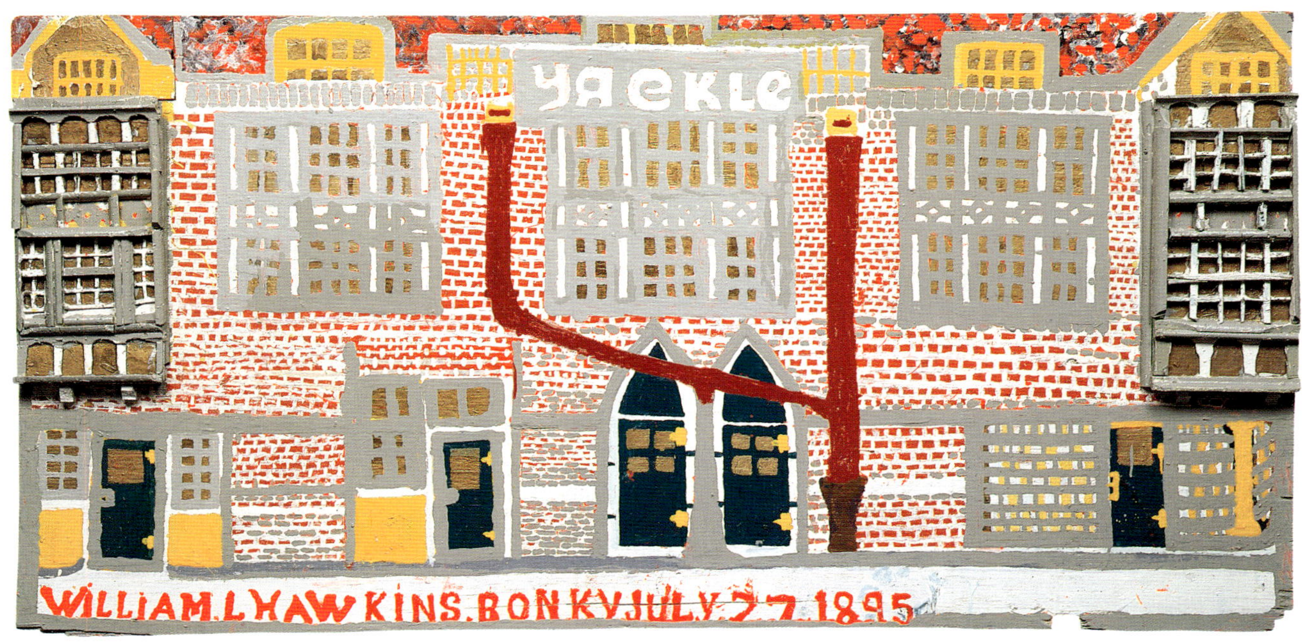

29

WILLIAM HAWKINS

Yaekle Building, ca. 1980

(cat. no. 119)

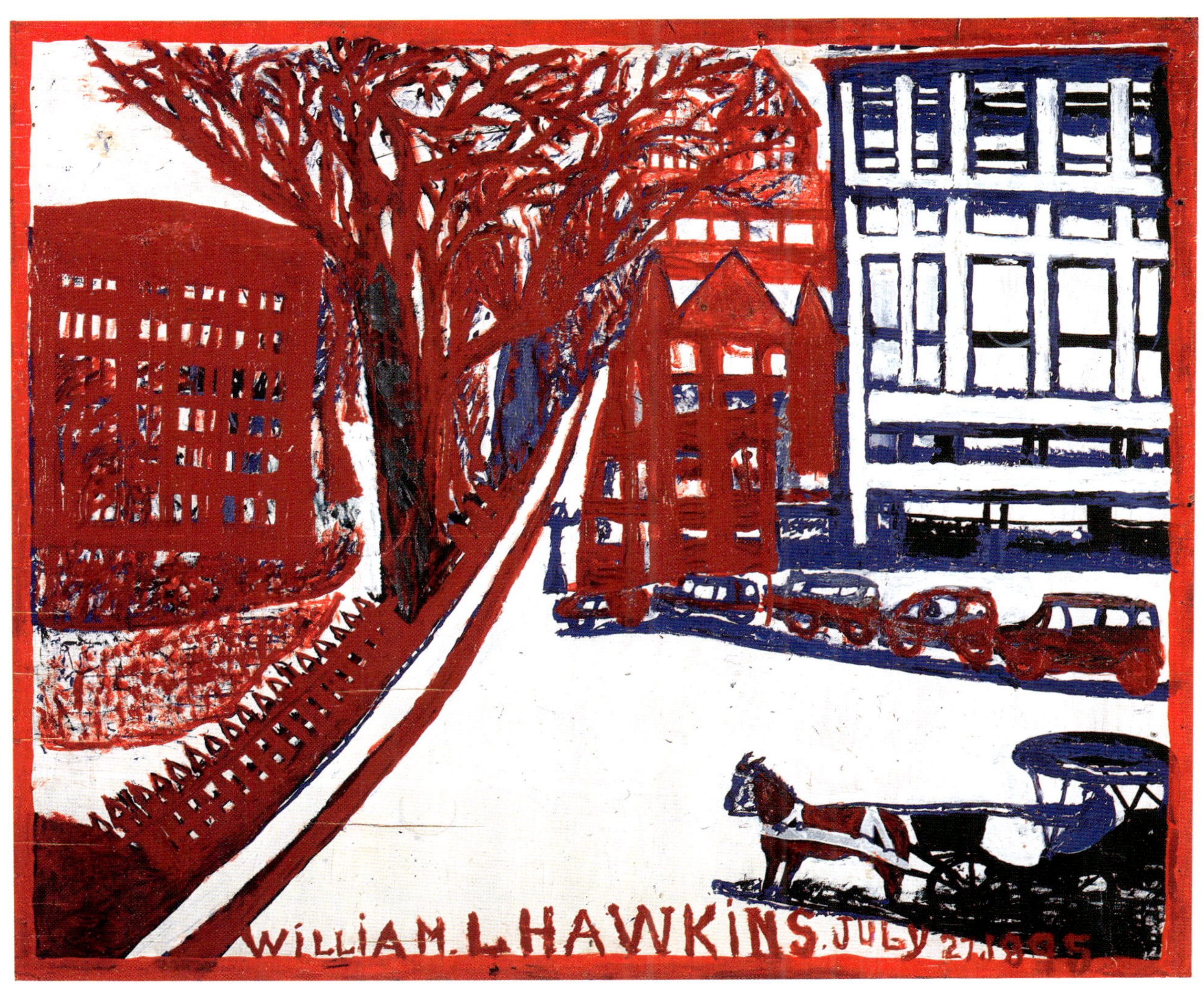

30

WILLIAM HAWKINS

Broad and High Streets, ca. 1982

(cat. no. 111)

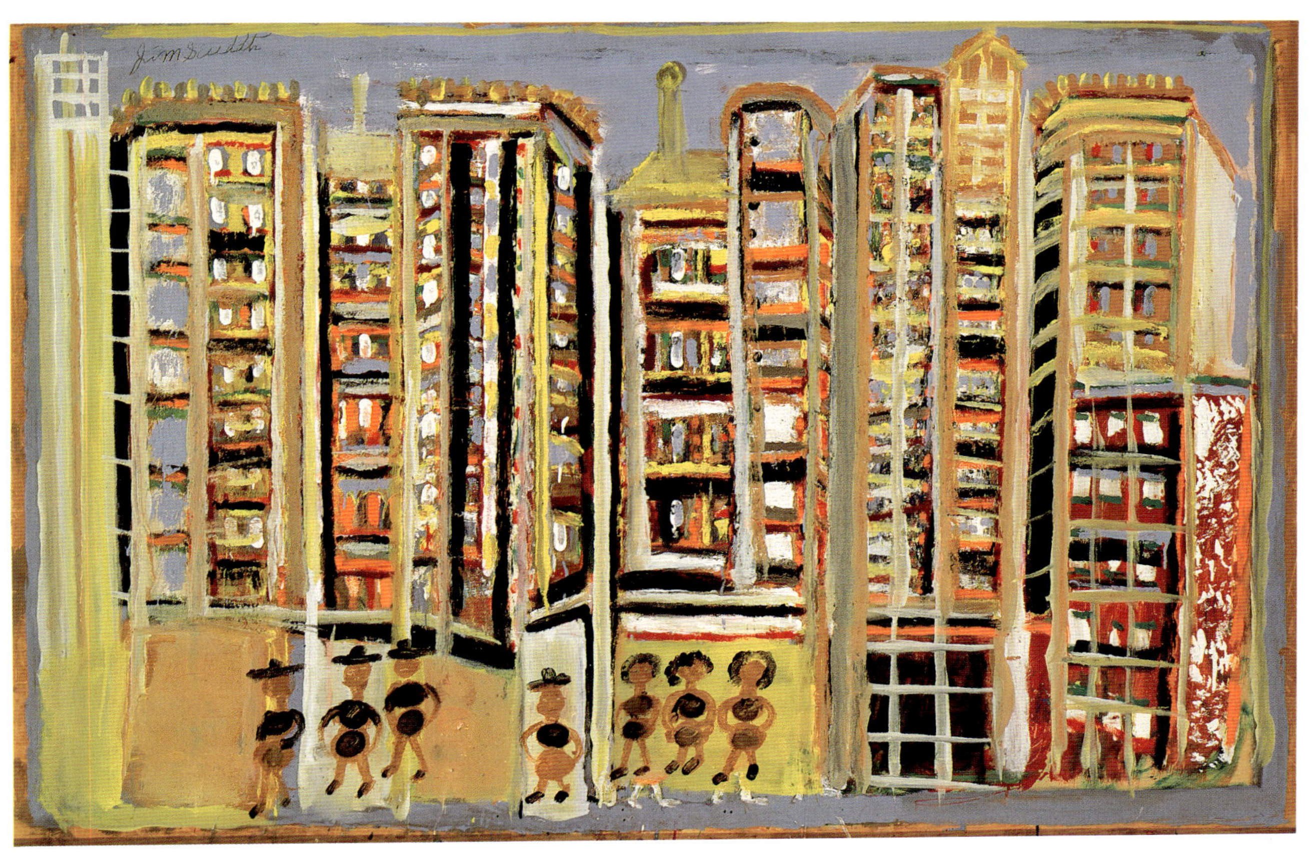

31

JIMMY LEE SUDDUTH

African-Americans Living in New York City, 1992

(cat. no. 218)

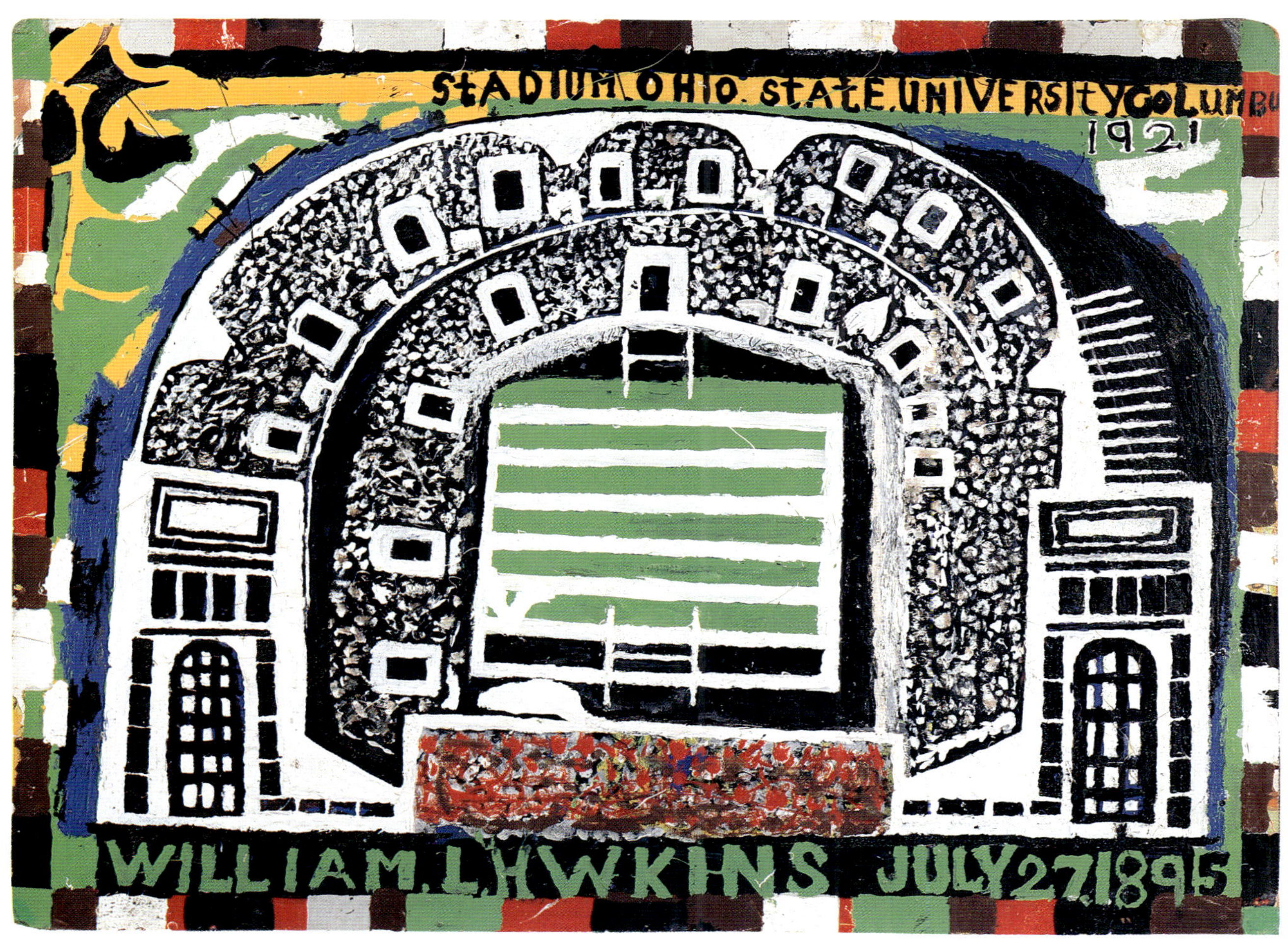

32

WILLIAM HAWKINS
Ohio Stadium No. 1, 1983
(cat. no. 116)

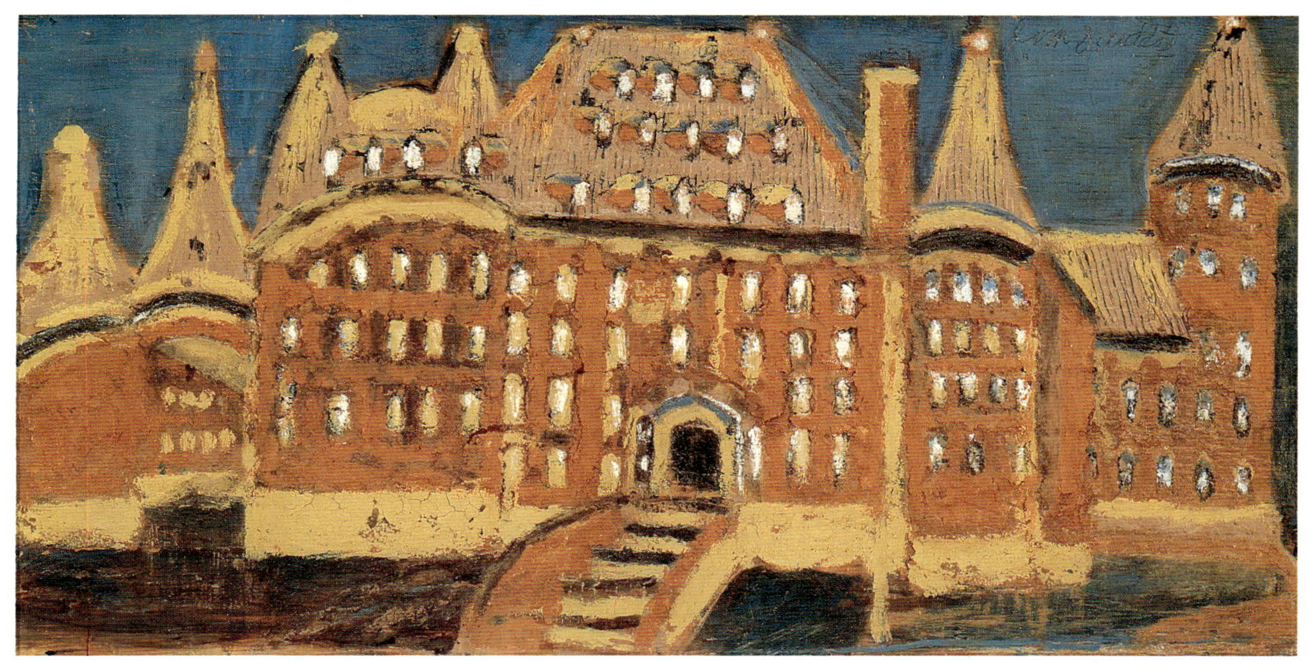

33

JIMMY LEE SUDDUTH

Fantastic Building, ca. 1970s

(cat. no. 221)

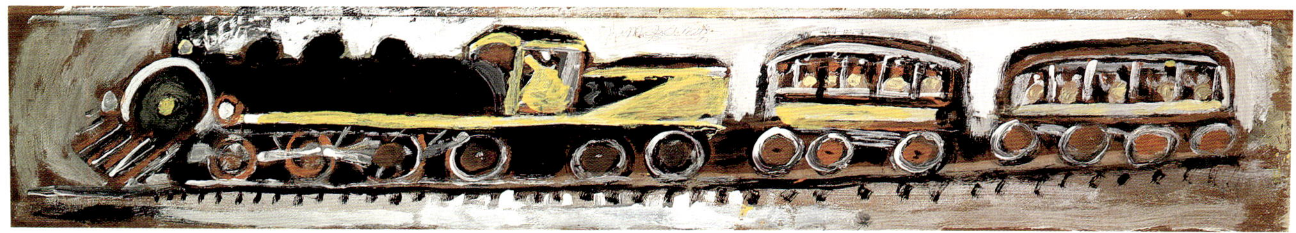

34

JIMMY LEE SUDDUTH

Train, 1988

(cat. no. 228)

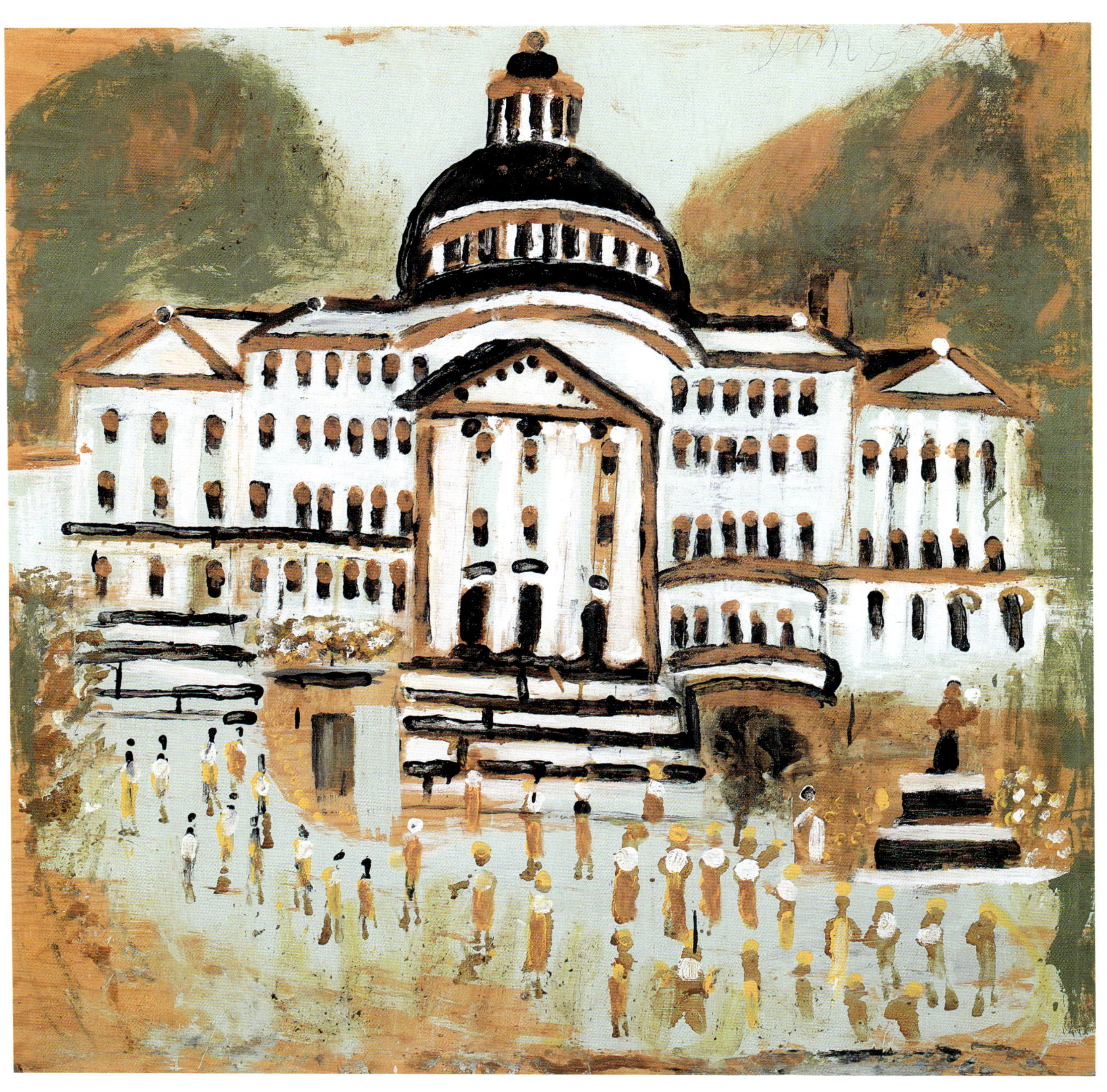

35

JIMMY LEE SUDDUTH

Mud Architectural of State Capitol, ca. 1989

(cat. no. 223)

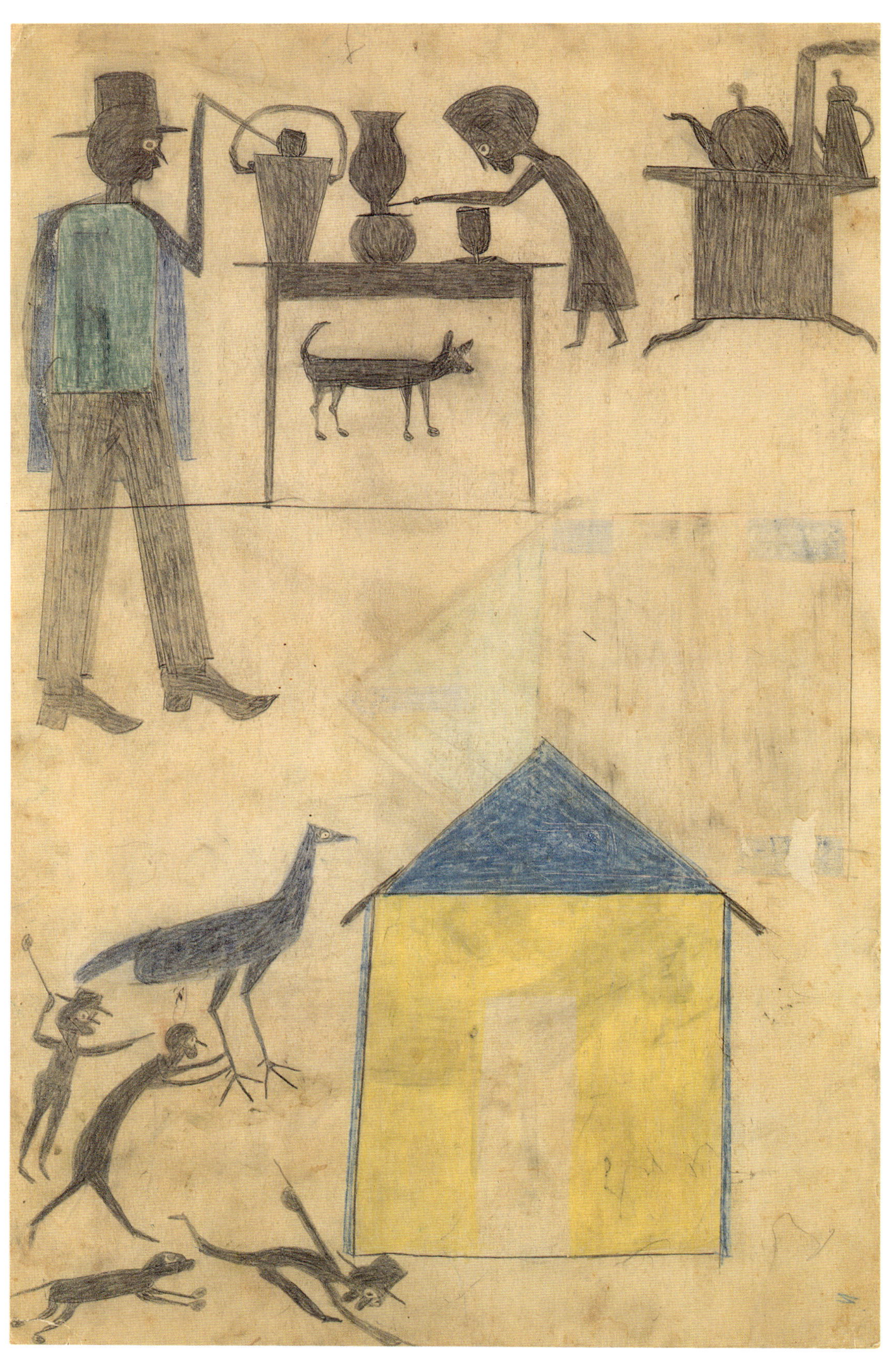

36

BILL TRAYLOR

Kitchen Scene, Yellow House, ca. 1939–42

(cat. no. 247)

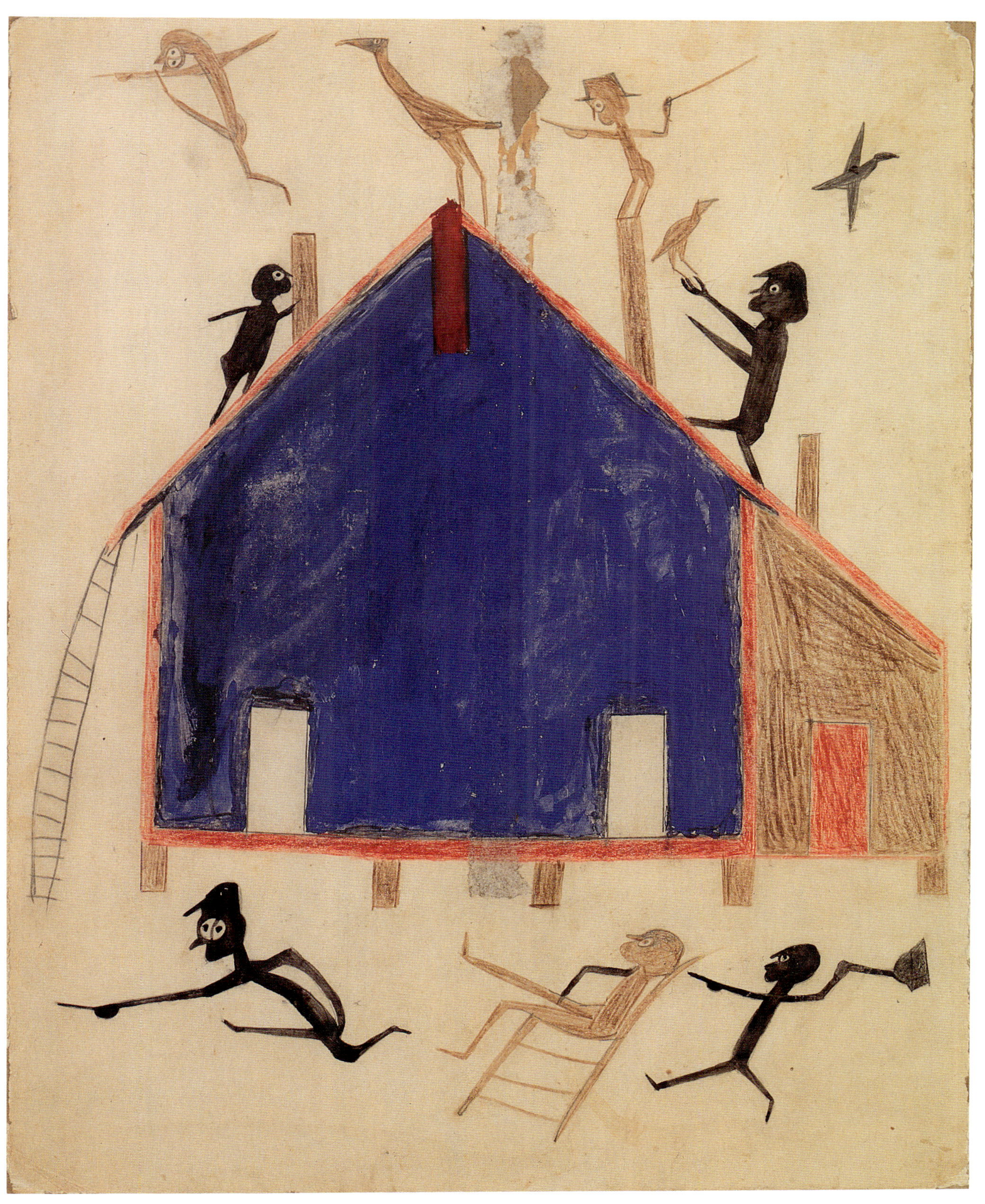

37

BILL TRAYLOR

Blue House with People, n.d.

(cat. no. 245)

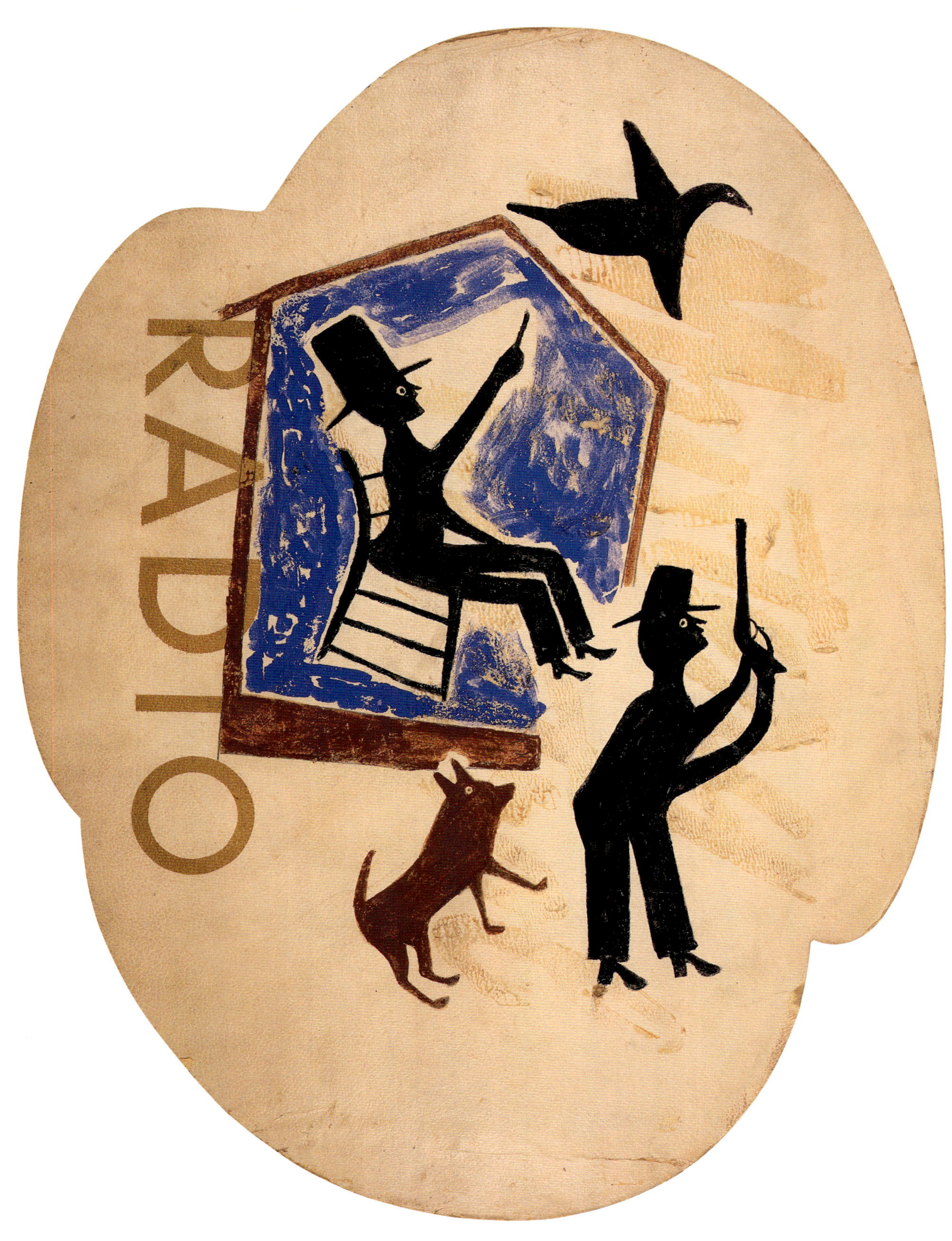

38

BILL TRAYLOR

Radio, ca. 1939–42

(cat. no. 253)

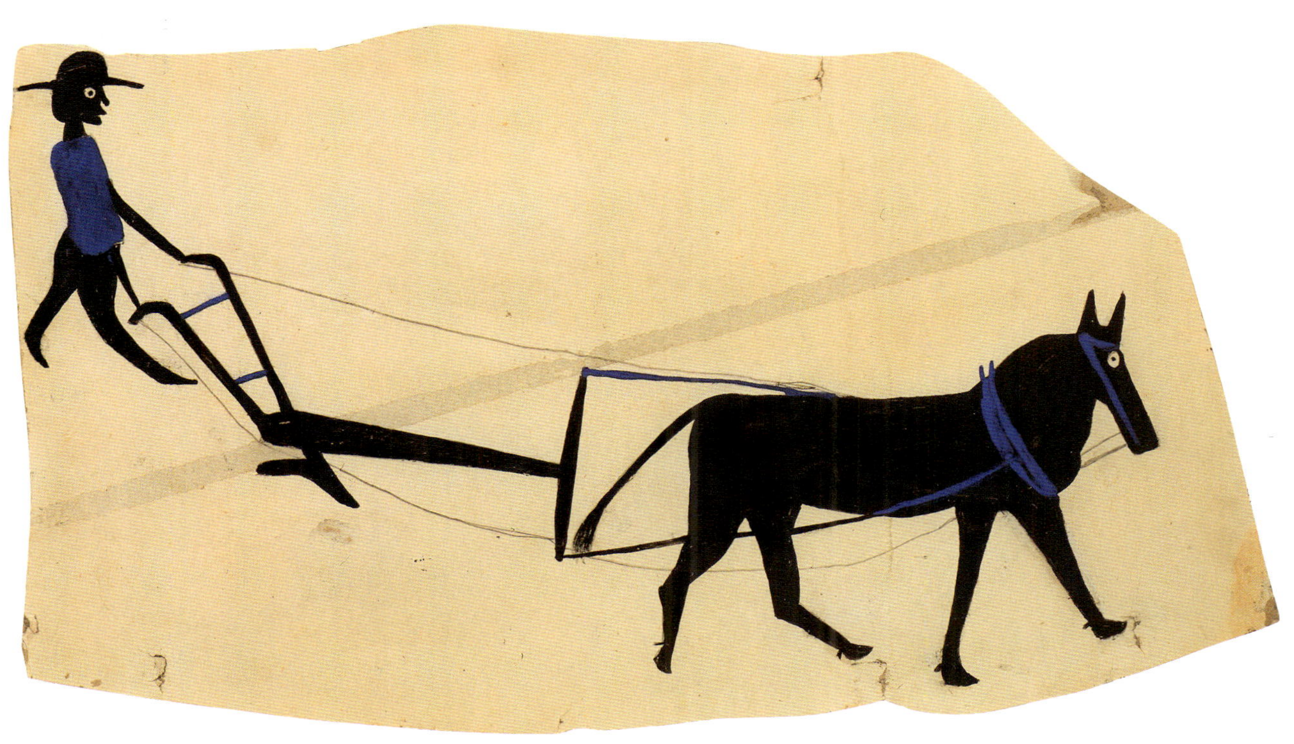

39

BILL TRAYLOR

Man with Mule Plowing, n.d.

(cat. no. 249)

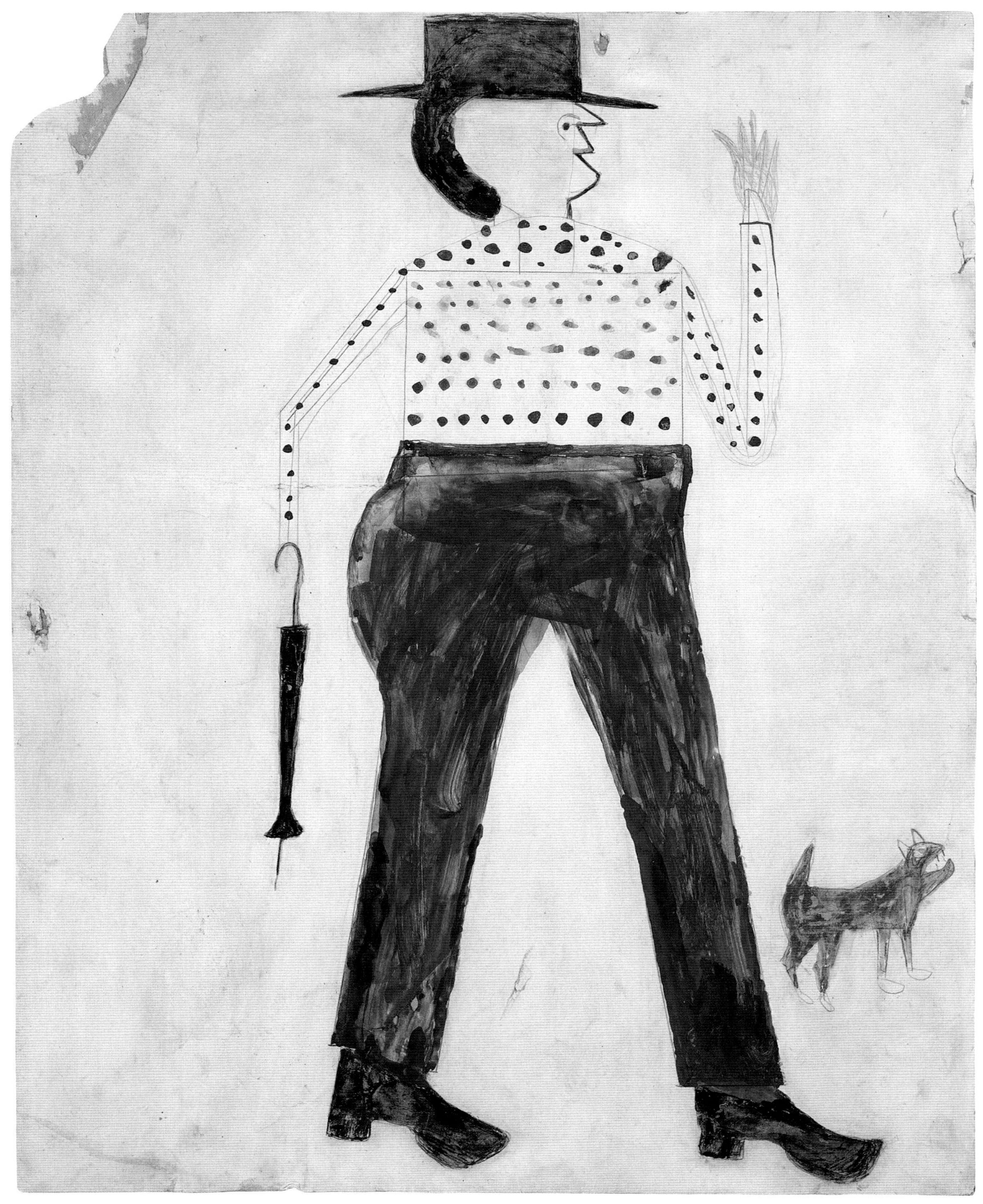

40

BILL TRAYLOR

Man in Blue with Small Dog, ca. 1939–42

(cat. no. 248)

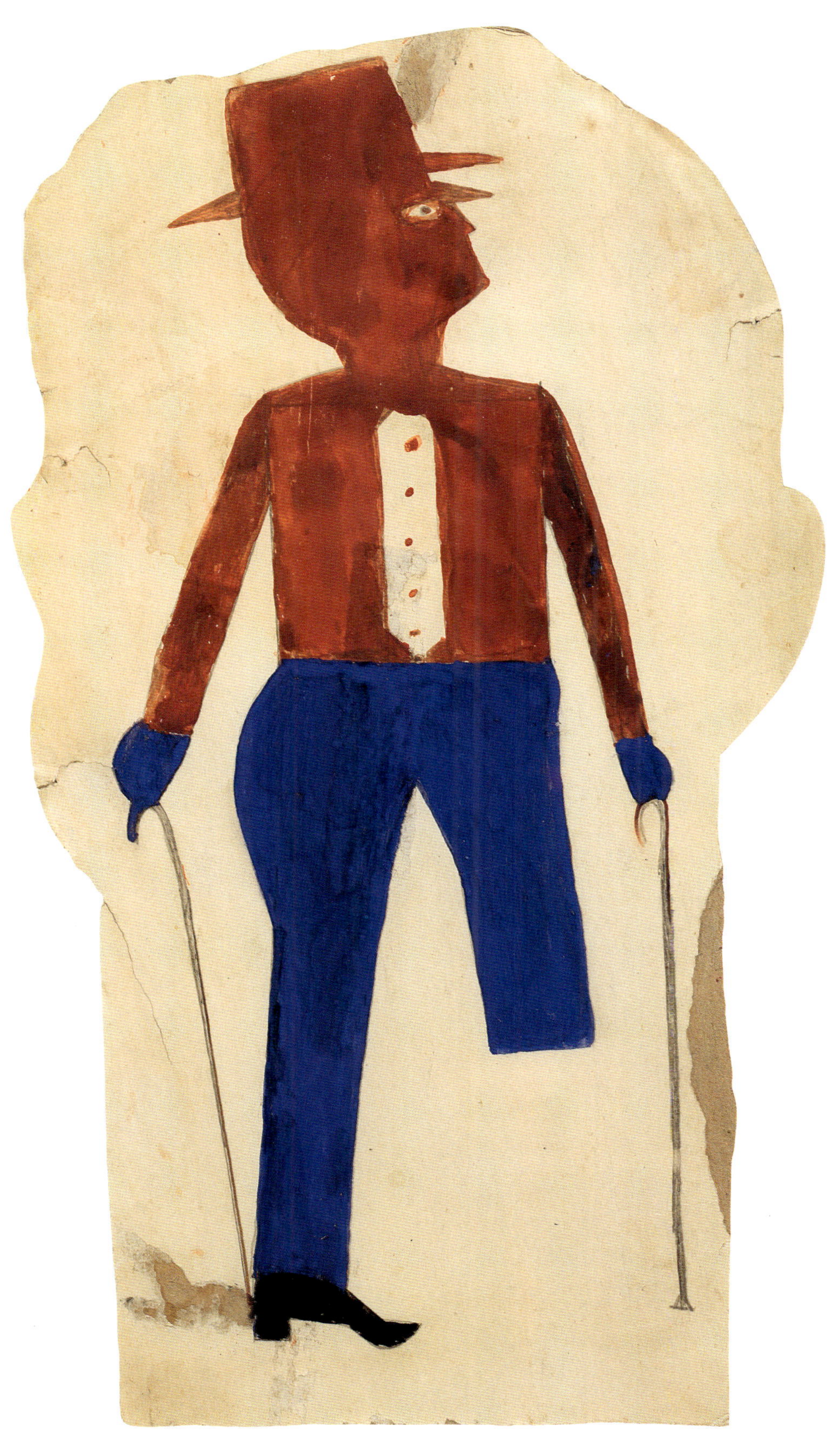

41

BILL TRAYLOR

Man with Two Canes, ca. 1940s

(cat. no. 250)

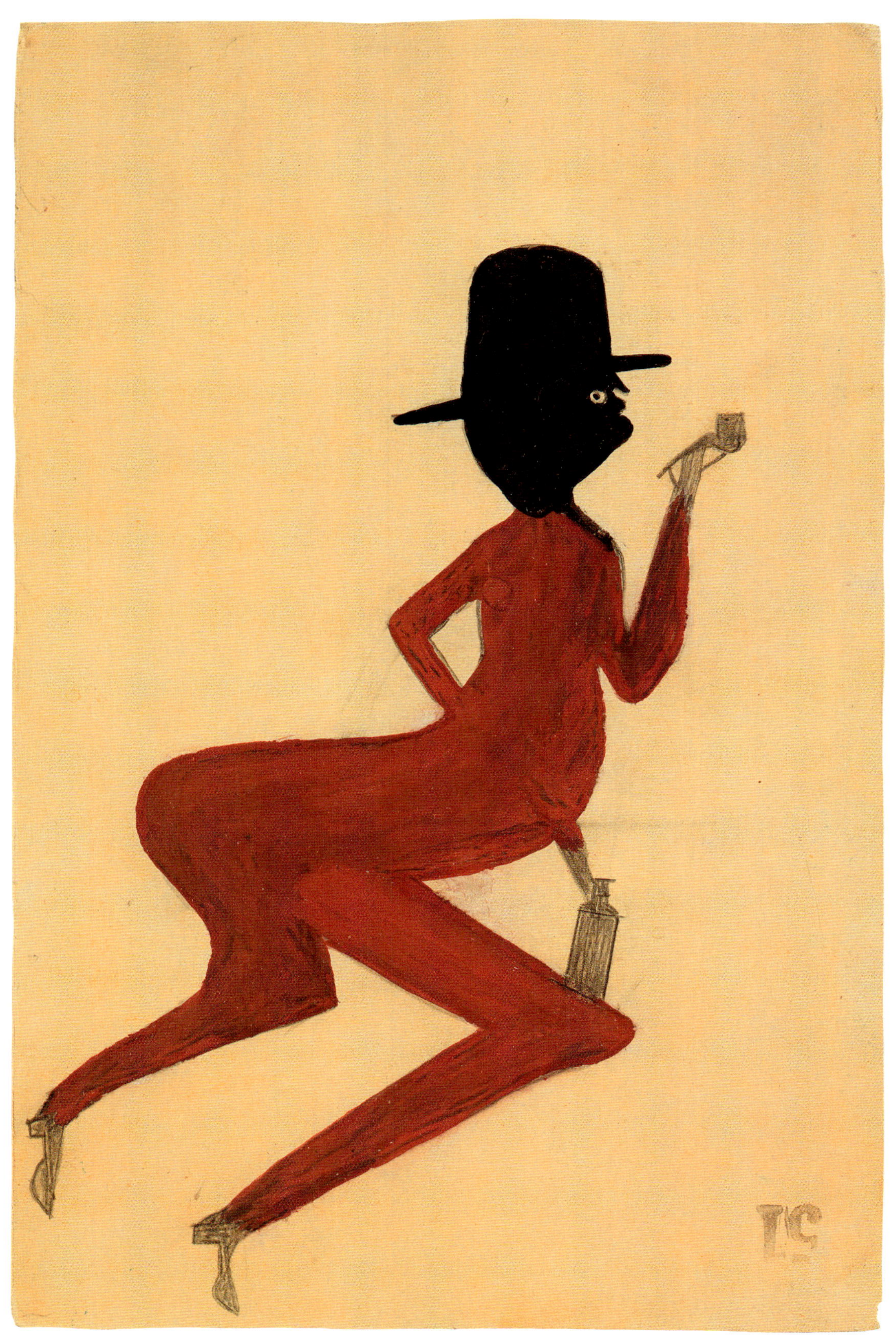

42

BILL TRAYLOR

Red Man, ca. 1939–42

(cat. no. 255)

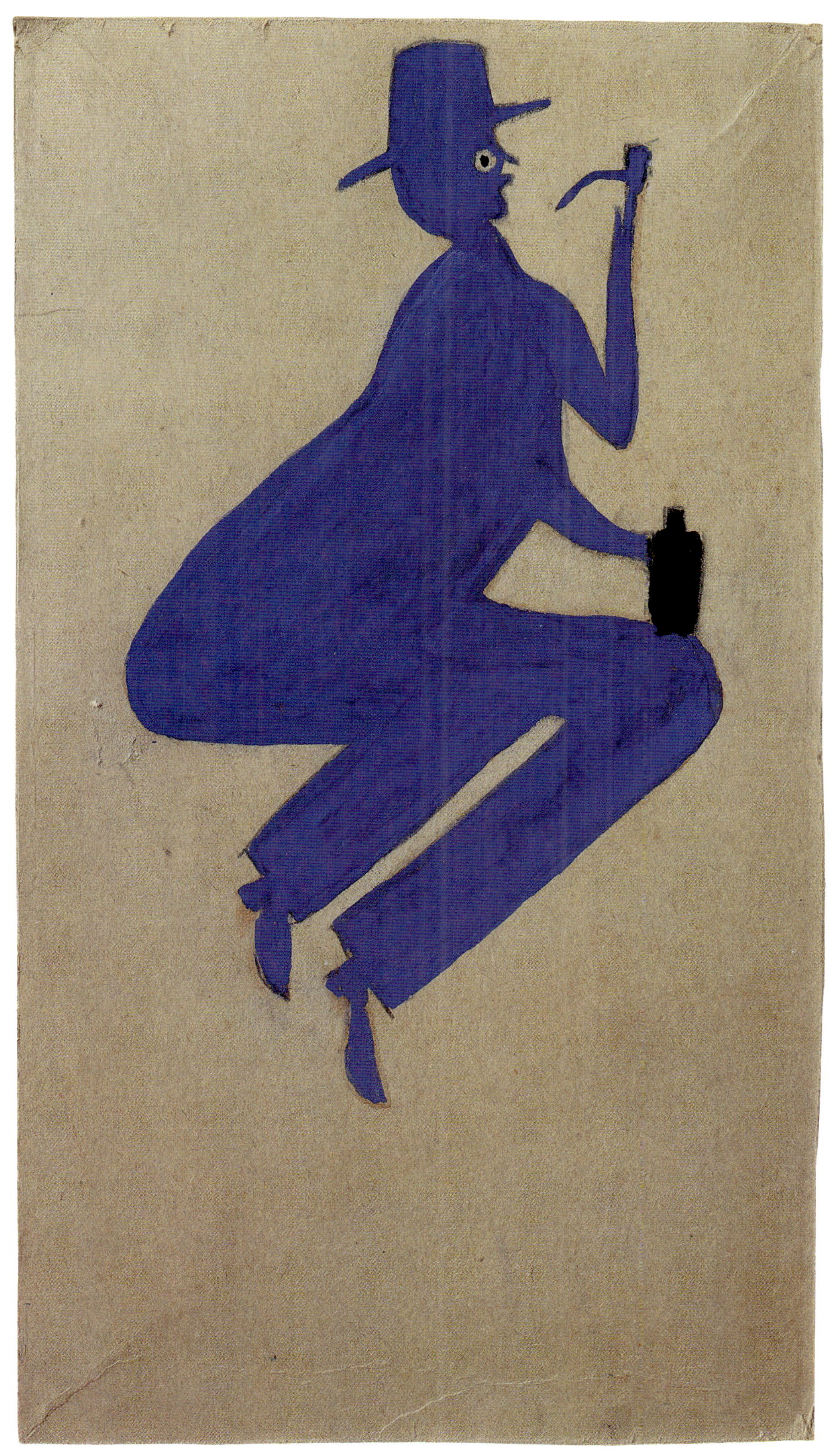

43

BILL TRAYLOR

Blue Man with Pipe and Bottle, ca. 1940

(cat. no. 246)

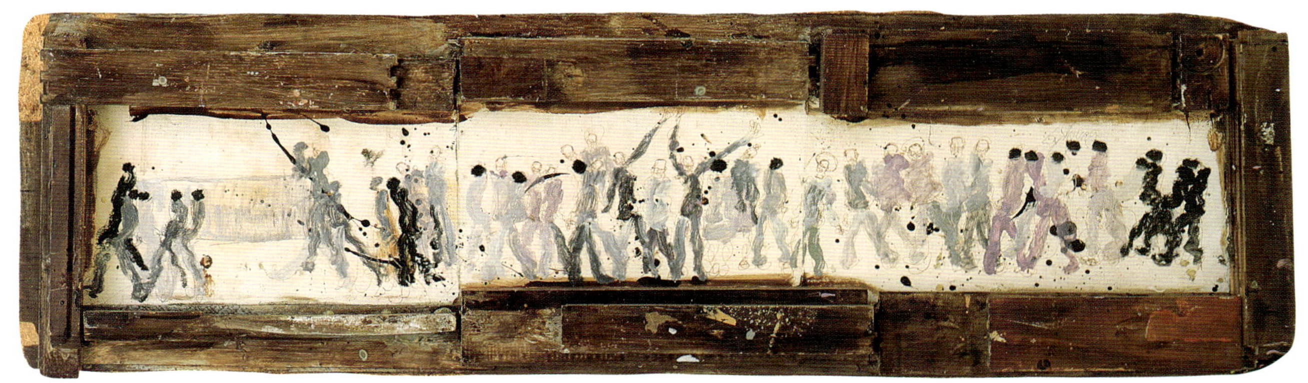

44

PURVIS YOUNG

Funeral Day Procession, ca. 1986–87

(cat. no. 266)

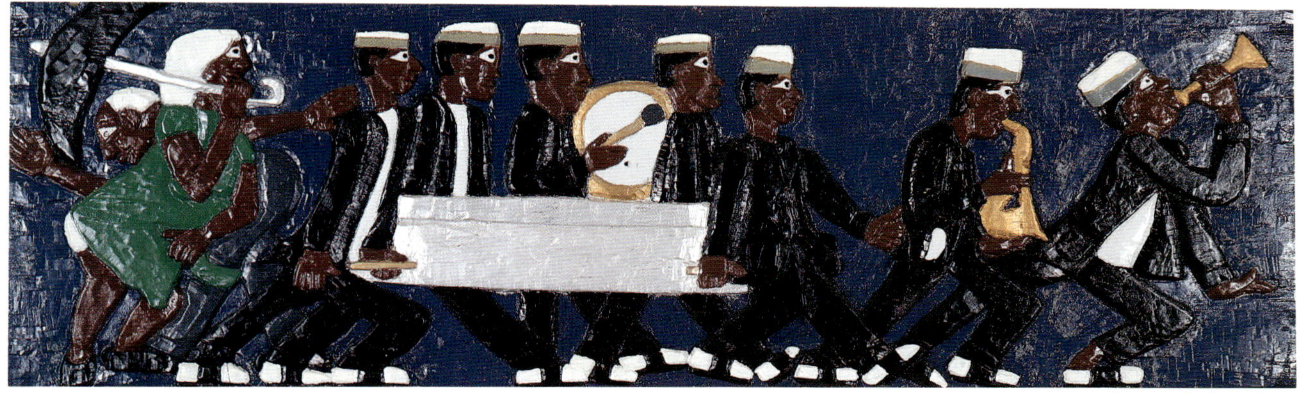

45

HERBERT SINGLETON

New Orleans Jazz Funeral, n.d.

(cat. no. 211)

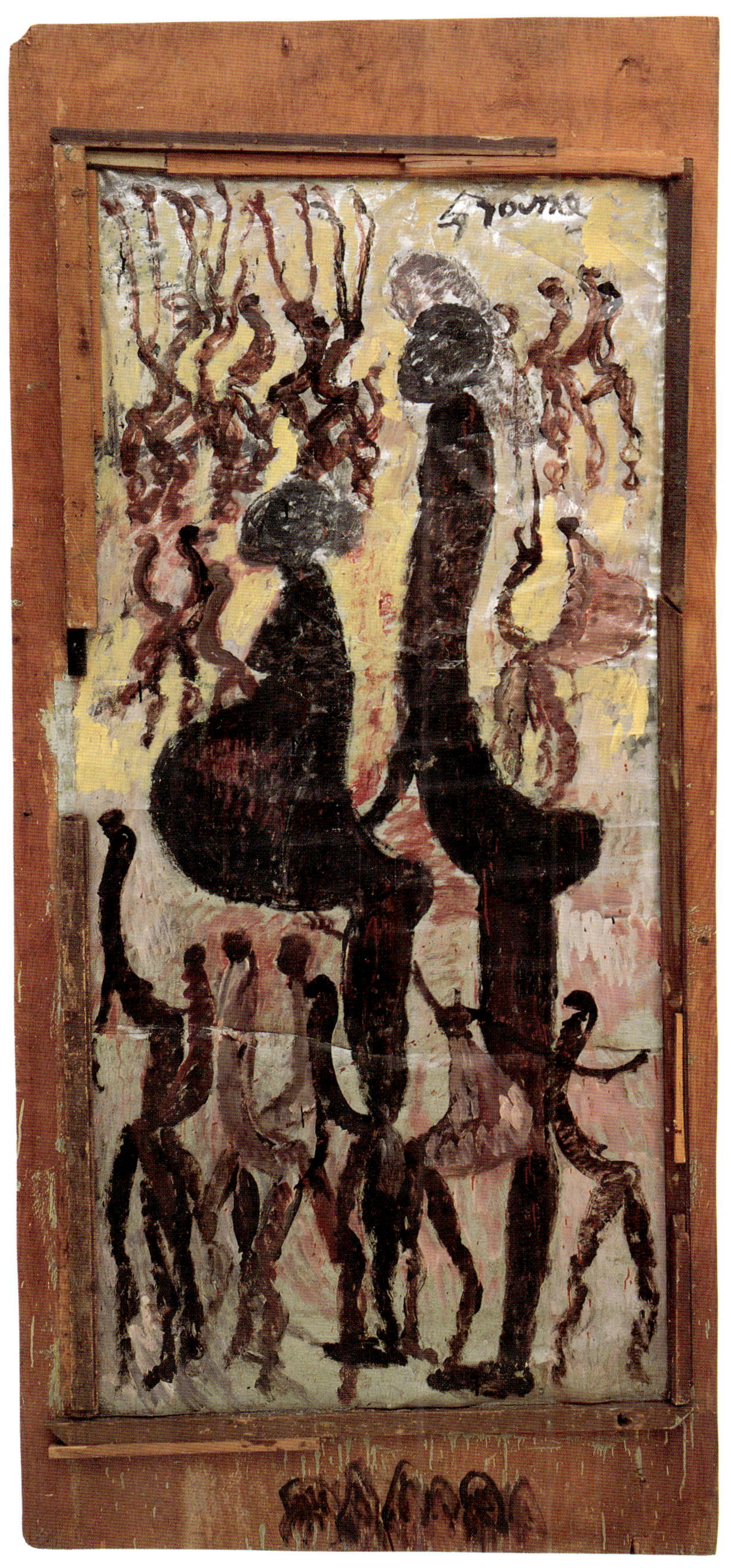

46

PURVIS YOUNG

Love Dance, n.d.

(cat. no. 268)

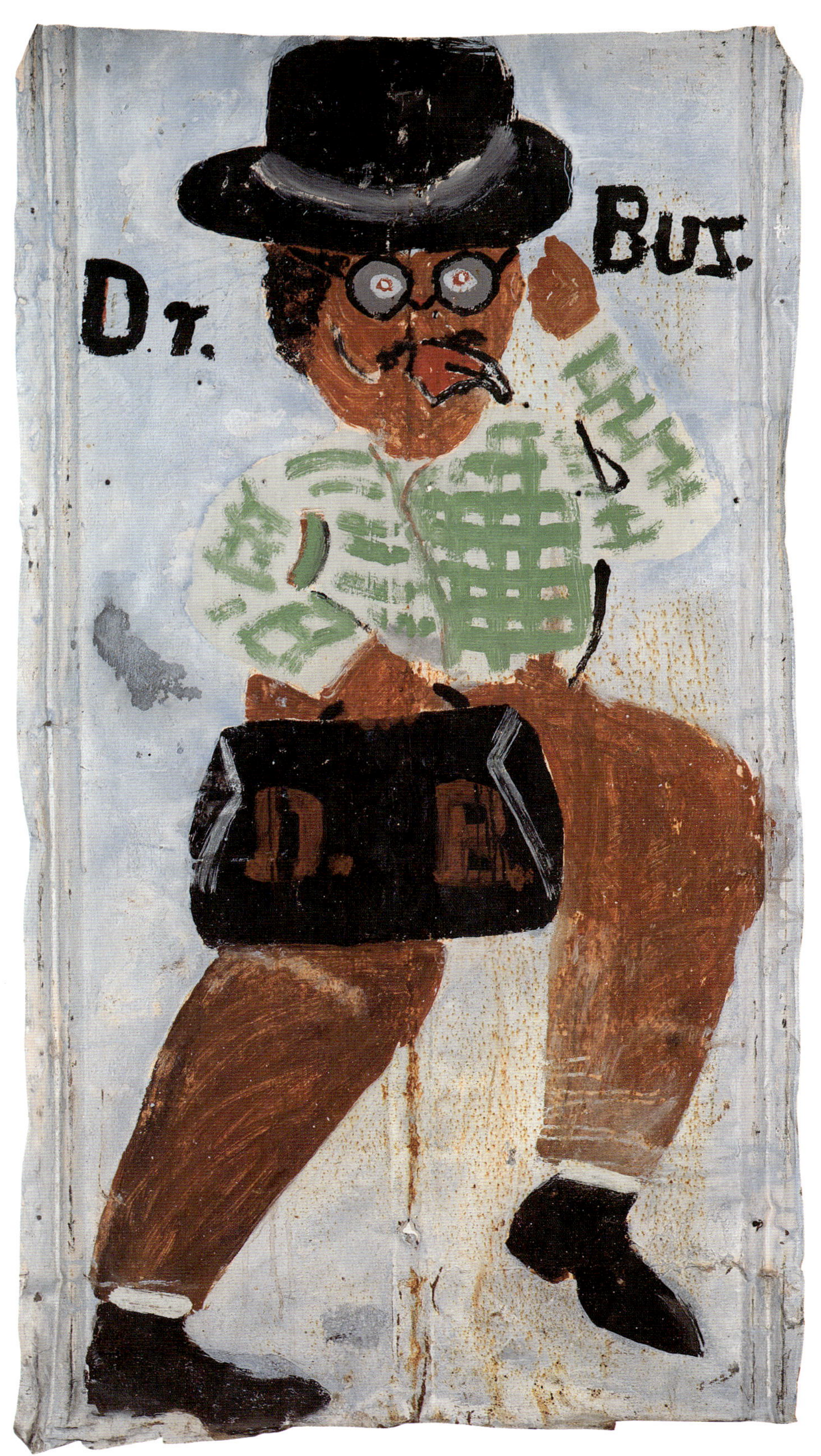

47

SAM DOYLE

Dr. Buz, ca. 1970s

(cat. no. 63)

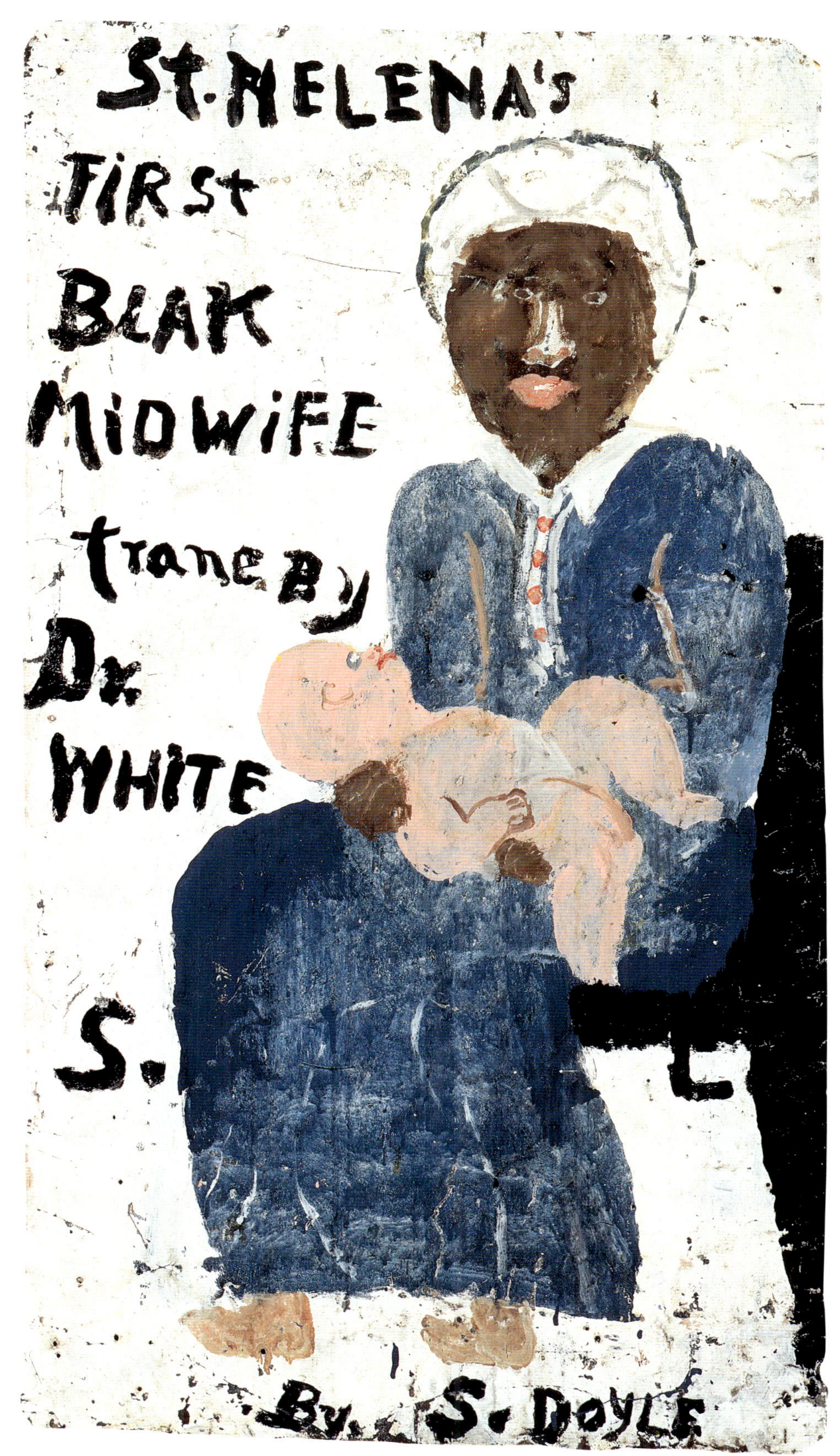

48

SAM DOYLE

St. Helena's First Black Midwife, ca. 1980

(cat. no. 69)

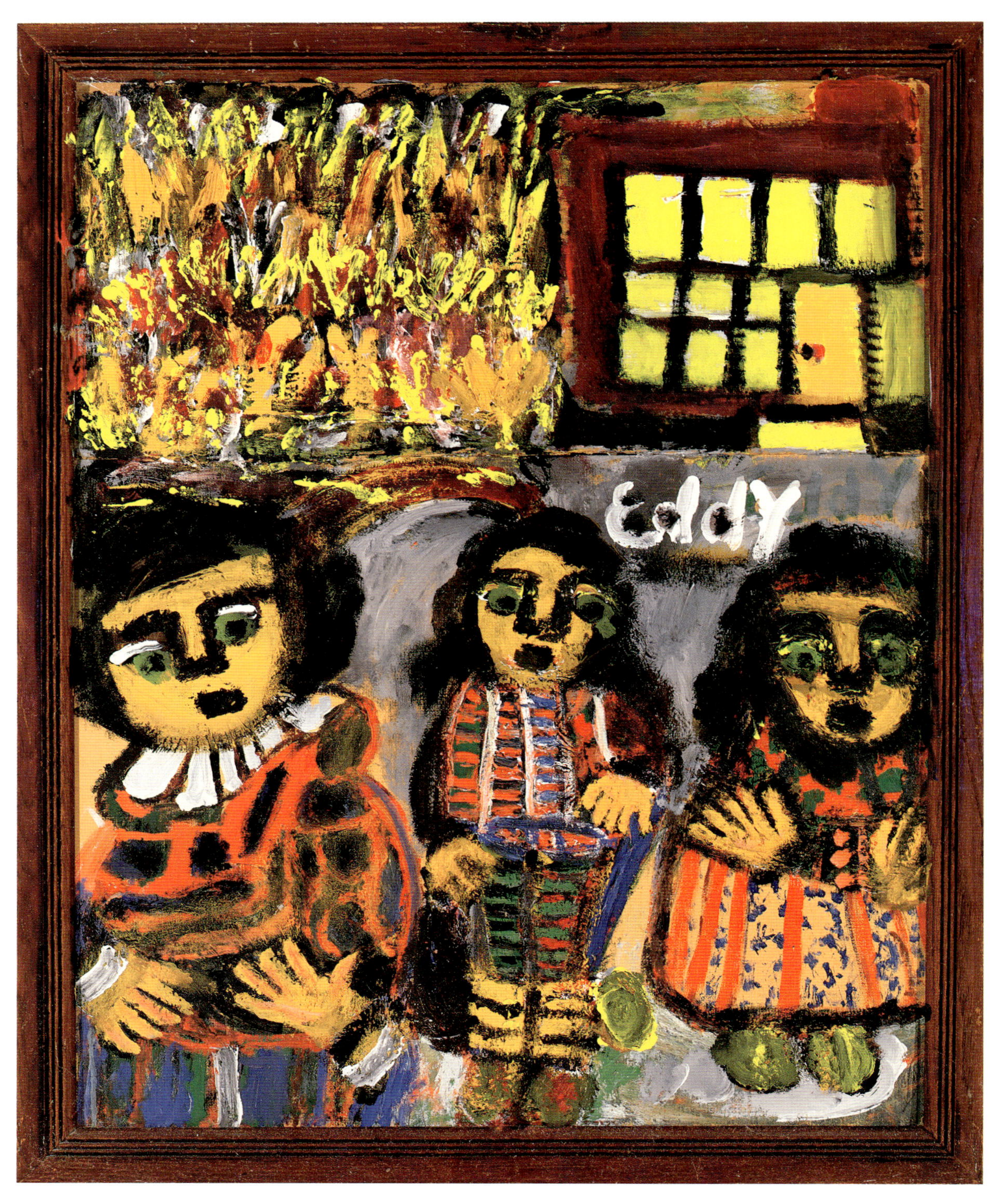

49

ED "MR. EDDY" MUMMA

Three Men and House, ca. 1978–82

(cat. no. 179)

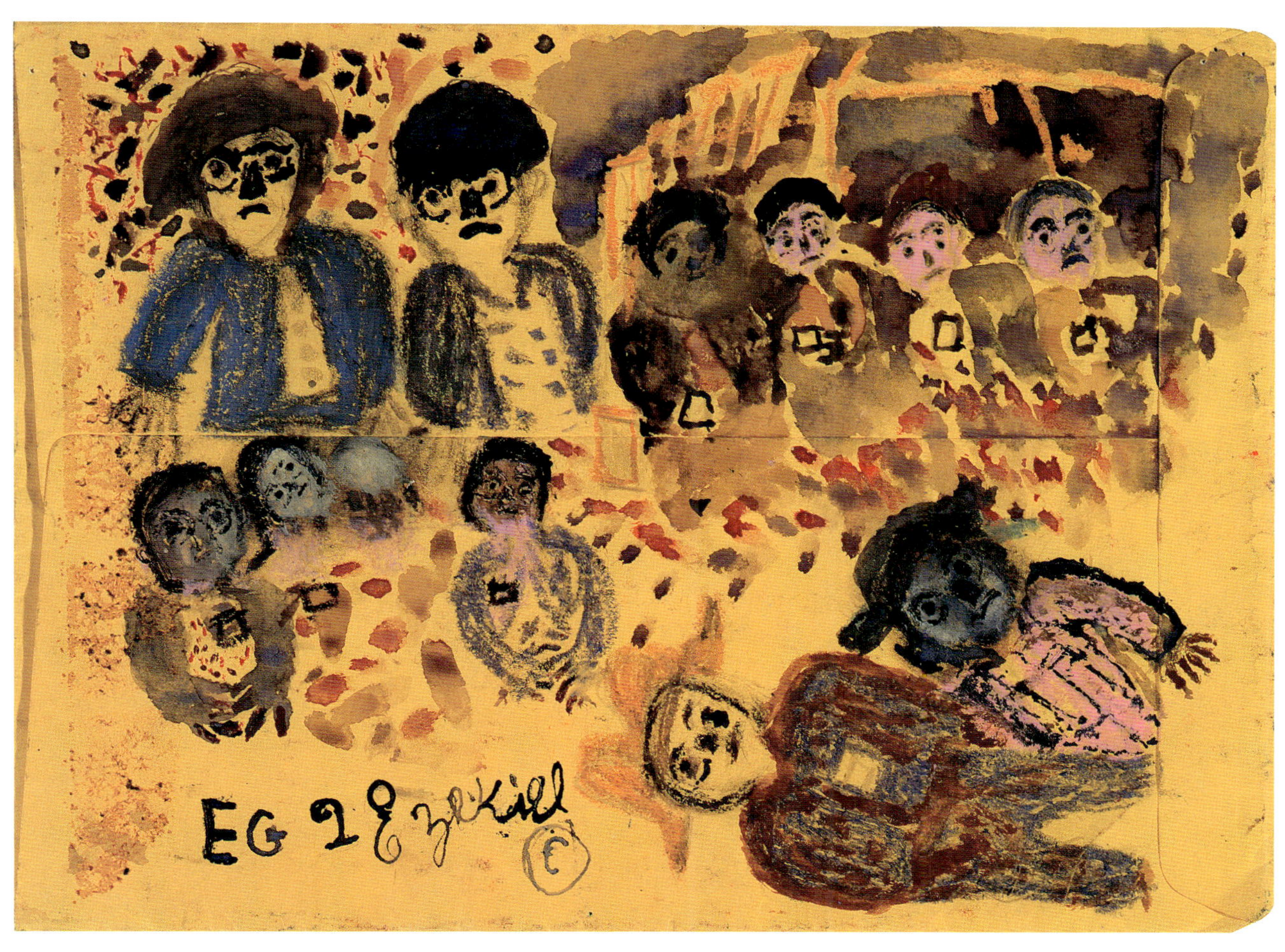

50

EZEKIEL GIBBS

Church Meeting, ca. 1986–87

(cat. no. 94)

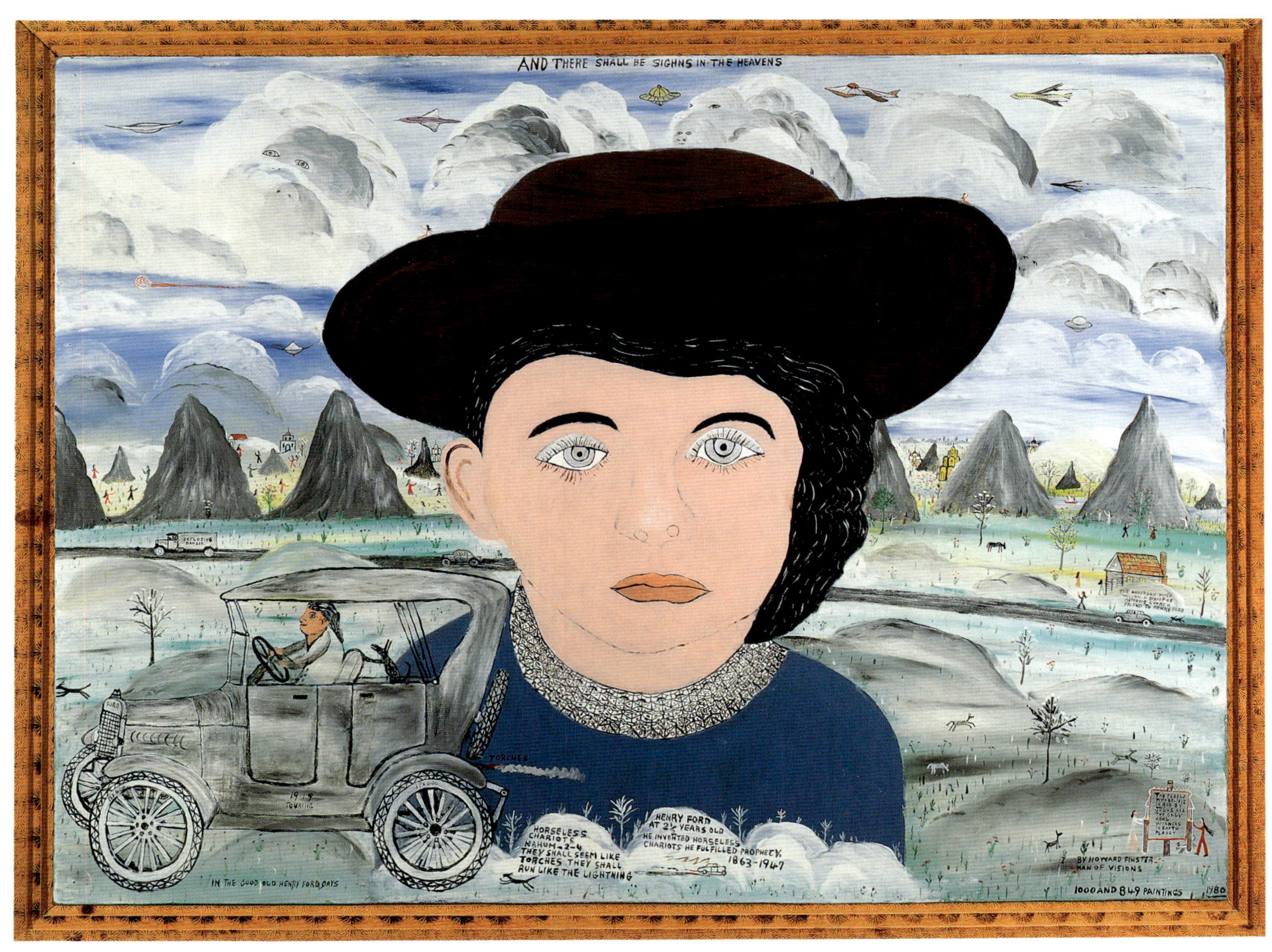

51

HOWARD FINSTER

Henry Ford at 2½ Years Old #1849, 1980

(cat. no. 90)

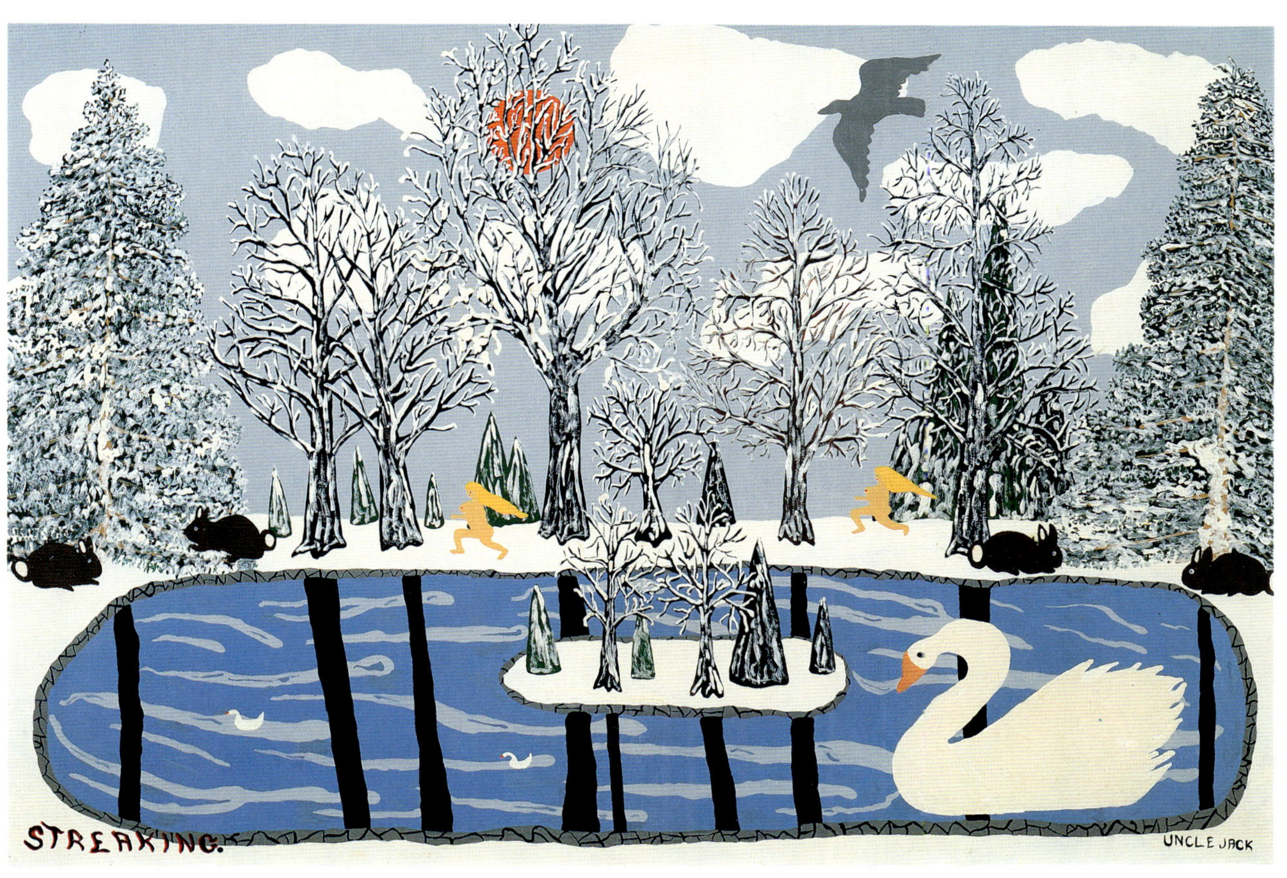

52

JOHN WILLIAM "UNCLE JACK" DEY

Streaking, n.d.

(cat. no. 52)

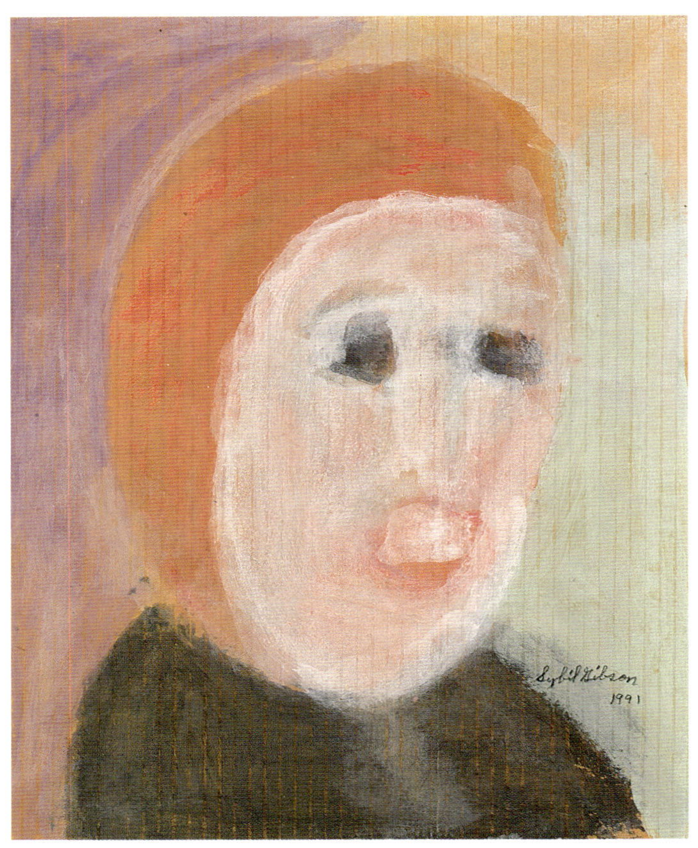

53

SYBIL GIBSON

Woman, ca. 1991–92

(cat. no. 100)

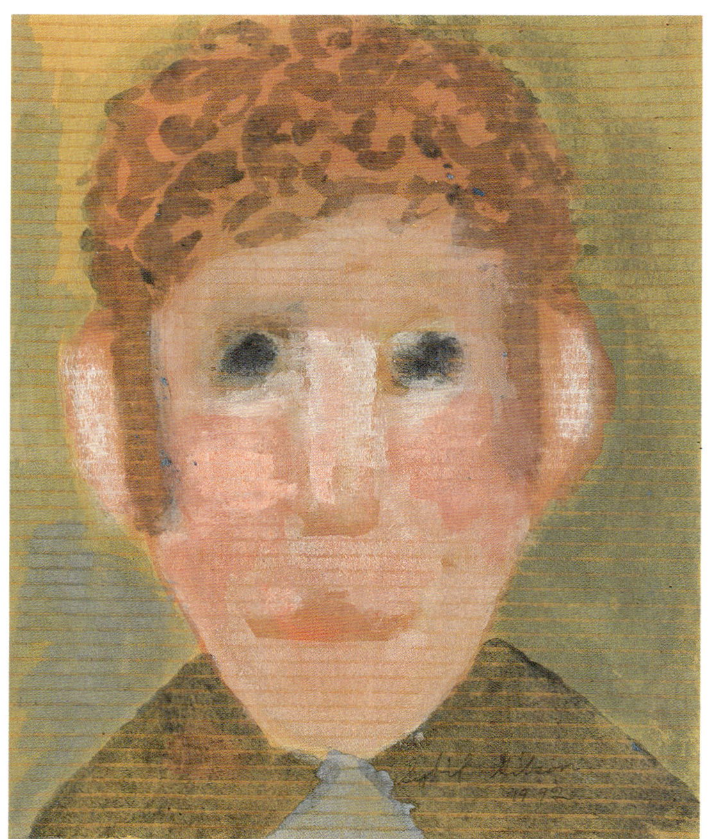

54

SYBIL GIBSON

Man, 1992

(cat. no. 99)

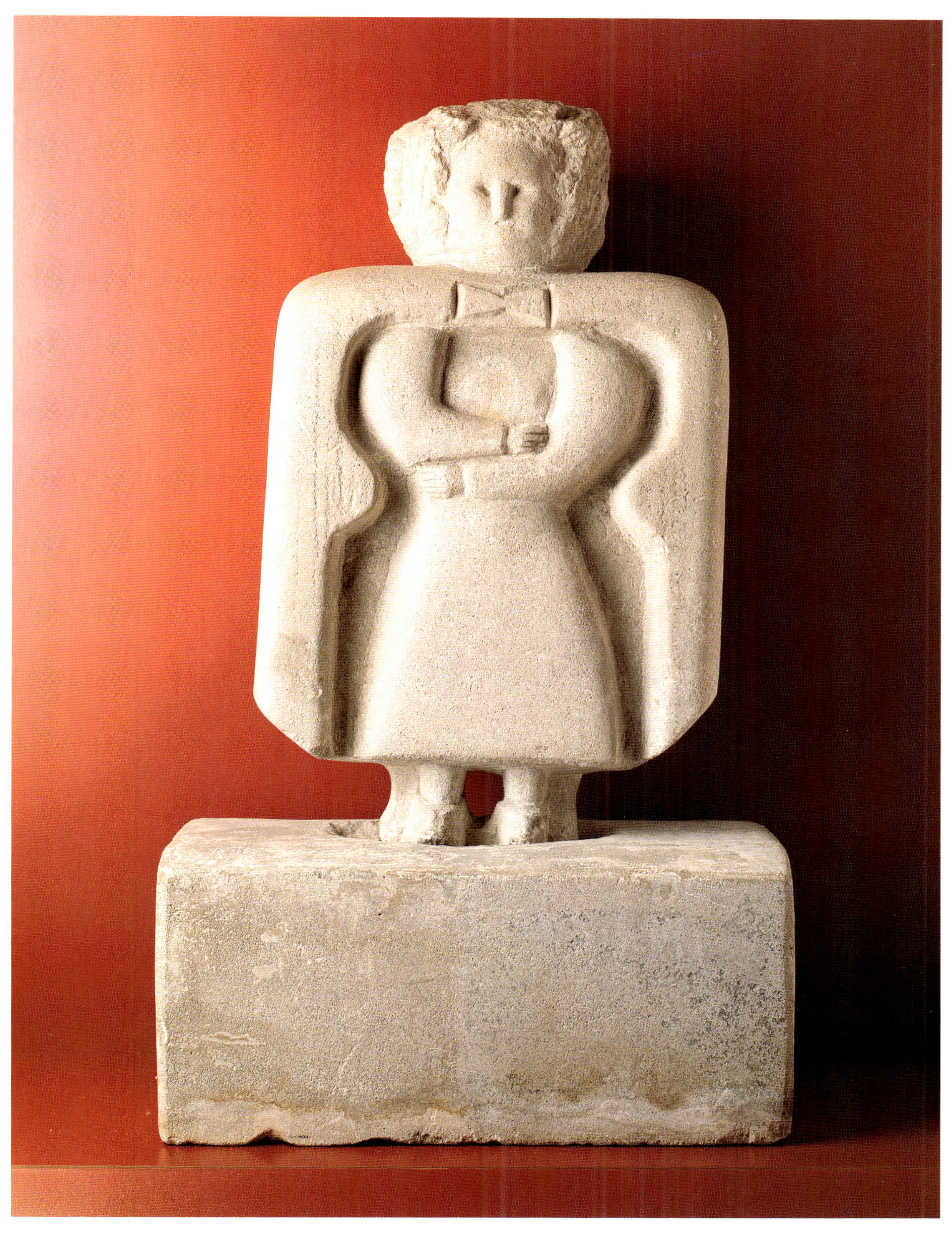

55
WILLIAM EDMONDSON
Girl with Cape, n.d.
(cat. no. 76)

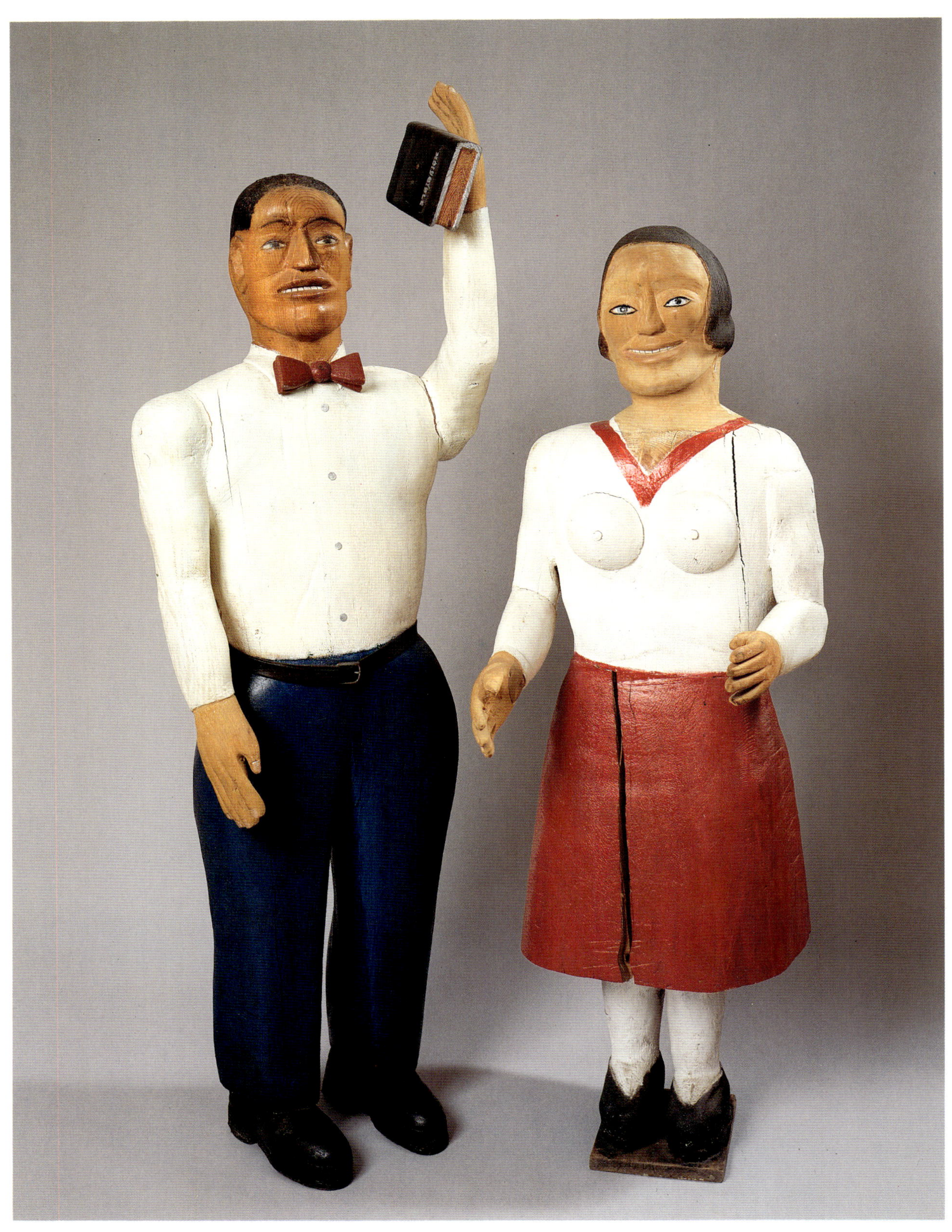

56

SHIELDS LANDON "S. L." JONES

The Preacher and Wife, ca. 1970s

(cat. no. 141)

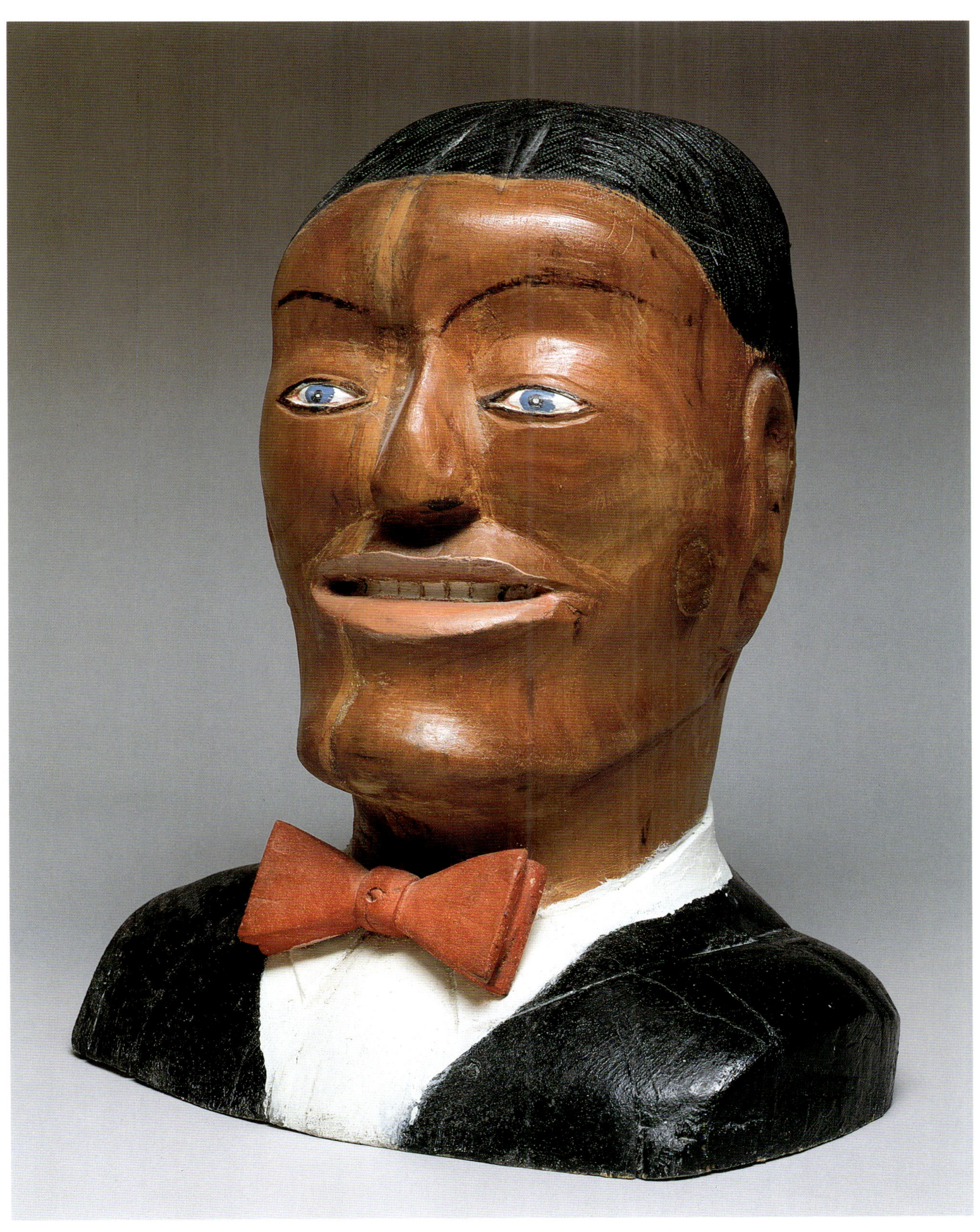

57

SHIELDS LANDON "S. L." JONES

Man with Red Bow Tie, 1983

(cat. no. 140)

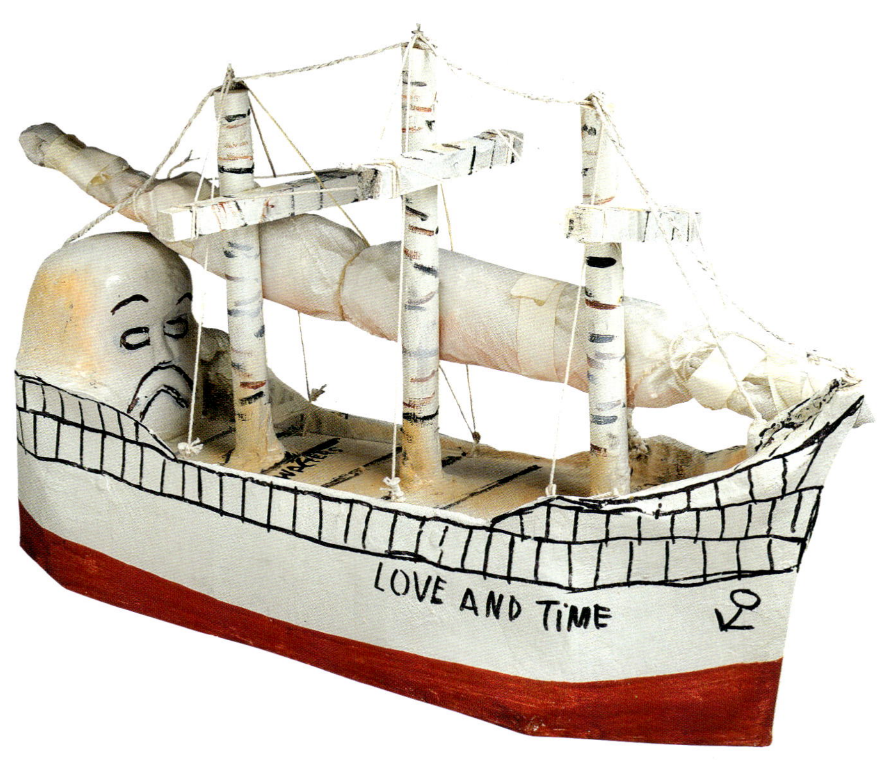

58

HUBERT WALTERS

Love and Time, 1989

(cat. no. 257)

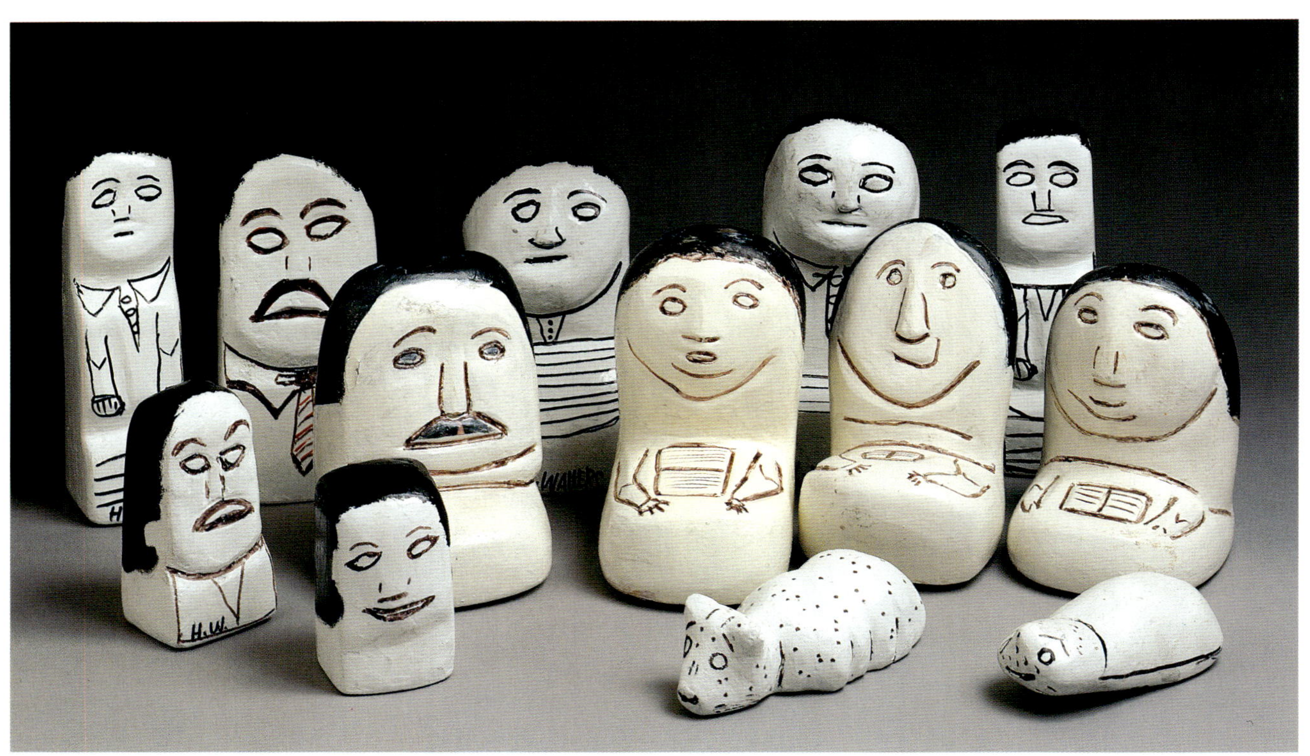

59

HUBERT WALTERS

Figures, ca. 1989–90

(cat. no. 256)

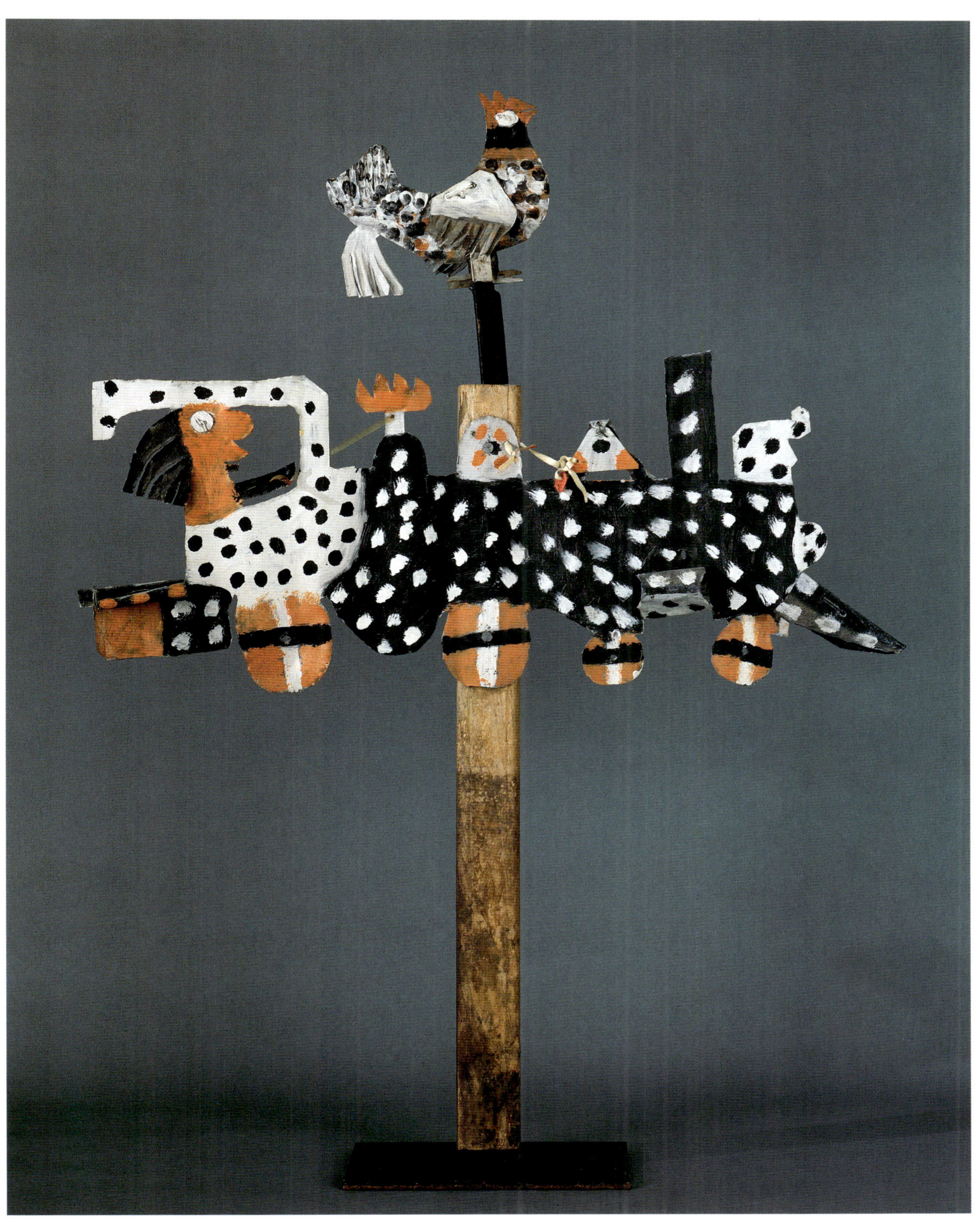

60

DAVID BUTLER

Locomotive Engine with Rooster, ca. 1980

(cat. no. 18)

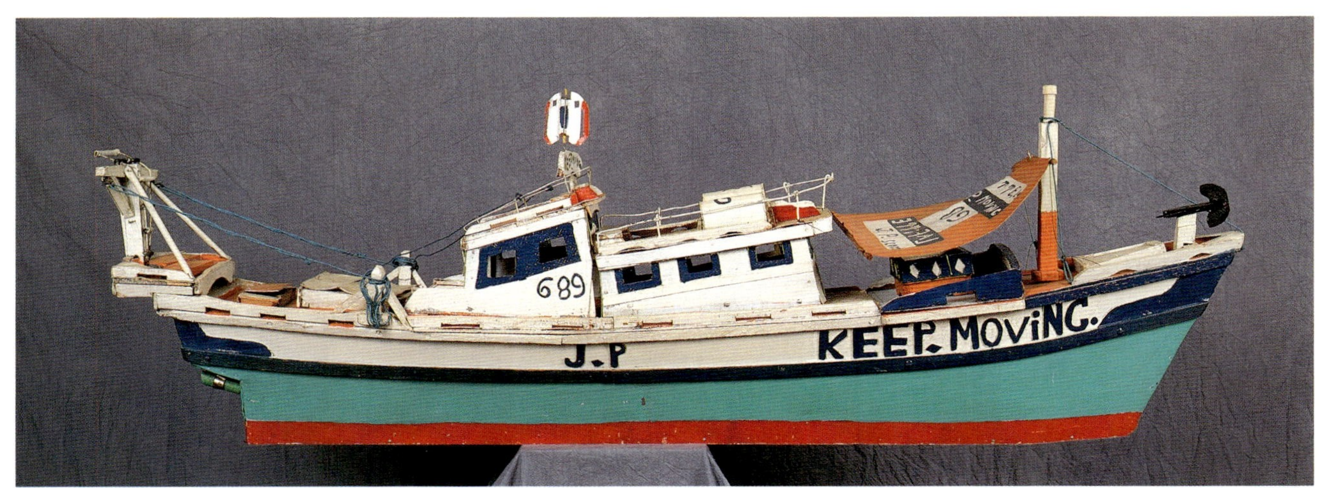

61

J. P. SCOTT

Keep Moving, ca. 1985

(cat. no. 202)

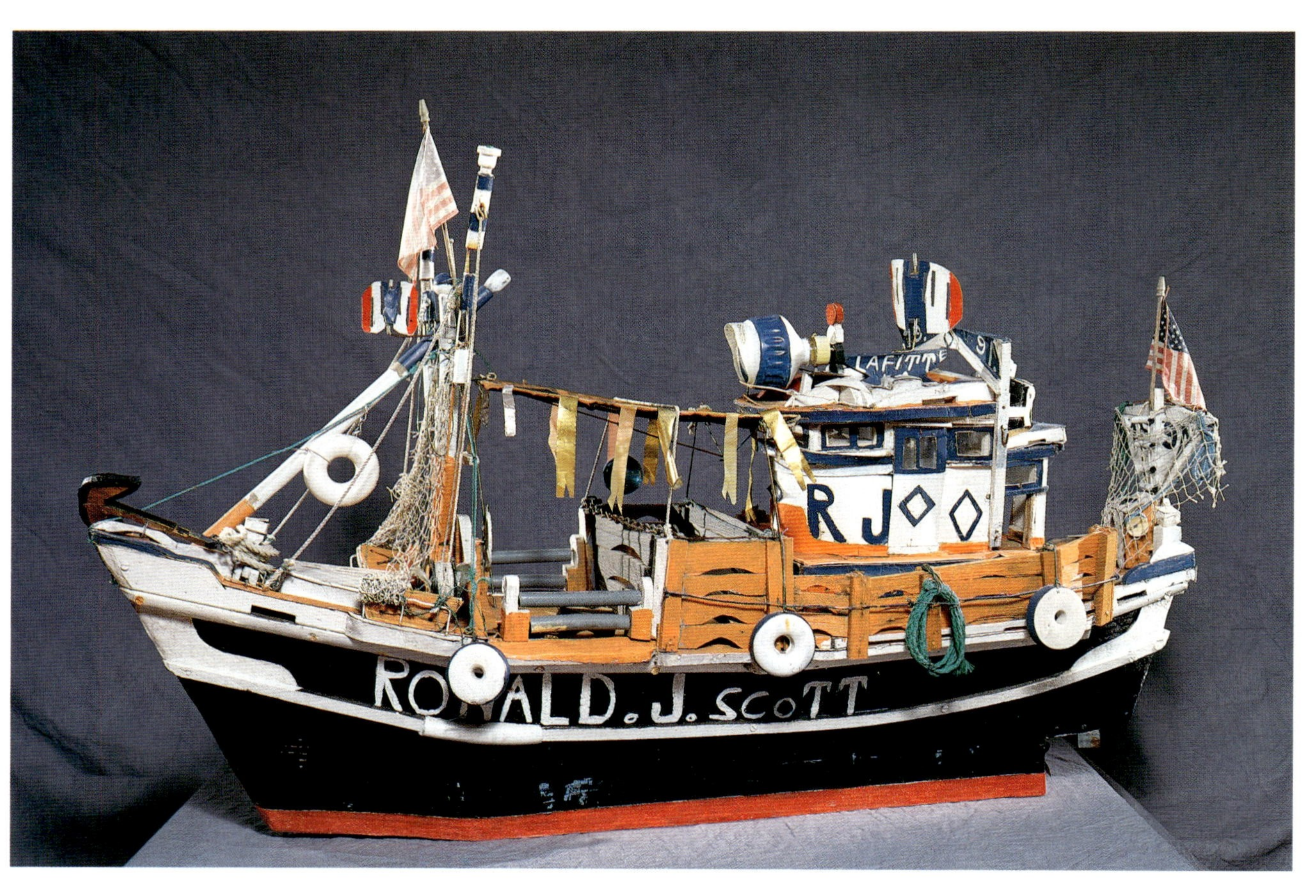

62

J. P. SCOTT

Ronald J. Scott, 1990

(cat. no. 205)

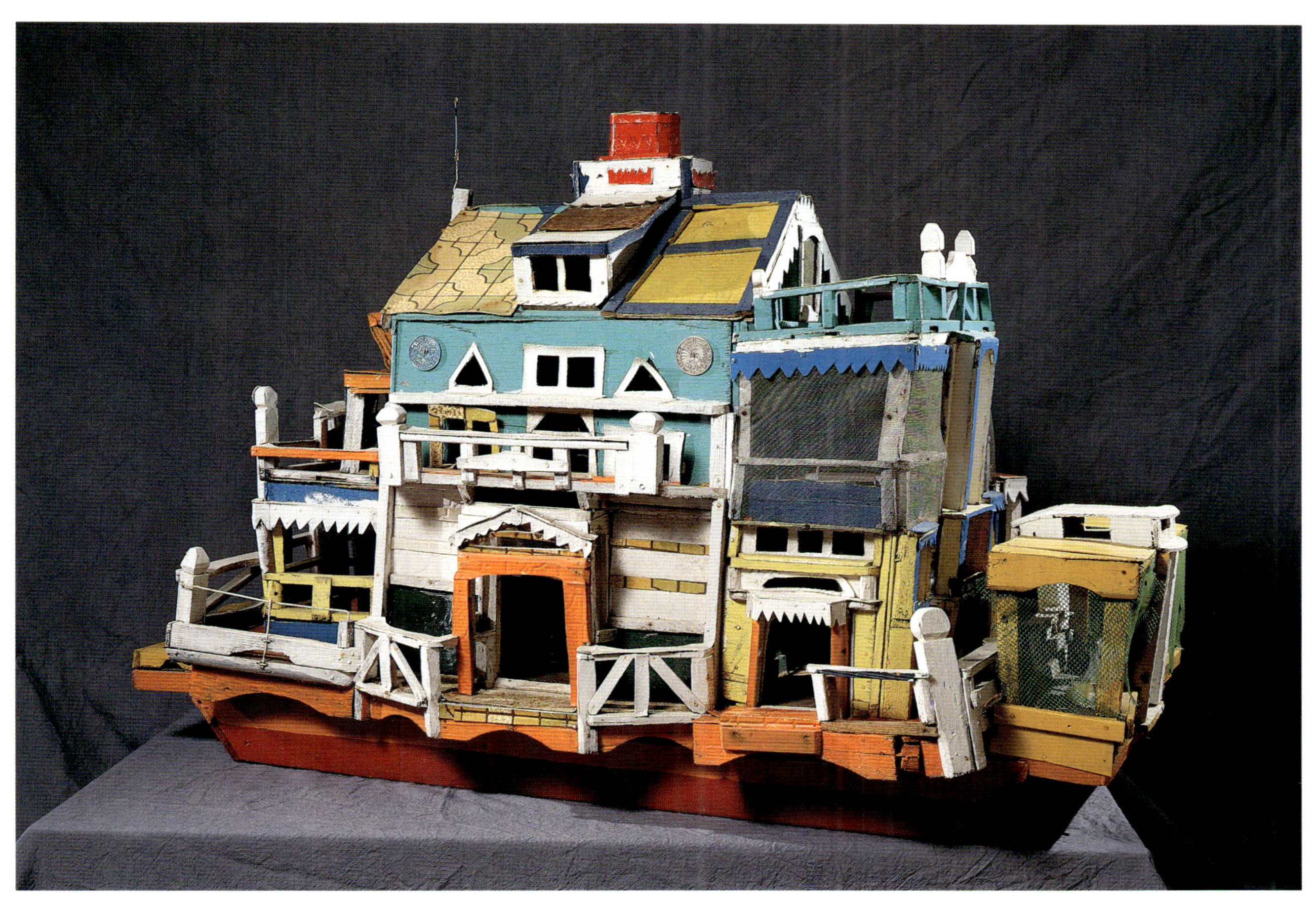

63

J. P. SCOTT

Quarter House, 1984

(cat. no. 204)

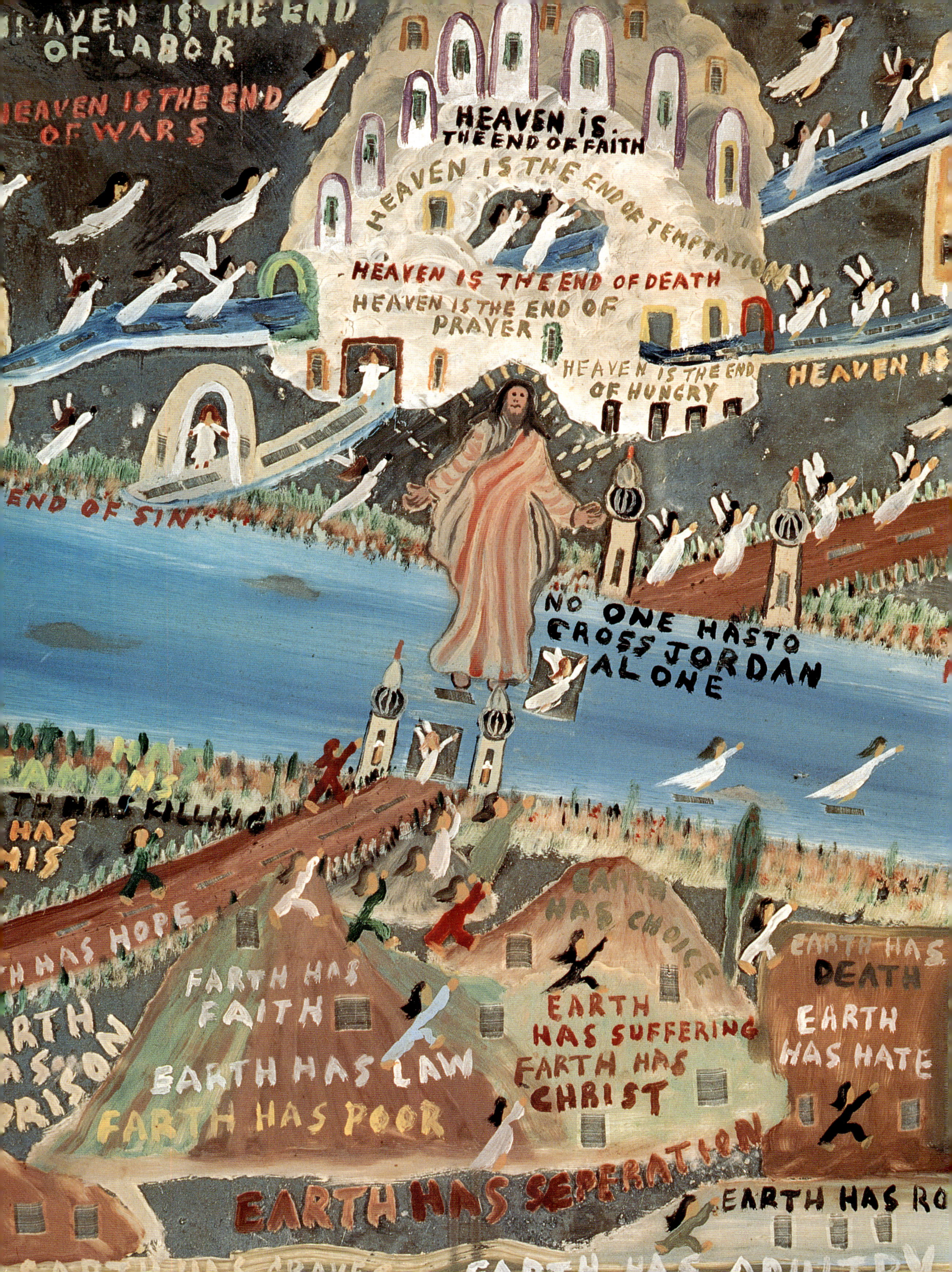
AVEN IS THE END
OF LABOR
EAVEN IS THE END
OF WARS
HEAVEN IS
THE END OF FAITH
HEAVEN IS THE END OF TEMPTATION
HEAVEN IS THE END OF DEATH
HEAVEN IS THE END OF
PRAYER
HEAVEN IS THE END
OF HUNGRY
HEAVEN IS
END OF SIN
NO ONE HAS TO
CROSS JORDAN
ALONE
TH HAS KILLING
H HAS HOPE
EARTH HAS
FAITH
EARTH HAS LAW
EARTH HAS POOR
EARTH
HAS CHOICE
EARTH
HAS SUFFERING
EARTH HAS
CHRIST
EARTH HAS
DEATH
EARTH
HAS HATE
EARTH HAS SEPERATION
EARTH HAS RO

RELIGIOUS AND VISIONARY IMAGERY

Religious and visionary imagery ranges from works that literally describe biblical chapter and verse to those reflecting an artist's internal vision. Some artists profess to be following instructions received from the Lord, in dreams, or via visions. Others are powerfully, often obsessively driven by unarticulated, internalized sources of inspiration.

In some sense, all self-taught artists might be described as visionary, as they each draw primarily on inner resources, and all work created from internal inspiration can be said to be motivated by a spiritual force, which may or may not be interpreted as a religious impulse. Regardless of definition, because religion and spiritual inspiration are so important in the southern way of life, it is hard to imagine a more fertile environment for the creation of religious and visionary imagery.

In the South, religious practice is dominated by evangelical Protestantism and is far more homogeneous and integral to daily life than in other areas of the country.[1] Evangelical groups emphasize the authority of the gospel and hold that salvation is gained by faith and grace, not by the performance of good works and sacraments. Daily choices made in the pursuit of personal salvation are conditioned by a rigid sense of "right" and "wrong," just as one's eternal reward is simply either heaven or hell. Requiring an intense affirmation of faith and stressing personal salvation, evangelical religions accentuate the individual's experience of a personally transforming faith through which God's grace fills one's life and being, beginning with individual spiritual conversion.[2]

Most evangelical southern Protestants, whether black or white, rural or urban, restrained or charismatic, Baptist, Pentecostal, or otherwise, believe in the Bible as the ultimate moral authority. They consider access to the Holy Spirit and thereby conversion to be direct; they uphold traditional morality as defined by their church; and because church authority is decentralized, they accept informal worship.[3] Each of these conditions finds a corollary, subtly or straightforwardly, in the work of many southern self-taught artists.

In the most literal, fundamentalist sense, and reflecting the centrality of the Bible, artists often visually depict the word of God through Old and New Testament narratives. Others portray their intimate experience of God's presence and his saving grace, which some perceive through revelations from the Lord, dreams, or inspired visions. Indeed, it is the expectation of divine revelation that provides a framework for the wealth of artists who claim their imagery is so inspired.[4] Everlasting redemption in heaven for those who followed the path of righteousness and eternal suffering in hell for sinners are frequent themes in self-taught religious art. The acceptance of personalized, informal forms of worship, founded on a common cultural fund of religious symbols, doctrines, and perspectives, also contributes to a plethora of religious and visionary imagery.

Church life and Old and New Testament stories are dominant themes. The appearance of biblical scenes, often literally interpreted, manifest the centrality of the Bible and the strict adherence to its word so prevalent in southern Protestant evangelical groups. From the Old Testament come stories of the creation, Adam and Eve, and Noah's ark; New Testament scenes center on the nativity, Christ's life, and the crucifixion. The struggle and dream of salvation is often based on narratives from the eschatological Book of Revelation, which stresses the second coming of Christ on Judgment Day when each individual's eternal life will be determined.

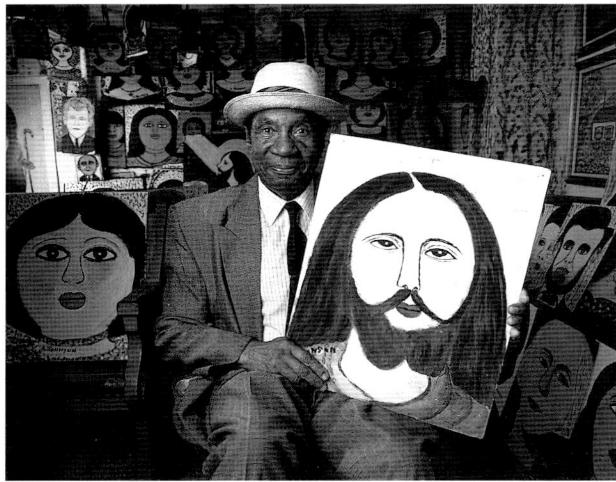

Fig. 1. Anderson Johnson, Newport News, Virginia, 1992. Johnson, a preacher, is surrounded by artworks that fill the interior of his home mission. Photo Thomas Daniel.

Many artists who produce narrative biblical subjects claim direct communication with God. Others simply tell Bible stories, commonly learned in childhood, Sunday school, or church. Some are lay preachers, often leaders of their own churches; others have no conventional religious affiliation. Self-proclaimed preachers abound in the ranks of self-taught artists, including Sister Gertrude Morgan, Howard Finster, Anderson Johnson, Rev. Benjamin F. Perkins, Rev. Johnnie Swearingen, Elijah Pierce, Josephus Farmer, Edgar Tolson, and R. A. Miller. Eddie Kendrick was an active church deacon. Those artist/preachers who founded their own churches usually decorated them with their own works of art. Anderson Johnson (fig. 1), for example, ingeniously fashioned an unconventional pulpit for regular use at Sunday prayer meetings from painted wood, egg cartons, styrofoam, rayon ribbons, house paint, nails, and plastic ice trays (pl. 65).

The pervasive impact of evangelical religion in the South is seen in roadside signs espousing messages of salvation. Scattered throughout the rural countryside, these signs are constant reminders of the omnipotence of the Lord and the need for personal salvation (fig. 2). R. A. Miller's placard, *Lord Love You* (cat. no. 167), is a handmade contemporary version of such a proselytizing sign. Made of painted, cut tin applied to a thin wooden cross, the work proclaims "Lord Love You" three times, a message reinforced by a winged angel whose presence suggests the wish for salvation. A preacher for more than thirty years, Miller is an ordained minister of the Free Will Baptist, and this evangelical declaration is inscribed on many of his painted tin drawings depicting angels, animals, creatures, and devils. Miller also places painted whirligig cutouts in

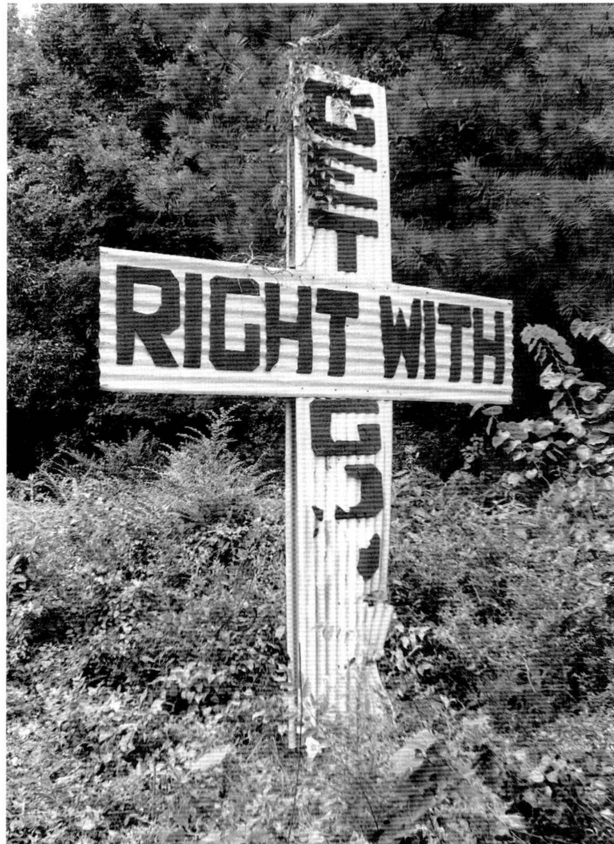

Fig. 2. "Get Right with God," Highway 72, North Alabama, 1992. Evangelizing roadside signs such as this are seen throughout the South. Photo Susan B. Lee.

his front and side yards where they catch the attention of walking or driving passersby. Of his imagery, he says, "Maybe the Lord wanted me to do this."[5]

The church, its activities, and its ministers are often portrayed in the art of the self-taught. In the South, going to church and worshiping, especially in black congregations, often provides religious fulfillment in itself.[6] Johnnie Swearingen, a self-proclaimed Baptist minister, recaptured the quintessential energy and fervor of his own black church services in *God Loves You* (pl. 77), painted in lively yellows, greens, and pinks.[7] His arm raised toward God, a preacher is surrounded by a gesturing, expressive choir, a diligent organist, and a rapt congregation. In *Sunday Camp Meeting* (pl. 76), Swearingen depicted a church that was the site of an annual revival meeting, a widely attended southern religious event as important to families for its social aspects as for the hope of conversion and spiritual rebirth. In *Church Scene* (cat. no. 27), Bernice Sims portrayed the church as a social center where congregants in small southern towns gathered at times other than Sunday services.

In *Dream House* (pl. 66), William Dawson's fanciful painted and sculpted record of a dream,[8] a black preacher stands at an architectonic podium. A painted landscape acts as a backdrop. This complex construction contrasts with the simplicity of William Edmondson's stone preacher, a robust and secure figure wearing a bow tie and holding a Bible (pl. 69).

The story of creation and of Adam and Eve's fall from grace are favorite themes. In an artistic equivalent to oral storytelling, Swearingen used multiple sequential scenes in *The Creation of the World* (pl. 105) to render the biblical account of the origin of man, from the creation of Adam and Eve to Abel's death at Cain's hand. In Raymond Coins's *Adam and Eve* (pl. 68), the figures and incised details appear as timeless as the chiseled river stone in which they are carved. The Garden of Eden is depicted in vibrant enamel model-airplane paints by John William "Uncle Jack" Dey (pl. 97) and in a charming painted wood assemblage by Carl McKenzie (pl. 103), in which Adam and Eve and the serpent pose beneath the tree of forbidden apples. Edgar Tolson's carved Adam and Eve, titled *Original Sin* (pl. 96), are participants in a ménage à trois, in company with the serpent that led to their downfall.[9]

Herbert Singleton adeptly carved the five panels of a six-foot door into scenes of a lion and a lamb in the garden; God's hand about to reach down to take a rib from Adam; Adam and Eve and the serpent; Adam and Eve's expulsion from the garden by God; and Cain slaying Abel. An inscription reads, "In the eyes of God true love covers all fault," a reference to God's forgiveness.

While Singleton often portrays biblical subjects based on his own detailed knowledge of these accounts, he expresses his skepticism of organized religion: "No matter if you're going to a preacher, a priest, a psychiatrist, a witch doctor, or a voodoo queen, you're only getting confidence by proxy. Can't nobody solve the problem but the person hisself."[10]

Noah's ark is another frequent subject of self-taught artists. Appealingly portrayed in carved high relief by Carl McKenzie (pl. 102), the crowded paired inhabitants of the ark, cheerily decorated with painted dots, swirls, and stripes, brim from within a boxlike structure. God's command that Noah gather the animals "two by two," with one of each sex to ensure regeneration, is suggested by the human figures, one dressed as a man, the other as a woman, and the pairs of animals. McKenzie's balanced format is emphasized by parallel snakes vertically framing the piece.

While McKenzie focused on the assemblage of animals gathered to survive the flood, William Edmondson interpreted the solid structure of the ark itself (pl. 72). Carved of gray limestone, his weighty, rectangular, symmetrical ark appears self-contained and secure, ready to weather the raging elements for forty days. Without a sign of human or animal life, Edmondson's ark is as austere as McKenzie's is crowded, vibrant, and colorful. Only the roughly chiseled, two-tiered base alludes to the angry sea on which the sturdy vessel will float.

A member of the Primitive Baptist Church, Edmondson carved in response to a vision from God: "First He told me to make tombstones; then He told me to cut the figures."[11] His sculpture was truly his service to the Lord: "Every time I try to read the Bible, or preach, the Lord takes my mind off it and tells me I got work to do."[12]

Johnnie Swearingen interpreted the story of Noah's ark (pl. 104) in a picture divided into four sections, each exploring a different facet of the tale—the building of the ark, the gathering of the animals against the chaotic raging waters, the turbulent flood, and the ark sailing on calm waters.

"I draw, sketch, and paint what I see . . . or visualize from a reading," said O. W. "Pappy" Kitchens.[13] Among his many sources was the Old Testament, and Isaiah's description of the peaceable kingdom (11:6) was perhaps one inspiration for *Peace in the Valley* (pl. 82), a beautiful, simple, pastoral landscape of a lion and lamb resting together. "Peace in the Valley," a well-known gospel song, might also have inspired Kitchens.[14]

New Testament subjects in general relate to the life and death of Christ. The nativity is shown in Josephus Farmer's realistic painted relief (cat. no. 83) and in David Butler's less literal, painted tin cutout (cat. no. 19). In *Handing the Keys to St. Peter* (pl. 84), William Hawkins skillfully designed a patterned composition dominated by vertical lines and bordered by white X's on black. Silhouettes of the central figures are brushed in textural, painterly strokes. Although here the color, often bold in Hawkins's work, is subdued, the imagery is dynamic.

Depictions of the crucifixion, a decisive moment of Christian theology, are plentiful. George Williams portrayed Jesus as a black man on a white painted wooden cross in his *Crucifixion* (pl. 94). If man was made in the image of God, as the Bible records, then it is natural for an individual to conceive Christ's figure like himself. Thus Williams and other African-Americans like William Hawkins, in *The Last Supper No. 6* (pl. 85), have rejected the Euro-American portrayal of a white savior.[15] Yet many other blacks have depicted a white Christ. Sister Gertrude Morgan, who considered herself to be spiritually married to Christ, has consistently painted him as Caucasian.

Edgar Tolson's *Crucifixion* (pl. 95), a bold, unpainted wood carving, reflects the New Testament account that places Christ on the cross between two thieves, one a sinner and the other a believer. In his dynamic *Crucifixion* (pl. 93), Jesse Aaron powerfully interpreted the figure of Christ from a single piece of found wood, which he cut with a chain saw and refined with woodworking tools. Even though Aaron's Christ is not attached to a cross, the identity of the piece is unmistakable. Sam Doyle's crucifixion scene, *I'll Go Down* (cat. no. 64), is painted on wooden slats tacked to a frame with a painted white fabric and wood backing, an unusual format for the artist.[16]

Southern evangelical Protestantism emphasizes heavenly salvation and the individual's responsibility for it, and thus many self-taught artists contemplate the future home of the soul in their works. In a densely calligraphic painting, Howard Finster asks *What Is the Soul of Man* (pl. 73). Finster identifies "three places for souls" in unambiguous terms that confirm the dogmatism of his evangelical roots: "earth for making a choice; hell for punishing and justice; heaven for rest, peace, and glory." Finster graphically represented the joys of passing from the trials of earthly life to the splendor of heaven in *No One Has to Cross Jordan Alone* (pl. 74).[17] The painting represents heaven and earth, separated metaphorically by the Jordan River, with inscriptions regaling the attributes of each realm: "Earth has robbery; earth has adultery; earth has suffering; earth has Christ" and "Heaven is the end of faith; heaven is the end of sins; heaven is the end of death. Heaven is the end of pain." Human figures surge along a highway leading to the river, where Christ oversees their transformation into angels that wing their way to the other side and heavenly redemption.

God's word is communicated through angels, celestial messengers who are intermediaries between God and human mortals.[18] Angels have been depicted by artists in human form for centuries, and self-taught artists, including Howard Finster, Clementine Hunter, Sister Gertrude Morgan, William Edmondson, Raymond Coins, Carl McKenzie, Johnnie Swearingen, R. A. Miller, and Eddie Kendrick, continue this tradition. Raymond Coins chisels their winged shapes and faces—to which he gives thick lips, prominent noses, and slanted, sometimes puffy eyes—from a blue, soft, speckled river stone, recovered from a neighbor's farm (pl. 90). William Edmondson claimed to have personal encounters with angels, which he experienced as a "swish of wings fluttering up under the eaves of my house."[19] Using limestone, as instructed by God,[20] salvaged from demolished buildings and curbs,[21] Edmondson made a number of freestanding angel sculptures. One winged female figure stands with crossed arms (pl. 89). Another is a timeless abstraction that can be read as either an angel or a cross (pl. 71). Made of four limestone blocks, this sculpture's trapezoidal torso, roundish head, and rectangular base create a powerful image at once specific yet suggestive of stone carvings of earlier centuries and other cultures.

In *Home Sweet Home* (pl. 78), Jessie and Ronald Cooper depict heaven and hell in a series of gentle celestial scenes painted on a solid storage trunk. On the inside lid, black and white worshipers stream along a path between two churches; according to Jesse Cooper, "We are all God's children."[22] Springing from within the trunk is the devil, who frequently lurks in the background of the Coopers' work, representing the omnipresent temptation of evil to all the faithful.

A deeply religious man and a deacon in his church, Eddie Kendrick portrayed his own ascension to heaven via contemporary modes of transportation, imagery that was most likely inspired by black gospel music. Since at least the turn of the century, gospel music has promulgated fast travel to heaven via train and, later, by airplane.[23] In Kendrick's Woods Temple Church, the congregation sang "The Gospel Train": "Come along my friends, come along and get aboard and ride this train."[24] This and other songs describing ascension to heaven via plane and train seem to have inspired Kendrick's expressive spiritual imagery. A peaceful, religious man whose work was influenced by his dreams, Kendrick created paintings and drawings that represented his concerns and hope for salvation. Kendrick said, "Jesus is my airplane and he'll never let me fall. He'll pick me up in an airplane on Judgment Day."[25]

In *This Plane Is Heaven Bound* (pl. 80), a colorful airplane, piloted perhaps by Christ, buoyantly ferries a full load of God-fearing passengers under the watchful eye of a full-bodied angel, typically present in Kendrick's work. In *This Is the Holy Train* (pl. 81) an angel hovers above a surrealistic train station and points to a long train, inscribed "This is the holy train," ascending from the building's roof to the heavens through clouds.

Sister Gertrude Morgan used similar imagery in *Train to New Jerusalem* (pl. 86), in which a locomotive steams across tracks bisecting the picture plane. Jesus and Sister Gertrude, pictured as the bride of Christ, enter New Jerusalem together. In another journey to salvation, Sister Gertrude preceded the words of Kendrick by some twenty years in *Jesus Is My Airplane* (private collection). Both churchgoers, the artists were most likely inspired by a gospel song of the same title, first recorded by a black singer, Mother McCollum, in 1930.[26] Sister Gertrude recorded the song herself in the 1970s on her album "Let's Make a Record: Sister Gertrude Morgan."

While the righteous find eternal life in heaven, the less fortunate and those lacking in faith are condemned to the suffering of hell, which southern self-taught artists express in fearful depictions of fire, brimstone, and devils. In Howard Finster's *Hell Is a Hell of a Place* (pl. 75), billowing, hot red flames engulf figures entwined in calligraphic admonitions such as "Vision of somewhere on hell's planet," and "You don't haf to go to hell."

Ronald and Jessie Cooper's *Praising the King: Kerosene Heater* (pl. 101) graphically displays the choice presented to each of us to be one of the saved or the damned[27] and the absolute dichotomy of heaven and hell. The upper three-quarters of a kerosene heater is covered with painted black and white figures, surrounded by clouds and angels, who raise their arms to praise the Lord. Ronald explains, "I put black and white people in heaven and hell. I feel like both races will be at both places."[28] Above the figures Christ welcomes with outstretched arms all who ascend to join him in heaven. The bottom of the heater, painted red, black, and white, conjures images of hell, and, indeed, when opened, the interior reveals a fierce-looking painted and carved devil surrounded by black and white sinners, scarred and suffering, in the very part of the heater where kerosene burns.[29] Members of a Pentecostal church, the Coopers are deeply religious and believe their work helps teach the Bible and attract "sinner people who don't believe in much, don't go to church or worship. . . . [It] might make them think about their own soul."[30]

Another work in which the material reinforces the subject is the Coopers' *Hell Bucket* (pl. 100). Made from an old pail once used to carry coal to fuel a fire, the work portrays the horrors of hell, with the devil himself rising above the pail's top in fiery red painted wood.

The proselytizing nature of evangelical Protestantism encourages public personal conversion and readily accepts self-proclaimed ministers who have received a call from the Lord. Many individuals, without the sanction of an established church, create their own small lay ministries, which become forums for the affirmation of faith, a major criterion for individual salvation. The self-taught artists who are preachers operate on the fringes of the church hierarchy; they are as out of the mainstream there

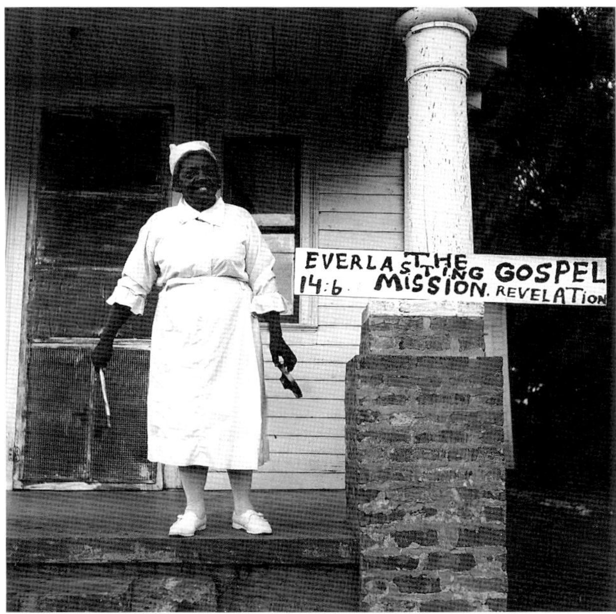

Fig. 3. Sister Gertrude Morgan, New Orleans, 1974. Sister Gertrude stands on the porch of her Everlasting Gospel Mission. The hand-painted sign on the post recommends a verse from the New Testament's Book of Revelation, one of the artist's chief sources of inspiration. Photo Guy Mendes.

as they are in the art world. Their method of using visual imagery to spread the word of God deviates from conventional proselytizing practices,[31] but their ministry work generally remains in keeping with church doctrine.

The comfortable marriage of southern evangelism and African-American spiritual traditions adds another dimension to the visionary phenomenon. In African lore, where spirits and the living mingle freely, visions are accepted.[32] Those self-taught artists connected with that tradition most readily acknowledge visionary experiences with the Lord, spirits, or other voices. Sister Gertrude reported a calling from a "strong, powerful voice," saying that "my heavenly father called me in 1934. . . . Go ye into yonder's world and sing with a loud voice. . . . You are a chosen vessel to call men, women, girls, and boys."[33] Morgan sought to fulfill her divine mission by going to New Orleans and becoming a street preacher with a fundamentalist sect. She later said, "It's sin I been working against, that's why I started the Everlasting Gospel Revelation [Mission]."[34]

Like other minister/artists such as Benjamin F. Perkins, Anderson Johnson, Josephus Farmer, Howard Finster, and Elijah Pierce, Sister Gertrude's art was created and probably used as a teaching device to enhance her missionary efforts. Her imagery derived from divine word, which once told her that she would become the bride of Jesus: "You are married to the lamb, Christ."[35] After her "marriage" to Jesus, Sister Gertrude consistently dressed and portrayed herself in white (fig. 3). Later the Lord instructed her to draw pictures of "the world to come—the New Jerusalem," the Christian paradise described in the New Testament's Book of Revelation.[36]

Reflecting those divine wishes, *Book of Revelation* (pl. 91) intersperses a patchwork of angels, animals, and humans with calligraphic passages from Revelation. This magnificently designed, complex composition, painted on a six-foot, horizontal window shade, displays Sister Gertrude's sensational skill as a colorist. *Book of Revelation*, as well as *The Lamb Standing on Mount Zion with His Company* (pl. 88) and *Way in the Middle of the Air* (pl. 18),[37] represents the artist's classic phase, shaped both by her maturity as a painter and by her switch to tempera and acrylic paints, which allowed greater spontaneity. These later works in a bright, bold, expressionistic style leave behind the delicate crayon strokes with which Sister Gertrude so beautifully delineated facial details and body gestures in *Christ Coming in His Glory* (pl. 87), an early work. In even later works such as *Self-Portrait with Jesus* (cat. no. 176), made after Sister Gertrude had experienced a partial loss of motor control and perhaps eyesight, her brushstroke and compositional style became looser.[38] But her work always entwines calligraphy, usually quoting Revelation, with her imagery of salvation themes, expressively depicted on such innovative but easily accessible materials as styrofoam meat trays, lamp shades, and cardboard.

The general comfort and acceptance of religious visions in the southern sectarian cultural environment provided for an easy transition from the literal acceptance of biblical miracles to sympathy for and responsiveness to personal internal visions, the source of visionary art. This milieu allowed for and, to a degree, enhanced the exceptional creativity of visionary artists, which finds expression in a number of unexpected visual forms and subjects, not all related to biblical imagery. Visionary objects range widely in style and subject, from the obsessively detailed drawings of Zebedee "Z. B." Armstrong, Minnie Evans, Henry Ray Clark, and Frank Jones to the loosely rendered abstractions of John "J. B." Murry, Hawkins Bolden, and Charlie Lucas, from the recognizable but abstracted images of Mary T. Smith to the personal, often unidentifiable symbolism of Juanita Rogers and Nellie Mae Rowe. Visionary images often challenge the reader to decipher an artist's internal ideation with little or no narrative information. Some visionary art depicts recognizable religious or biblical themes, but other examples are spiritual and nonrepresentational, inspired by divine revelations, visions, dreams, or internal creativity.

Compulsive detail and a repetitive geometrical, symmetrical style characterize the visionary art of Zebedee "Z. B." Armstrong, Henry Ray Clark, Frank Jones, and Minnie Evans. Armstrong's *1986 Weekly/Monthly Calendar* (pl. 118) is a rectangular block of painted wood, covered with a dense grid of red and black. The directional markings used by Armstrong—"top," "f" (for front), and "btms" (bottom)—give a clue to his job in a box factory. Two circles approximating clock faces dominate the composition, their hands pointing to letters representing the days of the week and numbers for the days of the month. The settings perhaps signal the date on which the world will end, an obsession of Armstrong's since 1972, when an angel reportedly informed him to "stop wasting your time because the end of the world is coming."[39] Armstrong's concern with the end of the world manifested itself in his statement, "When Gabriel blows his horn, everybody will rise, including the Titanic."[40]

Intricately and compulsively drawn in ink and felt-tip markers on both sides of a manila envelope, Henry Ray Clark's *The Magnificent Pretty Boy* (pl. 115) shares Armstrong's clock faces and obsessively filled surfaces. Its geometric shapes include a centrally positioned, architectural rendering inscribed with the artist's nickname, "The Magnificent Pretty Boy." Clark, who began to draw while in prison, said, "I truly believe that God helps me draw these pictures. . . . I feel like something or somebody is guiding my hand for me. They can lock my body up, but they can't lock up my mind. As long as my mind can create something beautiful to look at, I am a free man, and I will live forever in my art."[41]

Frank Jones, too, began his artistic career while incarcerated in Texas in 1964. Like Clark, Jones worked in a limited palette, usually red and blue, reflecting the pencils and standard-sized sheets of paper available to inmates. Jones was told by his mother at age six that he was born "with a veil over his left eye and that this veil would enable him to see spirits."[42] *Devil House* (pl. 117), a careful architectural drawing typical of his subject and style, contains varied spirits and devils. The enclosure of these frenzied yet benign figures within rigid compartments in effect stabilizes them, much like Jones's own prison cell undoubtedly regulated his behavior.[43] The ubiquitous clock at the top center alludes to how slowly time passes for the incarcerated. The large size, architectural elements, the clock and spirits, and the addition of green pencil to Jones's standard red and blue palette, identify this image as a mature work of the artist. He signed it, in his usual practice, "Jones SRMK" and included his prison number, "114591."

Minnie Evans's *Butterfly Design* (pl. 116) joyously and colorfully merges divinity and nature. Curvilinear, symmetrical renderings of angels with butterfly wings amid a profusion of floral designs combine the artist's central interest and influences, the Bible and nature. As a gate attendant at the Airlie Gardens Estate in North Carolina, Evans daily observed the unfathomable changing beauty, the work of the Lord, around her. In this image, the world of detail in the superbly colored flowers expands as one examines the painting more closely. The central pinwheel shape, resembling a zinnia or dahlia, is often seen in Evans's work, usually with the eyes of God peering out as in *Ark of the Covenant* (cat. no. 80). About her glorious use of color, Evans, a spiritual woman filled with dreams and visions, said, "Now we dreams, we talk of heaven, we think everything is going to be white. But I believe we're going to have the beautiful rainbow colors."[44]

Mary T. Smith says, "I believe in the Lord. . . . I thank the Lord all the way."[45] In *The Lord Is Head of the World* (pl. 99) she portrayed Christ and inscribed beside him the words of praise that are the painting's title. (Well-known verbal religious affirmations are often seen in Smith's work.)[46] Rendered in house paint on a piece of irregularly cut roofing tin, the broad, uneven brushstrokes of a bright but limited palette of green, red, black, and white typify Smith's distinctive style, which evokes a sense of joy and sometimes mystery.[47] For *I Was in a Wreck* (pl. 98), Smith assembled scraps of corrugated roofing tin in the shape of a human figure. Next to it a separate sign praises the Lord for her having survived a 1983 car crash—"I was in a rake, the Lord was for me."[48]

John "J. B." Murry, a quietly religious man, was instructed in a vision from God to spread his word through "spirit script,"[49] or scriptolalia, the visual equivalent of glossolalia, or speaking in tongues. Murry, illiterate, created in a trancelike state that he believed to be a direct communication with God, his hand moving "in a manner willed by His power."[50] Murry was a member of a southern Baptist church near Sandersville, Georgia, where speaking in tongues was not uncommon.[51] According to Murry, these columns of emotionally charged pencil and ink script could be deciphered only by the pure in spirit looking through a glass of "holy" water taken from a local well (fig. 4).

Murry's script is linear, rhythmic, and graceful. His works display an outstanding, varied design and a superb sense of color. In *Untitled* (pl. 120) an interior yellow ground supports the script. Black and red lines and dots form ghostlike shapes and images, which Murry sometimes referred to as bad folk: "Bad folk are people who don't act religion."[52] The more muted color scheme of *Untitled* (pl. 121) is executed in broad, thick lines of paint. A line of shifting color divides the work almost diagonally into an upper abstract composition and a lower figural one. In *Untitled* (pl. 119), thick colorful lines crowd the thin pencil script to the outer borders, where it encloses the work like a frame. From a formalist point of view, this work completely abandons the figure. Despite their visually abstract nature, Murry often mentioned themes of heaven and hell, good and evil, in explaining his works.[53]

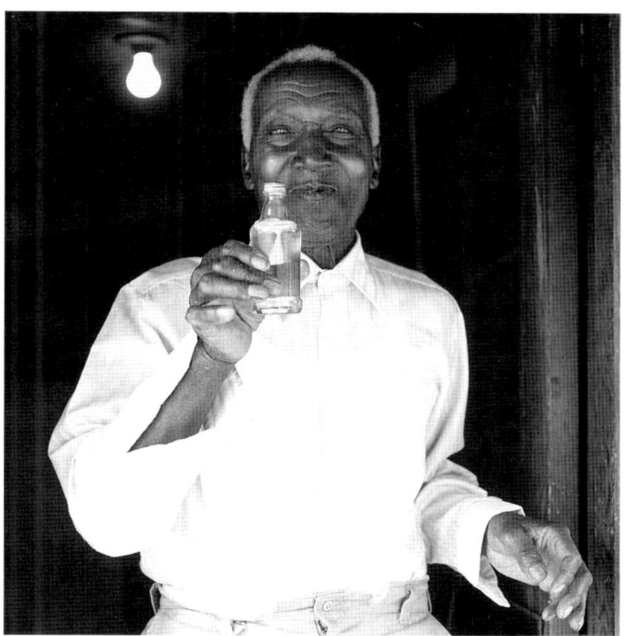

Fig. 4. John "J. B." Murry, near Wrens, Georgia, 1988. Murry holds a bottle of "holy water," which the Lord instructed him to look through in order to decipher his spirit writing (pls. 119–21). Photo © Roger Manley.

"Prophet" Royal Robertson combines futuristic imagery with patches of rambling calligraphy that bemoan his wife's departure about fifteen years ago, an overwhelming obsession in the artist's life and art. About his artwork, Robertson says, "That's a gift I got. I was having a vision . . . I call it spiritual travel."[54] The modernistic buildings of *Cute City Region* (pl. 114), resembling the oil refineries and rigs in nearby Morgan City, Louisiana, rise from an imagined landscape. A lone figure flies from a window into the sky. Robertson's inscription, with the heading "Them Far Away False Lover Affair Blues," explains: "Now we haven't nothing but to fly by us self alone." Robertson's deft incorporation of calligraphic text and images speaks of his years of experience as a sign painter.

Juanita Rogers was a compulsive artist-recluse whose primary link to the outside world was a black-and-white television. Her highly personal imagery sprang from her imagination and is not easily understood, but it was conditioned by what she saw on TV. The artist, however, identifies her inspiration as someone she calls "Stonefish" or "Stoneface," probably an imaginary figure. *Standing Creature* (pl. 112), typical of the early mud sculpture that Rogers called "funny bricks," is made of unfired clay textured with hair and grasses, and most likely reinforced with mule and cow bones. The roughly textured surface adds an earthy dimension to this otherworldly creature.

Sultan Rogers says that he sees "futures," when he dreams, images he proceeds to carve when he awakes: "I can make most anything I can imagine a future of."[55] In *Haint House* (pl. 125), nineteen spectral figures exit a two-story green house with a lamp emerging from its roof. The gruesome creatures' grossly exaggerated features—twisted mouths, satanic smiles of disproportionately large white teeth—unexpectedly shift to the animalistic: a snake hangs from one man's mouth; other figures have the heads of a snake, deer, or dog. In *Snake with Lady* (pl. 124), a carved snake, perhaps alluding to the serpent that tempted Eve, winds around a bikini-clad woman in what might be an imaginative twist on the garden of Eden story.

"I take stuff people recognize as being one thing and make a different use out of it," says David Strickland, a welder by profession.[56] *Big Bird* (pl. 127), Strickland's first welded sculpture, is a fantastical creation of unlikely scrap materials, including an air-conditioning duct left from an addition to the artist's house, a tricycle wheel, plumbing pipe, candlesticks, railroad spikes, and a garden fork. *Case Alien* (pl. 126) is an otherworldly figure, a contemporary looking robot fashioned from old farm equipment. Sinuous upright "hair" is made from a cotton duster manifold, complete with lights that are illuminated at night. The body is a Case tractor grill, its back is a shovel; other recycled materials are a tractor seat, disc planters, a Model-A steering assembly, chrome grease catchers, springs, and yard shears.

Nellie Mae Rowe took her artistic motivation from the Lord: "I just have to keep drawing until He says, 'Well done, Nellie, you have been faithful.'"[57] Her highly personalized, brightly colored pictures came from her fertile imagination and memories of a farming childhood in Georgia. Form and exquisite color take shape as flattened, carefully delineated imagery—peculiar animals (pl. 123) and oversized teapots (pl. 122)—which Rowe organized in vital, compact, and dense compositions. Rowe did not previsualize her paintings: "I draw what's on my mind. . . . I sit and look my paper over. It will come to me."[58]

William Dawson was sculpting totems long before he knew what they were: "I had never seen a totem. I was in the park one day. I was carving and a fellow came up and said, 'Oh, you make totems,' but I didn't know what they were. My wife looked it up in a book in a library, and sure enough, I was making totems."[59] Dawson was perhaps familiar with the cane carving tradition popular in his native Alabama early in the century. Sometimes inspired by dreams, his first totem carvings are of faces, male and female, black and white. Broad and rectangular, the faces display prominent, large white eyes and teeth. Some totems rest on a house base, perhaps drawn from Dawson's Chicago neighborhood; others are topped with carvings of birds (pl. 129).

Ralph Griffin, whose inspiration comes from found wood, said, "I look at a piece of wood and it tells me what it is."[60] Griffin worked from driftwood, roots, branches, logs, and tree stumps that he found in and along the Poplar Root Branch, a small stream that crossed his property in Girard, Georgia. According to his wife, Griffin, who thought his roots came from "ancient times," would "get the root from the water, wash it off and look at it. He would know what it was going to be."[61]

Screaming Lady (pl. 107) depicts a wide-eyed, alert, horrified face. Griffin cleverly inverted the stump so that the uneven, worn roots express blue hair standing on end and the nervous frenzy of the figure, which he accentuated by applying orange and red dots, white speckles, and a few tips of green. Griffin finds his imagery in the wood itself, each shape and surface of the wood imaginatively suits the needs of the image. In the case of *Screaming Lady*, Griffin saw a bird on the opposite side, guided by the different perspective offered from another angle. Two or more faces on different sides of a piece are common in Griffin's work.[62]

Bessie Harvey, who also uses opposing sides of found wooden objects to depict varied imagery, attributes her artistic vision to a special gift. "I have a vision," she says, "I have a gift. I can close my eyes and see things other people can't."[63] Harvey sought wood that expressed her idea. "I am not the artist," said Harvey. "Nature shapes my work. And God gives me a vision to see what nature has done."[64] Harvey also adds found objects to her painted wood such as bead eyes or wood shavings. In *Yellow Bird with Rider* (pl. 110) a beaked, long-legged bird, with painted wood shavings around its neck and tail, supports the attenuated figure of a black man, fashioned from a root. Harvey professes a strong interest in her African-American heritage, which she consciously expresses in her work: "Just about everything I touch is Africa. I think I'm of old African descent."[65]

Joseph Hardin's erotic imagery portrays visions and dreams of sexual experiences he probably never had because of arthritis that crippled him as a child.[66] *Untitled* (pl. 113), a depiction of a harshly styled, boldly colored nude female, conveys his frustrations; the woman's masklike face betrays his overwhelming preoccupation with the female body. Hardin depended on individuals who brought him supplies, and he decorated the walls of his otherwise monochromatic, institutional beige home with his hard-edged, exotic images.

Hawkins Bolden is quite literally a visionary artist. Blinded at age seven, he assembles found objects from his environment in Memphis according to his own internal vision. In *Untitled* (pl. 109) a large punctured pot, a wooden chair, and a pair of jeans, attached by wire and a chain, evocatively suggest a seated figure. Bolden's imaginative use of found materials would be notable even for a sighted artist.

The evangelical and cultural milieu of the American South of the last half-century—where religion's influence, even on secular life, was pervasive—readily allowed religious and visionary-inspired artists to flourish. The wealth and variety of their imagery, exceptional in its personal expressiveness, is a natural outgrowth of these circumstances and of the surroundings in which they lived.

NOTES

1. Charles Reagan Wilson, "Southern Religion and Visionary Art," *Mississippi Folklore Register* 25–26 (1992–93), p. 2. The article provides an excellent overview of this subject.

2. Ibid., pp. 7–8.

3. Samuel S. Hill, "Religion," *ESC,* p. 1270.

4. For an insightful discussion on this subject as it relates to African-Americans, see Joyce Ann Miller, "In the Handiwork of Their Craft Is Their Prayer: African-American Religious Folk Art in the Twentieth-Century South" (Master's thesis, University of Mississippi, 1992), p. 45.

5. Lisa Eller-Smith, "Ruben A. Miller's Windmill 300," *Folk Art Messenger* 4, no. 1 (Fall 1990), p. 10.

6. Hill, "Religion," p. 1272.

7. Stephanie Smithers, who owns this painting with her husband, observed that the church activity at Swearingen's funeral in 1993 mirrored that in *God Loves You:* Swearingen's church images clearly came from his own life experiences; Stephanie Smithers, interview, ARY, Oct. 1992.

8. Dawson told this to Jim Arient, one of the artist's earliest proponents and collectors of his work, interview, ARY, March 1993.

9. This portrayal of Adam and Eve was created by Edgar Tolson in response to an order from a French collector, who never picked it up. Tolson told Sal Scalero, the current owner, that he believed the Frenchman would prefer a risque version of the temptation. He himself wondered why anyone would want the "filthy thing"; Sal Scalero, interview, KAG, March 1993.

10. Robert Knott, *Diving in the Spirit* (Winston-Salem, N.C.: Wake Forest University, 1992), p. 13.

11. Louise LeQuire, "Edmondson's Art Reflects His Faith, Strong and Pure," *Smithsonian* 12, no. 5 (Aug. 1981), p. 51.

12. Ibid., p. 55.

13. William A. Fagaly, *1975 Artists Biennial Winners* (New Orleans: New Orleans Museum of Art, 1976), unpaginated.

14. Bill C. Malone, professor of history, Tulane University, interview, ARY, April 1993, provided this and other suggestions regarding the influences of gospel music.

15. Mose Tolliver and Clementine Hunter are among other African-American artists who have depicted a black Christ on the cross.

16. This unusual format is found in at least two other depictions of Christ by Doyle (private collections).

17. A gospel song, "I Won't Have to Cross Jordan Alone," might have influenced this work; Bill C. Malone, interview, ARY, April 1993.

18. Malcolm Godwin, *Angels: An Endangered Species* (New York: Simon and Schuster, 1990), p. 66.

19. LeQuire, "Edmondson's Art," p. 54.

20. Robert Bishop, *American Folk Sculpture* (New York: E. P. Dutton, 1974), p. 193.

21. Georganne Fletcher, ed. *William Edmondson: A Retrospective* (Nashville: Tennessee Arts Commission, 1981), p. 12.

22. Jessie and Ronald Cooper, interview, ARY, Dec. 1992.

23. Bill C. Malone, interview, ARY, March 1993.

24. E. H. Kendrick, cousin of the artist and a deacon in his church, letter, KAG, April 1993.

25. Eddie Kendrick, interview, KAG, Nov. 1992.

26. Bill C. Malone, interview, ARY, March 1993.

27. The Coopers' fundamentalist belief in the responsibility of the individual to attend to his or her own salvation is reflected in the title of a similar work, *Eternity Your Choice* (private collection).

28. Ronald Cooper, interview, ARY, Dec. 1992.

29. "A kerosene heater seemed like it would make a good hell because it's something that gets hot." Cooper has made similar scenes in a small number of both gas and electric heaters; ibid.

30. Ibid.

31. Hill, "Religion," p. 1243. According to Hill, southern religion does not often engender art because the visual sense is not thought (as speaking and hearing are) to be a likely conduit to the divine.

32. Lynne Adele, *Black History/Black Vision: The Visionary Image in Texas* (Austin: Archer M. Huntington Art Gallery, College of Fine Arts, University of Texas, 1989), p. 16.

33. Sister Gertrude Morgan, letter to Regenia Perry, May 1, 1973 (Gitter-Yelen papers).

34. Jane Livingston and John Beardsley, *Black Folk Art in America, 1930–1980* (Jackson: University Press of Mississippi; Washington, D.C.: Corcoran Gallery of Art, 1982), p. 100.

35. Chuck Rosenak and Jan Rosenak, *Museum of American Folk Art Encyclopedia of Twentieth-Century American Folk Art and Artists* (New York: Abbeville Press, 1990), p. 219.

36. Lynda Roscoe Hartigan, *Made with Passion: The Hemphill Folk Art Collection* (Washington, D.C.: Smithsonian Institution Press, 1990), p. 155.

37. "Way in the Middle of the Air," an inscription on the work, is also the title and refrain of a gospel song.

38. William A. Fagaly, interview, ARY, Feb. 1993. Fagaly, who organized Morgan's first one-person exhibition at the Museum of American Folk Art, New York, in 1973, graciously shared his thoughts on Morgan's stylistic development.

39. Rosenak, *Museum of American Folk Art Encyclopedia,* p. 40.

40. Zebedee "Z. B." Armstrong, as told to Tom Wells, who lived near the artist in Thompson, Georgia, interview, ARY, Dec. 1992.

41. William Steen, ed. *Avenues of Departure: Twelve Houston Artists* (New Orleans: Contemporary Arts Center, 1992), p. 13.

42. Adele, *Black History/Black Vision,* p. 41. Adele continues, "Children who were born with the veil, or caul—part of the fetal membrane—over their eyes were believed to have the power to see spirits and to communicate with them."

43. Ibid., p. 42.

44. Mitchell D. Kahan, *Heavenly Visions: The Art of Minnie Evans* (Raleigh: North Carolina Museum of Art, 1986), p. 9.

45. *Baking in the Sun: Visionary Images from the South* (Lafayette: University Art Museum, University of Southwestern Louisiana, 1987), p. 72.

46. A similar saying—"Christ is the head of this house. The unseen guest at every meal. The silent listener to every conversation"—was common enough to have been documented in a 1935 photograph of a home interior in Virginia; see "Post Master Brown, Old Rag, Virginia, 1935," in *The Depression Years as Photographed by Arthur Rothstein* (New York: Dover Publications, 1978), p. 10.

47. The occasionally rough strokes in Smith's work are the result of her habit of using stiffened, unwashed brushes.

48. Mary T. Smith related this story to Warren Lowe in 1983 when he purchased this object; Warren Lowe, interview, ARY, May 1992.

49. *Baking in the Sun,* p. 56.

50. Ibid., p. 56.

51. Andy Nacisse, longtime collector of Murry's work, interview, ARY, March 1993.

52. Ibid.

53. *Baking in the Sun,* p. 56.

54. *It'll Come True: Eleven Artists First and Last* (Lafayette, La.: Artist's Alliance, 1992), p. 63.

55. Rosenak, *Museum of American Folk Art Encyclopedia,* p. 263.

56. David Strickland, interview, ARY, Oct. 1992.

57. Judith Alexander, *Nellie Mae Rowe, Visionary Artist 1900–1982* (Atlanta: Southern Arts Foundation, 1983), p. 11.

58. Ibid., p. 9.

59. Jim Arient, "William Dawson: Chicago Carver," *Folk Art Messenger* 3, no. 2 (Winter 1990), p. 1.

60. Ralph Griffin, interview, ARY, Aug. 1991.

61. Loretta Griffin, Ralph Griffin's wife, interview, ARY, March 1993.

62. The phenomenon of two-faced figures in the work of southern self-taught artists has been ascribed to African tradition; Knott, *Diving in the Spirit,* p. 12. Griffin, in contrast to Bessie Harvey, did not consciously associate his work with African origins according to his wife, Loretta Griffin; interview, ARY, March 1993.

63. Rosenak, *Museum of American Folk Art Encyclopedia,* p. 152.

64. Robert Cogswell, "Two Tennessee Visionaries: Bessie Harvey and Homer Green," *Folk Art Messenger* 3, no. 2 (Summer 1991), p. 1.

65. Shari Cavin Morris, "Bessie Harvey: The Spirit in the Wood," *The Clarion* 213, no. 2/3 (Summer 1987), p. 46.

66. Andrew Glasgow, an early collector of Hardin's work, interview, ARY, March 1993.

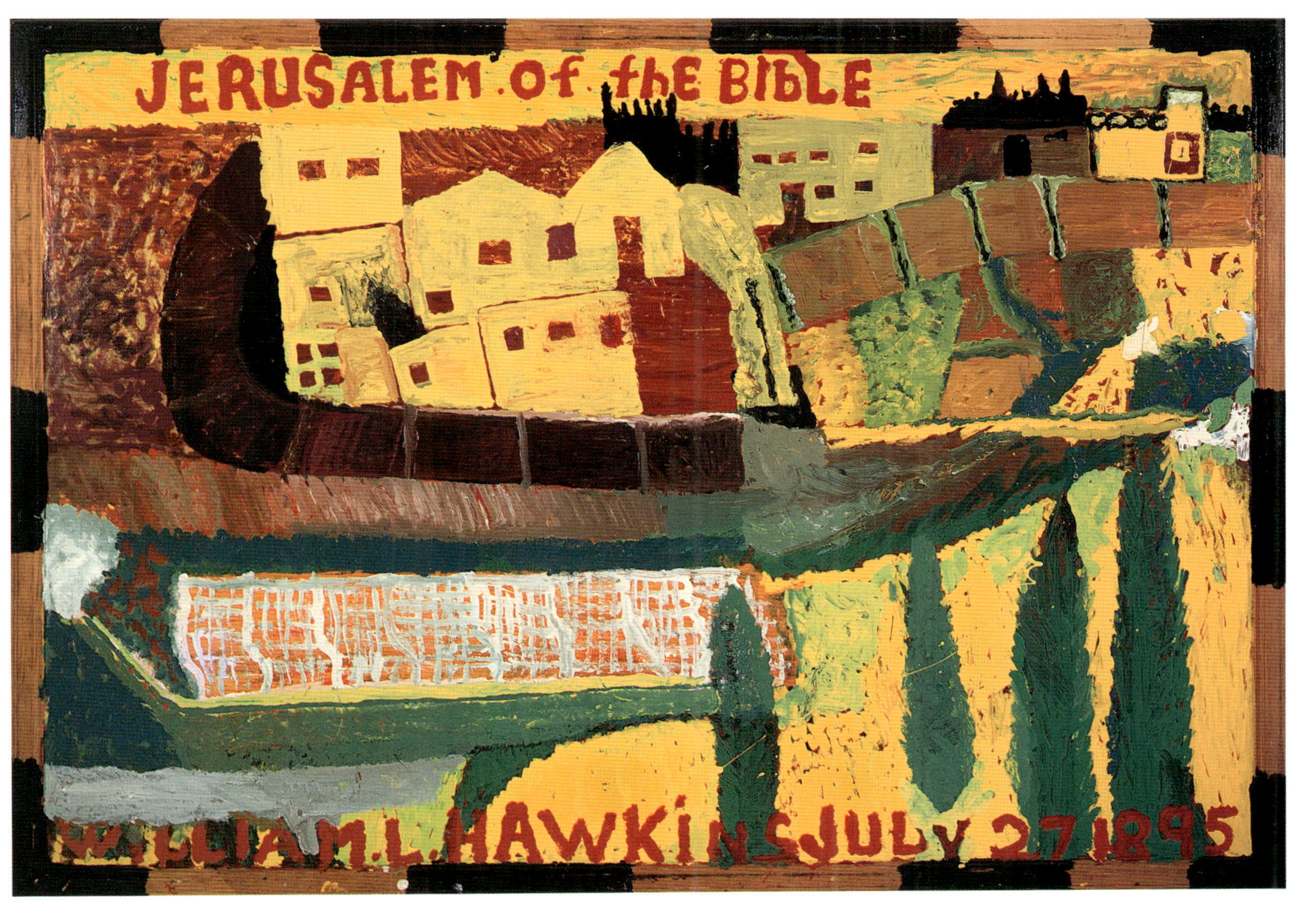

64

WILLIAM HAWKINS

Jerusalem of the Bible, 1984

(cat. no. 114)

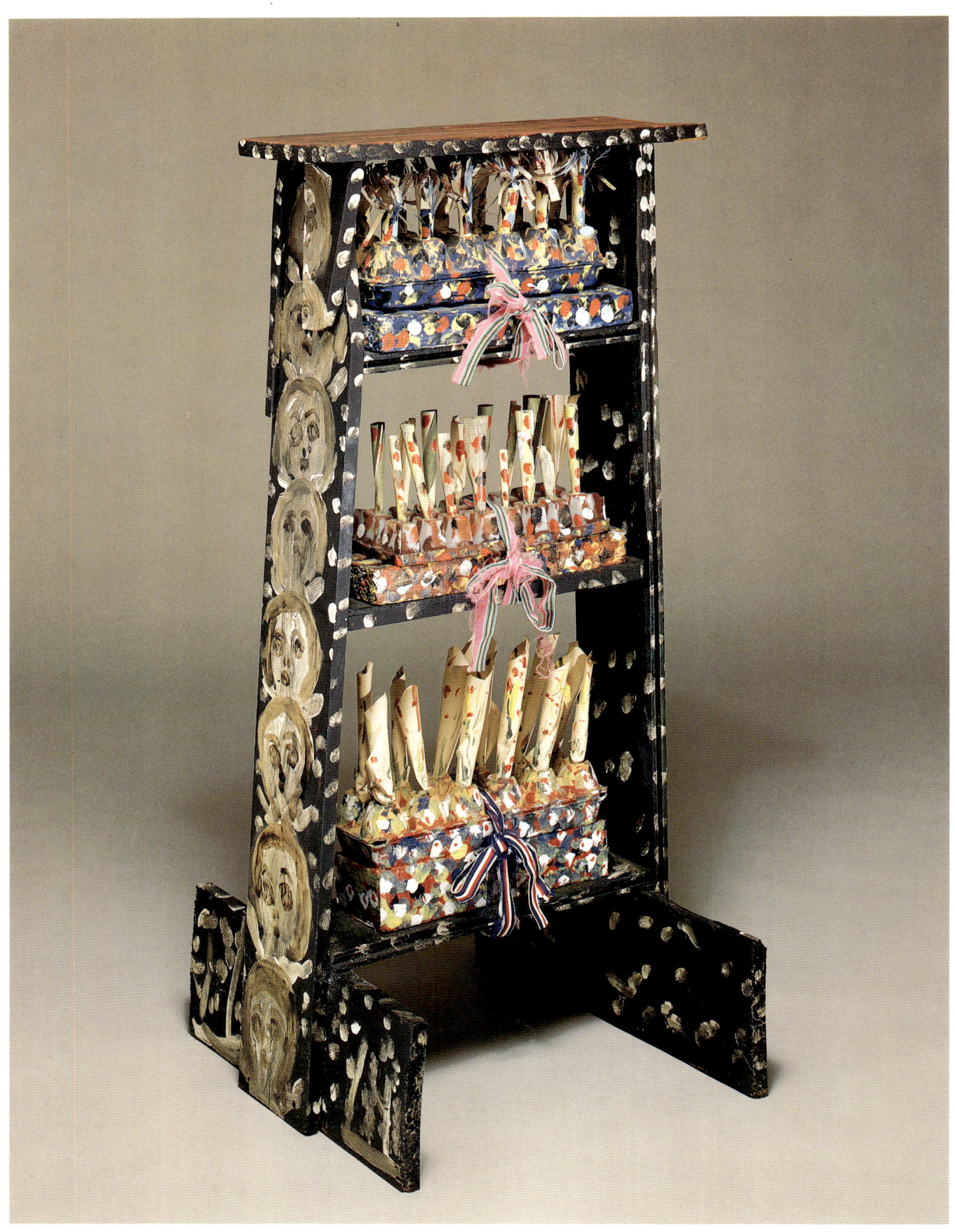

65

ANDERSON JOHNSON

Portable Pulpit, 1989

(cat. no. 133)

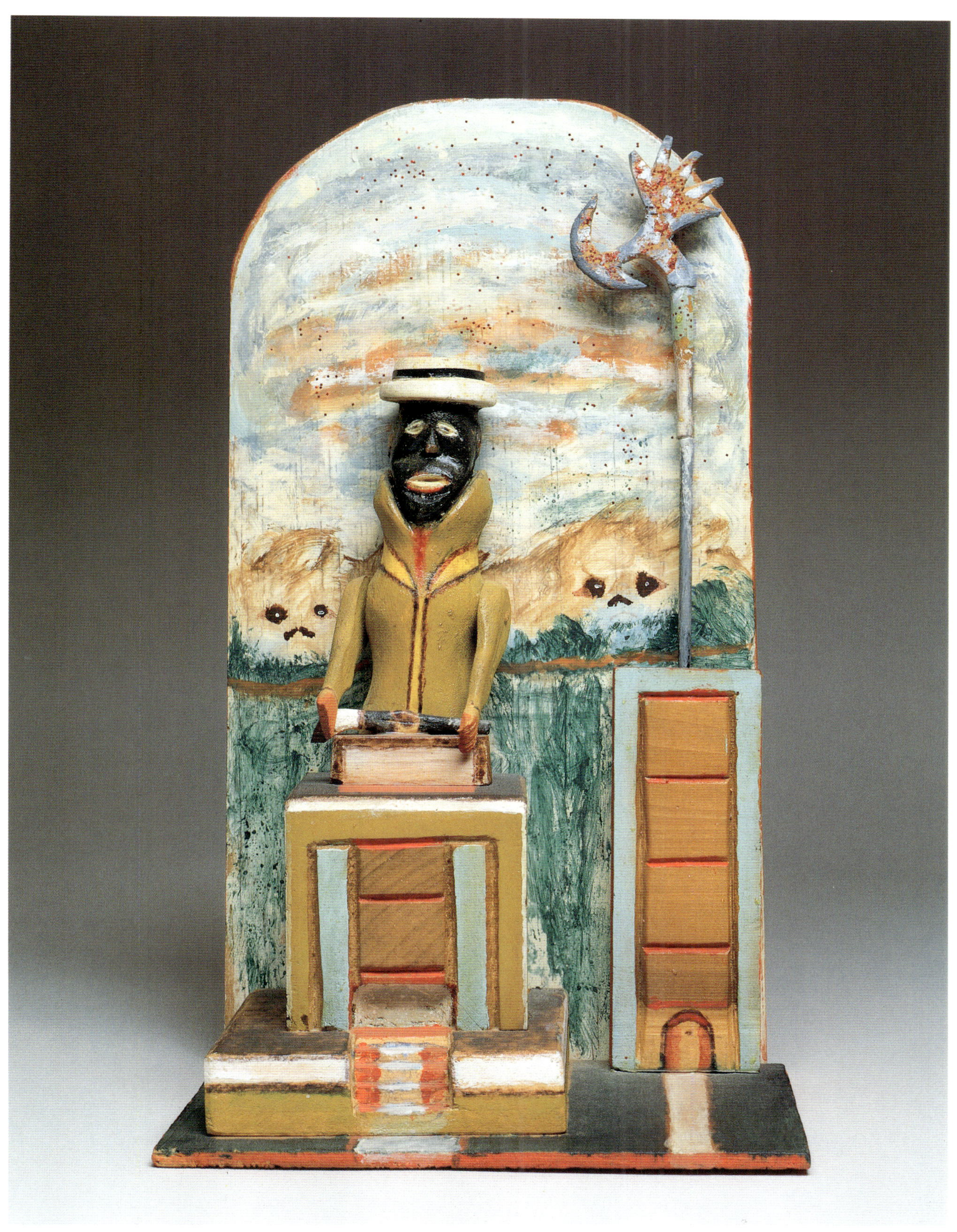

66

WILLIAM DAWSON

Dream House, 1977

(cat. no. 46)

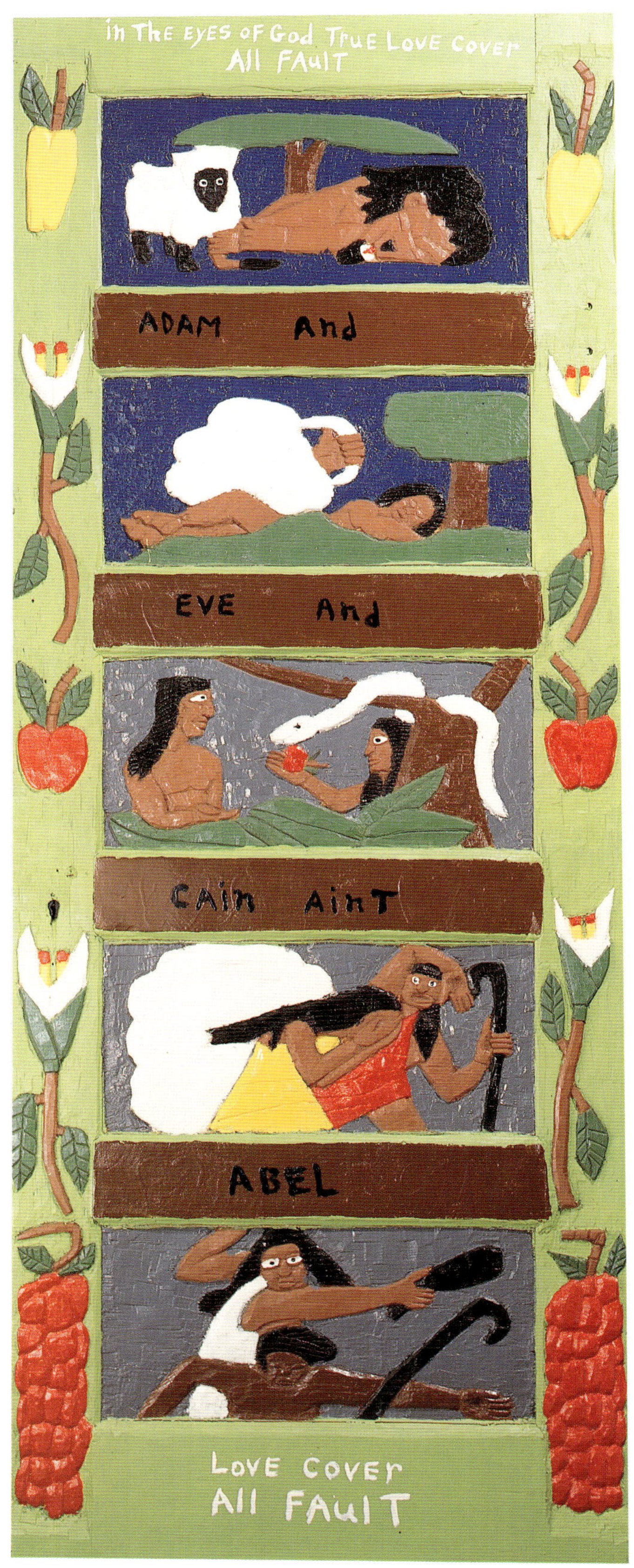

67

HERBERT SINGLETON

Adam and Eve, 1991

(cat. no. 208)

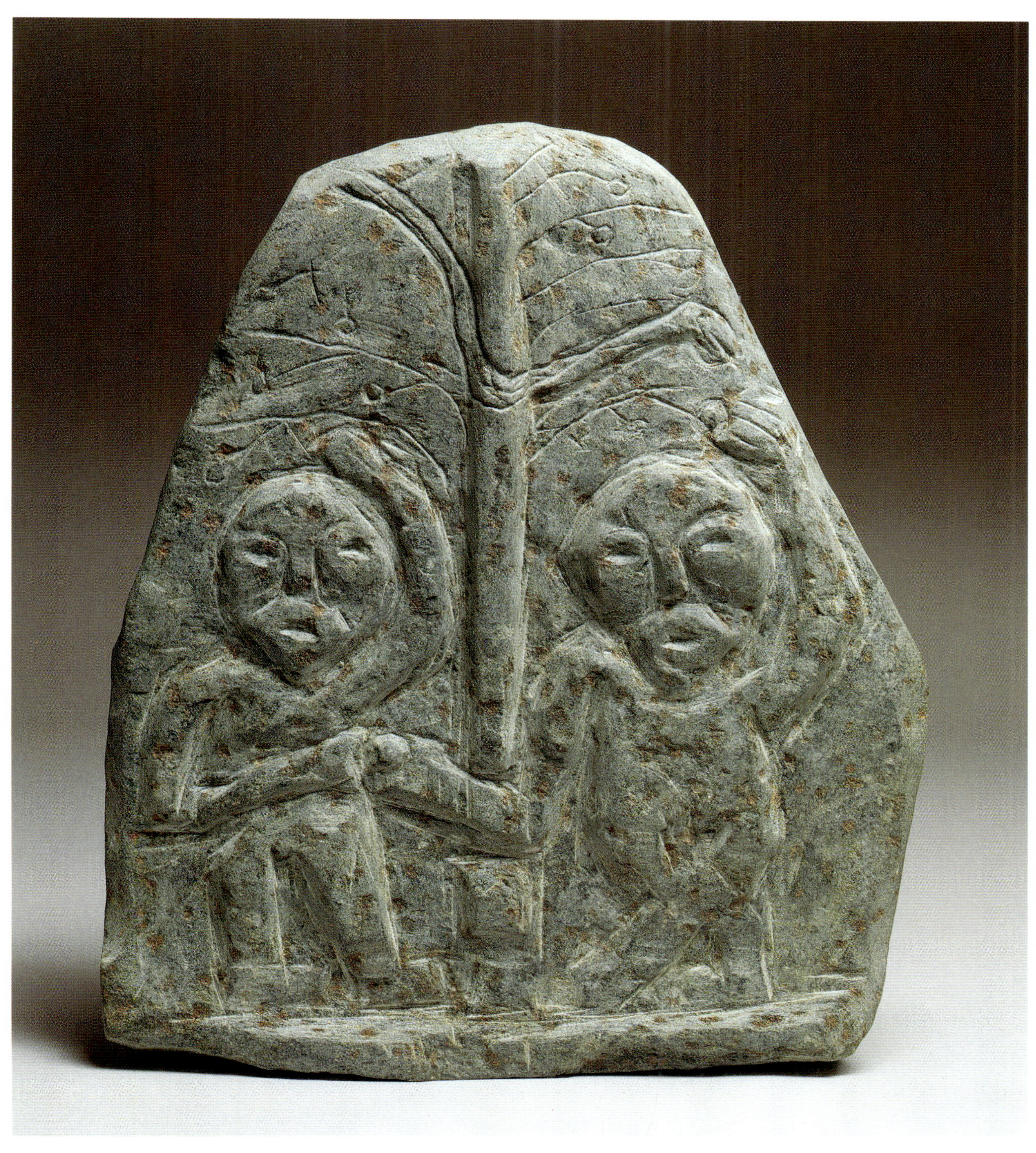

68

RAYMOND COINS
Adam and Eve, 1980
(cat. no. 28)

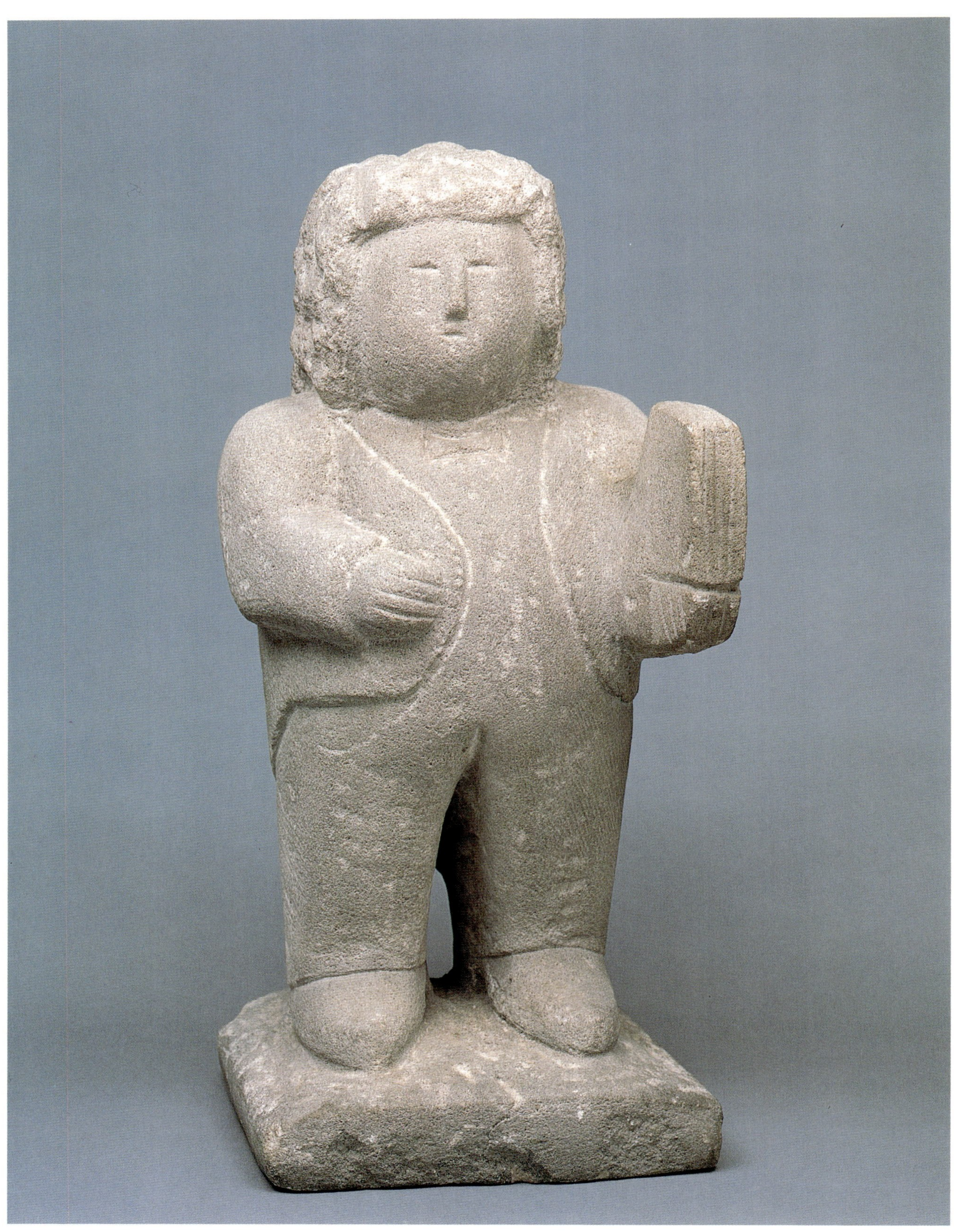

69

WILLIAM EDMONDSON
Preacher, ca. 1938
(cat. no. 78)

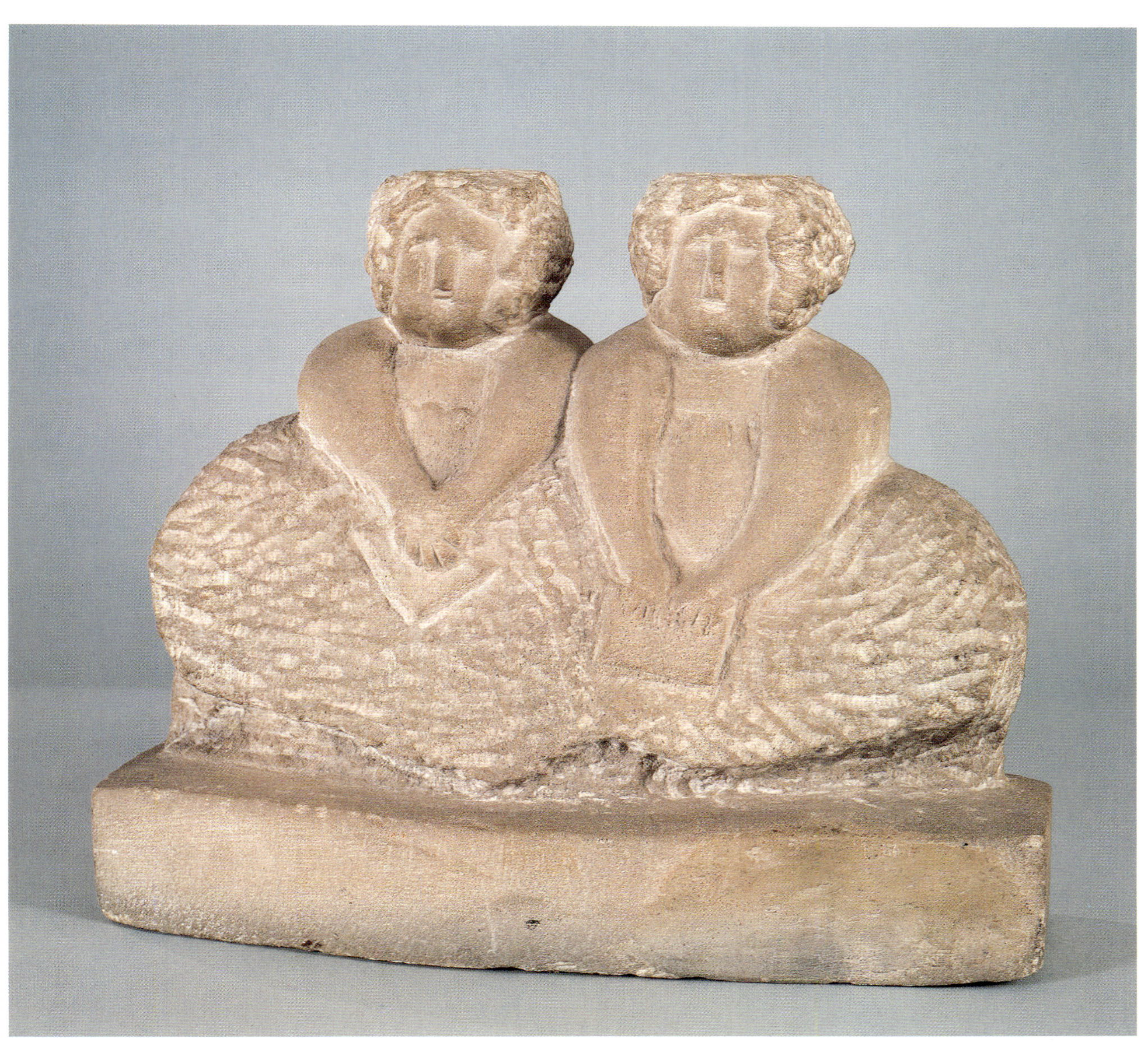

70

WILLIAM EDMONDSON

Choir Girls (Martha and Mary), ca. 1930–39

(cat. no. 75)

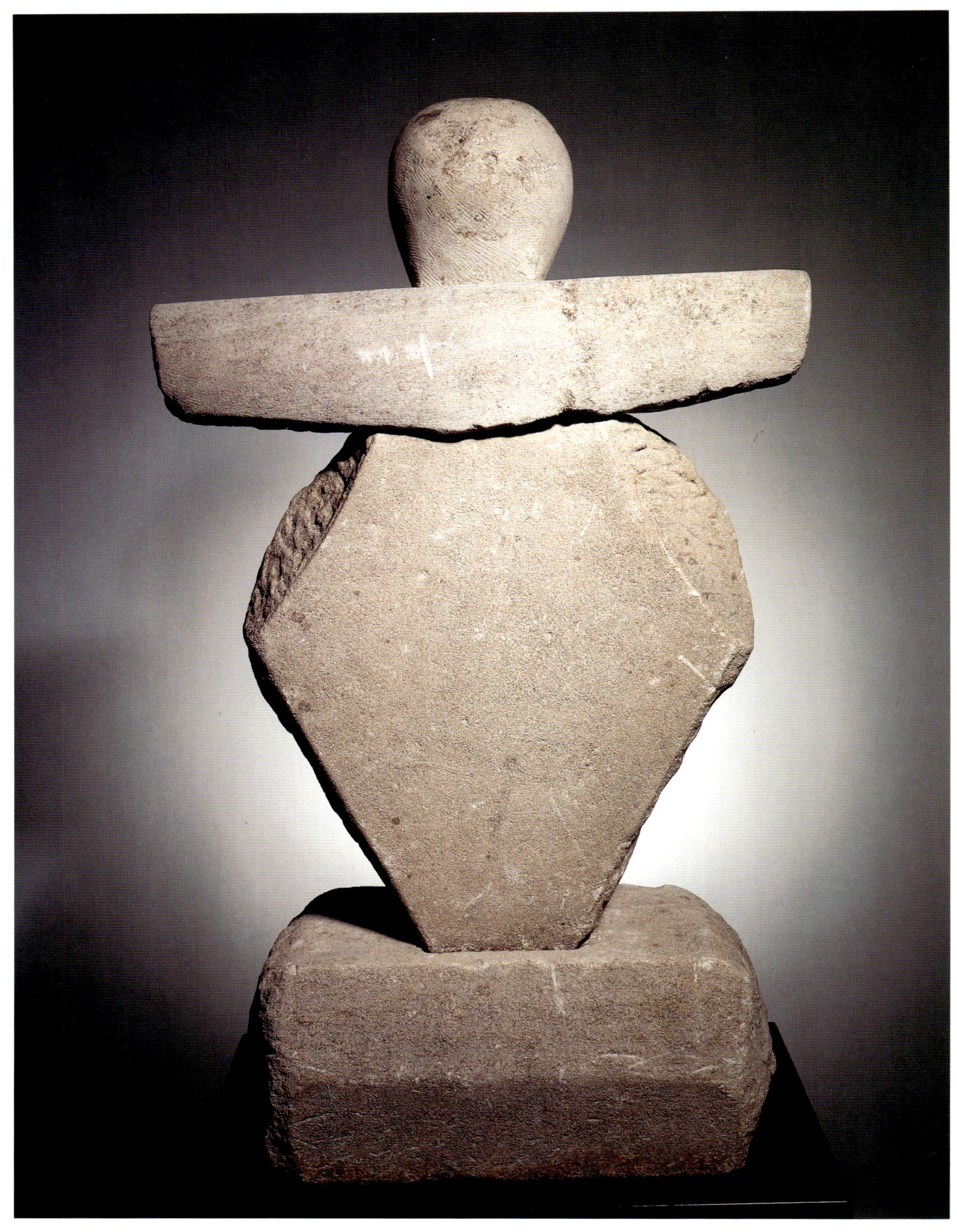

71

WILLIAM EDMONDSON

Angel, ca. 1930s

(cat. no. 72)

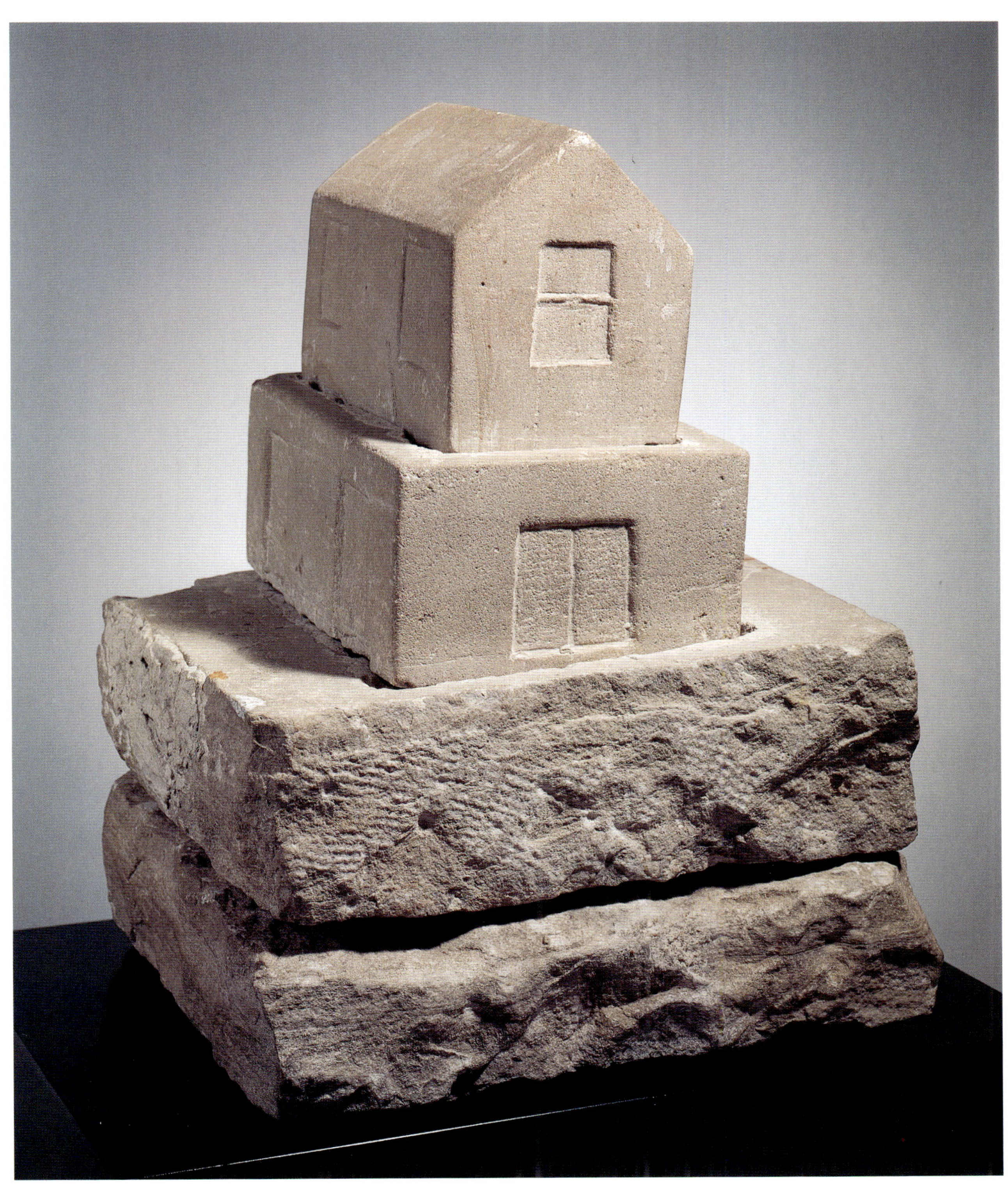

72

WILLIAM EDMONDSON

Noah's Ark, ca. 1930

(cat. no. 77)

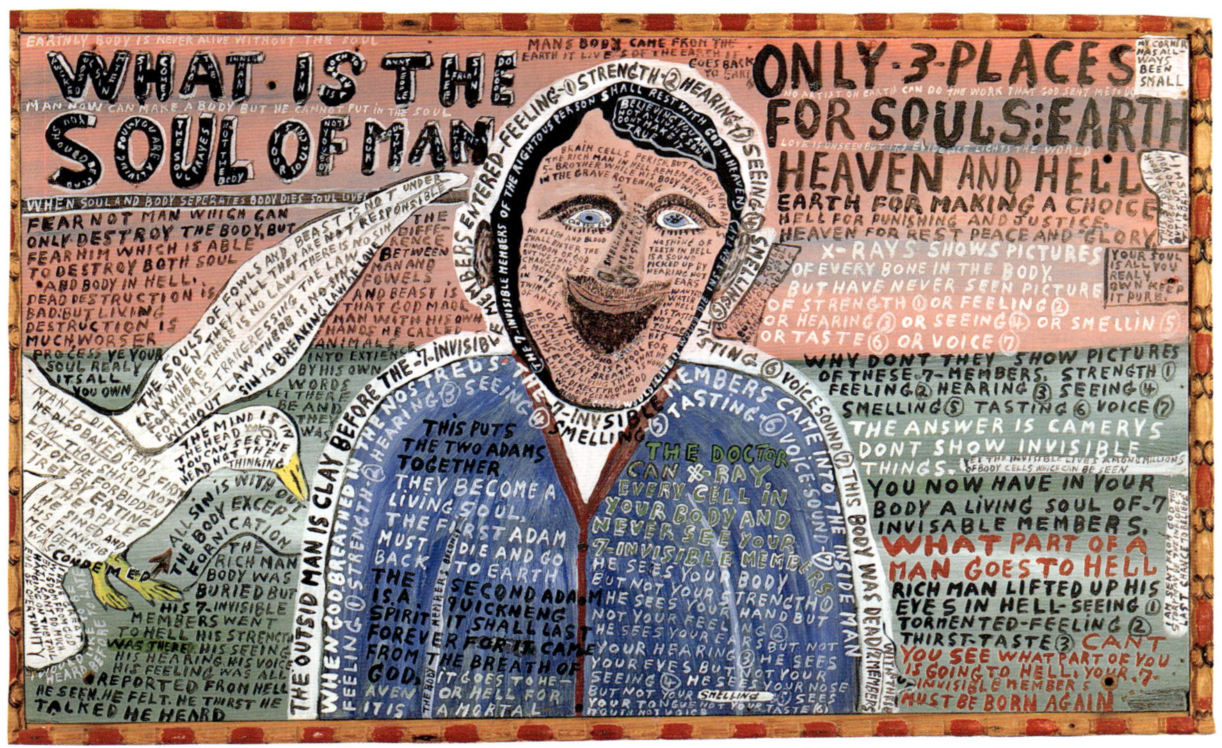

73

HOWARD FINSTER

What Is the Soul of Man, 1976

(cat. no. 92)

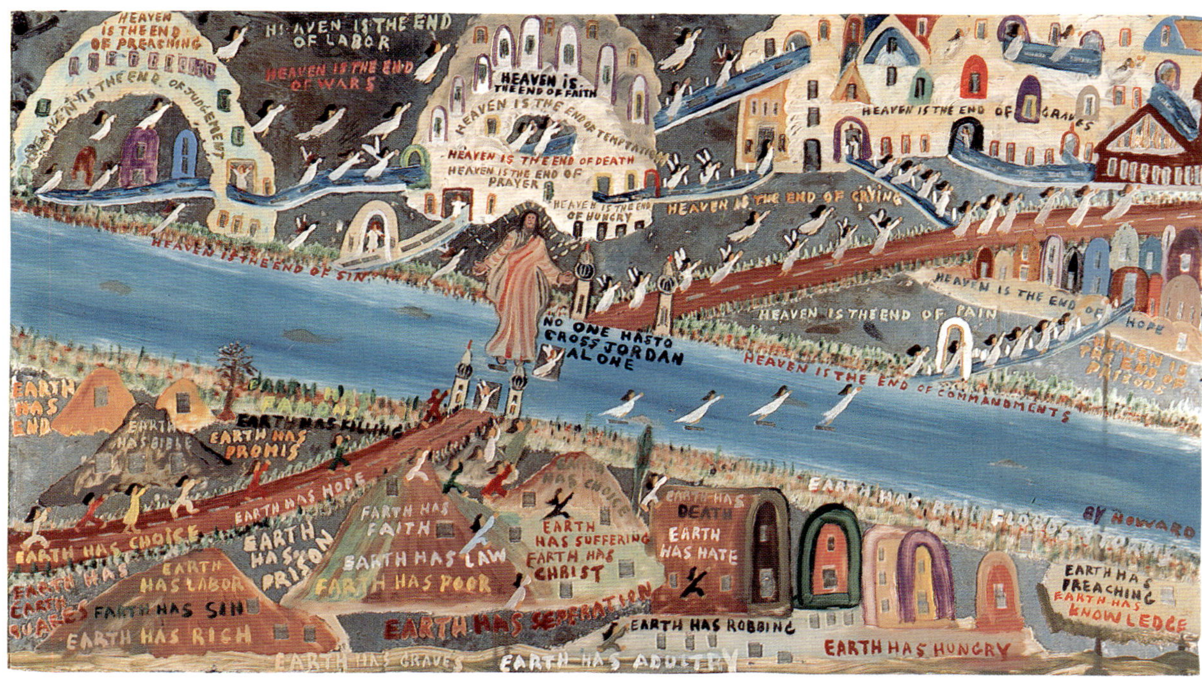

74

HOWARD FINSTER

No One Has to Cross Jordan Alone, 1976

(cat. no. 91)

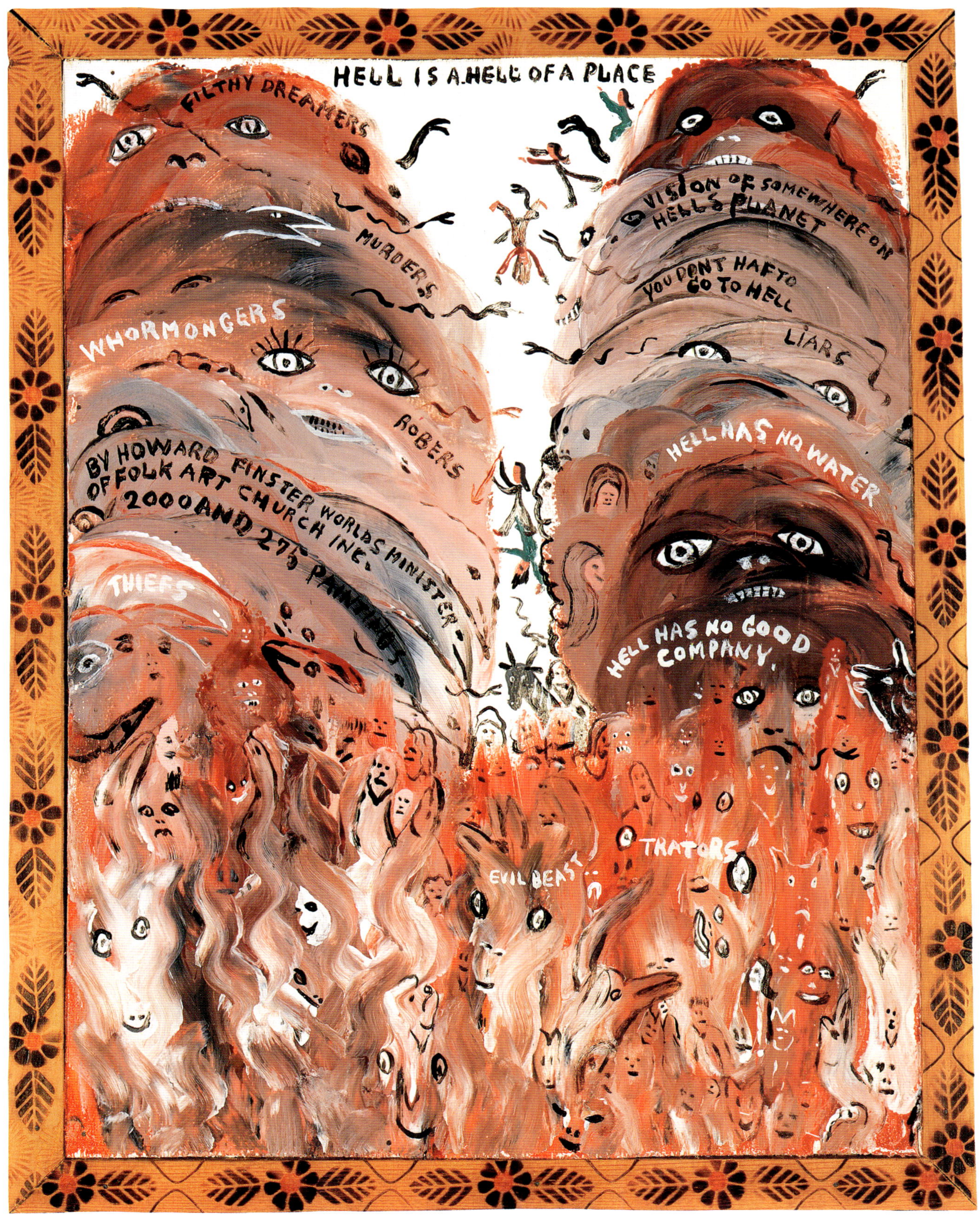

75

HOWARD FINSTER

Hell Is a Hell of a Place #2272, 1982

(cat. no. 89)

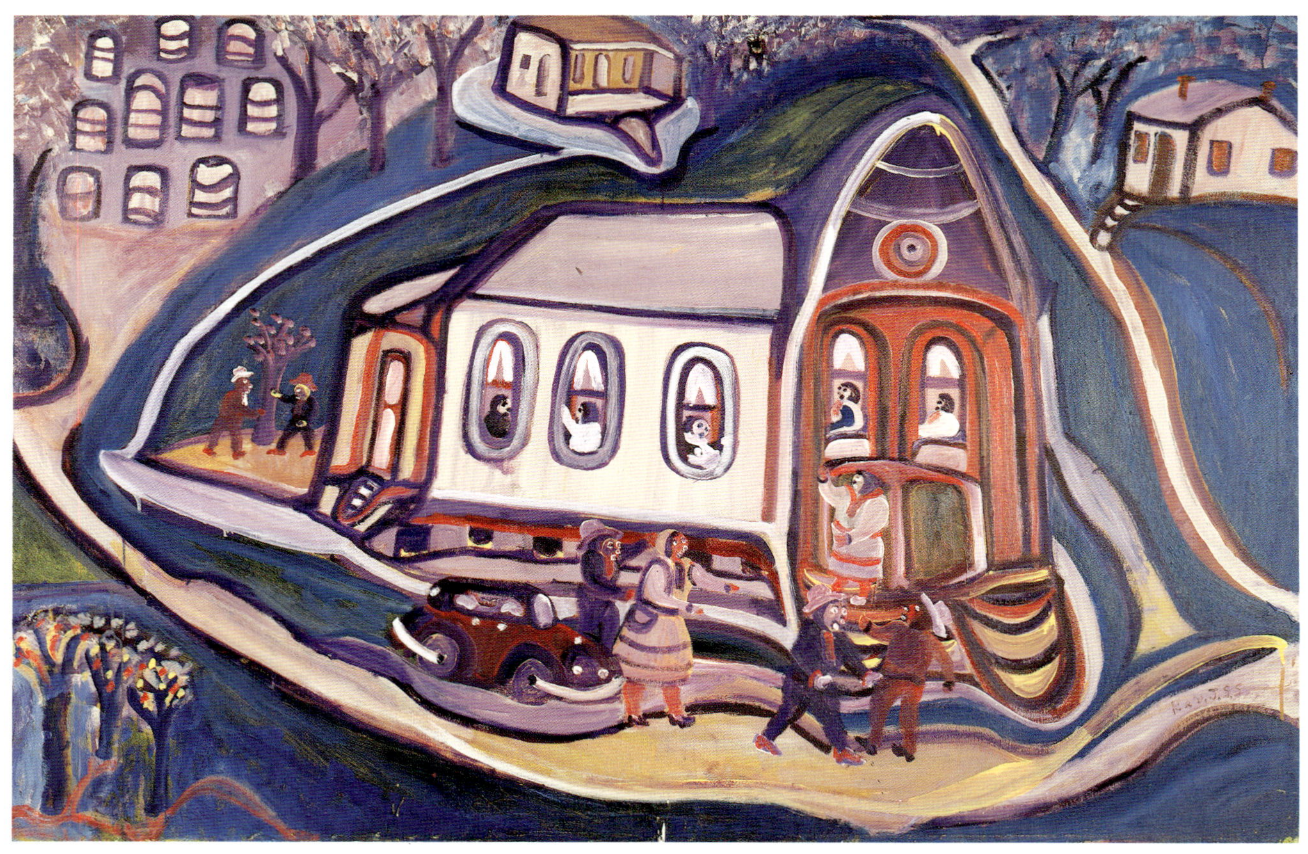

76

REV. JOHNNIE SWEARINGEN
Sunday Camp Meeting, 1991
(cat. no. 233)

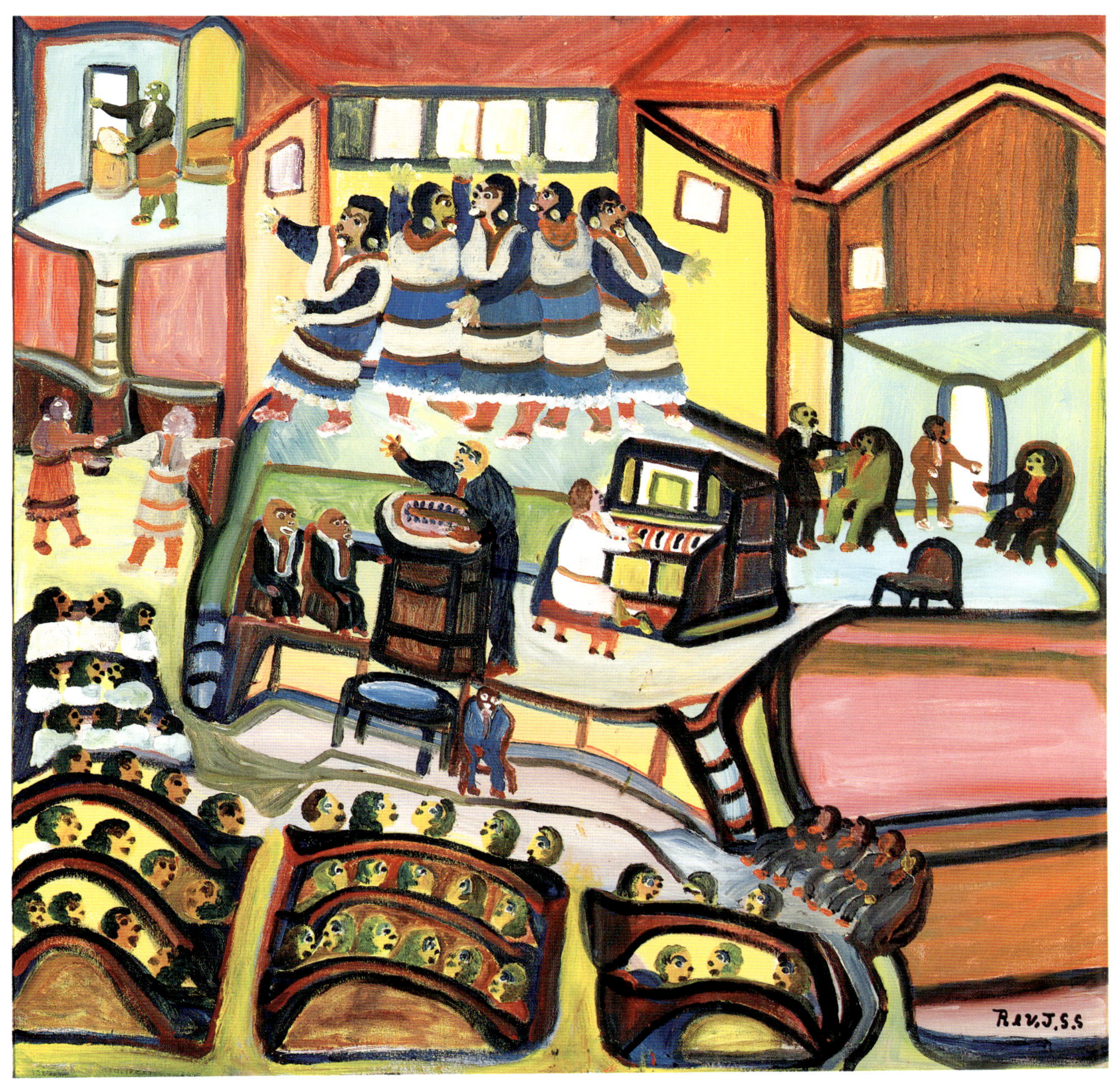

77

REV. JOHNNIE SWEARINGEN

God Loves You, 1991

(cat. no. 230)

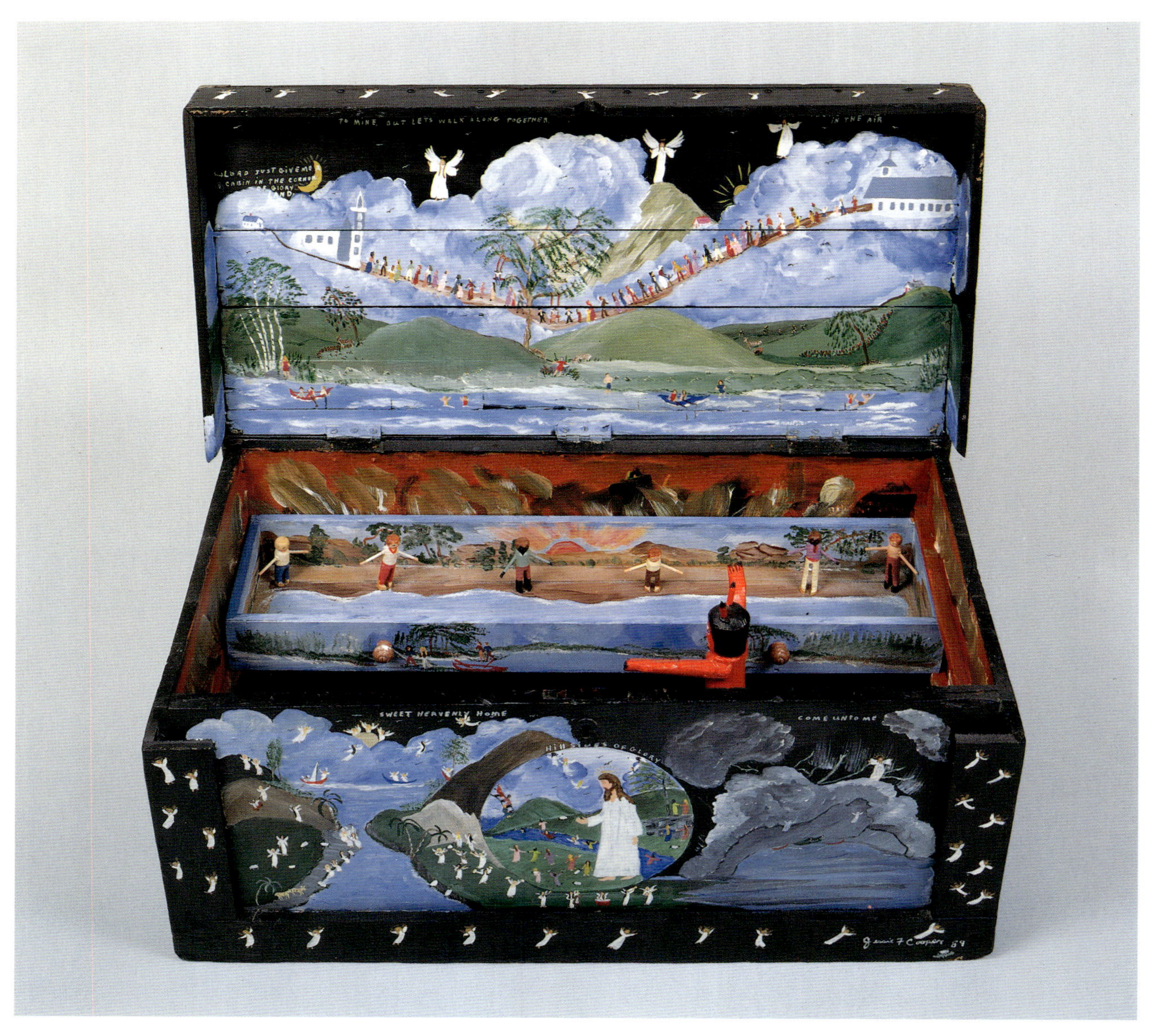

78

JESSIE AND RONALD COOPER

Home Sweet Home, 1989

(cat. no. 39)

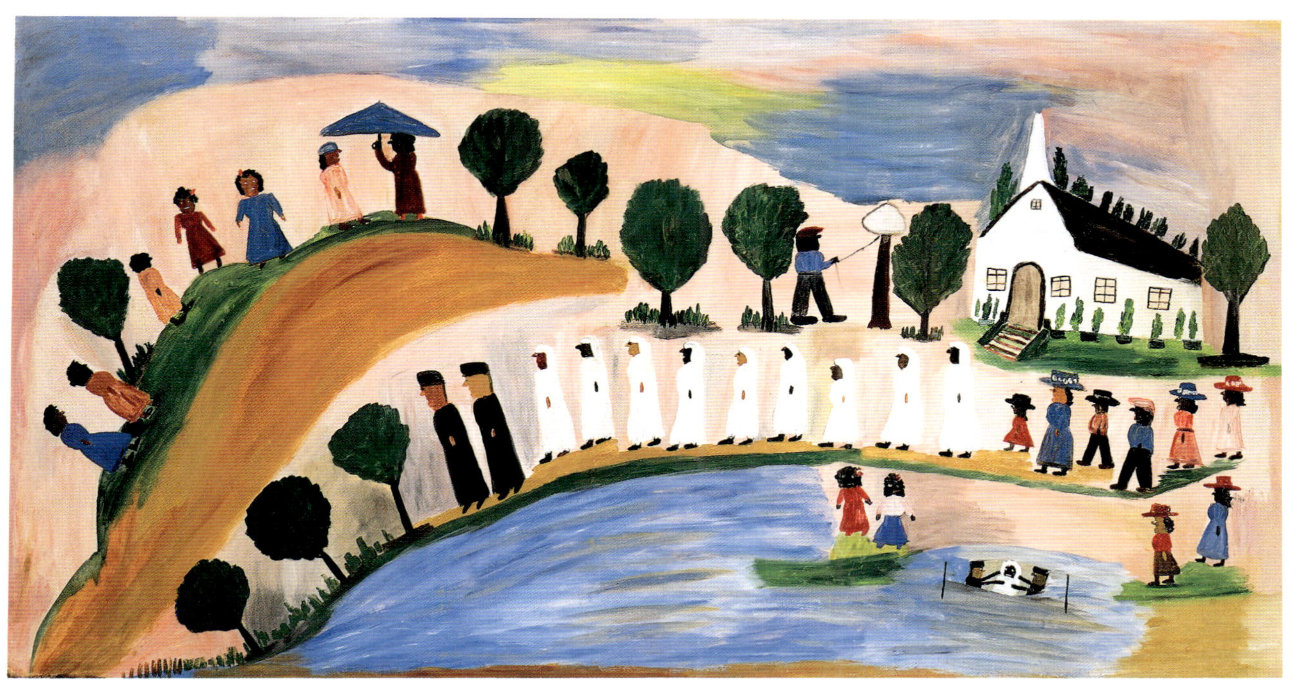

79

CLEMENTINE HUNTER

Panorama of Baptism on Cane River, ca. 1945

(cat. no. 124)

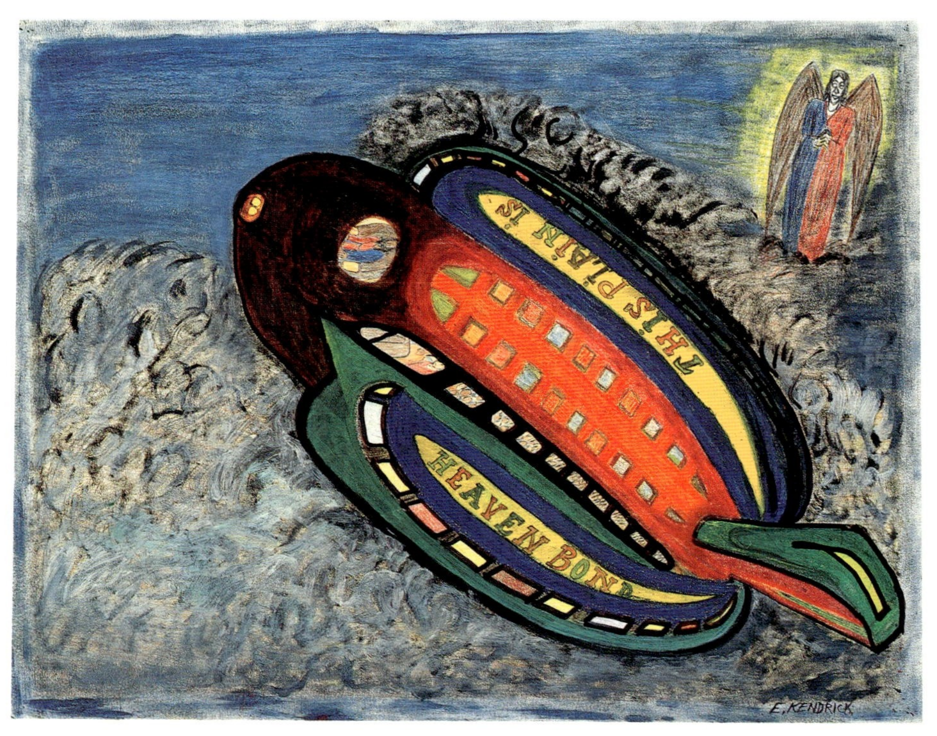

80

EDDIE KENDRICK

This Plane Is Heaven Bound, 1989–90

(cat. no. 144)

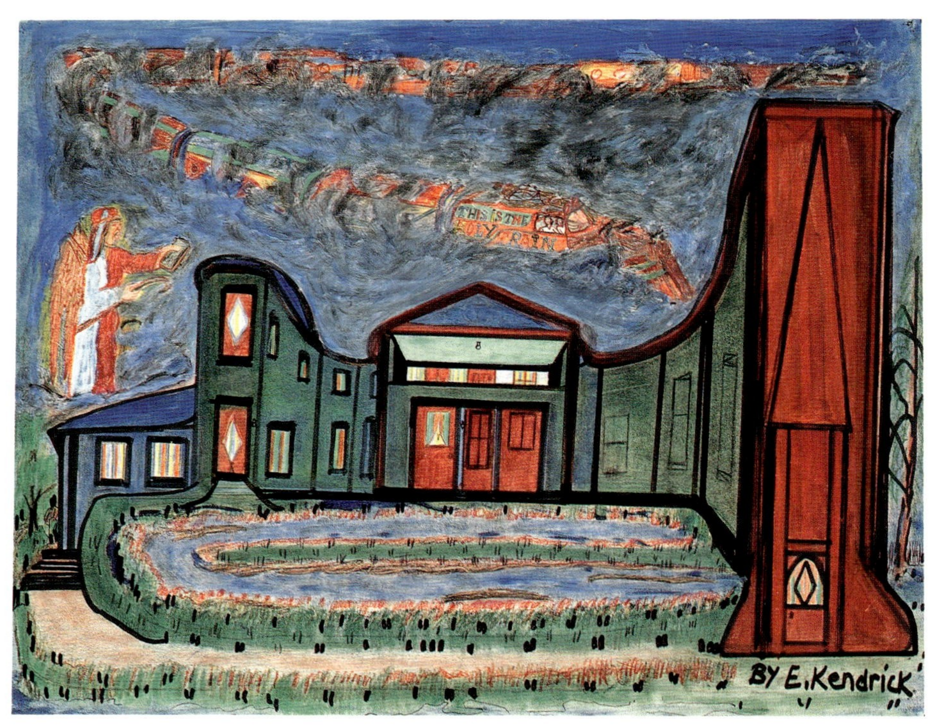

81

EDDIE KENDRICK

This Is the Holy Train, 1990

(cat. no. 143)

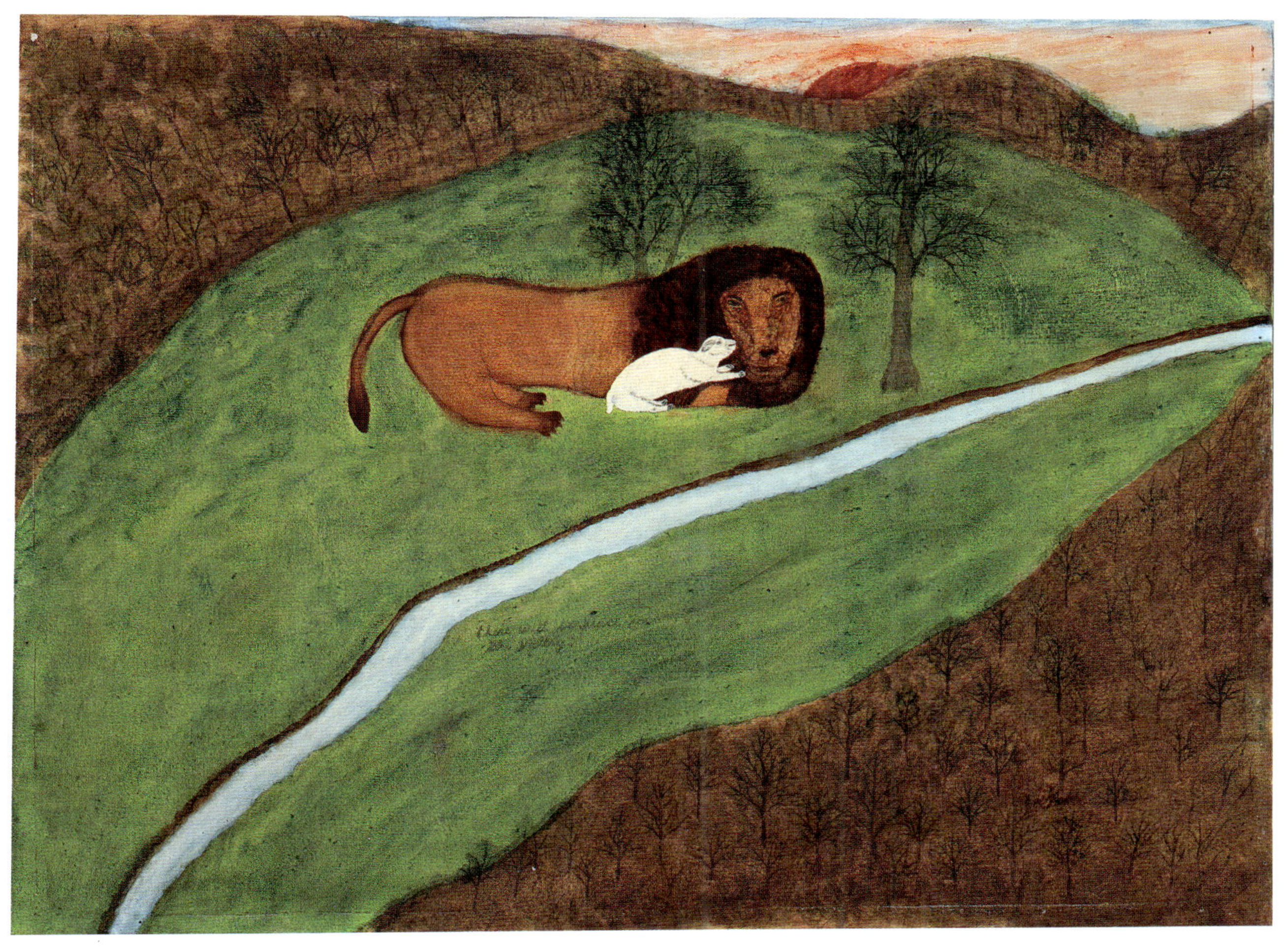

82

O. W. "PAPPY" KITCHENS

Peace in the Valley, 1977

(cat. no. 151)

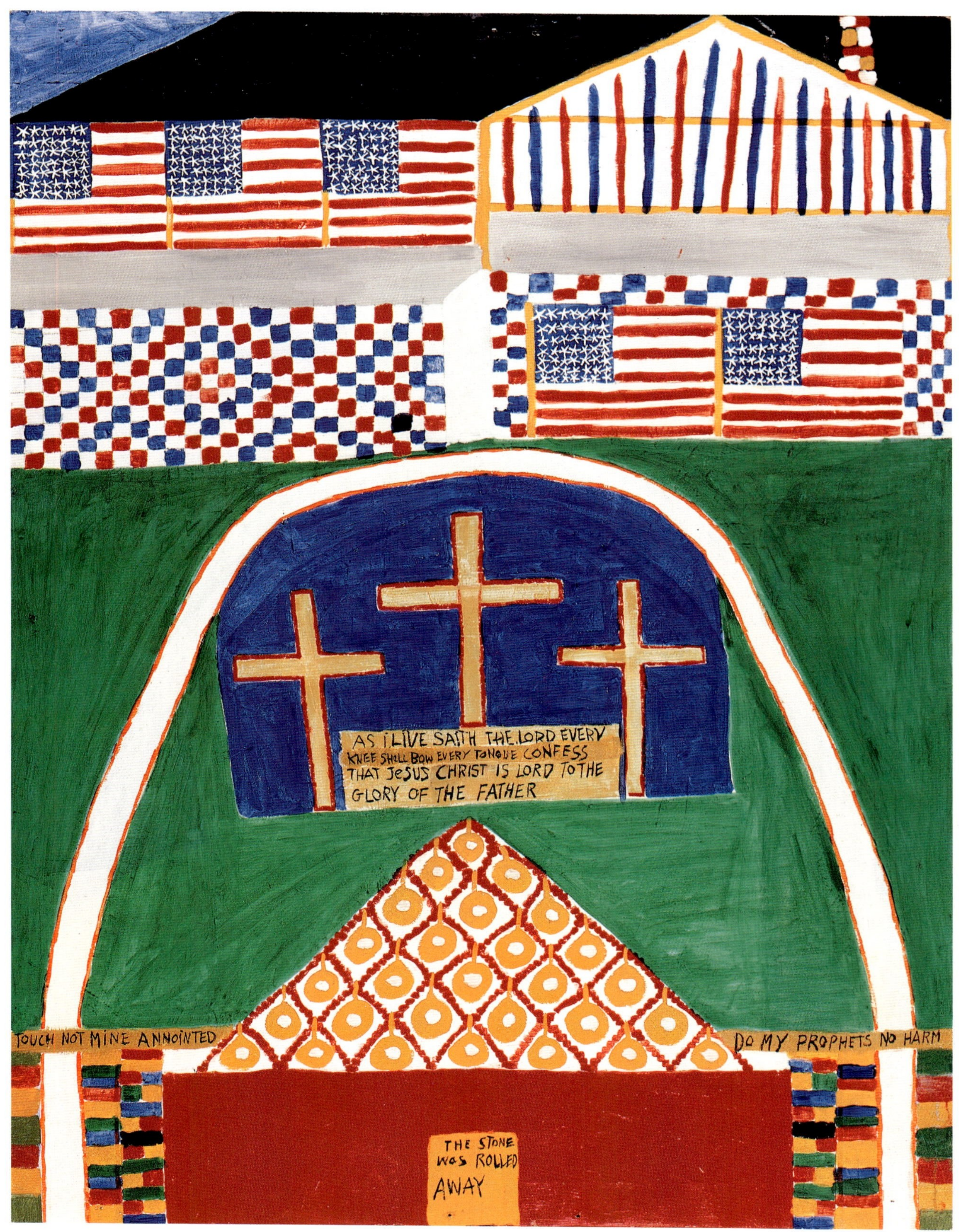

83

REV. BENJAMIN F. PERKINS

Homeplace, ca. 1985

(cat. no. 188)

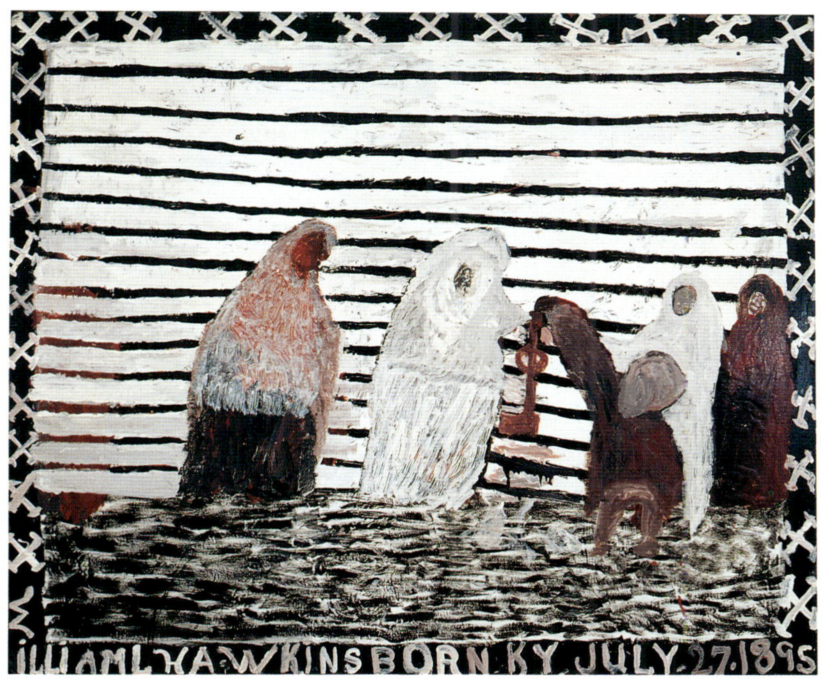

84

WILLIAM HAWKINS

Handing the Keys to St. Peter, 1989

(cat. no. 113)

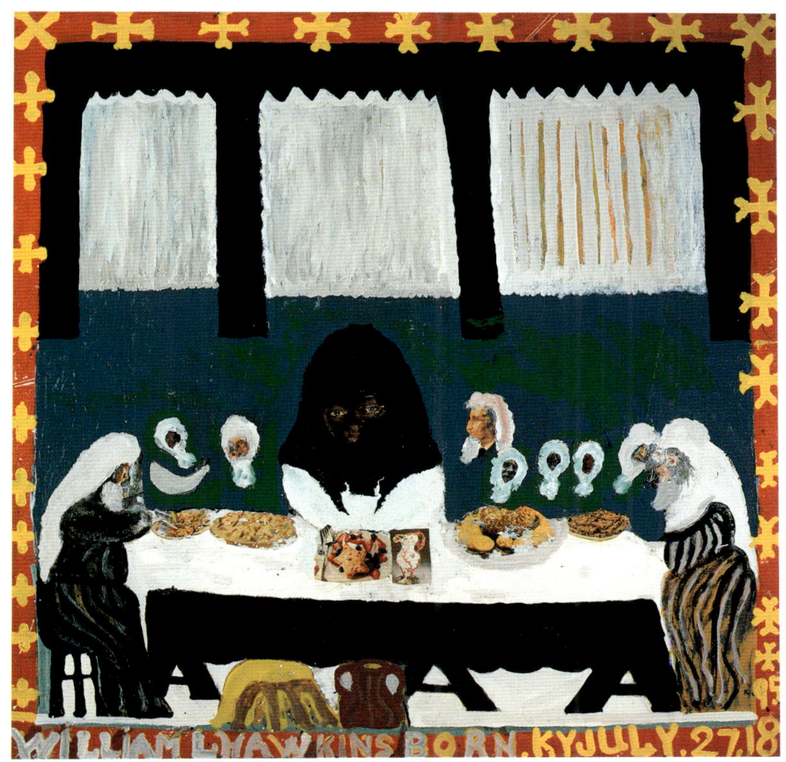

85

WILLIAM HAWKINS

The Last Supper No. 6, 1986

(cat. no. 115)

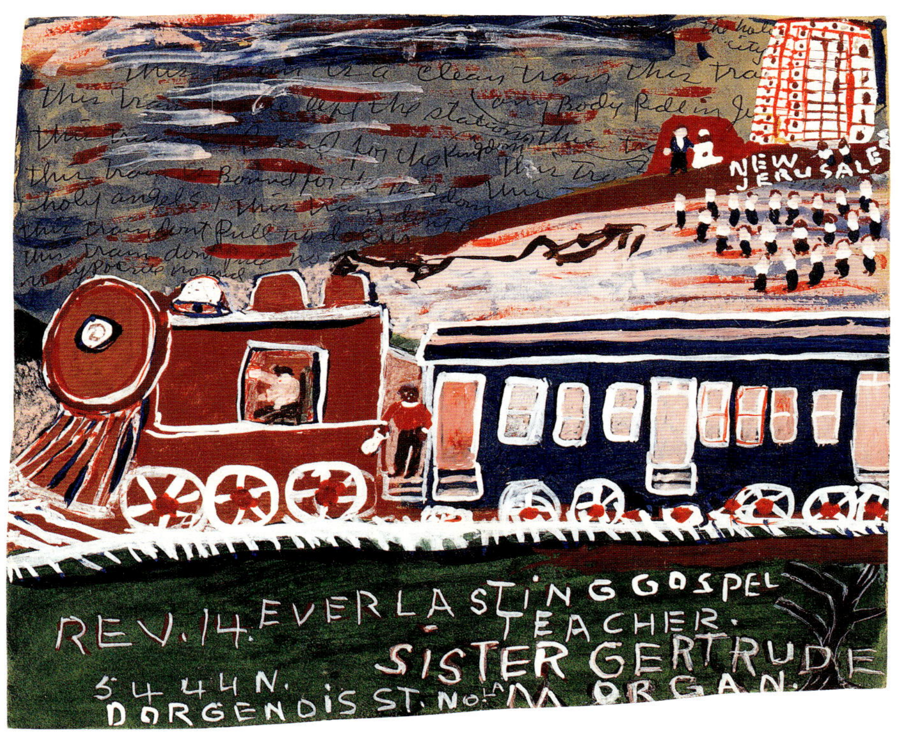

86

SISTER GERTRUDE MORGAN
Train to New Jerusalem, ca. 1970s
(cat. no. 177)

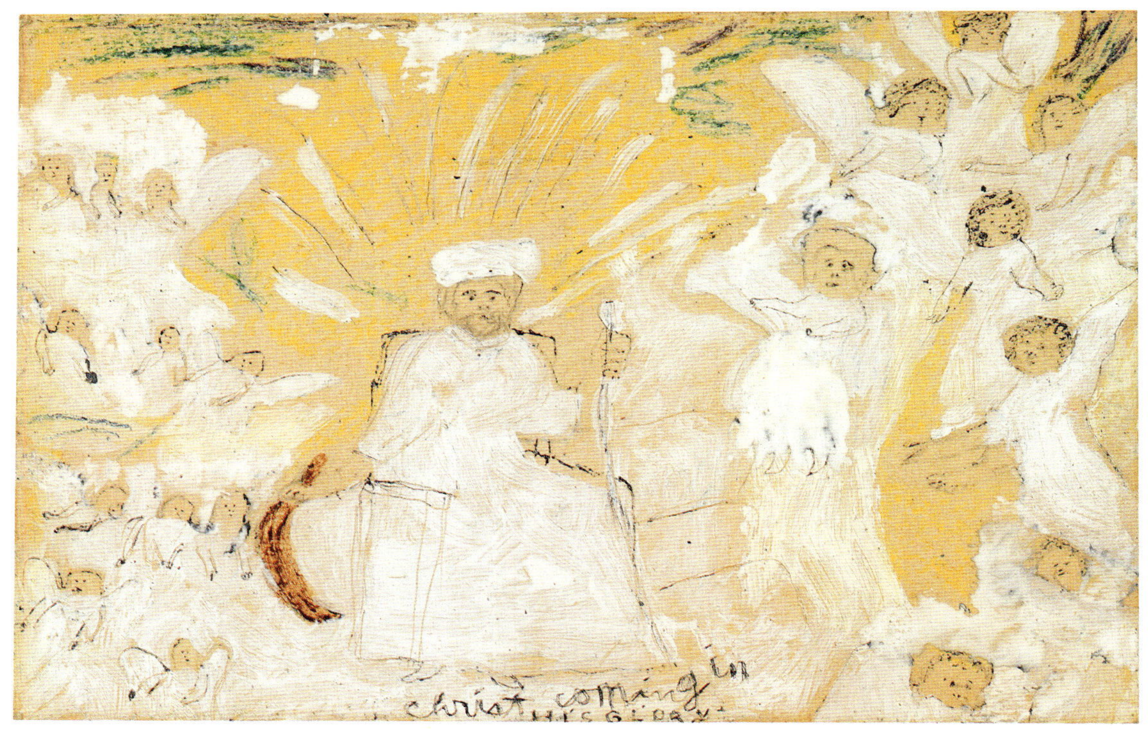

87

SISTER GERTRUDE MORGAN
Christ Coming in His Glory, n.d.
(cat. no. 171)

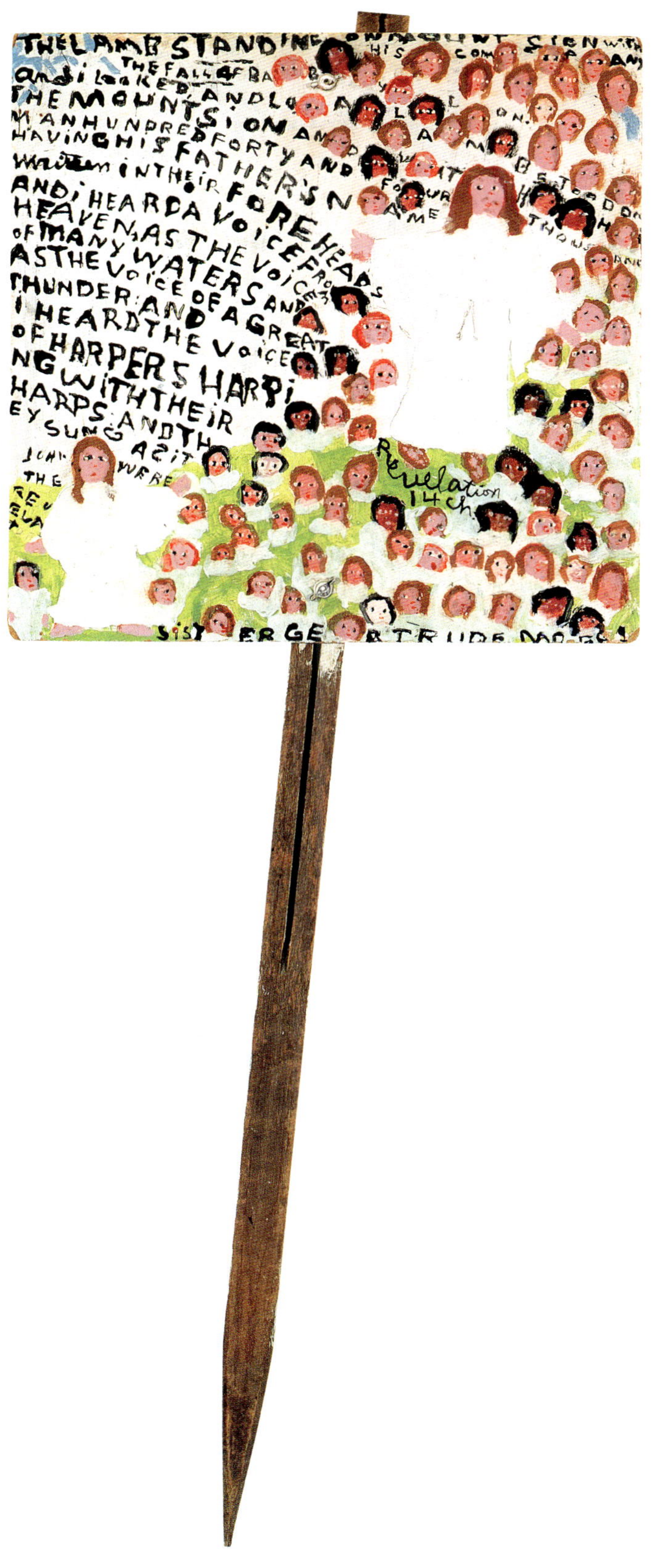

88

SISTER GERTRUDE MORGAN

The Lamb Standing on Mount Zion with His Company, n.d.

(cat. no. 173)

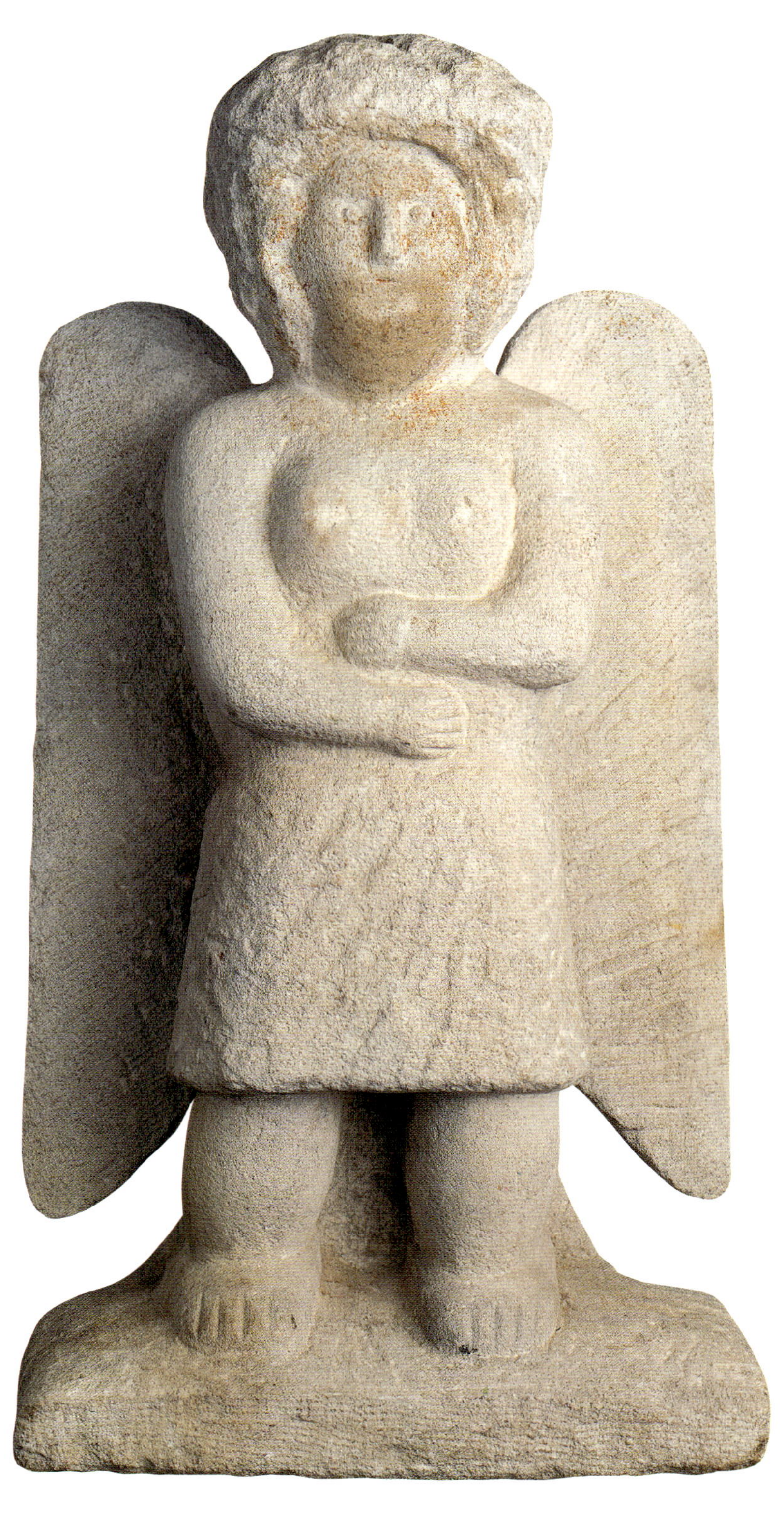

89

WILLIAM EDMONDSON

Angel, ca. 1940s

(cat. no. 73)

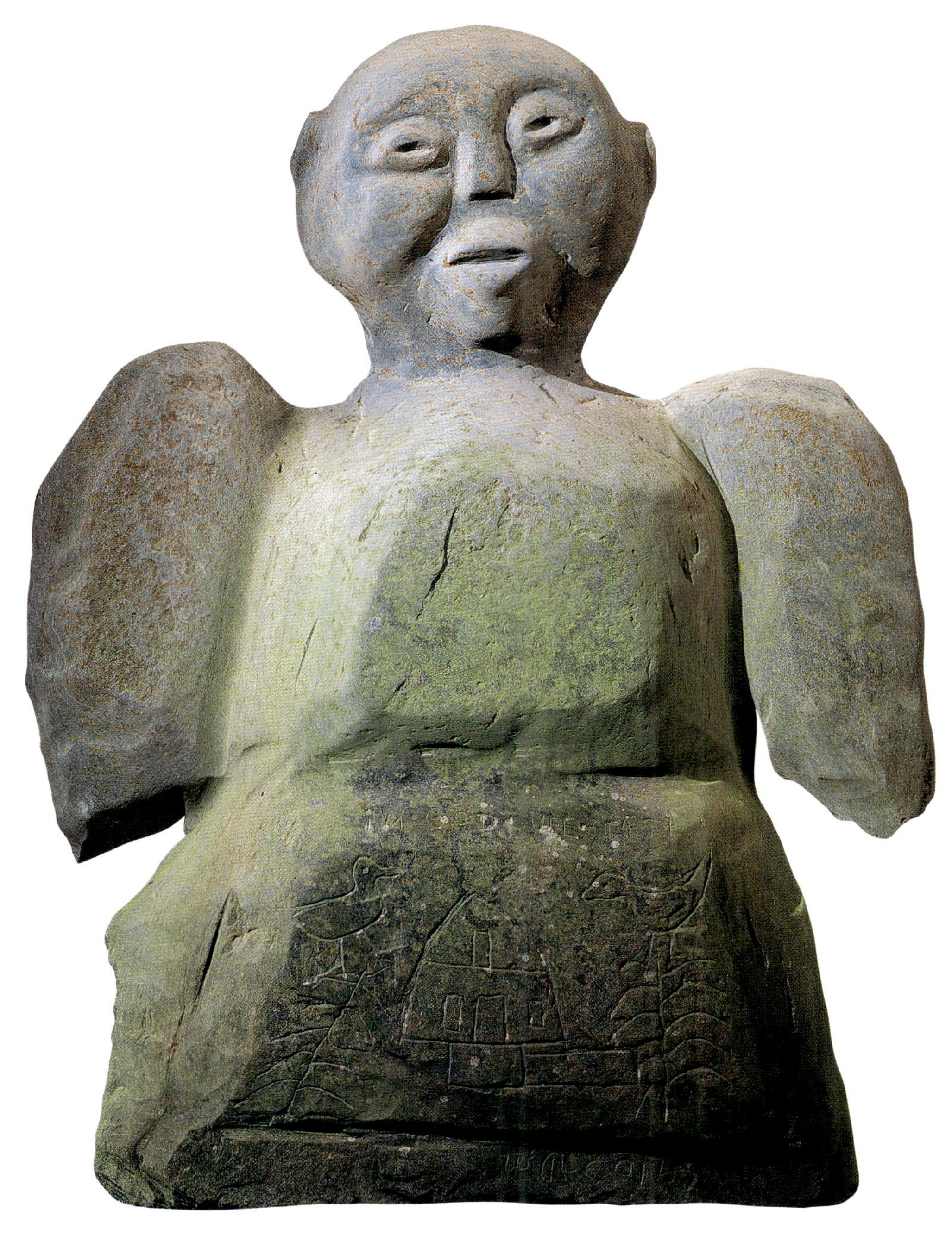

90

RAYMOND COINS

Angel, 1985

(cat. no. 30)

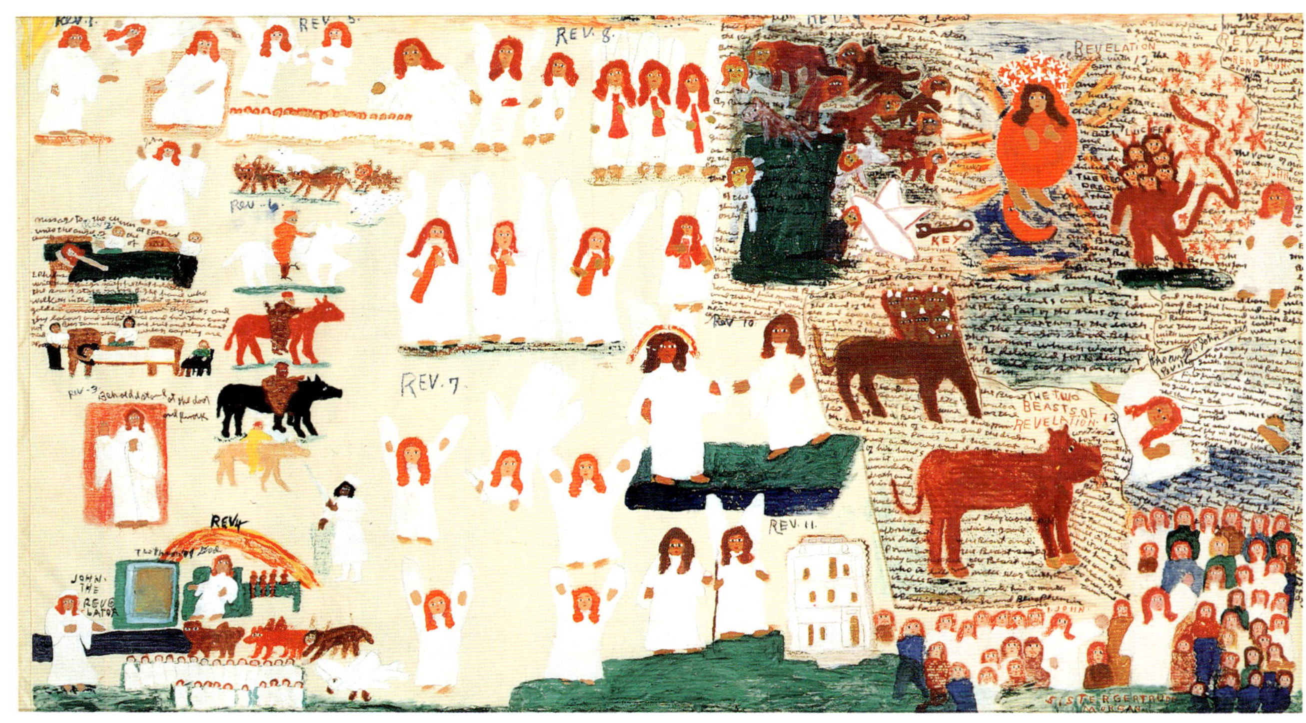

91

SISTER GERTRUDE MORGAN
Book of Revelation, ca. 1965–75
(cat. no. 169)

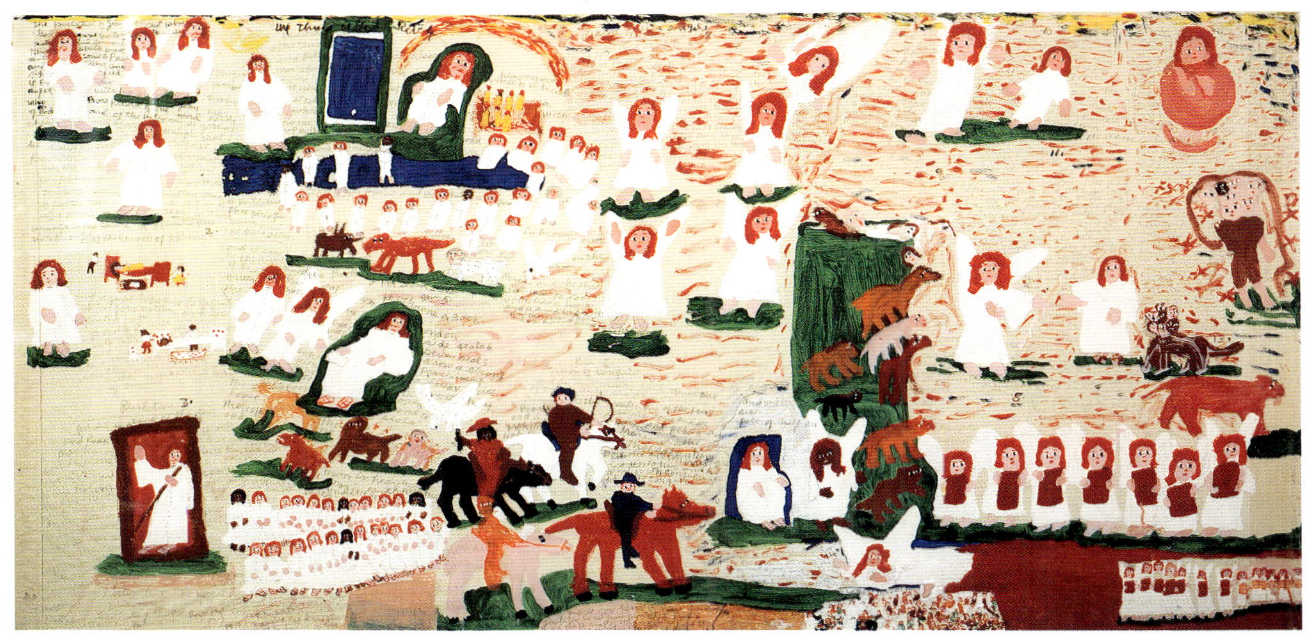

92

SISTER GERTRUDE MORGAN

Book of Revelation, ca. 1965–70

(cat. no. 168)

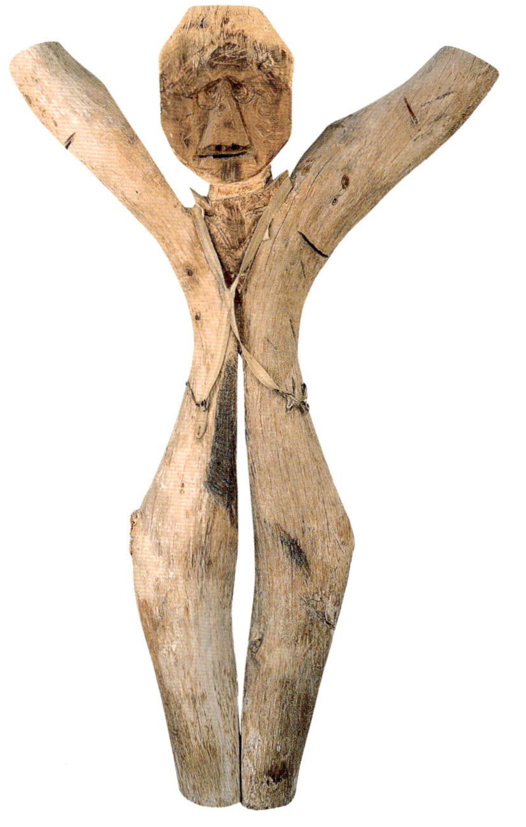

93

JESSE AARON

Crucifixion, n.d.

(cat. no. 1)

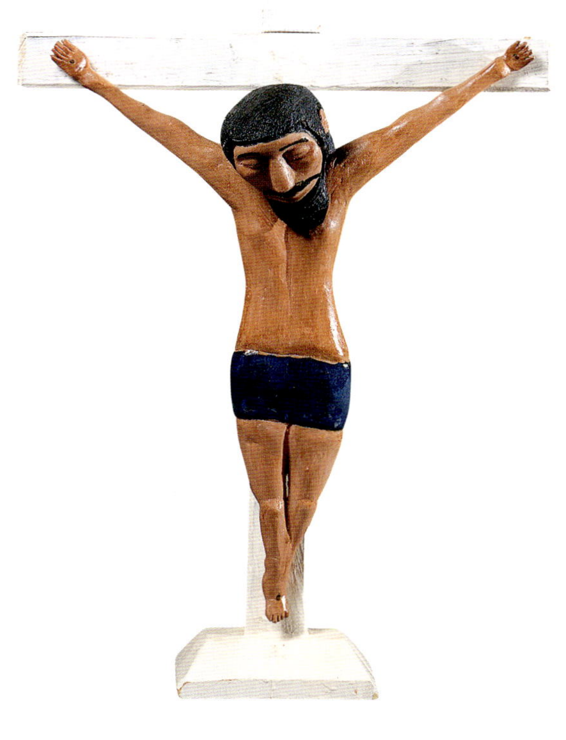

94

GEORGE WILLIAMS

Crucifixion, 1985

(cat. no. 262)

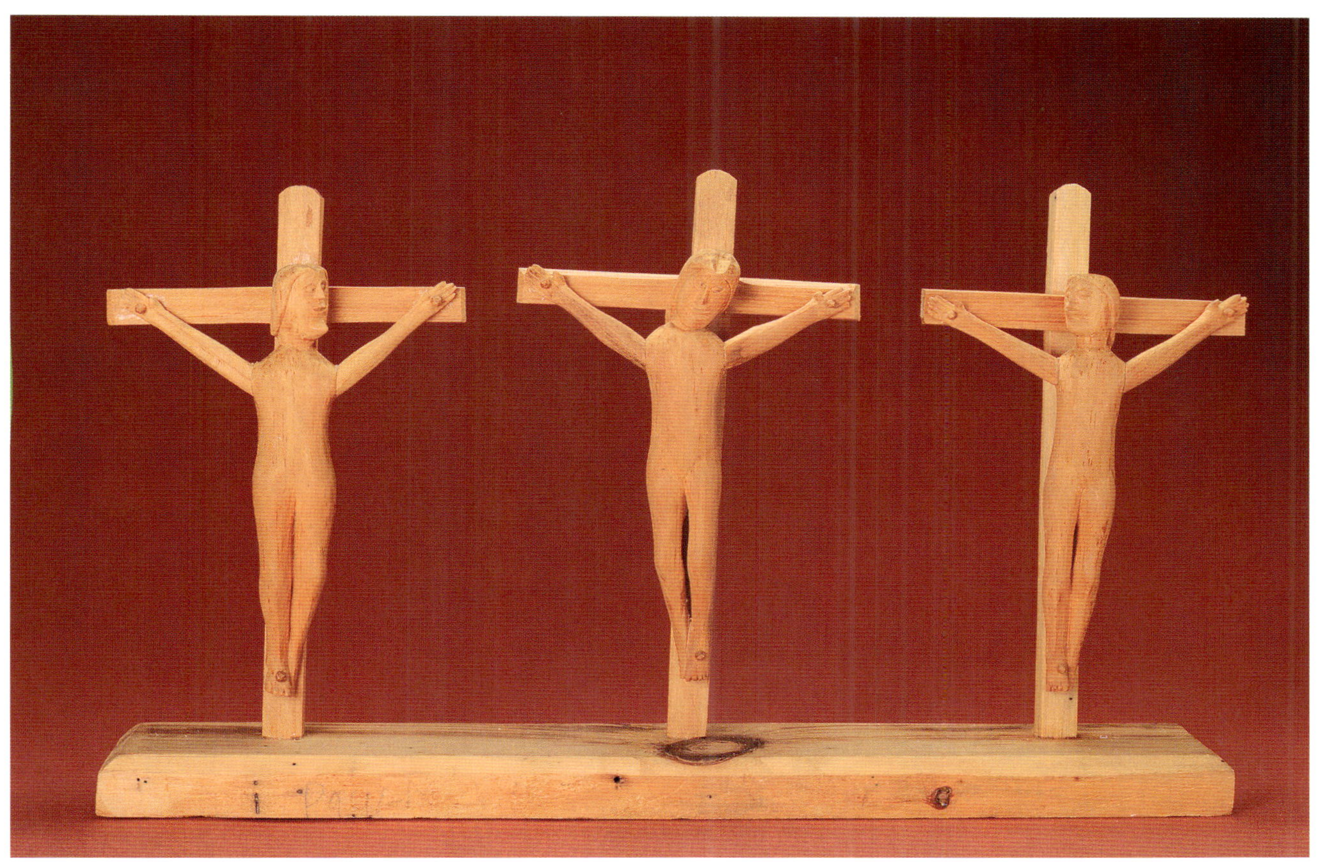

95

EDGAR TOLSON

Crucifixion, 1969

(cat. no. 242)

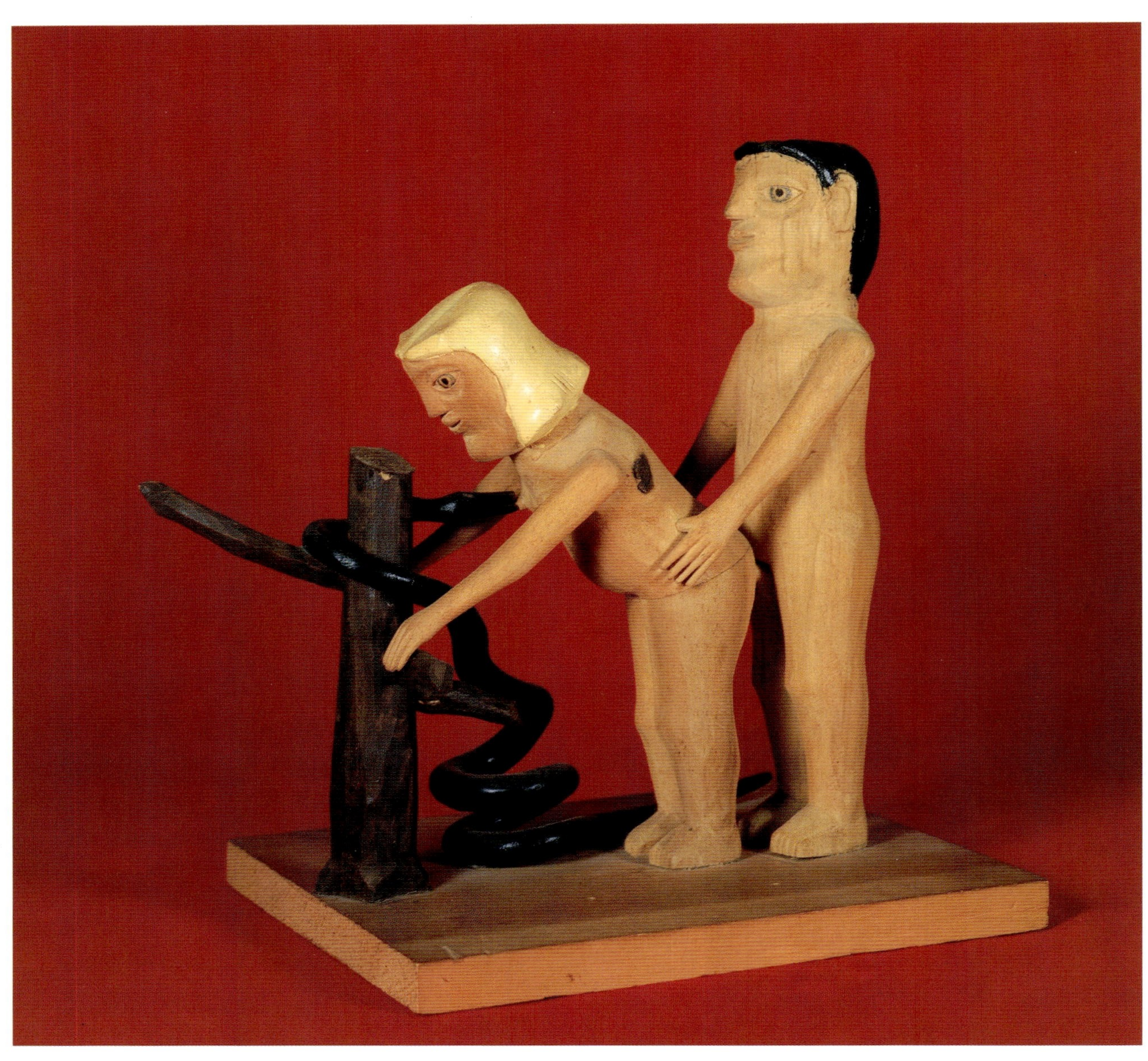

96

EDGAR TOLSON

Original Sin, 1976

(cat. no. 243)

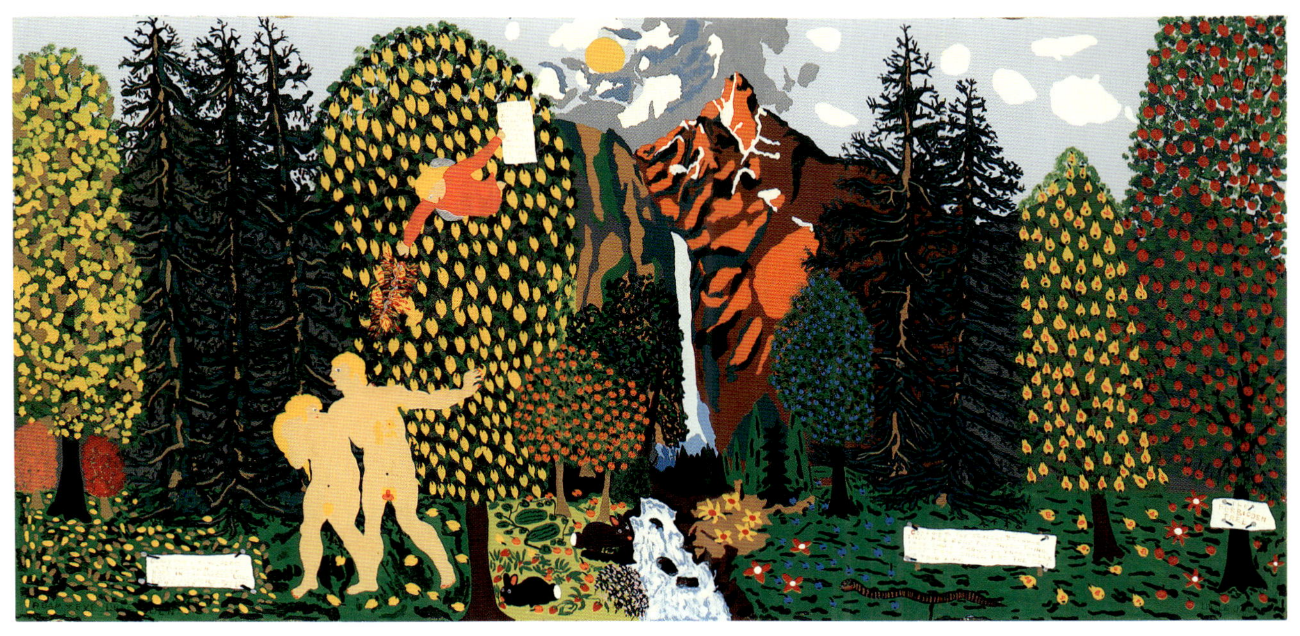

97

JOHN WILLIAM "UNCLE JACK" DEY

Adam and Eve Leave Eden, 1973

(cat. no. 50)

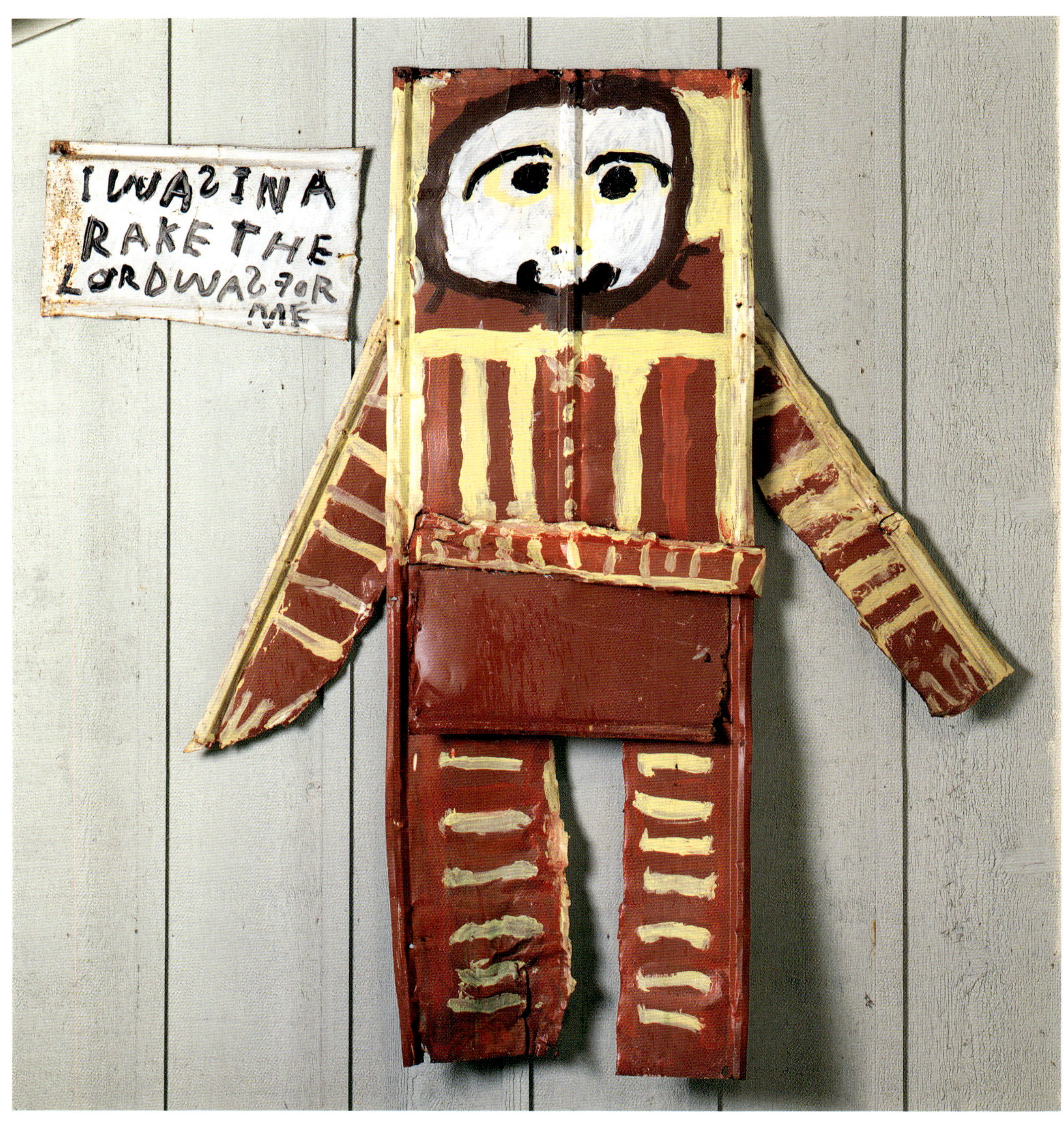

98

MARY T. SMITH

I Was in a Wreck, 1983

(cat. no. 213)

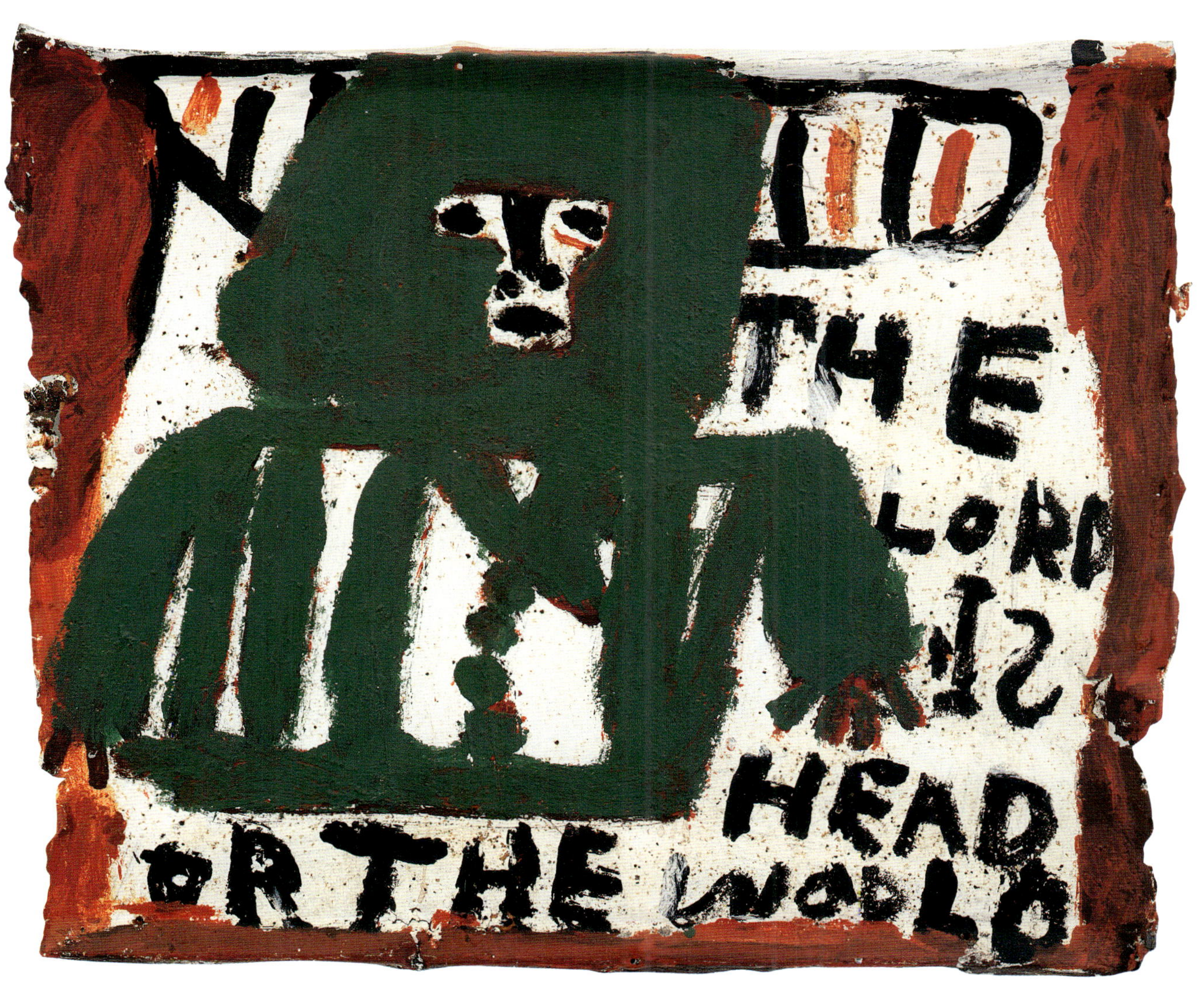

99

MARY T. SMITH

The Lord Is Head of the World, ca. 1983

(cat. no. 214)

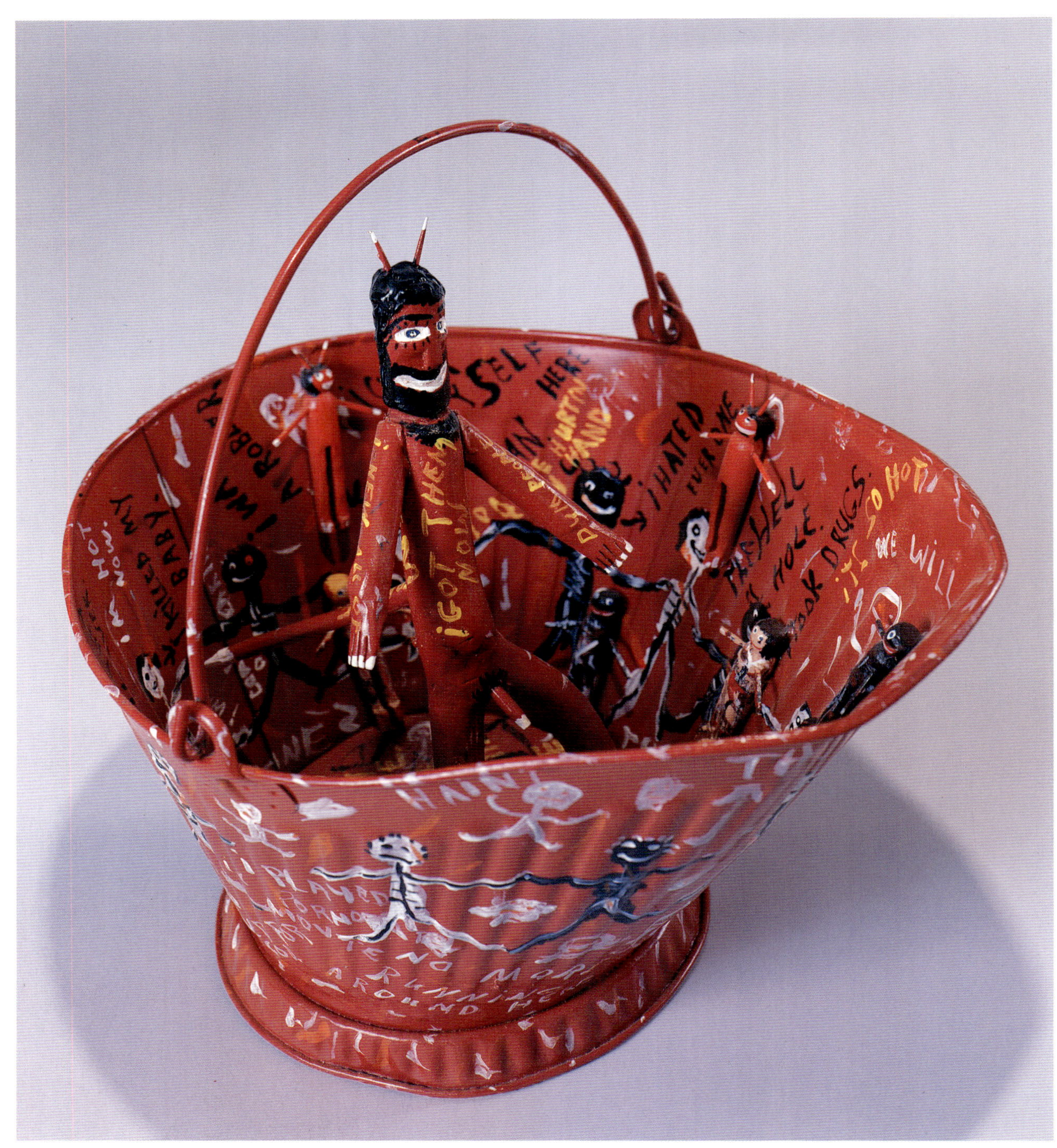

100

JESSIE AND RONALD COOPER
Hell Bucket, 1989
(cat. no. 38)

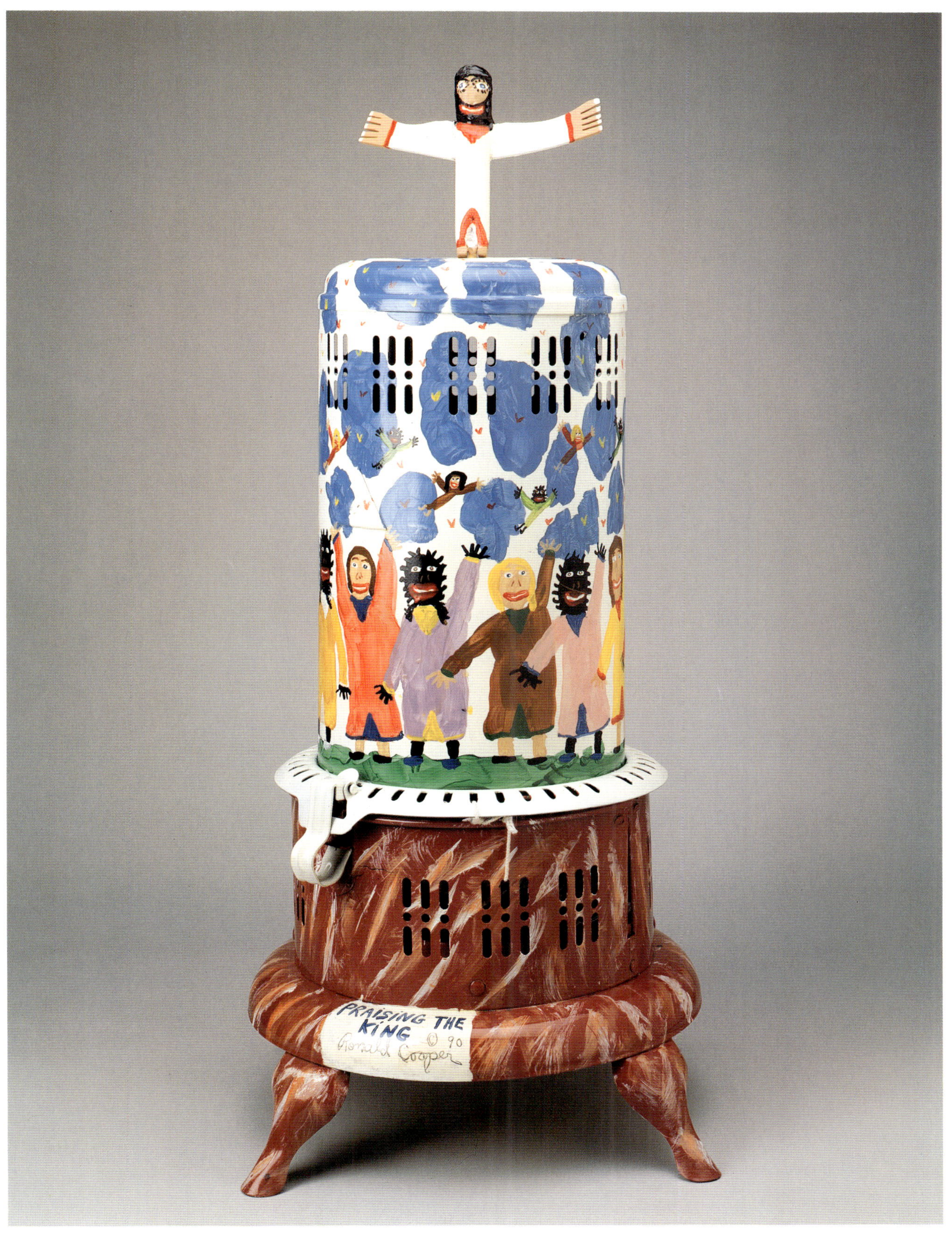

101

JESSIE AND RONALD COOPER

Praising the King: Kerosene Heater, 1989

(cat. no. 40)

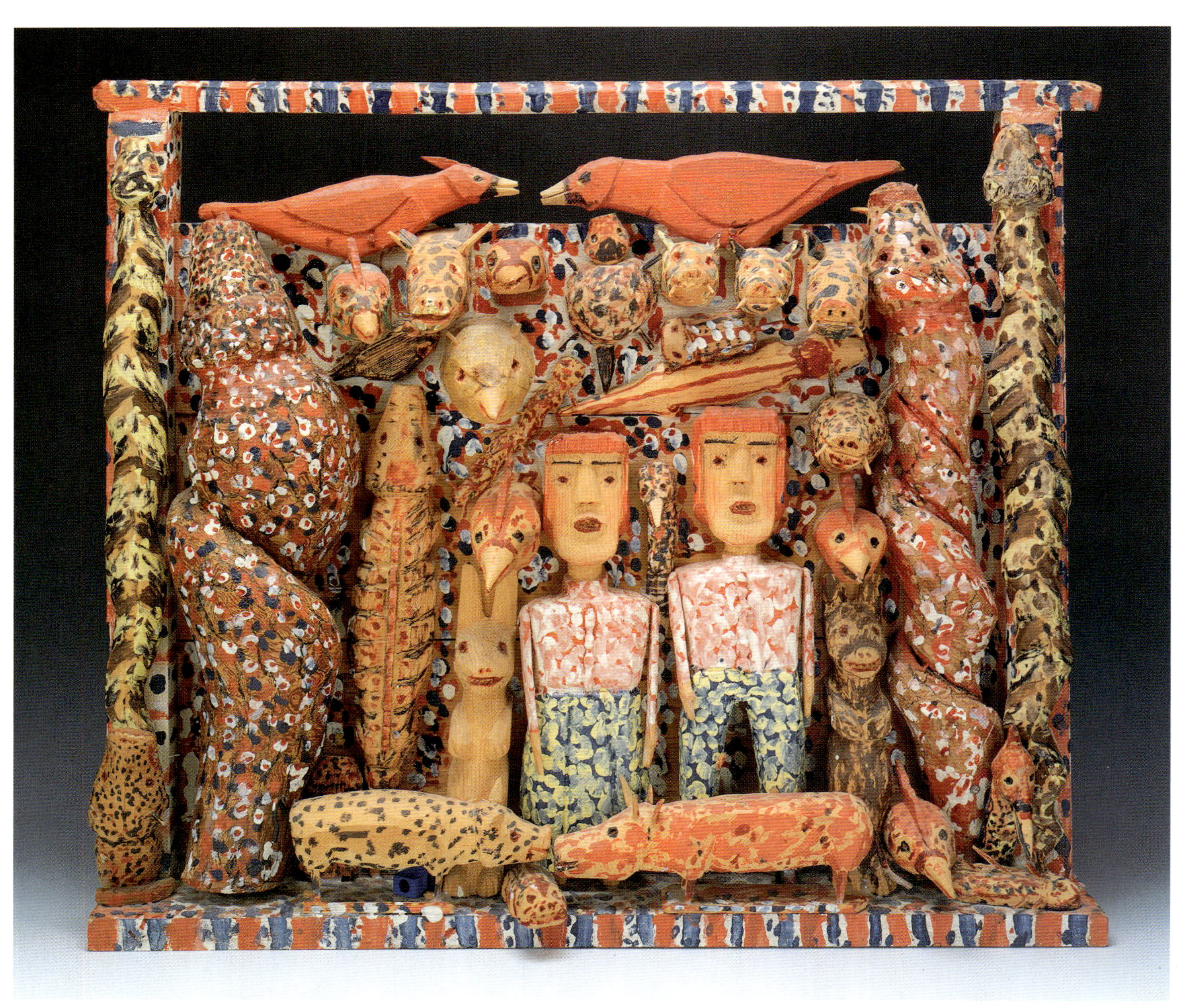

102
CARL MCKENZIE
Noah's Ark, 1987
(cat. no. 160)

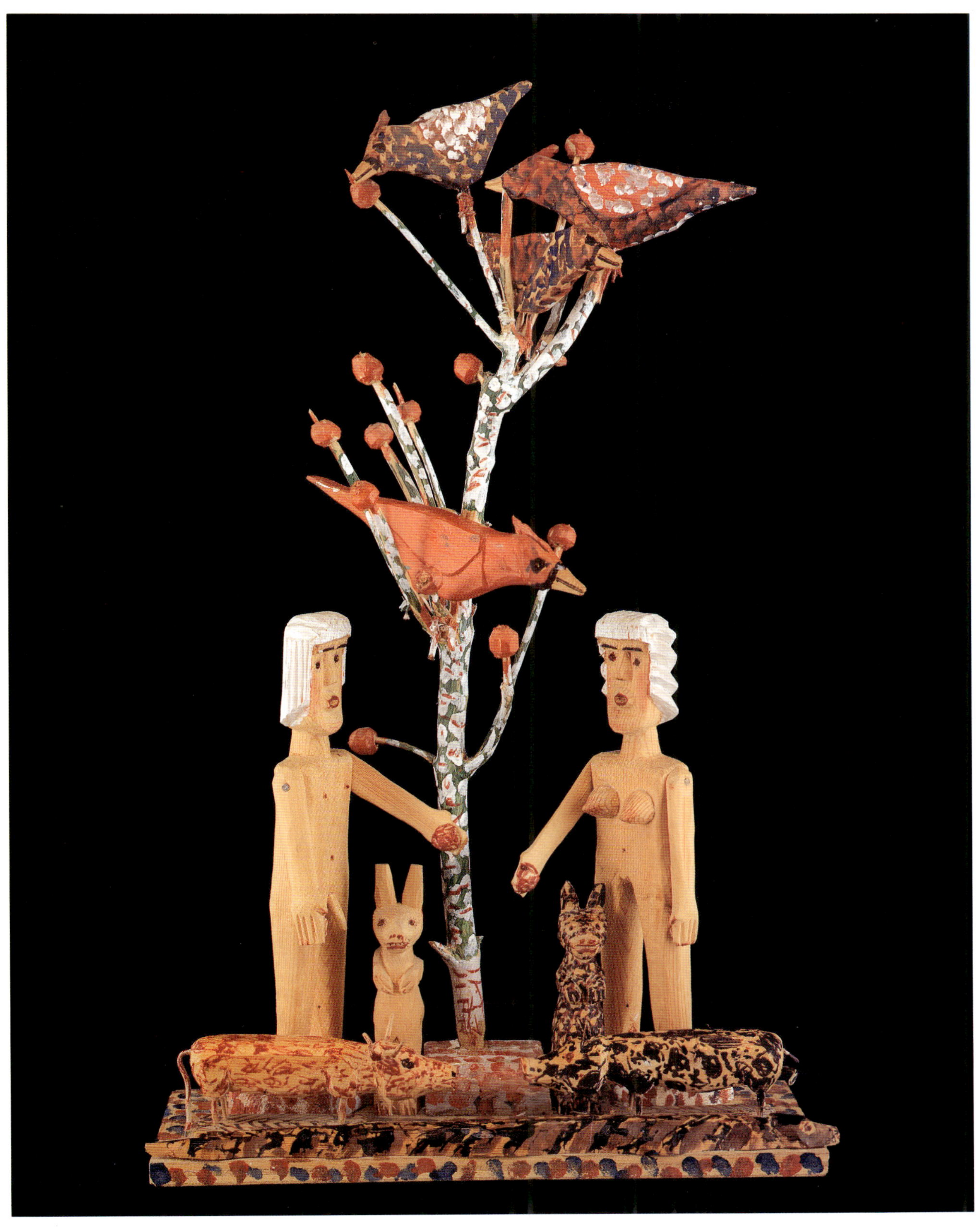

103

CARL MCKENZIE

Adam and Eve, 1987

(cat. no. 159)

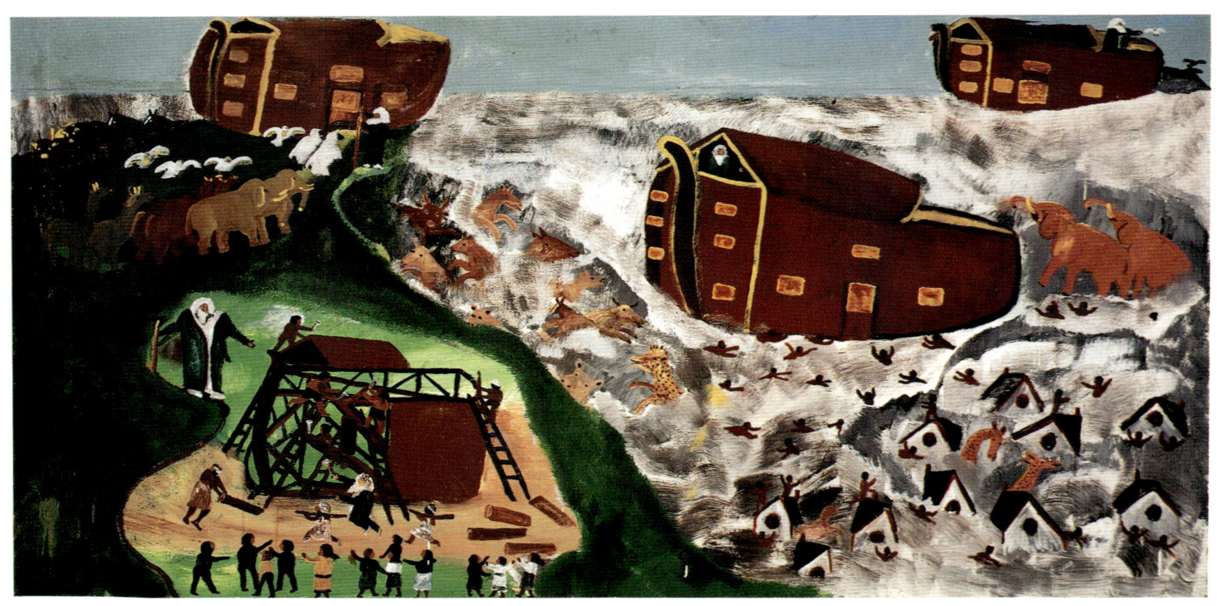

104

REV. JOHNNIE SWEARINGEN

Noah's Ark, n.d.

(cat. no. 231)

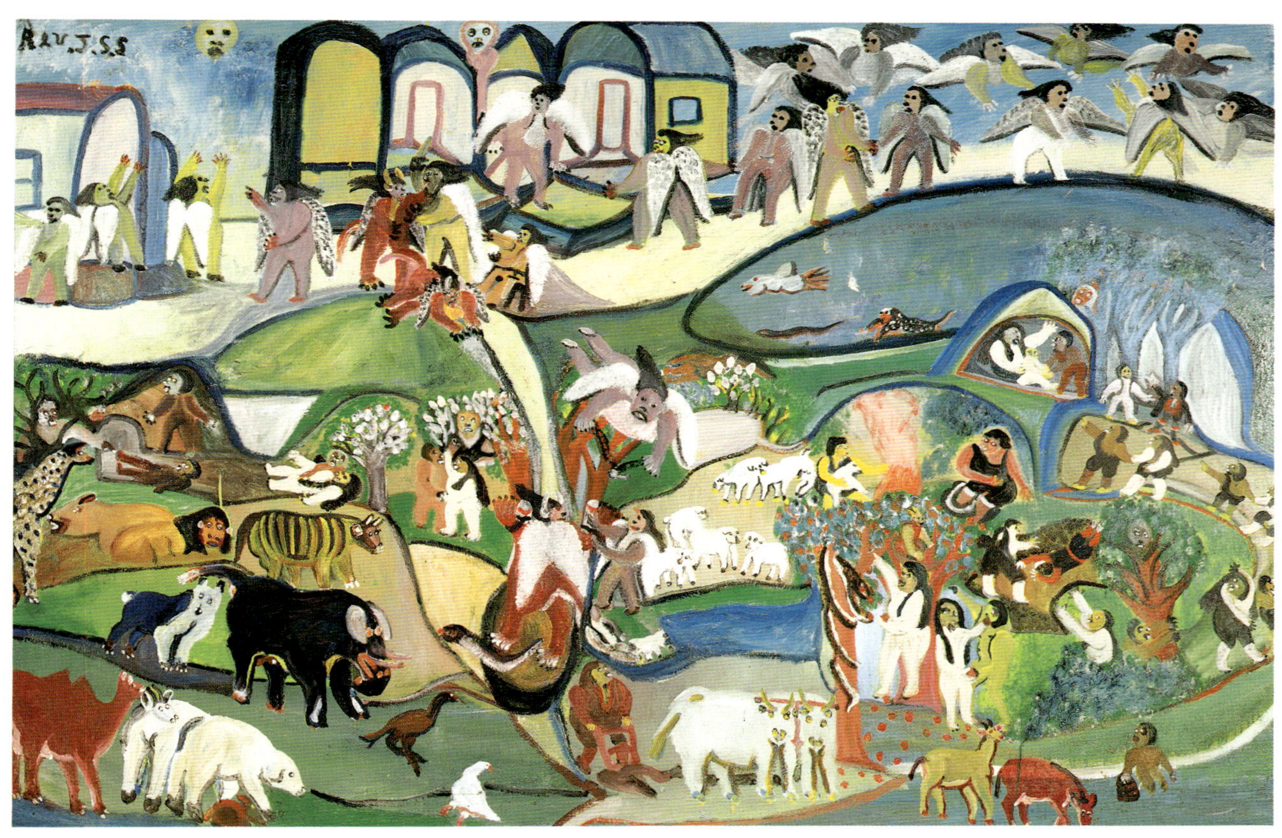

105

REV. JOHNNIE SWEARINGEN

The Creation of the World, 1990

(cat. no. 229)

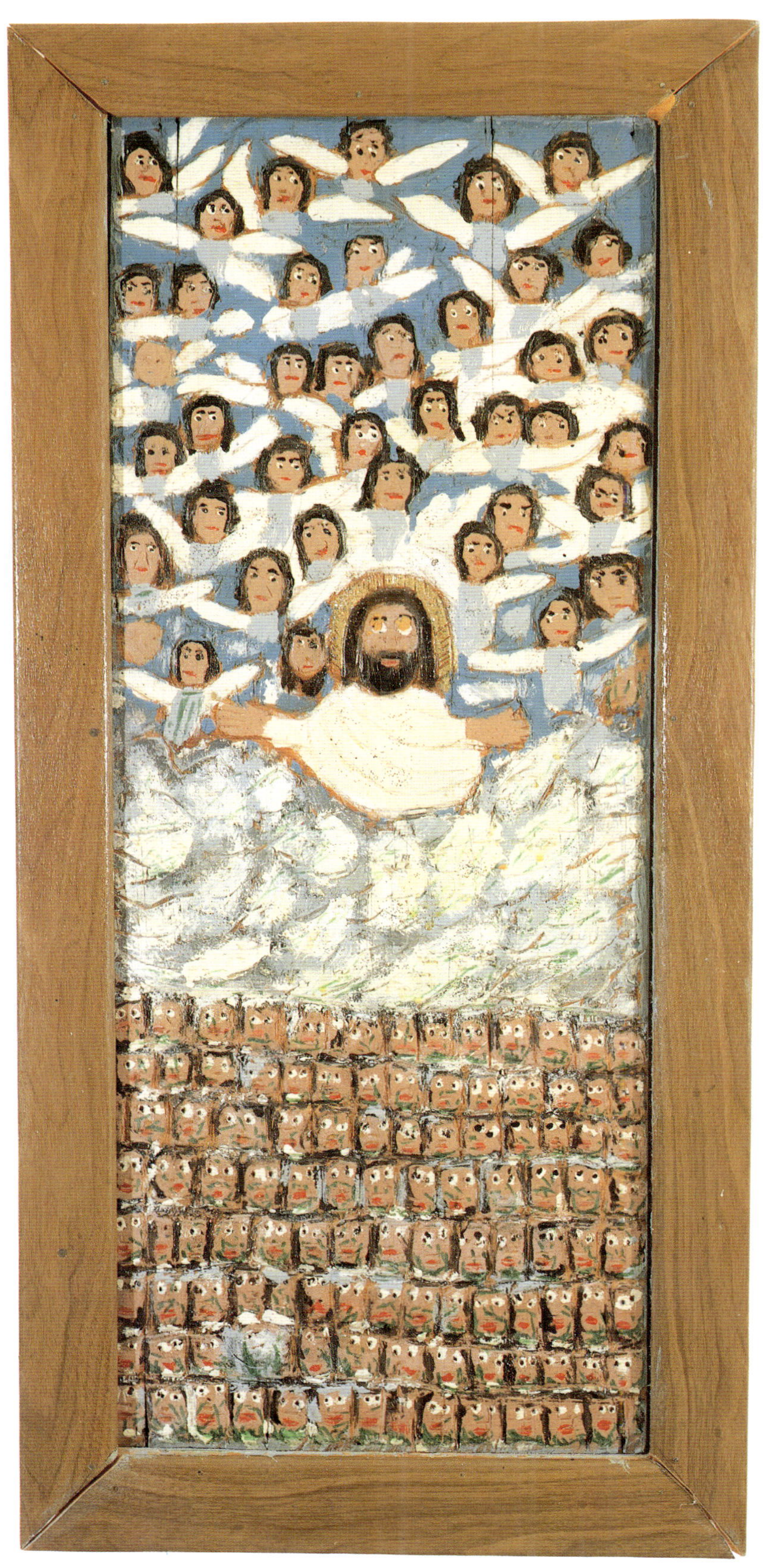

106

ELIJAH PIERCE

Jesus Is Coming Again, 1979

(cat. no. 189)

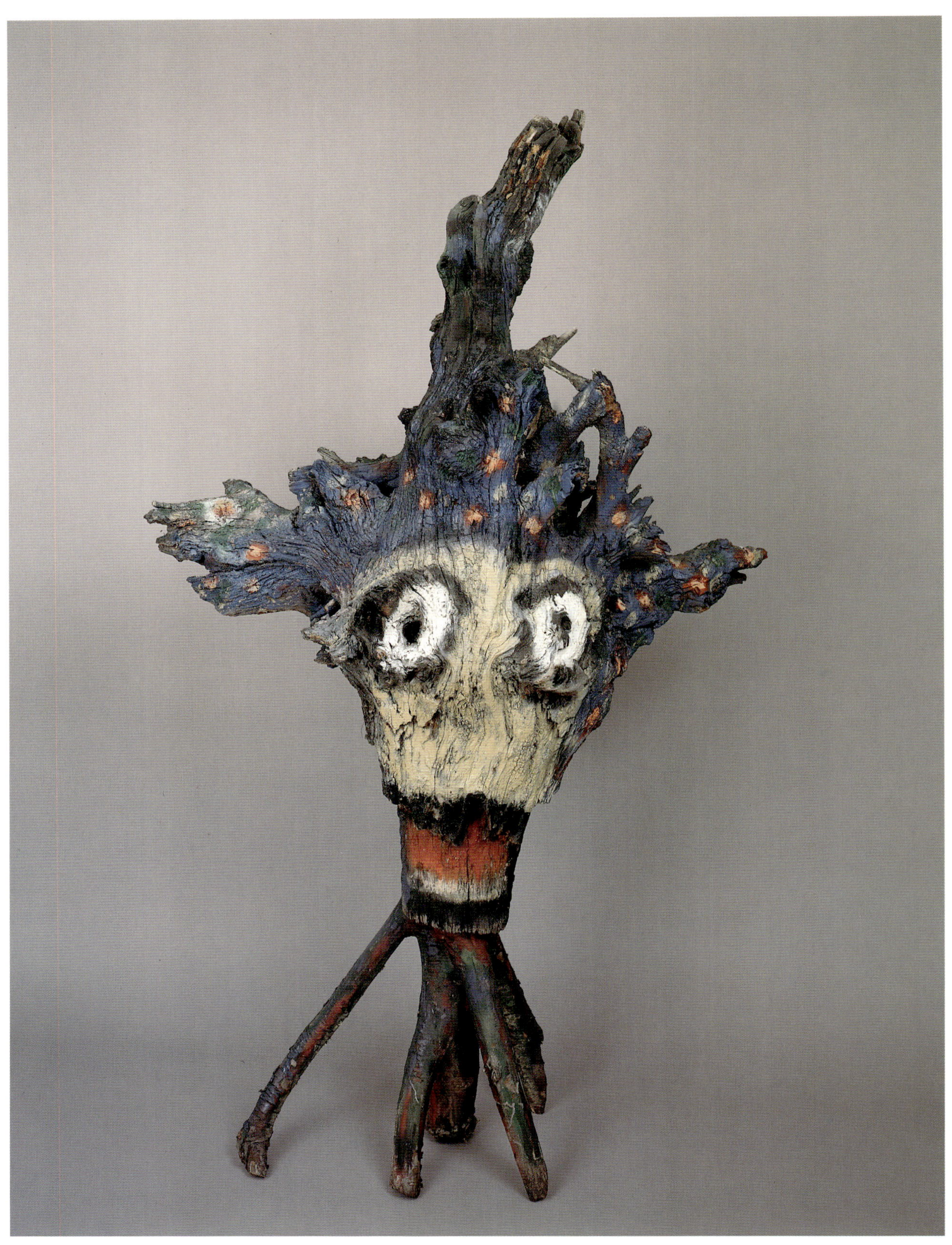

107

RALPH GRIFFIN

Screaming Lady, n.d.

(cat. no. 106)

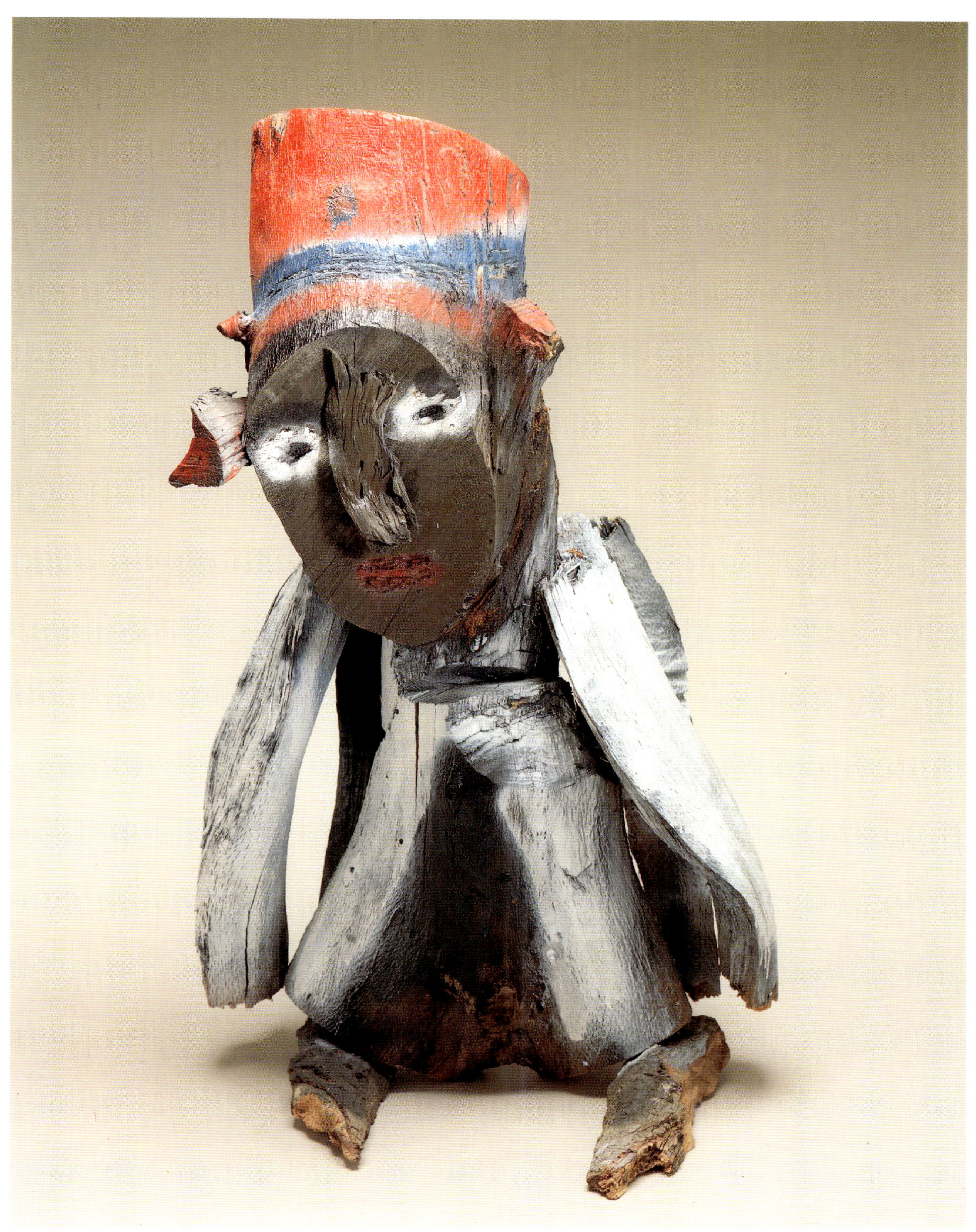

108

RALPH GRIFFIN

Gypsy, n.d.

(cat. no. 105)

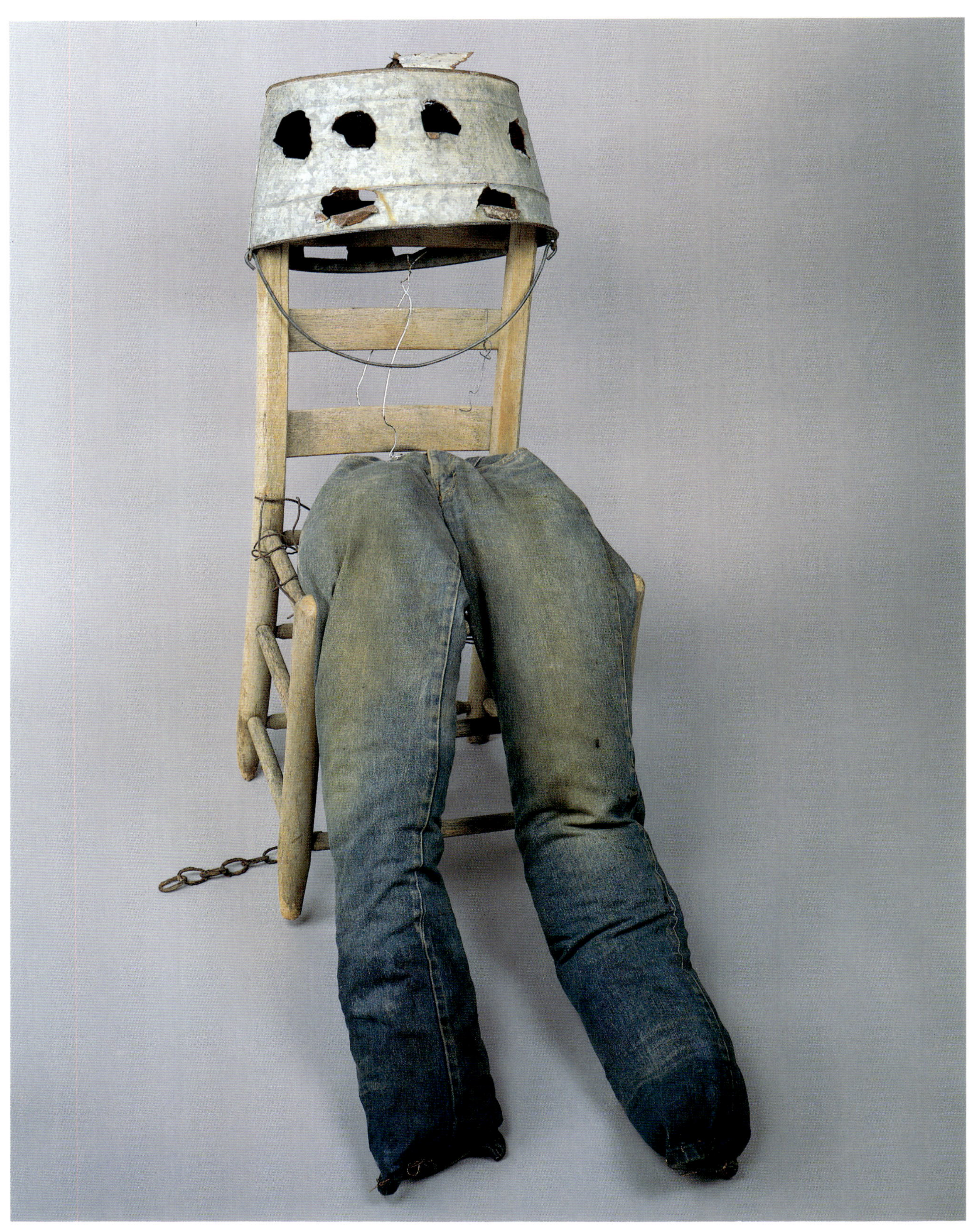

109

HAWKINS BOLDEN

Untitled, 1987

(cat. no. 14)

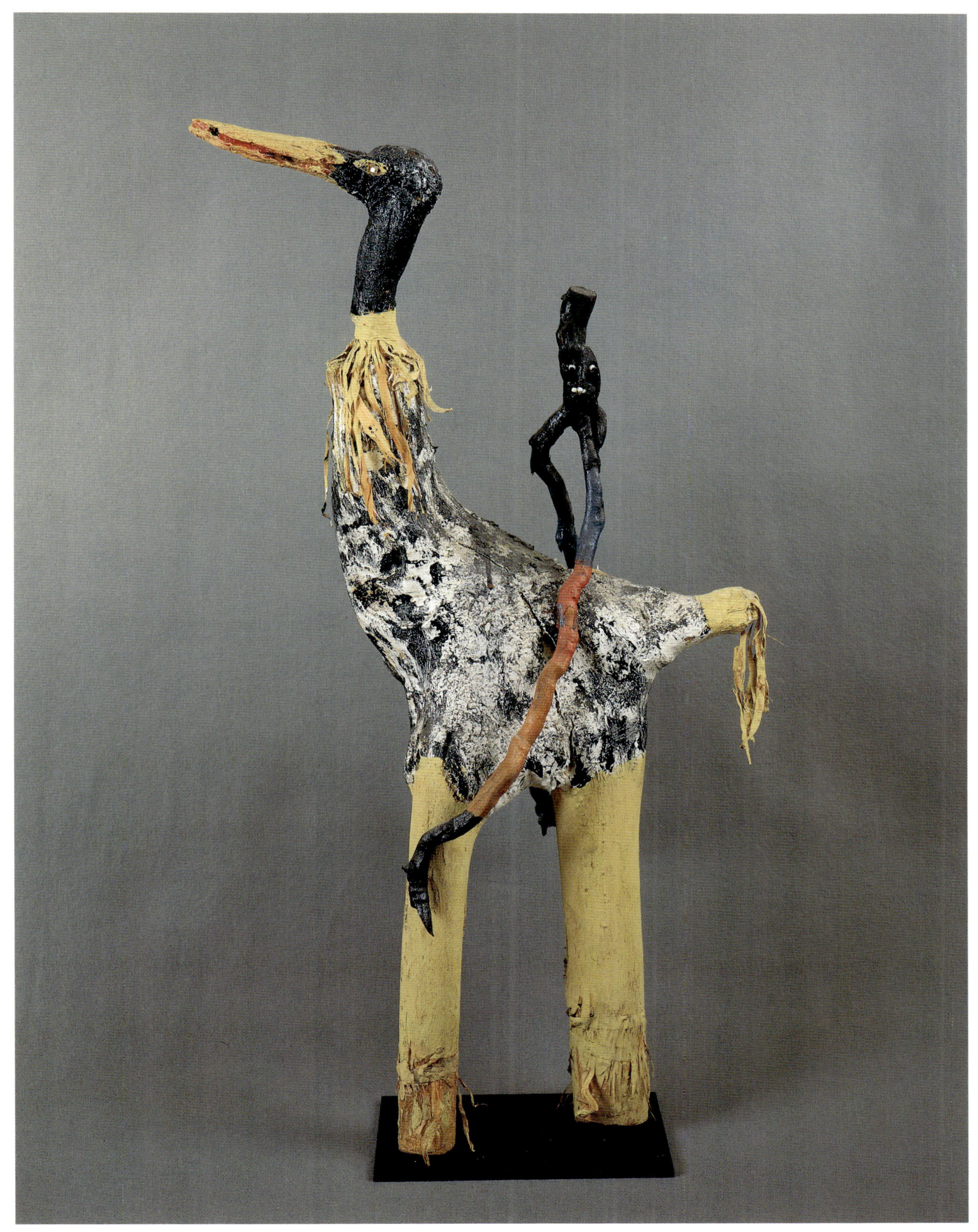

110

BESSIE HARVEY

Yellow Bird with Rider, n.d.

(cat. no. 110)

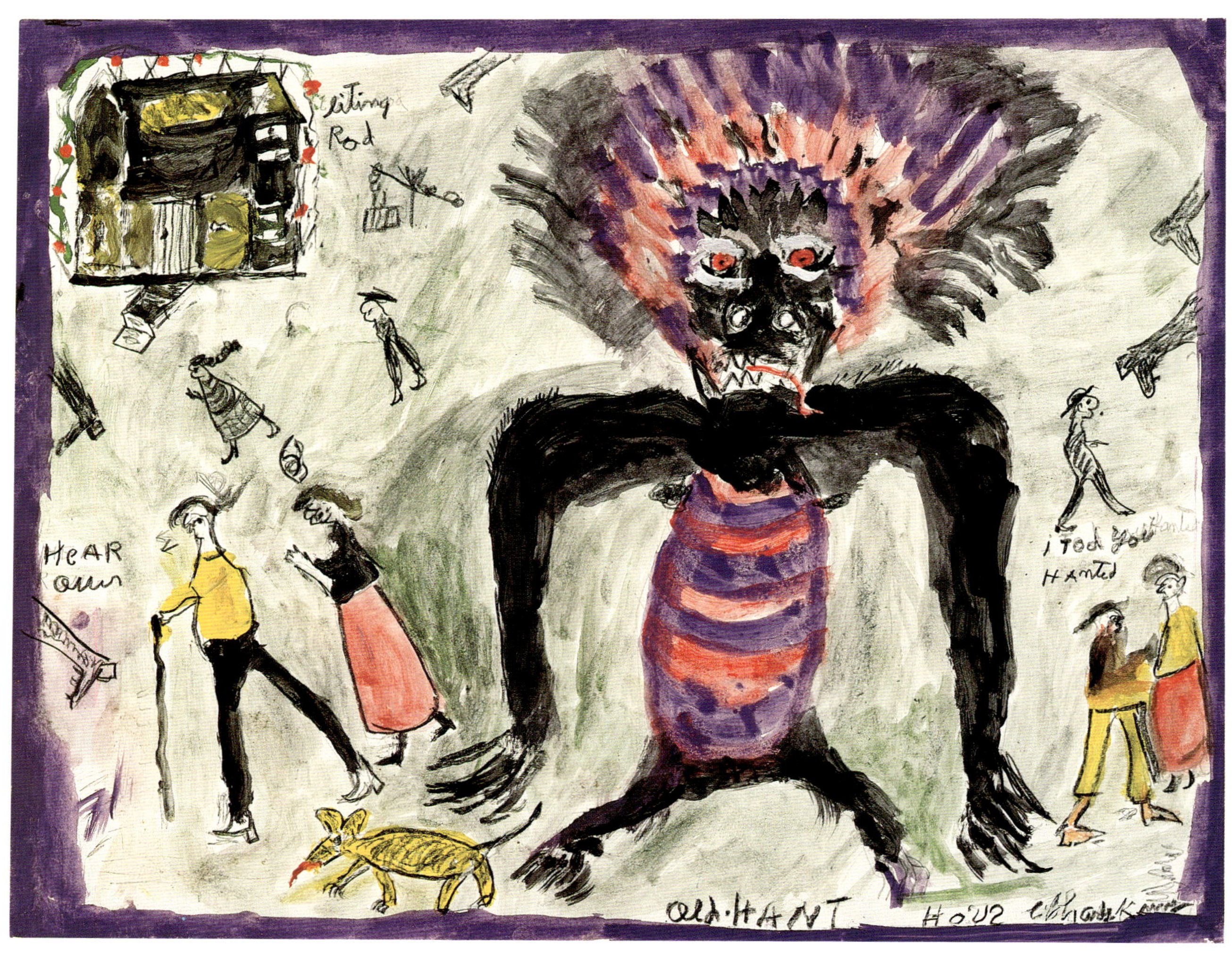

111

CHARLES KINNEY

Old Hant House, 1988

(cat. no. 149)

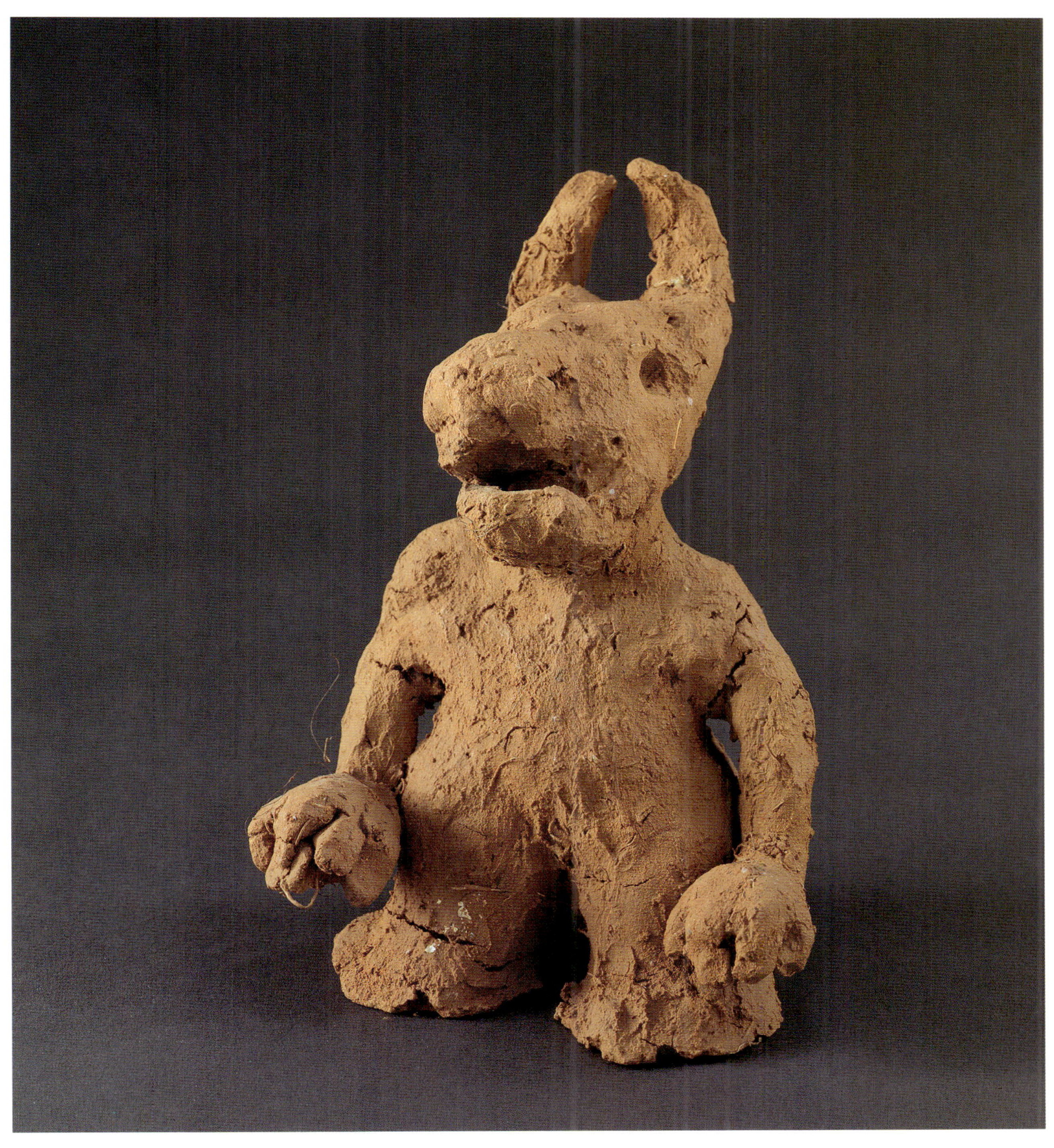

112

JUANITA ROGERS

Standing Creature, ca. 1980

(cat. no. 195)

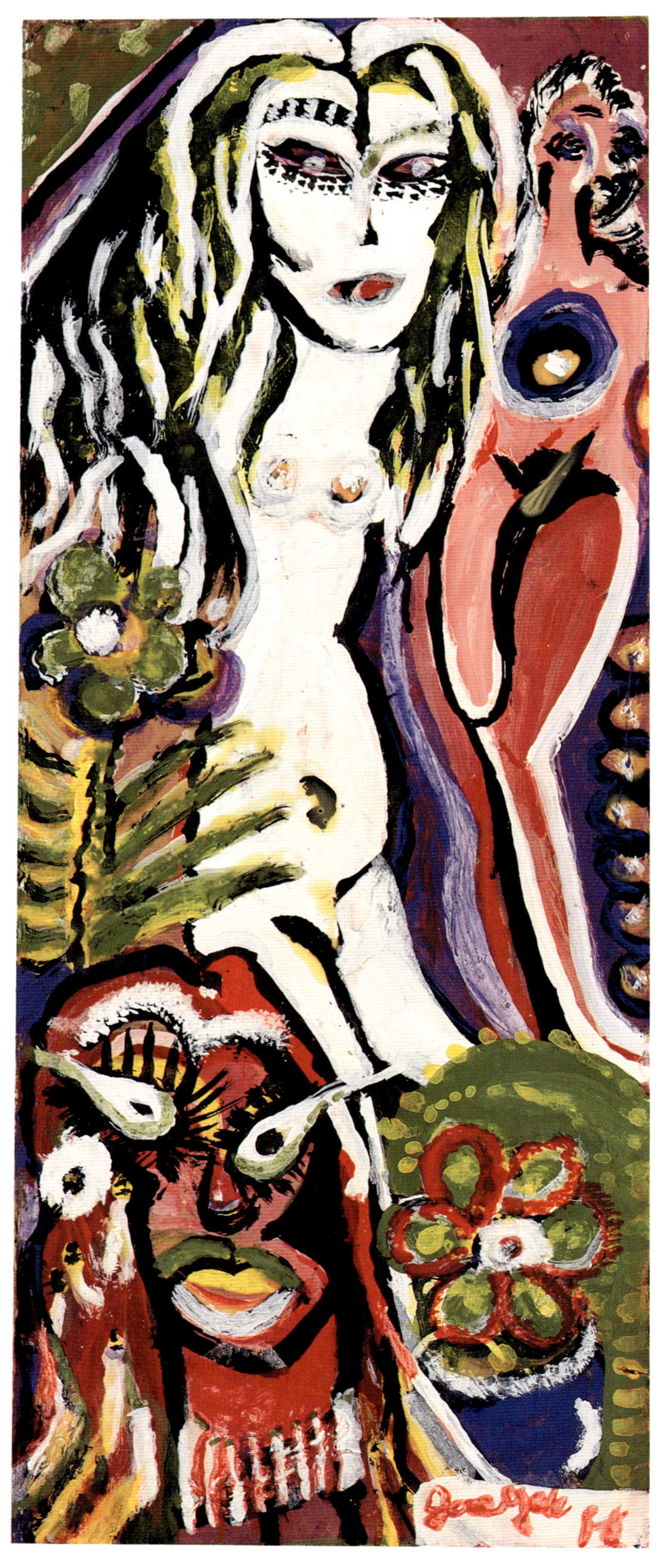

113

JOSEPH HARDIN

Untitled, ca. 1987

(cat. no. 108)

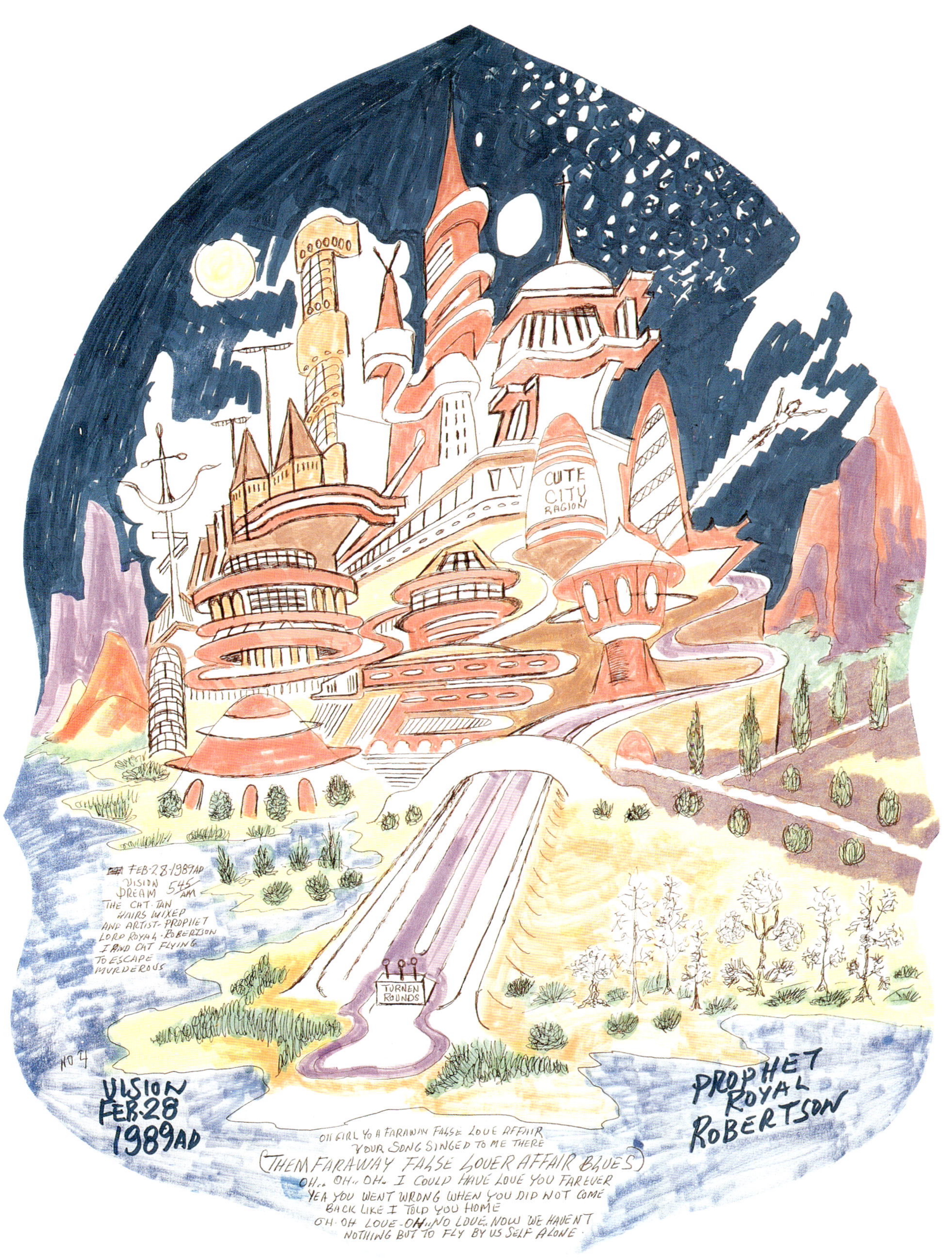

114

"PROPHET" ROYAL ROBERTSON

Cute City Region, 1989

(cat. no. 193)

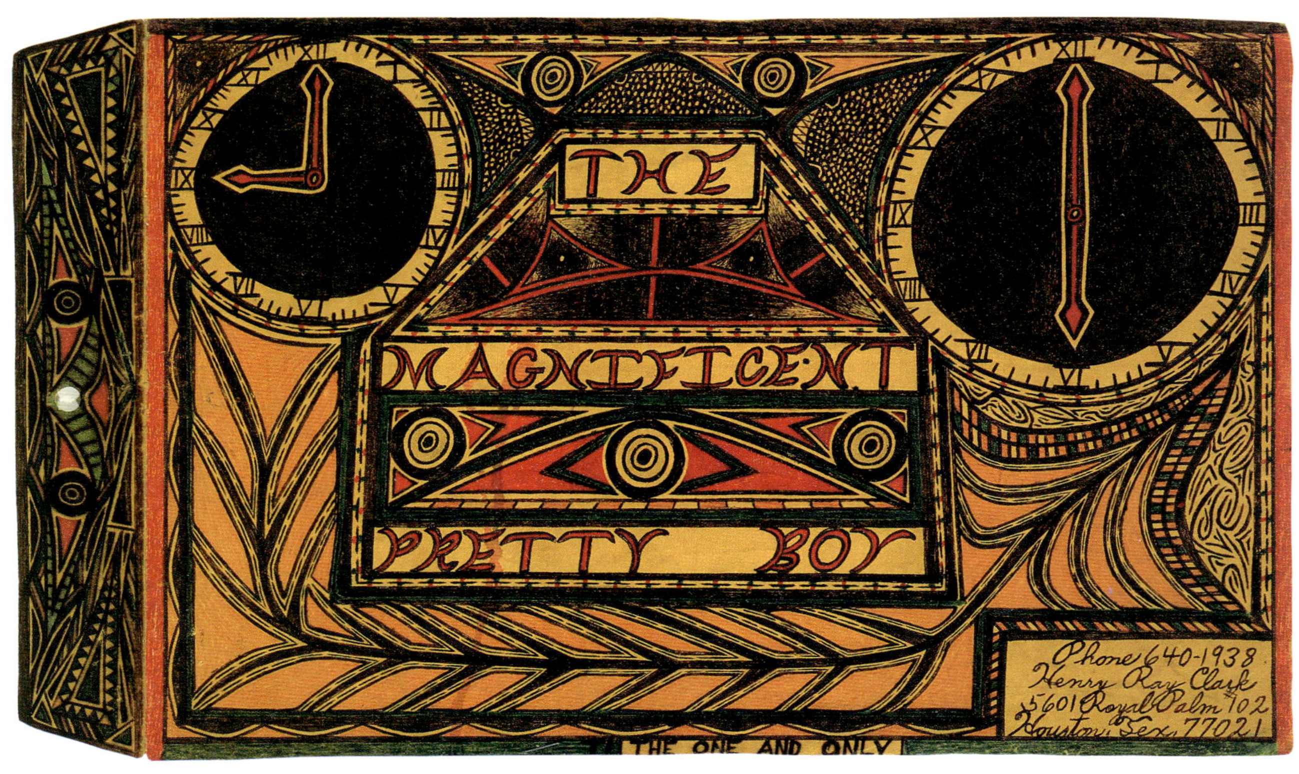

115

HENRY RAY CLARK

The Magnificent Pretty Boy, 1988

(cat. no. 27)

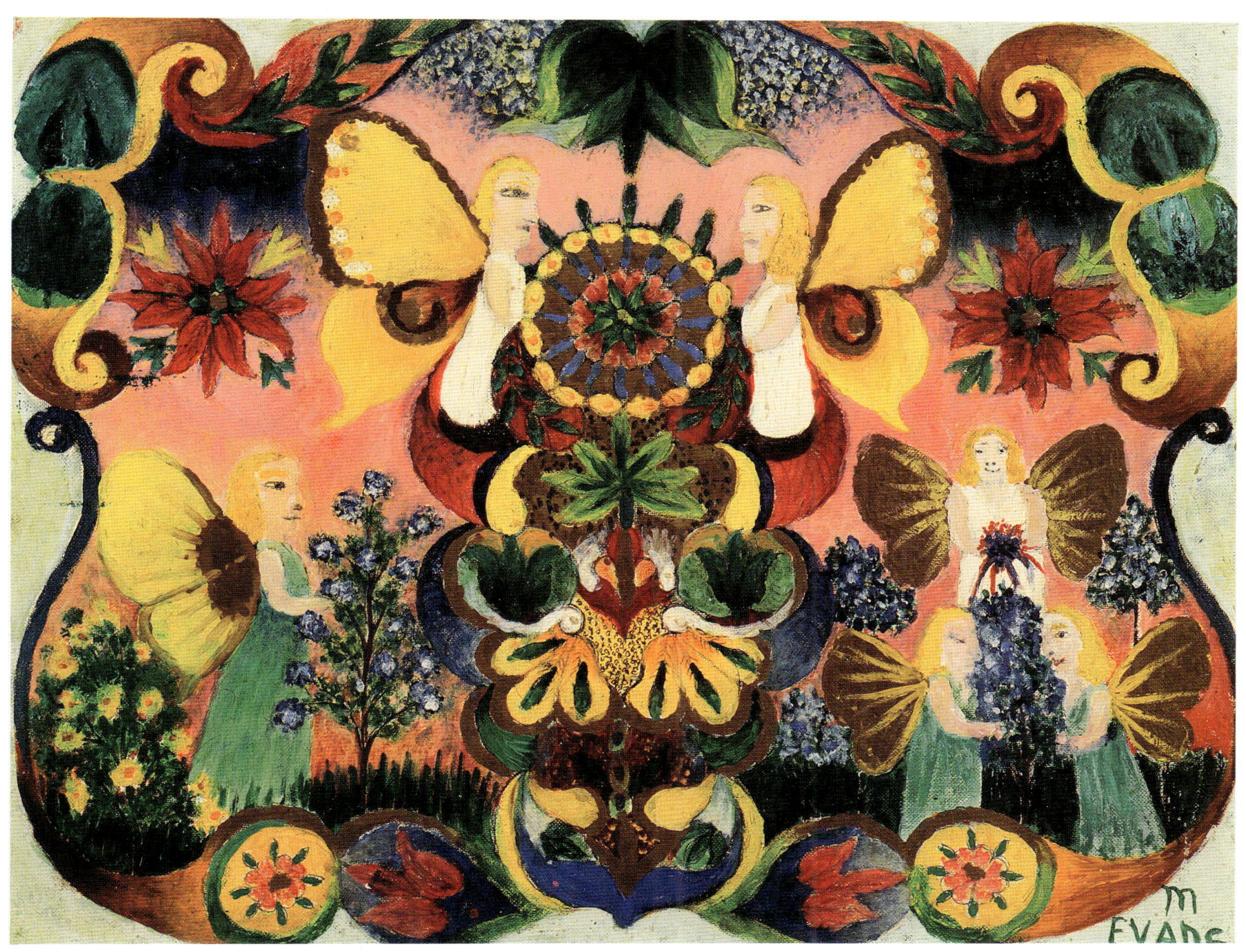

116

MINNIE EVANS

Butterfly Design, ca. 1965

(cat. no. 81)

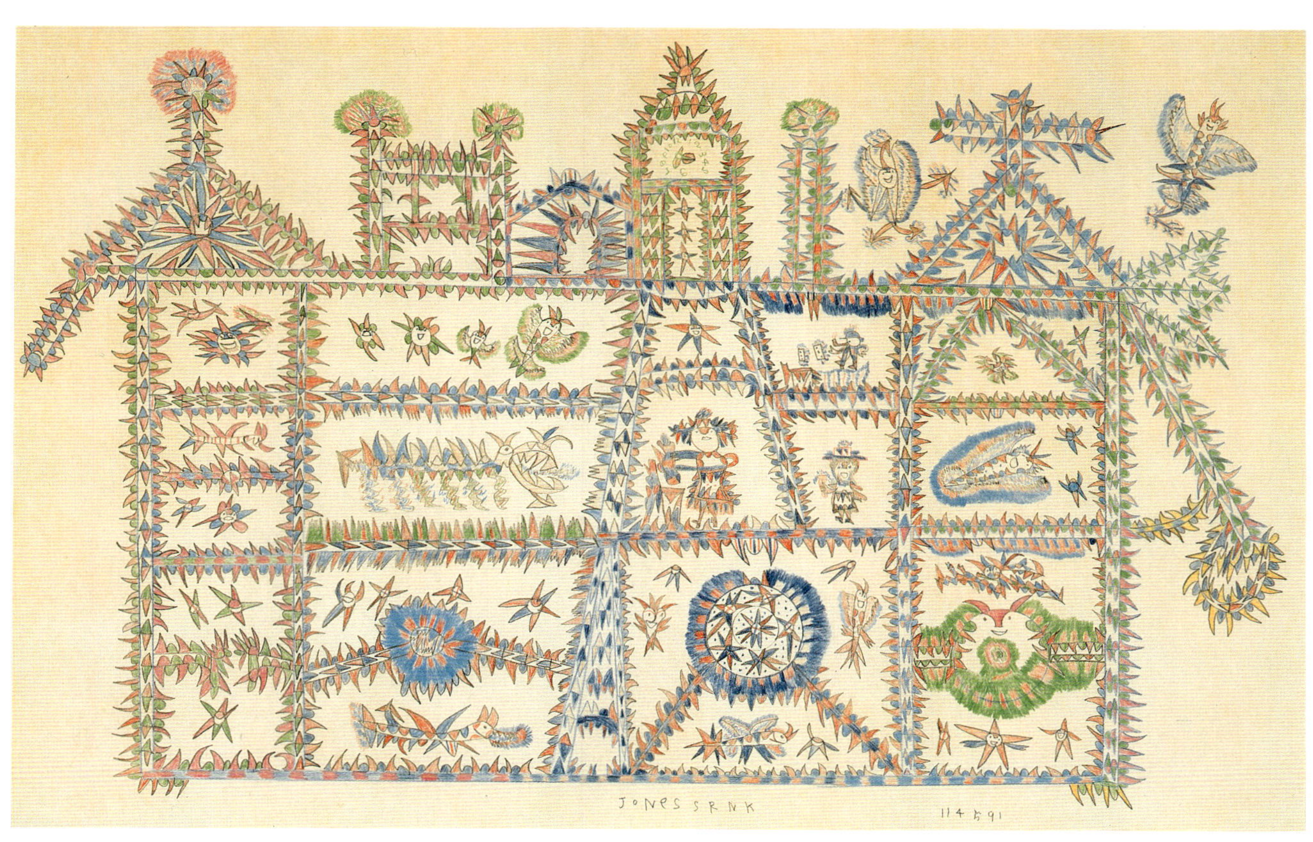

117

FRANK JONES

Devil House, ca. 1968

(cat. no. 138)

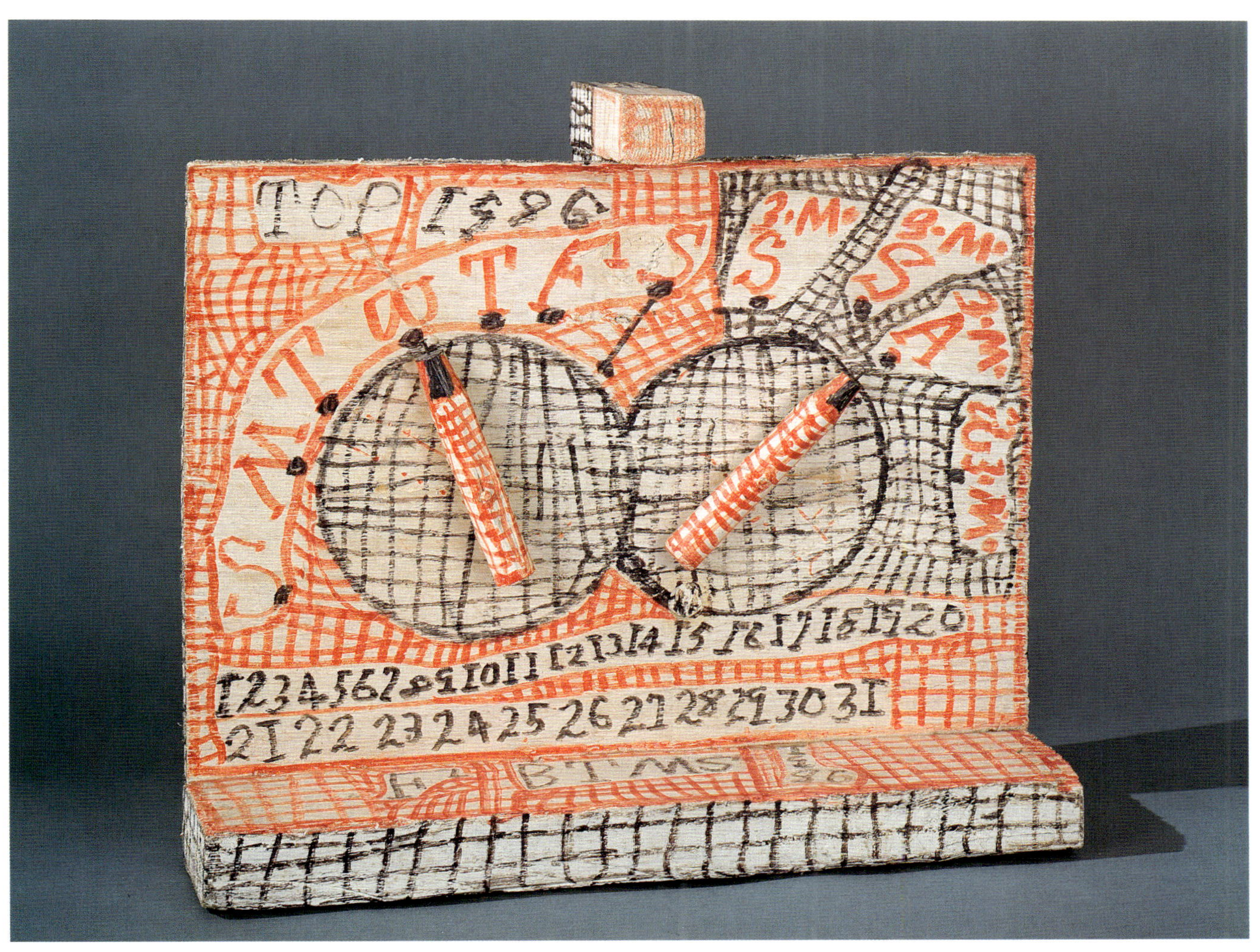

118

ZEBEDEE "Z. B." ARMSTRONG

1986 Weekly/Monthly Calendar, 1986

(cat. no. 4)

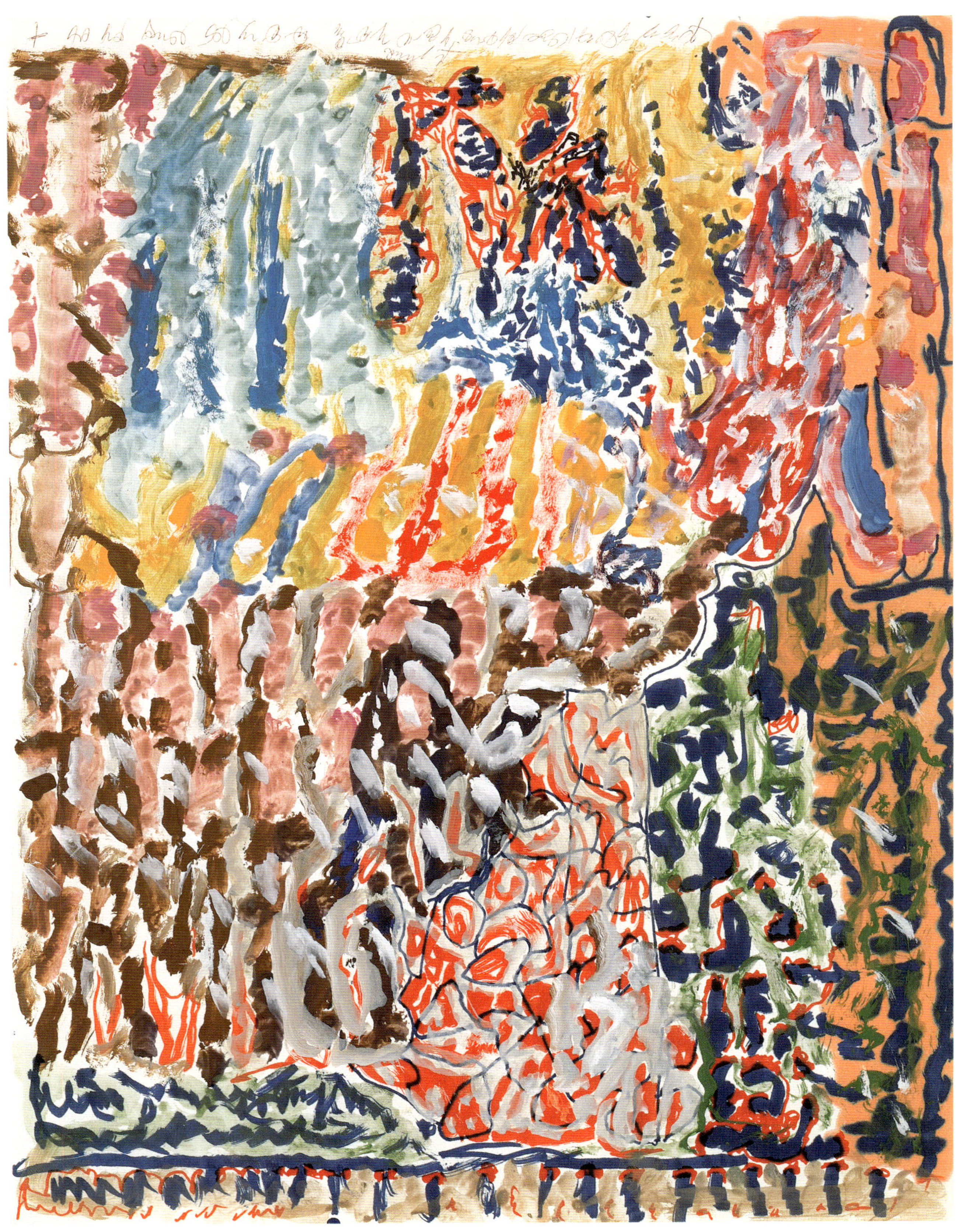

119

JOHN "J. B." MURRY

Untitled, ca. 1986

(cat. no. 183)

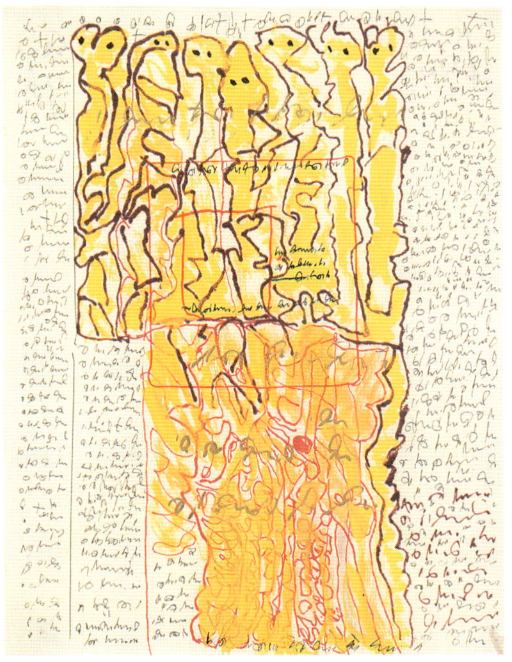

120
JOHN "J. B." MURRY
Untitled, ca. 1980
(cat. no. 181)

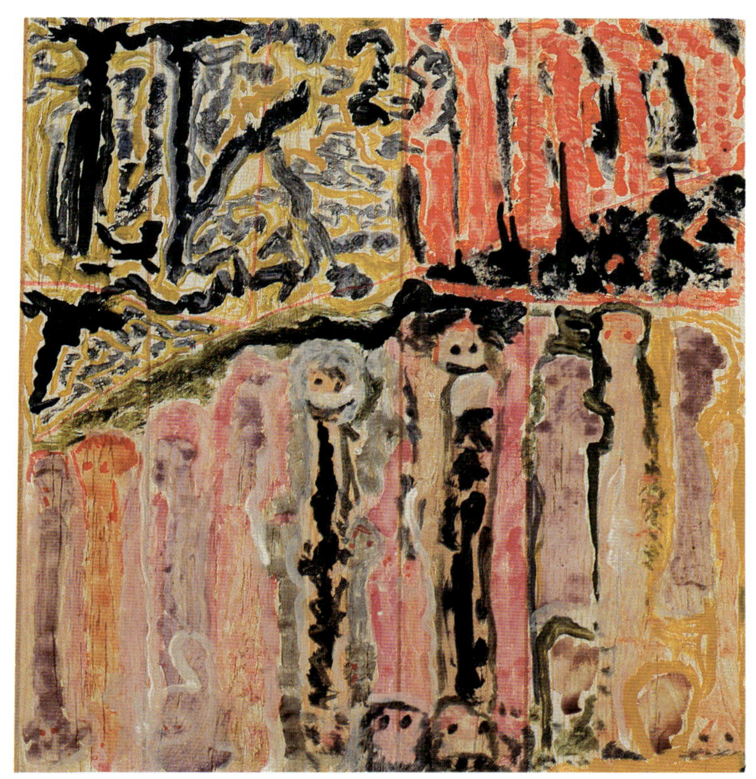

121
JOHN "J. B." MURRY
Untitled, ca. 1975
(cat. no. 180)

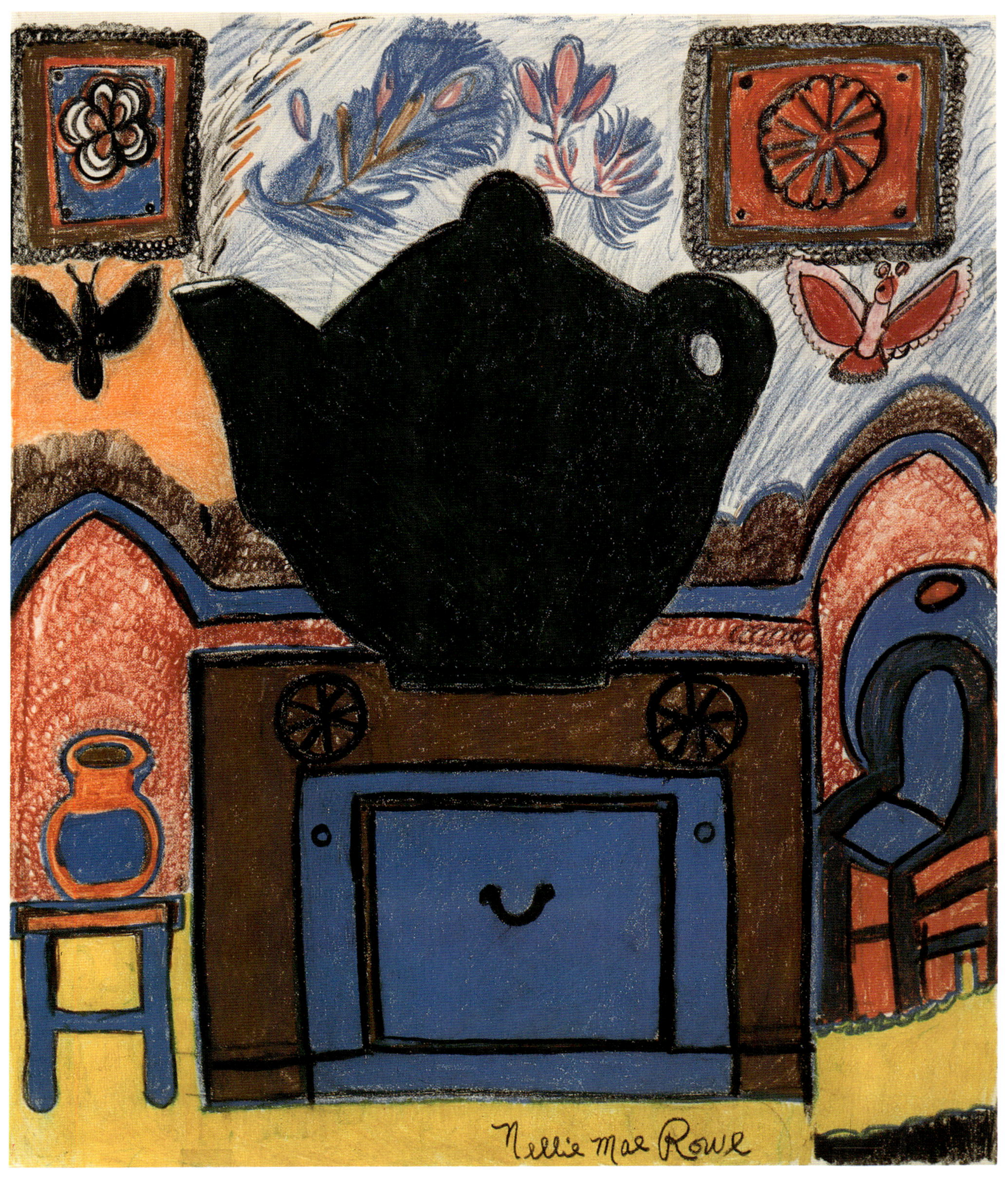

122

NELLIE MAE ROWE

Nellie's Teapot, ca. 1979–80

(cat. no. 200)

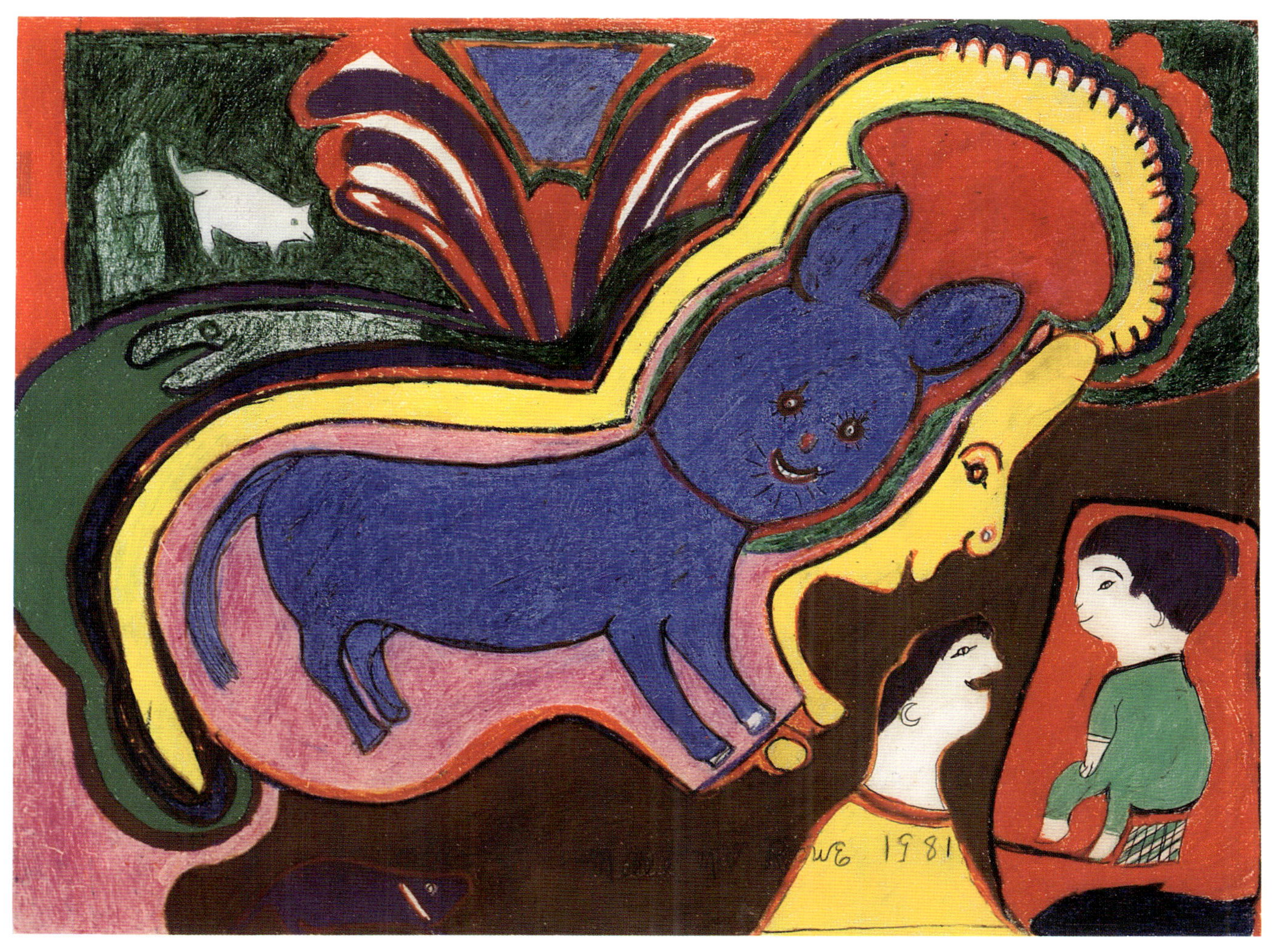

123

NELLIE MAE ROWE

Mother and Child, 1981

(cat. no. 199)

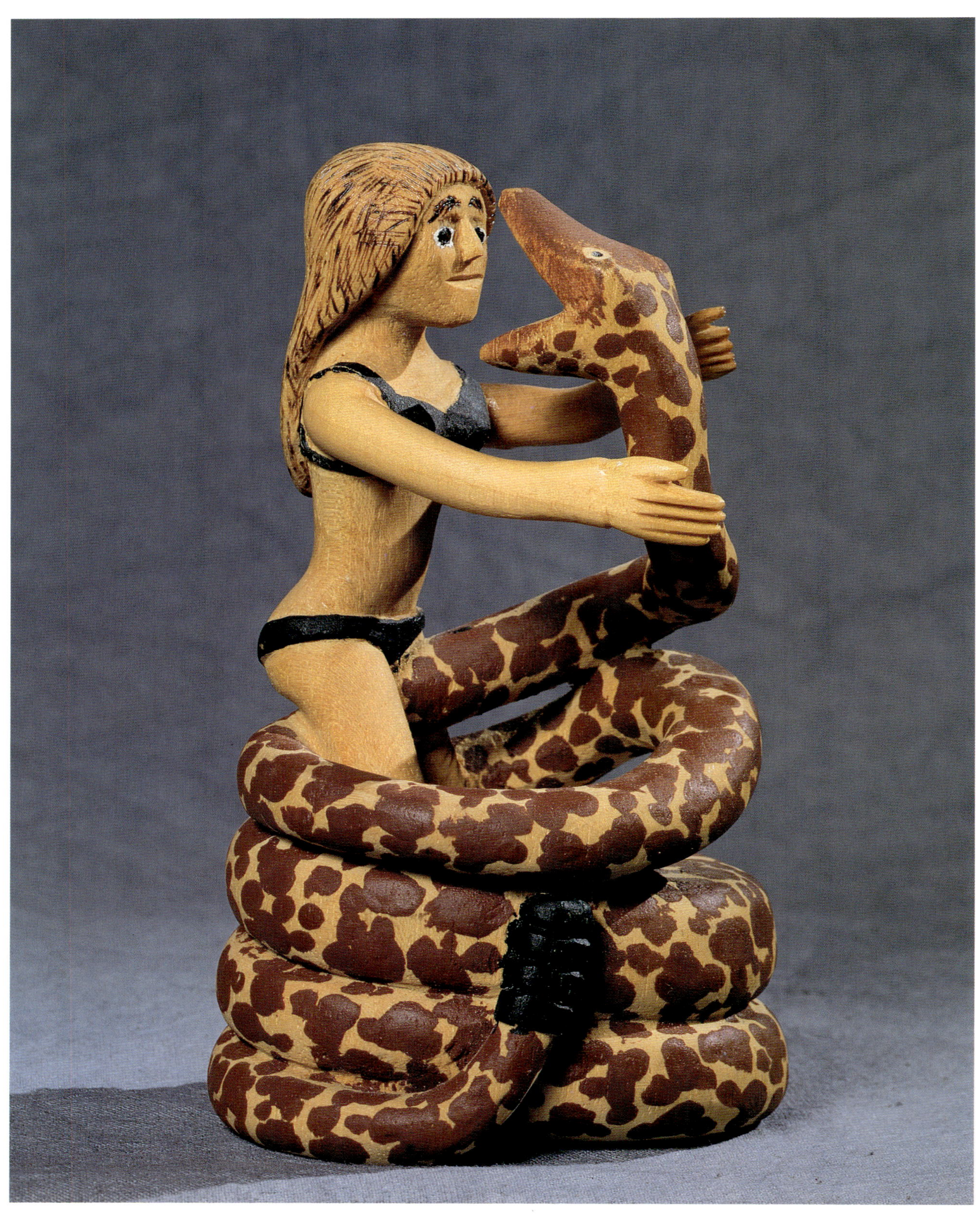

124

SULTAN ROGERS

Snake with Lady, 1991

(cat. no. 198)

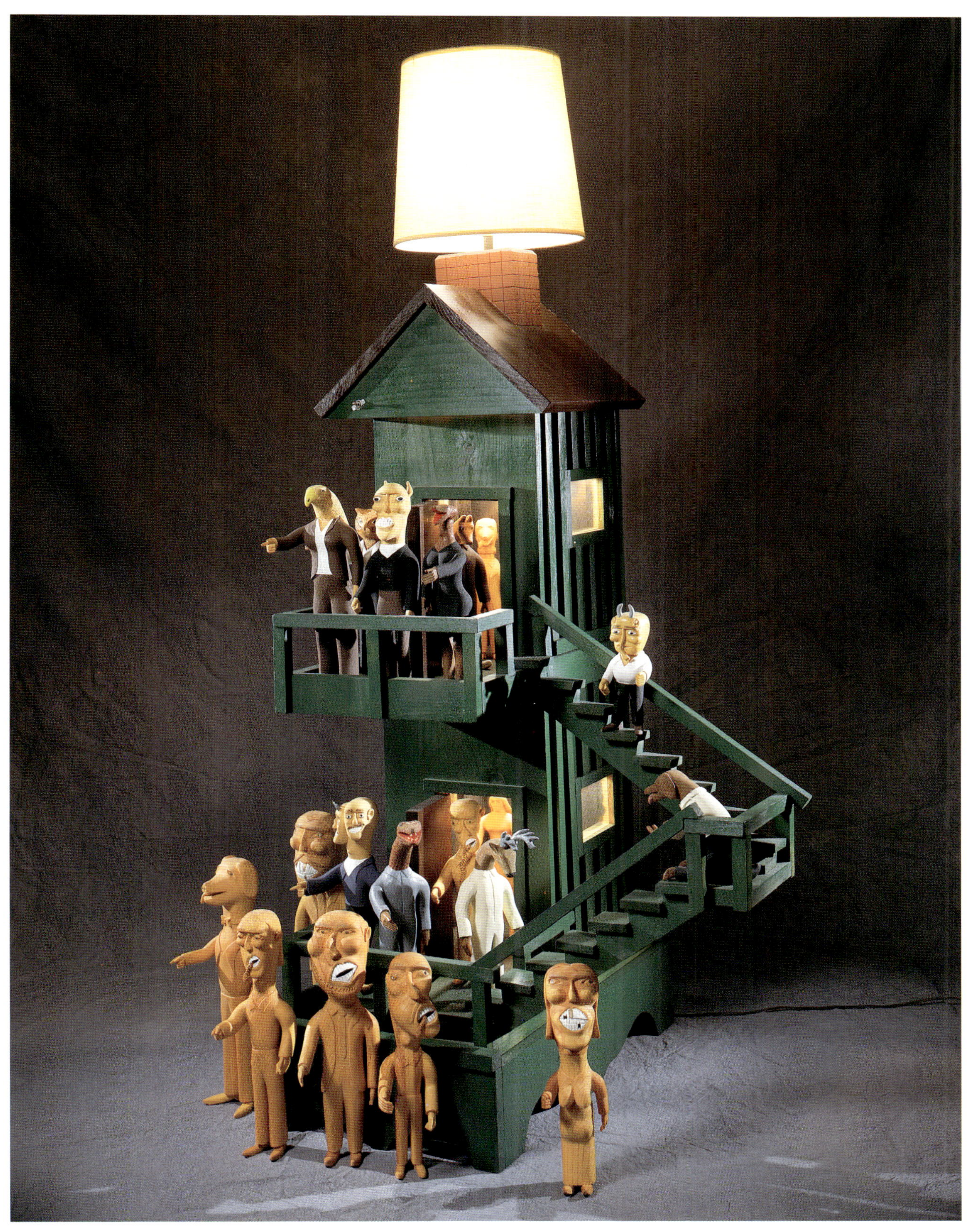

125

SULTAN ROGERS

Haint House, 1987

(cat. no. 196)

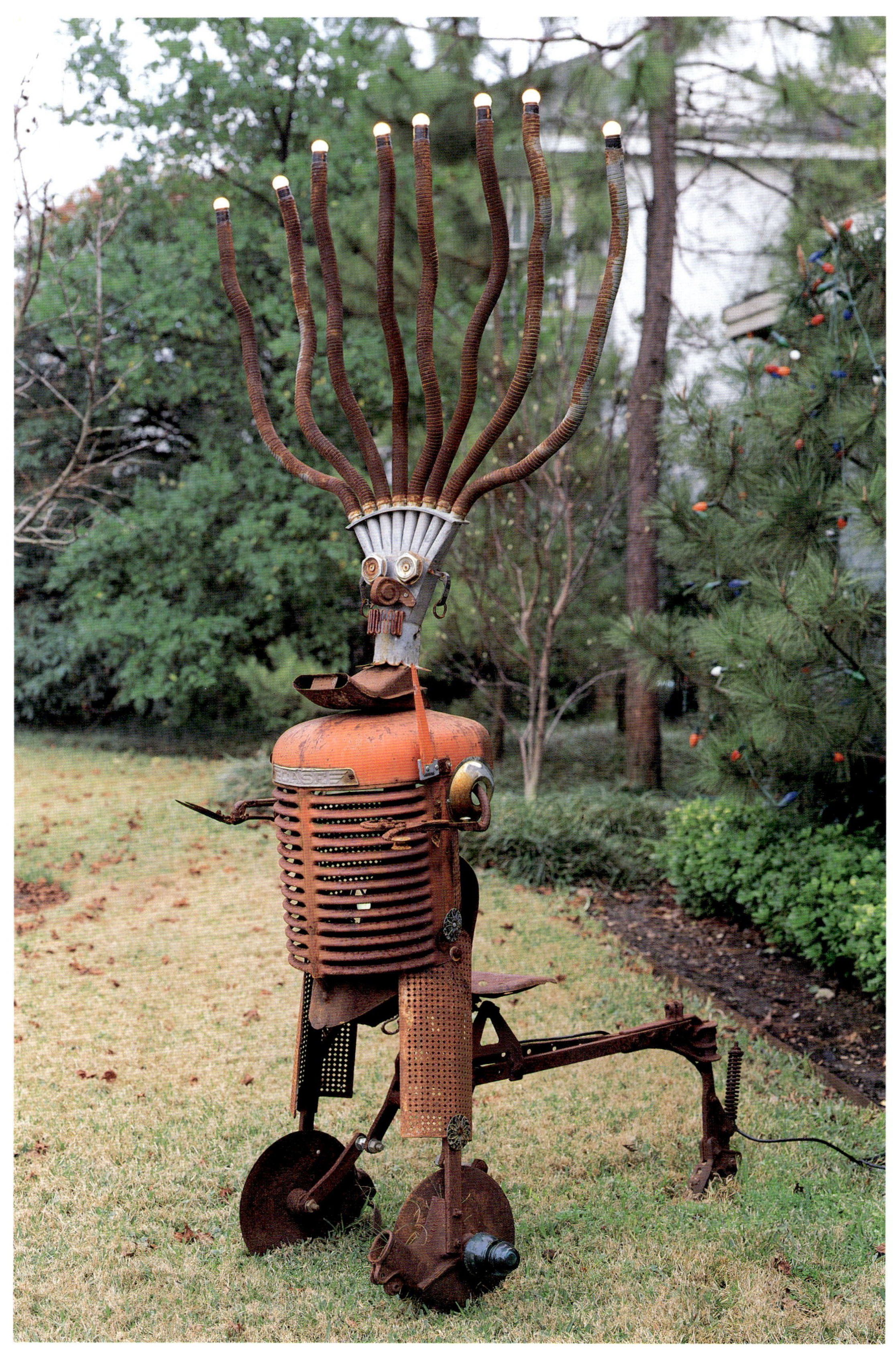

126

DAVID STRICKLAND

Case Alien, 1991

(cat. no. 217)

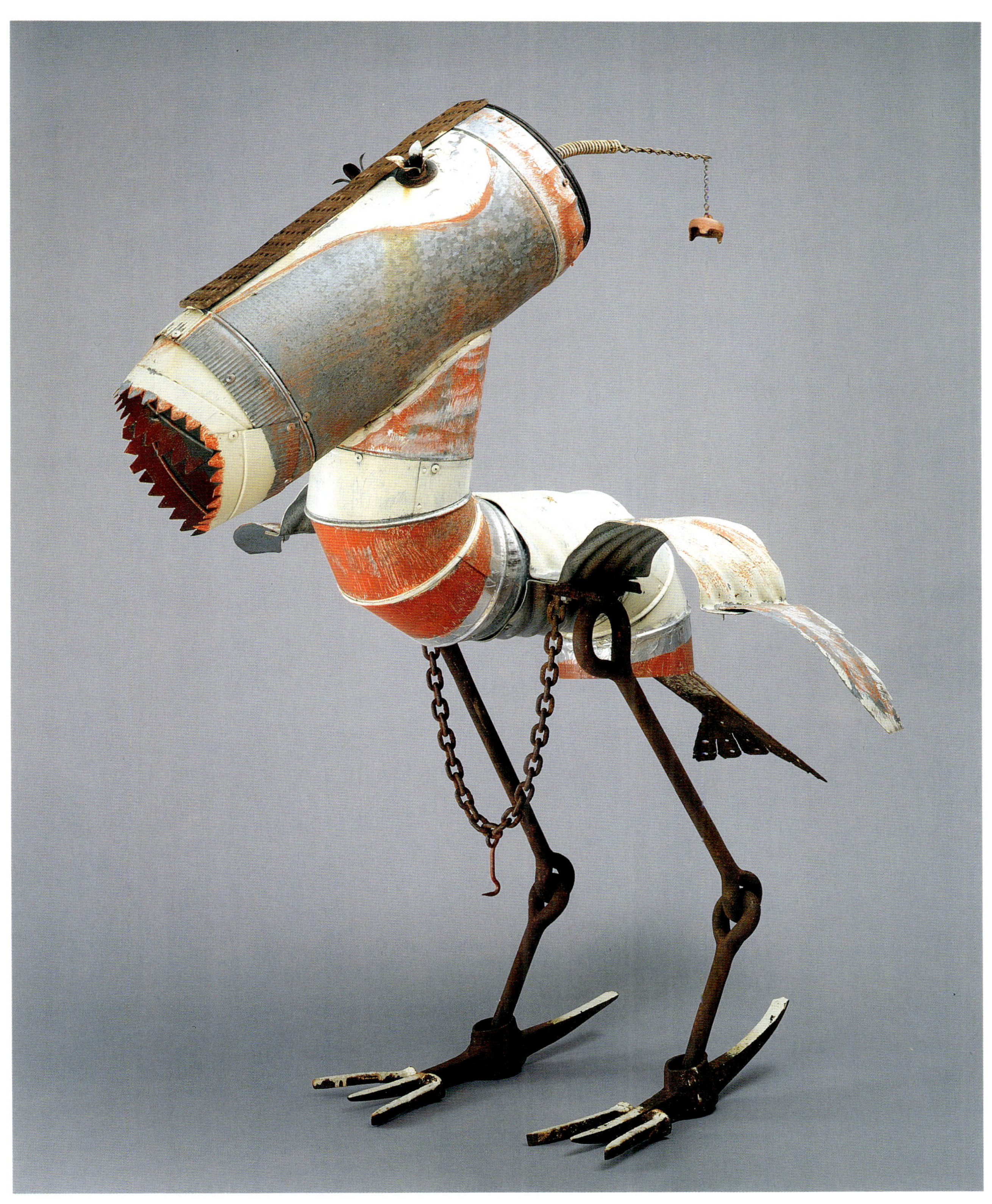

127

DAVID STRICKLAND

Big Bird, 1990

(cat. no. 216)

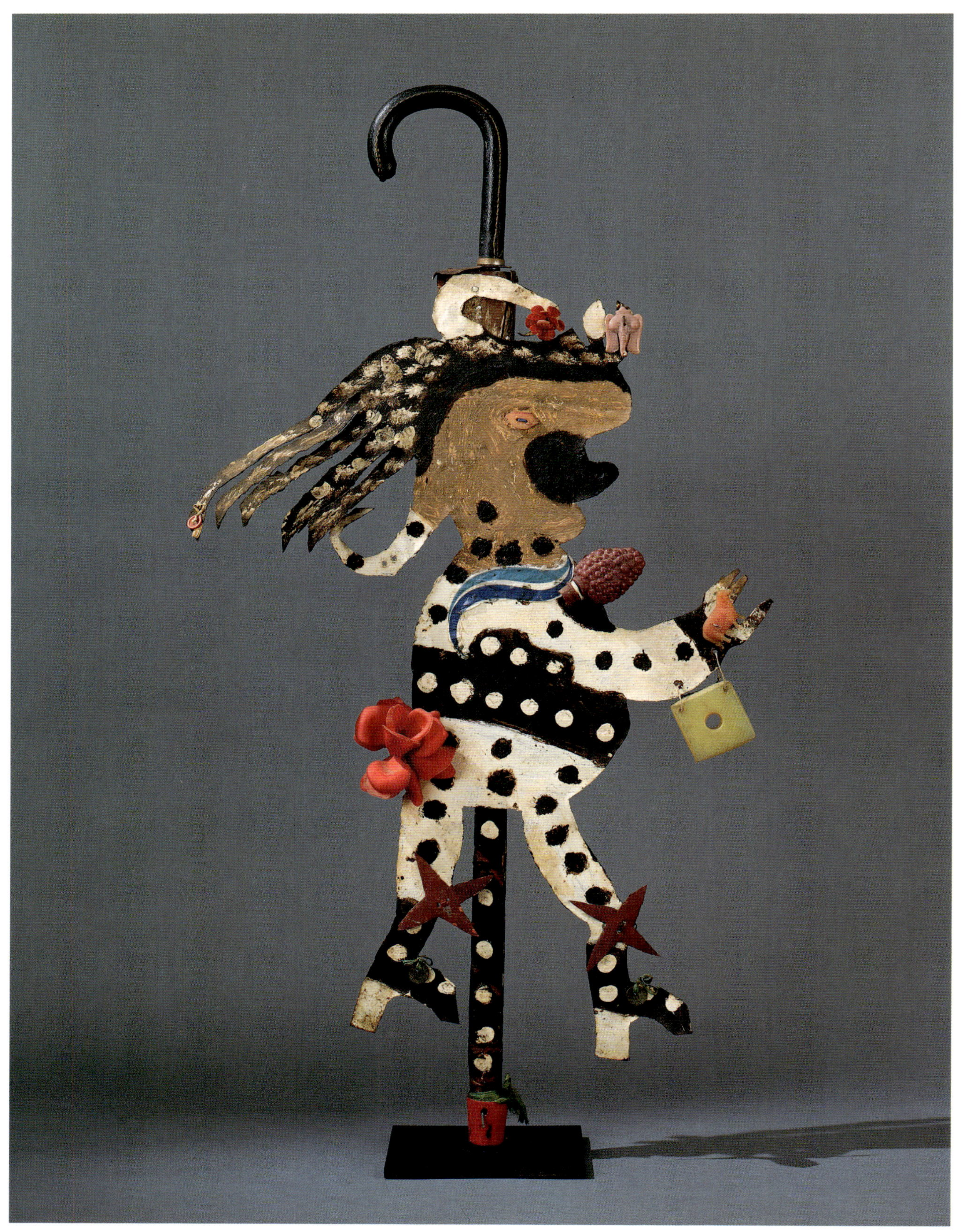

128

DAVID BUTLER

Walking Stick with Figure, ca. 1975

(cat. no. 22)

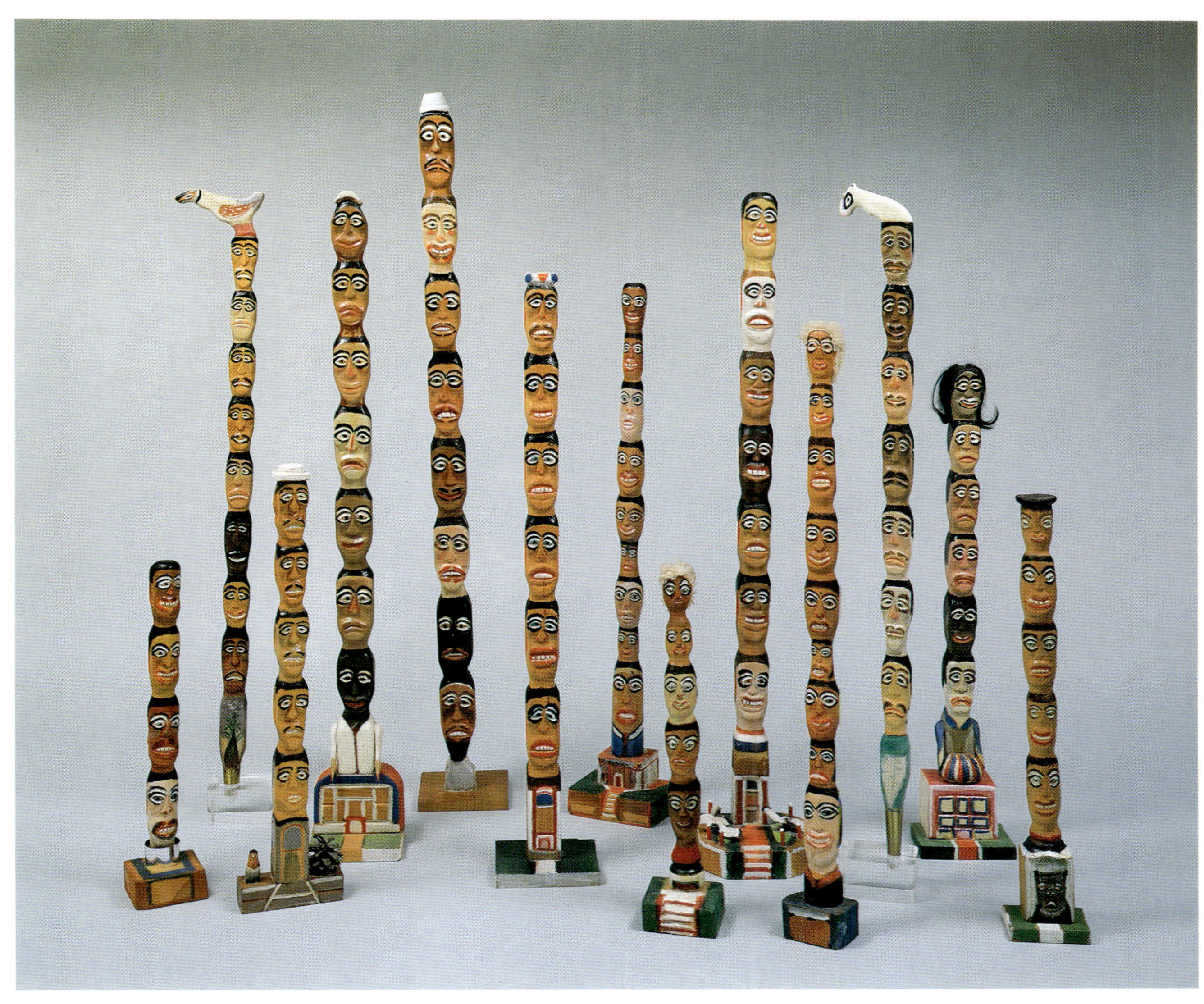

129

WILLIAM DAWSON

Assorted Totems, ca. 1980s

(cat. no. 43)

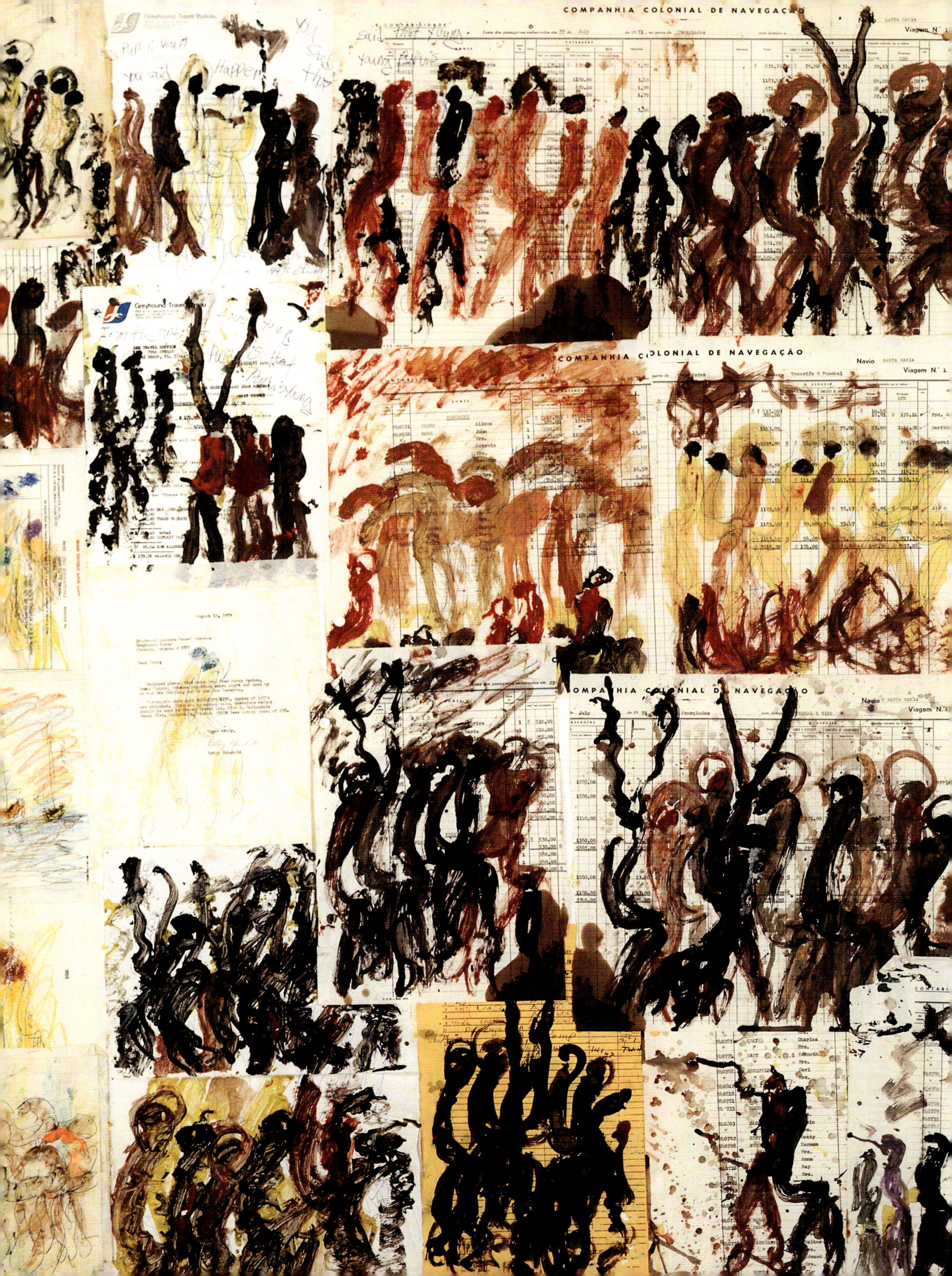

SOCIAL COMMENTARY AND POPULAR CULTURE

Self-taught artists are exposed through the media to national and global issues. Their immediate culture, however, is often based on an oral tradition, and thus their opinions and concerns about the larger world typically do not find expression in written forums. But the visual works of self-taught artists act effectively as windows to their personal points of view, which reveal a continuum of interests ranging from serious societal issues to icons of the purest popular culture.

Through the satisfying yet unthreatening outlet of their artwork, self-taught artists express to society-at-large their attitudes about sometimes controversial, painful, or inherently troubling situations. Particularly in the aftermath of the civil rights movement, open statements by African-Americans—of self-affirmation as well as discontent—have increased, and works by African-Americans make up the bulk of this section. Even though focused on events of national concern, these works are personal, bearing out the larger issues as experienced in the daily lives of the artists.

The socially attuned imagery of southern self-taught artists often focuses on racial problems yet extends to other concerns. The depictions range from slave auctions and Ku Klux Klan lynchings to the struggles of contemporary urban and ghetto life and poverty. Social commentary works by some artists document what they observe but often without consciously taking an activist point of view.

It should be noted, however, that white self-taught artists seldom overtly express social protest in their works. Poor southern whites have not been strangers to poverty or exploitation, and protest has not been absent from their experience, but nevertheless most have accepted, almost fatalistically, what life has presented to them. Instead of protesting the social environment through artwork, white self-taught artists are more likely to comment on life's trials through religious imagery, where the pursuit of salvation promises a better life after death.[1]

But African-Americans have long battled for equality in their daily lives. Nearly half the artists in this exhibition were born before 1910, within two generations of the conclusion of the Civil War. Some black artists have direct family links with slavery. For example, Bill Traylor was born into slavery in 1854, and Steven Ashby, William Edmondson, Josephus Farmer, Ezekiel Gibbs, Elijah Pierce, Clementine Hunter, and Nellie Mae Rowe had at least one parent who was a freed slave. A pervasive oral tradition about slavery was passed down through families in the form of folktales and music. But most of all, the artists' own life experiences of segregation and racism sensitized them to social inequities.

Slavery was one of the world's most pernicious institutions, but it could not entirely strip slaves of their individuality, dignity, and self-expression. It is a testament to the ongoing strength of the human spirit and the African-American race that so many descendants of slaves today express themselves in distinctive individualistic vocabularies as creative self-taught artists.

With both a father and grandfather who had been slaves,[2] Josephus Farmer could draw on personal family experience to imagine a slave auction. Farmer's exquisitely carved and painted relief *Abraham Lincoln and the Slave Auction* (pl. 133) follows a group of slaves from the auction block to emancipation. At the left a sinuous line of carved, nearly freestanding black men, women, and children moves through the intertwining negative space toward an auctioneer who points to a woman and four children about to be sold.[3] To the right is the white facade of the Lincoln Memorial, with

President Lincoln, the great emancipator, seated above an incised inscription, "With one stroke of his pen, he set the slaves free. 1809–1865." The dates give the years of Lincoln's birth and death, and Farmer's incorporation of them into the image is characteristic of his habit of creating a historical framework in his work, particularly in his renderings about the South. The inscription "Auction of slaves 1780s, SC" might be a reference to an event in South Carolina, which Farmer could have read about in his frequently used source, the *American Heritage Illustrated History of the United States*.[4] The Reverend Farmer often cross-referenced historical data with a biblical quote, as he considered southern black history to be parallel to biblical history, and he sought biblical accounts to explain the events of his daily life.[5] In this piece "PS 68:31," carved above the slaves at the top left and beneath the slave auction block, probably refers to a Psalms verse.

A beautifully carved, serpentine gold rope binds the slaves together and contrasts with their dark skin and muscular physiques. Farmer humanized his slave figures by delineating individual body types and activities. Some tote baskets on their heads; a woman carries a child on her back; another gracefully bends toward three figures who scoop water into their mouths. The detail of the incised brick base upon which the auctioneer stands, the delineated baskets, the serrated greenery, and the multicolumned Lincoln Memorial all show Farmer's skillful hand.

Sam Doyle's *Slave* (pl. 130) chronicles the experience of one black man. Seen from behind, centrally positioned on a pale aqua background, a slave is chained to a wall by his legs and arms. Irregular, red brushstrokes on his black skin, blood from a recent whiplash, and a bright yellow loincloth call attention to the powerlessness of his sturdy body. The most striking feature of this work is the commanding anonymity of the slave. Doyle, who typically portrayed the distinguishing characteristics of local heroes (pls. 8, 47, 48), here, by the absence of individuality, suggested the plight of the slaves as depersonalized property. Like Farmer's, Doyle's knowledge of these experiences came through his family history, as his grandfather was a freed slave.

Thornton Dial, Sr., symbolized the trauma of the journey from Africa to America in *Slave Ship* (pl. 134), an early large, painted sculpture from 1987. Fashioned from painted cut metal, wood, wire, industrial compound, and water-based paint, the ship is decorated predominantly in marine colors. Black and white wavy lines on sea blue simulate water and waves. Irregular sails, made of cut tin scraps, complement the design in their painted dot pattern of black, tan, and blue-gray. On the side of the ship, Dial projected a two-dimensional scene of slaves below deck. Four African women, their hair billowing around them,[6] are bound by a painted metal chain that leads the eye through the composition. Between the women are three much smaller figures, black men held by the same painted chain, their bodies fashioned from tin and projected from the flat painted surface. At the rear Dial painted a rape scene, with a white man lying atop a black woman; this inhuman violation, committed directly under the ship's American flag, happened all too often both on the slave ship and later on the southern plantation.

Dial once commented that the white woman and the black man were both slaves, insinuating that neither had the white man's apparent sexual freedom.[7] "Life is a struggle," says Dial, whose commentary expands beyond the scope of his own experience as a rural black Alabaman. Dial, who was born in 1928, witnessed the peak and the collapse of institutionalized segregation. He believes the struggle of the black man applies to all mankind: "The colored man doesn't have freedom like he should have but the white man is also struggling for money and freedom. Freedom is for everyone."

Over the past five years, the tiger has been a major element in Dial's large paintings and drawings and has come to symbolize the struggle for freedom, because, as he observes, "Man has to struggle like the animal." Dial's tiger can also be considered a metaphor for Perry "Tiger" Thomason, "a white-skinned black man" who, as leader of CIO Labor Union 1466, fought in the 1960s for the rights of union workers in the artist's hometown of Bessemer, Alabama.

In *The Longest Tail Tiger in the United States* (pl. 136), a tiger is outlined with thickly painted, broken black lines. Within it and all around it, the chaos of struggle is revealed in a web of textured, intertwining, curvilinear lines of brown, black, red, blue, and white. Dial juxtaposes his depictions of the tiger with portrayals of a bird representing freedom, as in *Life Go On* (pl. 135). The bird, says Dial, "is flying free. . . . [and] is like a white man because he's free."

Urban life and its struggle are portrayed in the works of Herbert Singleton and Purvis Young. Born in the 1940s, both African-American artists formulated the content of their work from their awareness of the civil rights movement, black consciousness, and ghetto poverty.

Herbert Singleton, who lives on the outskirts of New Orleans, began carving at age seventeen. His first pieces were walking sticks, which he sold to

Big Hat Willie, a notorious New Orleans pimp, and other drug dealers to pay off personal debts.[8] Singleton, a streetwise yet spiritual and engaging man, continues to make walking sticks, along with carved totems up to ten feet high, narrative wall plaques, carved doors, and tree stumps highlighted with enamel paint.

In *Behind the Eight Ball* (pl. 132), a white man lunges toward a black man, pressing a flaming red torch against his outstretched hand. The black man's right leg is clinched by a biting dog; his left leg is chained to a billiard eight ball. The scene symbolizes the struggle of the black urban male who strives on many levels to get out from "behind the eight ball." This street phrase, common for blacks and whites, derives from the game of pool and means having the odds against you, a view consistent with Singleton's portrayal of a white man's position of empowerment over a black man.

Singleton's highly energized, taut, and compact use of space emphasizes the tension of the scene, and solid, bright colors accentuate the relief's key subjects. The stark white suit and hat of the pursuer suggest the garments of a plantation owner, but the well-dressed, knife-wielding black man seems to be an urban dweller, not a field hand. That the white man threatens but never actually touches the black man suggests the sophisticated manner in which prejudice exists today.

Singleton inscribed his sentiments on the work: "My affliction have brought me to shame. I am among a nation of people that have no mercy on the hearts and souls of black people. I can only say this is a good night to die." Singleton, who served "twenty years in prison on and off,"[9] sees himself as a savvy observer of life as it is.[10] His imagery often focuses on the daily struggles of life in ghetto neighborhoods, the source of his experience.

In Singleton's horizontal wall relief, *Catch Me If You Can* (pl. 131), two hooded men with a noose in hand pursue a black man, who seems to taunt them from behind a tree. The carved, textured surface bears the creative mark of his individual hand. The solid yellow background contrasts with the dark-colored tree and black-skinned man, while the red cuffs and hood of the Ku Klux Klan members balance with the victim's red shirt. The bent shape of the rope and noose echoes that of the branches and trunk of the tree.

Singleton's lynching scene suggests a lyrical dance with death. The black man smiles, believing he can beat it, as Singleton himself might have done (he says that *Catch Me If You Can* is based on personal experience).[11] Aesthetically powerful yet elegantly simple, the scene is touched with irony but little fear. Many whites once believed that the threat of lynching deterred black crime,[12] but Singleton treats this serious subject with satire: "The more amusing, the better the piece comes out because you be laughing at what you be creating, though it's really a serious thing."[13]

Purvis Young, who grew up in an urban Miami ghetto in the Overton area, says that "the street is life."[14] And it is from the street that he finds the source of his imagery: "I go down there in the environment. I go down there and look at the people. I like to walk among the peoples, ride my bike with the peoples, and listen to the peoples."[15]

Purvis constructed his first public mural in 1973, when he attached hundreds of painted plywood panels to the sides of dilapidated buildings on an Overton street, veiling the harsher reality of the surrounding ghetto. Within less than a decade, Young had developed such a reputation that he was commissioned to create murals for the Metro-Dade Public Library (1983), the Culmer/Overton Branch Library (1984), and a local Metrorail station (1986).

Young sometimes both chronicles and protests the phenomena he observes, for he himself is, on occasion, a man of protest.[16] He has developed his own recurring symbolic imagery. Clusters of sinuous, rhythmic vertical lines rising to the sky represent the uplifted arms of individual figures that protest unemployment, crime, and other social ills as they seek to escape their ghetto bondage. "Each figure," says Young, "tells a story."[17]

In Burial over the City, upstretched arms of calligraphic lines rise above a cluster of buildings, lifting a corpse to the heavens (pl. 142). With crosses and a crosslike canvas top, the work's format suggests a spiritual connection. When asked if he was religious, Young responded that he "looked up in the sky, to tell Him thank you. I don't listen to man too much."[18] Similar attenuated figures appear in *Peoples and Boats* (pl. 145), a collage of disparate works which creates a rhythmic whole, and in *The Boat People* (pl. 143), a painted six-foot door that alludes to the arrival of Haitian refugees in Miami in the 1980s. Depicted rising en masse from boats in a misty but fiery orange, black, and subdued gray field, these pulsating figures typify Young's excellent use of gestural line and expressive color.

In *Angels over the City* (pl. 144), the looming heads of two figures dominate the canvas as they hover over a cluster of city buildings. The pain of the city is portrayed in the tearful look of the angels, recalling Young's comment that "sometimes I go and cry when I hear what happens to people."[19] Such figures with oval faces, looming over a dense cityscape, typically represent sources of hope and inspiration to the artist. Young's painterly brush and uniquely constructed frames make aesthetically superb statements on contemporary subjects.

Archie Byron described an inhospitable street environment in his sculpture titled *Despair* (pl. 140). An unusual combination of built-up sawdust, glue, and paint, this molded figure of a homeless person speaks, through one man's expression, of the plight of contemporary ghetto life. The artist, a former Atlanta city councilman, is fully aware of the despair of the underprivileged. He exhibited this work in city hall while trying to pass legislation on behalf of the homeless.

A white artist whose imagery reflects an awareness of social issues is Miles Carpenter. He carved *Wounded Knee* (pl. 141) in 1973, when Native Americans were demonstrating at Wounded Knee, South Dakota, in commemoration of the 1890 massacre of 220 Indians by the U.S. cavalry.[20] In Carpenter's sculpture, which is carved, painted, and clothed, a young man stands on crutches, his right leg severed above the knee. The artist intended that the angelic, peaceful face (which shows no signs of Native American heritage) and the "wounded knee" would show "man's humanity and inhumanity to man in one piece."[21]

Charlie Lucas is a deeply spiritual, philosophical man whose social commentary focuses on humankind's disregard for nature. In *Mother Nature Stood Up to Take the World Back Cause Man Has Abused Her Body* (pl. 139), pastel tones record the artist's personally conceived environmental symbolism. Lucas described the work's imagery: "Mother Nature shows that man comes in and dumps the nuclear waste and created a spot in the earth. Man pushed the trees away so that the birds didn't have nowhere to lay the egg."[22] One bird holds an egg in its mouth, unable to find a nesting site because the earth's landscape has been altered by man's harmful actions. The sleek, green woman at the left represents nature; behind her the outline of a man's body represents humankind's disruption of natural forces.

The lines between political, historical, social, and cultural phenomena blur in the face of the media machine, where everything becomes entertainment. Even presidents are cultural figures who, to succeed, must transform themselves from simple politicians into icons, much as Roosevelt, Kennedy, and Reagan did. Self-taught artists live amid the blitz of popular culture—television, magazines, books, advertisements, travel brochures, popular songs, postcards—and its imagery appears in their work. Their popular culture artworks usually contain easily recognizable subject matter, which the artist uniquely interprets and imbues with personal meaning.

Howard Finster drew on images from popular culture as part of his overall missionary plan to spread the word of God. His artworks have featured Elvis Presley, Hank Williams, the Talking Heads, and various U.S. presidents, but one of his most frequently rendered images from the late 1970s to the present is a painted wooden cutout of a Coca-Cola bottle. In an early example (pl. 148), human figures, each drinking from a Coke-shaped bottle, sparsely cover a plain field. Beneath the bottle's cap, the artist inscribed, "Eat drink and be merry for tomorrow ye may die."

This cutout probably served as a prototype for similar Coca-Cola cutouts produced since the 1980s in multiple copies,[23] which ensured a wider audience for Finster's religious message. Finster later combined popular culture images with religiously oriented words and symbols in the Coca-Cola cutouts. One such work (private collection) depicts a church and a Model T car and reads, "Millions of church folks drink Coke and drive home safely." An inscription at the bottom rim of the Coke bottle—"the bottom is as low as you can go"—ties his evangelical philosophy to his popular culture imagery.

Elvis Presley, the best-known southern entertainer of the twentieth century, is widely represented in the work of self-taught artists. Finster's large Elvis cutout is identified by the singer's signature black pompadour hairstyle and elongated face (pl. 147). James Harold Jennings also represented him (pl. 149). Born in Mississippi and raised in Tennessee, Elvis made seminal contributions to the creation of rockabilly, an unmistakably southern sound that synthesized rock and roll, hillbilly, and white and black gospel music with the blues.[24]

Sam Doyle depicted musician Ray Charles, wearing his hallmark sunglasses, on irregular shaped tin marked "Rae" on the top left corner (cat. no. 68). The color scheme is limited; the white background and white suit contrast with Charles's dark face and the brown piano. Charles, a major rhythm-and-blues musician, blended gospel with pop and the blues, and successfully incorporated country and western music into his sound.[25]

Television entertainers provided a visual source for Jimmy Lee Sudduth. His portrayal of comedian Red Skelton is simply designed on a small scale in muted earth tones (pl. 151), while his depiction of the pop star Cher is more colorful and decorative (cat. no. 219).

Black professional athletes served as symbols of immense national pride for African-Americans. Jackie Robinson, painted on tin with house paint by

Sam Doyle, was the first black baseball player to enter the major leagues in 1947 (cat. no. 65). Joe Louis, considered one of the twentieth century's greatest boxers, was the second black heavyweight champion of the world, from 1937 to 1949.[26] Sam Doyle made a full-figure painting of Louis, in boxing shorts and gloves, identified by his nickname, Brown Bomber (pl. 152). Due to his "clean living" and "God-fearing ways," southern blacks viewed Louis as a significant hero and a cultural icon.[27]

Taken in historical perspective, the popular culture icon can in fact become an agent for social change. The Reverend Jesse Jackson recently commented on the importance of the black athlete as a trailblazer who becomes part of the African-American consciousness: "Athletes led the way for social transformation. . . . Joe Louis taught us we can fight back with dignity and conquer."[28]

NOTES

1. Bill C. Malone, professor of history, Tulane University, shared his insights on this issue with ARY, March 1993.

2. Joanne Cubbs, *The Gift of Josephus Farmer* (Milwaukee: Milwaukee Art History Gallery, University of Wisconsin, 1982), p. 8.

3. The medium brown skin of Lincoln, the auctioneer, and his two attendants is probably a result of Farmer's available paint combined with yellowing varnish and not due to any complex racial statement on the artist's part; Joanne Cubbs, interview, ARY, March 1993.

4. Cubbs, *The Gift of Josephus Farmer*, p. 25.

5. Joanne Cubbs, interview, ARY, Feb. 1993.

6. Barbara Archer, curator, Arnett collection, interview, ARY, Feb. 1993.

7. This and subsequent quotes are Thornton Dial, Sr., interview, KAG, Feb. 1993. Dial, an African-American, spent the first thirty years of his life in the segregated town of Bessemer, Alabama, and well understood this phenomenon.

8. Singleton says that if he were not working with A. J. Boudreaux, his dealer, he would be making walking sticks or "something for protection" to beat up people; interview, ARY, Jan. 1992.

9. Herbert Singleton, interview, ARY, Jan. 1992.

10. Robert Knott, *Diving in the Spirit* (Winston-Salem, N.C.: Wake Forest University Fine Arts Gallery, 1992), p. 13.

11. A. J. Boudreaux, Singleton's dealer, interview, ARY, Feb. 1992.

12. Eighty-two percent of all lynchings since 1882 occurred in the South; 84 percent of southern victims were black, and more than 95 percent of the victims were male; see William I. Hair, "Lynching," *ESC*, p. 173. By 1945, when Singleton was born, lynching occurred only infrequently, and by 1950 it had virtually ceased.

13. Herbert Singleton, interview, ARY, Jan. 1992.

14. Cesar Trasobares, "Purvis Young, Me and My People" (Miami: Main Library–Metro Dade Cultural Center, 1989), unpaginated.

15. Purvis Young, interview, ARY, May 1992.

16. Young was once arrested for protesting the Vietnam War; ibid.

17. Purvis Young, interview, KAG, Feb. 1993.

18. Young says he does believe in a supreme being, but not Christ or Buddha specifically, although both figures appear in his imagery; ibid.

19. Purvis Young, interview, ARY, May 1992.

20. Accounts of the Wounded Knee demonstrations were widely published in 1973. According to Jeff Camp, Carpenter's longtime dealer, the artist was an observer more than a social activist, but he was moved by the demonstrators' arguments; interview, KAG, Feb. 1993.

21. Ibid.

22. Charlie Lucas, interview, ARY, Aug. 1992.

23. I am grateful to Tom Patterson, author of *Howard Finster: Stranger from Another World* (New York: Abbeville, 1989), for corroborating this fact and for the information that, since at least the early 1980s, the artist's family members have aided Finster by cutting the shapes from a template (designed by Finster) and applying a base coat of paint. Finster might then paint as many as five to ten cutouts at a time.

24. Stephen R. Tucker, "Elvis Presley," *ESC*, p. 1077.

25. Robert Bowman, "Ray Charles," *ESC*, p. 1049.

26. Randy Roberts, "Boxing," *ESC*, p. 1214.

27. Ibid.

28. "Rights Leader Calls Sports Teaching Tool," *USA Today*, Feb. 26, 1993, p. 1.

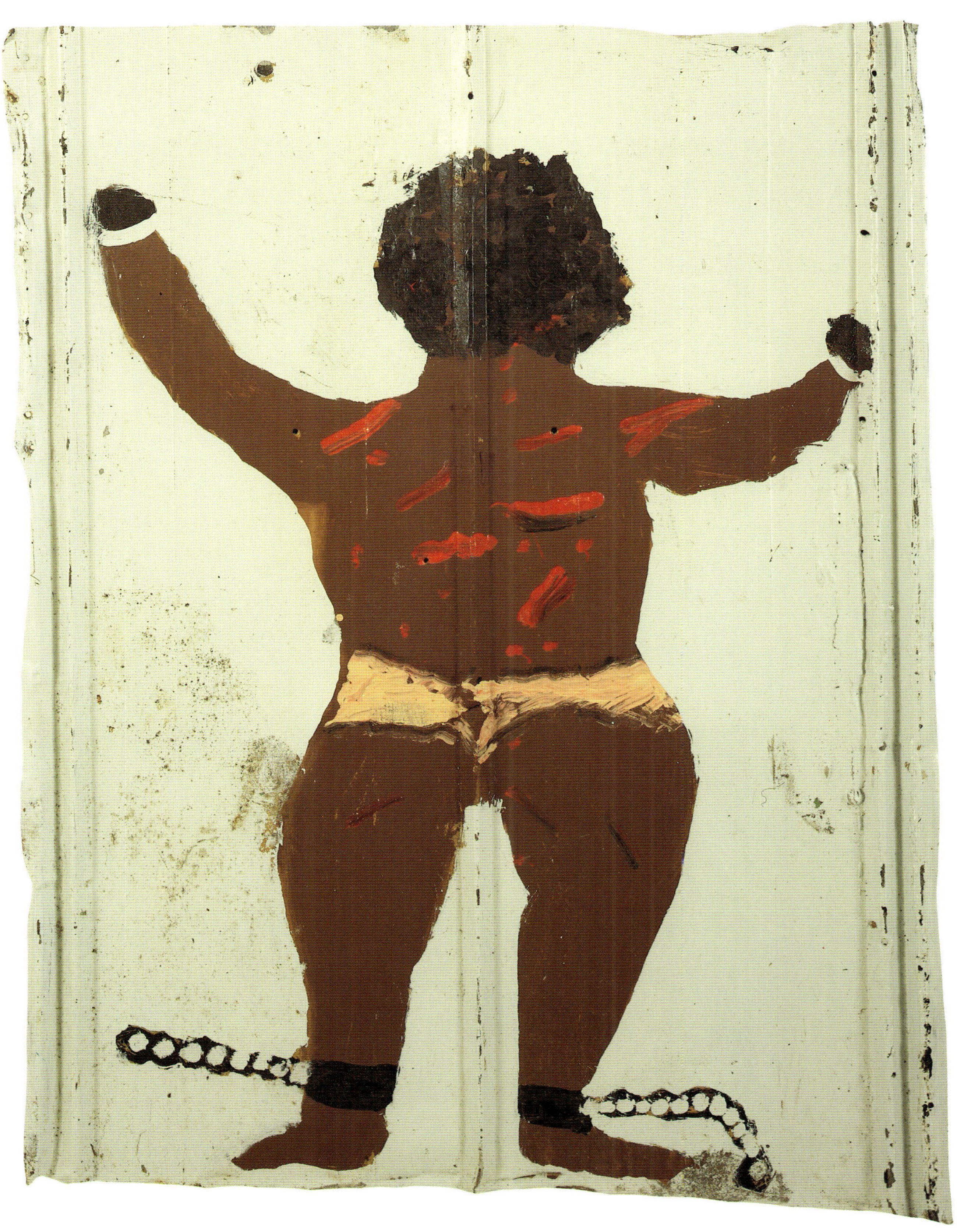

130

SAM DOYLE

Slave, n.d.

(cat. no. 70)

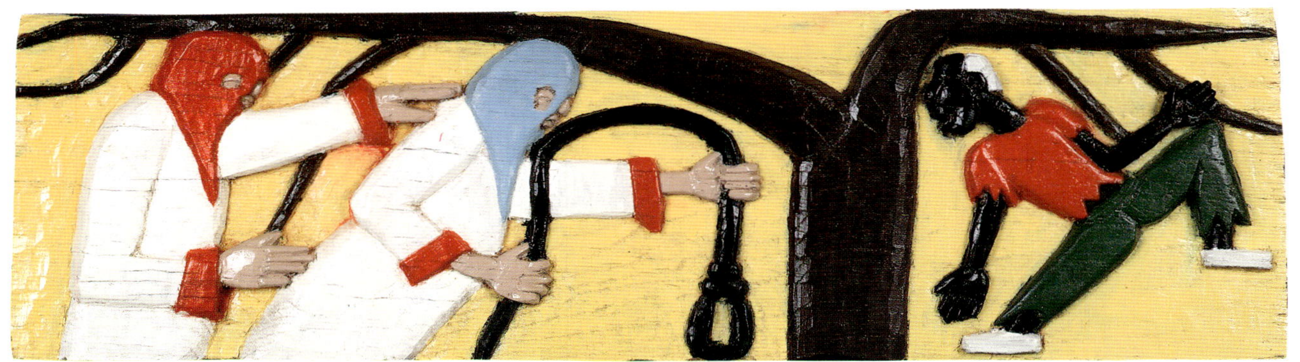

131
HERBERT SINGLETON
Catch Me If You Can, 1989
(cat. no. 210)

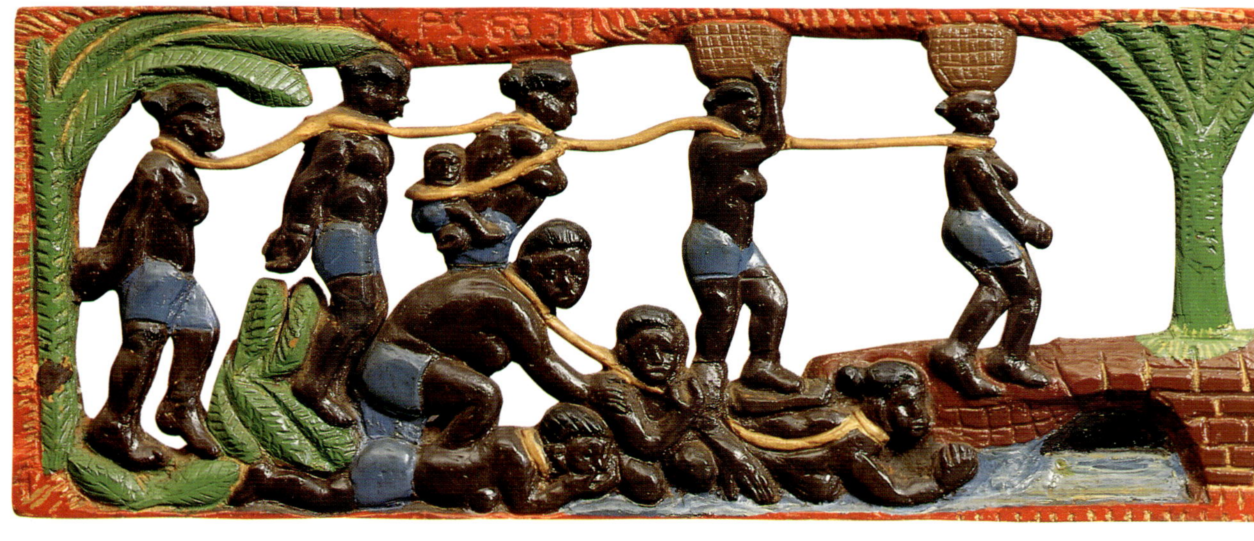

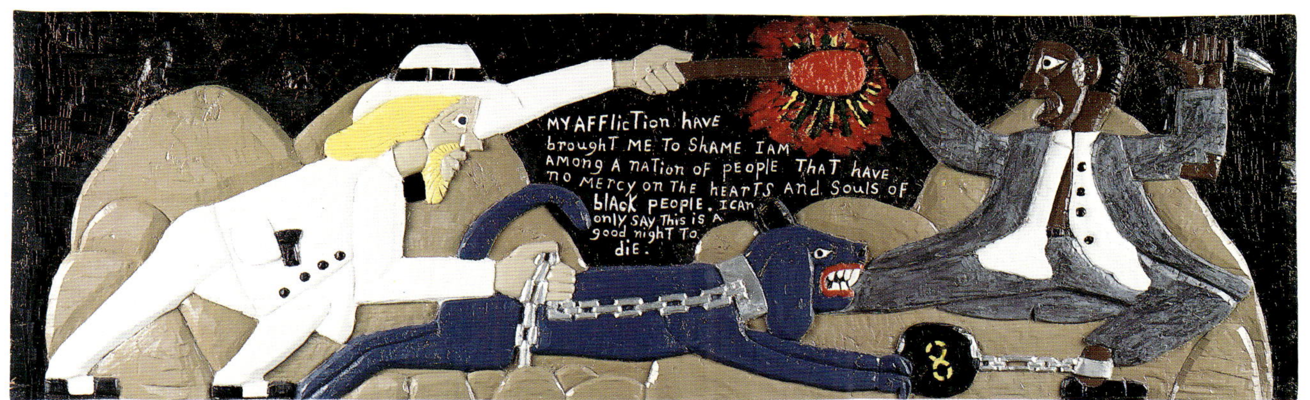

132

HERBERT SINGLETON

Behind the Eight Ball, 1991

(cat. no. 209)

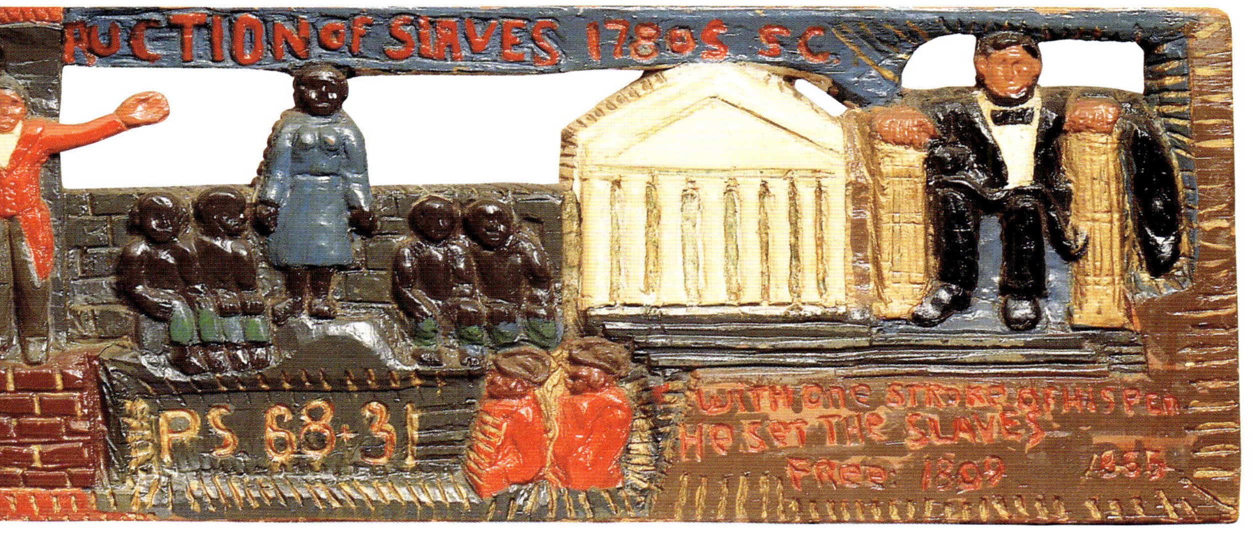

133

JOSEPHUS FARMER

Abraham Lincoln and the Slave Auction, ca. 1979

(cat. no. 82)

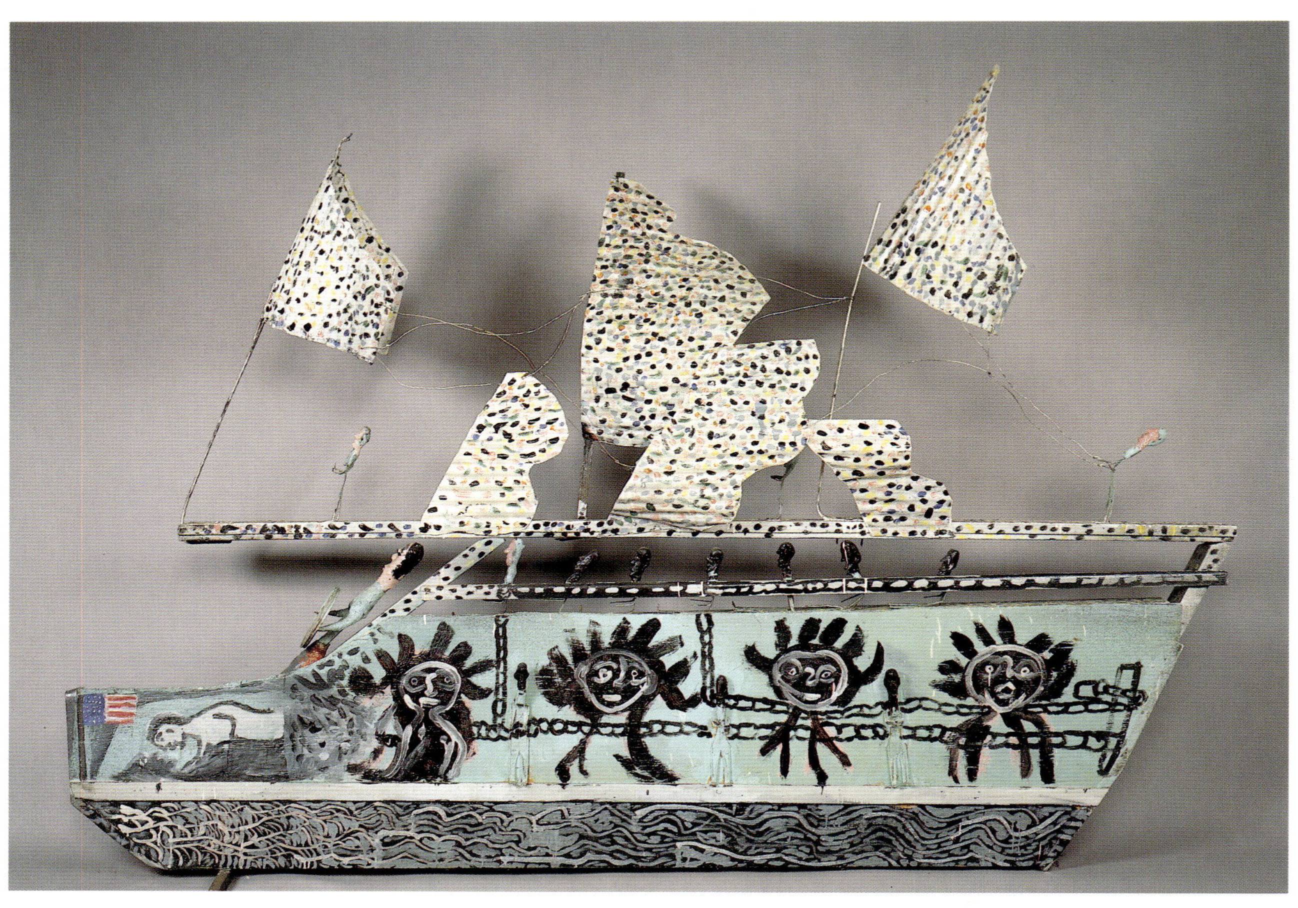

134

THORNTON DIAL, SR.

Slave Ship, 1987

(cat. no. 59)

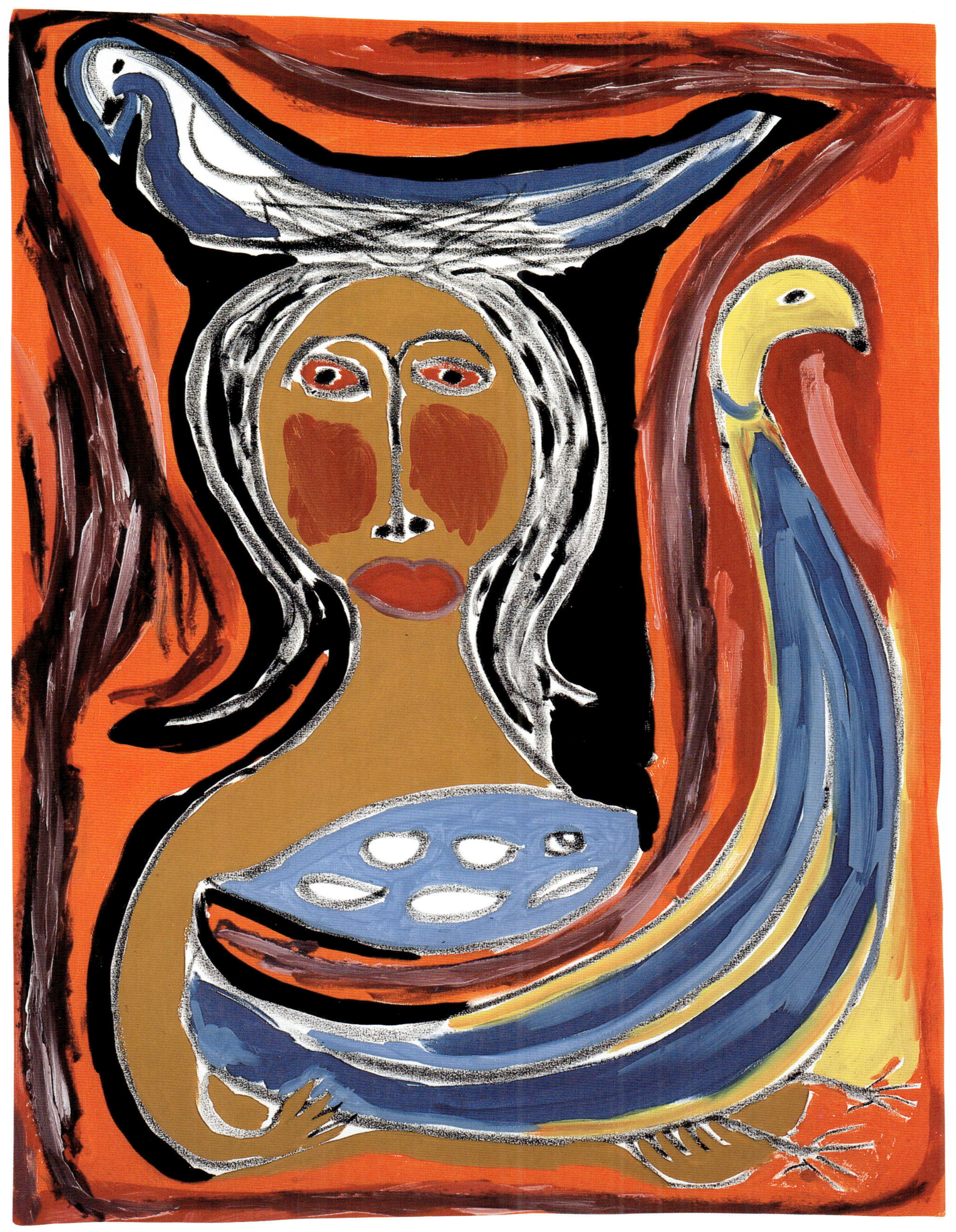

135

THORNTON DIAL, SR.

Life Go On, 1990

(cat. no. 55)

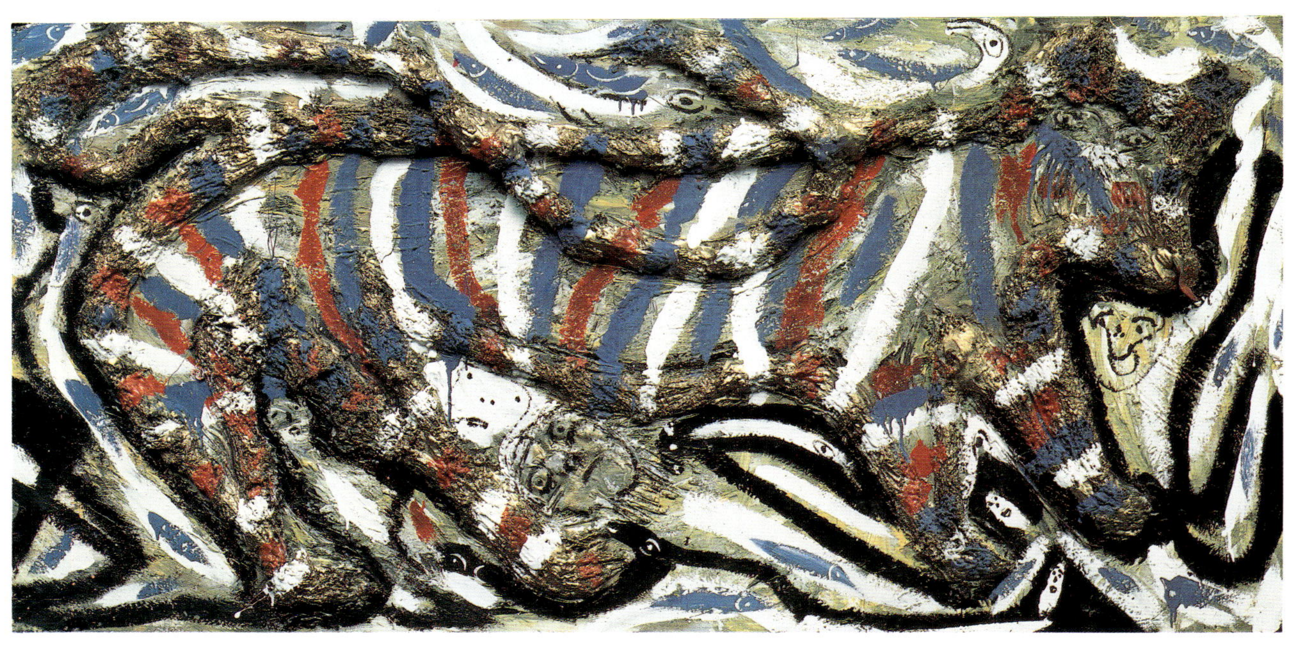

136

THORNTON DIAL, SR.
The Longest Tail Tiger in the United States, 1989
(cat. no. 56)

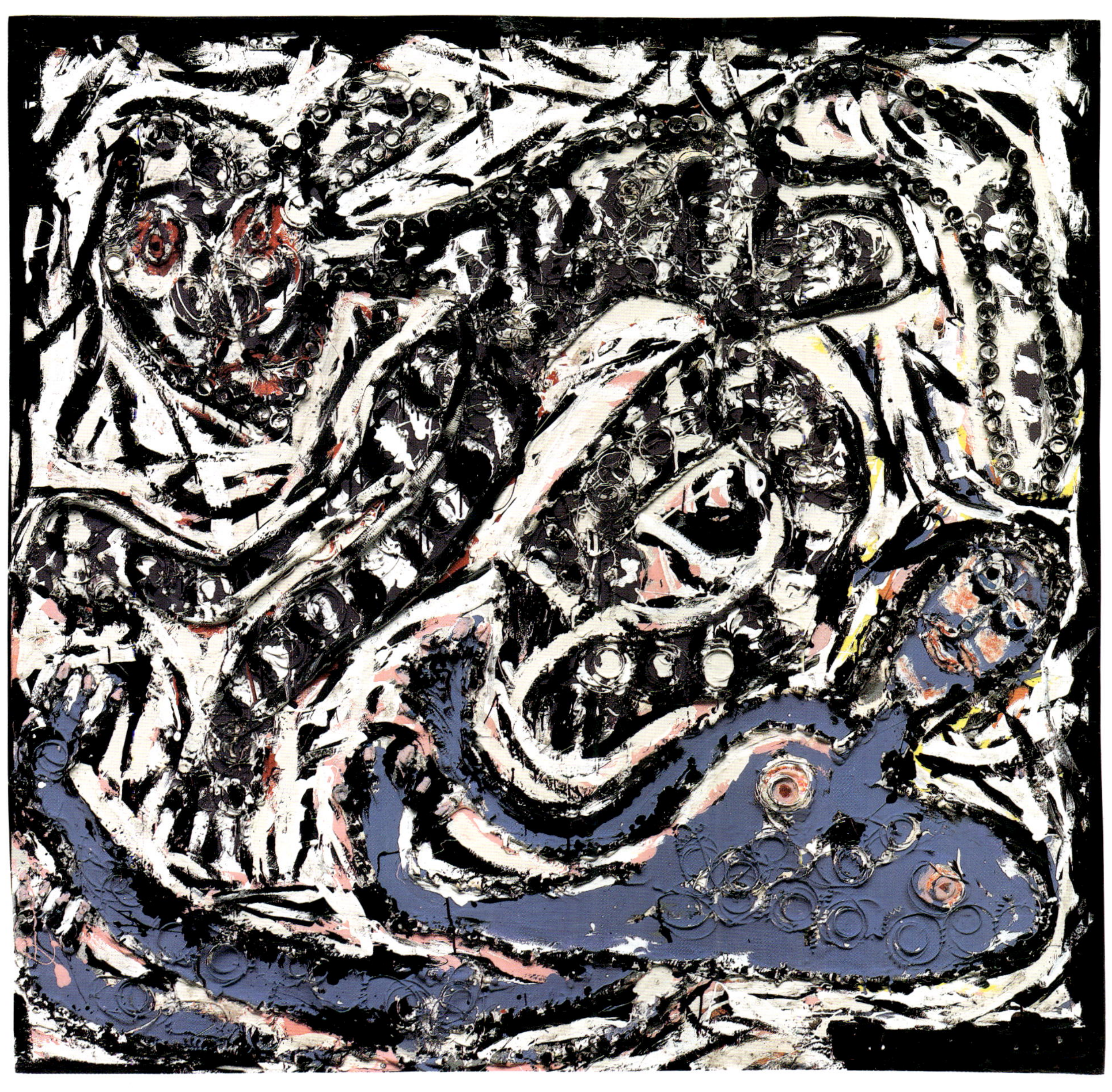

137

THORNTON DIAL, SR.
Rolling Mill: Steel Is the Master, Lady Is the Power, 1992
(cat. no. 58)

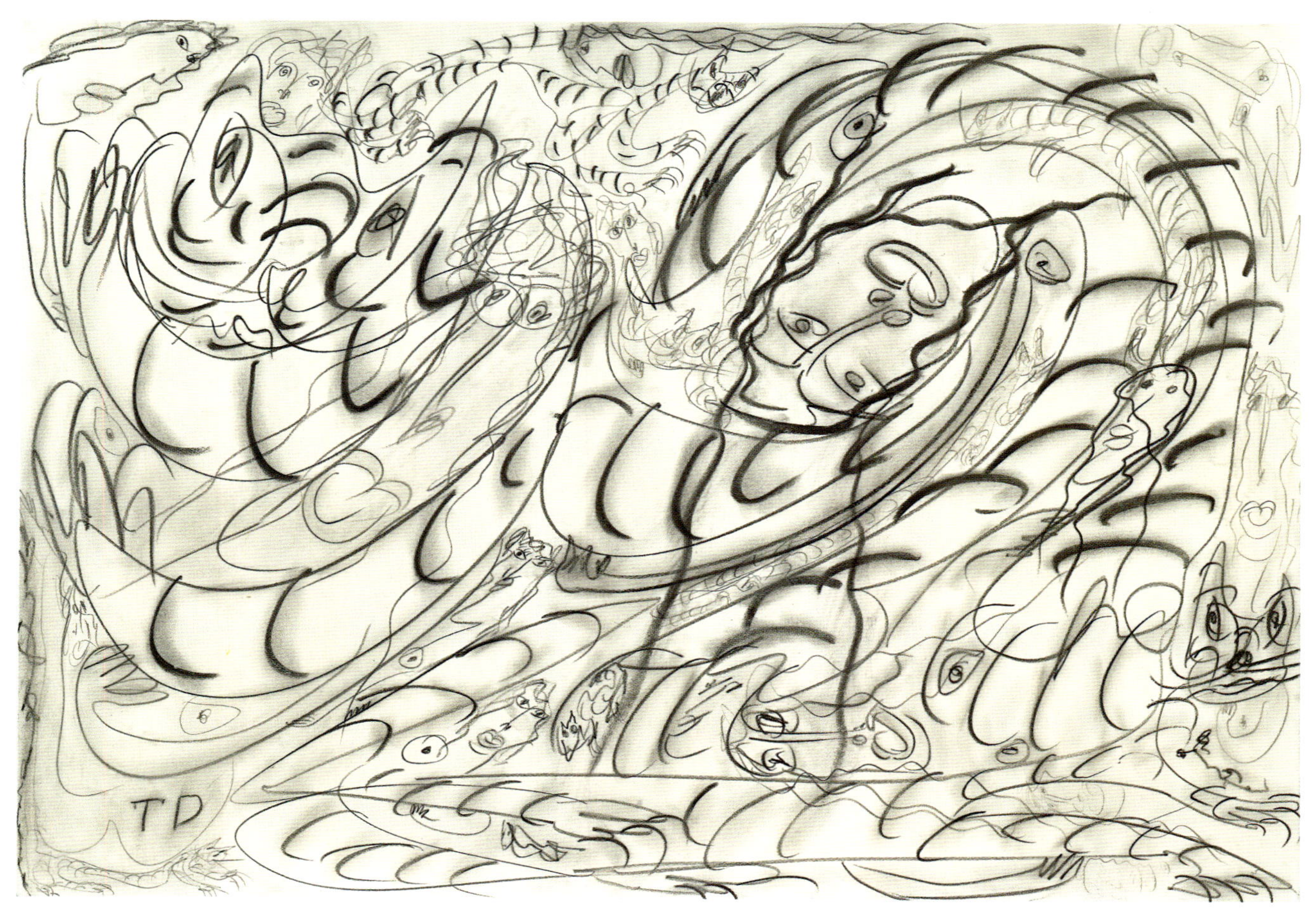

138

THORNTON DIAL, SR.
Eyes on the Business, 1992
(cat. no. 53)

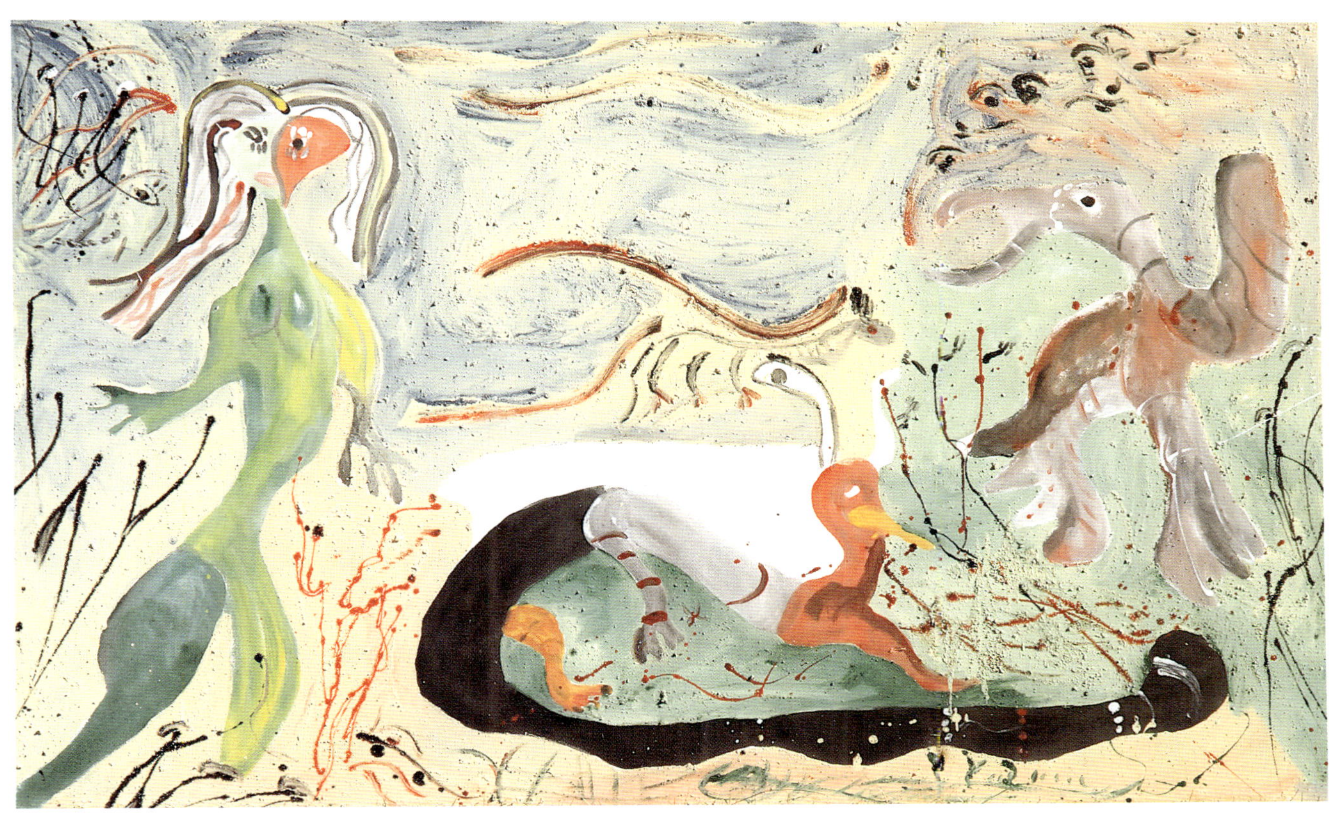

139

CHARLIE LUCAS

Mother Nature Stood Up to Take the World Back Cause Man Has Abused Her Body, n.d.

(cat. no. 158)

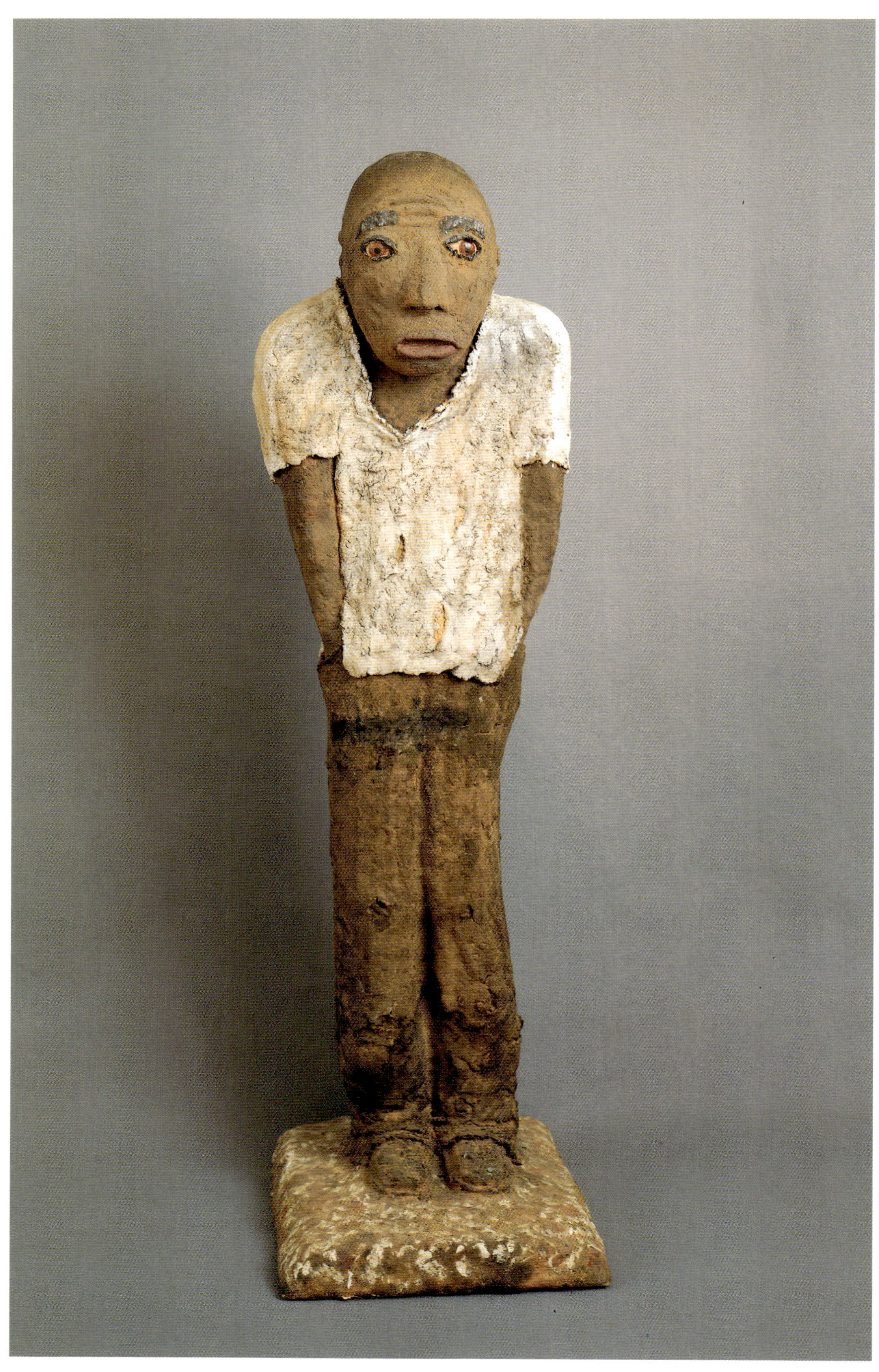

140

ARCHIE BYRON

Despair, 1984

(cat. no. 24)

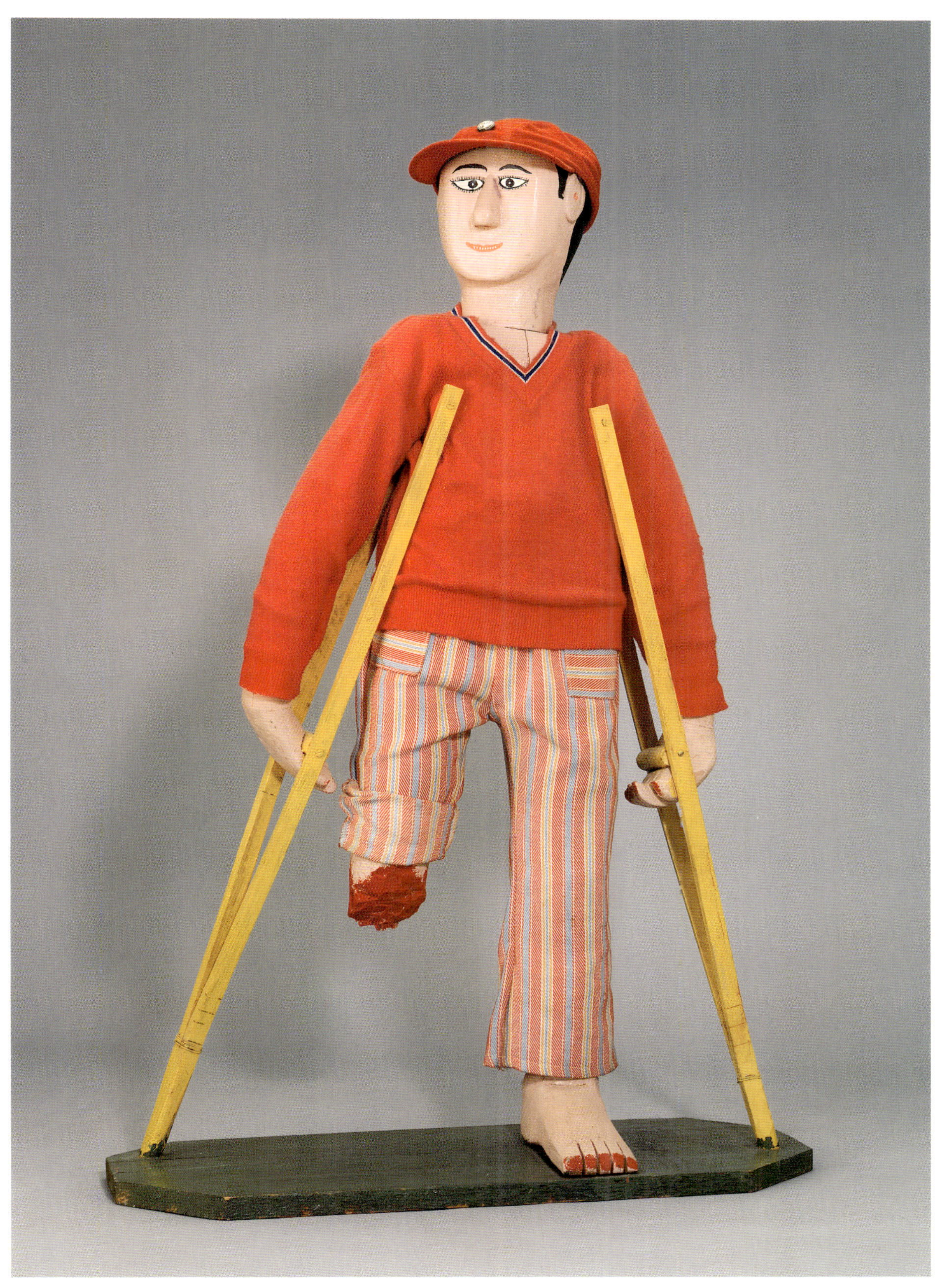

141

MILES CARPENTER

Wounded Knee, 1973

(cat. no. 26)

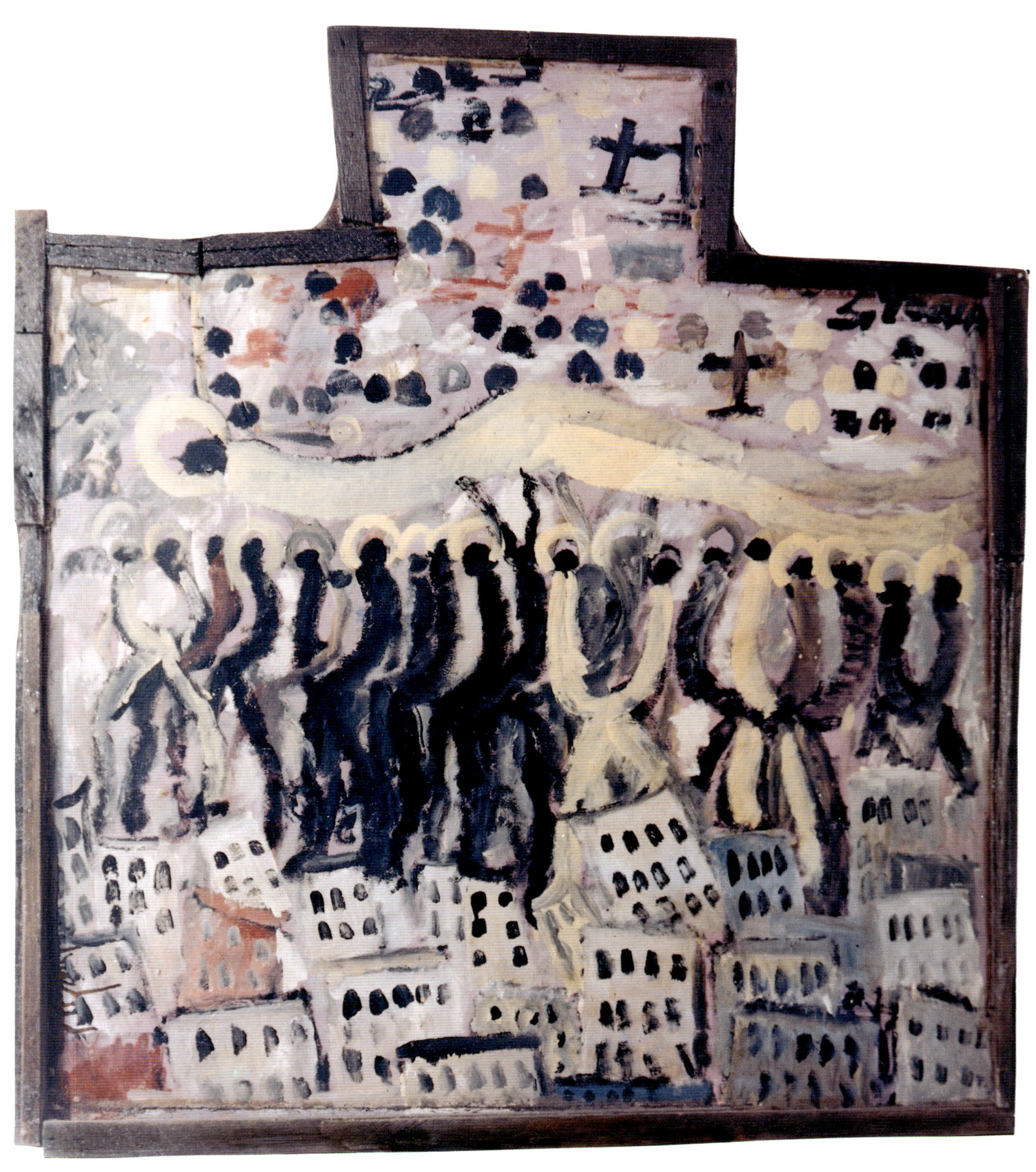

142
PURVIS YOUNG
Burial over the City, 1988
(cat. no. 265)

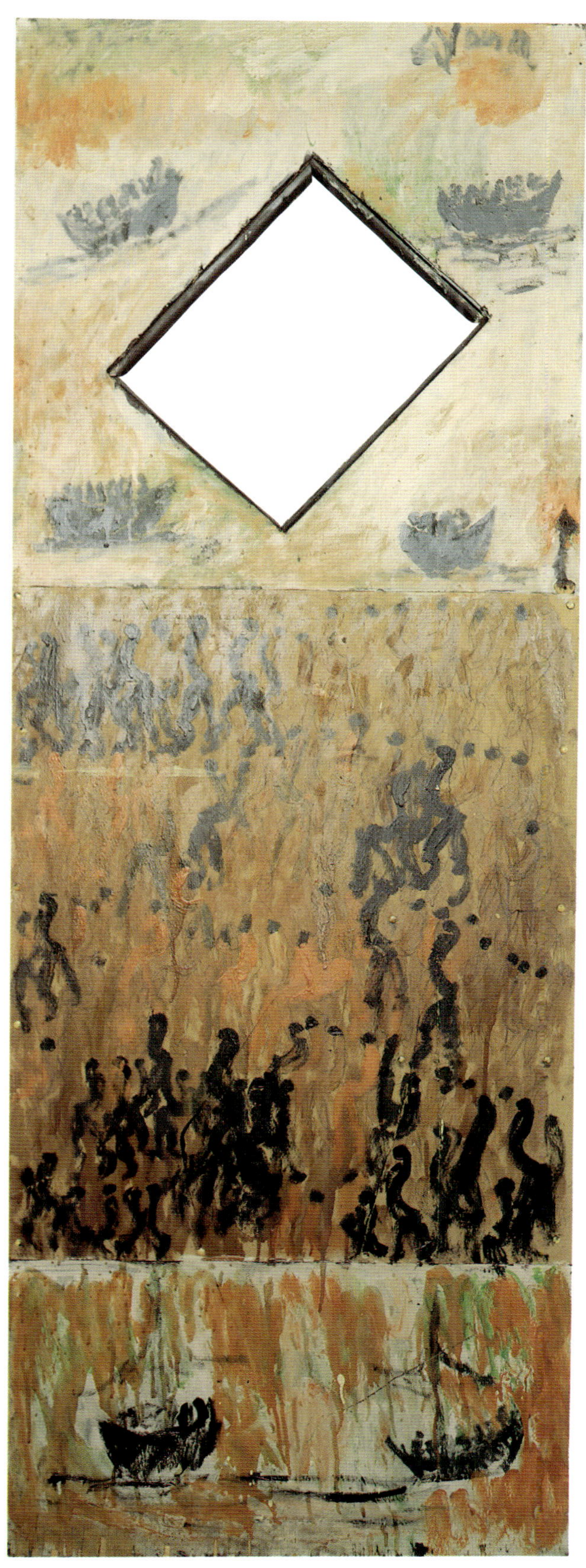

143

PURVIS YOUNG

The Boat People, n.d.

(cat. no. 264)

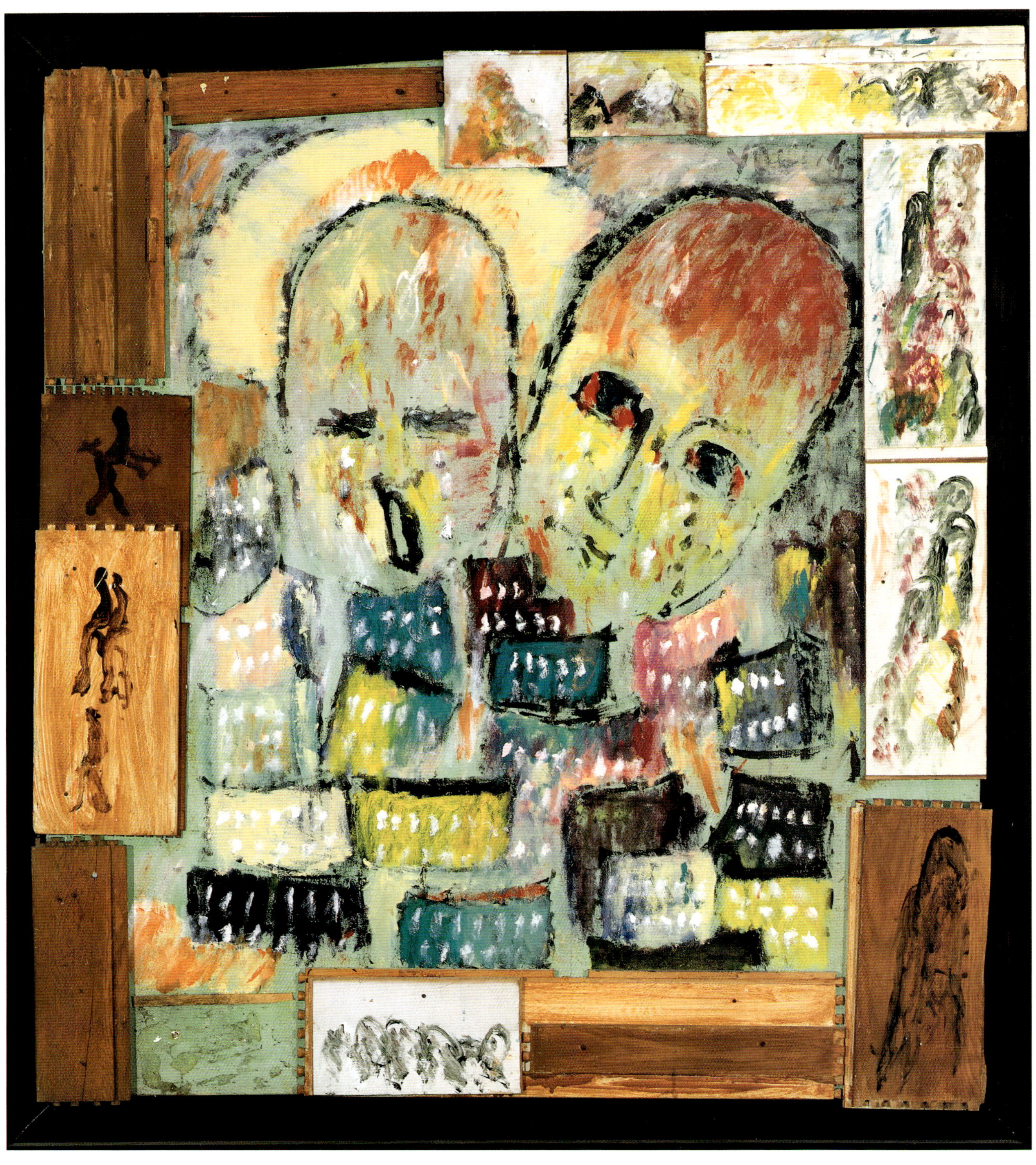

144

PURVIS YOUNG

Angels over the City, 1989

(cat. no. 263)

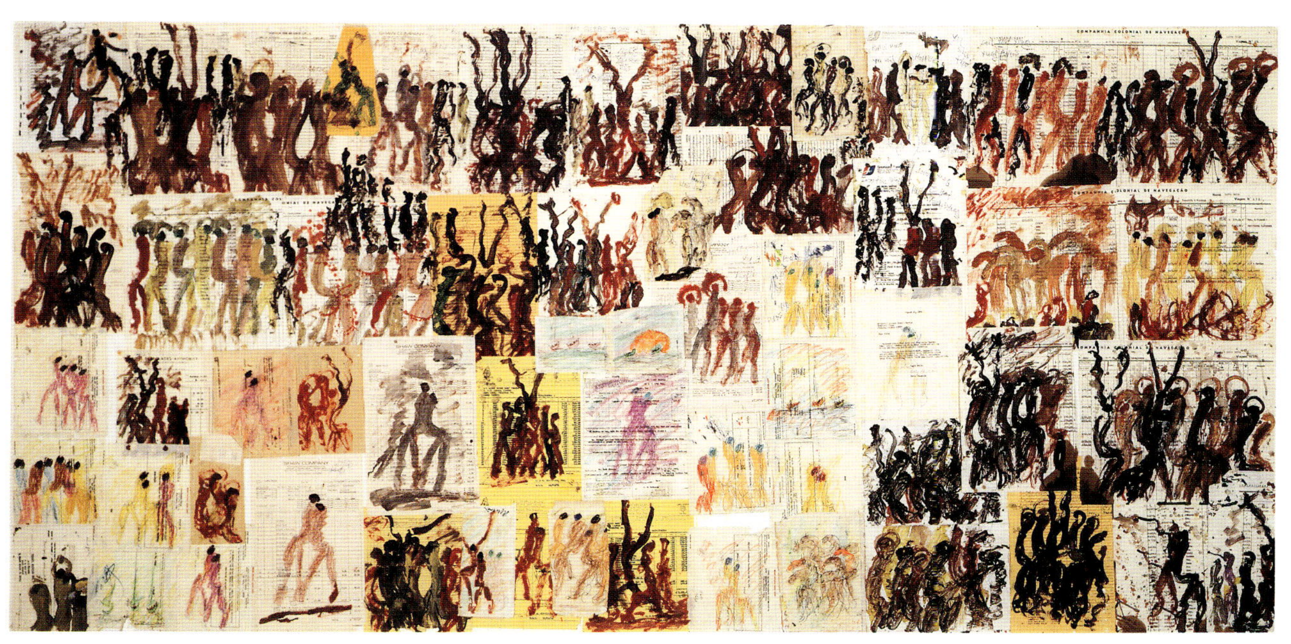

145

PURVIS YOUNG

Peoples and Boats, 1991

(cat. no. 269)

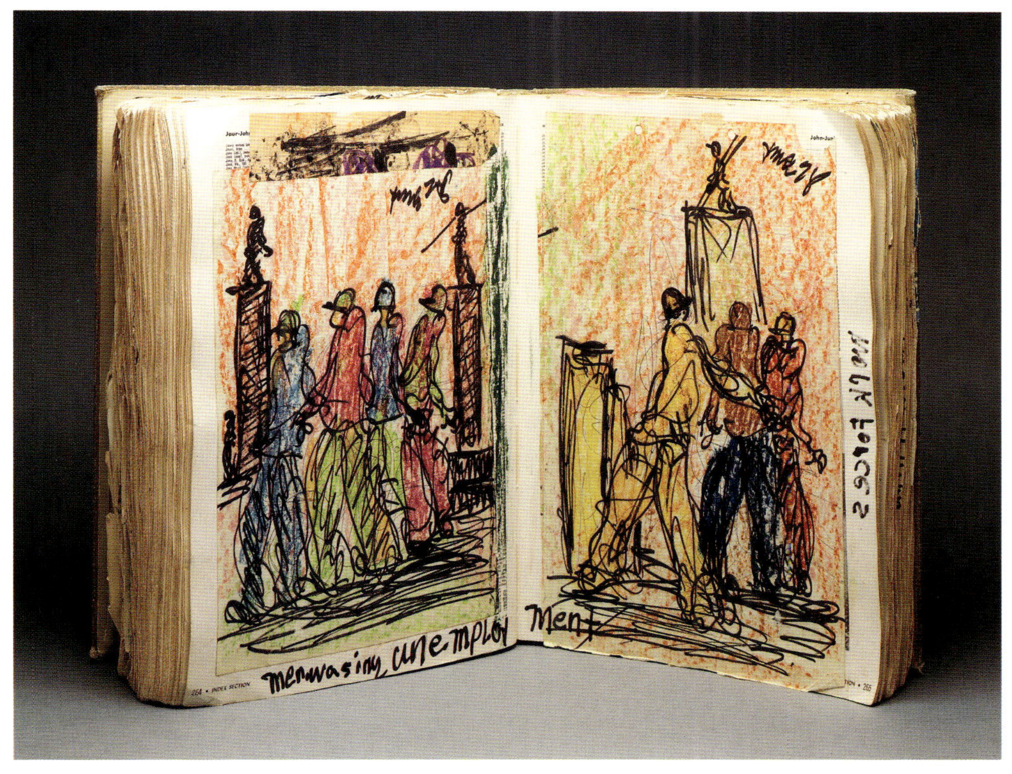

146

PURVIS YOUNG

Unemployment, 1982

(cat. no. 270)

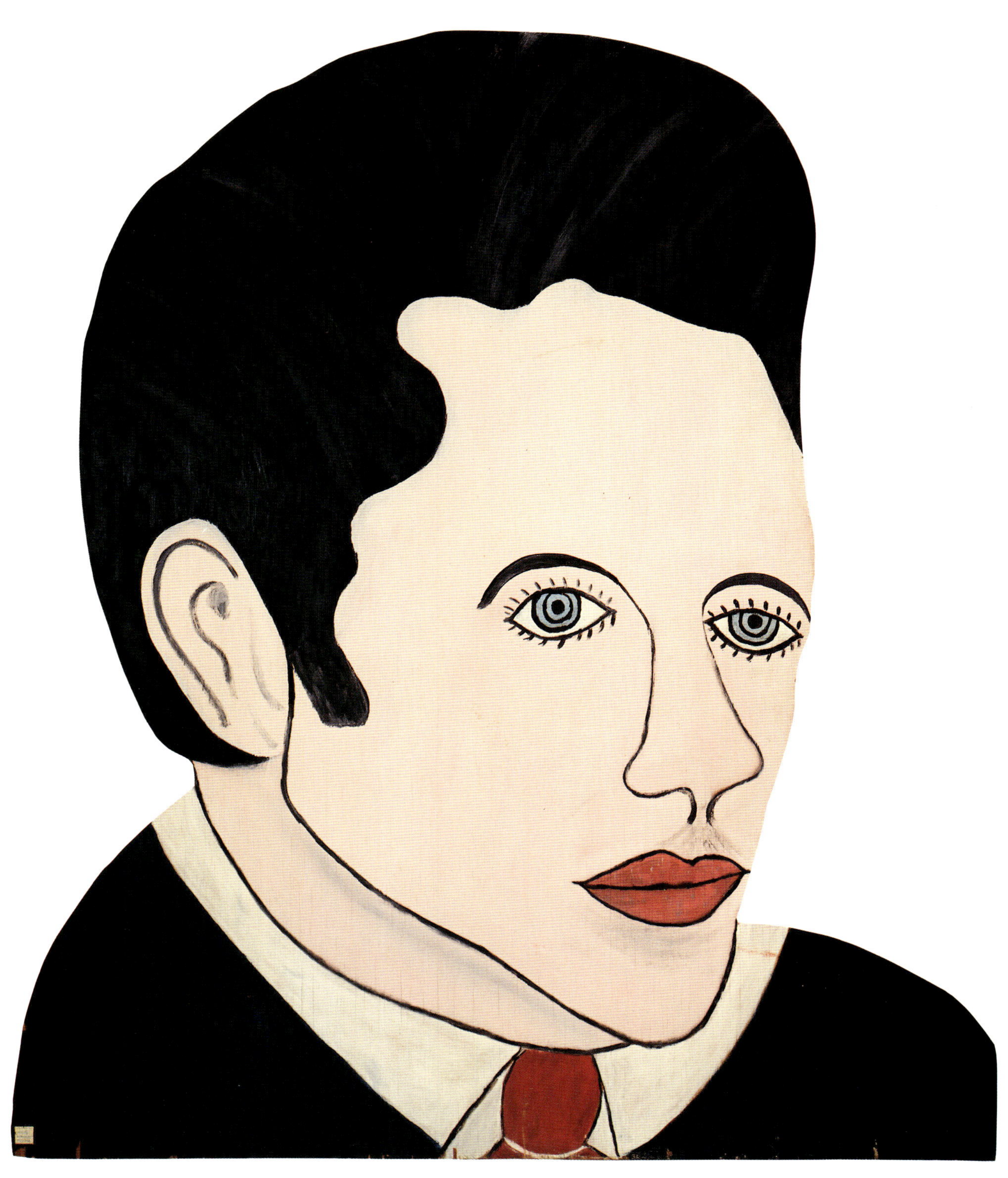

147

HOWARD FINSTER

Elvis, 1977

(cat. no. 87)

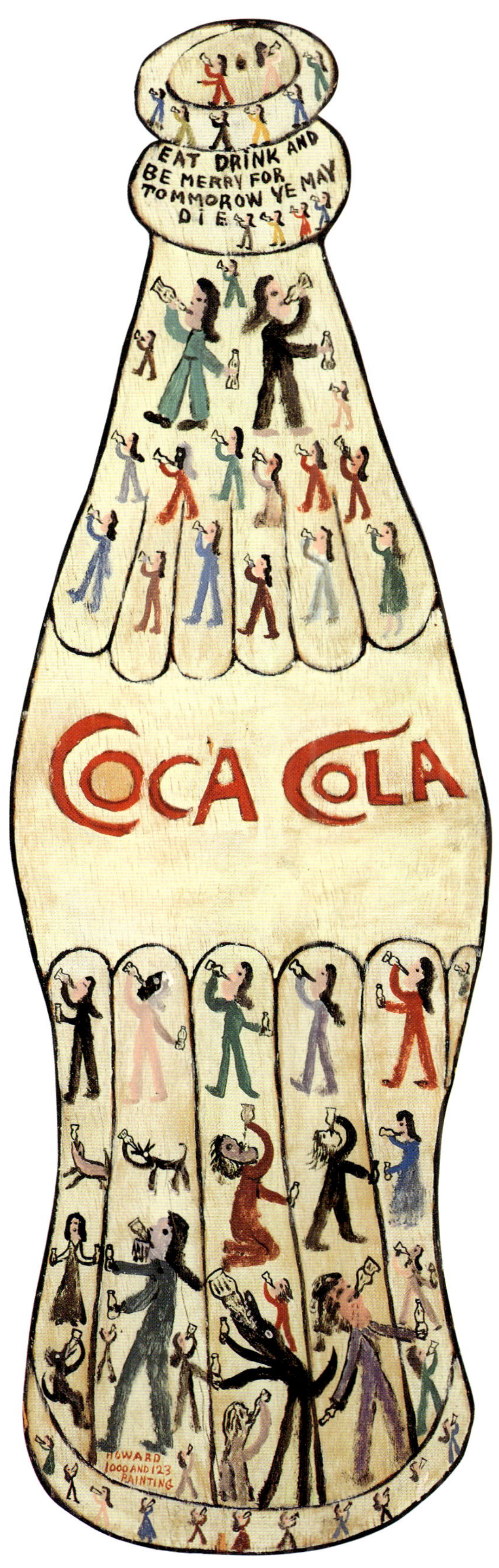

148

HOWARD FINSTER

Coca-Cola #1123, 1977

(cat. no. 85)

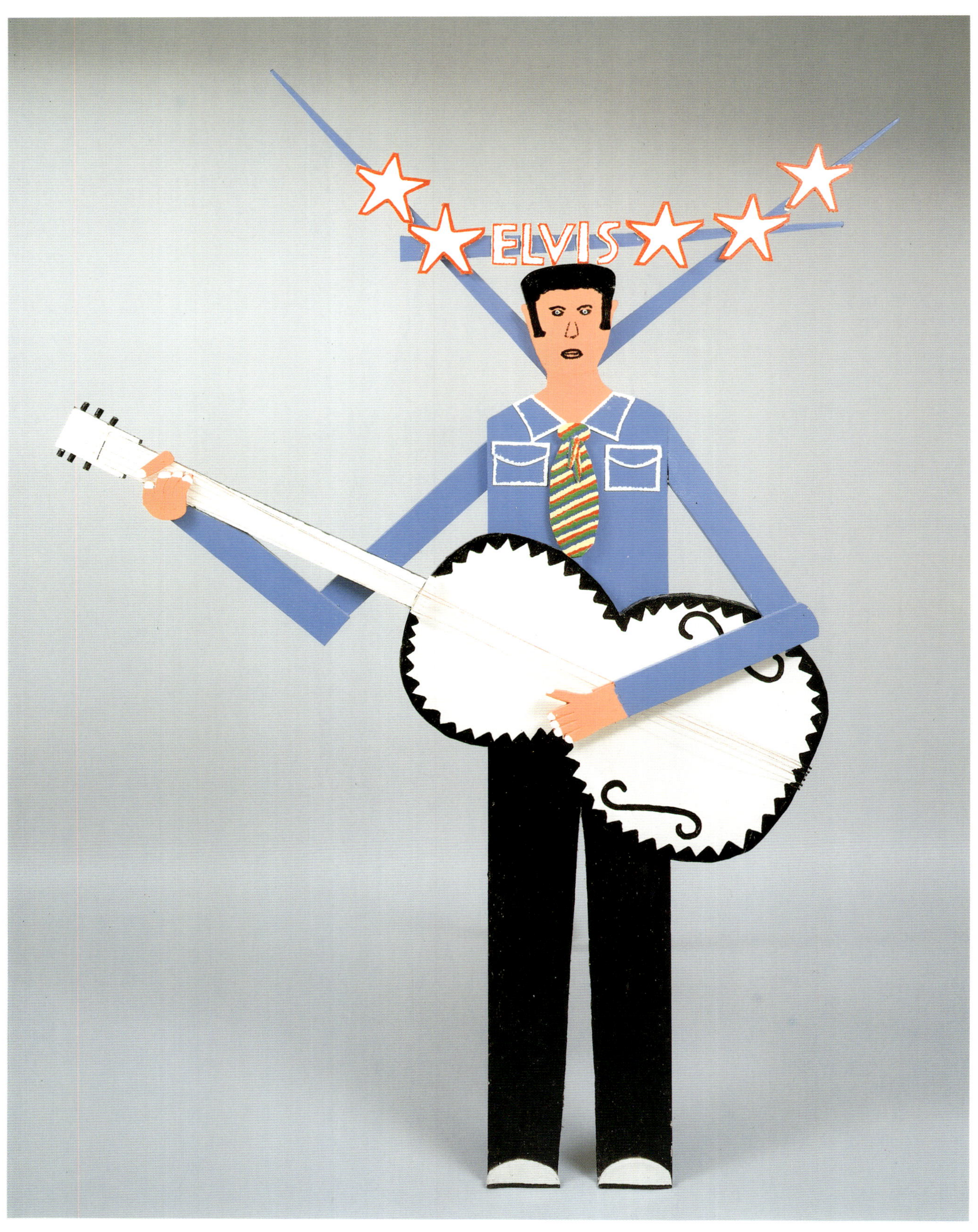

149

JAMES HAROLD JENNINGS

Elvis, 1987

(cat. no. 130)

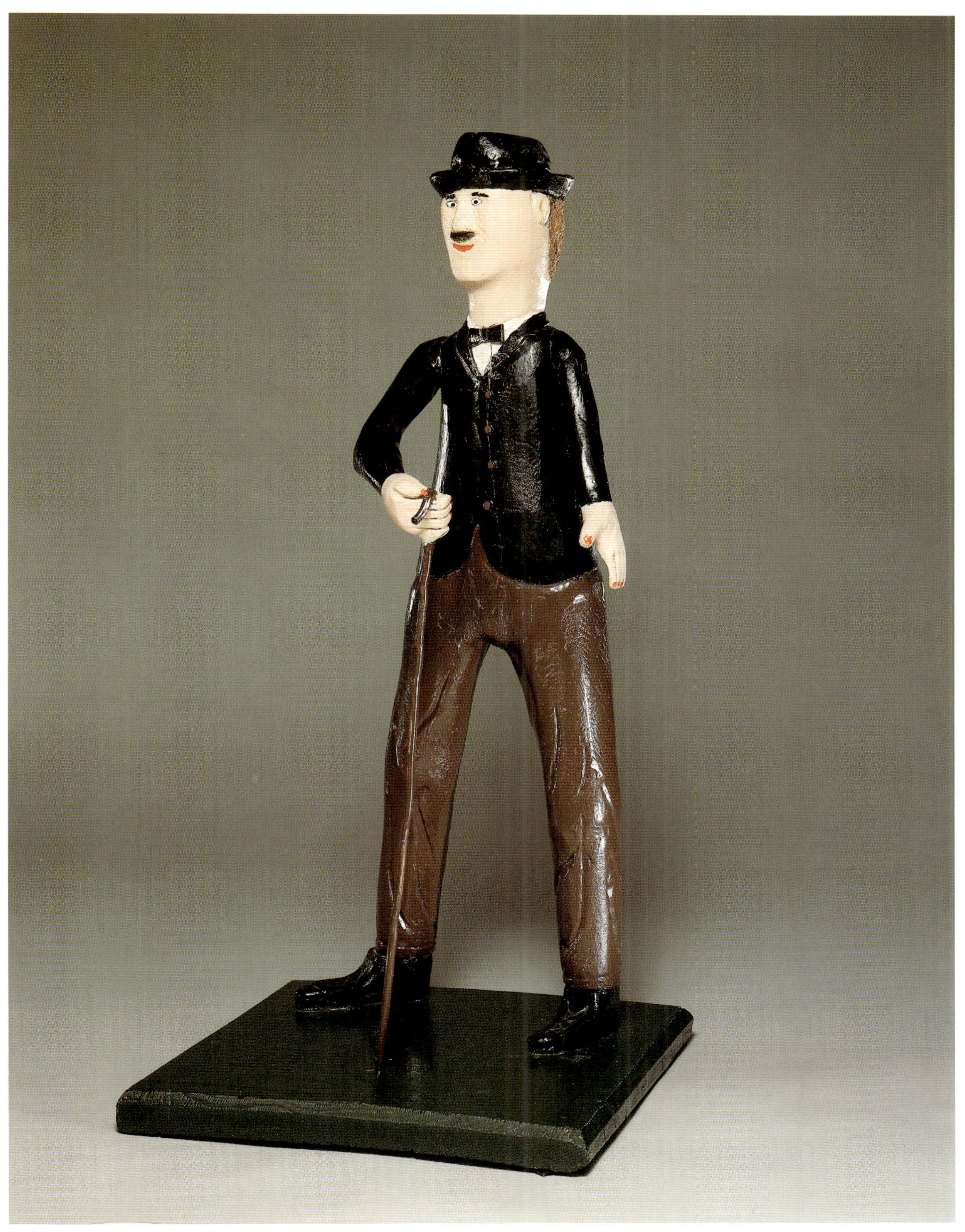

150

MILES CARPENTER

Charlie Chaplin, 1981

(cat. no. 25)

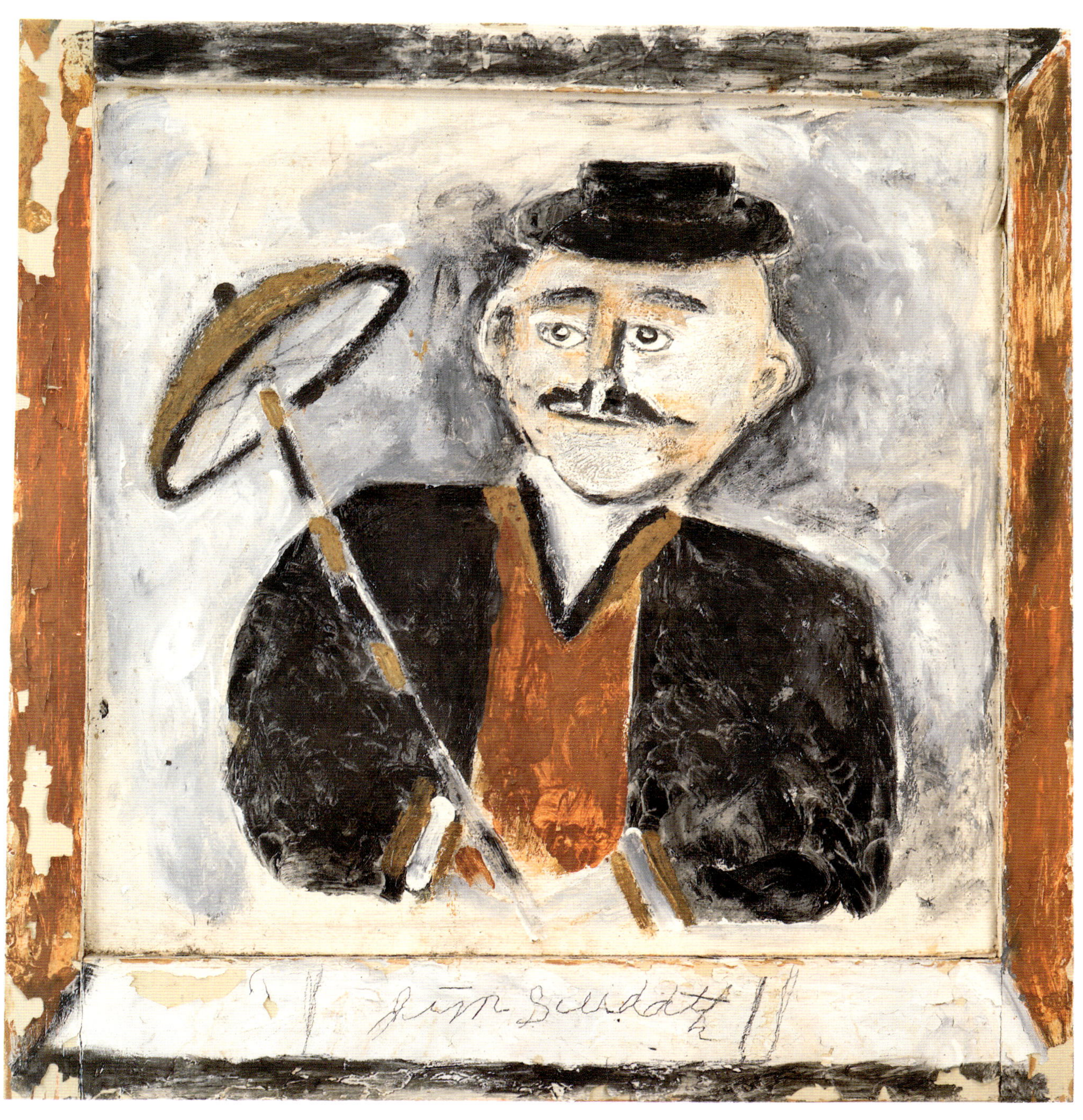

151

JIMMY LEE SUDDUTH

Red Skelton, ca. 1970s

(cat. no. 224)

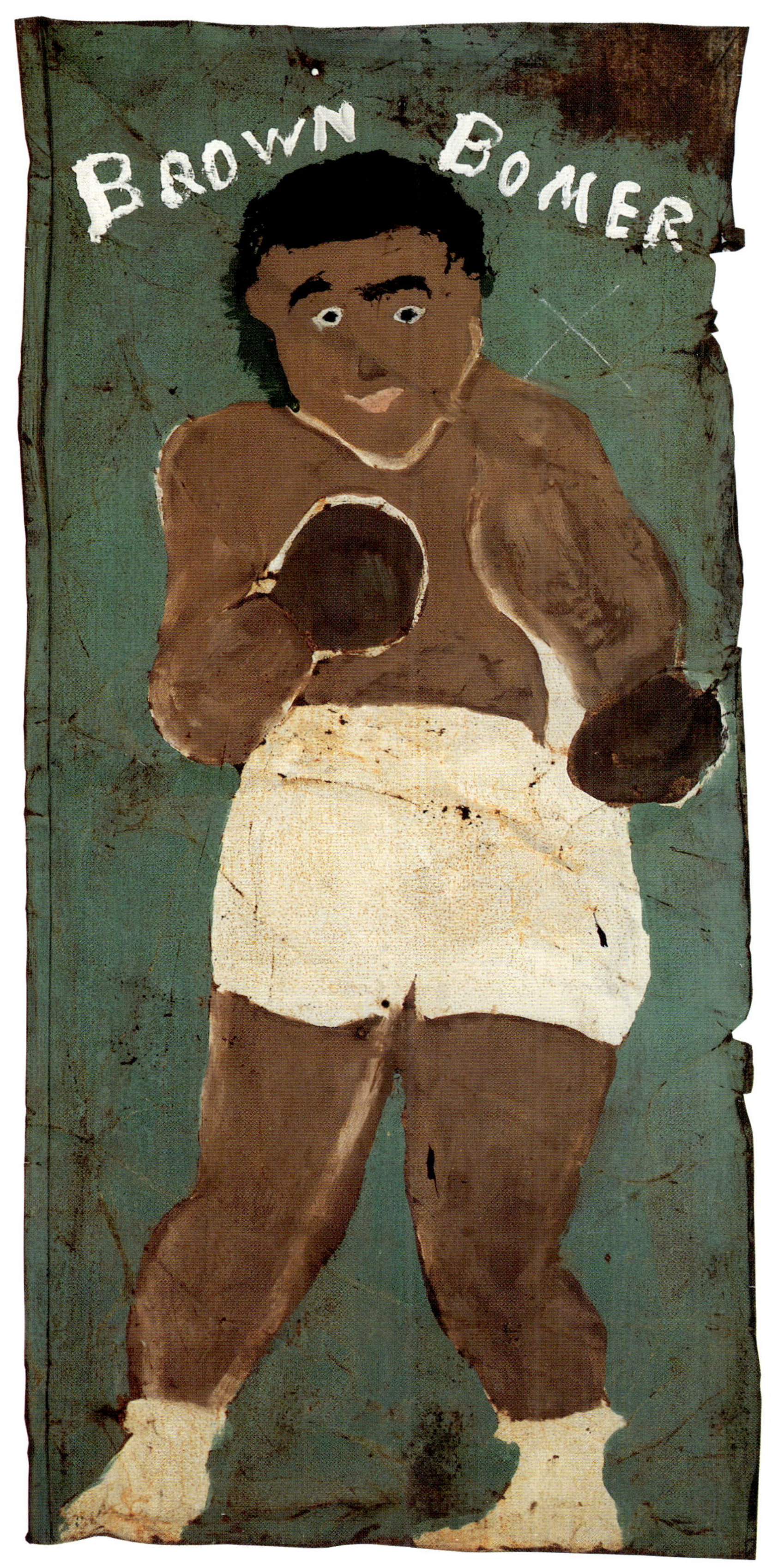

152

SAM DOYLE

Brown Bomber (Joe Louis), 1979

(cat. no. 62)

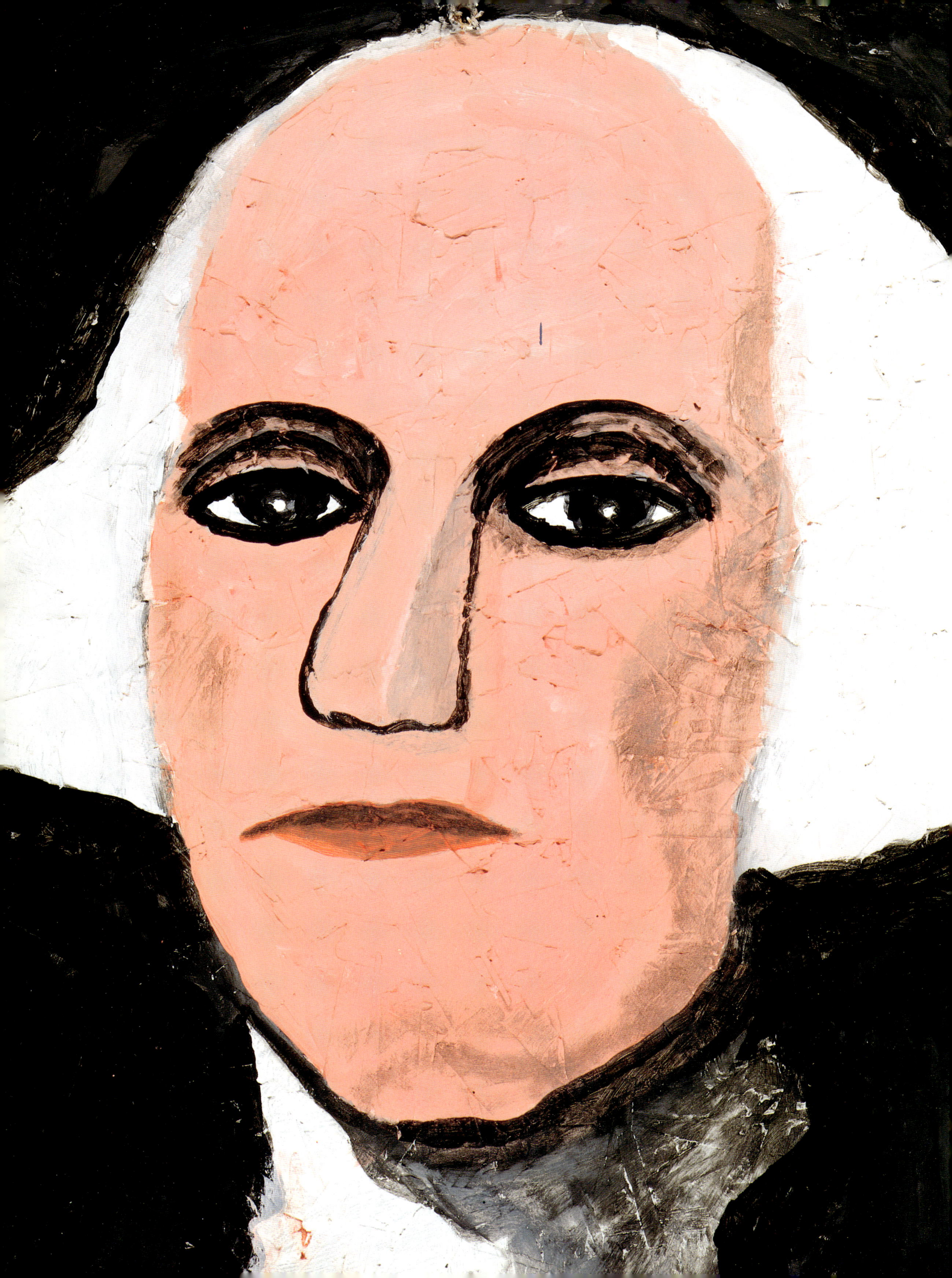

PATRIOTISM

The patriotism of the South, like its regionalism, is characterized by pride, loyalty, and honor, three attributes that have successfully built a strong sense of southern identity. This region, so insistent on retaining its separateness, looks fervently beyond itself in its duty to America. Twentieth-century self-taught artists in the American South have channeled these characteristics into numerous patriotic expressions.

Many southern patriotic works of the past half-century are based upon ubiquitous national symbols that date back to our nation's early history. They include the Statue of Liberty, dedicated in 1886; the American flag, adopted in 1777; Uncle Sam, first popularized as a graphic image by political cartoonist Thomas Nast in the 1860s; the eagle, incorporated into our national seal in 1782; and the Liberty Bell, rung in 1776 to commemorate the signing of the Declaration of Independence. Historical expressions of patriotism are revealed in images of the presidents, especially George Washington and Abraham Lincoln. In the twentieth century, emerging heroes like John F. Kennedy, Robert Kennedy, and Martin Luther King assume prominence, too, in a limited number of patriotic works.

The presence of national symbols in the work of self-taught artists indicates how ingrained these emblems are in their daily lives. Patriotic symbols, like the imagery of popular culture, directly reflect the common culture and shared visual resources that affect everyone's daily lives, despite differing backgrounds and perspectives. Such broader influence can be difficult to discern in the work of self-taught artists because they focus on self-expression and personal experiences. Nonetheless, their patriotic images, usually single figures, are painted from commonly viewed sources and portrayed in easily recognizable but individualistic styles. The depiction of actual details varies according to the interest, manner, and medium of each artist.

Patriotic imagery is seen in the work of both white and black southern self-taught artists, but for southern blacks, in particular, patriotism presents complex issues. African-Americans not only have been required to fight for their nation but have insisted on it as a right that demonstrates both their loyalty and manhood. Nevertheless, after both world wars they returned to a homeland that did not offer them equal treatment. Yet, as artist Thornton Dial, Sr., has said: "Blacks are as patriotic as whites, because they were born in the U.S. This is their country and they fought for their country."[1]

A gift from France, the Statue of Liberty stands valiantly in New York Harbor with her outstretched arm welcoming the tired and the poor, "the huddled masses yearning to breathe free," in the well-known words of poetess Emma Lazarus inscribed on the statue. Since her dedication in 1886, Lady Liberty has symbolically sanctioned the immigration of millions, and she has come to represent not only freedom and hope but one of our nation's greatest strengths, its pluralism. In the South this is seen in the makeup of its early population—a special gumbo of African-Americans, Native Americans, and Caucasians of European descent, primarily Scotch, Irish, French, German, and English.

Many African-Americans came to this country through enforced slavery, not by choice. That some African-Americans, despite their struggles, portray the Statue of Liberty in their artwork with respect reflects the power and universality of her symbolism. Indeed, Miss Liberty represents the hope of true freedom and equality for all.

Among self-taught artists who have depicted the Statue of Liberty are Raymond Coins, Ulysses Davis, William Hawkins, Rev. Benjamin Hunter, James Harold Jennings, Carl McKenzie, Leslie Payne, Rev. Benjamin F. Perkins, Elijah Pierce, Jimmy Lee Sudduth, Sarah Mary Taylor, James

Henry "Son" Thomas, and George Williams. Each rendering of the statue possesses readily identifiable features, usually a crown and an outstretched arm with a torch (sometimes abstract), yet each image reflects an artist's personal style and individual interpretation.

Jimmy Lee Sudduth's larger-than-life two-dimensional *Statue of Liberty* (pl. 172) is made of adeptly blended earth-toned mud, a natural chalky substance, and dabs of yellow paint on plywood. The enlarged outstretched arm reinforces the verticality of the elongated image and its vital but earthy, grounded character. Steps at the statue's feet ascend symbolically to liberty. Sudduth had identified Liberty as a woman by adding breasts, an indication of a waistline, and a painted necklace. By portraying her as an African-American, Sudduth expressed his personal identification as a patriotic black American with the principle of liberty for all.

Leslie Payne energized the regal but static original by transforming her into a dazzling, spirited, and feminine image on brightly painted tin (pl. 153). Lady Liberty's curvilinear hourglass figure is accentuated by the sassy placement of her hand on a small waist, above very rounded hips. Vibrant, distinctive primary colors—red, yellow, and blue—activate the work's surface, which is further bedazzled by applied costume jewelry. This lively and colorful portrayal in man-made materials contrasts with the subdued but solid appearance of Sudduth's image of natural mud on wood.

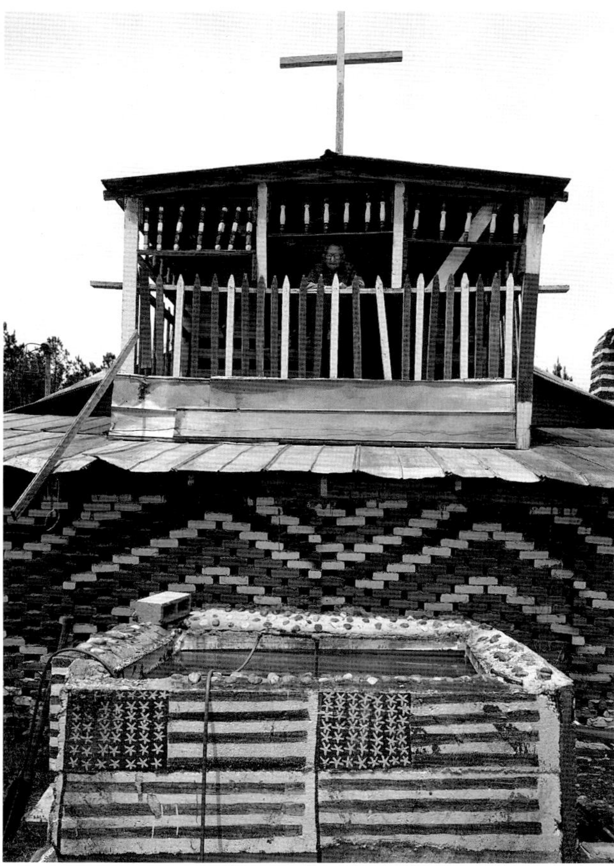

Fig. 1. Benjamin F. Perkins, Bankston, Alabama, 1988. The red, white, and blue American flags and bricks of Perkins's home, church, and bell tower, with a cross on top, represent the artist's principal themes: love of country and freedom of worship (pl. 83). Photo Marcus Schubert.

Sarah Mary Taylor's Statue of Liberty quilt features a lively arrangement of eighteen silhouettes of Miss Liberty (pl. 166). Taylor's playful sense of color, pattern, and design, as seen in her drawings (pl. 182), translates superbly into her expressive fabric constructions. Taylor, who had made string and patch quilts, started to make picture quilts, sometimes influenced by media images, after she began drawing on paper. "I would draw and then cut quilts by my drawings," said Taylor.[2] About her Statue of Liberty quilt, Taylor said: "I saw a Statue of Liberty [in the local newspaper]. I told one of my customers. . . . He sent me a big picture of the Statue of Liberty. I copied it, cut out one drawing, and made a pattern by it. I cut each Statue of Liberty by the same pattern."[3]

Raymond Coins's interpretation of the statue is solid and serious (pl. 167). The statue rises in carved relief from a stone slab. Uniting patriotic, domestic, and religious imagery, her figure is flanked by a crucifixion on one side and a house and tree on the other.

Rev. Benjamin F. Perkins rendered a flat and boxy two-dimensional gold Liberty as one of several images painted on a recycled child's portable toilet (pl. 163). The overall pattern of her garment is formed by an inscription, applied in red paint: "Miss Liberty welcomes those persecuted, sick, hungry, to the land of liberty to pursue Happiness. This is America." Red accents on a blue background with white stars allude loosely to the American flag.

Perkins was himself deeply affected by the sight of the imposing statue when he returned to the United States in the mid-1920s as a young marine after a three-month tour of duty abroad. Sixty-five years later, at the age of eighty-seven, Perkins recalled: "We were sailing into New York . . . and I was in the engine room. . . . The captain called for the crew to come on deck. We went up to the captain to look and straight ahead was the most beautiful sight I've seen in my 87 years [and] that was the Statue of Liberty—not a cloud in the sky, not a moon up, just stars. And then when I began painting, I remembered that night."[4]

A pastor in his own church (Heartline Assembly Church of God), Perkins, who cherished the American freedom to worship according to one's choice, often combined patriotic and religious imagery with calligraphy. Besides the rendering of Liberty,

All-American Potty depicts a church and the flag, above which Perkins inscribed the Pledge of Allegiance. On another work (private collection), he inscribed: "The United States is great because our flag stands for freedom to worship God according to the dictates of our heart's desire." Perkins's consistent representation of word and image is clearly linked to his evangelical mission. "All of my works have a message," says Perkins. "For me, if art don't tell me anything, it's not art."[5]

Perkins also has made numerous paintings of the American flag, rendered fairly realistically with fifty stars and thirteen stripes. Occasionally he overlays a map of the United States or Statue of Liberty on the work.

In 1990 and 1991, Howard Finster made a series of nontraditional American flag paintings superimposed with images of cultural heroes or religious patriarchs such as Henry Ford, Abraham, and Christ. Like Perkins, Finster's patriotic imagery is linked to the artist's evangelical beliefs, and he also interlaces words with images. One flag, for example, is inscribed: "Let all religions be free."[6]

The red, white, and blue and the stars and stripes of the American flag conjure up such strong patriotic sentiments that they were the likeliest colors and motifs to garb the figure of Uncle Sam, an equally evocative symbol of patriotism. Earnest Patton, a Kentucky carver, portrayed a stern, purposeful Uncle Sam figure, in painted wood, wearing a navy jacket and hat and red-and-white striped pants (pl. 165).[7] R. A. Miller's Uncle Sam, *Blow Oscar*, a large cutout figure painting on tin (pl. 164), has a double meaning. Miller lives above a Georgia highway on a hill decorated with whirligigs visible to passersby. His cousin Oscar identifies himself when driving past by wildly blowing his horn. What began as a private message to his cousin gained a more widely understood patriotic significance by virtue of the red, white, and blue design.

Since becoming a part of the national seal in 1782, the eagle has come to signify the strength of our country. Raymond Coins's carved wooden eagle stands upright, solid and rigid (cat. no. 33). Minnie Black's fanciful eagle on painted gourd is charming in its awkwardness (pl. 170), and Willie Massey's eagle, painted on cardboard from an orange crate, suggests a warm, whimsical familiarity with nature (pl. 171).

Considering the South's strong regional identity, surprisingly few patriotic symbols have emerged that are uniquely southern. The Confederate flag, the most obvious emblem, is rarely chosen as a subject. R. A. Miller occasionally depicts the Confederate flag, but this seems to be a rare example among a handful of others.[8] Black artists, understandably, are not likely to use the icons associated with the South's support of slavery during the Civil War except in images of protest; the reasons that white artists do not often use its imagery are unclear. Perhaps for some the Ku Klux Klan's recent adoption of the Confederate flag as its own is a deterrent, as association with the Klan could transform the flag's meaning from a representation of the loyalty of southern states to a symbol of racism.

Civil rights heroes Martin Luther King, John F. Kennedy, and Robert Kennedy are often featured as a triad in clocks, posters, and photographs found in many southern black homes (see p. 51, fig. 8). But self-taught artists depict these political champions less frequently than one might expect. The limited number of artworks devoted to civil rights leaders seems unusual given the prevalence of other representations of them within the culture. Some self-taught artists who have portrayed these heroes include Elijah Pierce and William Hawkins, each of whom has portrayed the Kennedy brothers and Martin Luther King. Ulysses Davis has carved an elegant mahogany bust of Martin Luther King (pl. 160) as well as one of John F. Kennedy for his Presidents series. Josephus Farmer has depicted King and Kennedy, whom Farmer regarded as "the greatest president and the man responsible for civil rights."[9] But with the exception of Ulysses Davis, who is known for his political and patriotic images, few of these artists have emphasized this subject matter, as patriotic imagery in general does not dominate the field of self-taught art.

Nonetheless, within the extant body of work, depictions of the nation's first president are plentiful. George Washington, as a leader in America's struggle for freedom from England, has come to embody the ideals upon which our nation was founded. He has been widely portrayed in the work of self-taught artists throughout the South, from his home state of Virginia to the Mississippi Delta. Howard Finster, Jimmy Lee Sudduth, Mose Tolliver, Earnest Patton, Archie Byron, Ulysses Davis, James Henry "Son" Thomas, Glassman, Anderson Johnson, and Noah and Charles Kinney, to name a few, have captured Washington's familiar features in a variety of materials and interpretations.

Washington's overwhelming popularity as a portrait subject can be attributed in part to the easy accessibility of his image on the $1 bill. The portrait recorded there, based on the painting by the eighteenth-century fine artist Gilbert Stuart, has become the basis of our shared vision of Washington's appearance.[10] Washington's picture often hangs in schoolrooms, and his aura was probably memorable even to those with limited schooling. The well-known portraits of Washington and, later, of Abraham Lincoln, by mainstream artists and photographers provided self-taught artists with a model of how a two-dimensional portrait is traditionally made. Their own portrait compositions of these two presidents usually feature a single, bust-length subject, which is frequently centered.

James Henry "Son" Thomas depicted Washington using local materials: clay and soft, white unginned cotton from the Mississippi Delta (pl. 169). His technique and materials give Washington the appearance of an older man, in contrast to Howard Finster's painting on canvas of a younger, dark-haired Washington, a portrait typical of Finster's tendency toward stylized features.

Charles Kinney's George Washington is shown to the waist, dressed in military gear (pl. 156). At his side is a green tree with red cherries, a hatchet, and the words "cut cherry daw," referring to the president's famed apocryphal admission as a young boy that he had cut the cherry tree down.

Glassman fashioned a portrait of Washington from bits of broken glass found on the street which he attached to a wooden board with freshly applied house paint to form a silhouette (pl. 168). Next to the president, the artist inscribed the adage, "Honesty is the best policy," and, above him, he outlined the Liberty Bell, an icon rarely depicted by southern self-taught artists.

Anderson Johnson's Washington is painted on composition board, which produces a highly textured effect (pl. 155). The black background strongly contrasts the white shirt, pink face, and white hair. The modulated black background too is carefully integrated with the figure's dark coat. Typical of Johnson's portraits, this one is direct, strong, and bold, portraying his subject's distinctive personality. Washington's piercing visage is strengthened by large expressive eyes.

Johnson also painted a portrait of Abraham Lincoln (pl. 154). Held in high esteem by many blacks for his role in the abolition of slavery during the Civil War, Lincoln was frequently portrayed by self-taught artists. Johnson's portrait is created from solid areas of black and white, in reverse arrangement from his painting of Washington. Here a painted white background and a white triangle of shirt accentuate the form and darkness of Lincoln's hair, beard, and jacket. Lincoln's image was accessible through its presence on the $5 bill. Whereas Washington's likeness was preserved through portrait painting, Lincoln benefited from the early stages of photography, an art form that allowed multiple copies of his image to be distributed in his lifetime, primarily through the work of the well-known photographer Matthew Brady.[11]

Some other self-taught artists who have captured Lincoln's likeness include Sam Doyle, Vernon Burwell, Charles Kinney, Earnest Patton, Archie Byron, Ulysses Davis, James Henry "Son" Thomas, Josephus Farmer, George Williams, and Glassman. Burwell, for example, depicted a full-length standing portrait of Lincoln, complete with stovepipe hat and topcoat, in concrete (pl. 158). Despite the unlikeliness of the medium, Burwell's Lincoln has a somewhat soft appearance and is true to his tall and lanky figure. Doyle painted a full-length figure of the president in *Lincoln at Frogmore* (pl. 159), executed in house paint on a six-foot window shade. A lanky, bearded Lincoln addresses an audience of slaves, his black outfit contrasting with the green landscape and clear blue sky.

Doyle's father reputedly told his son that Lincoln secretly visited him and other former slaves (by then freed men) at their home at Frogmore, on St. Helena Island off the coast of South Carolina, to enlist them in the Union forces.[12] Whether Lincoln actually visited Frogmore has not been historically documented, but Doyle's depiction is a direct example of an oral history tradition passing down from generation to generation. Unlike other iconic Lincoln portraits, in Doyle's the president is contextualized according to the artist's family tradition. Doyle's personal history is linked to his patriotic expression, a tendency that is emblematic of most patriotic works by self-taught artists.

NOTES

1. Thornton Dial, Sr., interview, KAG, Dec. 1992.
2. Sarah Mary Taylor, interview, ARY, April 1993.
3. Ibid.
4. Rev. Benjamin F. Perkins, interview, ARY, Nov. 1991.
5. *In/Outsiders from the American South* (Montgomery, Ala.: Montgomery Museum of Fine Arts, 1992), unpaginated.
6. Christopher Murray, *Howard Finster American Flag Paintings* (Washington, D.C.: Govinda Gallery, 1992), p. 16.
7. Patton's work was influenced by Edgar Tolson, who also carved Uncle Sam figures.
8. R. A. Miller, interview, ARY, Aug. 1992.
9. Joanne Cubbs, *The Gift of Josephus Farmer* (Milwaukee: Milwaukee Art History Gallery, University of Wisconsin, 1982), p. 26.
10. Stuart painted Washington twice from life, in 1795 and model for subsequent portraits of Washington; Stuart himself is thought to have made seventy versions of it; Milton W. Brown, et al., *American Art: Painting, Sculpture, Architecture, Decorative Arts, Photography* (Englewood Cliffs, N.J.: Prentice-Hall; New York: Harry N. Abrams, 1979), pp. 139–40.
11. In an early example of popular culture at work, Lincoln attributed his election to Matthew Brady's campaign portrait of him, sold widely as a *carte-de-visite*; see Naomi Rosenblum, *A World History of Photography* (New York: Abbeville Press, 1984), pp. 63, 191.
12. Sam Doyle, as told to Louanne Laroche, a longtime collector and dealer of Doyle's work, interview, ARY, Dec. 1992.

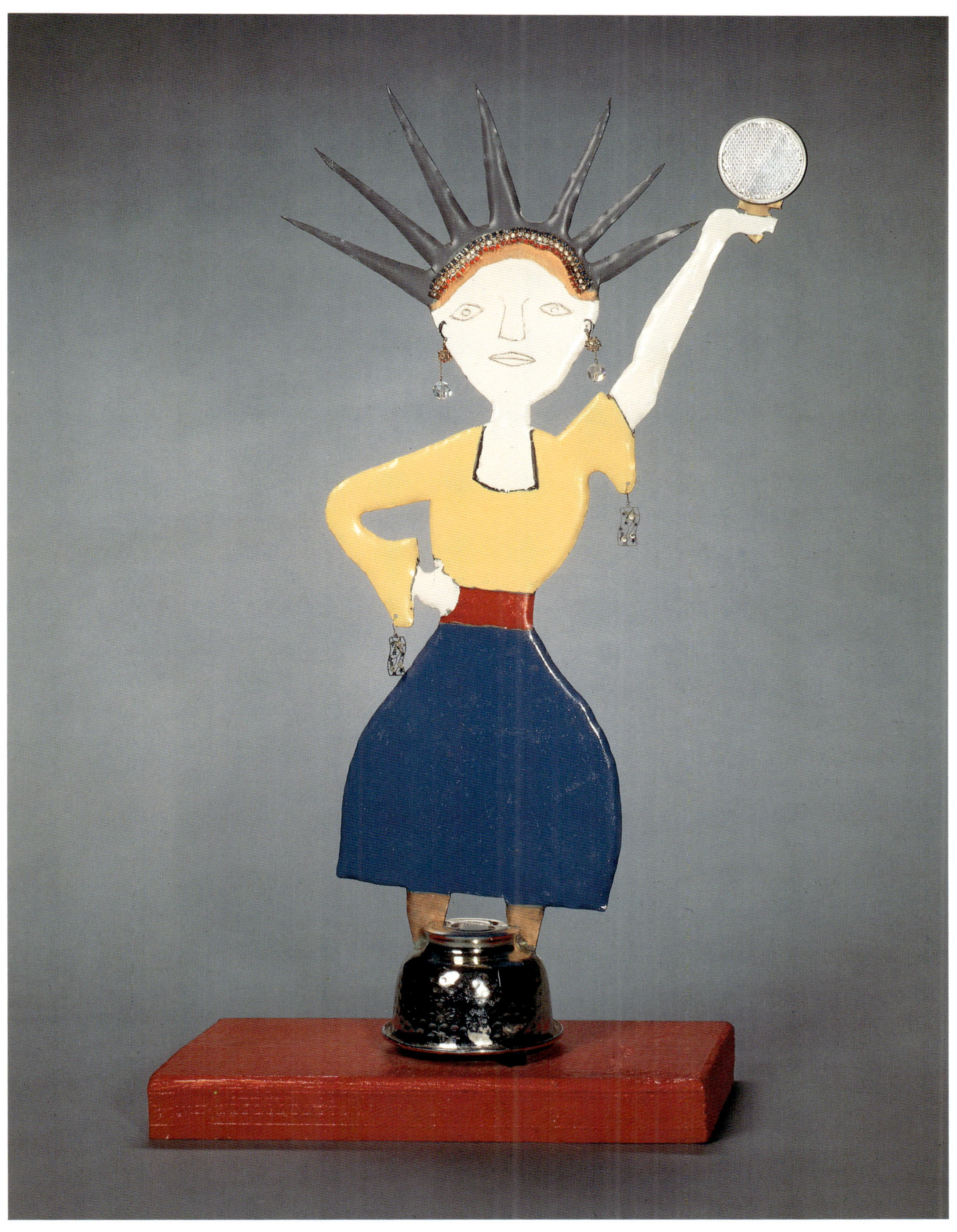

153

LESLIE PAYNE

New York Lady, ca. 1970s

(cat. no. 185)

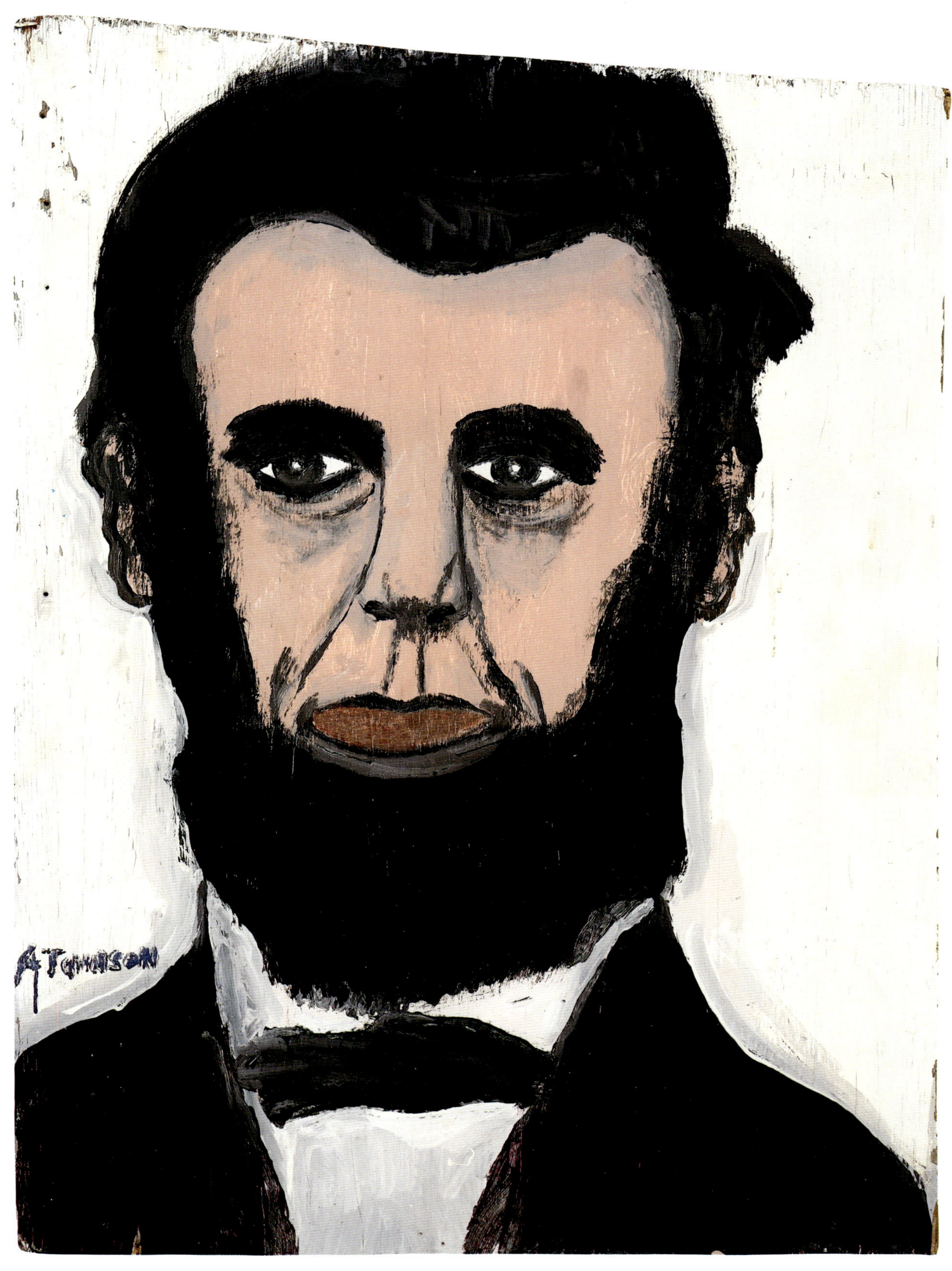

154

ANDERSON JOHNSON

Abraham Lincoln, 1989

(cat. no. 131)

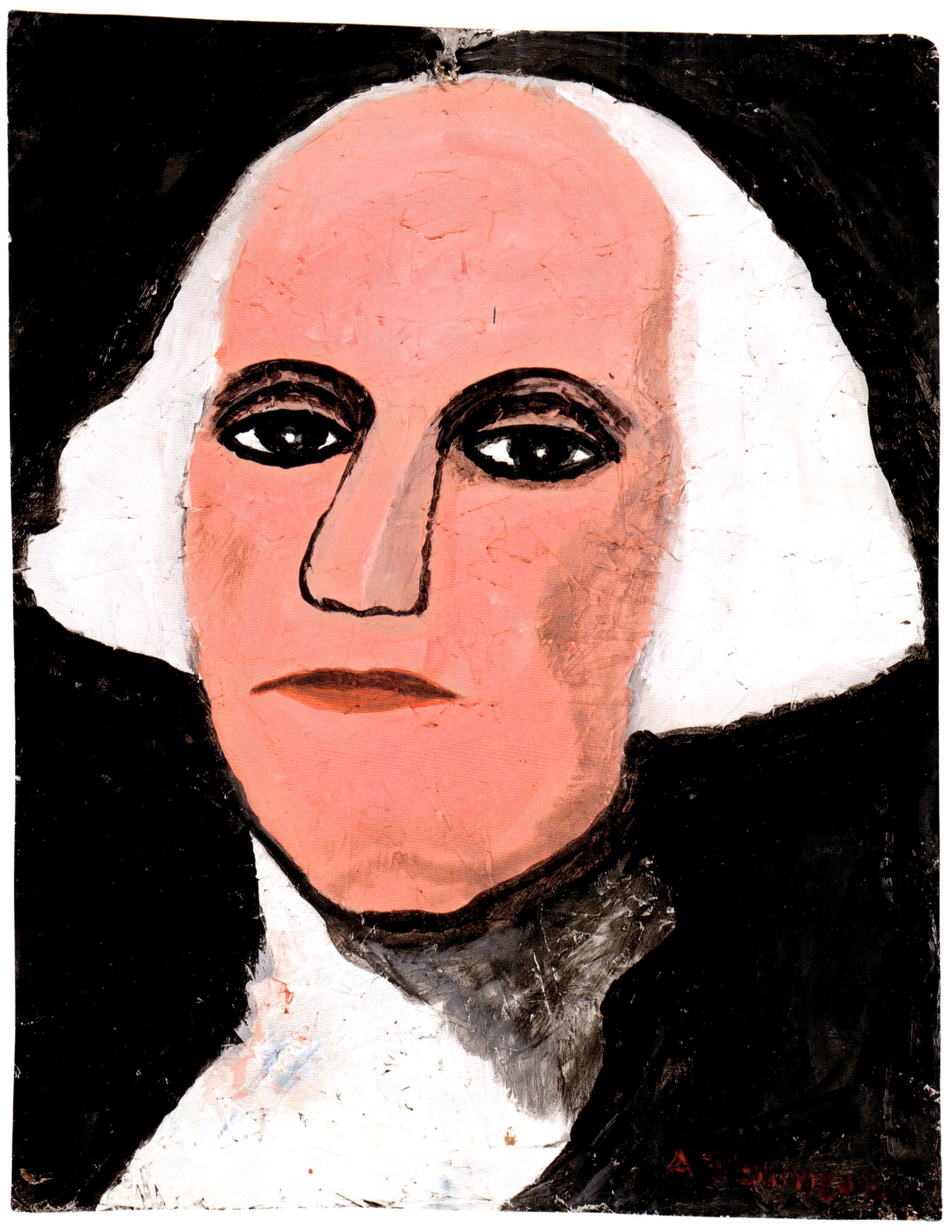

155

ANDERSON JOHNSON

George Washington, ca. 1985

(cat. no. 132)

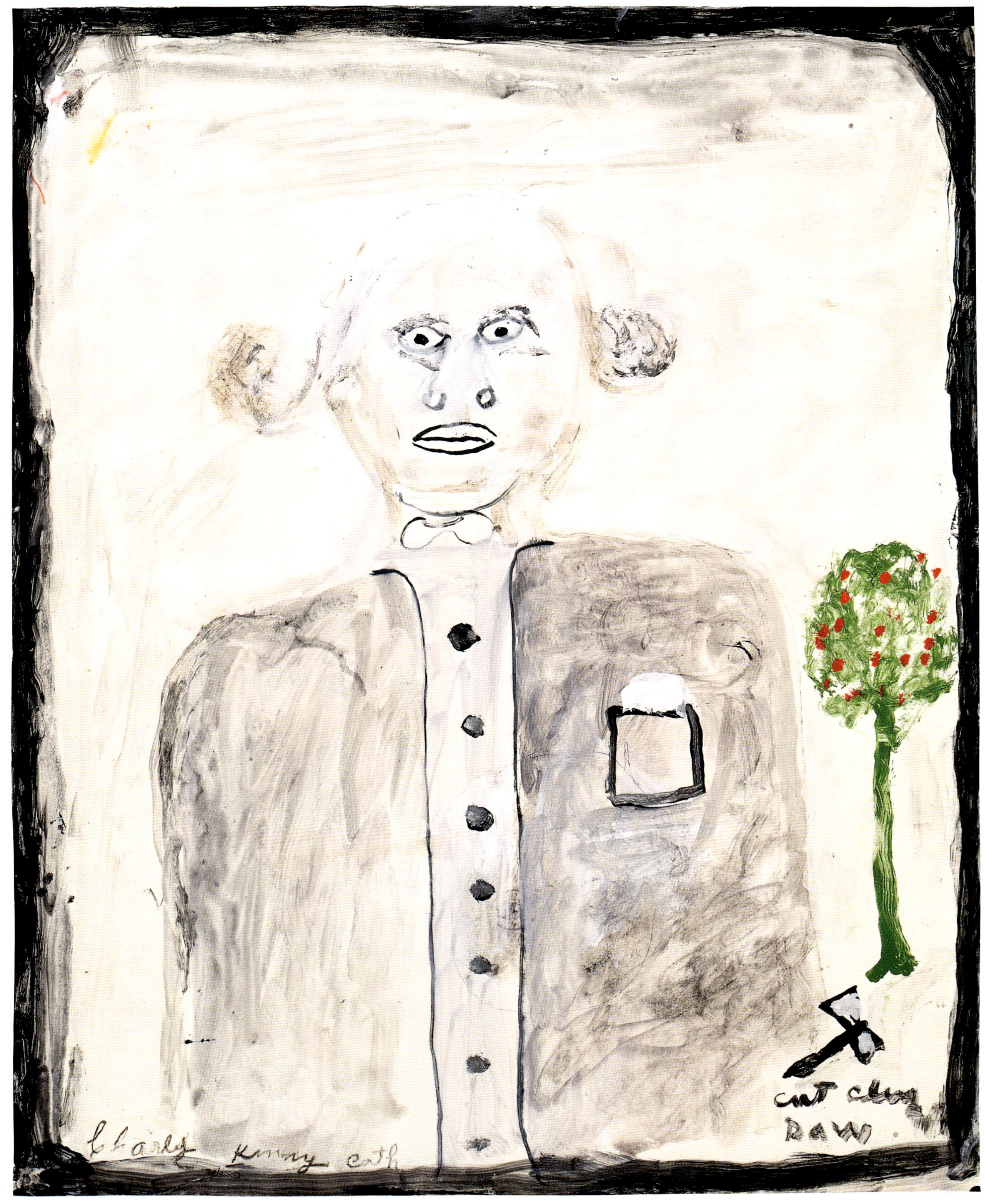

156

CHARLES KINNEY

George Washington, 1990

(cat. no. 147)

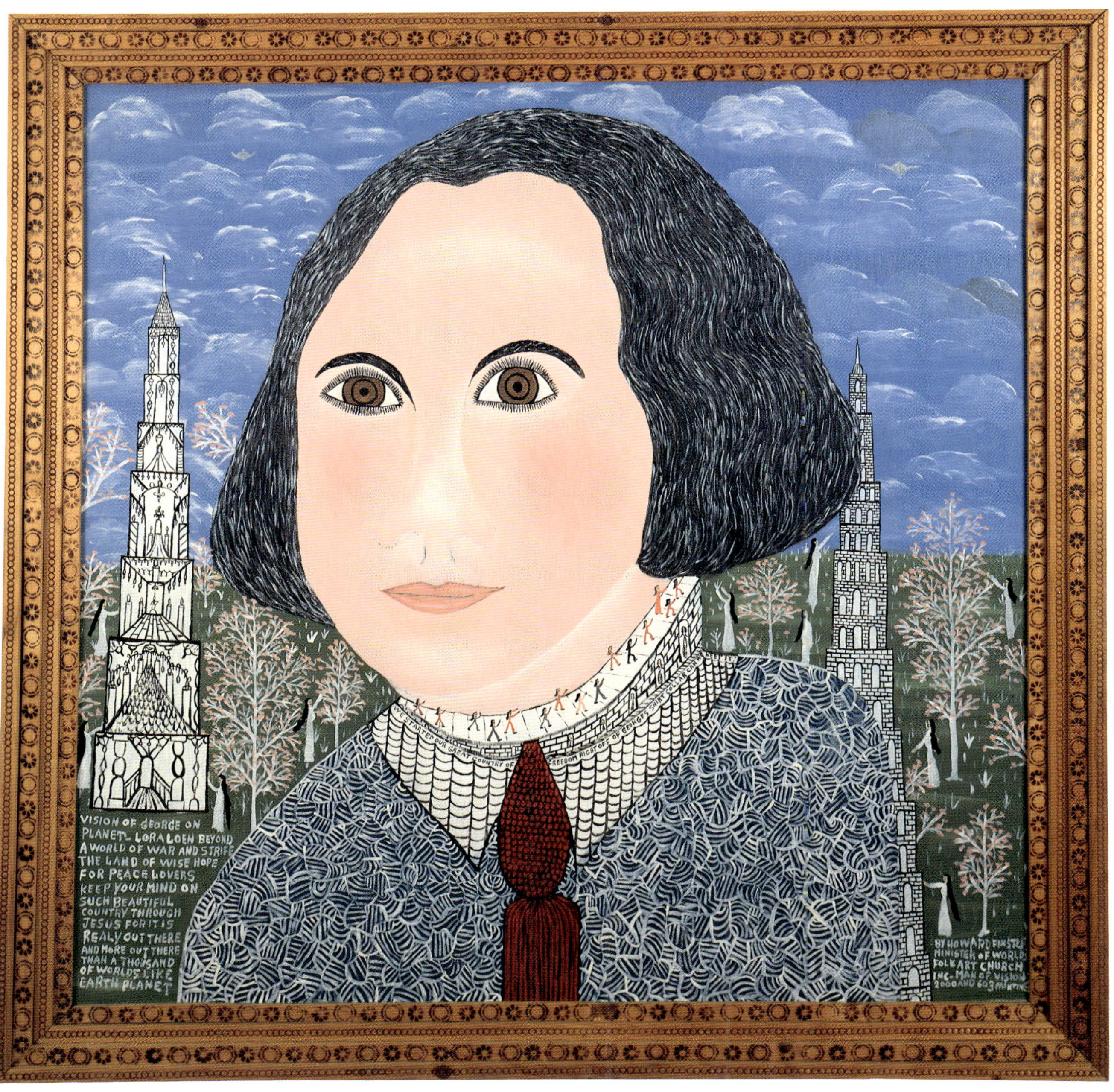

157

HOWARD FINSTER

George Washington #20603, 1982

(cat. no. 88)

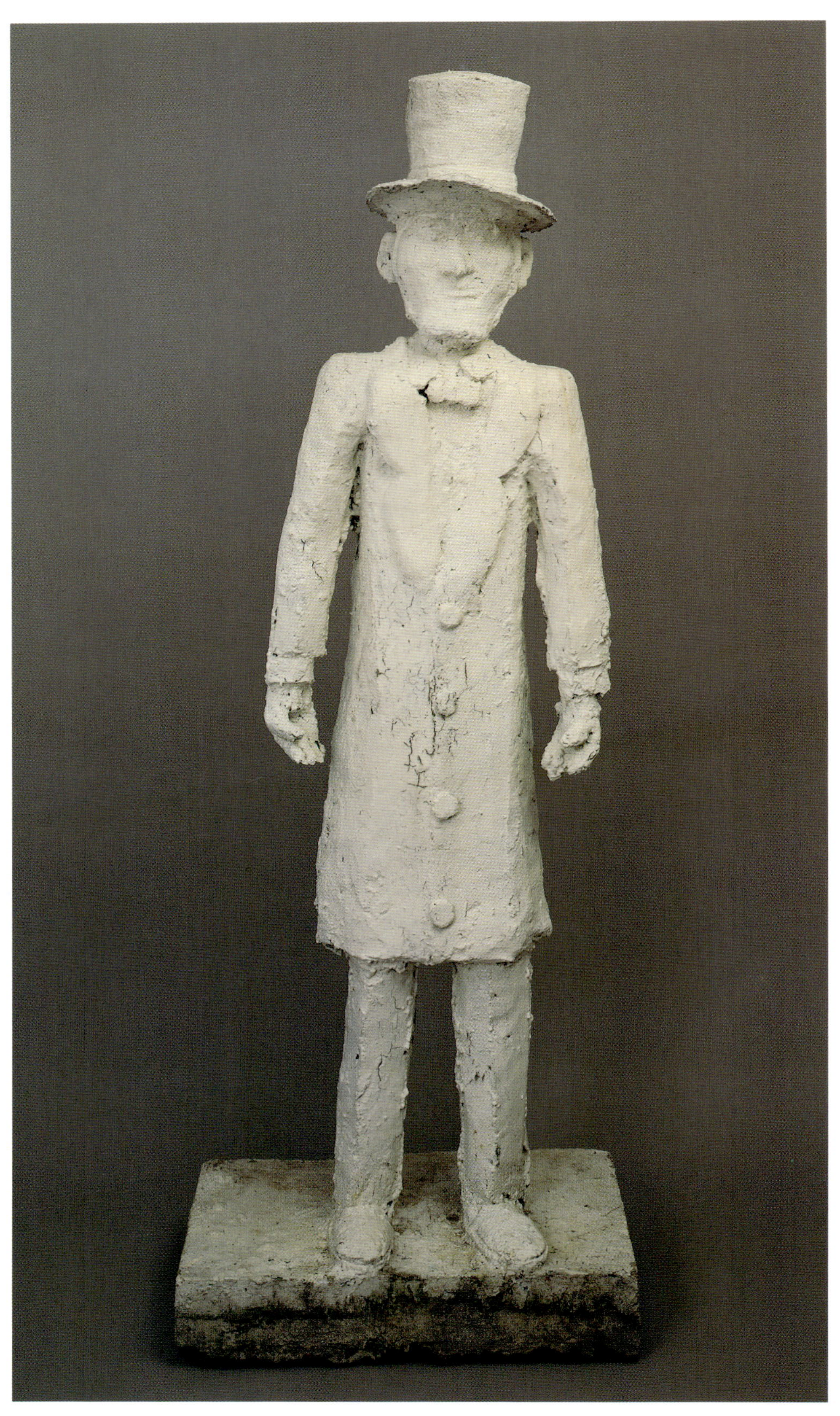

158

VERNON BURWELL

Abe Lincoln, n.d.

(cat. no. 15)

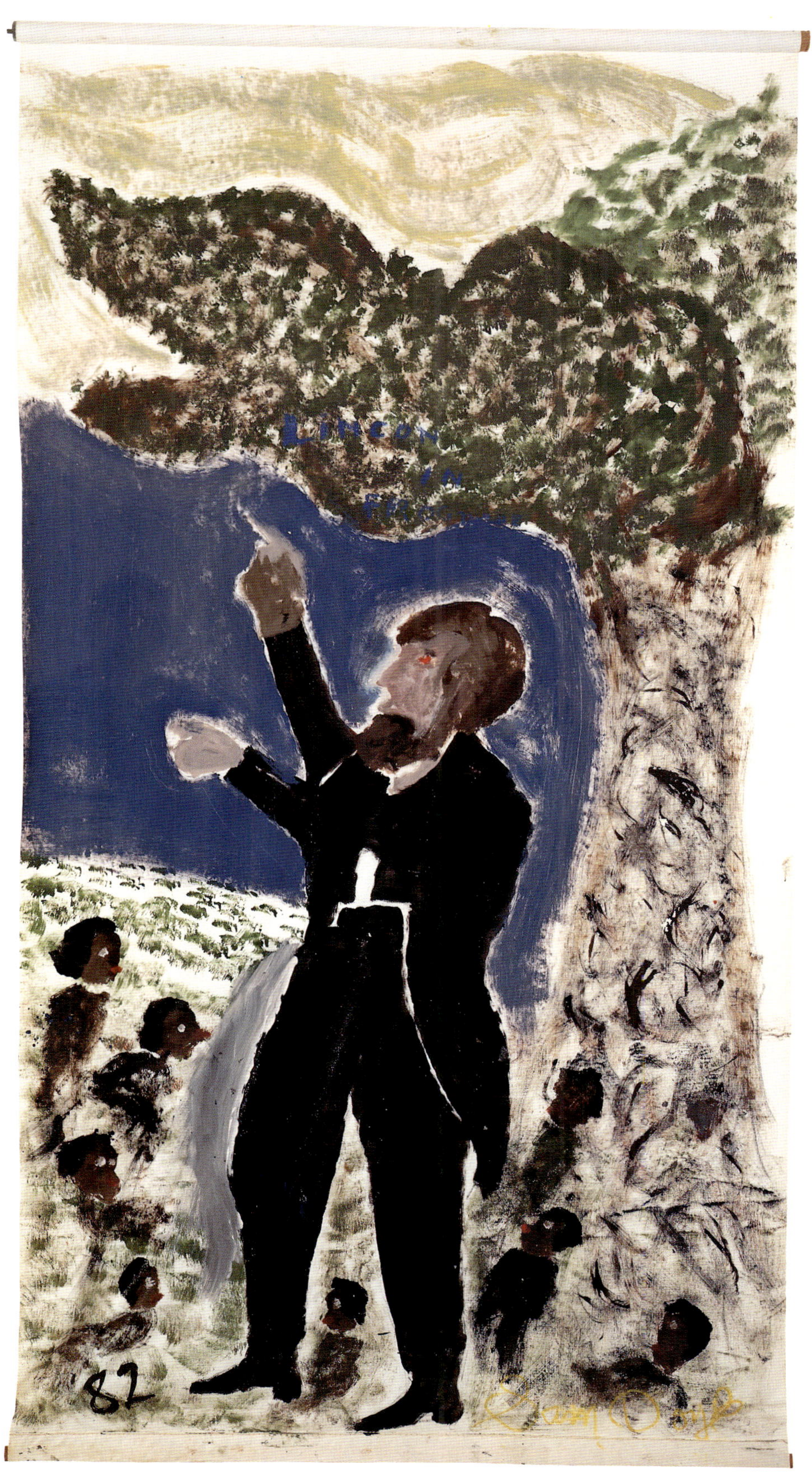

159

SAM DOYLE

Lincoln at Frogmore, 1982

(cat. no. 67)

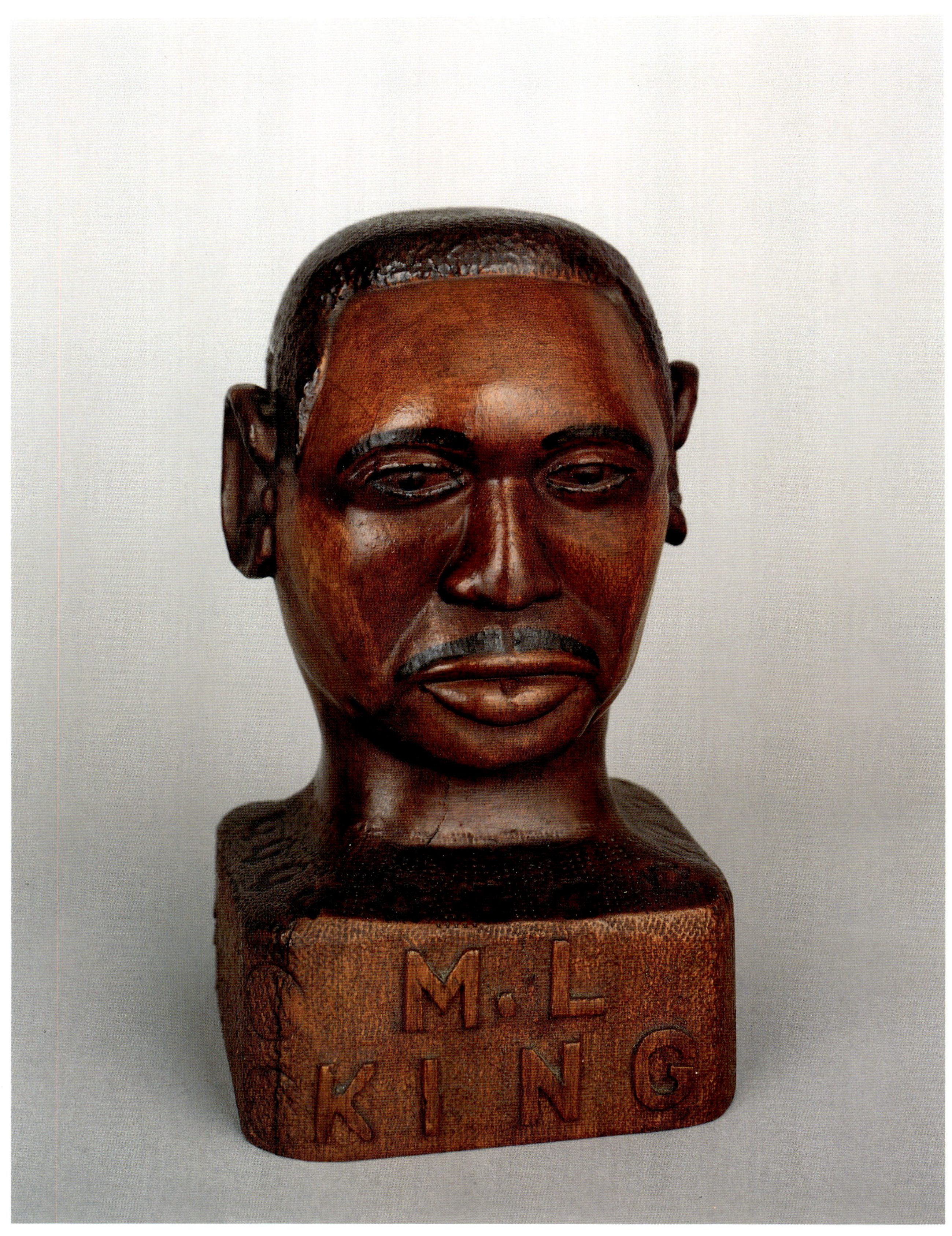

160

ULYSSES DAVIS

M. L. King, n.d.

(cat. no. 42)

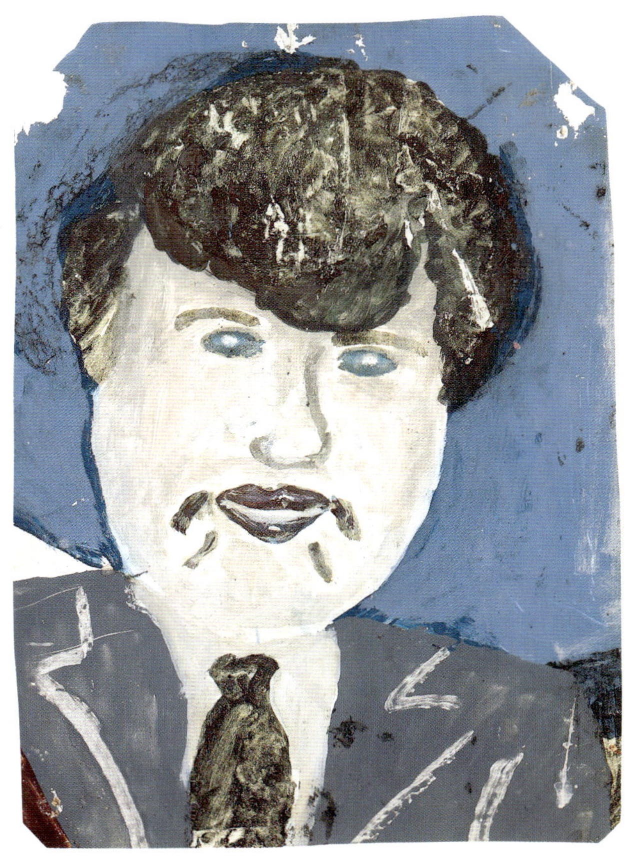

161

SAM DOYLE

Bobby Kennedy, ca. 1980

(cat. no. 61)

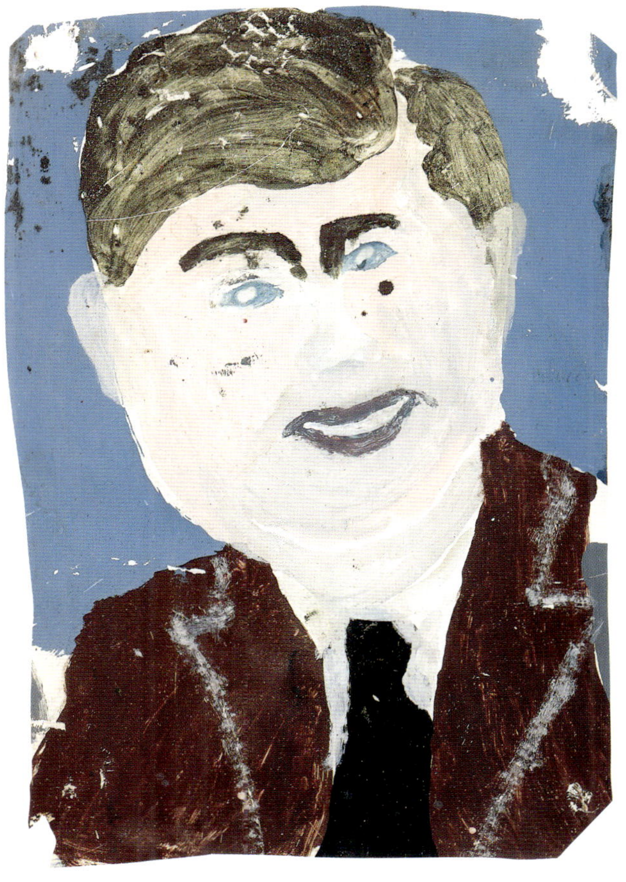

162

SAM DOYLE

John F. Kennedy, ca. 1980

(cat. no. 66)

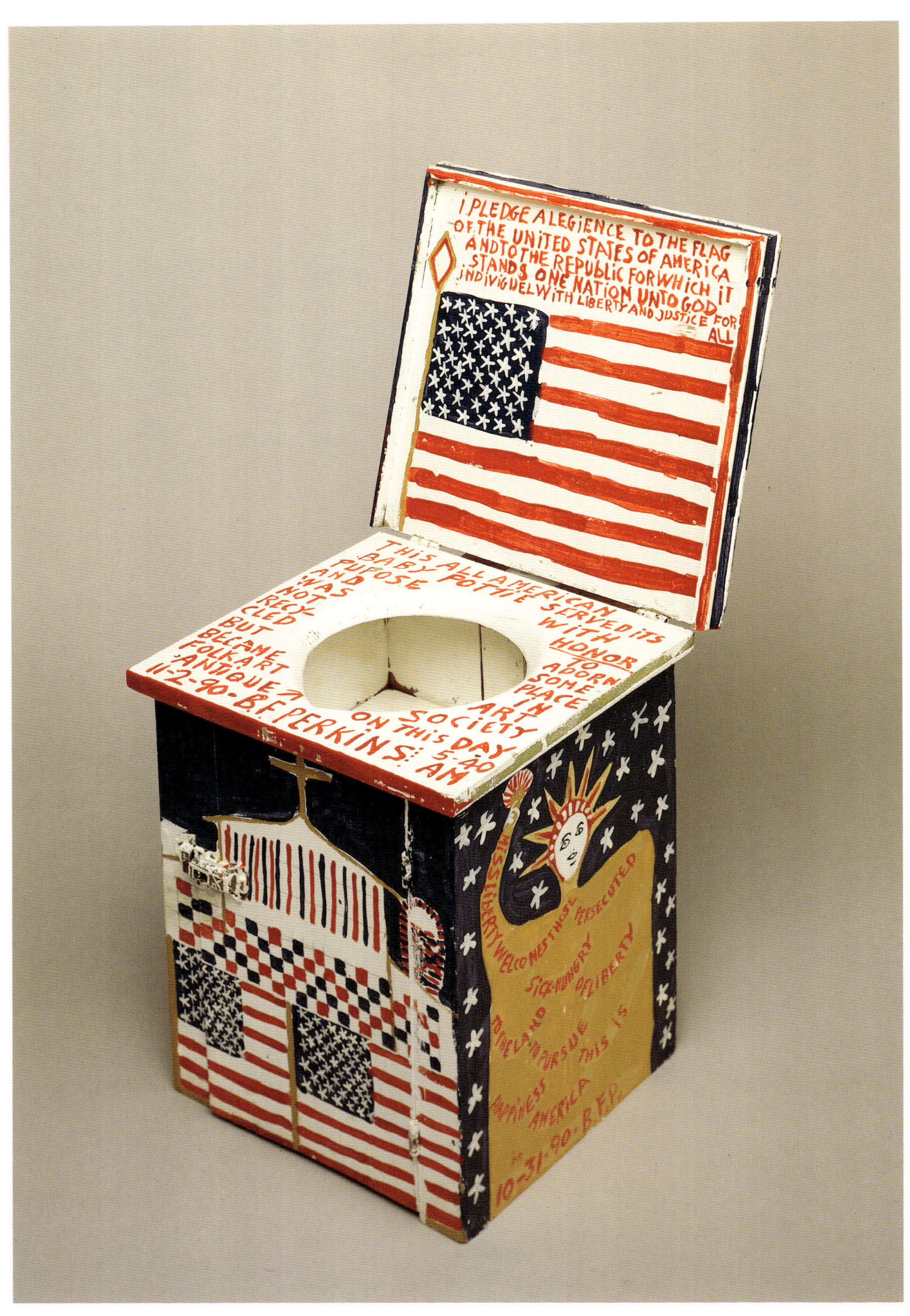

163

REV. BENJAMIN F. PERKINS

All-American Potty, 1990

(cat. no. 186)

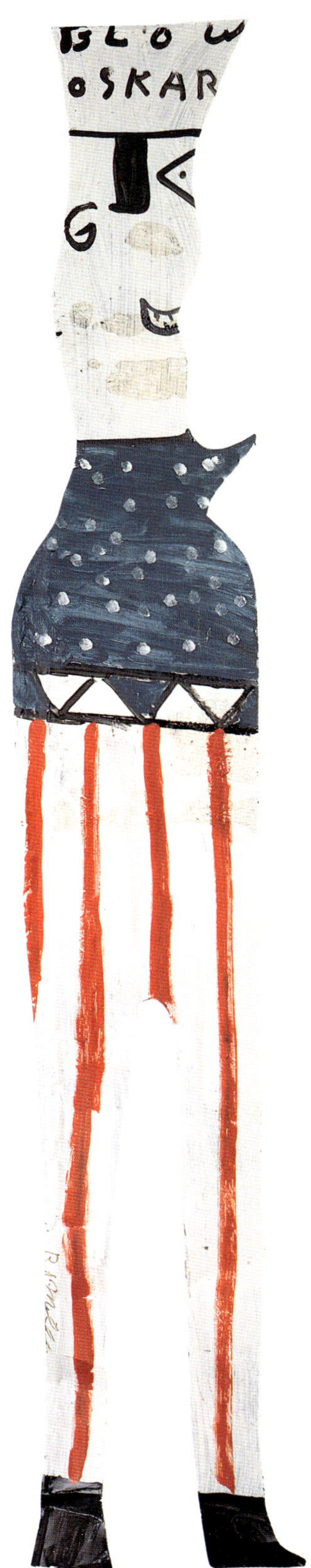

164

R. A. MILLER

Blow Oscar, ca. 1989

(cat. no. 166)

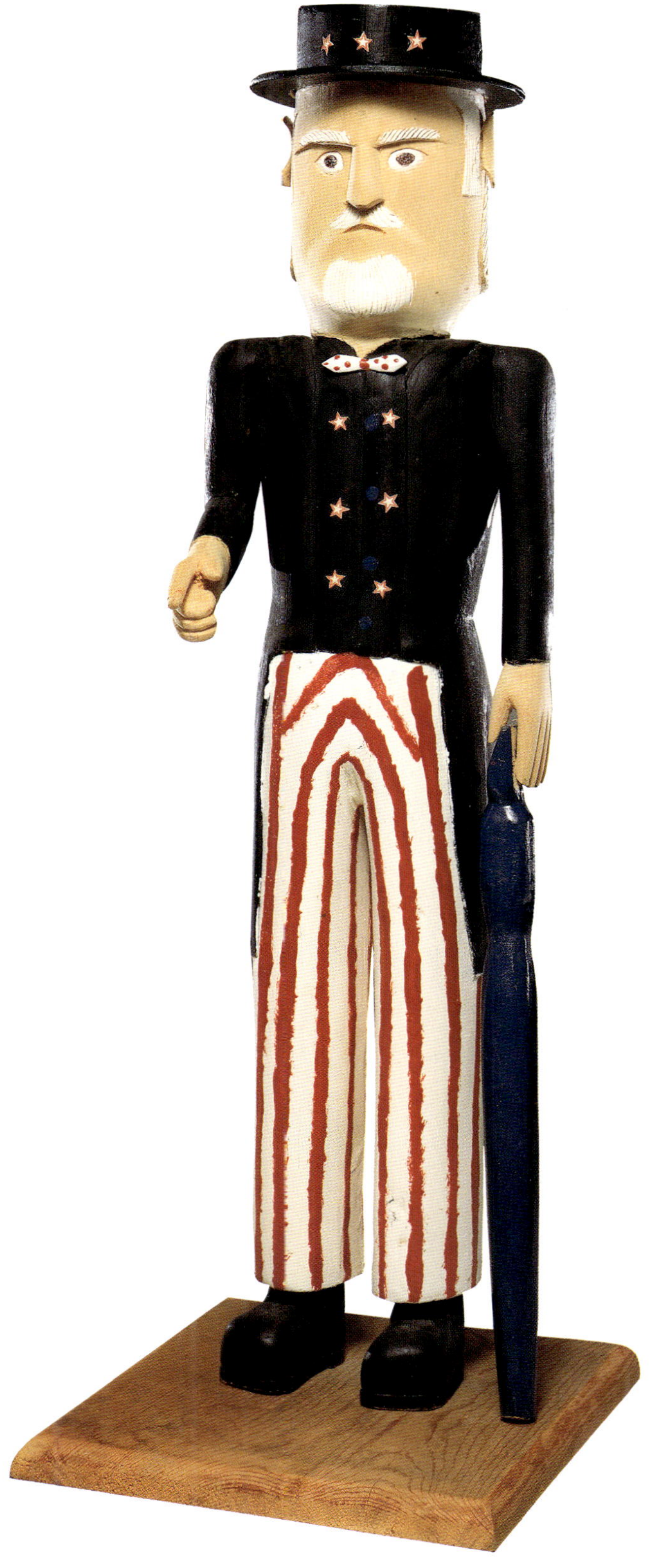

165

EARNEST PATTON

Uncle Sam, 1987

(cat. no. 184)

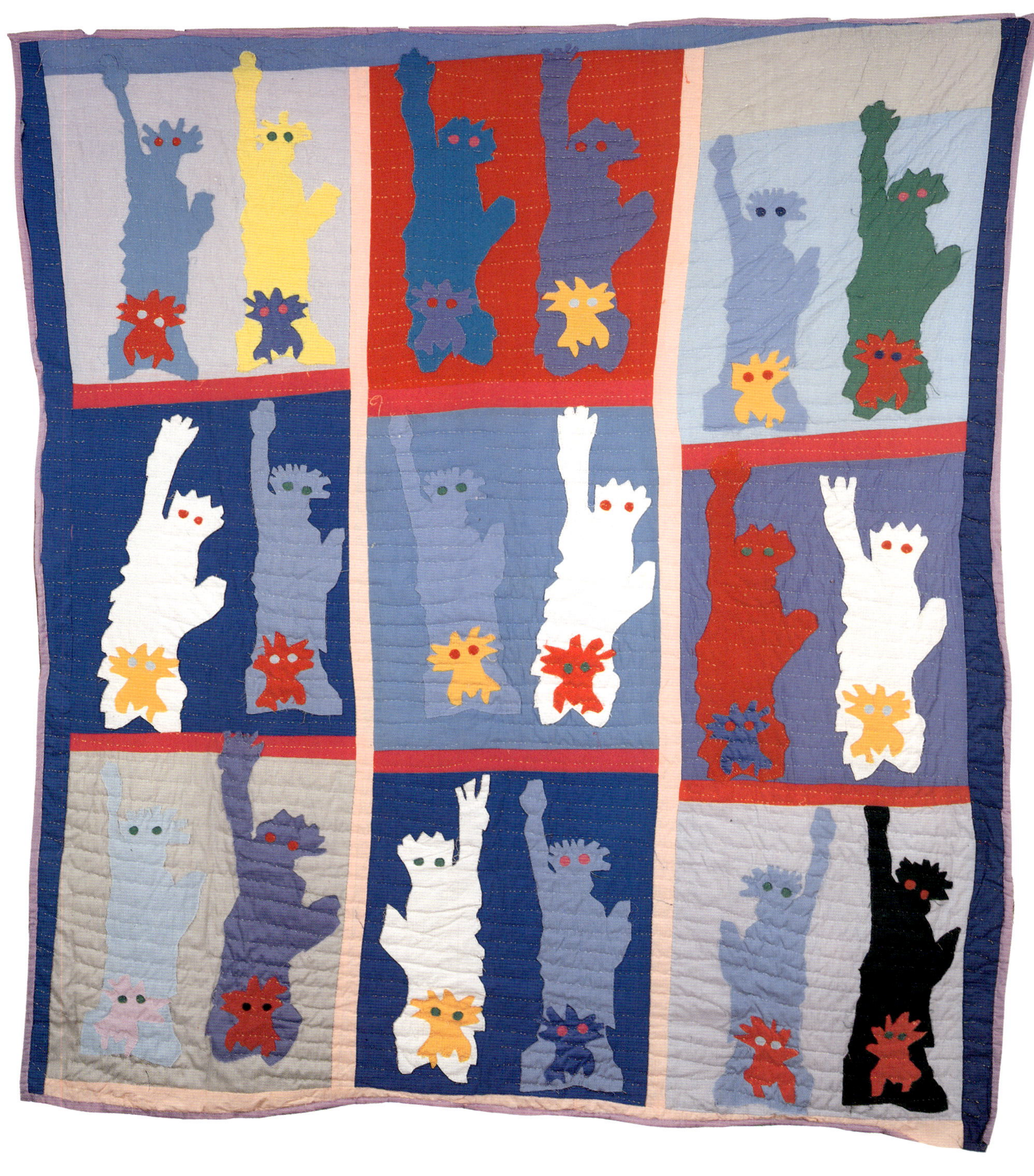

166

SARAH MARY TAYLOR
Statue of Liberty, 1988
(cat. no. 235)

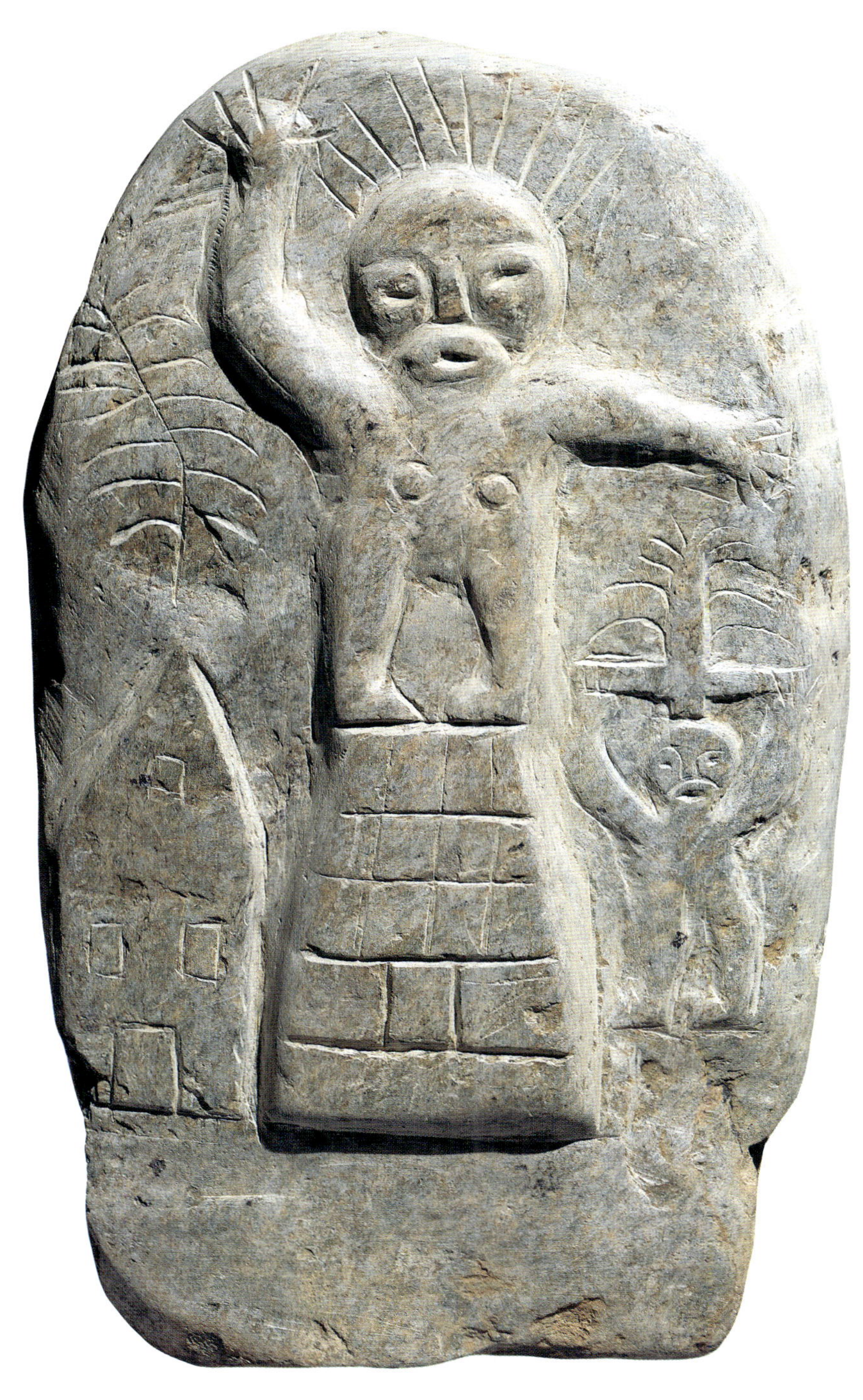

167

RAYMOND COINS

Statue of Liberty, 1988

(cat. no. 37)

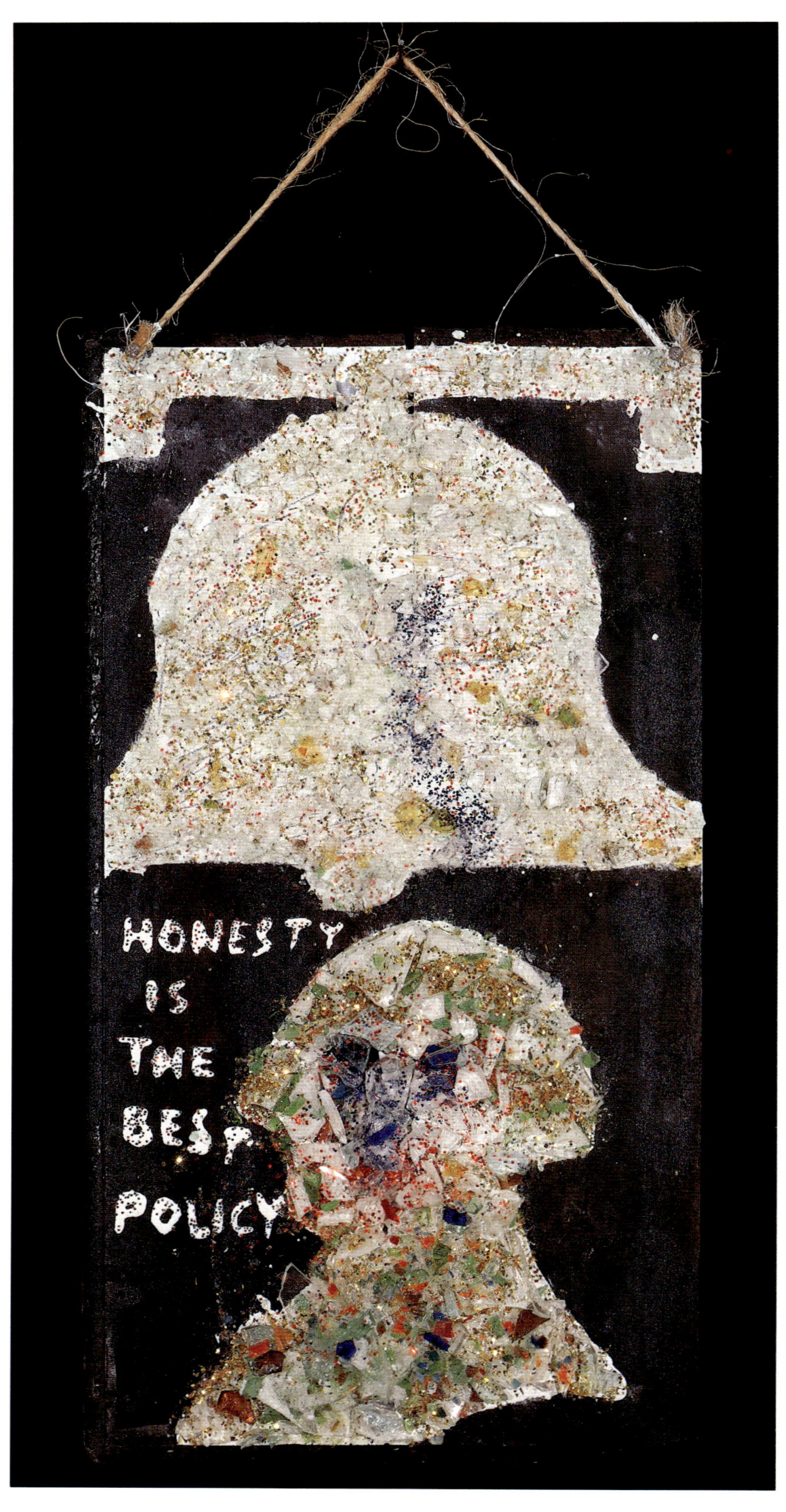

168

GLASSMAN

Honesty Is the Best Policy, ca. 1990

(cat. no. 101)

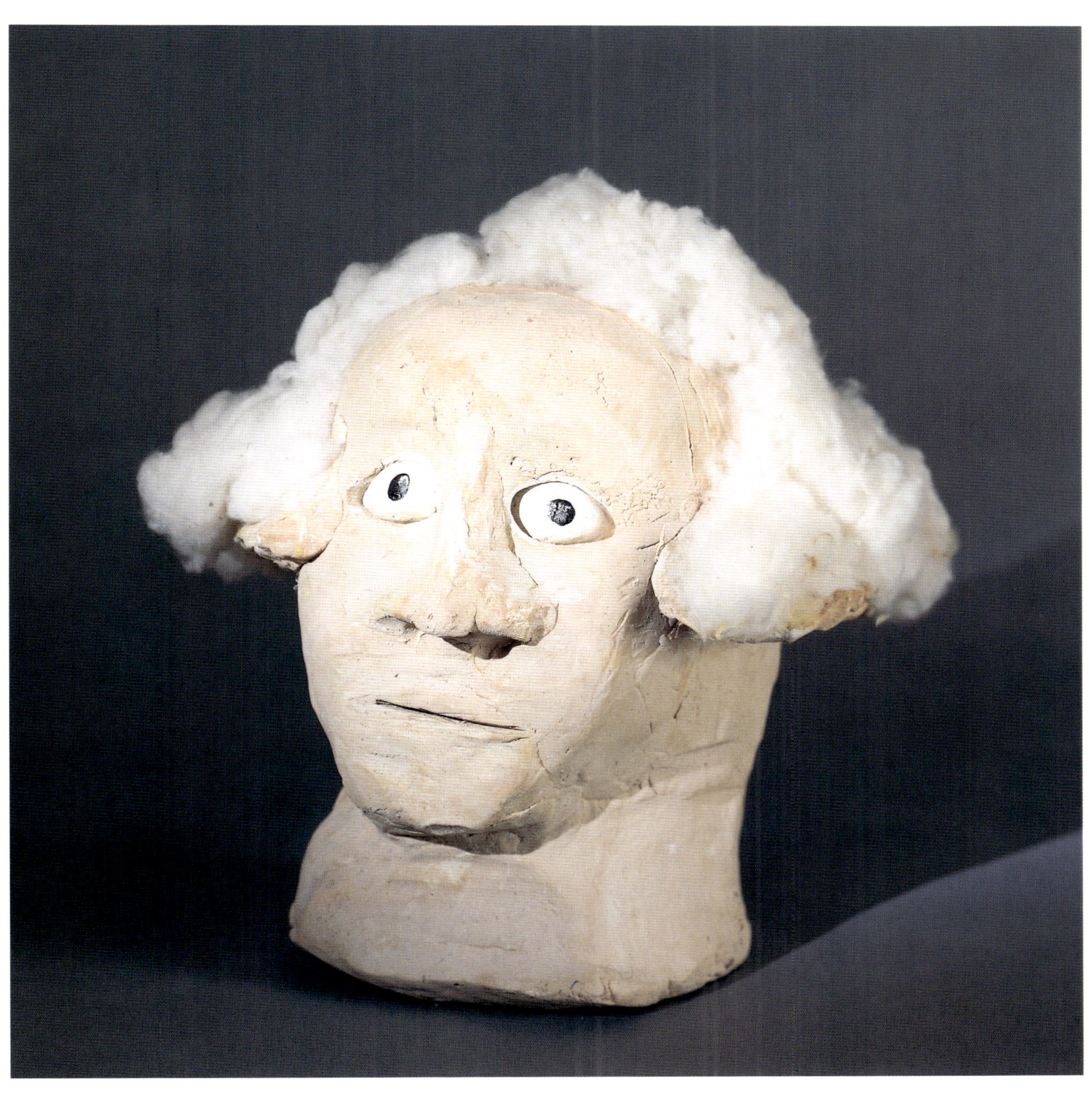

169

JAMES HENRY "SON" THOMAS
George Washington, 1984–85
(cat. no. 236)

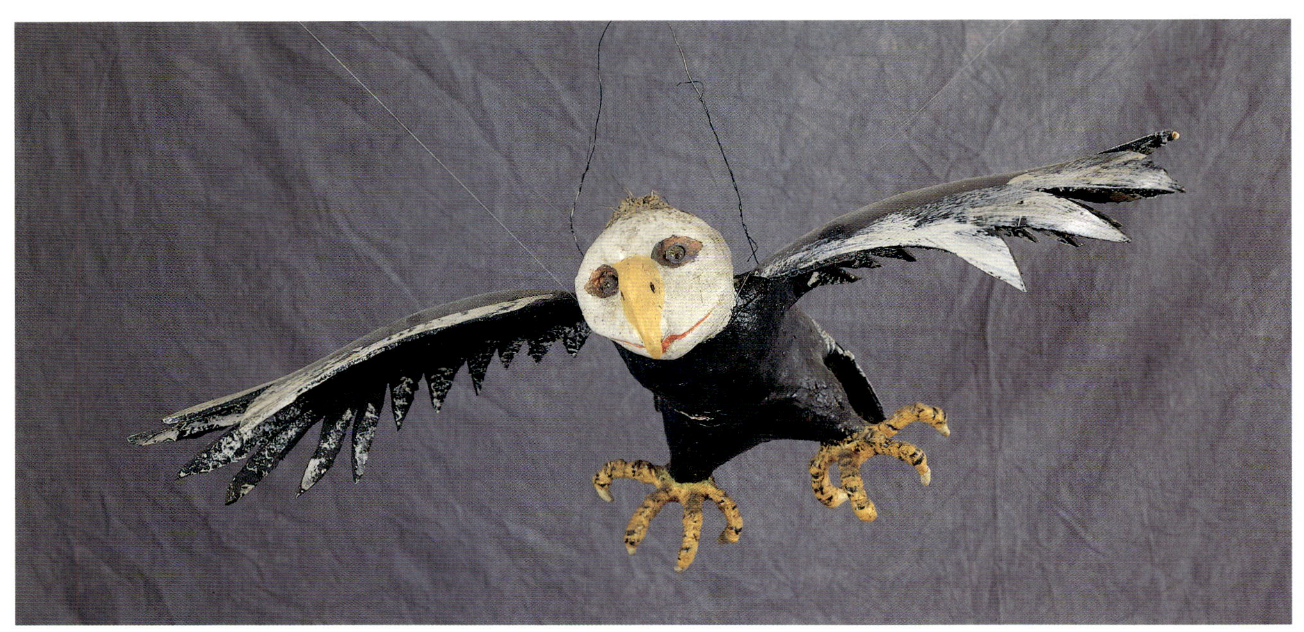

170

MINNIE BLACK

Bald Eagle, n.d.

(cat. no. 12)

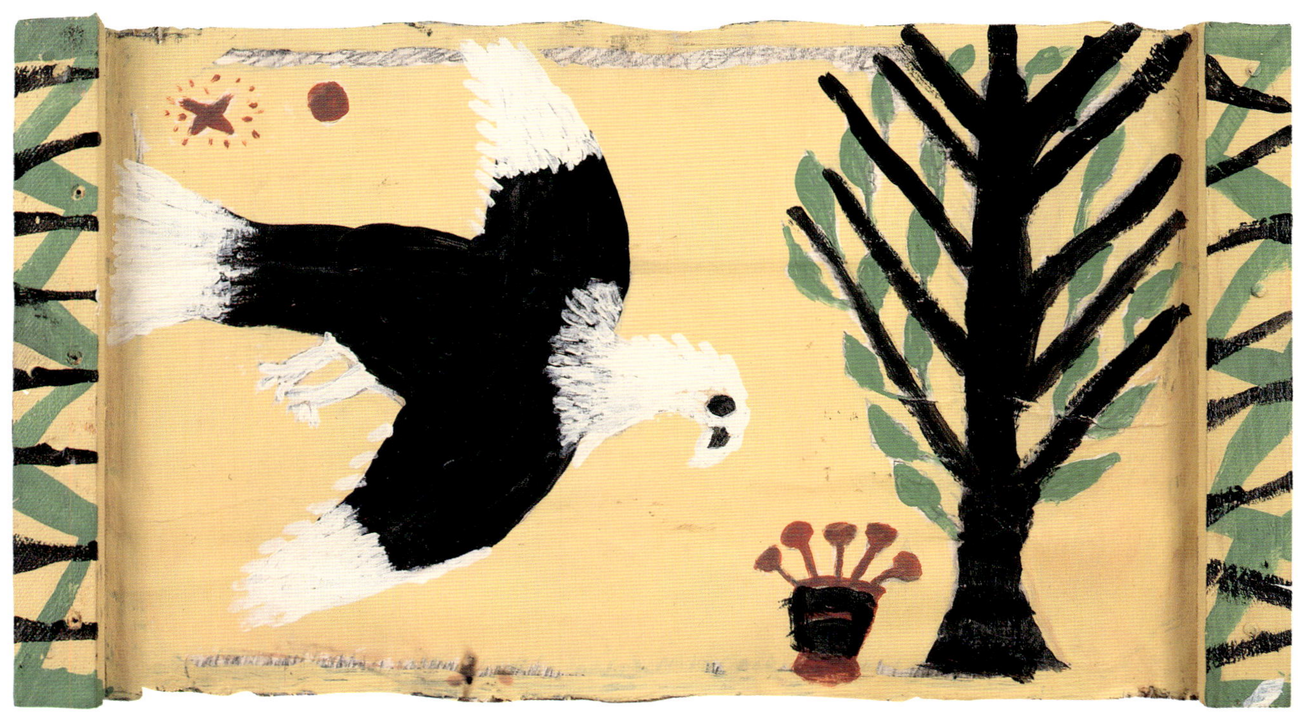

171

WILLIE MASSEY

Eagle, 1989

(cat. no. 162)

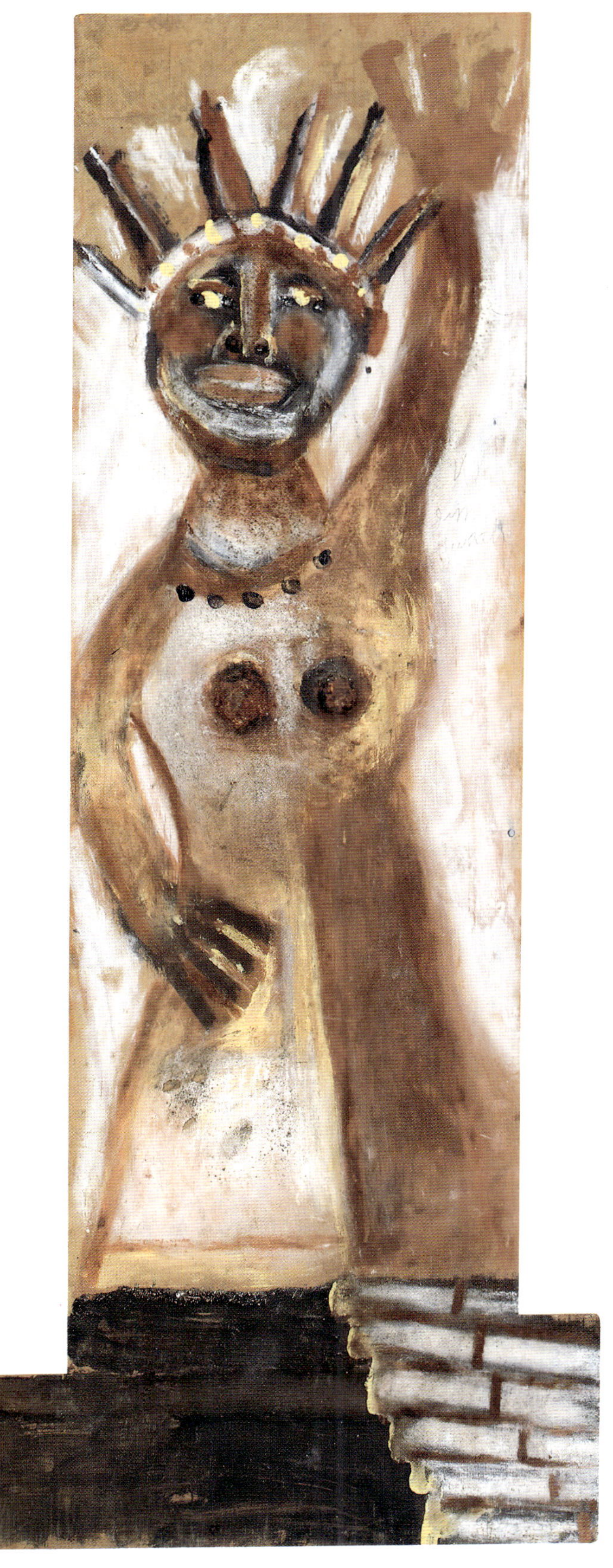

172

JIMMY LEE SUDDUTH

Statue of Liberty, 1991

(cat. no. 226)

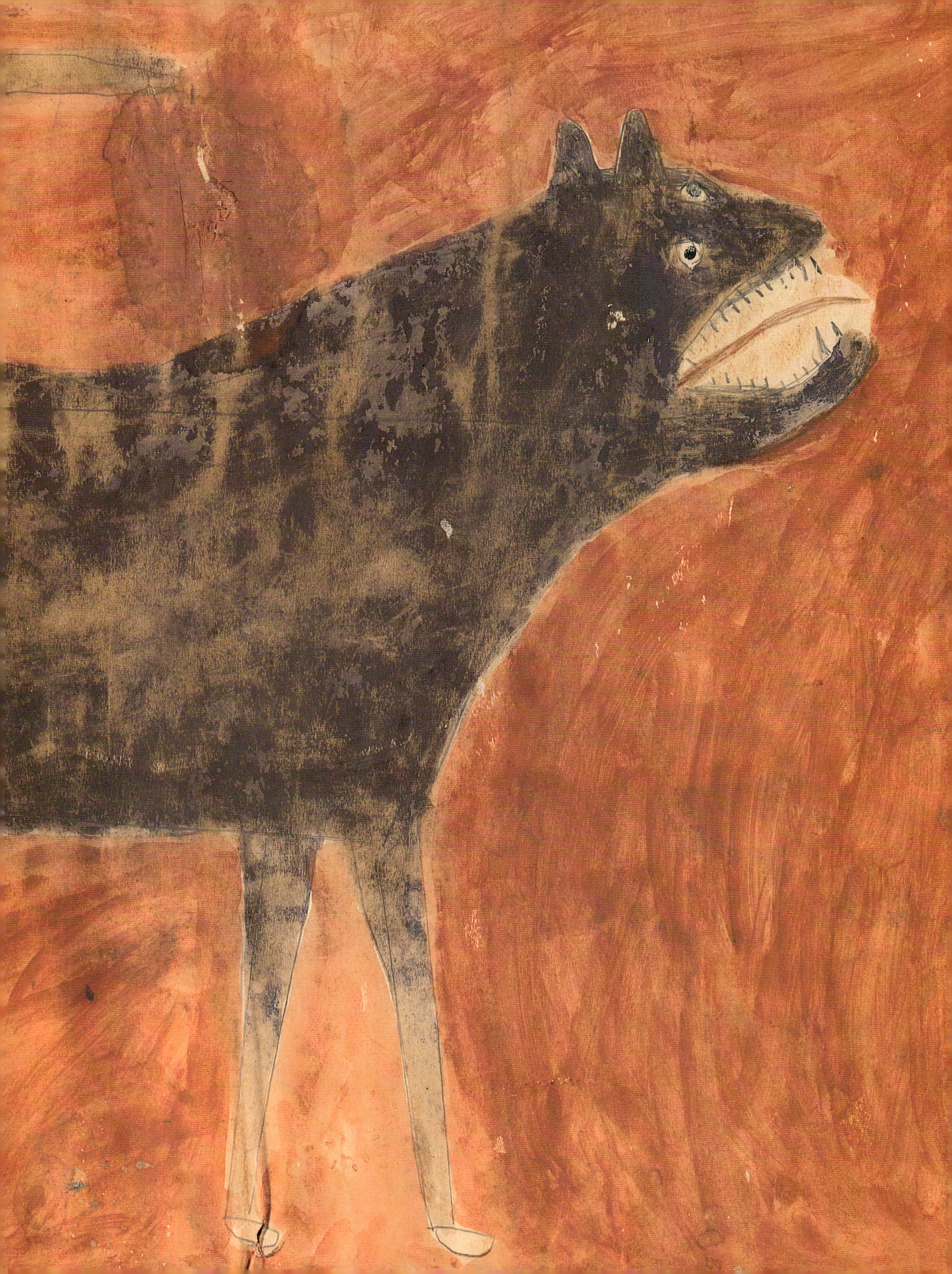

NATURE

The South remained predominantly rural until the 1950s, when with the decline of farm work, factory jobs drew people from sparsely populated areas into towns and urban communities. Implicit in this rural existence was an awareness of, proximity to, and affinity for nature. Farming afforded consistently close contact with the land and animals.

The majority of artists in this exhibition spent their childhoods in rural settings, where animals were more numerous than people. Even those who left southern farms for the urban North or for the towns and cities of the South tended to later recollect the intimate bond they forged with nature in their early years.

William Dawson lived in Chicago from the 1920s yet drew upon his memories of rural Alabama in his drawings of animal life. William Hawkins and Elijah Pierce also demonstrated a keen interest in animals based on their early Kentucky and Mississippi associations. Bill Traylor, who spent only the last years of his long life in Montgomery, Alabama, interspersed his urban drawings of people with animal sketches that revealed his reminiscences of the country.

In interpretations ranging from the realistic to the whimsical, these artists depict what they see around them. Birds, fish, frogs, and lizards were common sights to rural dwellers, as were working farm animals and pets: horses, mules, cows, pigs, and dogs. Wild, prehistoric, exotic, and imaginary animals were also rendered, their forms and characteristics freely interpreted from magazines and books, television programs, or visits to the zoo or circus. Just as animals are prominent in the oral storytelling tradition of both African-Americans and whites, they commonly appear in the artwork of southern artists.

Sparsely populated rural areas attracted a multitude of birds which also are plentiful in the work of self-taught artists. "I did birds because people asked for them," said Mose Tolliver, "but now I do them all the time without asking."[1] The artist grew up on an Alabama farm, the son of a sharecropper, and later was a tenant farmer himself. He often created images of birds, trees, turtles, fish, and other animals. On a pair of symmetrical headboards (pl. 183), Tolliver created a natural treed environment for his birds, ducks, and an owl. Short, energetic brushstrokes and a limited palette create a lively sense of motion. One headboard depicts three birds moving in flight toward the edges of the picture plane. In the other, more static scene, a centrally positioned, stationary owl is flanked by a pair of standing ducks. Tolliver's mastery of compositional design is well displayed by the cleverly opposed qualities of these complementary works.

Echoing Tolliver's staid owl and ducks, Eddie Arning's *Two Geese* (pl. 184) is static, stylized, and refined. After 1966 Arning began to collect illustrations and advertisements as starting points for his distinctive imagery. *Two Geese* was inspired by a two-page illustration in *Sports Afield* magazine,[2] which Arning transformed from a realistic rendering into a singular, highly patterned work that only minimally resembles the original.

In Arning's composition the geese stand in profile, the curve of one head and beak gracefully tucked under the other. They pose on an island of yellow-green whose shape elegantly echoes the contours of the birds' heads. The artist characteristically interpreted the natural feathers by a stylized patterning in blue and white and gray and white. The birds' bodies seem almost to rest on a row of green trees whose verticality emphasizes the horizontal line of the geese. Another upright row of trees recedes into the background. Arning, who typically eschews negative space, filled the remaining picture plane with rapid, dark green strokes. A consummate colorist, Arning contrasted his rich green tones with touches of red in each tree and on the beaks and feet of the geese.[3]

Willie Massey's imperfect yet charming aesthetic is seen in his two-story *Birdhouse: Blue and Pink* (pl. 180), complete with roof and painted window. Two arched openings, roughly fashioned from painted wooden fruit crates, provide nesting spaces for birds. Triangular cut vents at the four front corners circulate air and illustrate the artist's knowledge of the requirements of birdhouse design.[4] A bird made from tin foil is perched on the rooftop; the head of another bird, of painted wood with a protruding plastic eye, peers out from the upper balcony. Massey often shaped birds from the tin foil that originally covered the hot dinners delivered to him by Meals on Wheels.[5] He might then paint and wrap the bird with black masking tape. Painted walnuts dangle from three levels, one from an orange Elmer's glue top and another from a black plastic top. Massey's fascination with birds and nature is an intuitive outgrowth of the nearly seventy years that he worked on a Kentucky farm. He made his birdhouses for actual use, hanging them from trees, where art enthusiasts first saw them.

Birdhouses are popular in the southern landscape, where migrating birds flock in the winter. David Butler's painted wooden *Birdhouse* (cat. no. 16) is a multistoried construction that resembles a small house. Rev. Benjamin F. Perkins fashioned birdhouses from dried gourds by hollowing out their natural forms and painting them (looking much like *Gourd* [cat. no. 187]). Similar unpainted gourd birdhouses were once a familiar sight in the South.

William Edmondson's regal *Birdbath* (pl. 185), static and solid, is a rectangular and symmetrical limestone structure. At the opposite rims of its saucer, two life-size birds are poised, drinking water as if to beckon other birds. Edmondson's *Talking Owl* (pl. 186) is a streamlined, totemic creature. Incised lines indicate eyes, mouth, and wings; all other features are suggested by Edmondson's powerful, volumetric carving.

Homer Green's *Totem Pole* (pl. 196) is characteristic of the artist's sculptural style. Three carved owls stand one on the other, their bodies and outstretched wings decorated with dabs of colored paint.[6] A poor farmer in rural Tennessee, Green began to carve after retiring in 1981. His first images were farm animals, especially oxen and horses, and later he made more eccentric critters—giraffes, penguins, buzzards, alligators, and owl totems.[7]

Green reportedly first got the idea for his totems almost thirteen years ago. "I was looking at some telephone poles. I got out there with my chain saw and said, 'I'm going to make something of it.'"[8] He now saws his totems from cedar tree limbs and later refines them. The owl wings are individually cut and carved, then painted and glued or nailed onto the body of the totem. Within each outstretched wing Green painted a silhouette of a four-legged animal. Although the color scheme of each owl varies, a vertical stripe of primary yellow marks the beak of each face and unifies the vertical structure, transmitting the feeling of joy and freedom characteristic of Green's work.

The Green work titled *Black Angel* (cat. no. 102) refers to the fanciful buzzards that protect from vandals the menagerie of painted wooden animals grazing on the artist's lawn. "Buzzards will take care of anything,"[9] said Green. "I enjoy people a-comin', but I don't enjoy these here rogues a-comin'. . . . I feel like I'm in the penitentiary. I can't go nowhere."[10] A sign (private collection) that was once in Green's yard exhibits his fear of vandalism: "Private Property. Stay out. Caught on my land you'll be shot cause my black angels are hungry."[11]

R. A. Miller's rooster, hen, other birds, and animals were cut from single pieces of flat tin (pl. 197). Bold strokes of green and red on yellow simulate a turkey's feathers; red is used for the crown, beak, and tail feathers of a white rooster. Similar cut tin images and windmills, usually painted in solid colors, are also the basis of Miller's outdoor whirligigs, which he fastens on top of ten-foot posts.

Like Miller, David Butler has created painted tin roosters, but his *Two Roosters and Two Hens* (pl. 202) is more animated. A rooster with green wings seems about to peck at something on the ground; another bird turns to look back at its tail. Butler's feathered, painterly brushwork aptly simulates the feathers of a live bird. Butler adds a third dimension to the hand-cut, flattened, corrugated tin by attaching smaller pieces of tin with coat hangers and wire for wings, eyes, and legs, and by cutting tail feathers to fan out into a sculptural image. Butler, too, places his works on whirligigs, but his are more complex than Miller's, and they often combine objects that interact when the whirligig is in motion.

Raised on a Kentucky farm, William Hawkins recalled the days of his youth in *Two Horses* (pl. 181), a masterful image of horses running side by side. The motion of the horses moving gracefully through the painting and even a sense of fantasy are beautifully conveyed. Although known for his cityscapes and architectural scenes, Hawkins made his most personal statements in his depiction of animals. He preferred above all the horse, which he rendered with intense respect. Hawkins traced his immense fondness for horses back to farm life; as a child he had become adept at raising and breeding horses, which to him symbolized "everything . . . pure and noble."[12]

Sarah Mary Taylor's *Horse* (pl. 182) is a fanciful, animated sketch. The forward thrust of the horse is emphasized by an intense frenzy of red markings on the horse's face, mane, and front leg. Looser, swift red strokes fill in the rest of the body, and a combination of yellow, brown, orange, and green pencil marks compose the background. Known as a quilt maker, Taylor for some time has kept sketchbooks of drawings (with horses among them) that have inspired her quilt imagery and served as design templates.[13]

Large Wire Horse (pl. 204) by Charlie Lucas is at once proud and arrogant. Its frame is constructed entirely of scrap banding once used to tie shipments of lumber together. "I try to show . . . the movement of a graceful horse. When I ride . . . you won't see me, you only . . . see the horse."[14]

Lucas lives in rural Alabama on an acre of land outside Montgomery. Roughly half of his welded imagery depicts often recognizable animals with a modernist's sensibility for negative space. These and other assemblages of figures and bicycles, made of old car parts, found scrap metal, and sometimes bits of farm equipment, adorn his rustic environment. Of *Cow* (pl. 205), Lucas, a family man with six children, said, "The cow is the provider. It gives nourishment. I want all kids to have nourishment from the cow. . . . The cow doesn't serve one person, it serves everybody."[15] Lucas's spare, evocative cow is made from rusted metal, a material whose old and new functions he sometimes links philosophically. The cow's head is made from parts of a car engine, the legs are old gas pipes dug up from the ground, and the hips are made of springs.

Lucas includes a bicycle rim in many of his works, as seen in the stomach of *Cow*, to honor his great-grandfather, a blacksmith. Lucas explained, "I saw him fix a wooden wagon wheel. . . . He cut down a tree, turned it down to make a spoke on a wheel. It was like art to me."[16]

Steven Ashby's *Bull* (pl. 194) is a whimsical construction. A profile cutout, the bull turns its head toward the viewer with a strong but docile look. Ashby added a braided hemp tail and a few hemp strands to the animal's penis. He indicated the bull's scrotum with a hanging painted nut.

Bill Traylor, who moved from the plantation on which he lived for most of his life to Montgomery in his old age, sometimes recalls plantation days in his artwork. *Double Goat* (pl. 188) and *Red Dog* (pl. 187) are two of the largest known works by Traylor. The double image of a goat, with two bodies but only four legs, is brushed in brown hues. In *Red Dog* the menacing mood of the large fierce dog, with open mouth, bared teeth, and tense tail, is accentuated by the surrounding red background.

Pig (cat. no. 252), drawn by Traylor with bold black lines, represents one of the most common animals on the southern farm. In the rendition by Minnie and Garland Adkins, *Sow with Piglets* (pl. 179), three piglets stand in a row under the mother's teats. The sow's expression is remarkably ferocious, with piercing eyes, open red jaw, and sharp white teeth. The Adkinses share the tasks of making their animals—Garland finds wood of an appropriate shape and approximates the animal's form with his chain saw; Minnie refines the details with carving and painting.

Dixie, the Barking Dog (pl. 176) by Jimmy Lee Sudduth captures an exuberant, friendly bird dog, whose somewhat silly expression contrasts with the fierceness of Bill Traylor's dog. Dixie, according to Sudduth, was fifteen years old when he painted her. She lived on a blind black man's farm and "had as much sense as a person had."[17] Her body pushes at the borders of the painted frame; her open jaw and one hind leg indeed go beyond it. The dotted pattern of the dog's coat is repeated in the frame's design of alternating smudges of black, white, and brown.

Willie Massey's *Lizard* (pl. 174) is a friendly fellow. His black body, vividly seen against a vibrant red background, clings to a rocky outcropping of flat orange and brown. Massey worked on the back side of stretched commercial canvases, bought by a niece at J. C. Penney. Massey saw the wood stretcher as a ready-made frame,[18] which he here painted orange with bold dashes of purple.

Raymond Coins's *Frog* (pl. 199) resembles a docile backyard pet. Carved from blue-gray river stone, this work in its stark beauty and simplicity resembles the sculpture of Arp or Brancusi. Another Coins work, *Bear* (pl. 200), is carved from a greenish stone with ocher undertones. Although not a bear hunter, Coins saw bears in the North Carolina mountains. The artist never knew what he would carve: "I'd have a feeling I would cut something. Whatever was on my mind, I'd cut."[19]

Many artists were inspired by more exotic animals seen outside their natural settings (in zoos, the circus), in magazine or poster reproductions, or on television. Some creatures they simply imagined. Noah Kinney once recalled, "I saw the Cincinnati Zoo some years ago. I started carving them lions and tigers."[20] *Tiger* (pl. 178), carved with a pocketknife and brightly painted in orange and black, prepares to lunge. The cat's legs are tensed, ready to spring, and his upright ears and extended tail suggest his alertness. Another aggressive beast, in William Hawkins's *Tasmanian Tiger No. 2* (pl. 193), roars as he emerges from a painted background. The built-up facial area, of enamel and cornmeal modeling paste with attached painted wood "tusks," extends beyond the Masonite and board picture plane and contributes to the impression of the animal's ferocious forward motion. Hawkins not only knew farm animals from his days in Kentucky but also probably saw exotic animals in circus posters and at the circus itself, which periodically visited his town.[21] In his later years Hawkins turned to *Smithsonian* magazine for much visual inspiration, exemplified by the direct influence that a photo in the August 1985 issue had on *Tasmanian Tiger No. 2*.[22]

In *"Cheter" Cat* (pl. 173) Charles Kinney placed a jungle beast in a delicate, peculiar landscape with a cactus, a manicured tree, and a mountainous background reminiscent of the eastern Kentucky hills near Kinney's tobacco farm. Kinney's cat, soft and unthreatening, stands in profile, peering frontally. A light application of greens, blues, and browns on a vinyl window shade created the painting's muted surface.

Willie Massey's *Spotted Cat* (pl. 175) is a docile feline. With a white-tipped tail and toes, and a tufted ruff on its face, the orange and black cat has an almost sporty look.

Elijah Pierce's carved *Leopard* (pl. 177) is a languid spotted beast. His stance is relaxed compared to Kinney's lunging tiger or Hawkins's frightful *Tasmanian Tiger No. 2*. Pierce's leopard seems more like a sad dog, similar to the canine he depicted in *Little Boy and His Dog* (cat. no. 192). Like the majority of Pierce's later freestanding animals, *Leopard* stands with his head turned to face the viewer.[23] As a young boy, Pierce first carved animals from his Mississippi farm environs. Later, when his wife praised his carving of an elephant, Pierce promised to carve a whole zoo for her. Identifying his diverse sources of inspiration for his animal carvings, Pierce said, "I began carving every animal that I ever saw in the circuses and in the parades and in the street carnivals—cows and horses and dogs and squirrels and any kind of animals that I could think of. Sometimes I'd see some animal in a paper or in a magazine and I'd carve it."[24]

"I like to carve animals because I love animals," said Linvel Barker,[25] whose sleek *Giraffe* (pl. 201) has almost the refined look of a machine-made piece. Barker worked in linden, a light-colored wood that grows on his farm in eastern Kentucky. Barker shaped the unpainted giraffe by hand with electric power tools, then finished it with a pocketknife and sander. Barker remembers seeing a giraffe at the zoo in Brookfield, Illinois, north of Chicago, near where he worked before retiring back to Kentucky. "We went there quite a bit; I fed giraffes peanuts from my hands."[26]

A painter with a wonderful sense of color and texture, Clyde Jones made *Penguins* (pl. 198) after a trip to New York and a visit to the Bronx Zoo. Jones thickly painted the shape of each penguin on a large board, which he then incised with a chain saw. Jones also sculpts from tree limbs, roots, and stumps, which he cuts and assembles, adding found or used objects such as nails, plastic, spools, or film containers. Jones has a clearly independent sense about his work. For example, *Whale* (cat. no. 137) was green and white when selected for this book; soon after, when photographed, it was red. *Porcupine* (pl. 208) is a daunting assemblage of wood and spiky textile spools that creates a bizarre rendition of the quilled animal.[27] In *Pelican* (pl. 209), the Louisiana state bird stands tall, proud, and with a strikingly distinctive aura.

Prehistoric dinosaurs enter the imagination of self-taught artists, as seen in Charlie Lucas's *Bondo* (pl. 191). "The dinosaur has been extinct so long. I want to bring him back. I see the dinosaur as a favorite puppy. Ever since I was young, I liked the dinosaur."[28] *Bondo* is made from an old car hood whose surface has been reworked with Bondo, a liquid fiberglass used to smooth out dents in car bodies. "*Bondo* says you patch up things and change the whole image of it. If something was broken, Bondo could replace it and make it sleek and beautiful. It is just a repair kit, almost like plastic surgery. . . . Bondo is like makeup."[29] The rich orange surface had previously been painted three or four times. Lucas, formerly a car mechanic, cut the basic black lines of the dinosaur with a torch to uncover these remnant layers of painted color and then accented the creature with staccato dabs and strips of white paint.

In his New Orleans home, Willie White, too, fancied dinosaurs as colorful, boxy horselike creatures. Frequently repeated images in White's work, his dinosaurs are imaginatively rendered. In *New Orleans Dinosaur* (pl. 213) the beasts are surrounded by other recurring elements in White's vocabulary—fantastic bald-headed eagles with double wings, spheres for planets, an alligator, and an upright tomato plant. Dinosaurs and a planet also appear in White's *Creole Tomatoes* (pl. 212), which refers to the locally grown tomatoes considered to be a special treat in New Orleans.

White's love of animals and plants probably stems from his childhood on a Mississippi farm. White's whimsical, dynamic, simplified imagery is flat, bold, and textured. He builds form with large patches of primary color applied to glossy poster board, and creates texture and linear pattern with felt-tip marker strokes. Both images are beautifully arranged and balanced, filling the entire field with color. Highly decorative, White's images are often inspired by dreams.

David Butler's *Windmill with Man Riding Flying Elephant* (pl. 203) is a fantastical whirligig. A man dangling a yellow plastic cube rides a yellow elephant, with black stripes and matching yellow button eyes, whose flapping, painted tin wings are attached with hinges. A whimsical Ferris wheel with seats revolves in the wind.

Minnie Black's glossy, painted *Critter* (pl. 195), assembled from gourds, might have been inspired by one of her primary visual sources—*National Geographic* magazine or the Discovery Channel. Black "gets her mind on an animal, chooses the suitable gourds for the head, feet, body, and tail, and cuts them with a utility knife."[30] She joins the gourds and their cut pieces with Sculptamold, a fast-binding cement, and paints them with acrylic or spray paint.[31]

Surprisingly, relative to the portrayal of animals, pastoral landscapes are less frequently seen in the work of self-taught artists, except for memory painters like John William "Uncle Jack" Dey or Philo Levi "Chief" Willey. Occasional examples are seen in the paintings of Jimmy Lee Sudduth, William Dawson, Charles Kinney, O. W. "Pappy" Kitchens, and Ezekiel Gibbs; Howard Finster sometimes sets a portrait study in a landscape environment, as in *Henry Ford at 2½ Years Old #1849* (pl. 51).

Joe Louis Light's landscape *Hard to Beat* (pl. 207) is a contemporary visual statement with the austerity and purity of a work by Georgia O'Keeffe. Flat patches of often solid, bold color are outlined in heavy black lines. The expansive landscape has no human or animal life (frequently the case in Light's abstracted scenes) but contains a sparse sampling of real and imagined plant life with spiritual overtones. A cactus stands in the central vista; from the fingers of a white hand grow a few willowy orange flowers; other flowers thrive along the work's bottom edge; and a single fine blossom rises on the left. Light's brushwork is mostly flat, as in the red and brown mountains and the blue lake, with a few painterly strokes of white for clouds and green for the foreground.

Still lifes of flowers, common in the Western tradition of art history, are rare in the work of self-taught artists. But they are not uncommon in the work of Clementine Hunter and Joe Light, as seen in his *Erection Flower* (cat. no. 153), where a single, central flower is the painting's focus. Sybil Gibson makes floral drawings in soft, ethereal pastels on hand-washed and unglued grocery bags. Her wispy strokes and fragile colors are often enhanced by the rippling texture and color of the unevenly shaped bags, as in two works of flowers in a vase (pls. 210, 211). Gibson's impressionistic brush, unusual in the world of self-taught artists, can have a haunting, enchanting quality (pls. 53, 54). Some other artists who occasionally incorporate flowers and plant life set within an overall compositional pattern include Mose Tolliver, Nellie Mae Rowe, and, more often, Minnie Evans.

The natural and animate subjects recorded by many southern self-taught artists reflect their true love of nature and their preoccupation with animal and plant life. Their tendency to look to the natural world verifies the importance of their everyday surroundings to the content of their work.

1. Mose Tolliver, interview, ARY, Nov. 1991.

2. Arning's source for this drawing was a color rendering by Tom Dolan illustrating the article "Blue Goose: Enigma of the North" in the May 1967 issue of *Sports Afield* (pp. 44–45); see Barbara R. Luck and Alexander Sackton, *Eddie Arning: Selected Drawings, 1964–1973* (Williamsburg, Va.: The Colonial Williamsburg Foundation, 1985), p. 41.

3. Ibid., p. 16.

4. Aarne Anton, American Primitive Gallery, interview, ARY, April 1993.

5. Ann Miller, longtime collector of Massey's work, interview, KAG, April 1993.

6. Although Green painted his totems in solid colors (see cat. no. 102), he typically created a spotted surface with dabs of colored paint in response to his wife's encouragement; see Robert Cogswell, "Two Tennessee Visionaries: Bessie Harvey and Homer Green," *Folk Art Messenger* 4, no. 4 (Summer 1991), p. 3.

7. Robert Hicks, longtime collector of Green's work, interview, KAG, April 1993.

8. Homer Green, interview, ARY, Dec. 1991.

9. Ibid.

10. Cogswell, "Two Tennessee Visionaries," p. 3.

11. Robert Hicks, interview, KAG, April 1993.

12. According to Gary Schwindler, who discusses the artist's relationship with horses, Hawkins made almost twenty horse paintings and included the horse as a motif in many other works; see "William L. Hawkins: A Biography," unpublished ms., pp. 212, 323–31.

13. Sarah Mary Taylor, interview, ARY, March 1992.

14. Charlie Lucas, interview, ARY, Aug. 1992.

15. Ibid.

16. Ibid.

17. Jimmy Lee Sudduth, interview, ARY, Aug. 1992.

18. Willie Massey, interview, KAG, Oct. 1989.

19. Raymond Coins, interview, KAG, July 1991.

20. Chuck and Jan Rosenak, *Museum of American Folk Art Encyclopedia of Twentieth-Century American Folk Art and Artists* (New York: Abbeville Press, 1990), p. 174.

21. Hawkins remembered from his youth, probably while living in Kentucky, a parade of the Ringling Brothers and Barnum and Bailey Circus and noted having seen Jumbo the elephant; see Schwindler, "William L. Hawkins," pp. 348–49.

22. The article on the Tasmanian tiger, entitled "Is This Toothy Relic Still on Prowl in Tasmania's Wilds?" (*Smithsonian* [Aug. 1985], p. 117), included a still shot of the carnivorous wolflike marsupial from a 1920s zoo film. Its huge jaws and teeth reach toward the viewer, its head and body loom toward the camera, and its back legs and hindquarters are foreshortened, just as in Hawkins's depiction. According to Gary Schwindler, Hawkins made four depictions of Tasmanian tigers.

23. *Elijah Pierce: Woodcarver* (Columbus, Ohio: Columbus Museum of Art, 1992), p. 171.

24. Ibid., p. 83.

25. Linvel Barker, interview, ARY, June 1990.

26. Ibid.

27. Jones, a mill worker for ten years, lives in Bynum, North Carolina, the site of a large textile mill.

28. Charlie Lucas, interview, ARY, Aug. 1992.

29. Ibid.

30. Black's nephew drives a truckload of 50 lb. bags of Sculptamold from Indianapolis, Indiana, to Kentucky twice a year; Minnie Black, interview, KAG, Oct. 1992.

31. Ibid.

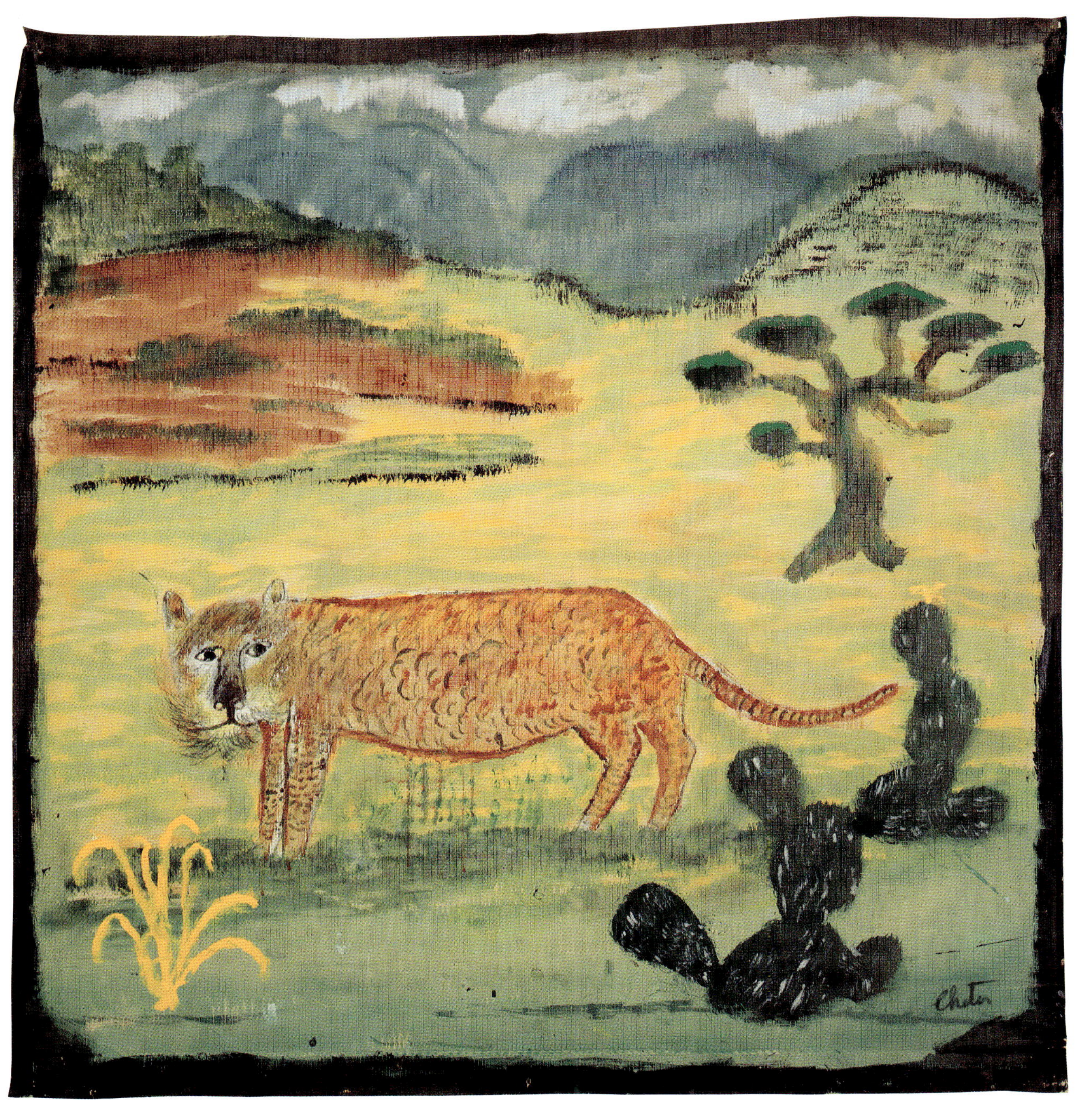

173

CHARLES KINNEY

"Cheter" Cat, 1978

(cat. no. 145)

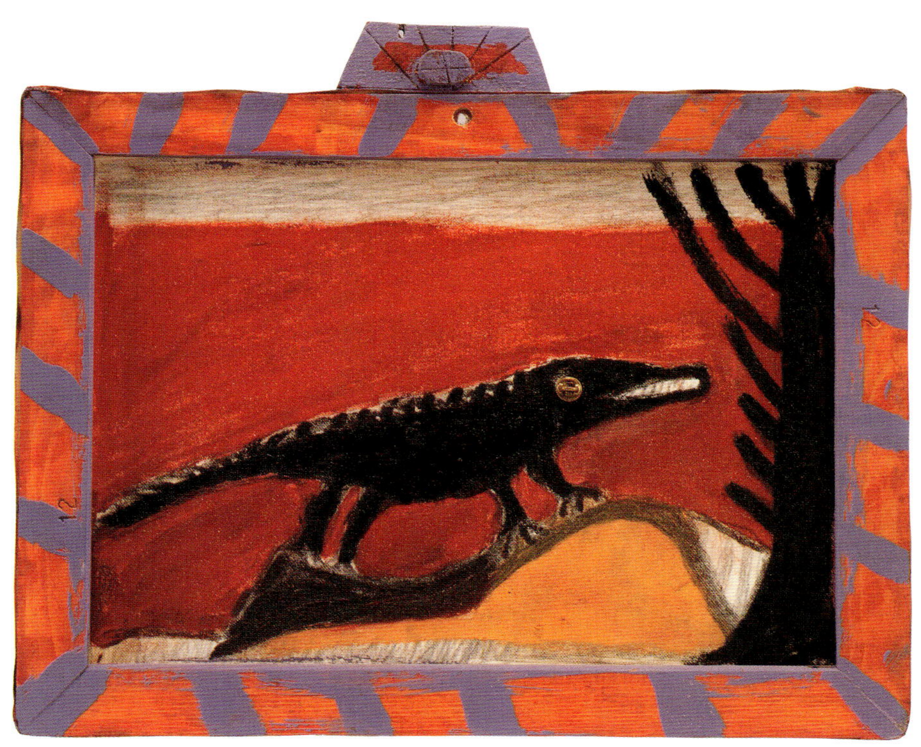

174

WILLIE MASSEY

Lizard, 1989

(cat. no. 163)

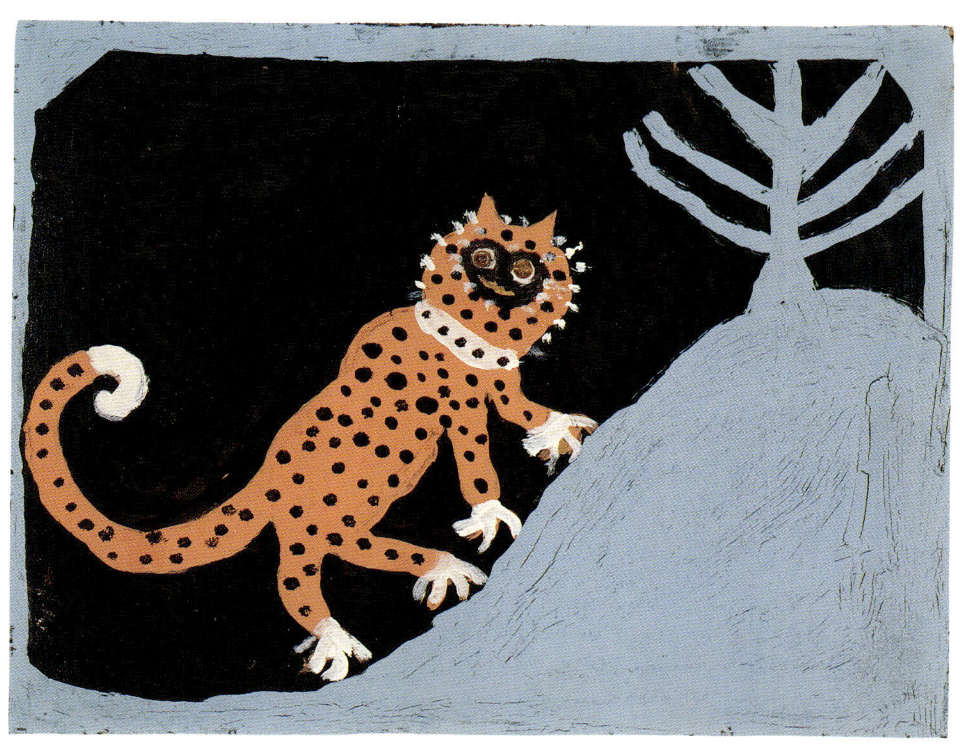

175

WILLIE MASSEY

Spotted Cat, 1989

(cat. no. 164)

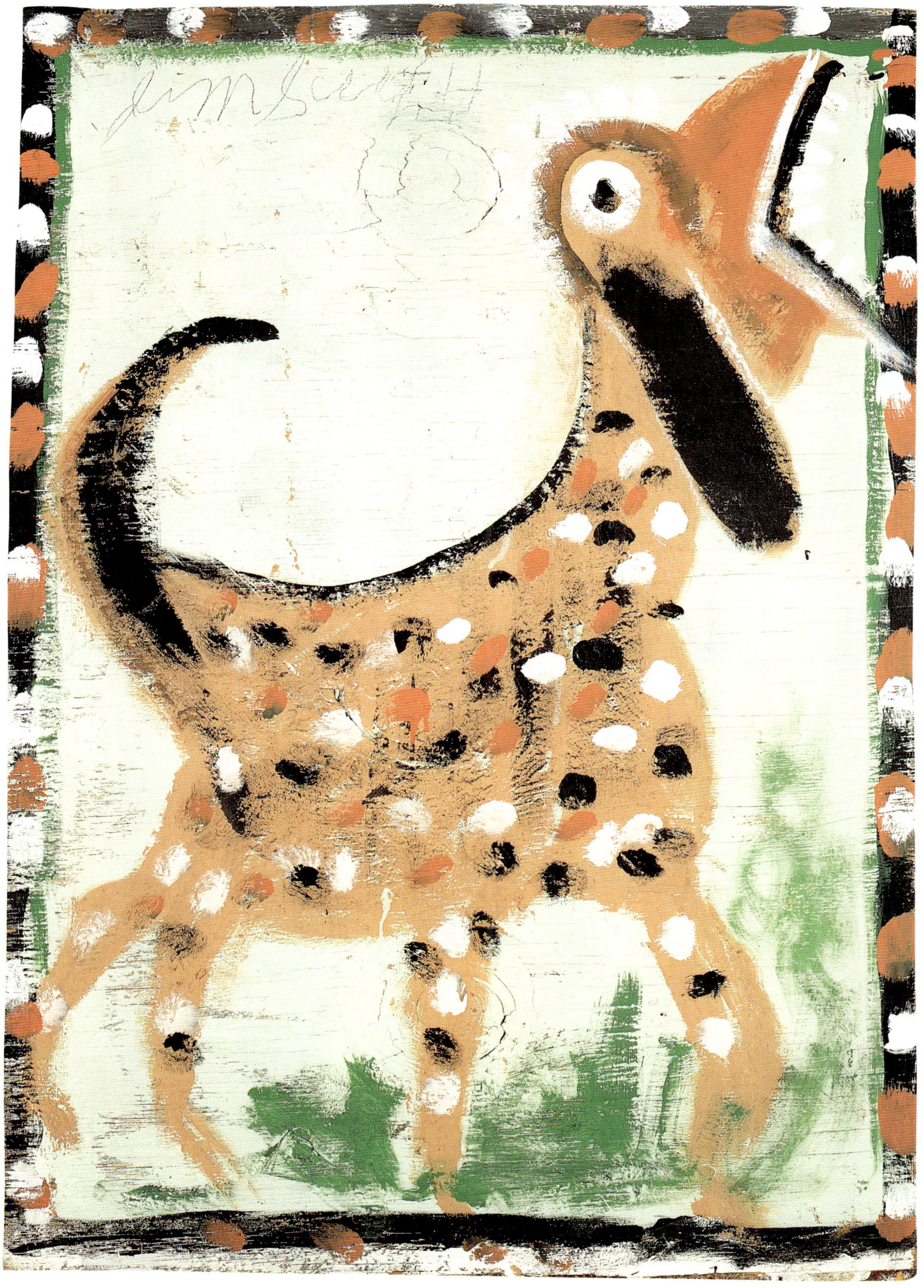

176

JIMMY LEE SUDDUTH

Dixie, The Barking Dog, 1990

(cat. no. 220)

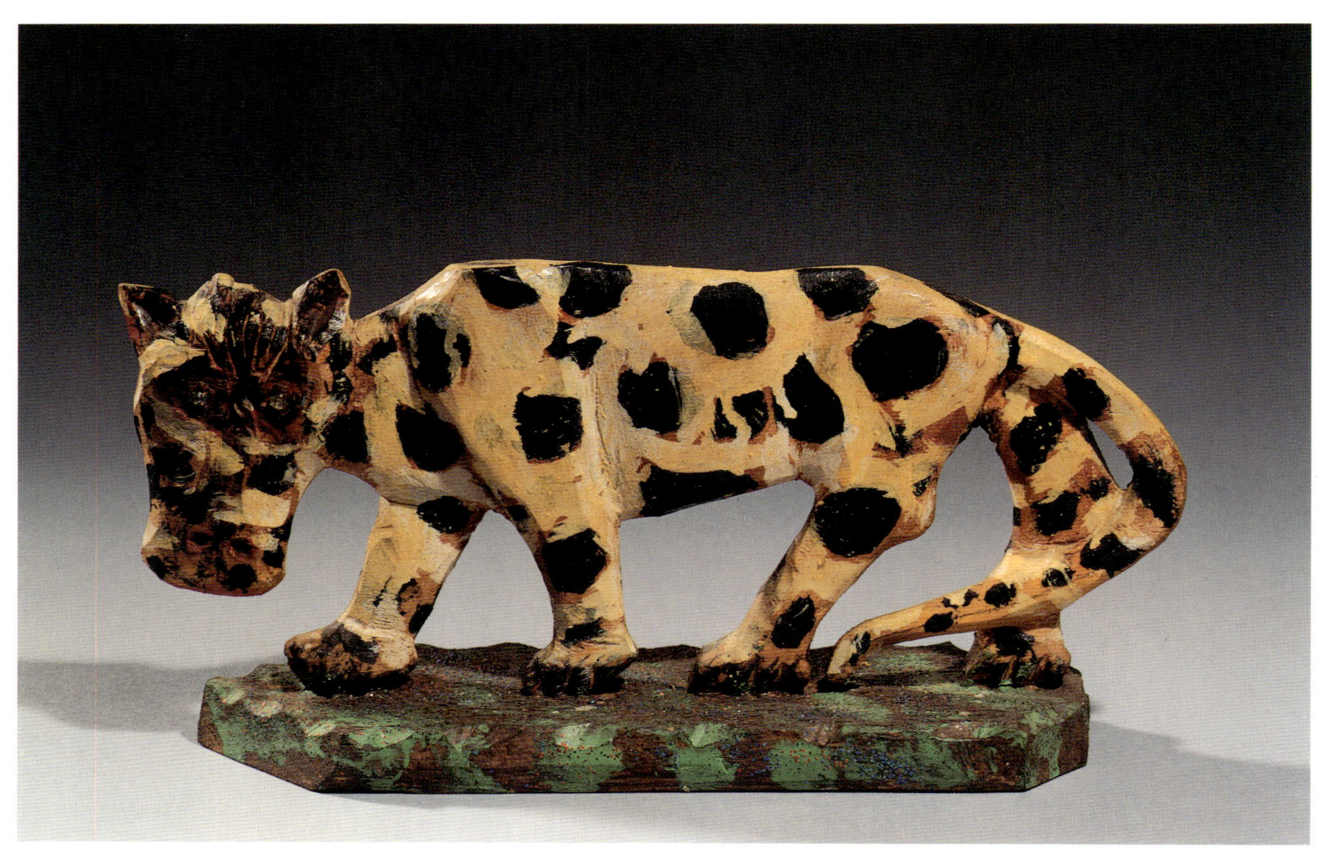

177

ELIJAH PIERCE

Leopard, 1978

(cat. no. 191)

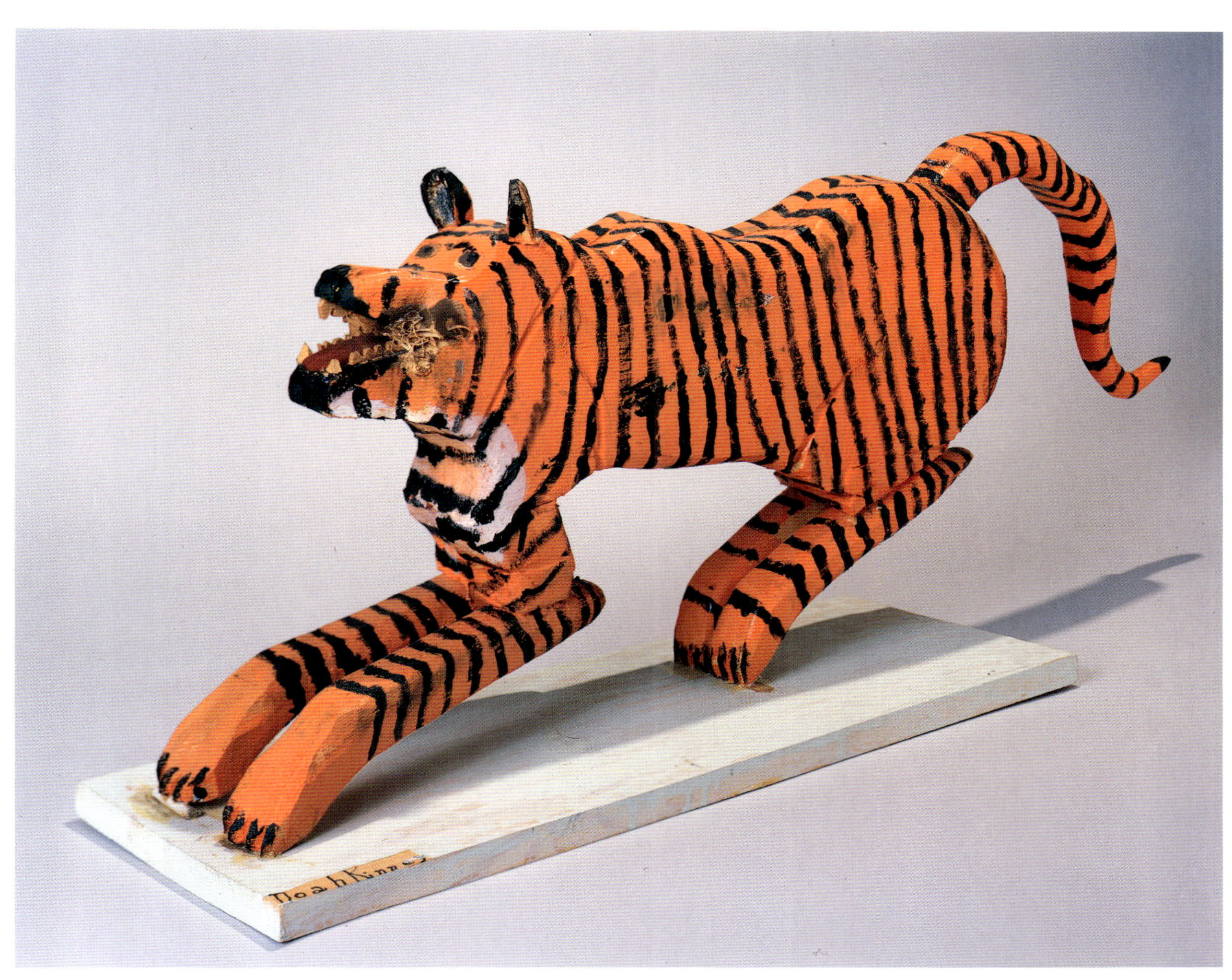

178

NOAH KINNEY

Tiger, 1987

(cat. no. 150)

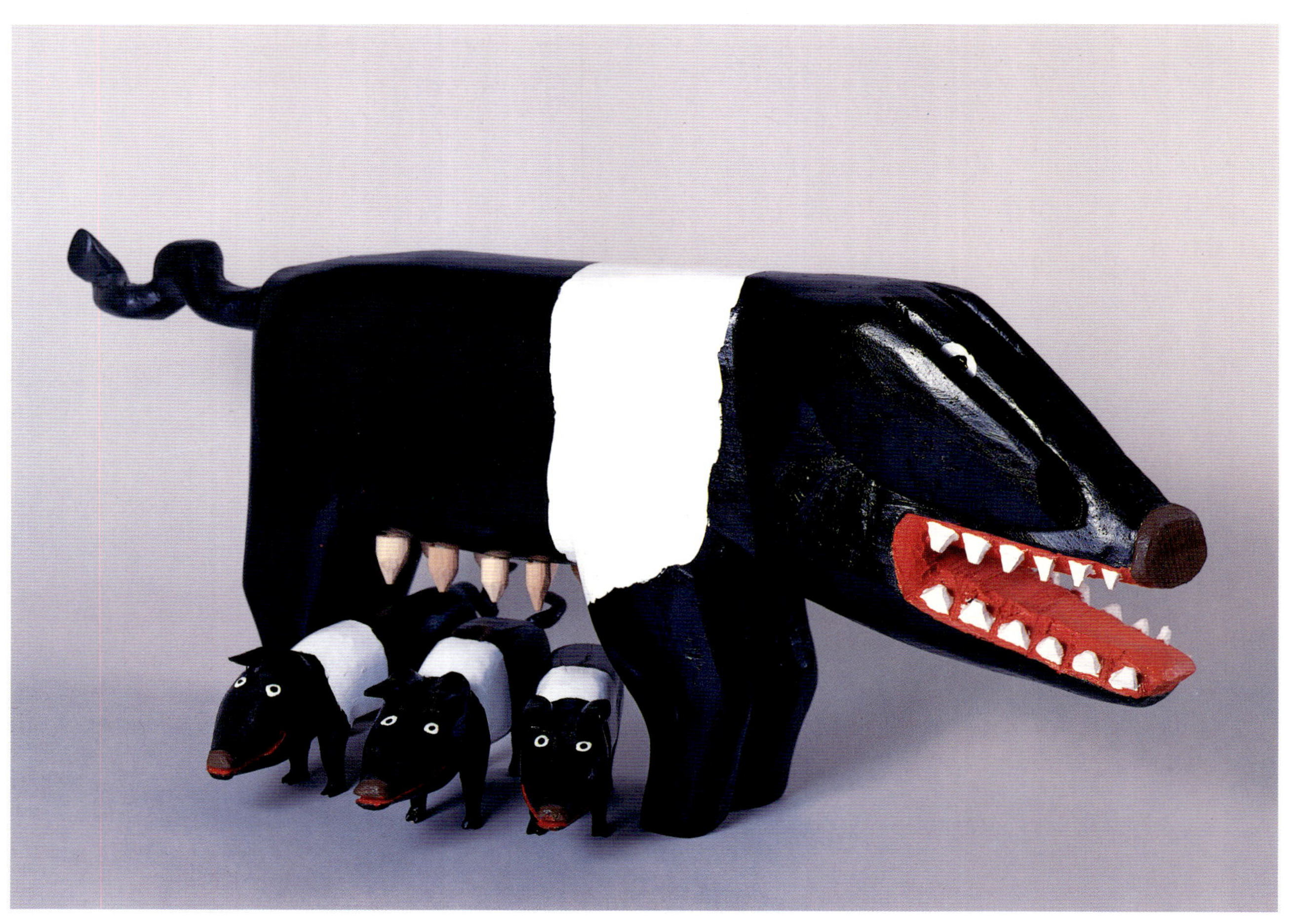

179

MINNIE AND GARLAND ADKINS

Sow with Piglets, 1990

(cat. no. 3)

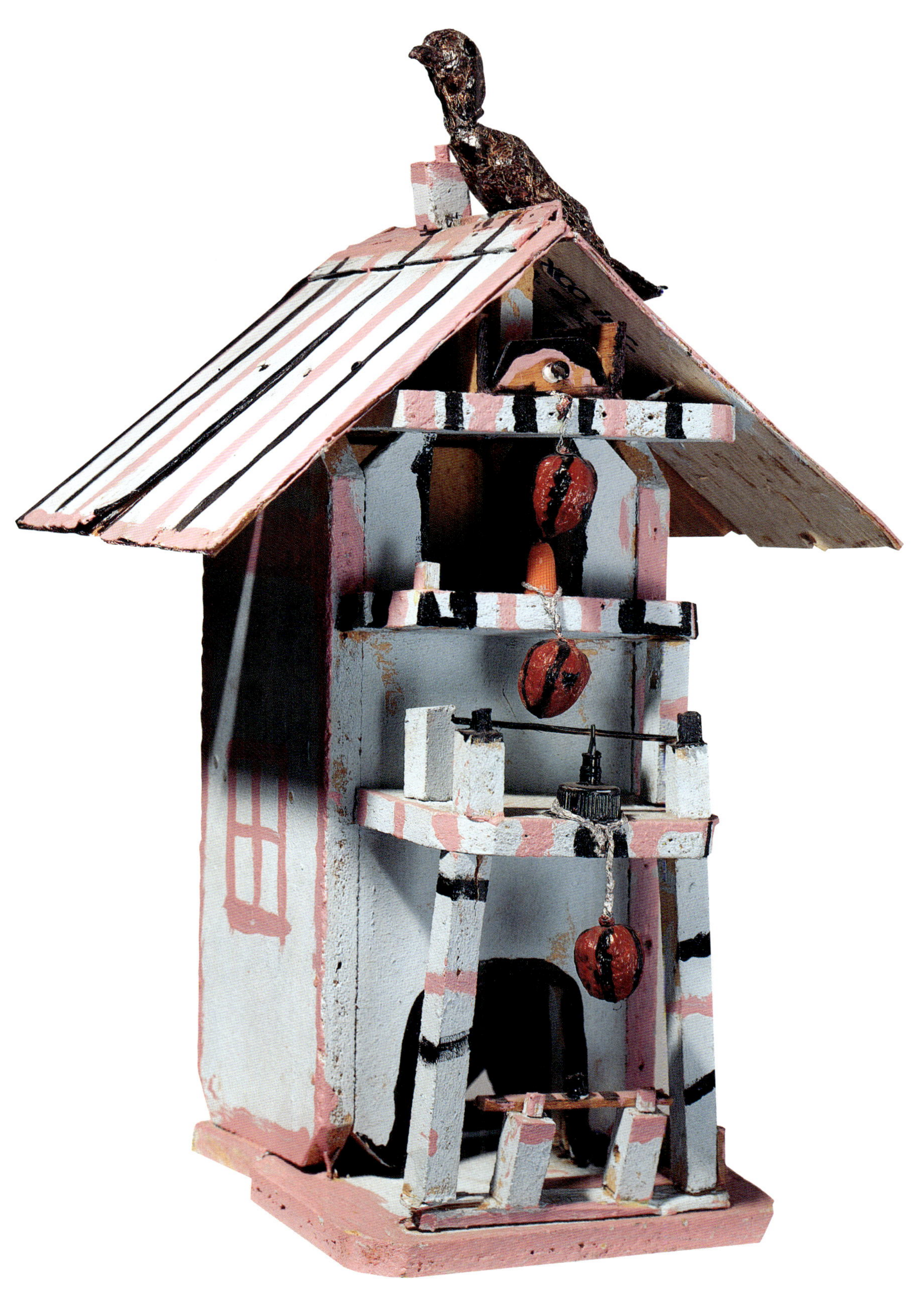

180

WILLIE MASSEY

Birdhouse: Blue and Pink, 1989

(cat. no. 161)

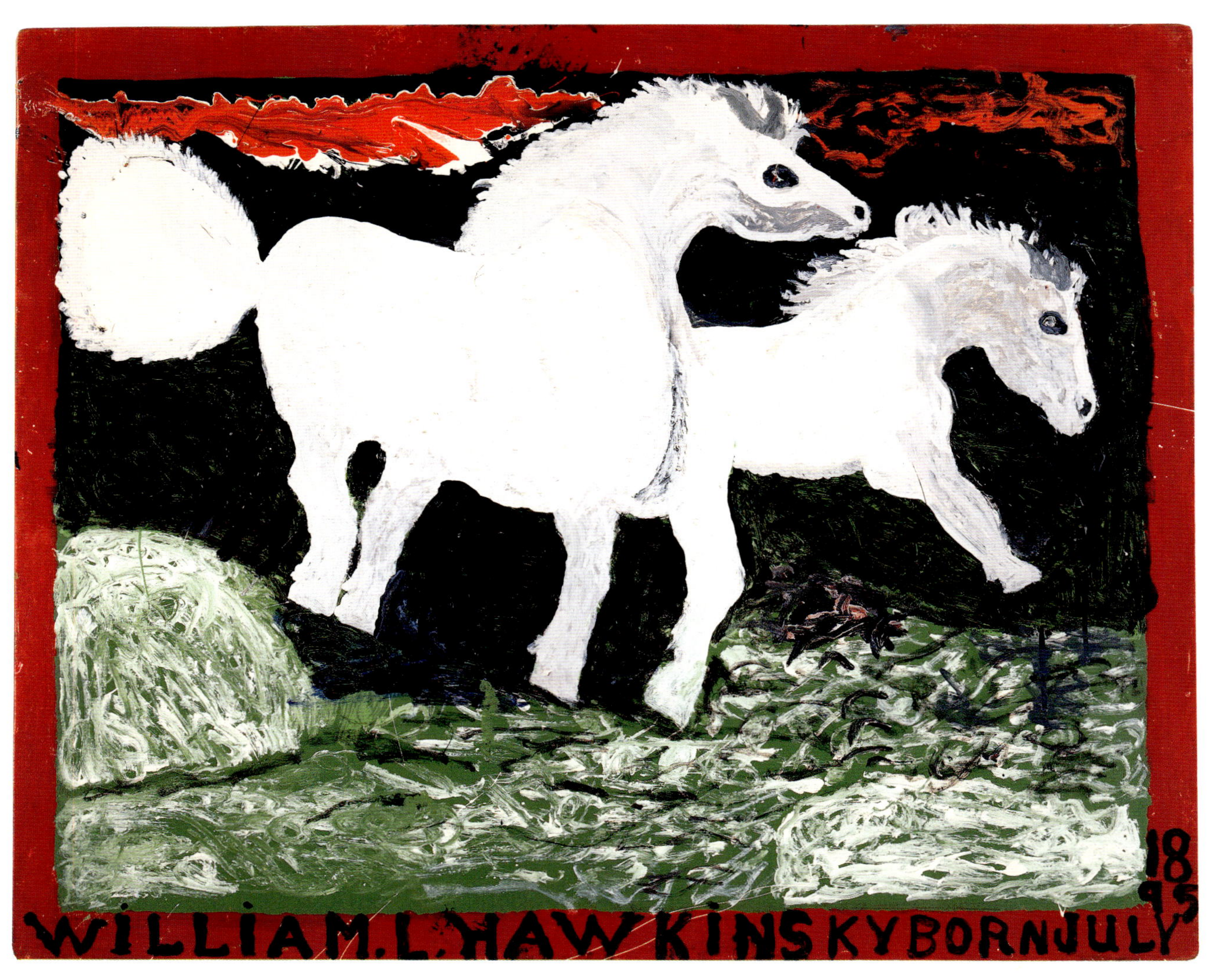

181

WILLIAM HAWKINS

Two Horses, 1984

(cat. no. 118)

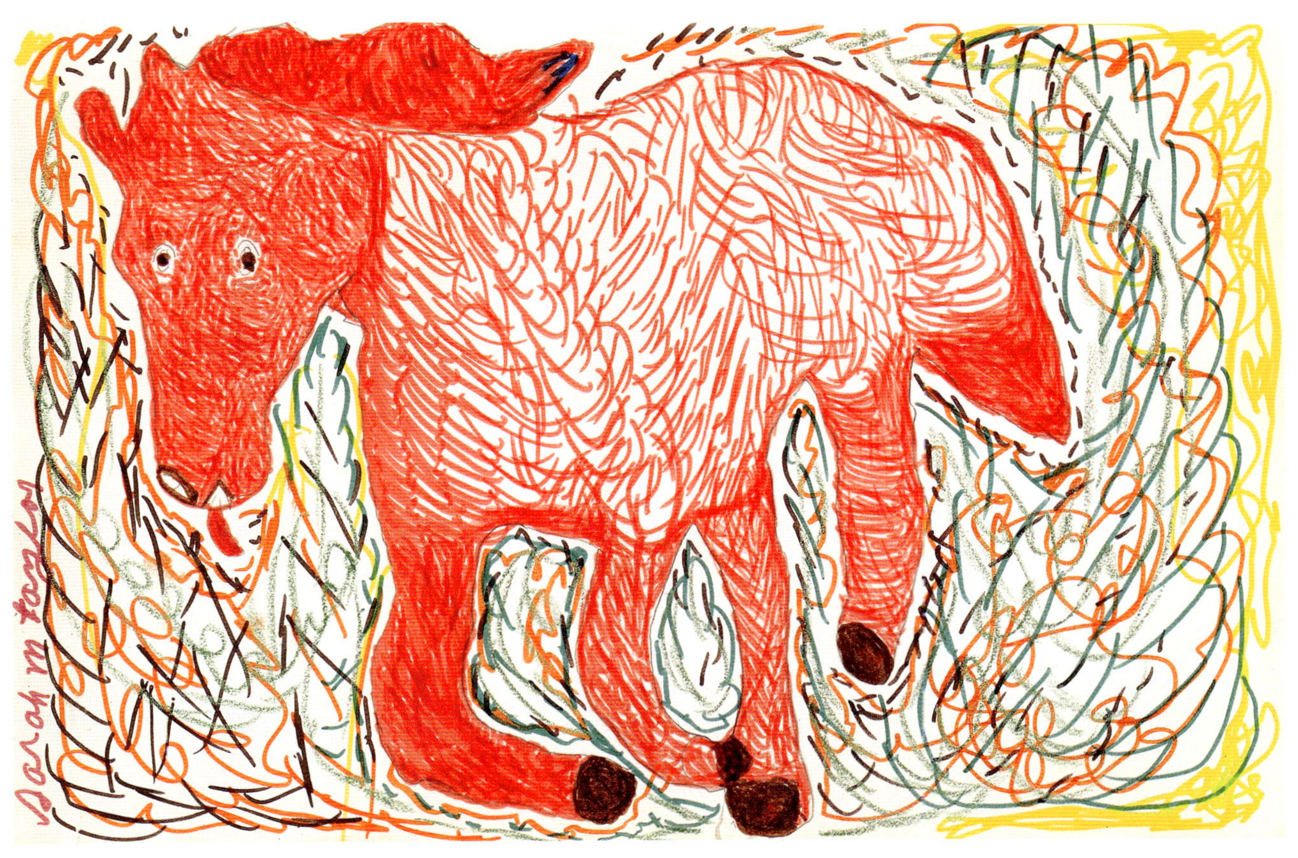

182

SARAH MARY TAYLOR

Horse, 1988

(cat. no. 234)

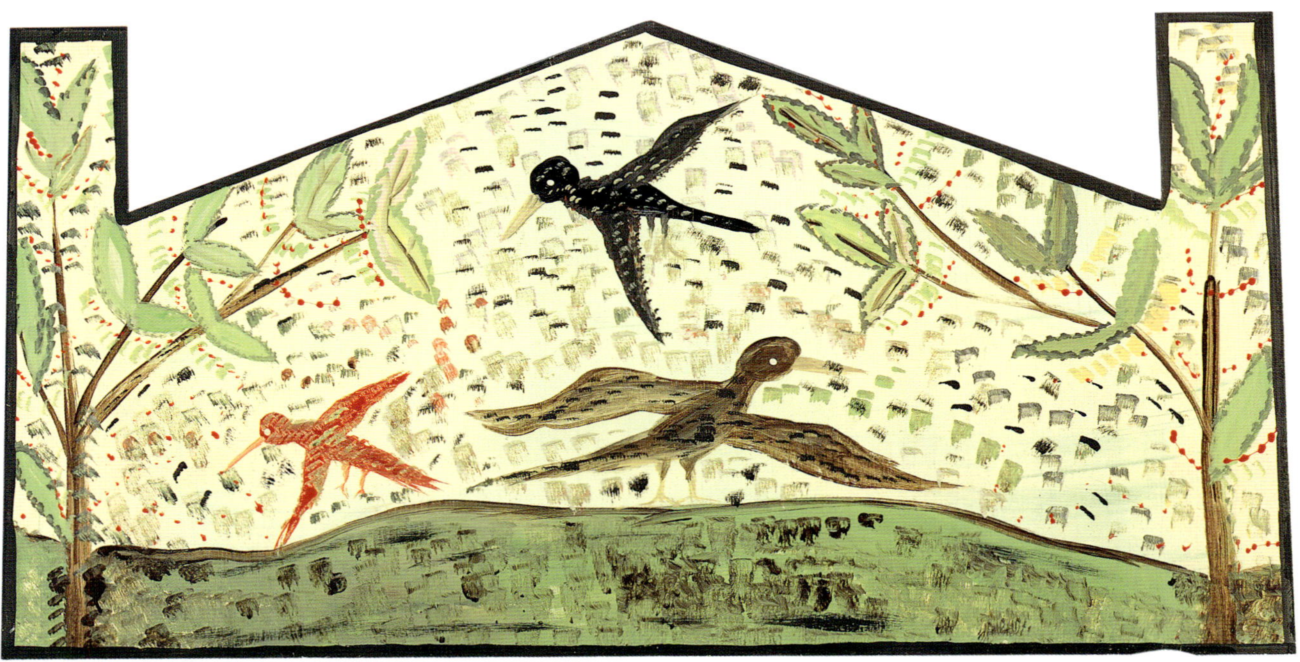

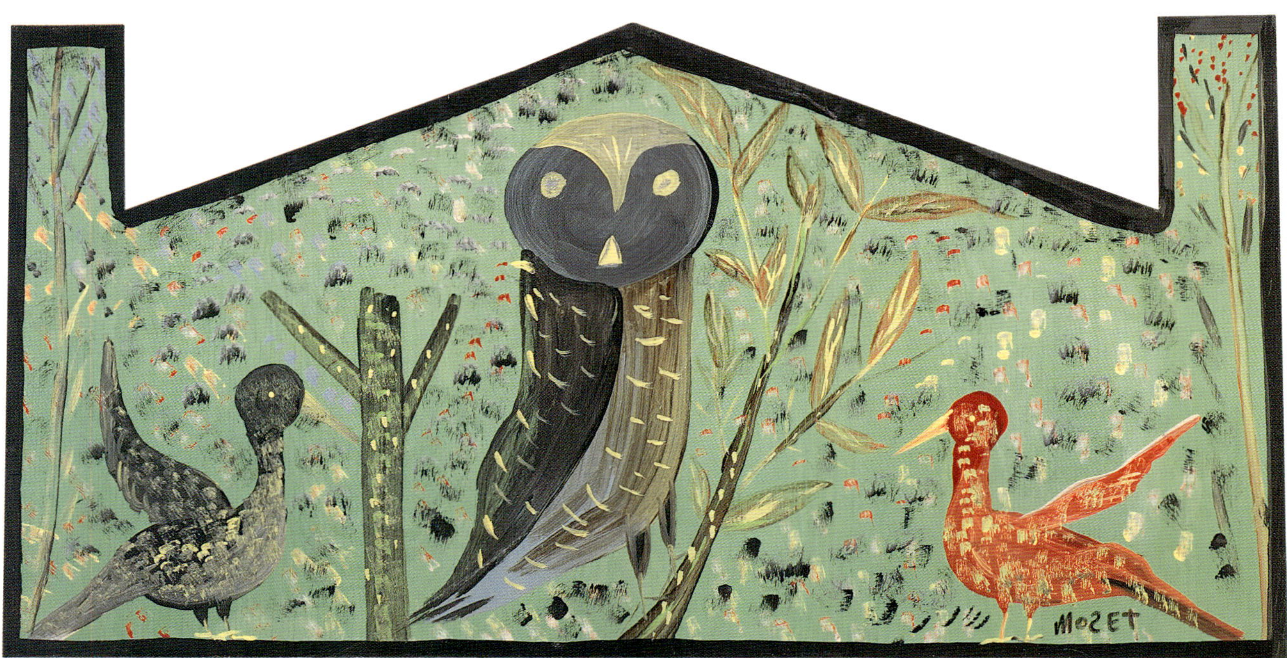

183

MOSE TOLLIVER

Headboards, 1987

(cat. no. 238)

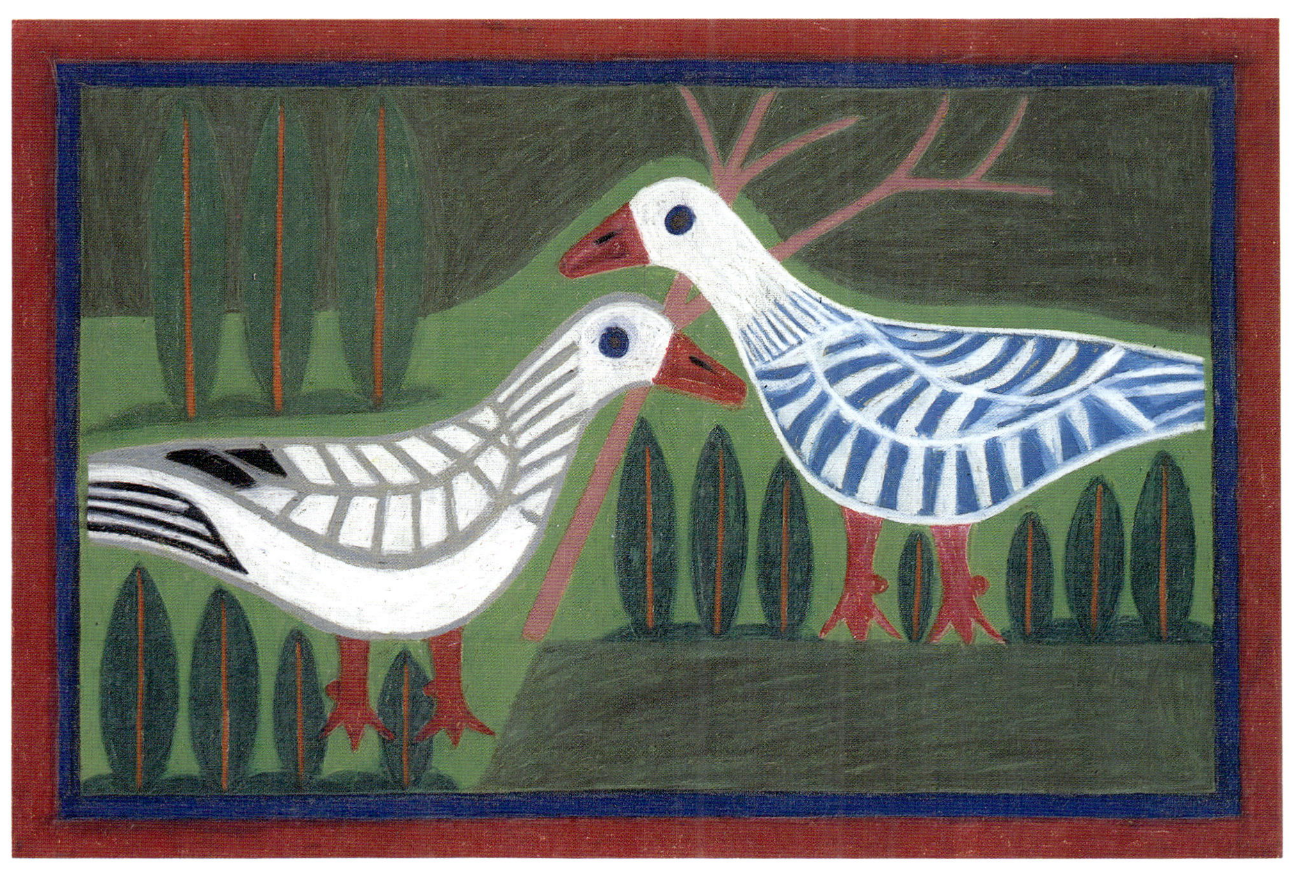

184

EDDIE ARNING

Two Geese, ca. 1970

(cat. no. 6)

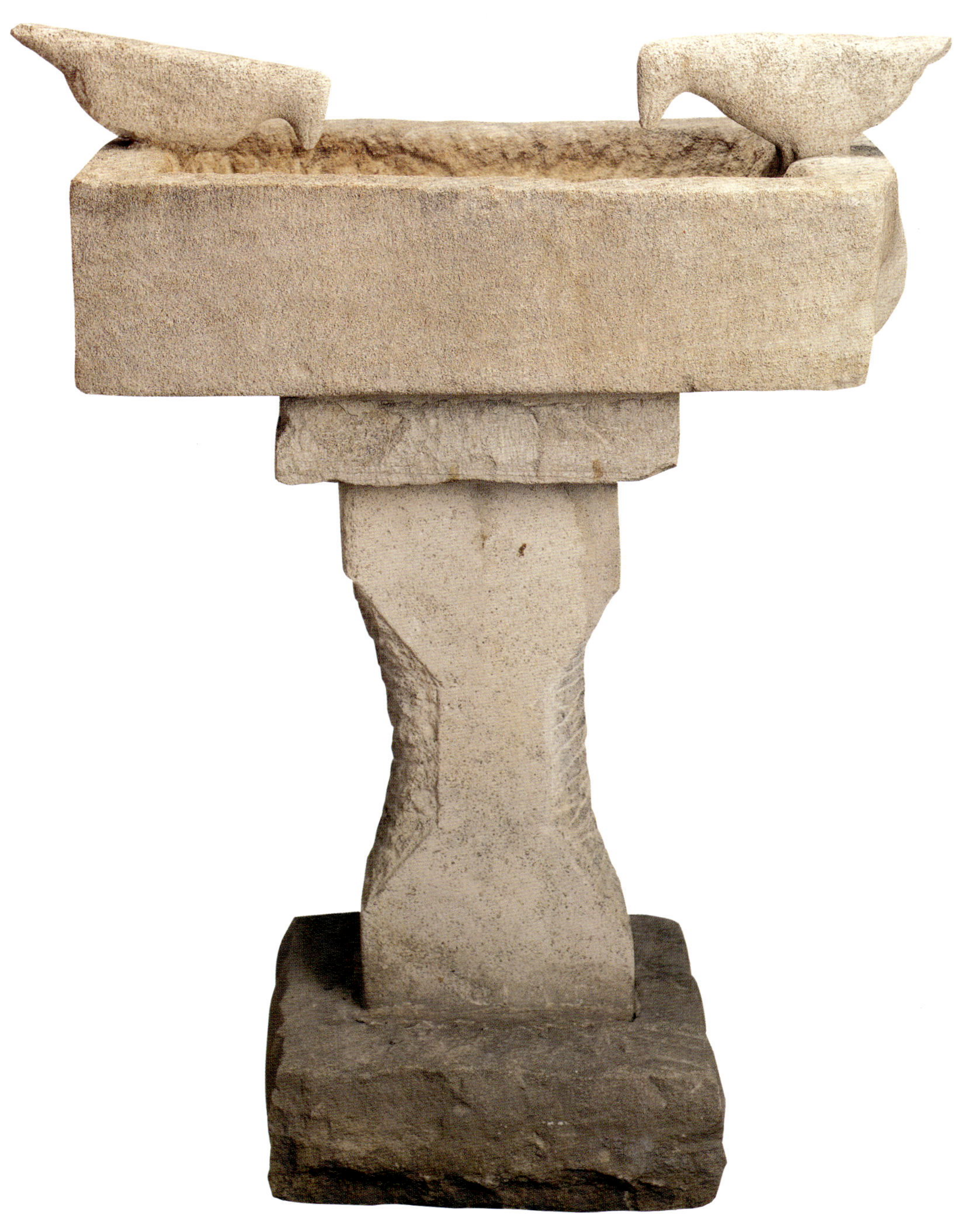

185

WILLIAM EDMONDSON

Birdbath, ca. 1940s

(cat. no. 74)

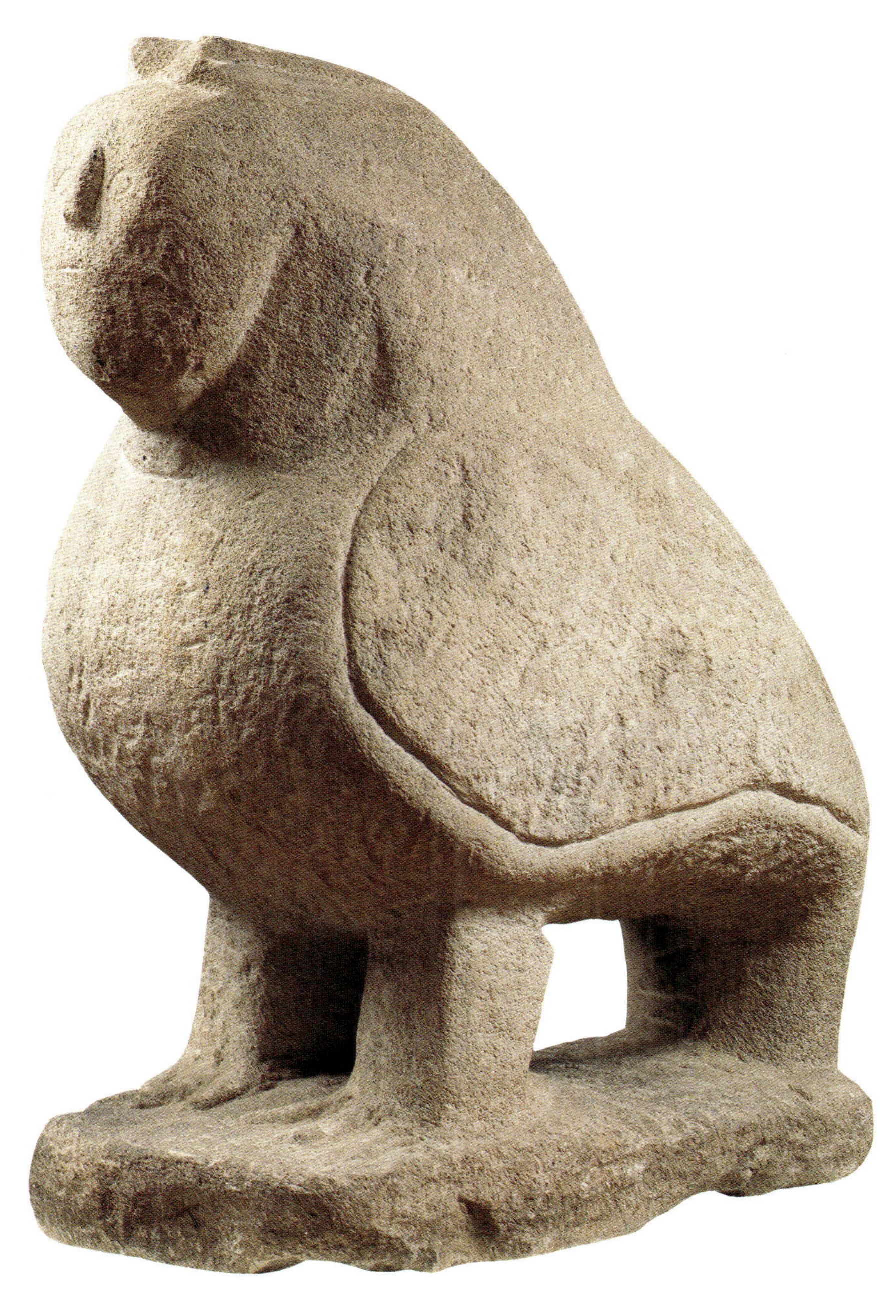

186

WILLIAM EDMONDSON

Talking Owl, 1937

(cat. no. 79)

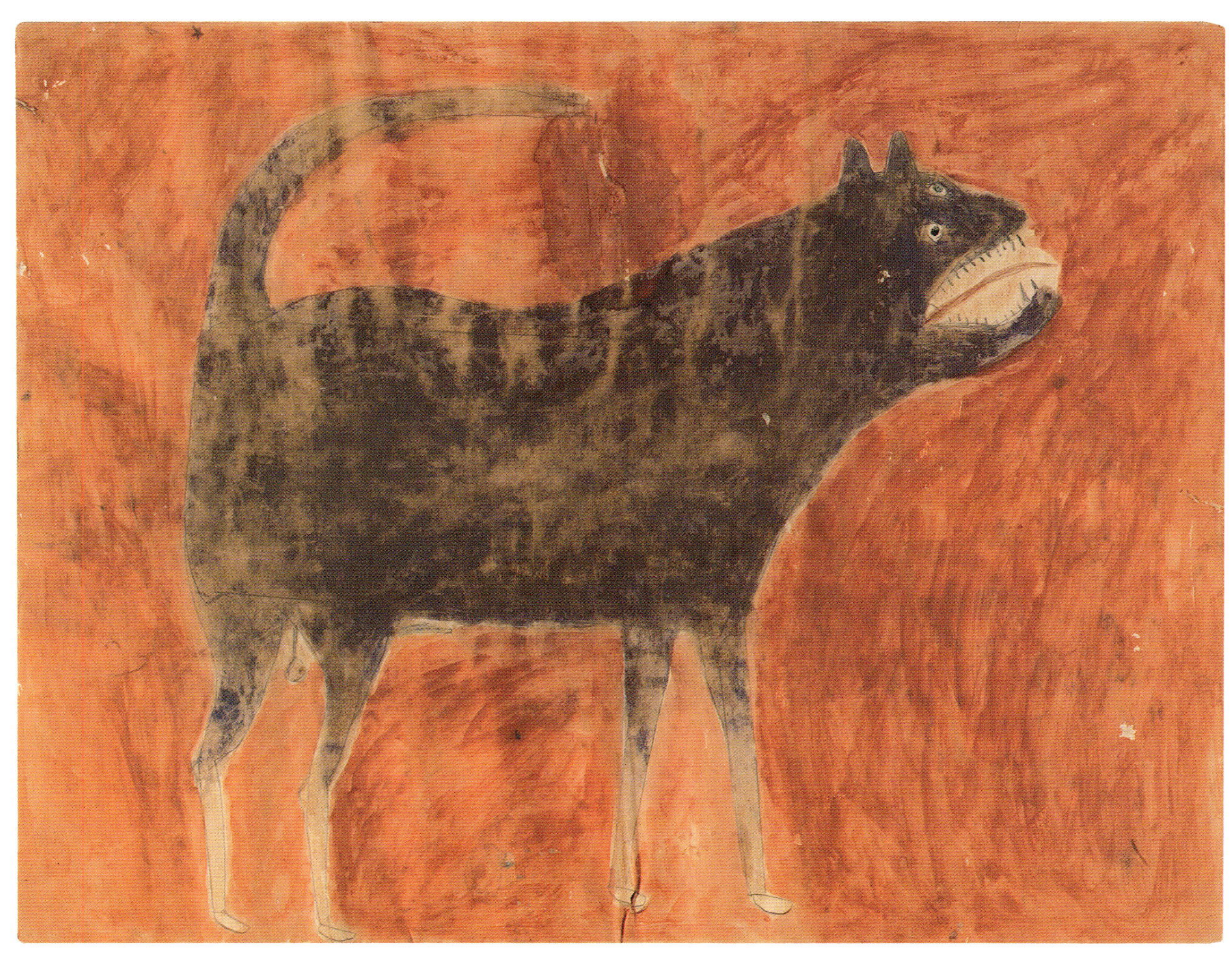

187

BILL TRAYLOR

Red Dog, 1939–42

(cat. no. 254)

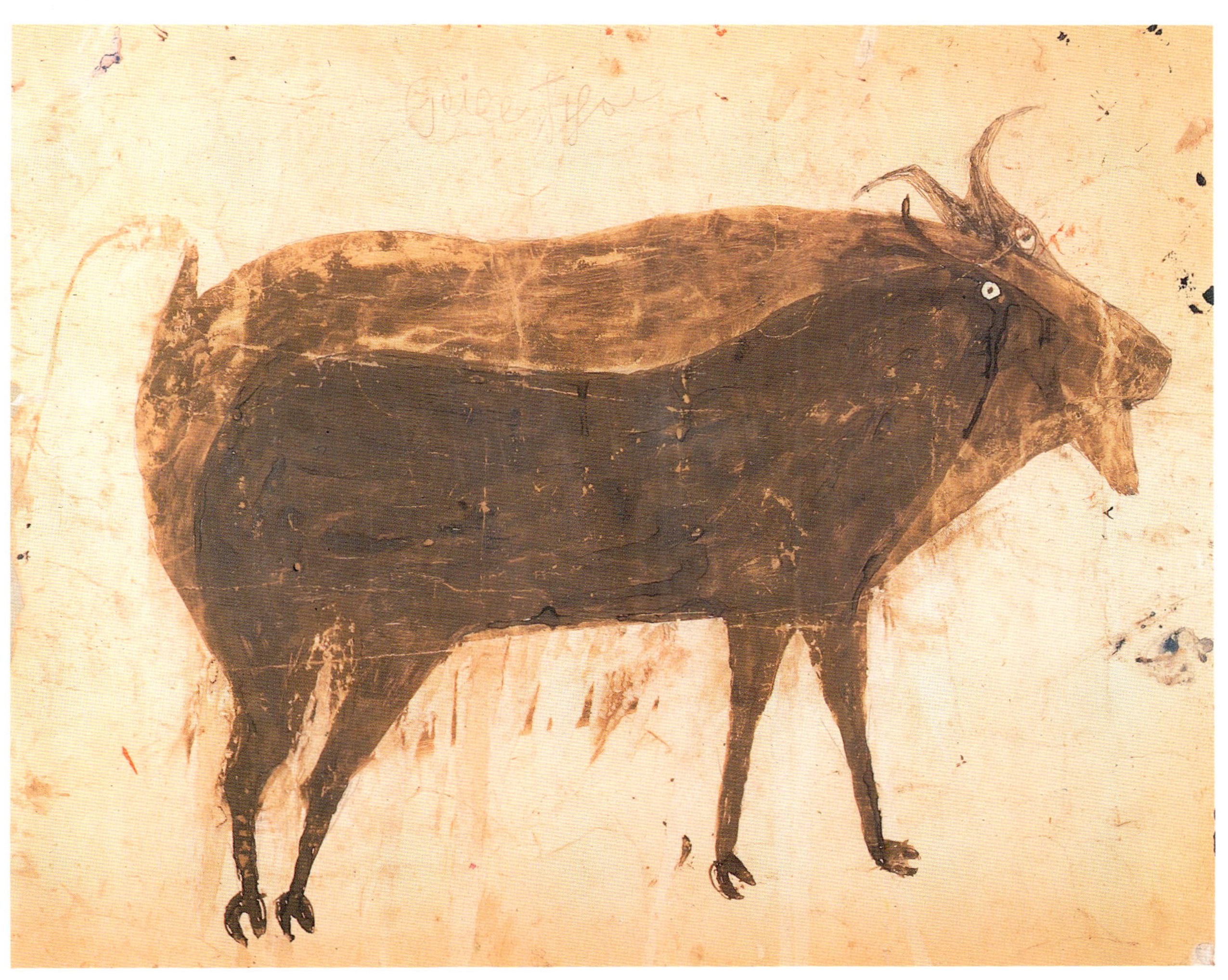

188

BILL TRAYLOR

Double Goat, ca. 1940–42

(cat. no. 251)

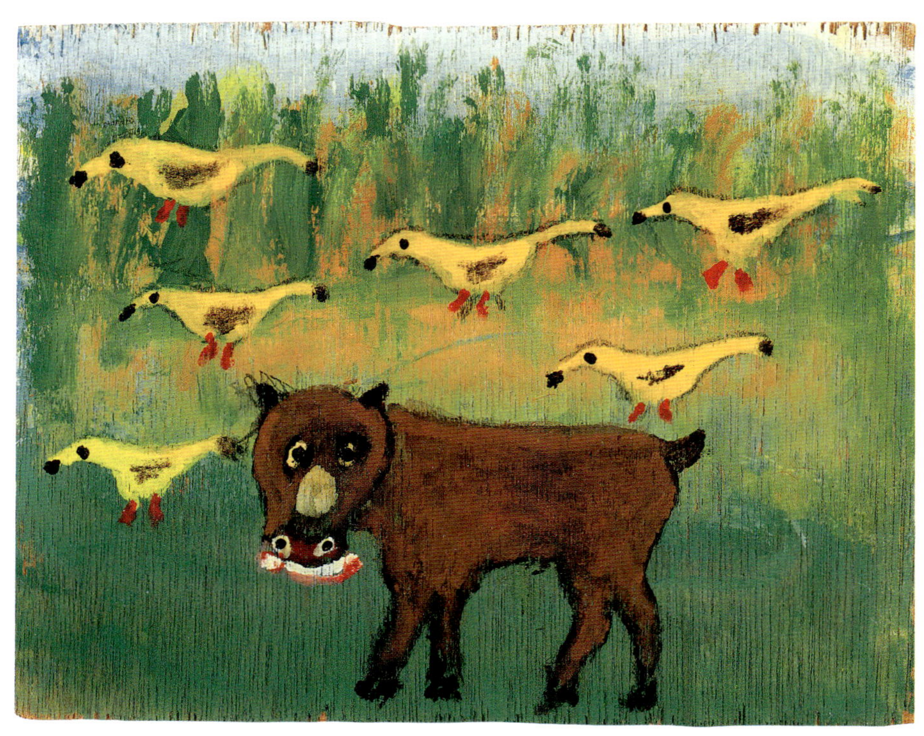

189

WILLIAM DAWSON

Dog with Six Yellow Birds, 1982

(cat. no. 45)

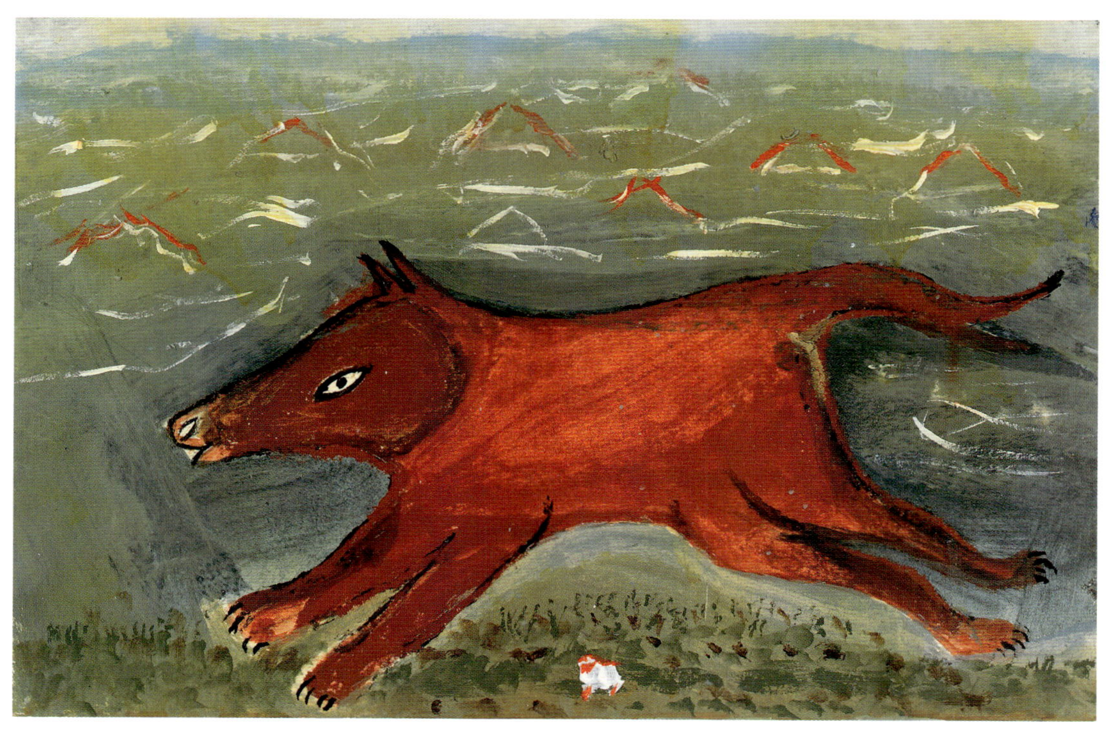

190

WILLIAM DAWSON

Red Fox, 1981

(cat. no. 47)

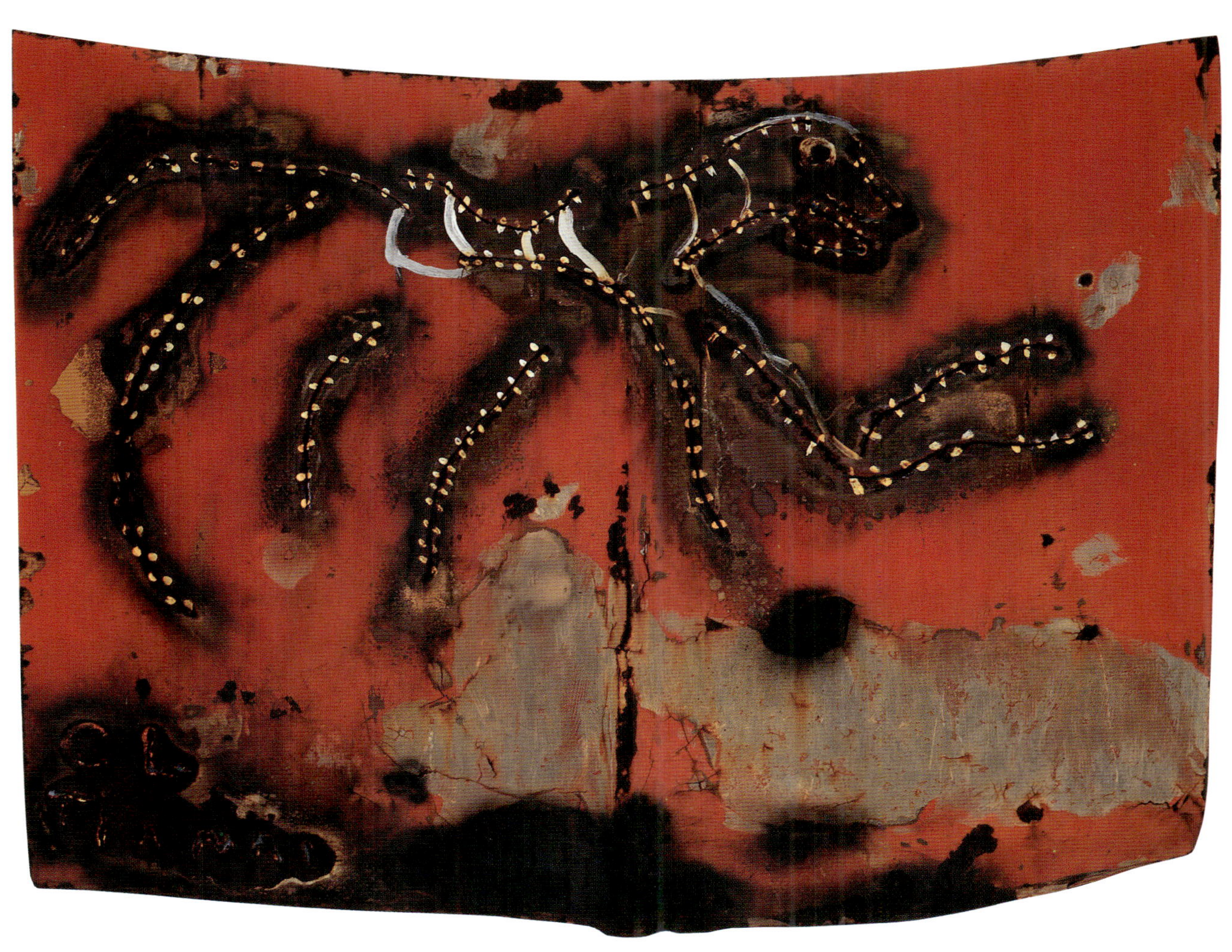

191

CHARLIE LUCAS

Bondo, 1989

(cat. no. 155)

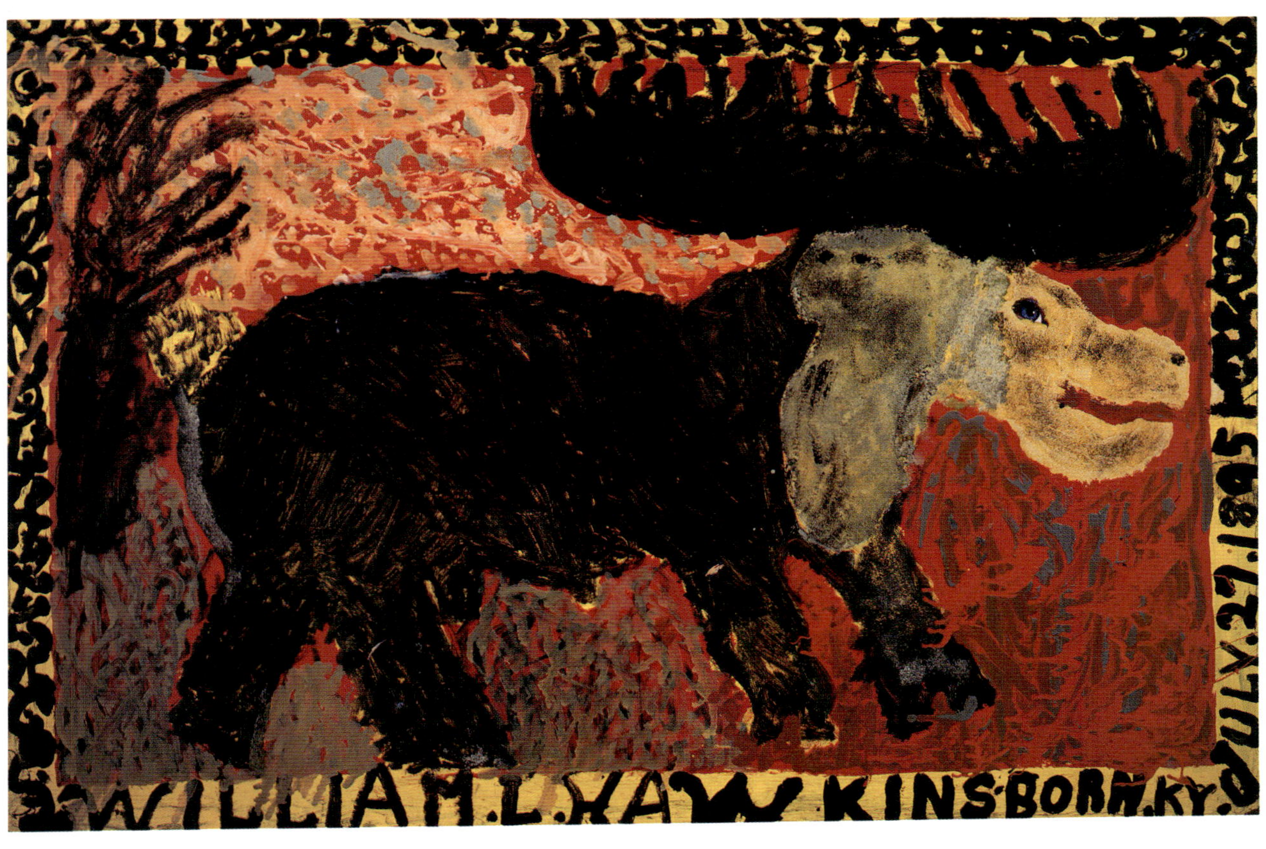

192

WILLIAM HAWKINS
Bull Moose, 1988
(cat. no. 112)

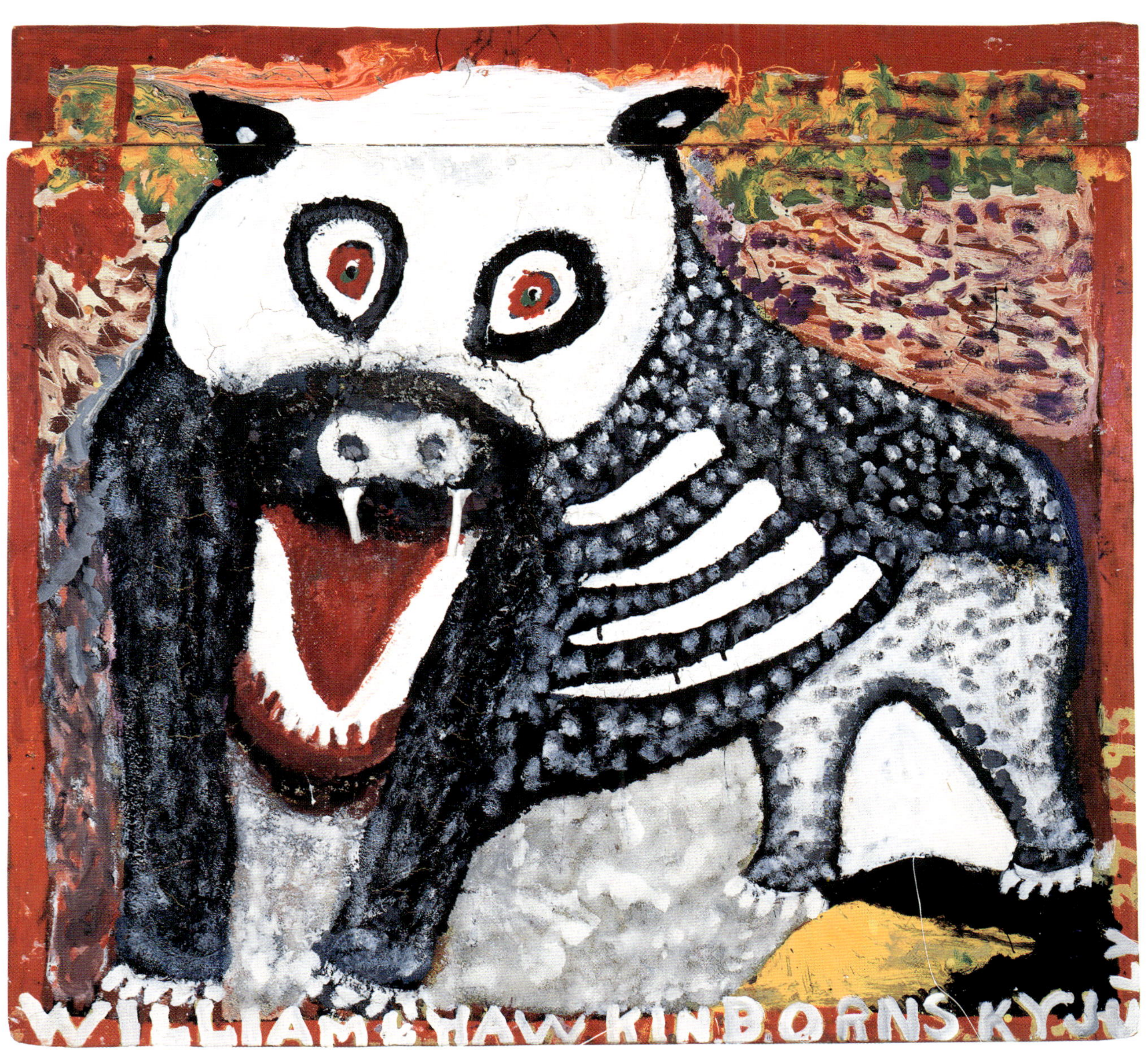

193

WILLIAM HAWKINS

Tasmanian Tiger No. 2, 1986

(cat. no. 117)

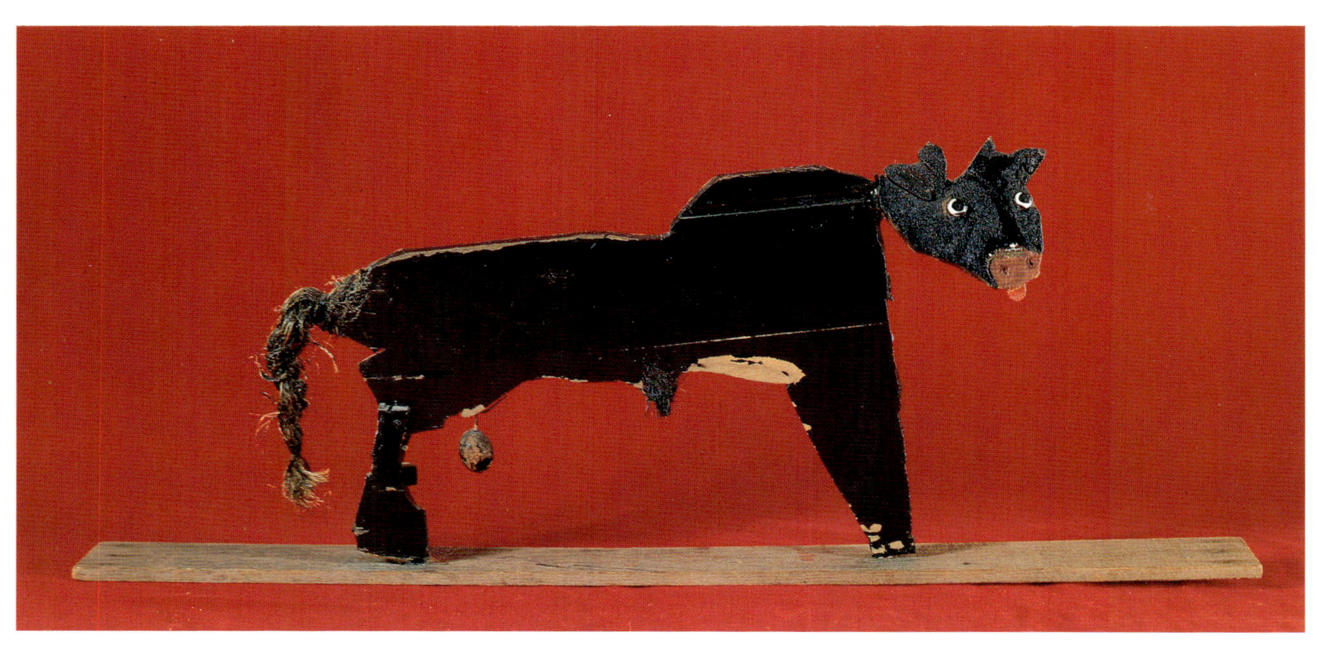

194

STEVEN ASHBY

Bull, 1978

(cat. no. 7)

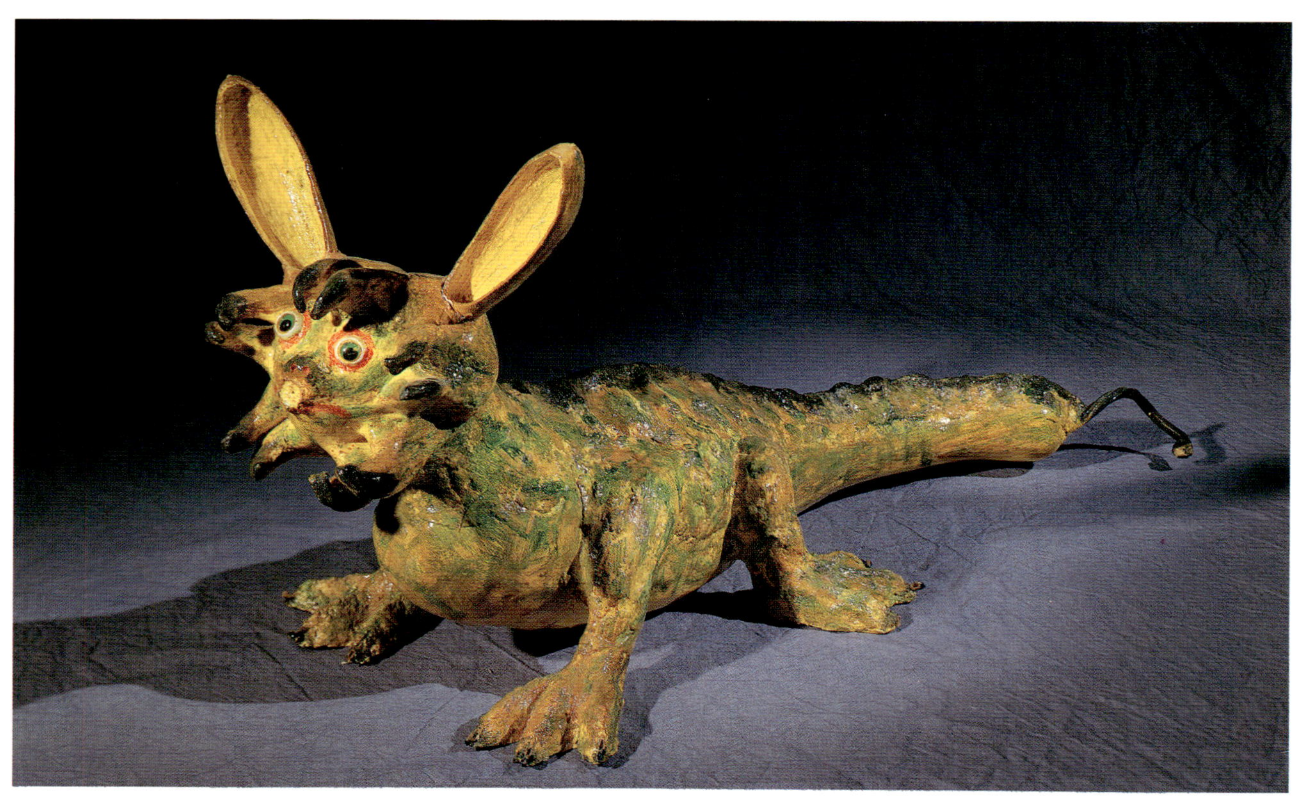

195

MINNIE BLACK

Critter, 1990

(cat. no. 13)

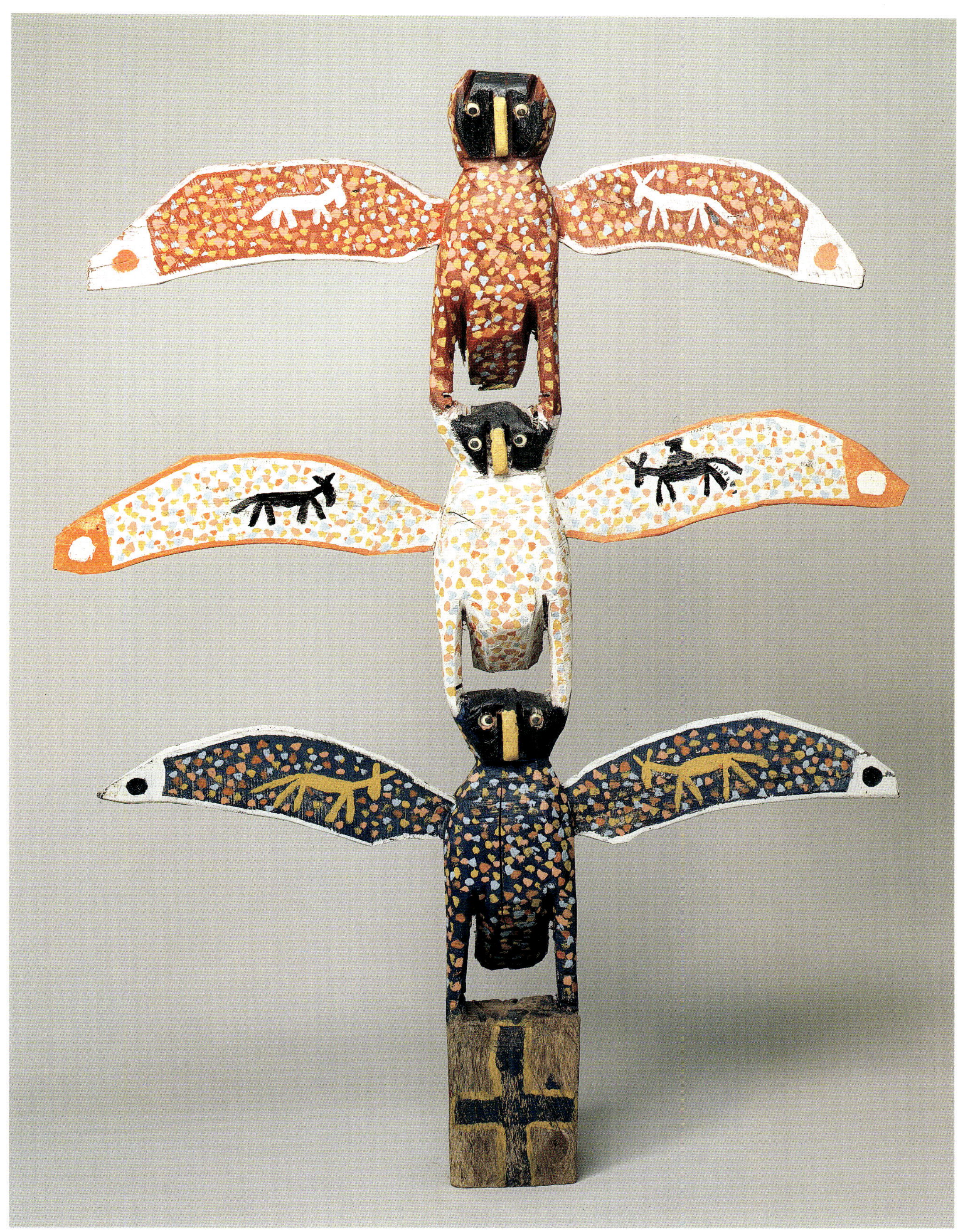

196

HOMER GREEN

Totem Pole, 1987

(cat. no. 103)

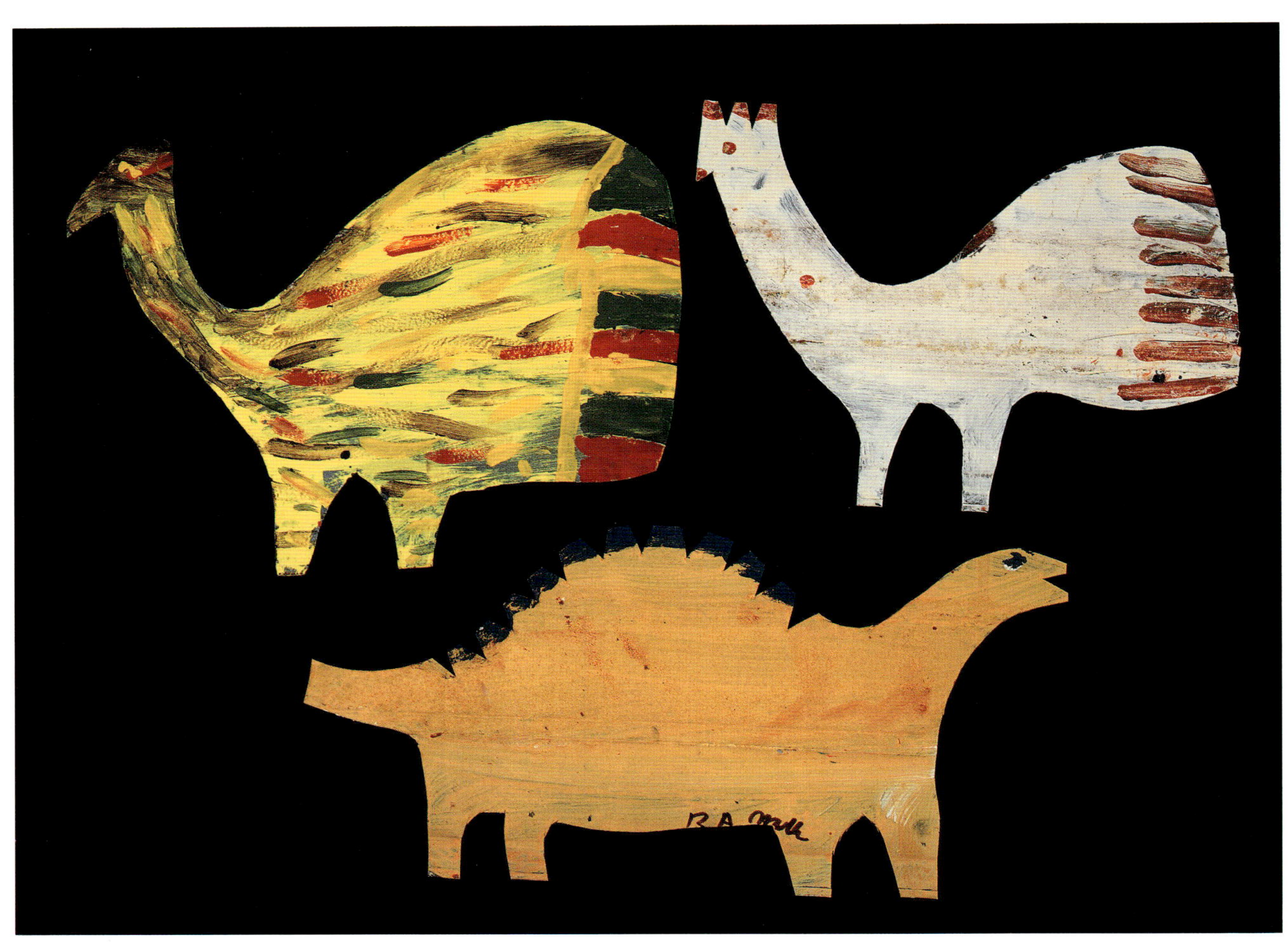

197

R. A. MILLER

Assorted Animal Cutouts, 1988

(cat. no. 165)

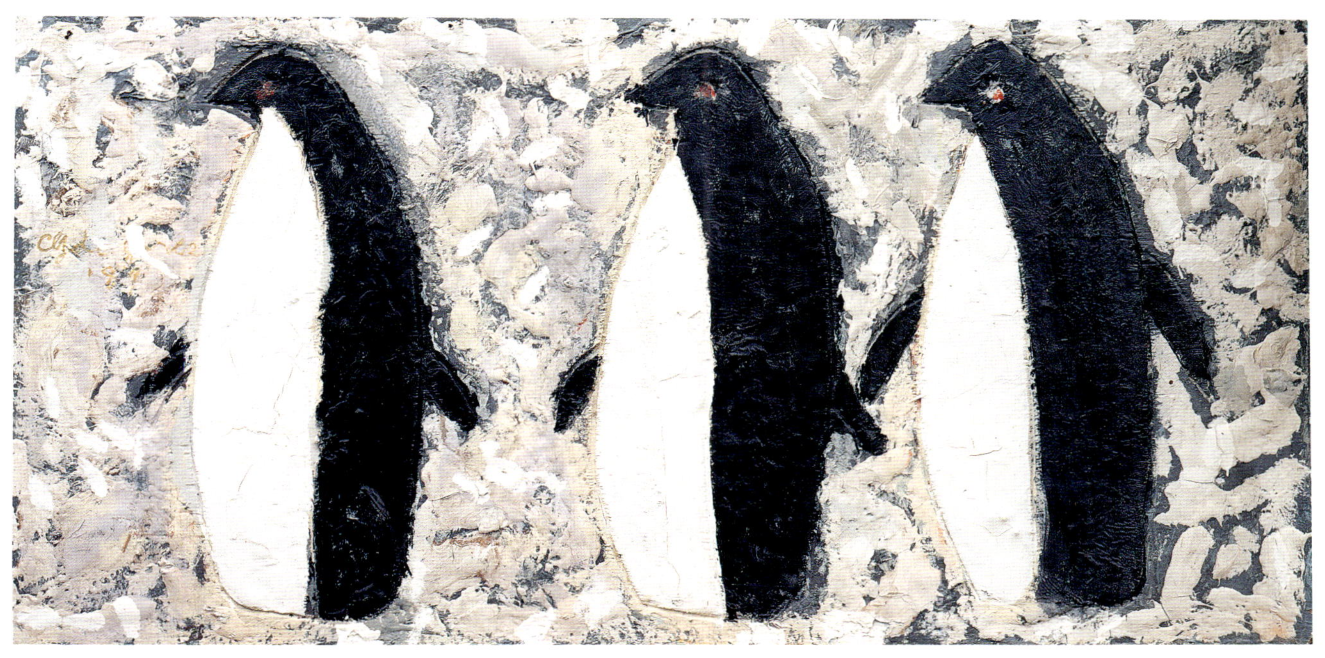

198

CLYDE JONES

Penguins, 1989

(cat. no. 135)

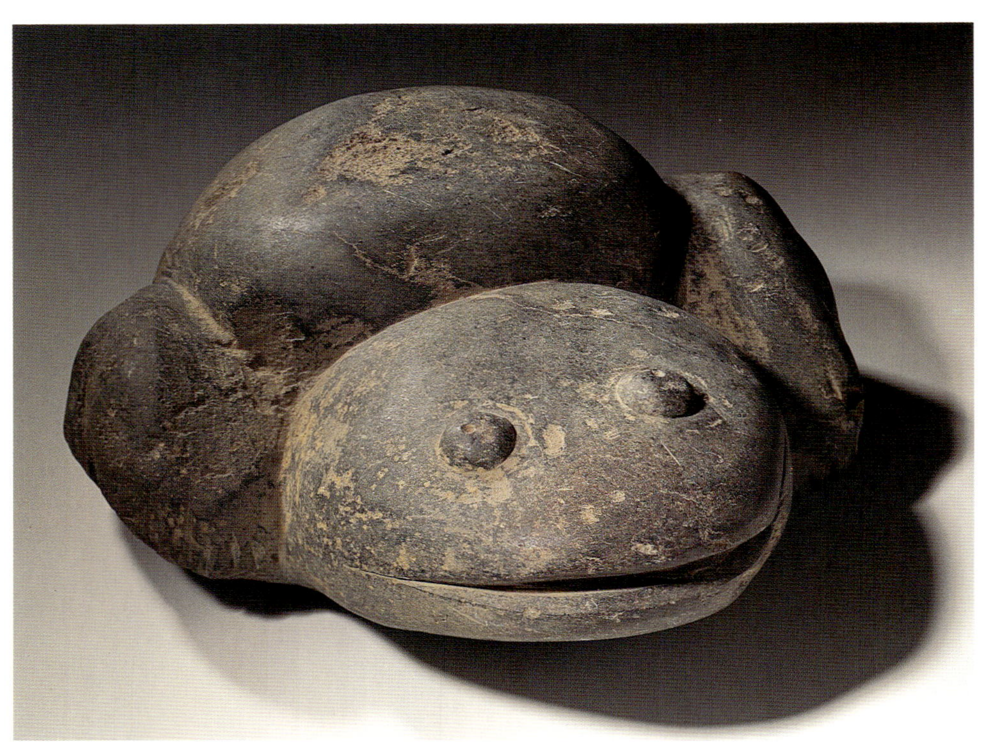

199

RAYMOND COINS

Frog, 1961

(cat. no. 34)

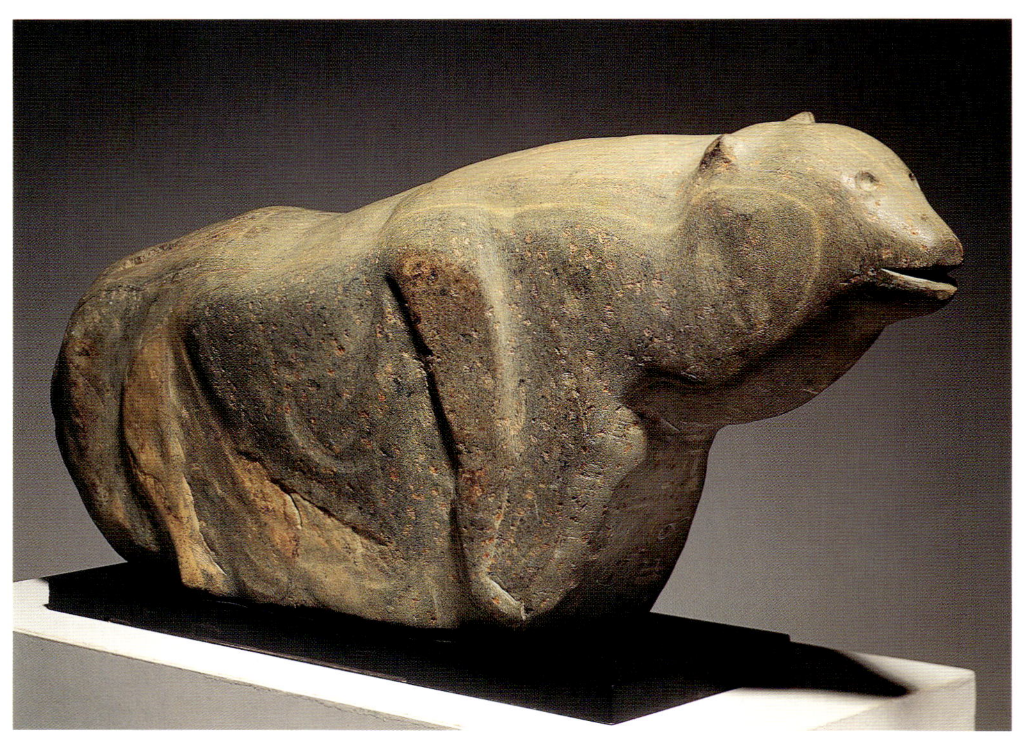

200

RAYMOND COINS

Bear, 1987

(cat. no. 31)

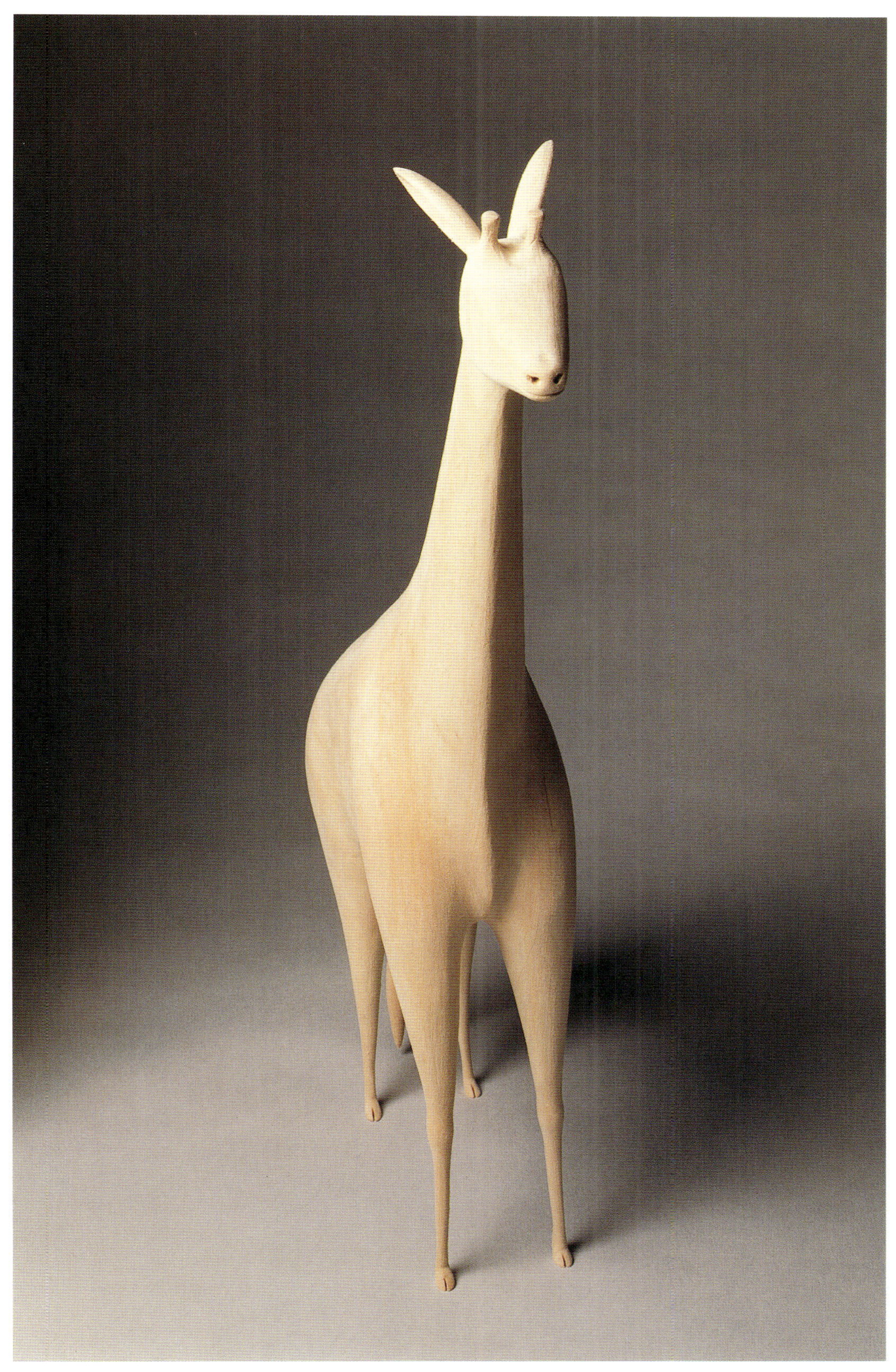

201

LINVEL BARKER

Giraffe, 1991

(cat. no. 10)

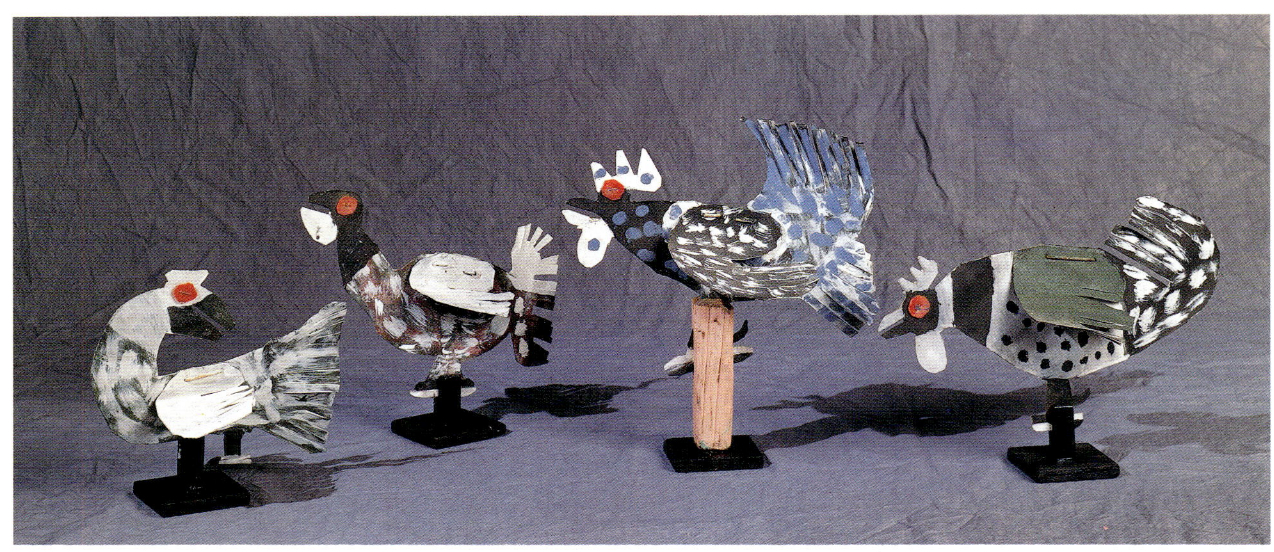

202

DAVID BUTLER

Two Roosters and Two Hens, 1979

(cat. no. 21)

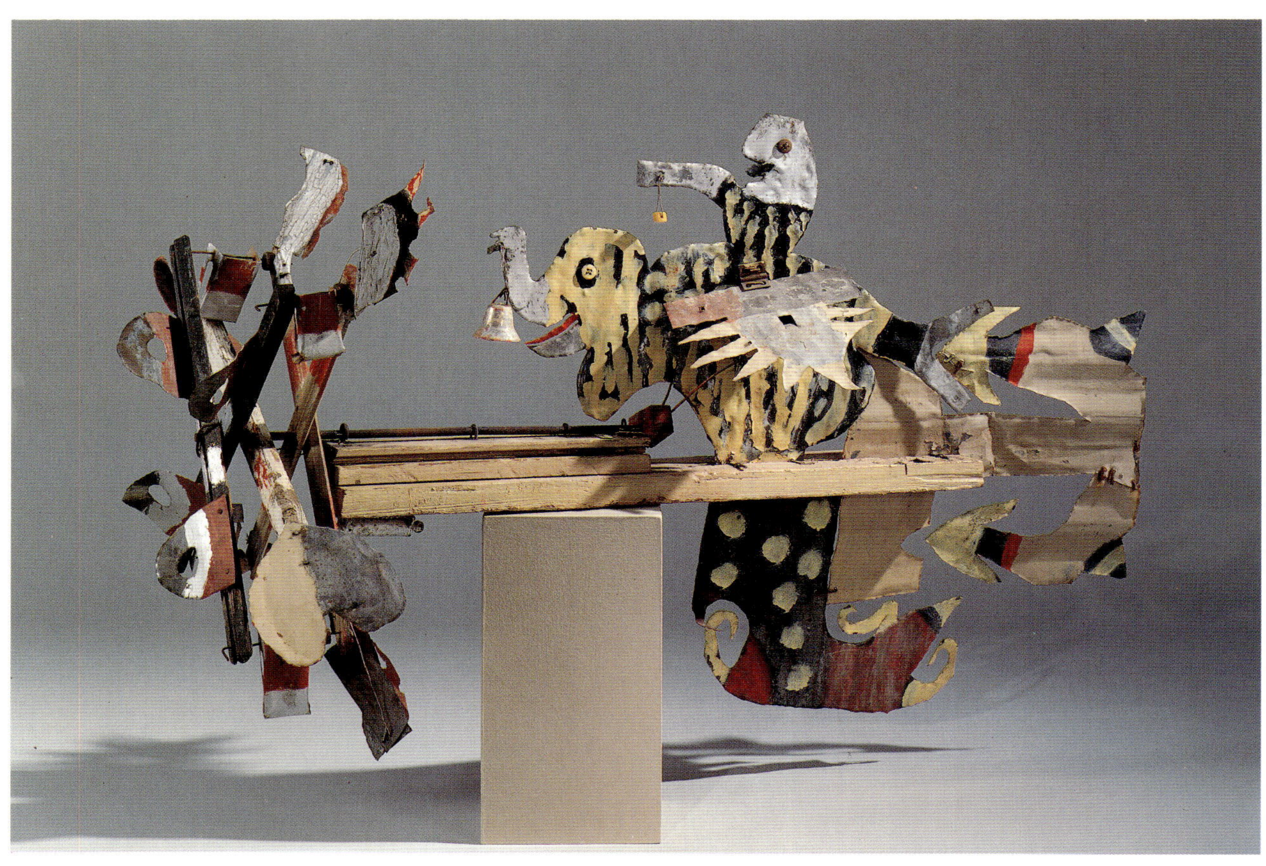

203

DAVID BUTLER

Windmill with Man Riding Flying Elephant, 1975

(cat. no. 23)

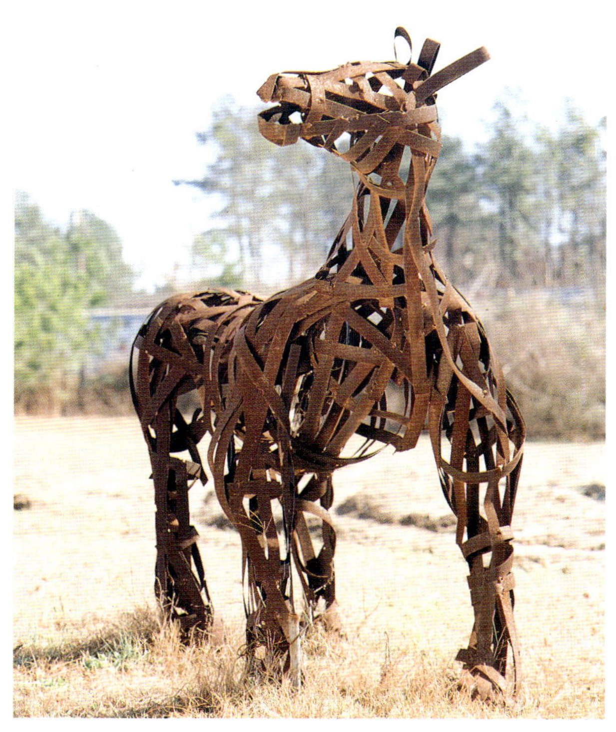

204

CHARLIE LUCAS

Horse, n.d.

(cat. no. 157)

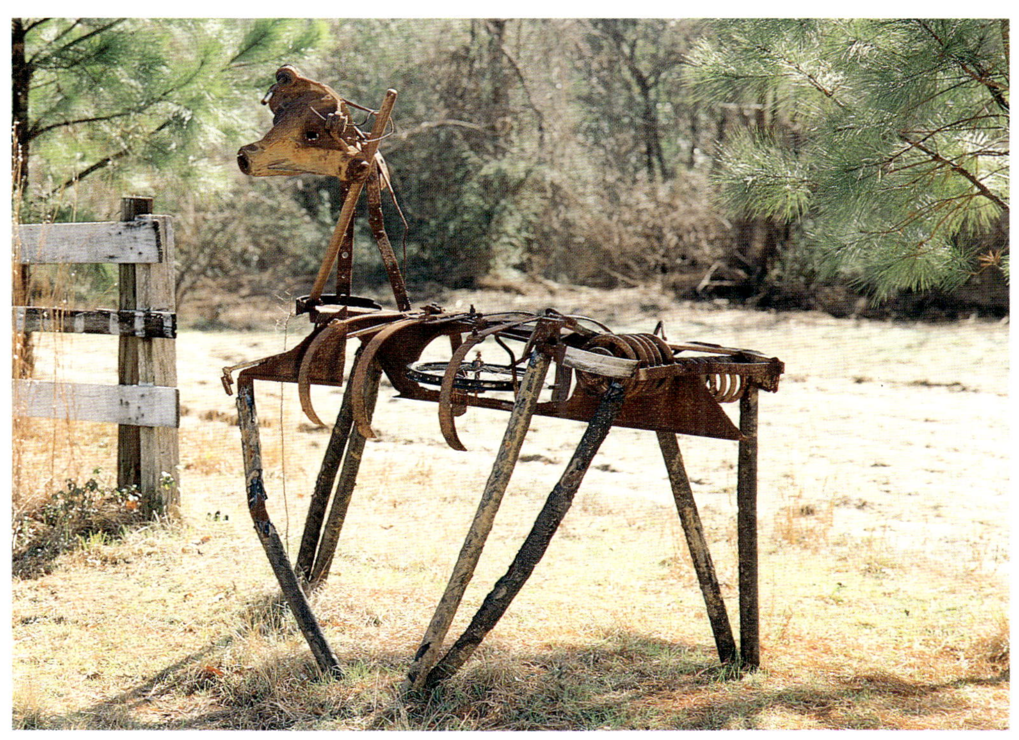

205

CHARLIE LUCAS

Cow, n.d.

(cat. no. 156)

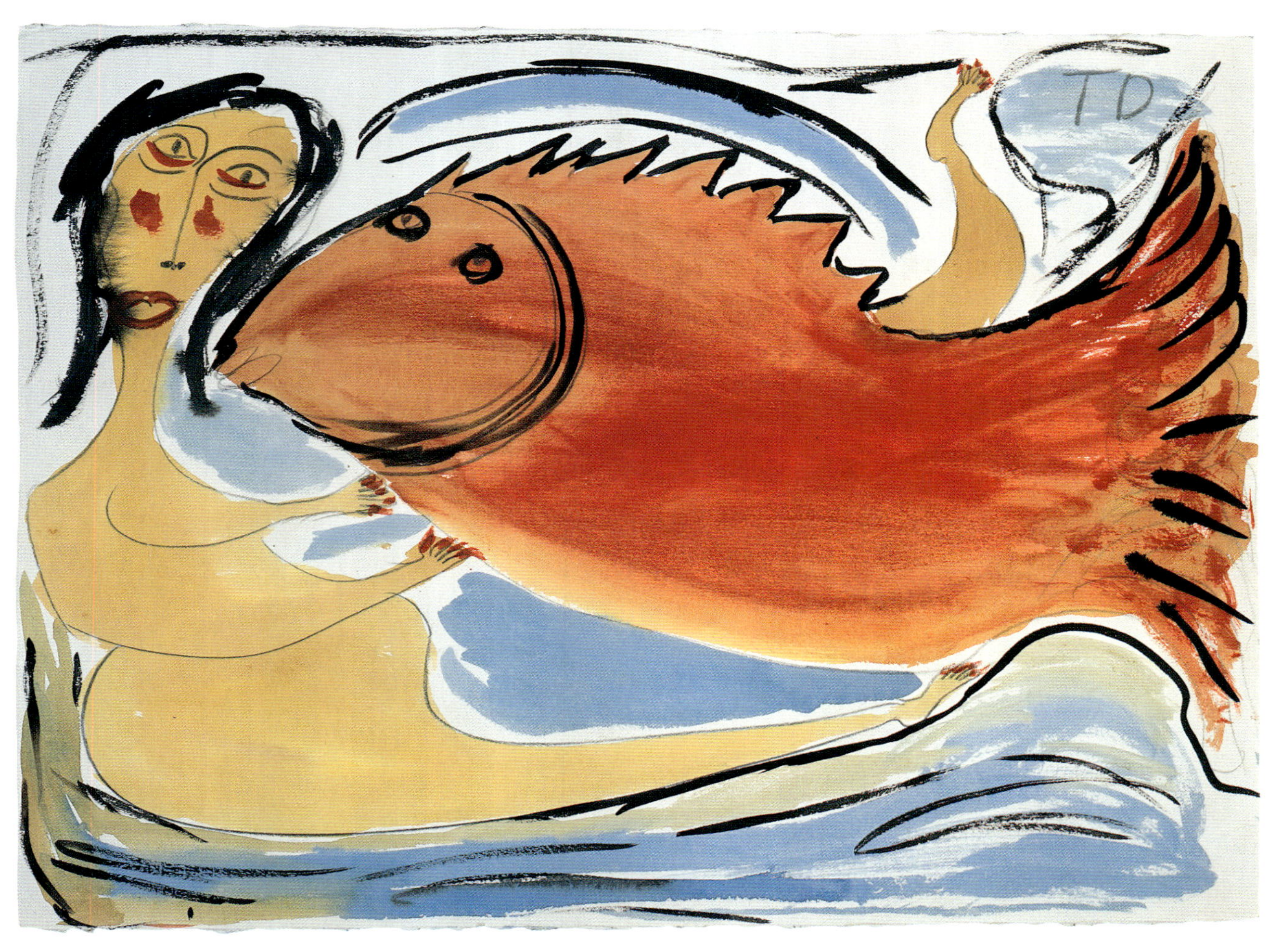

206

THORNTON DIAL, SR.

Fishing for Love, 1990

(cat. no. 54)

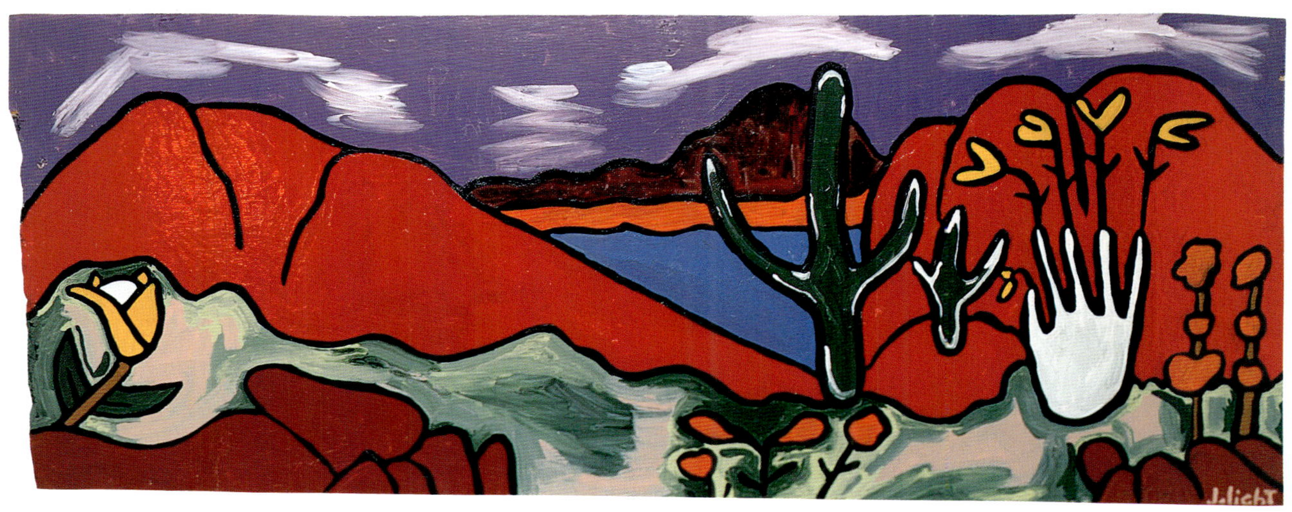

207

JOE LOUIS LIGHT

Hard to Beat, 1988

(cat. no. 154)

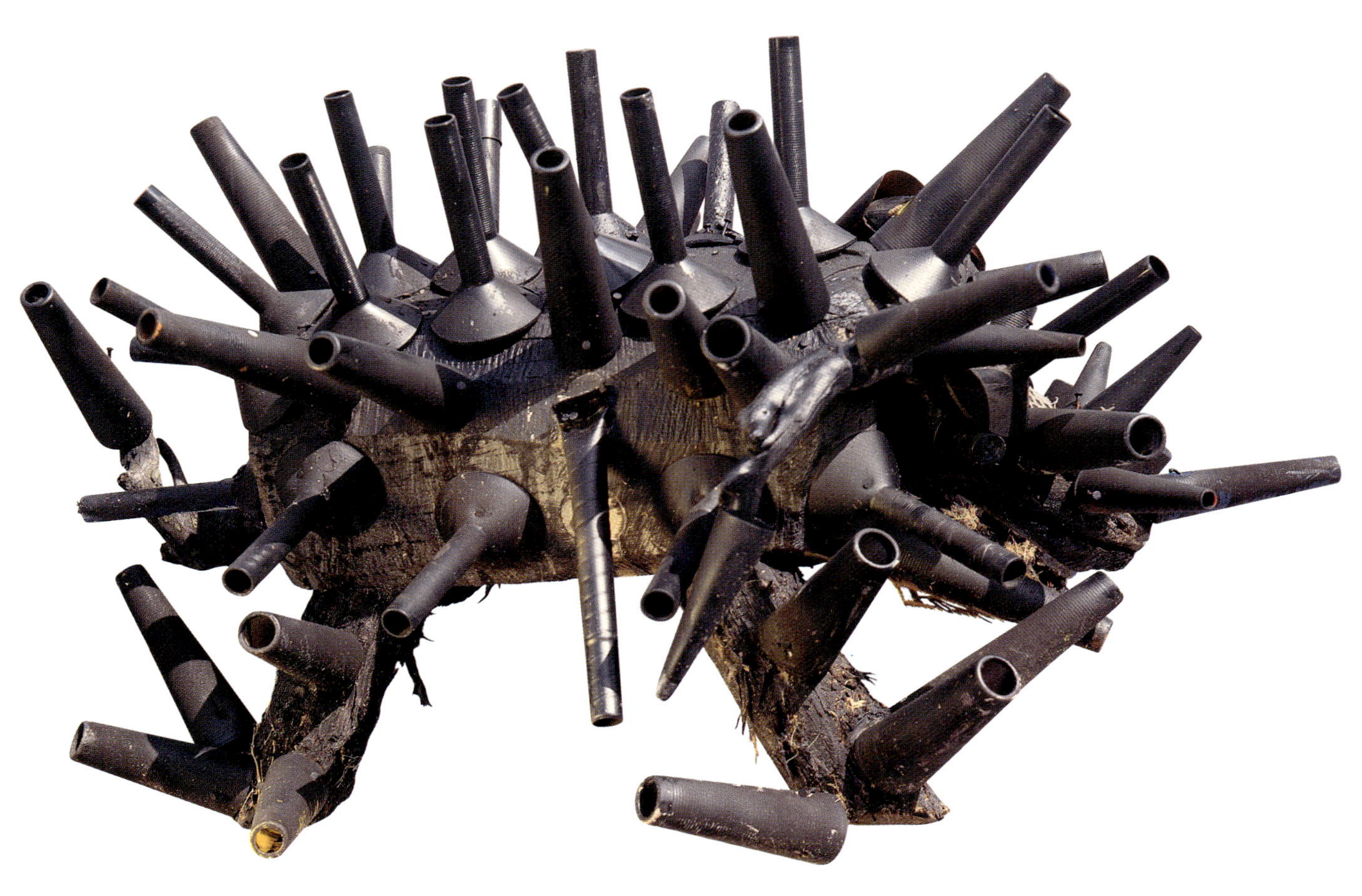

208

CLYDE JONES

Porcupine, 1989

(cat. no. 136)

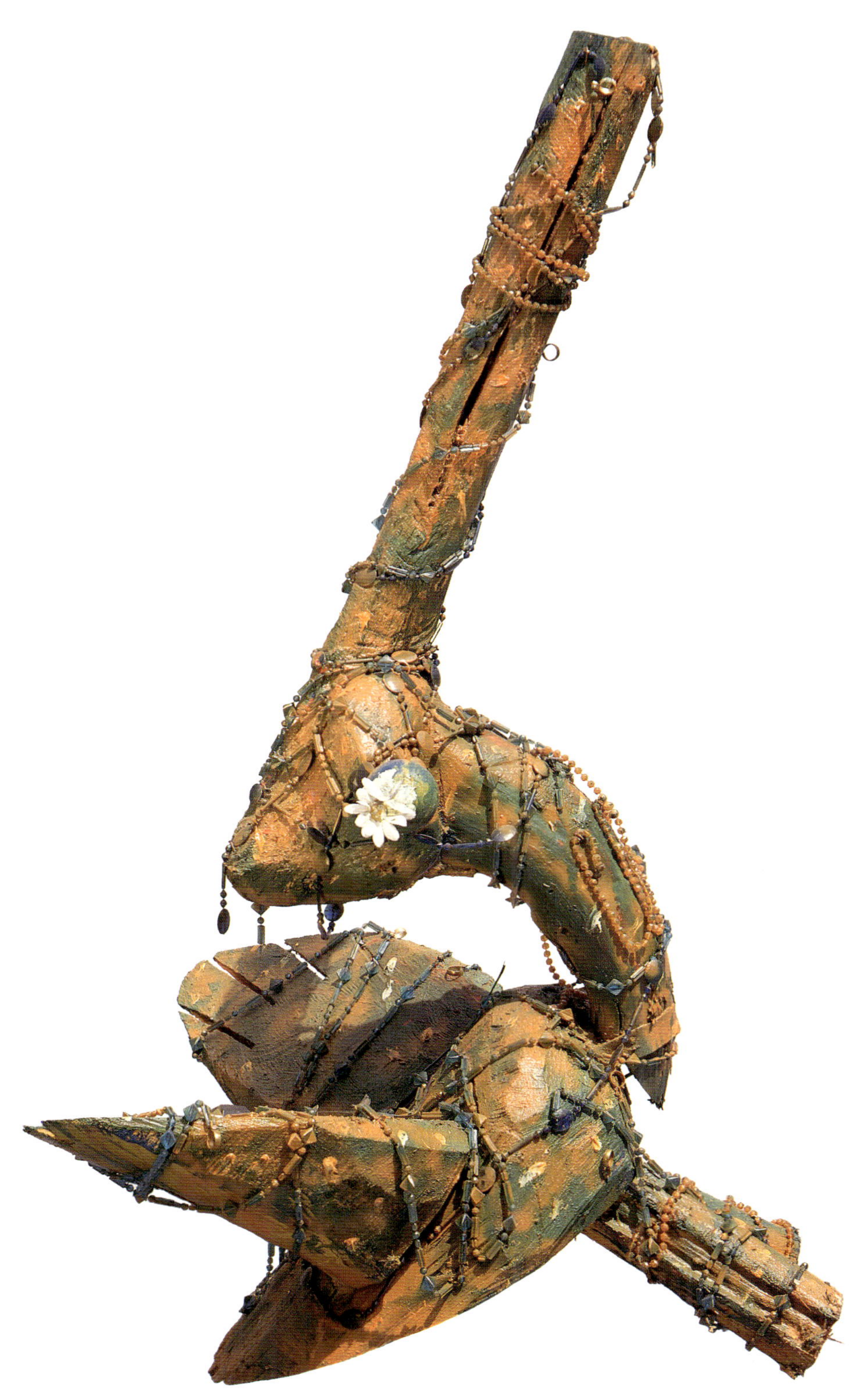

209

CLYDE JONES
Pelican, 1989
(cat. no. 134)

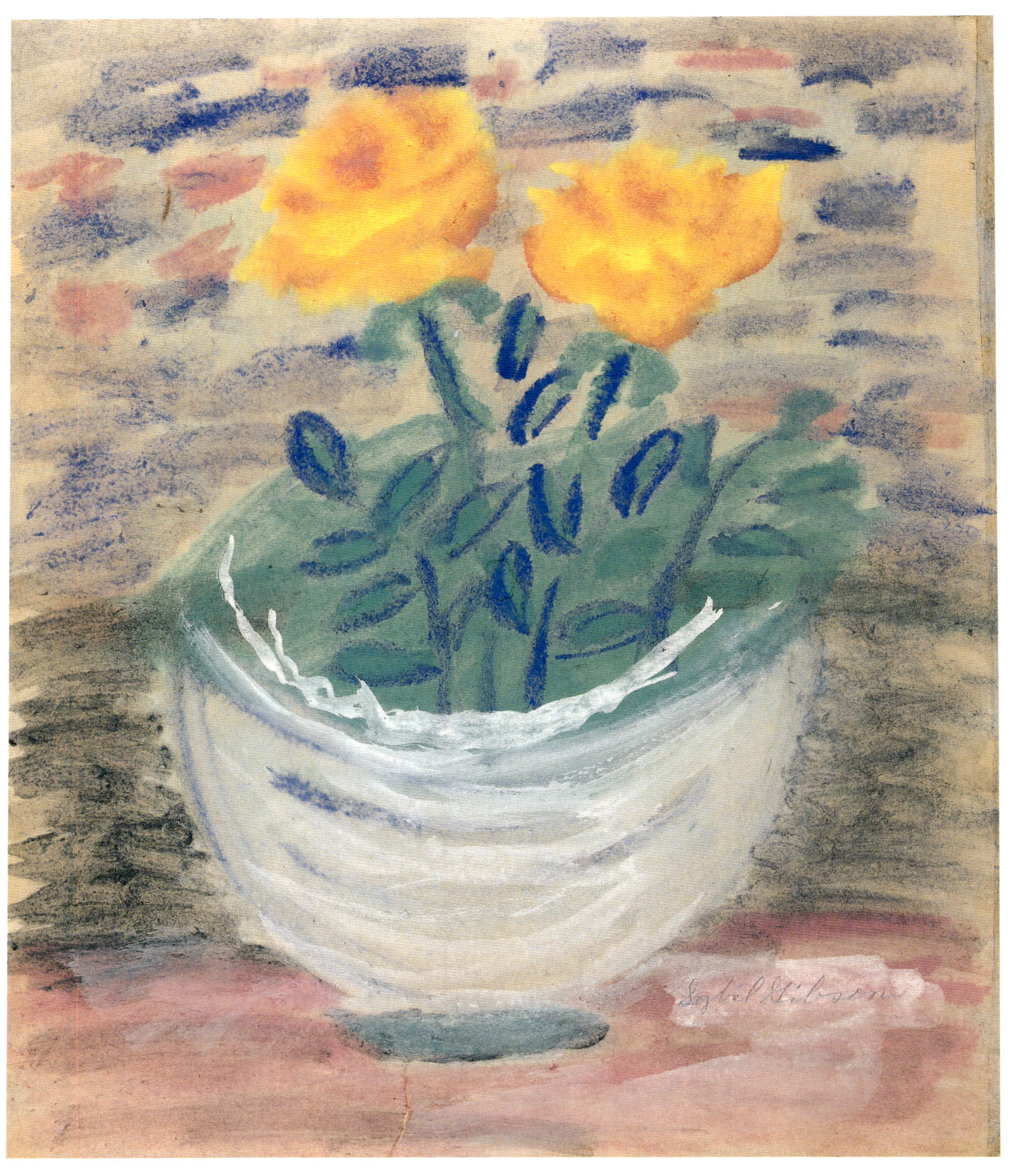

210

SYBIL GIBSON

Flowers in White Vase, n.d.

(cat. no. 98)

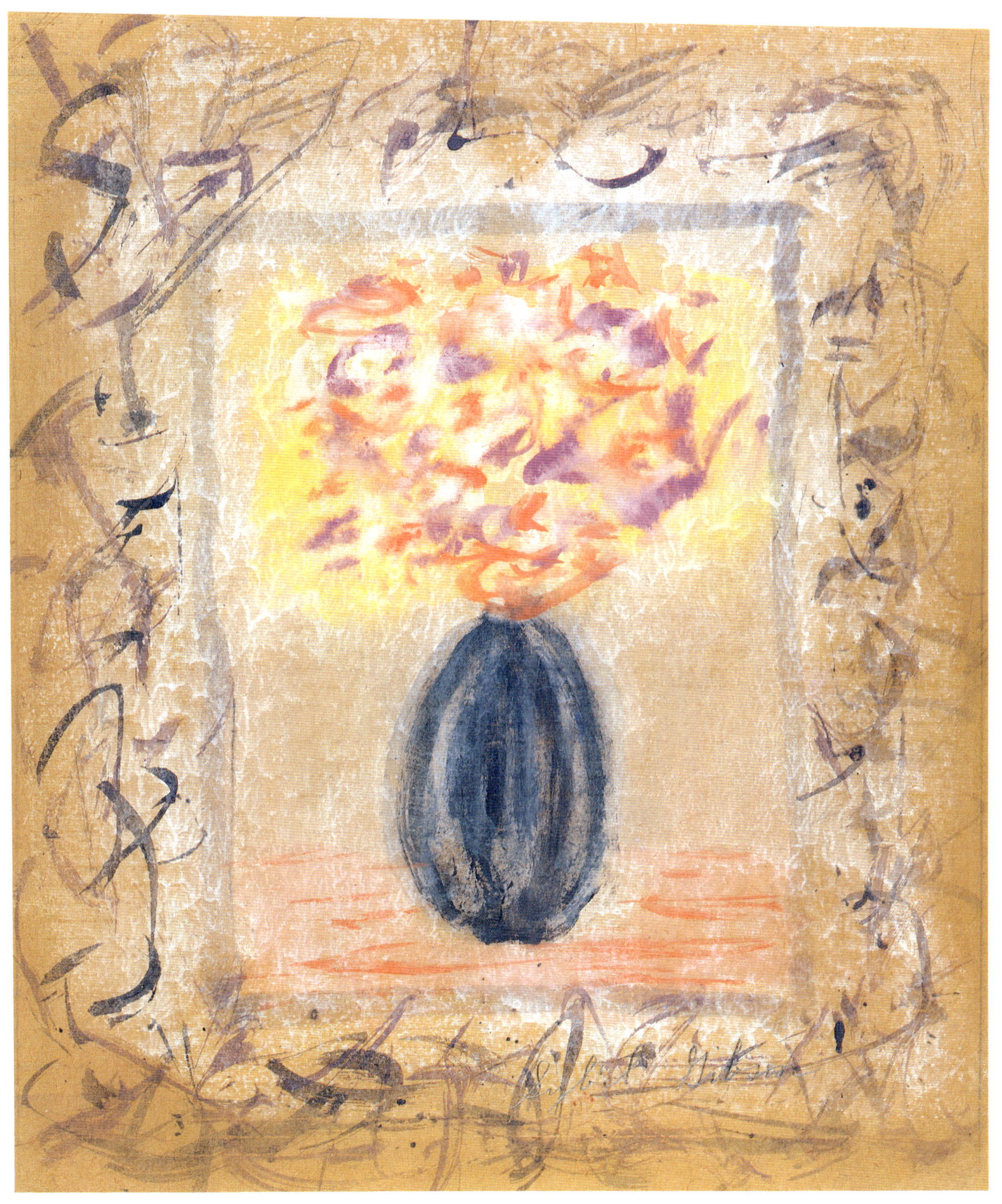

211

SYBIL GIBSON

Flowers in Black Vase, n.d.

(cat. no. 97)

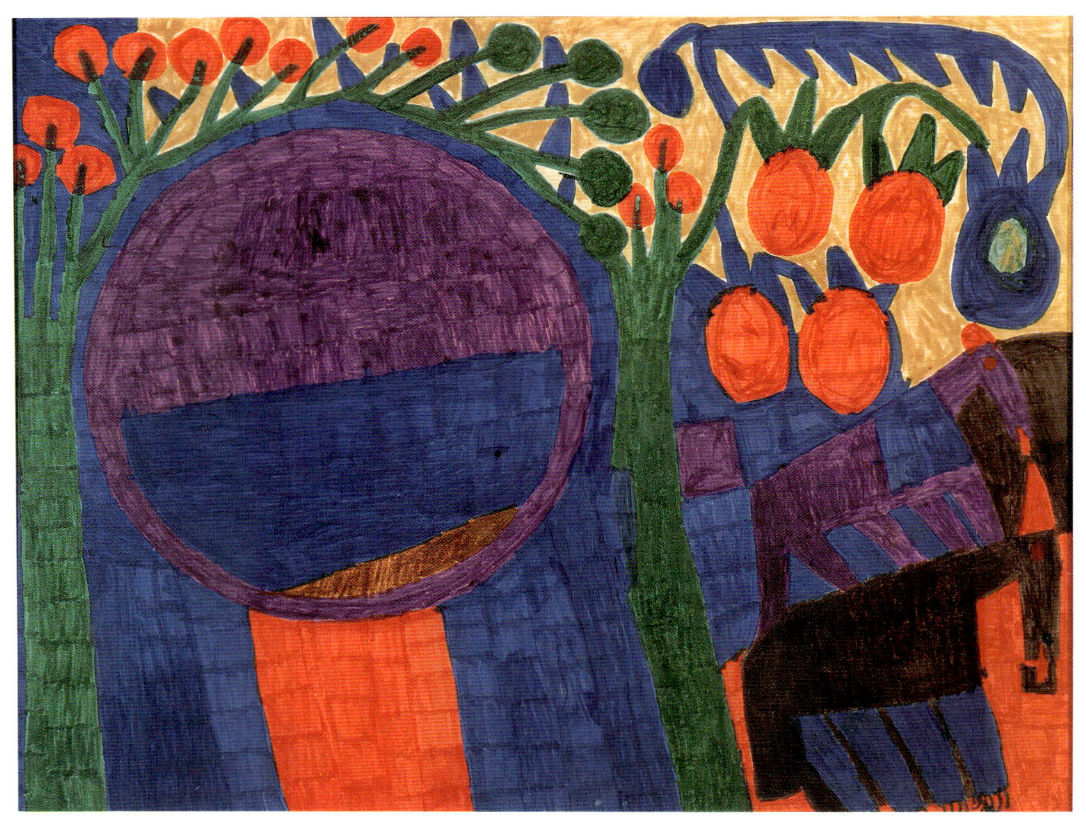

212

WILLIE WHITE

Creole Tomatoes, ca. 1988–89

(cat. no. 258)

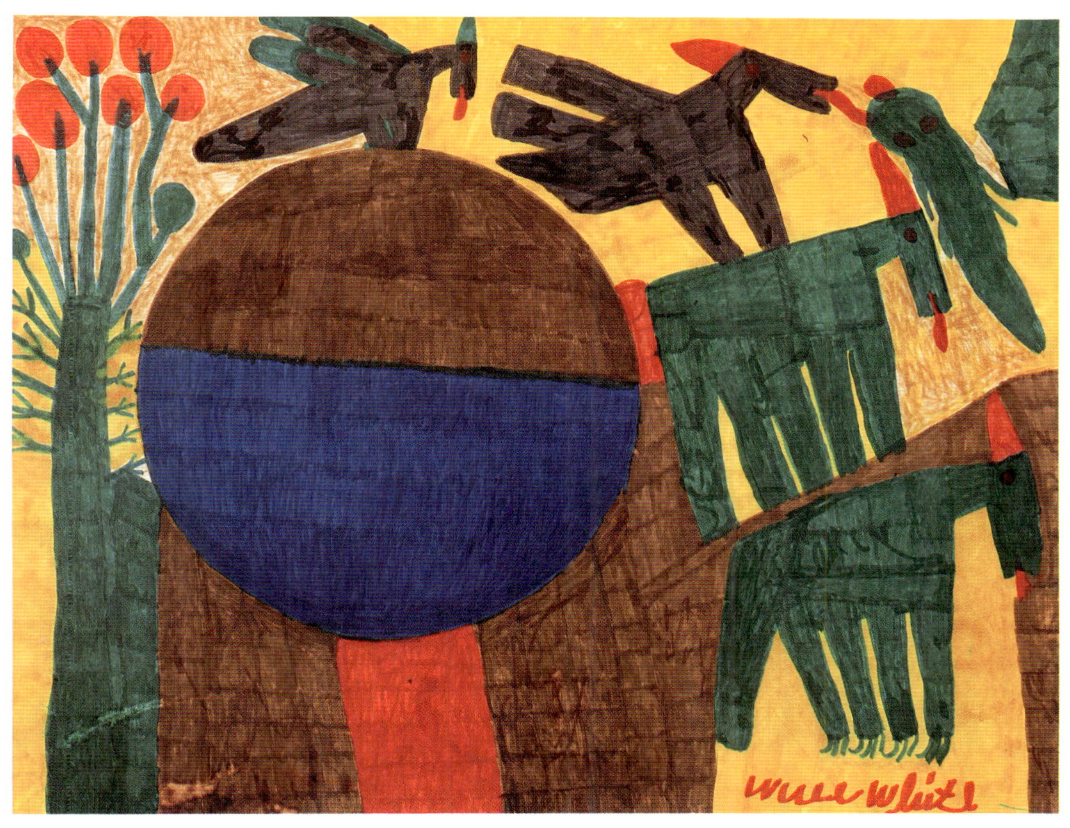

213

WILLIE WHITE

New Orleans Dinosaur, ca. 1988–89

(cat. no. 259)

ARTISTS' BIOGRAPHIES

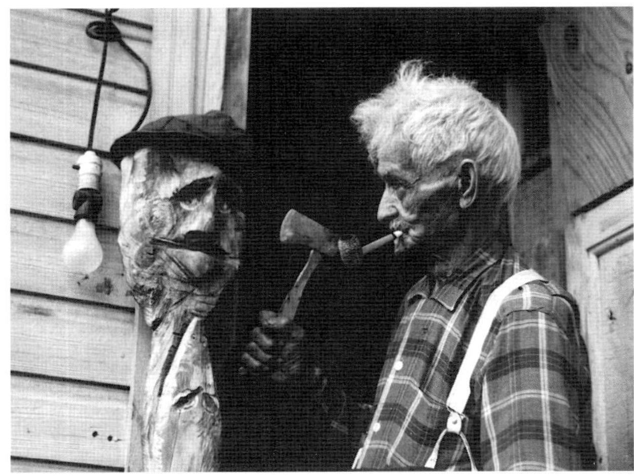

JESSE AARON

1887–1979

"I can see faces on anything. I can look at a tree stump and know just how it is gonna look 'fore I start."

Aaron was born of black and Seminole Indian descent in Lake City, Florida. The first of eleven children, he left school in the first grade to work as a farmhand to support his siblings. In his early twenties, he apprenticed at a bakery and later operated several bake shops. Aaron worked on a tomato farm for several years and in the early 1930s worked as a cook in Gainesville, Florida. In the 1960s, Aaron retired to care for his disabled wife and started a nursery, which failed. Unemployed, Aaron prayed repeatedly to God for the right job.

Inspired by God, Aaron began to liberate human and animal forms from wood. Preferring cypress and cedar wood, Aaron employed chain saws to rough out the forms; hammers, chisels, and knives to finish off the image; and drills to produce the eyes. Untouched by stain, varnish, or paint, the surface was often burned to alter its color and texture. Occasionally Aaron adorned the finished carvings with plastic eyes and found objects. The sculptures range in size from a few inches to larger than life-size.

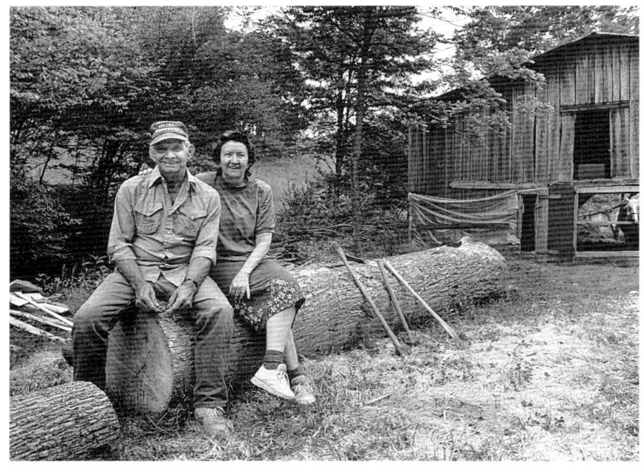

MINNIE ADKINS

B. 1934

GARLAND ADKINS

B. 1928

Minnie and Garland Adkins are husband-and-wife artists from Kentucky. Minnie spent her youth on her father's tobacco farm; she whittled whenever she had the chance. After she and Garland were married, they lived for several years in Ohio. Minnie carved animal figures that she sold at local flea markets, but not until they moved back to Kentucky did she begin to carve full-time.

Minnie inspired Garland to take up carving, and today the Adkinses often work as a team. Garland roughs out a general shape, usually an animal or a religious scene, from a piece of local wood, and Minnie carves the finishing details. She sometimes paints the figures but often leaves the natural finish.—*D.P.*

Armstrong was born in Thomson, Georgia. He attended McDuffie County schools through the eighth grade, and as his father had done, he worked for most of his life as a field hand, picking cotton. After his wife's death in 1969, Armstrong went to work for a box factory, retiring in 1982.

About 1972 Armstrong had a vision of an angel, who prophesied the end of the world and urged him to stop wasting time. Armstrong diligently created calendars indicating days, weeks, and months of the year to predict this cataclysm. He made these calendars from wood, nailed together into irregular boxes; from paper or cardboard; and from functional objects, including mailboxes, urns, and vending machines. Armstrong painted the objects white and superimposed a grid pattern and lettering with red and black felt markers. The calendars vary in shape and size: the flat ones measure from 6 by 11 inches, while the largest box is an actual wardrobe.

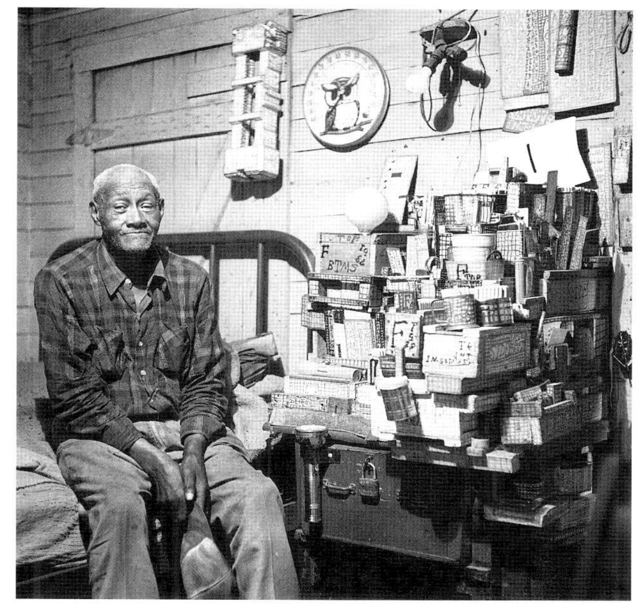

Zebedee "Z. B." Armstrong

1911–1993

Eddie Arning was born in a small German farming community near Austin, Texas. He lived and worked on his family's farm until his mid-twenties, when he began to experience bouts with mental illness. In 1934 he was committed to a mental institution; he remained there for thirty years. In 1964 he was released to a nursing home. It was then, at the age of sixty-six, that he began a decade of artistic output.

Arning worked with crayons or oil pastels on paper. Early subjects were objects from everyday life: animals, plants, farm implements, automobiles, windmills, and musical instruments. Later he used scenes and advertisements from magazines as inspiration. Arning stopped drawing in 1973.—*D.P.*

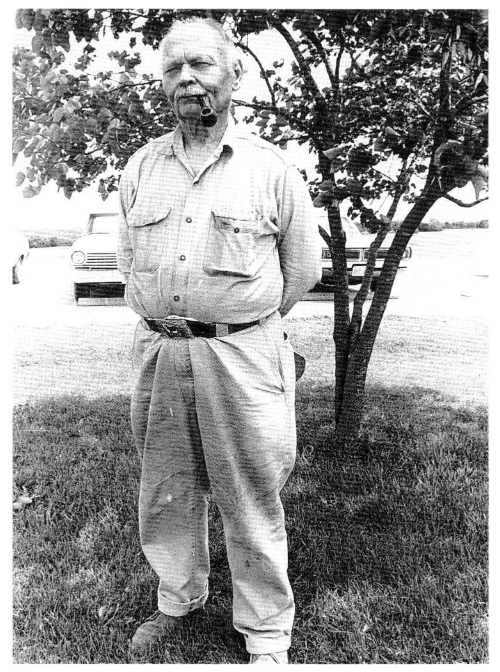

Eddie Arning

B. 1898

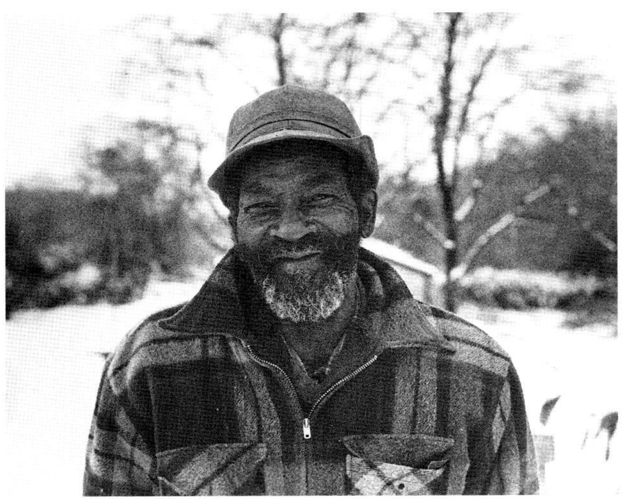

Steven Ashby

1904–1980

"I kept thinking about it. I dreamed about it. I just had to do it."

Ashby, born in Delaplane, Virginia, spent his entire life in Virginia's Fauquier County. His father was a freed slave laborer on a farm where Ashby also worked. He was a farmhand all his life, except for a brief period as a waiter. Although Ashby may have produced carvings throughout his life, his retirement and the death of his wife in the early 1960s intensified his activity.

Ashby's subjects were inspired by his agrarian surroundings and by dreams. His work ranges from small plywood figures to life-size representations of men and women formed from lumber or tree trunks. He enhanced the sculptures with model-airplane paint and frequently adorned them with clothing and found objects, often explicitly indicating gender. Ashby arranged his pieces in his yard and suspended them from the trees.

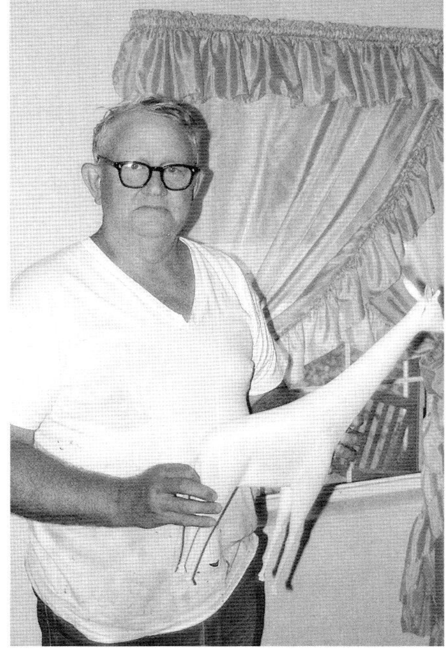

Linvel Barker

B. 1929

"When I was growing up I'd whittle things and give them to people."

Barker was born in eastern Kentucky, and as a young man, he hitchhiked throughout the country. For more than thirty years he lived in Indiana, working as a technician at a steel mill. He later moved back to Kentucky, where he became reacquainted with Minnie Adkins, a self-taught artist who encouraged him to carve. Paying meticulous attention to detail, Barker carves from linden, which he sands to a finely finished surface. Although Barker is a preacher, with a small nondenominational congregation, he does not carve religious subjects; instead, he creates images of animals.

"In 1947 a stray gourd appeared alongside my driveway. I had a gourd garden, so I just started making things out of 'em."

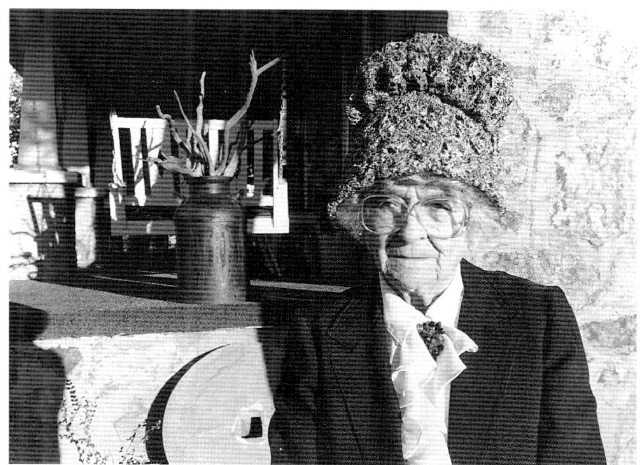

Minnie Black

B. 1899

Born Minnie Lincks in Laurel County, Kentucky, Black was raised on her father's cattle farm. She attended Kentucky schools—Annville Institute for eight years and Sue Benette College for one year. Although Black had aspired to be a teacher, she married and devoted herself to her family. Her husband ran a grocery store in Bernstadt, Kentucky, and she began to explore the artistic possibilities of her gourd garden.

Guided by the original shapes of the gourds, Black creates portraits, prehistoric images, fantastic and prosaic animals, and biblical and political figures. Black organized a senior citizens band that played instruments made from gourds. After her husband retired in the late 1960s, she converted his grocery store into Minnie Black's Gourd Craft Museum.

Black cuts gourds into sections, and joins the pieces with nails or glue to create new shapes. She builds them out with clay, plaster, and papier-mâché and uses Sculptamold to cover the joints and add features. Black preserves the natural color of the gourds, painting them only lightly.

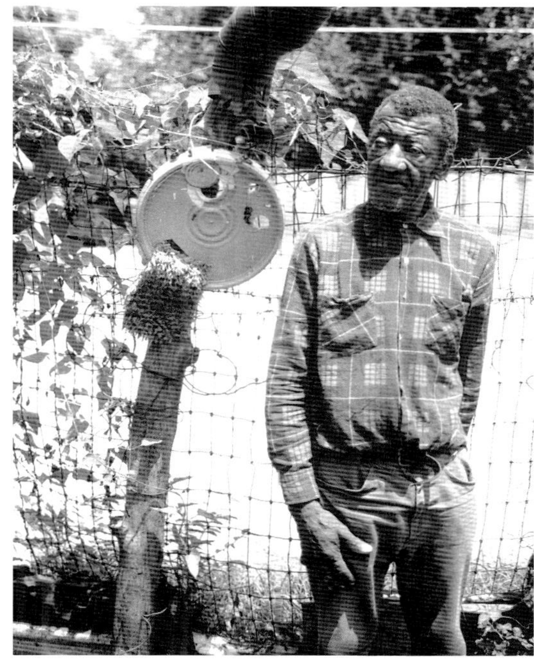

Hawkins Bolden

B. 1914

Born in Memphis, Tennessee, Bolden resides near the neighborhood where he was raised. Although he has been blind since the age of five, he has made things all his life. With his brother, Bolden assembled radios from discarded parts. An avid gardener, he earned his living by cultivating lawns and cleaning alleys and vacant lots.

Bolden has created a menagerie of assemblages to serve aesthetic and utilitarian functions in his garden. He scavenges his material, often pans and wash tubs, which he punctures and connects with wire, carpet strips, and wood to produce both simple and complex anthropomorphic forms.

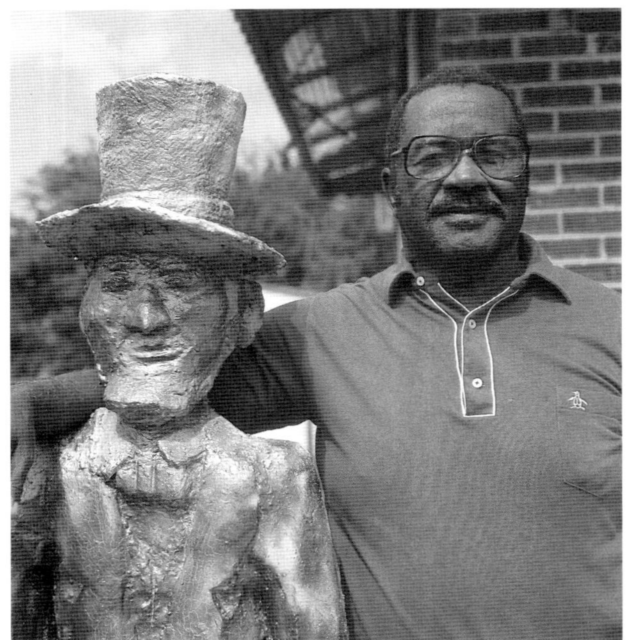

"Soon after my retirement in 1976, I got a little sick and wanted to do something. I went down into the cellar and made a statue."

Born and raised in Rocky Mount, North Carolina, Burwell attended school through the eleventh grade. At the age of nineteen, he began raising tobacco as a cash crop on the farm he inherited from his father. In the early 1940s, he gave up full-time farming and began to work for the railroad, starting as a laborer and working his way up to mechanic and sheet metal worker. In 1976 he retired from the railroad and began making artworks.

Burwell created concrete sculptures in his basement and carport. His subjects were his friends, heroic images, biblical characters, images from newspapers and television, animals, and anthropomorphic figures. Burwell applied a mixture of lime, sand, gravel, cement, and water with a trowel to an armature of steel rods, clothes hangers, and pipes. He finished the work by thickly applying outdoor house paint to the dry concrete.

VERNON BURWELL

1916–1990

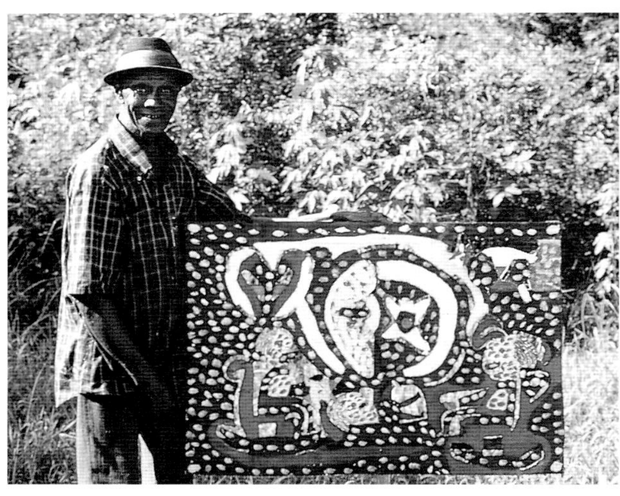

David Butler is the oldest of eight children born to a carpenter father and a missionary mother. After leaving school at an early age, Butler cut grass, built roads, and labored in sugar cane fields. During his adult life, he worked in sawmills until an on-the-job injury in the 1960s forced his retirement.

Soon after his accident, Butler began to make painted, snipped tin sculptures. Inspired by God to decorate his immediate environment, the artist covered his yard with vividly painted mermaids, flying elephants, cowboys, religious scenes, fish, trains, and other fanciful subjects, many of which first appeared to him in dreams. Many of his works have moving parts and often incorporate found objects into their design.—*D.P.*

DAVID BUTLER

B. 1898

"I swept up a half box of sawdust to take to the Dumpster and then decided to experiment with it."

Born in Atlanta, Georgia, Byron left high school in 1946 to join the navy. In 1949 he returned to Atlanta and finished high school. Byron later attended trade school and worked as a bricklayer until he was recruited by the Fulton County sheriff's department in 1961. He founded in Atlanta the first black-owned private investigation firm in the United States. He was elected as council member for the city's ninth district in 1981 and served until 1990.

Byron's first artworks were root sculptures; later, he developed his signature molded pieces, which are formed of sawdust combined with solvent and glue. Recently Byron has executed near-life-size sculptures from wood and adhesive materials. He paints the surface and writes an explanation of the meaning of each piece. Byron's works vary in subject matter, composition, texture, and color; many of his images are social and political statements, or anatomical studies.

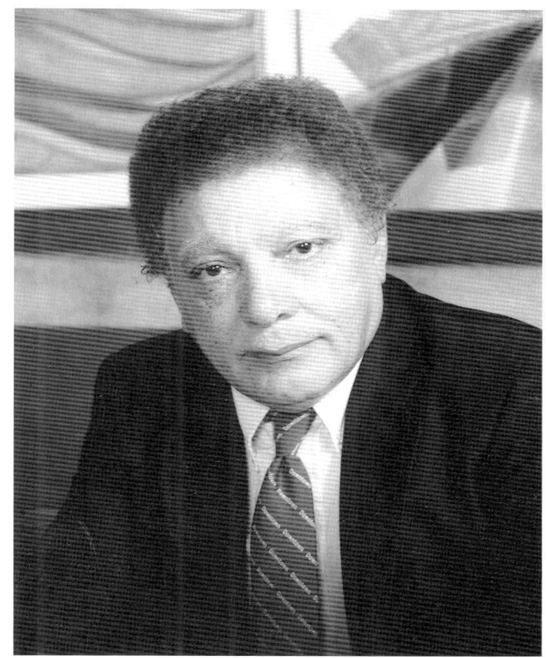

Archie Byron

B. 1928

"There's an old story about wood and it's true . . . that there's something in there, under the surface of every piece of wood."

Carpenter was born in Brownstown, Pennsylvania, in Lancaster County, and received eight years of formal education. In 1901 his father moved the family to Waverly, Virginia, and began operating a lumber mill. At twenty-three years of age, Carpenter established his own lumber mill, and beginning in 1916, he and a friend operated an outdoor summer theater for five years. Carpenter retired from his lumber business in 1955 and opened a roadside icehouse and produce stand.

Carpenter began whittling with his pocketknife after World War II, when business at his mill was temporarily slow. His wife encouraged him to continue carving, and he carved actively from 1955 on, except for the three years before his wife's death in 1966. With a pocketknife and simple hand tools, Carpenter fashioned fanciful animals, famous people, and fantastic creatures from boards, roots, and driftwood. He derived the ideas for his creations, which he painted with enamel, from the original shape of the wood.

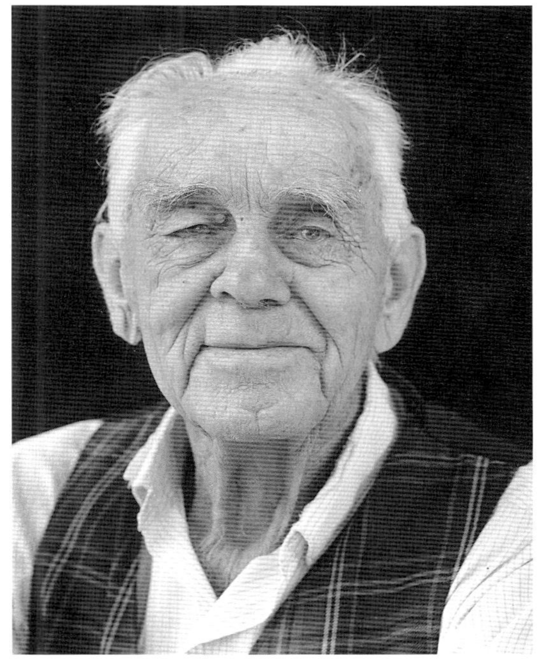

Miles Carpenter

1889–1985

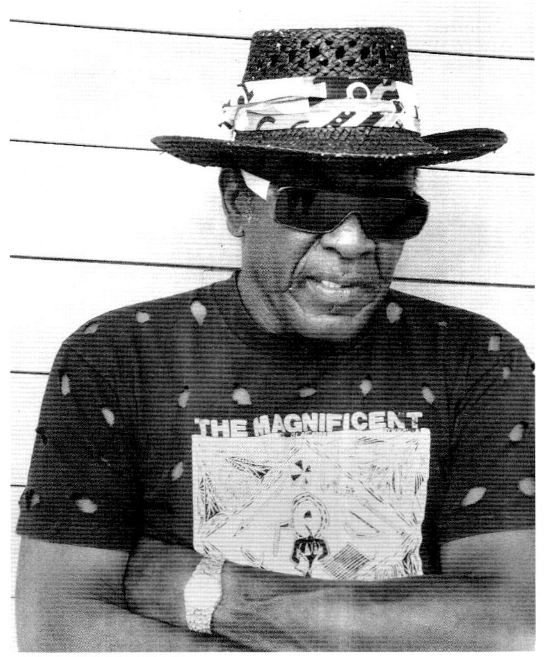

Henry Ray Clark

B. 1936

"As long as my mind can create something, I am a free man."

Born in Bottley, Texas, Clark dropped out of school at the age of fourteen to pursue the attractions of gambling in Houston's third ward. Although he worked periodically for his father, who managed a construction company, and in various other professions, including plumber, plasterer, cement mixer, and carpenter, Clark at the same time was involved with hustling, gambling, and pimping. These vices led to a series of convictions, one for attempted murder and two for possession of narcotics. While serving his first jail term in 1977, he began to draw to occupy his time.

Clark's visionary drawings are kaleidoscopic designs of intensely colored geometric patterns and images of fantastical men, women, and creatures. Initially, Clark drew on whatever he could salvage from prison trash, including requisition forms and manila envelopes; later he acquired good-quality drawing material. His mixed-media drawings are executed with ink, pen, and pencil, in green, black, red, yellow, and purple hues, and range in size from 9 by 12 inches to 18 by 30 inches.

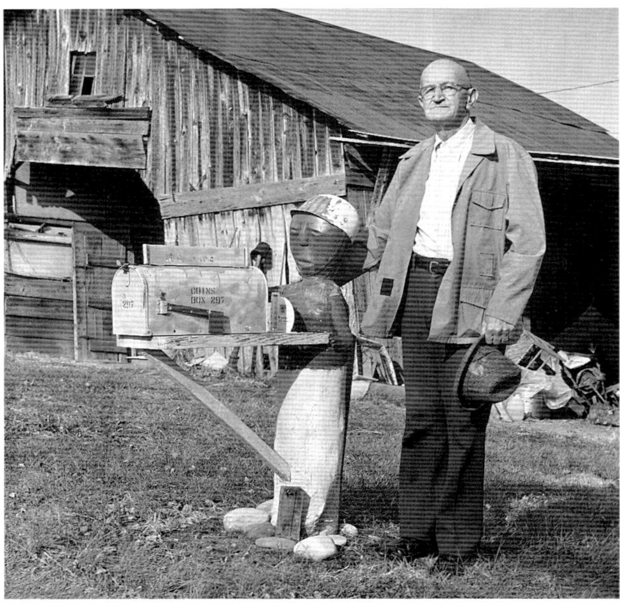

Raymond Coins

B. 1904

"I'd cut what was on my mind and never think of a thing that was going on in the world. Someone could walk or talk to me and not have any effect. I'm amazed at myself getting that much good feeling from cutting stone."

The son of subsistence mountain farmers, Coins was born in southern Virginia. When he was ten years old, his father purchased a farm in North Carolina and moved the family there. After completing the fifth grade, Coins assisted with the field work. He worked as a hired field hand until, in 1950, he was able to purchase a small farm of his own. Coins grew tobacco, corn, wheat, oats, and rye and worked in the winter as a floorman at tobacco warehouses.

Coins was inspired to carve after he retired in 1968. He shapes local river rocks and woods with a chisel and axe. Coins began by carving Indian tomahawks and arrowheads; later, he fashioned animals, human busts, bas-relief stone carvings of his religious dreams, and a variety of other images suggested by the natural form of his material. He prefers white, speckled, and blue soft river stone and cedar. The works vary in size from several inches to almost life-size.

"After my accident, I had nightmares where walking snakes chased me. I carved the snakes and put them in hell, where I was living."

The Coopers were married in 1949 in Flemingsburg, Kentucky, where they managed a country store until financial problems caused them to move in search of work. In Marion, Ohio, Ronald worked on a General Motors assembly line, and Jessie was a supermarket cashier. In 1984, after Ronald suffered two heart attacks and a near-fatal car wreck, the Coopers returned to Flemingsburg and took up art to escape their troubles.

While recovering from his injuries, Ronald began to carve, and Jessie continued an interest in drawing and began to paint in collaboration with Ronald. Although both artists decorate old wood furniture with house paint, Jessie usually paints the objects that Ronald carves. Their works are primarily biblical scenes and depictions of the struggle between good and evil. Ronald carves preachers, snakes, devils, and ghosts. Although their work is serious in subject, the message is frequently seasoned with humor.

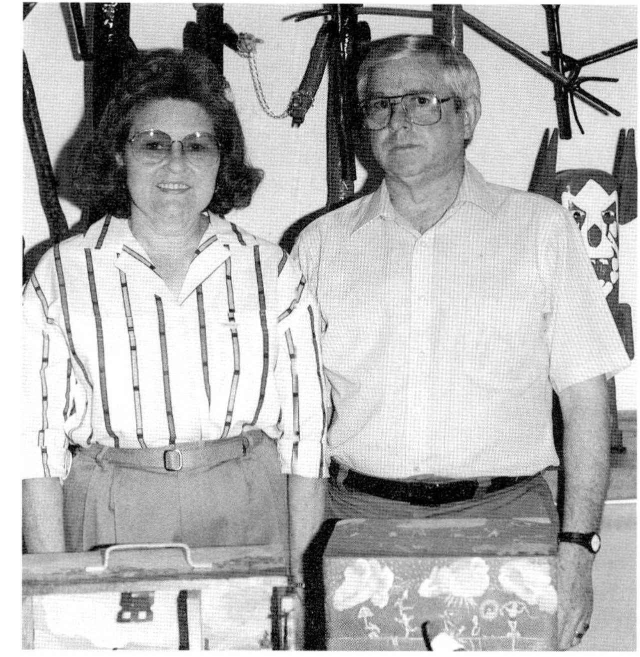

Jessie Cooper — Ronald Cooper

B. 1932 — B. 1931

Harold Crowell, the son of a Methodist minister, has been mentally handicapped since birth. He had his first experiences with art as an activity when his mother gave him paper and pencils to keep him occupied during church services. Since being institutionalized in 1975, he has been encouraged to paint as therapy.

Crowell is a prolific painter who creates vivid images of animals, plants, people, and religious and imaginary scenes. He usually employs a bright palette, and his style can range from realistic to abstract.—*D.P.*

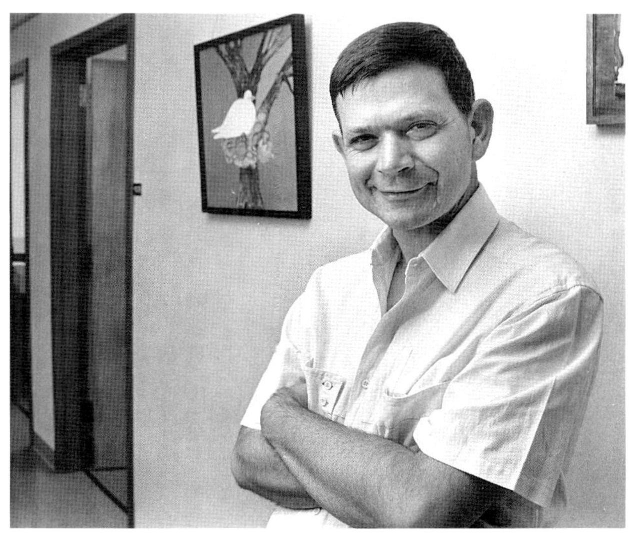

Harold Crowell

B. 1953

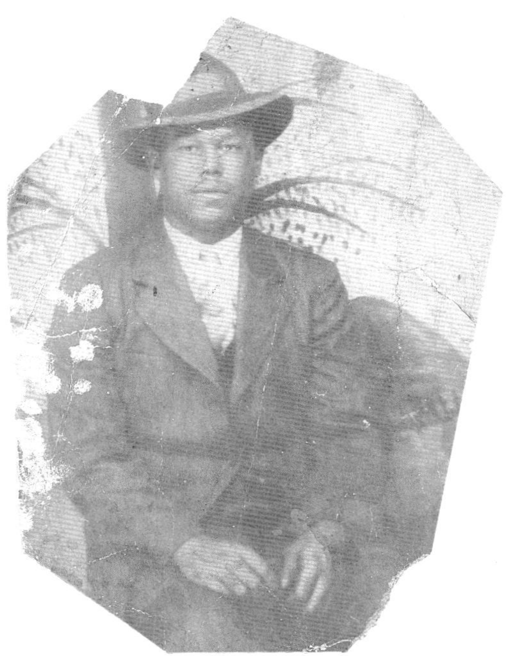

Ulysses Davis

1913–1990

"I'm an American, so I carve the Presidents. Whether you like them or not, they built the country."

Davis was born in Fitzgerald, Georgia. Because of family financial pressures, he left school after the fourth grade to work as an assistant in the local railroad office; in 1942 Davis was transferred to Savannah. When the railroads began to decline in the early 1950s, Davis was laid off. Consequently, he took up barbering and wood carving, both of which he had learned in his youth.

Davis furnished his barbershop with framed reliefs and freestanding sculptures that he had carved from various woods with a hatchet and chisel. His subjects were largely religious themes; human figures, particularly political icons, and especially U.S. presidents; fantastical creatures; and lizards. Davis imprinted floral motifs in the wood with brands that he chiseled on bolt heads. He applied paint sparingly in a limited palette of white, black, and occasionally red. Davis frequently decorated his pieces with glitter, rhinestones, and sequins, all of which he called "twinklets."

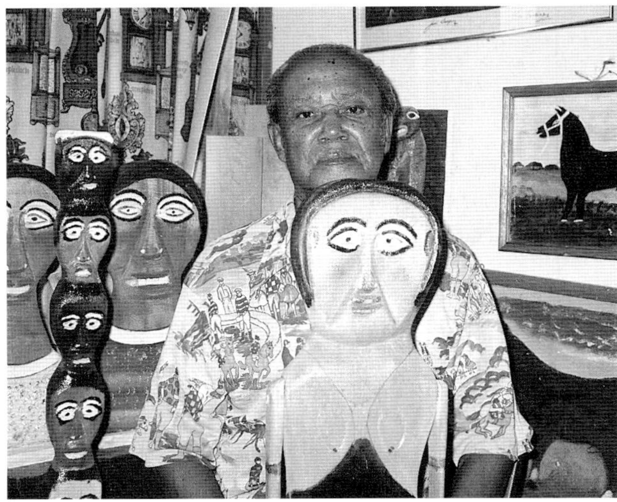

William Dawson

1901–1990

"I had always been good with my hands . . . but when I retired altogether, I needed something to do, so I began whittling."

Born in Huntsville, Alabama, Dawson was raised on his family's farm and attended school through the fifth grade. He moved to Chicago in the early 1920s and worked for a produce distributor for thirty-five years, eventually becoming the manager of operations.

After his retirement in the mid-1960s, Dawson enrolled in adult education classes in ceramics and painting but found them too regimented. He began to carve instead and, more recently, returned to painting. At first using discarded wood, often old chair and table legs, he created totemlike sculptures, human and animal figures, and multimedia assemblages. His subjects derive from the Bible, current events, television, and folktales and imagined subjects. Each carved piece is painted with enamel, varnished, and occasionally decorated with glitter, animal bones, feathers, hair, stones, or shells. Most of his figures are carved in the round and have strongly outlined facial features and prominent eyes and teeth. Dawson roughed out his figures with a coping saw and detailed them with wood files and a drafting knife. His carvings range from a few inches to 4 feet in height.

"Sometimes a picture just doesn't look like it's level, and then I have to put something on to anchor it—something like a cow or a rabbit."

Dey was born in Phoebus, now Hampton, Virginia. During his school years his part-time job as a newspaper carrier supplemented his mother's income. Dey dropped out of school in 1930 and subsequently supported himself as a trapper and a lumberjack in Maine. In 1934 he moved to Richmond, Virginia, worked as a barber, and in 1942 became a policeman. After his retirement from the force, at the age of forty-three, Dey began to paint.

Often symbolic, humorous, and fanciful, Dey's illustrations include imaginative adventures and autobiographical scenes. He occasionally introduced into his compositions subjects from television and figures seen in popular Christian literature and newspapers. He often traced his images from templates for a meticulous, uniform appearance. Dey layered pure hues of model-airplane enamel on wood or plywood. His pieces range from a few inches to almost 30 inches tall.

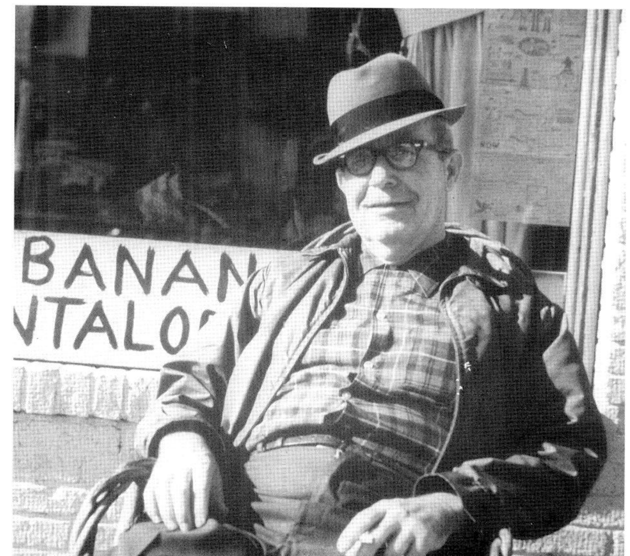

JOHN WILLIAM "UNCLE JACK" DEY

1912–1978

"I can't read and spell but I got a mind and I can speak with any man. I might say something in my art that somebody ain't never heard before."

Born in Emmel, Alabama, Dial never knew his father. At ten years of age he was sent to live with his aunt, and when she died three years later, he went to live with his grandmother in Bessemer, Alabama. After completing the fourth grade, Dial began to support himself. For almost thirty years he was employed at the boxcar factory in Bessemer and also took side jobs in construction and maintenance, commercial fishing, and farming. He operated his own cafe and raised crops and animals on vacant lots throughout the community. In 1984 Dial and two of his sons began making wrought-iron lawn and patio furniture in a workshop in their backyard.

Dial left the family business in 1987 to make art. Through paintings and assemblages, he comments on contemporary social issues, particularly race, freedom, love, responsibility, women, and sexuality. He represents these themes with symbolic human and animal forms, such as tigers, birds, and fish. Dial uses oil-base and water-base paints in bold colors. He forms his assemblages from salvaged materials, cutting and welding tin and other metal, and combining tree roots, wood, bottles, carpet, and plastic. His pieces measure up to 6 by 9 feet.

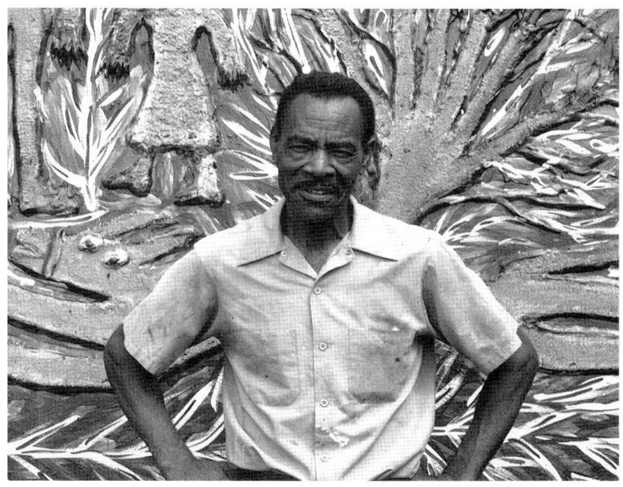

THORNTON DIAL, SR.

B. 1928

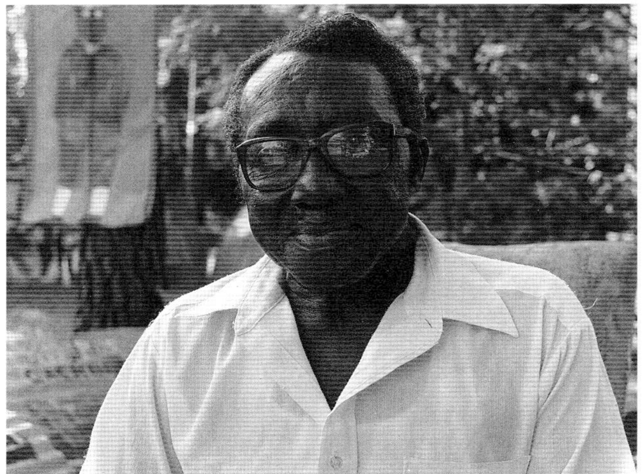

Sam Doyle

1906–1985

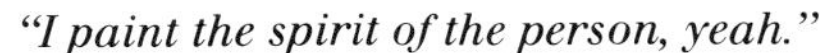

"I paint the spirit of the person, yeah."

Doyle was born on St. Helena Island, South Carolina. His parents, the descendants of freed slaves, were farm workers. Doyle attended Penn School, a private vocational school run by northern whites for the island's black children. He dropped out after the ninth grade and took a job as a clerk at a local store. From 1930 to 1950, he was a porter in a wholesale store in Beaufort, South Carolina, and later worked in a laundry at the Parris Island Marine Corps base. He retired in the late 1960s, and although he continued to work part-time, he considered painting his principal profession. He was most active as an artist in the 1970s and 1980s.

Doyle's images often document the rich folklore and traditions of St. Helena's African-American culture. In addition, he rendered local and national figures, including sports, political, and popular culture heroes. Doyle painted predominantly with enamel or latex house paint on large sheets of cut roofing tin. He also occasionally made animal sculptures from driftwood, roots, tar, and found objects. Doyle displayed many of his pieces in his yard. His works measure as large as 6 by 10 feet but average 2 by 4 feet.

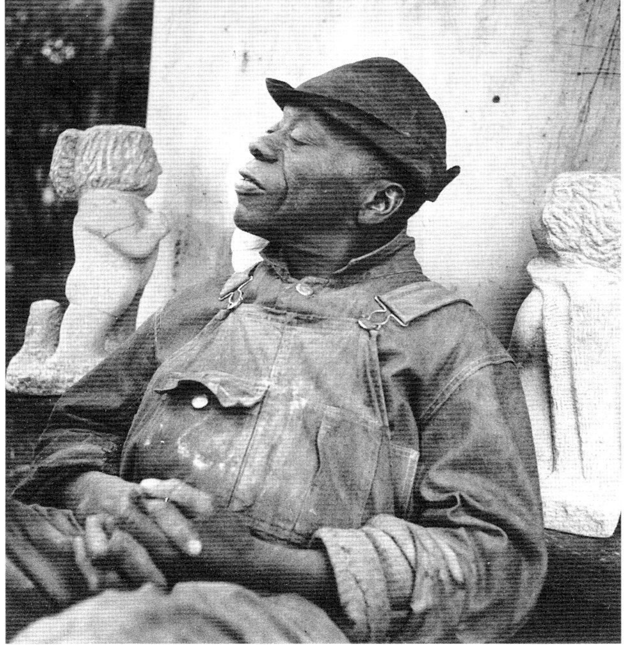

William Edmondson

1870–1951

"I do according to the wisdom of God. He gives me the mind and the hand, I suppose, and then I go ahead and carve these things."

Edmondson was born to former slaves in Davidson County, Tennessee. While residing in Nashville, he worked as a farmhand, as a laborer at a railroad yard, and, after a disabling accident, as a janitor at a women's hospital. Edmondson had little formal education, and he was left unemployed after the hospital closed in 1931. A devout follower of the Baptist Primitive faith, he had a vision in 1932 in which God commanded him to carve tombstones.

Edmondson began carving memorials, tombstones, and tombstone decorations commissioned by blacks for the local church graveyard. He later carved realistic and imaginative animals, religious figures, and images of workers. Edmondson used limestone from demolished buildings and created chisels from railroad spikes. His carvings range from small birds to larger pieces 25 inches in height. Edmondson is remembered as the first black artist to have a one-man show at the Museum of Modern Art in 1937.

"In a dream it was shown to me what I have to do, of paintings. I never plan a drawing."

Born into poverty in Long Creek, North Carolina, Evans, nee Jones, was raised in Wilmington, North Carolina, by her grandmother. After completing the fifth grade, she went to work as a "sounder," or hawker, of seafood from the Delaware Sound. In 1908 Evans moved to Wrightsville Beach, North Carolina, with her mother and grandmother. She was employed as a domestic for several years, and in 1948 she became gatekeeper at Airlie Gardens, near Wilmington, where she began to sell her artworks to visitors.

Evans composed ethereal images derived from the Bible and mythology, combined with floral motifs. She used ink, graphite, wax crayon, and, after 1950, oil paint on canvas board or paper. Most of her works are relatively small, ranging from 4 by 6 inches to 20 by 23 inches; however, after visiting an art museum in 1966, Evans began making larger works, occasionally creating collages from fragments of her earlier pieces.

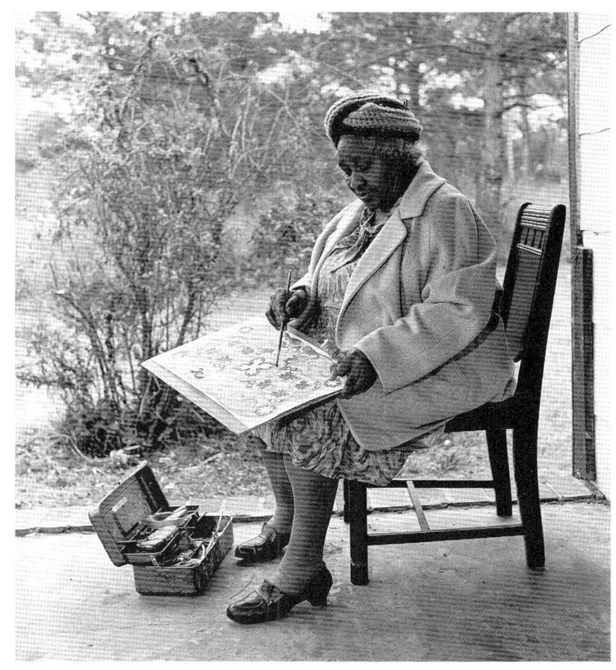

MINNIE EVANS

1892–1987

"My carving? It's just a gift, a gift from God."

The descendant of a slave, Farmer was born in Gibson Courts, near Trenton, Tennessee, and moved with his family to Humbolt, Tennessee, about 1900. Although he occasionally attended school, he spent most of his youth working on farms. In 1917 Farmer moved to East Saint Louis, Illinois. In 1922, shortly after being baptized, he was ordained as a Pentecostal minister and became a street evangelist. Farmer founded the El Bethel Apostolic Church in 1931 in South Kinloch, Missouri. In the 1940s he moved to Milwaukee, obtained a job as a hotel porter, and opened a storefront church. He retired from secular employment in 1960.

Farmer had made colorful canvas banners as preaching tools a decade before his retirement, after which he began to create reliefs with biblical and historical subjects and dioramas documenting his rural memories. Farmer's early wood reliefs were carved with a utility knife from redwood and mahogany; later, he adopted more sophisticated wood-carving tools, including an electric drill, and used softer woods, particularly pine. The dioramas are assemblages of carvings, cloth, plastic, canvas, and assorted objects. Farmer partially paints the wood with enamel and frequently attaches rhinestones or other items to the surface. The wood reliefs are about 20 by 35 inches and the dioramas are about 24 by 24 by 10 inches.

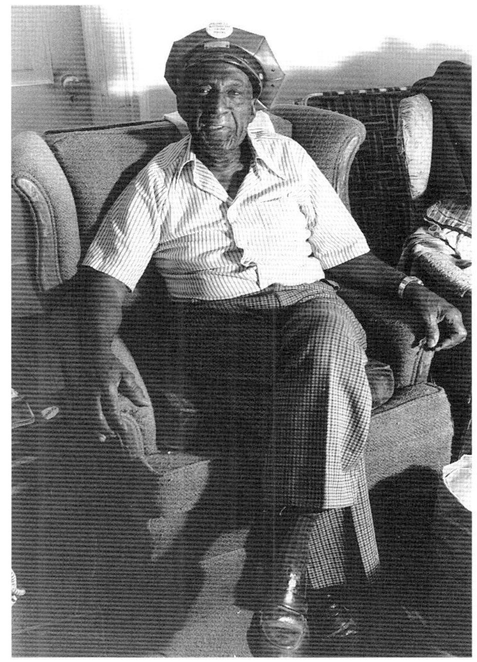

JOSEPHUS FARMER

1894–1989

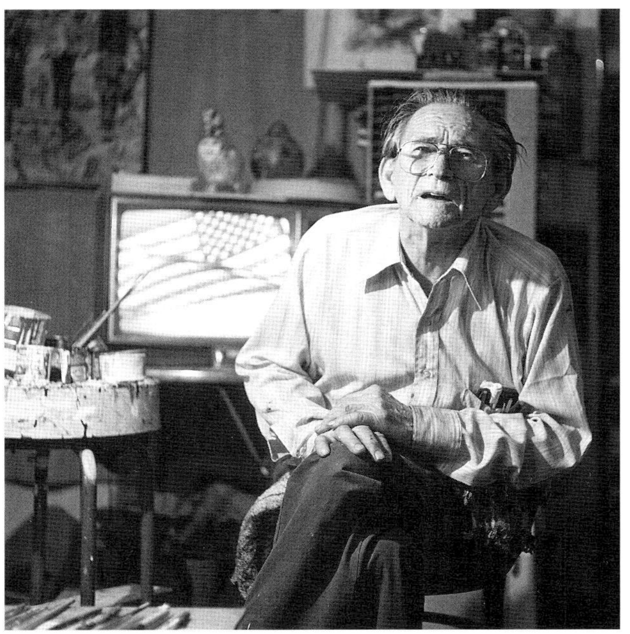

Howard Finster

B. 1916

Finster, the youngest of thirteen children, completed six years of school. As a teenager he began to preach, supplementing his meager minister's salary with a series of odd jobs. In the early 1960s, Finster, at God's command, began to convert a swampy plot of land around his house into what he eventually called the Paradise Garden, which was intended to represent each of mankind's inventions. In the early 1980s, Finster bought and decorated a church on an adjoining piece of land.

In 1976 Finster was commanded by God to paint sacred art. Most of his works are covered with calligraphy meant to instruct the viewer on religious themes. Heaven, hell, angels, Noah's ark, and the Jordan River are common subjects, but Finster does secular works as well that feature American heroes and popular culture figures.

Finster paints on plywood, canvas, or gourds using paint, enamels, or oils. He creates his three-dimensional works from found materials.—*D.P.*

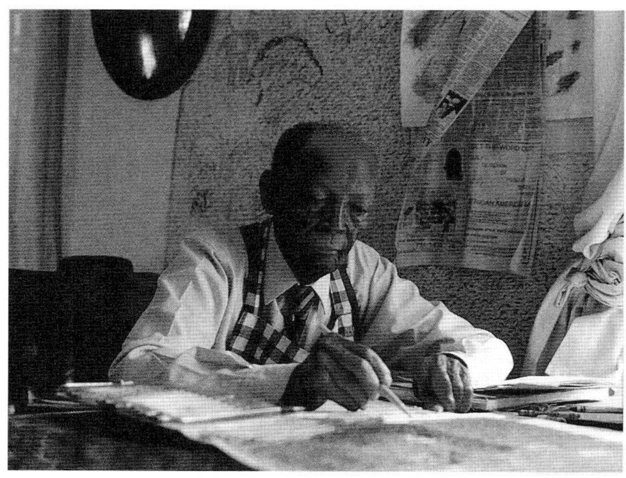

Ezekiel Gibbs

1889–1992

"Don't call the roll. Don't call the roll until I get there. I may be crippled. I may be blind and not see, but I am going to stand right here until I shake hands with thee."

Born in Fort Bend County, Texas, Gibbs lost both his parents before he was six years old. His memories of them are few, but he was told that his father came from Africa and his mother was a Cherokee Indian. Gibbs was sent to live with an uncle in Richmond, Texas, then stayed with a farm family near what is now Katy, Texas. At twelve years of age he returned to Richmond. Because there were no schools in the area that accepted people of color, Gibbs did not receive a formal education. As an adult, he made his living sharecropping and raising animals and vegetables. A religious man, Gibbs was a member of the Vernon Missionary Baptist Church for more than fifty years and served as a deacon.

Gibbs began painting and drawing in 1972, after his wife died. His subjects are drawn from his life experiences, including farming, gardening, church life, animals, family members, and friends. Using watercolors, pencil, wax crayons, and oil pastels, Gibbs transformed available materials, including scraps of paper, old letters, and paper grocery bags, into works of art.

"My life is my work, I live to work."

Gibson, born Sybil Aaron in Dora, Alabama, graduated from Jacksonville State College with a degree in biology. She taught elementary school in Cordova, Alabama, until the mid-1940s; she later lived in Jasper, Alabama, and now resides in Florida. Gibson began to draw on Thanksgiving Day, 1963, making Christmas wrapping paper out of brown paper bags. The favorable response to her efforts encouraged Gibson to pursue her art.

Gibson began to produce decorative drawings with an atmospheric, lyrical quality. Inspired by childhood memories, she depicts the faces of men and women, flowers, multiple portraits, animals, and girls in frilly dresses. Gibson paints with tempera, pastels, and house paint on old guitar cases, mirrors, newsprint, and, most frequently, brown paper bags that she hand washes to unglue and flatten. Her pieces range from 9 by 12 inches to about 15 by 20 inches.

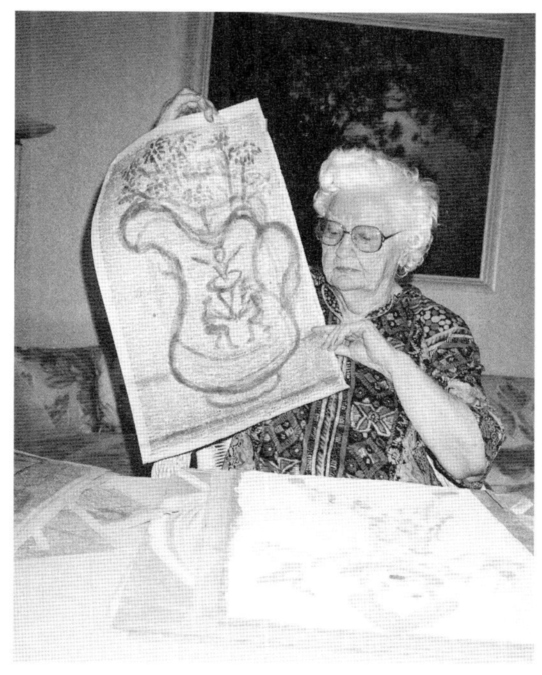

Sybil Gibson

B. 1908

The artist known by the epithet Glassman was born in Moundsville, West Virginia, to Polish immigrant parents. He attended school until the age of fourteen or fifteen, then worked to help support his family. He spent much of his working life at a Bethlehem Steel plant in Baltimore. He served in the navy during the Korean War. About 1983 he began to make art as a pastime.

Glassman creates roadside signs that communicate messages to the public. Symbolic elements represent his ideas, inspired by the Bible and the Constitution, concerning independence, self-sufficiency, and freedom. Using paint as an adhesive, Glassman applies foraged, broken glass and crockery to boards, doors, shutters, mirrors, and other flat surfaces. Occasionally he adds glitter, marbles, tinsel, car reflectors, or air fresheners. Glassman completes his pieces by adding printed messages, biblical quotations, or song titles.

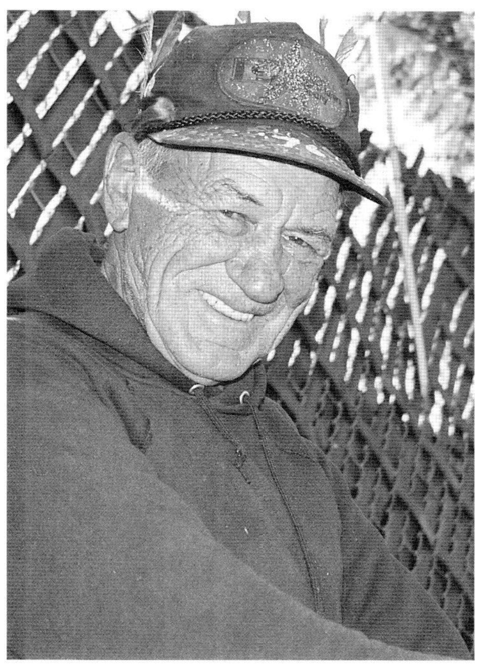

Glassman

B. 1925

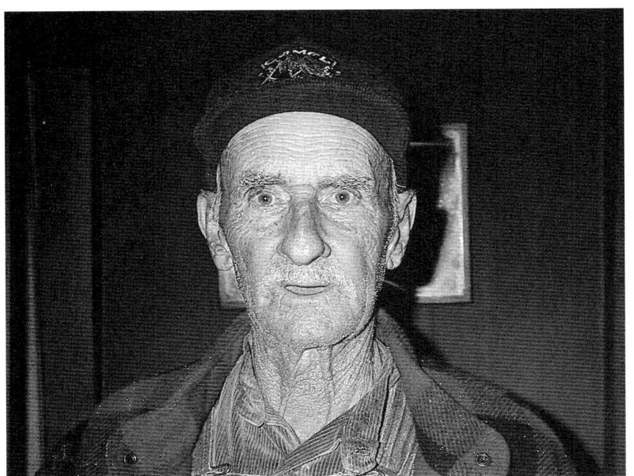

"After I retired, I just got out there and started working with a chain saw."

Green, born in rural Tennessee, worked at many jobs, including carpenter, farmer, blacksmith, dairyman, factory worker, and utility lineman. He retired in Beech Grove, Tennessee, and began creating art in the early 1980s.

To pass time, Green began to carve small objects in cedar and later fashioned larger objects with a chain saw. He carves images of ordinary birds, turtles, pigs, and cows as well as exotic species and dinosaurs. Utilizing bright paints, he gives his carvings a richly dappled surface. Green displays a carnival of creations on his property, attracting many admirers and prospective buyers.

Homer Green

B. 1910

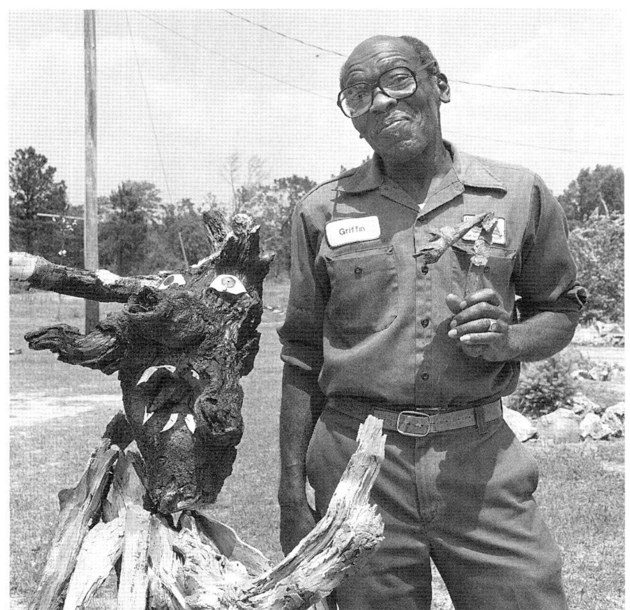

"I look at a piece of wood and it tells me what it is."

Born in Girard, Georgia, Griffin attended school through the ninth grade. He worked on his family's cotton farm until he was thirty and subsequently traveled throughout the coastal southern states and central Georgia, supporting himself at a variety of jobs. Griffin returned to Girard in the mid-1960s and was employed as a janitor for twenty-three years. Although he began making sculptural assemblages about 1980, he did not devote himself to art full-time until his retirement in 1989.

Griffin worked in his front yard, creating biblical and fantastical figures, animals, and masks from driftwood and roots collected from a stream running through his property. Griffin nailed the forms together and painted the faces of his images. He sometimes used spray paints. His assemblages range in height from 5 inches to 5½ feet.

Ralph Griffin

1925–1992

Born in Bessemer, Alabama, Hardin suffered from juvenile arthritis from the age of seven. His pain and inability to walk forced him to quit school at the age of fourteen. He began to experiment with painting on his bedroom walls, depicting Indians, cowboys, animals, fantastic creatures, and erotica. Later he transferred these impressions to paper. The last years of his life were spent in a government housing project for the handicapped in North Birmingham.

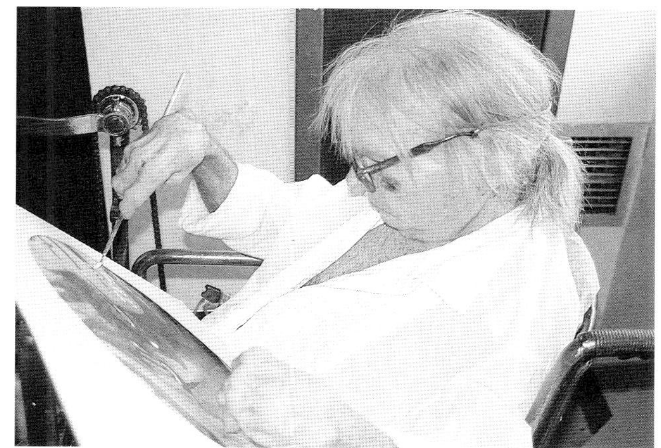

Joseph Hardin

1921–1989

"When I was a child I had these strange things I'd see and feel and now I'm puttin' them in wood."

Born Bessie Ruth White in Dallas, Georgia, Harvey was married at the age of fourteen. She was mother to eleven children, and with only a fourth grade education, she had to struggle to provide for her family. At the age of twenty-one she began working as a domestic and was employed in Knoxville, Tennessee, about 1960. From the late 1960s until her retirement in 1983, she worked as a housekeeper's aide at a hospital in Alcoa, Tennessee.

Late in her life, tormented by recurring visions of faces, Harvey began to make doll-like sculptures. The anthropomorphic forms that she constructs from found materials and her clay figures express her visions, profound religious beliefs, and powerful sentiments about her African-American heritage. Because Harvey preserves the natural form of the tree branches, stumps, and roots that she uses, her figures are often highly abstracted. The pieces are frequently embellished with hair, glass eyes, feathers, jewels, and splotches of paint.

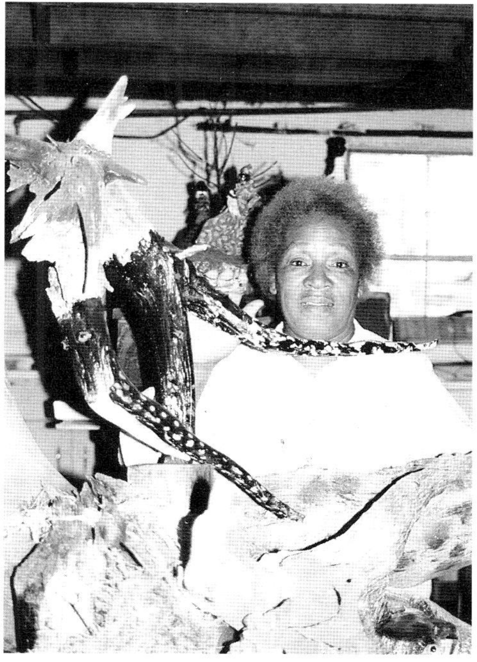

Bessie Harvey

B. 1929

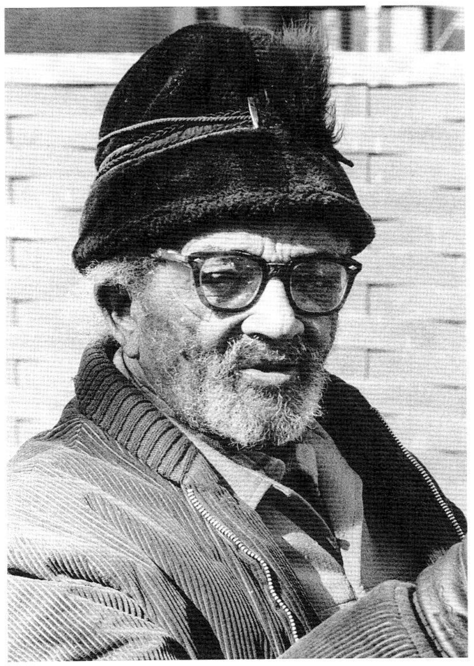

William Hawkins

1895–1990

"Now, everyone today, they got to go to school to draw! I've been drawing all my life . . . anything I see, just come to me."

Hawkins, born and raised on a farm near Lexington, Kentucky, attended school for three years and subsequently farmed, shucked corn, and broke horses. In 1916 he moved to Columbus, Ohio. There Hawkins drove trucks, labored on construction projects, and worked for a steel-casting company in the 1920s after serving in the army in France. After retiring, he invested his energy in his artwork.

Using photographs and illustrations for inspiration, Hawkins painted dramatic images of buildings and animals; he occasionally depicted biblical subjects. Scavenging his materials, Hawkins painted on sometimes torn and irregular Masonite and plywood. He used one brush to apply semigloss enamel paint, mixing the colors directly on the panel. Hawkins frequently attached found objects to his paintings to build up their surfaces and framed them in cast-off pieces of wood molding or by simply adding a painted border. His paintings are large, measuring up to 7 feet.

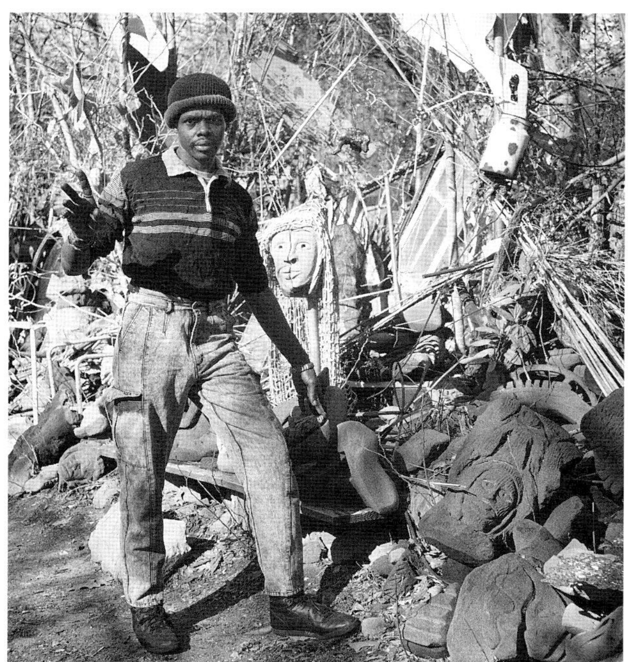

Lonnie B. Holley

B. 1950

"My environment is always changing and evolving like a garden that needs tending."

Holley was born in Birmingham, Alabama. He attended school through the seventh grade, spending much of his youth in foster homes and reform schools. At fourteen years of age, Holley ran away to Louisiana; he later moved to Florida and Ohio, then returned to Birmingham. During this period, he worked primarily as a short-order cook. In 1977 Holley lost two nieces in a house fire, and suffering from personal anguish, he attempted suicide. Holley prayed to God for an alternative solution to bring him from his grief.

Inspired by God, Holley created two tombstones for his deceased nieces and subsequently began to make small abstract images of animals, faces, and figures for children. Employing discarded saws, knives, kitchen utensils, and nails, he carves from an industrial material similar to sandstone. Holley has explored Islam, Christianity, and spiritualism and has educated himself in African philosophy. His yard houses an environment of carvings, paintings, and sculptures assembled from salvaged materials. His pieces range in height from a few inches to 9½ feet.

"Soon as I light my lamp, a whole lot of things start goin' 'cross my mind and 'fore I know it, I'm gettin' 'em down on paper."

Hunter, the descendant of a slave, was born on a cotton plantation near Cloutierville, Louisiana. She only briefly attended a Catholic school. When she was a teenager, her family, following the demand for farm labor, moved to Melrose plantation, near Natchitoches, Louisiana. She went to work picking cotton and later hoed corn and harvested sugar cane. In the late 1920s she moved out of the field and into full-time domestic duties.

While on the plantation, Hunter made dolls for the children, sewed clothes, wove baskets, made quilts, and created hand-tied lace curtains. In the 1940s she was inspired by a visiting artist to take up painting, through which she began to document her life experiences on Melrose plantation. Hunter depicted scenes of work, play, and religion and occasionally rendered still lifes, domestic animals and portraits. She worked with house paint, oil paint, and watercolors on any available material, including cardboard boxes, brown paper bags, wine bottles, paper, and canvas. Although she painted a few mural-size pieces, her works are typically no larger than 20 by 30 inches.

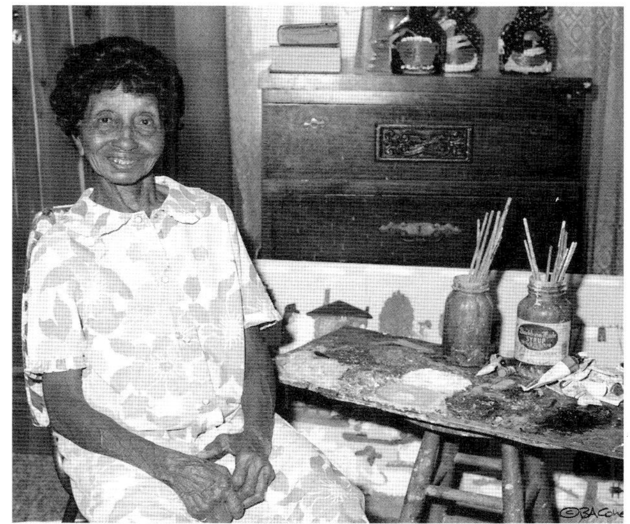

Clementine Hunter

1886 / 87–1988

"Anything I can make out of wood I just make. I just sit down whittling and chopping and making it."

Hunter was born in Taylor, Texas. His father died when Hunter was an infant, and he was raised in his grandparents' home. In 1918 Hunter and his mother moved to Dallas. He attended school and took various jobs, including fourteen years at a drugstore. In 1936 Hunter entered Southern Bible College and later attended Bishop College. He pastored in Sherman, Texas, for eight years and in Texarkana, Texas, for thirteen years. In the 1960s, Hunter became the senior minister at the True Light Baptist Church in south Dallas.

In the 1930s, a horoscope that said he was artistic inspired Hunter to use his talent. In addition to preaching and teaching school, he periodically fashioned colorful walking sticks, covered-wagon lamps, animal toys, trains, ships, and figurines. Hunter worked with collected wood, popsicle sticks, wood shavings, paint, and glue.

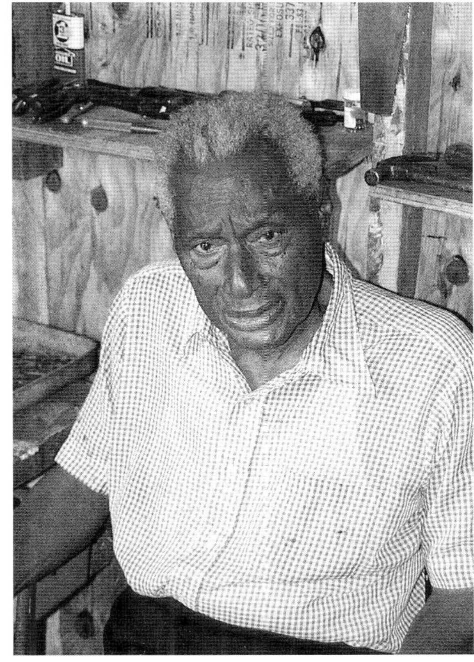

Rev. J. L. Hunter

B. 1905

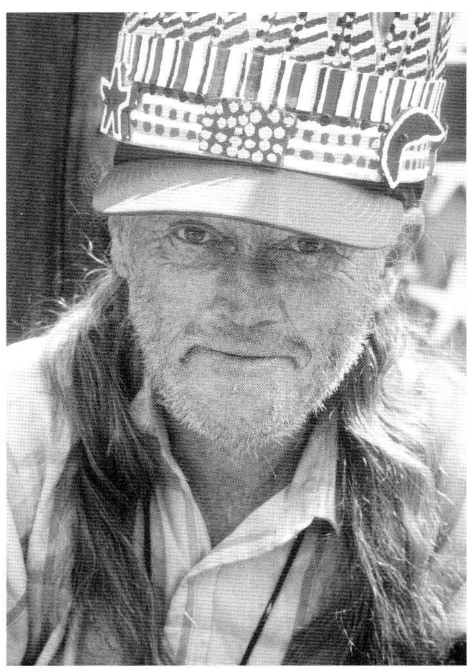

James Harold Jennings

B. 1931

Jennings has lived all his life in rural North Carolina. Dropping out of school after fifth grade, he was taught at home by his schoolteacher mother. In addition to her instruction, he avidly read dictionaries, encyclopedias, *Popular Mechanics*, and *National Geographic*. These sources provided a diverse, if eccentric, education for the artist, traces of which can often be found in his art. Jennings worked for a short time on his family's tobacco farm. Later, he was a night watchman and a movie projectionist, but he left that job in 1968 after his nerves "went bust."

The death of Jennings's mother in 1974 was apparently a catalyst for his artistic impulses. He began using scrap lumber to make whirligigs, windmills, Ferris wheels, Indians, Amazon women, angels, and an assortment of animals, all of which he painted in bright colors and assembled in his yard.

Color is the outstanding feature of Jennings's work; every piece is vividly painted, usually with primary colors. He draws his subjects from books, magazines, and dreams.—*D.P.*

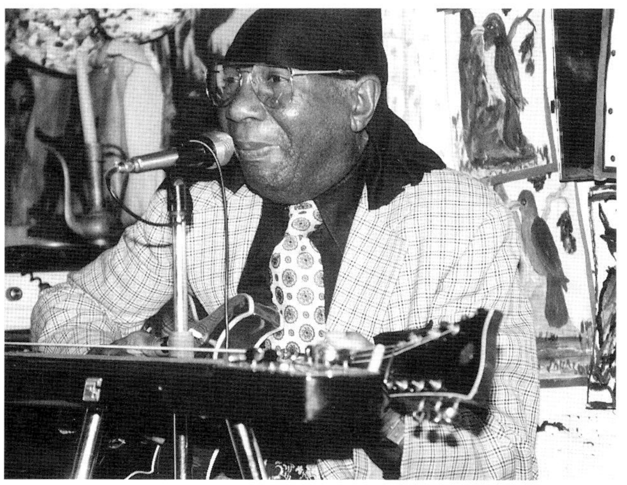

Anderson Johnson

B. 1915

"I am a creator. I like to take nothing and make something of it. That's the way of the Lord."

Johnson was born and raised in Lunenberg County, Virginia. At the age of eight, while working in his father's cornfield, he had a vision that began his lifelong pursuit to preach the word of God. Johnson had almost no formal schooling, but he was well versed in Bible studies. At twelve years of age, he began preaching from church to church and left home at sixteen to become a pastor for a small New Jersey congregation. Johnson later traveled throughout the United States, preaching in churches and on street corners. In the early 1970s, he contracted a paralyzing illness and moved to Newport News, Virginia.

Recovering from his paralysis, Johnson believed he had been healed by God and converted the first floor of his living quarters into a mission, which he decorated with colorful paintings of biblical, political, and national heroes; visionary images; calligraphy; and landscapes. His paintings, often hung one atop another from floor to ceiling, covered the entire room, collectively creating one composite work. Johnson paints on discarded salvaged material, including irregular boards, cardboard, paper, canvas, boxes, rotting wood, discarded formica tabletops, trinkets, and plastic bottles, in addition to his own walls.

"It's still a hobby to me. It just exploded and has gone every which way."

Born in North Carolina, Jones grew up on a farm by the Rocky River. He attended school intermittently, and in 1956 he moved to a small company town to work in a textile mill. He later worked as a day laborer, construction worker, and pulpwood logger. In 1979, while recovering from a leg injury, Jones occupied himself by carving. Jones lives on a small pension and creates artwork to entertain people, particularly children.

Inspired by shapes in his wood pile, Jones sculpts with a chain saw. He nails roots and stumps together to create animals, fanciful creatures, and human figures, which he often paints. Jones incorporates into his sculptures gourds and found objects such as bottle tops, film containers, plastic flowers and fruit, old springs, and tires. He displays the menagerie on his property and refers to it as his "Jungle Boy Zoo." In 1987 he began painting with enamel and oil-based paint on plywood and paneling.

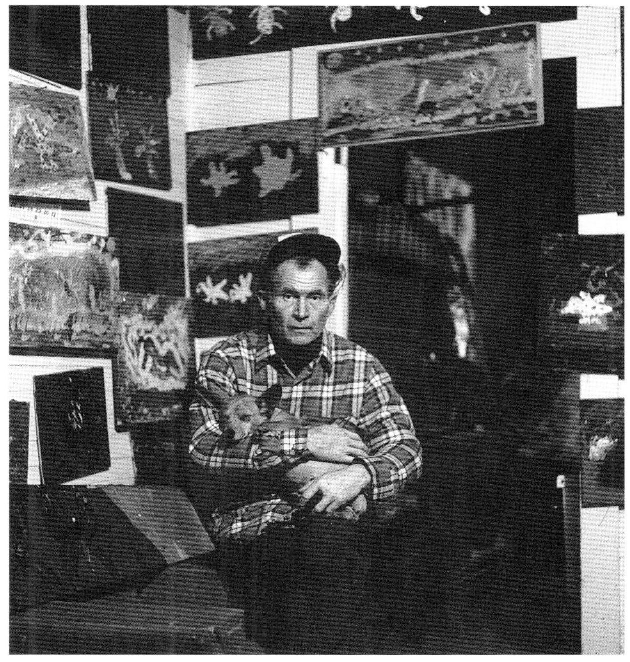

Clyde Jones

B. 1938

Born in Clarksville, Texas, Jones, of black and Indian descent, was abandoned by both his parents by the age of six. He believed, in the African-American tradition, that the caul or "veil" that covered his left eye at birth gave him the power to see and communicate with spirits or "haints." He worked as a farm laborer and a yardman, hoboing from town to town by train. In 1941, he was sentenced to his first of three prison terms, which kept him incarcerated for most of his life.

Jones began his artistic career in 1964 while incarcerated in Texas. He expressed his beliefs and experiences through his own visual language, which blended African-American cultural traditions and personal visions. Preferring red and blue colored pencils, he executed his drawings on paper, in sizes ranging from 4 by 6 inches to 2 by 3 feet.

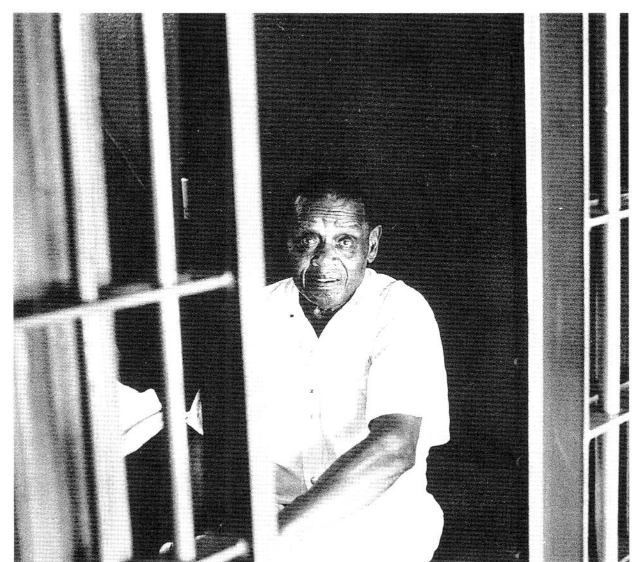

Frank Jones

CA. 1900–1969

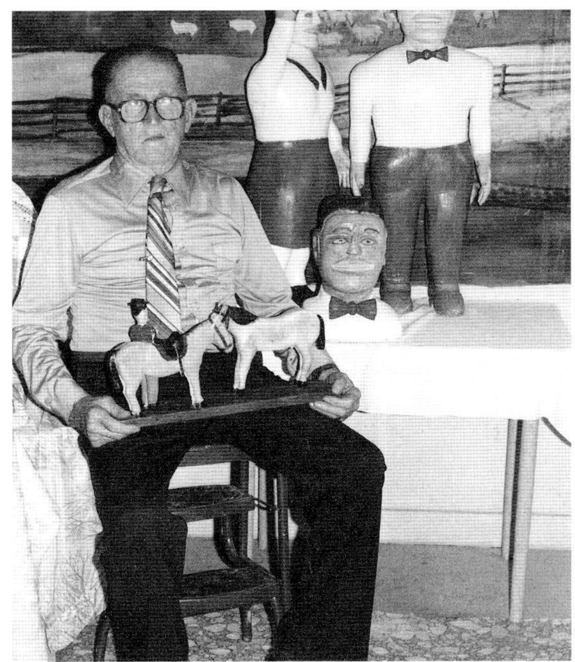

Shields Landon "S. L." Jones

B. 1901

"Waiting for my dog, Dan, to sniff out game, I'd find me a piece of buckeye, and carve a squirrel or a bird."

Jones was born in Indian Mills, West Virginia. As soon as he was old enough to raise a hoe, he assisted his father, a tenant farmer and part-time lumberjack. He also learned the backwoods skills of hunting and trapping. He whittled with his first barlow knife to occupy time while hunting. Jones quit school in the eighth grade, and in 1918 he lied about his age and was hired to lay track for the Chesapeake and Ohio Railroad Company. In 1967 he retired as shop foreman of the company and took his pension.

After the death of his wife in 1969, Jones resumed his boyhood hobby of carving. He moved to Pine Hill, West Virginia, and built a workshop where he made small carvings of rabbits, dogs, and horses, and, later, larger carvings of kinfolk, friends, and coworkers. Jones selects his wood carefully, preferring yellow poplar, black walnut, and maple. He roughly shapes a log with a chain saw, refines the form with chisels and a rasp, executes delicate details with his knife, and highlights the carvings with paint. Jones also makes drawings related to his sculptures. The carvings reach almost 5 feet; most of his drawings are 9 by 11 inches.

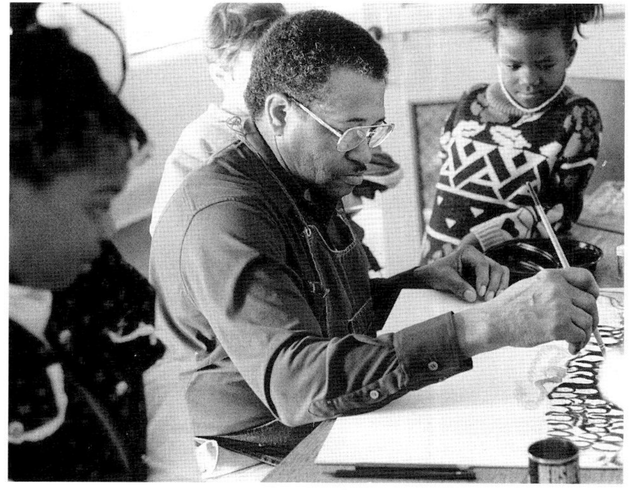

Eddie Kendrick

1928–1992

"Jesus is my airplane and he'll never let me fall. He'll pick us up in an airplane on Judgment Day."

Born in Stephens, Arkansas, Kendrick was the first of thirteen children. He was raised on a farm and attended school through the seventh grade. Kendrick showed a strong interest in art during his youth. He worked as a school custodian in Little Rock, where his talents were first recognized by a teacher. A deeply religious man, he was made a deacon in his church in 1986.

Experiencing visions from God in his dreams, Kendrick was charged to create religious paintings. His subjects included landscapes, portrayals of contemporary life, and visionary images; in all instances, empyreal beings supervise the scene and calligraphic inscriptions identify it. Kendrick used pencils, crayons, watercolors, and occasionally oil paints in works ranging from 8 by 10 feet to 20 by 28 inches.

"I used to make this stuff outta clay, you see, and bake it. . . . And painting—well, it was just like falling off a log after doing all that."

Kinney was born in Lewis County, Kentucky, and was raised on his family's tobacco farm, where he resided all his life. He attended school through the third grade. A birth defect prevented Kinney from doing strenuous work, but he helped on the farm throughout his life, performing light chores and earning money by baking pies, cutting hair, and creating split-oak baskets. He did not become a prolific artist until he retired from farm work in the mid-1970s.

Kinney was primarily concerned with storytelling; through his paintings he communicated religious stories and "haint" tales. He painted pictures of animals and nature, farm and biblical scenes, local myths, legends, and patriotic figures. His works, on poster board, are typically 22 by 28 inches, with larger paintings 30 by 30 inches.

Kinney also fashioned human and animal figures, which he made from clay and baked in the oven. His 3-foot-tall puppets danced and appeared to play music when operated with a foot pedal.

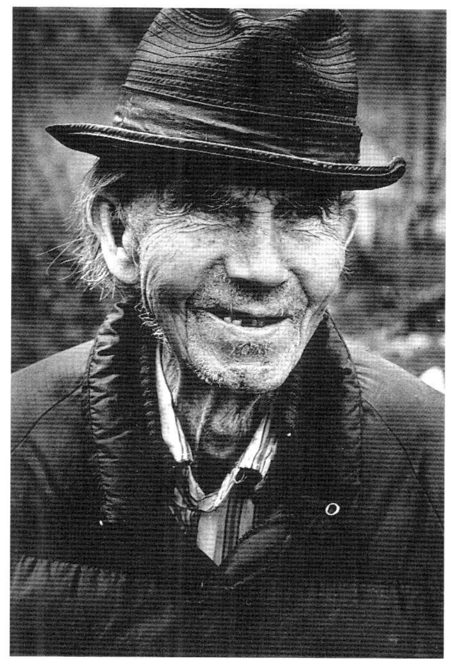

Charles Kinney

1906–1991

Kinney spent his entire life with his brother Charles on the family tobacco farm in Toller Hollow, Lewis County, Kentucky. He attended school through the eighth grade and subsequently worked on the farm until a heart attack forced him to retire in 1975. He then turned to art.

Kinney had drawn since his childhood, and began to carve around 1970. He made wood carvings of old farm equipment, sawmills, human figures, and familiar animals as well as exotic ones that he saw in the Cincinnati zoo. Kinney carved yellow poplar and white pine with a saw and a pocketknife. He used wood putty to assemble his pieces and painted them in bright colors. His larger carvings, including figures of lions and tigers, are 3 feet tall.

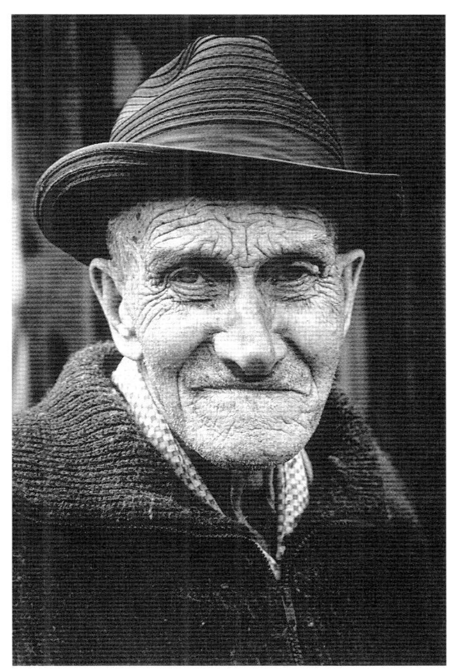

Noah Kinney

1912–1991

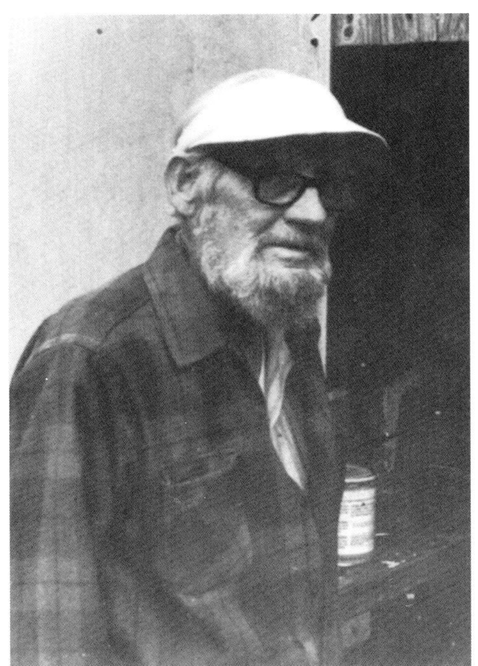

"Art is like a tree, having many branches, such as music, dancing, writing, painting . . . as well as many crafts and trades."

Kitchens was born between Hazelhurst and Crystal Springs, Mississippi. He attended school through the eighth grade in Hazelhurst and then hoboed through the South to find work. In the 1940s he settled in Jackson, Mississippi, where he owned a construction company and a house-moving business. He retired in 1970 and, inspired by his son-in-law's artistic talent, devoted the remaining years of his life to painting.

A storyteller, Kitchens communicated in his paintings events from his past and his views on political and social issues. He frequently included printed materials or a self-portrait of himself as narrator. Kitchens derived inspiration from the Bible, photographs, conversations, newspapers, magazines, books, television, and a crystal ball. He drew on paper and canvas with an oil and acrylic wash. Most of his pieces are 11 by 13 inches; some are as large as 30 by 50 inches.

O. W. "Pappy" Kitchens

1901–1986

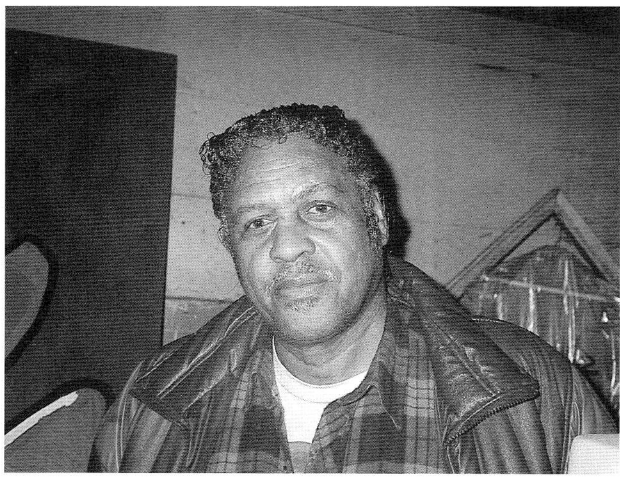

"I'm awake now, but I wish I had been awake before I went through all of this to learn."

Light was born in Dryersburg, Tennessee. He attended school until the eighth grade and worked on a farm throughout his youth. In 1951 he enlisted in the army; after being discharged because of a self-inflicted arm injury, Light engaged in illicit activities. He was incarcerated in the Nashville penitentiary from 1954 to 1955, and again from 1960 to 1968. During his second prison term, Light converted to Judaism and changed his ways. He traveled throughout the South, eventually settling in Memphis, where he sold housewares at flea markets.

About 1975 Light began to produce paintings, driftwood sculptures, assemblages, and signs advocating moral behavior and Old Testament beliefs. He also expresses his views on political, social, and racial issues. Light applies house paint to scavenged driftwood, old television sets, hubcaps, and other found objects. His largest works are about 4 by 7 feet.

Joe Louis Light

B. 1934

"He [God] slowed me down to where I stop running and turn my hand to what I was meant to do."

Born in Birmingham, Alabama, Lucas grew up in a family that supported itself with skilled crafts: blacksmithing, basket making, quilting, ceramics, and needlepoint. Lucas left home at fourteen and found employment as a construction worker and then truck driver. Curious about the outside world, by 1968 he had moved to Miami, where he supported himself by breeding shrimp. Lucas found city life overwhelming and returned to Alabama. In 1984 he underwent surgery after injuring his back and was confined to his bed for a long period.

During his convalescence, Lucas occupied himself by making small wire sculptures and rediscovered his youthful fascination with shaping metal. When he was once again on his feet, he began creating large pieces. Lucas welds found materials into complex metal assemblages resembling larger-than-life (sometimes 8-feet-tall) animals and people. In addition, he produces colorful semiabstract paintings with house paint on canvas and used boards.

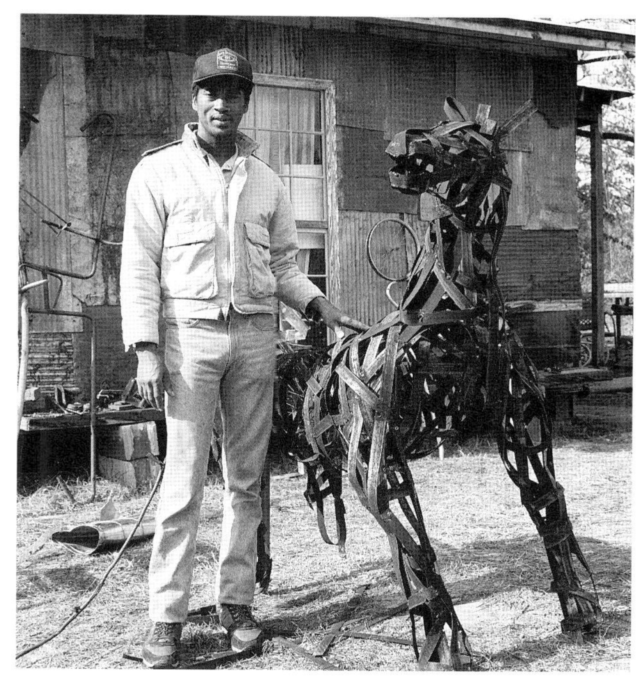

Charlie Lucas

B. 1951

Born in Campton, Kentucky, McKenzie learned to whittle from his grandfather at the age of ten. Having no formal education, he started out as a farmhand in Ohio. McKenzie later worked at a steel plant and an iron and coal company in Middleton, Ohio; labored in the coal mines in Hazard, Kentucky; was employed at the steel-rolling mills in Newport, Kentucky; and for seventeen years drove a lumber truck. He retired in the late 1950s and subsequently has carved full-time for income as well as pleasure.

McKenzie repeats many of his themes, which include the Statue of Liberty, waitresses, barnyard animals, biblical scenes, and groups of devils. He prefers white pine or birch and embellishes the surfaces with graphite, colored pencil, felt marker, and acrylic house paint, often adding metal, twigs, plastic, or other found objects. With brushes that he makes from split twigs, McKenzie applies bright paint in thick, layered splotches. His carvings range in height from 6 to 33 inches.

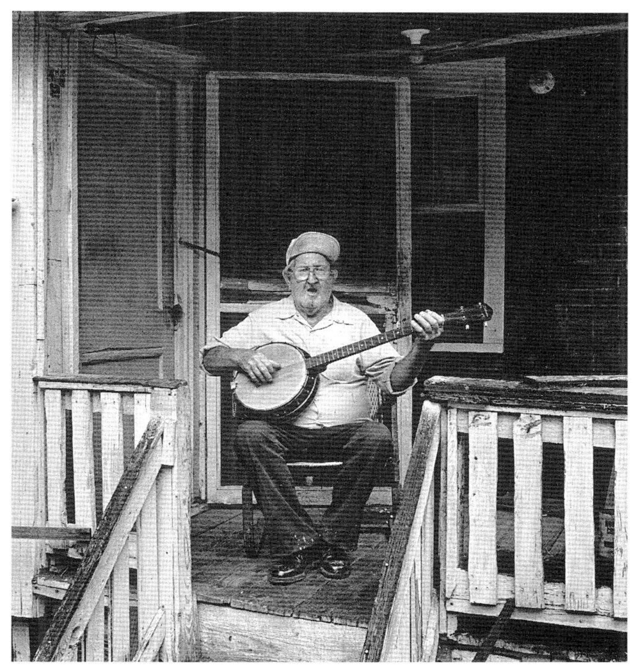

Carl McKenzie

B. 1905

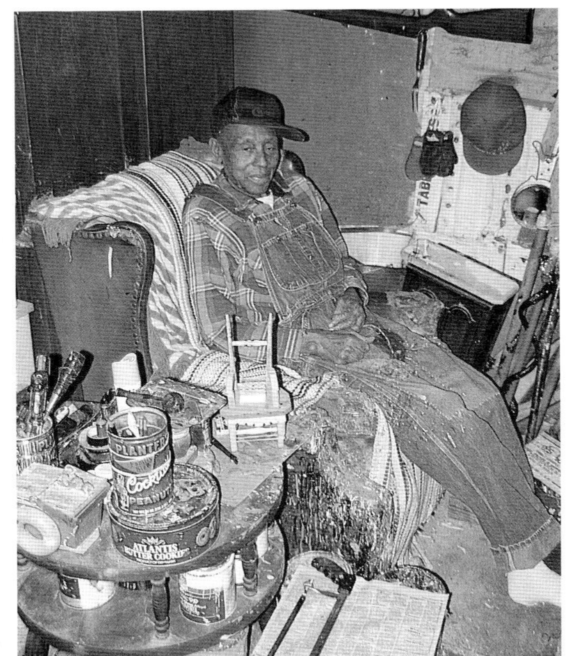

Willie Massey

CA. 1908–1990

"Whatever I take a notion to make, I just start on it and it wind up what it'll be."

Massey was born in Brown, Kentucky, and attended high school there. He worked for nearly seventy years on a local farm for the Bohannan family, who later deeded him his house in gratitude for his services. Massey began to create sculptures and paintings shortly after his wife died in 1955. Suffering from rheumatism, he retired from farming and devoted himself entirely to producing art.

Massey created colorful multilevel birdhouses from old boards. He embellished them with fanciful wingless birds, often fashioned from aluminum foil, and bright shiny enamel paint. In addition to his sculptures, he painted animals on the reverse side of stretched canvas and decorated the stretcher as a frame. Massey often applied aluminum foil and buttons to the surface of his paintings. His birdhouses measure as tall as 3 feet, and his paintings are about 15 by 20 inches.

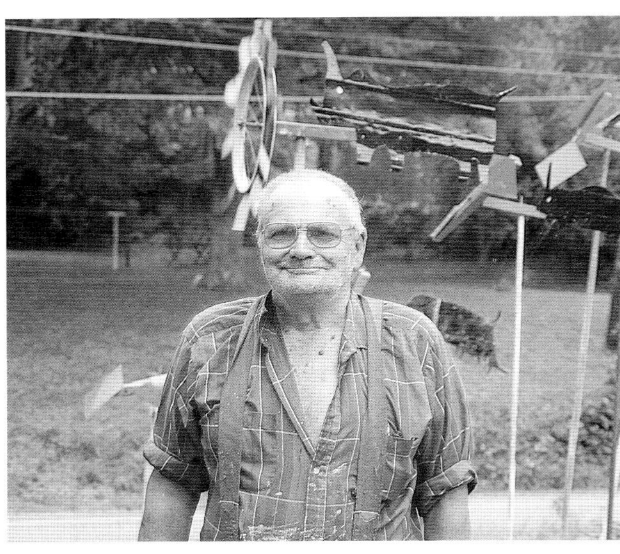

R. A. Miller

B. 1912

Miller resides on the property in Hall County, Georgia, where he was born and raised. He labored as a farmer and cotton mill worker, and is an ordained minister in the Free Will Baptist Church. After being stricken by glaucoma, he retired and began to create artwork to spread his spiritual message.

As a young boy, Miller made windmills, or "fluttermills," out of cornstalks. More recently he has made tin cutouts, whirligigs, and drawings on boards, paper, and tin. Miller flattens discarded gutters with a hammer, cuts out silhouettes of animals and figures, and embellishes the images with enamel paint; he attaches these to his windmills and whirligigs or displays them as individual cutouts. In addition, Miller creates drawings on Masonite with enamel and felt-tip markers. Both art forms often integrate images and words, such as his spiritual message, "Lord love you." His drawn and cutout subjects are frequently inspired by television or are fanciful representations of his life.

"He [Christ] have taken me out of the black robe and crowned me out in white. We are now in revelation. He married me, I'm his wife."

Morgan was born in Lafayette, Alabama. She went to elementary school and was an active member of the Southern Baptist Church. In the mid-1930s, a voice charged Morgan to begin preaching. In 1939 she moved to New Orleans and preached in the streets. She helped found an orphanage and chapel, and in the late 1960s she established the Everlasting Gospel Mission. Morgan adopted the all-white garb of a bride of Christ and painted or covered many of her furnishings in white. She began painting actively in 1956 and increased her artistic output after the orphanage was destroyed a decade later in a hurricane.

Morgan created vibrant apocalyptic paintings, often inspired by the Book of Revelation. She developed a calligraphy to transcribe spiritual messages that she believed were composed by God, and sold the messages and drawings to finance the mission. Morgan painted on paper, plastic, cardboard, board, and utilitarian objects, including window shades, a guitar case, folding fans, and a megaphone. She outlined her subjects with pencil and pen and filled them in with acrylic, watercolor, pastel, crayon, or tempera. Although there are a few large works, most are smaller than 12 by 20 inches.

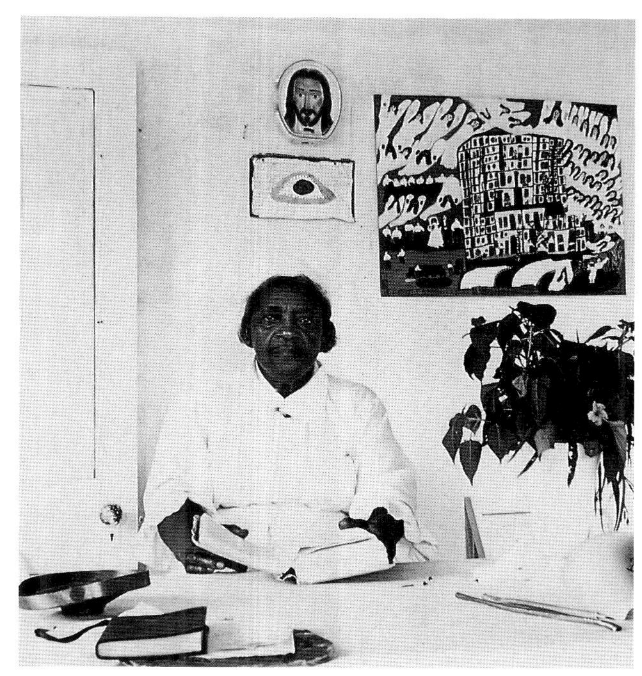

Sister Gertrude Morgan

1900–1980

Mumma was born in Milton, Ohio, and is of Pennsylvania Dutch (German) descent. After attending school through the eighth grade, he traveled the country, acquiring whatever employment was available. In 1941 Mumma settled on a small farm near Springfield, Ohio, and raised vegetables. Later, he and his wife started an antique and junk business. After his wife's death in 1966, Mumma retired from farming and moved to Gainesville, Florida, to be near his daughter.

In 1969, Mumma joined the Council for Older Americans, a senior citizens group, and, encouraged by his daughter, attended his first art lesson. Although he failed to meet the instructor's expectations and did not return, Mumma continued to paint, covering every wall of his home with his creations. In addition to landscapes and animals, his most common subject is a three-quarter bust of a round-faced, large-eyed man holding his hands against his chest. Mumma painted with acrylic on plywood or Masonite, often using both sides of the surface. He frequently ornamented his finished paintings with frames made from scraps of wood and plastic. Most are 12 by 15 inches, but some are as large as 40 by 60 inches.

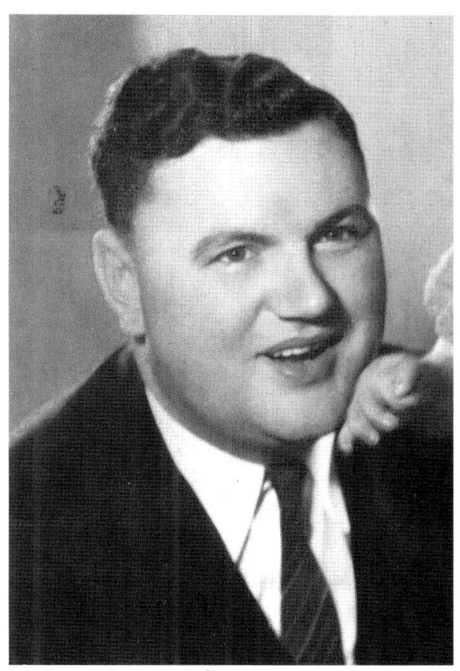

Ed "Mr. Eddy" Mumma

1908–1936

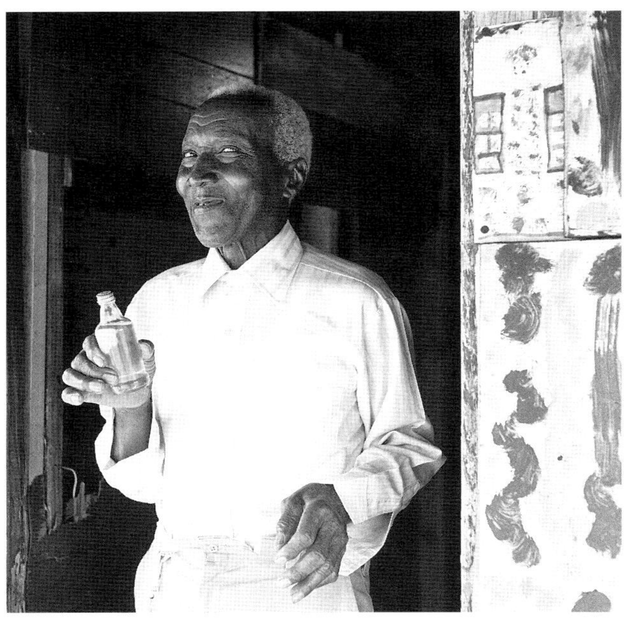

John "J. B." Murry

1908–1988

"When I started I prayed and I prayed and the Lord sunk a vision from the sun."

Murry was born in Sandersville, Georgia. Lacking a formal education, he worked from childhood to the age of sixty-five as a sharecropper and farm laborer in rural Glascock County, Georgia. In the late 1970s, after disabling his hip, Murry had a religious experience that he later communicated through a personal "spirit script."

Murry created drawings and paintings that used an expressive calligraphy to preach a spiritual message. This script, which he interprets by looking through a bottle of "holy water," incorporates ghostlike characters and meandering designs. Initially Murry drew on scraps of paper or whatever material he found at hand; later he was provided with drawing materials, including colored pencils, watercolors, pastels, marking pens, and high-quality paper. Black, red, and blue are the predominant colors of Murry's pieces, which are as large as 24 by 18 inches.

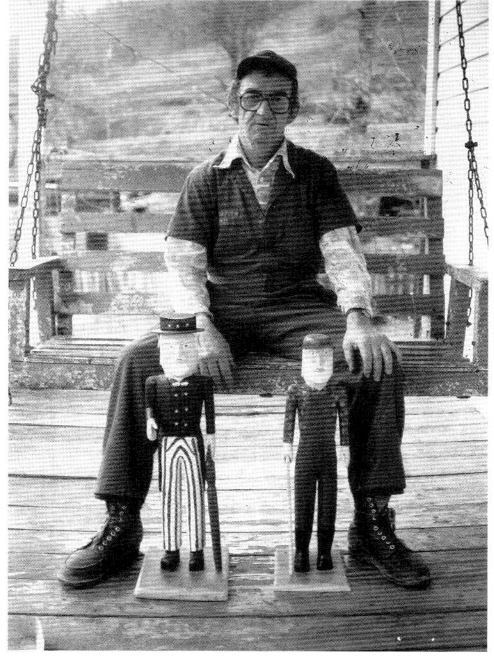

Earnest Patton

B. 1938

"I get it pictured in my mind. I enjoy figurin' somethin' out and makin' it my way."

Born in Holly Creek, Kentucky, Patton quit school after the second grade to work on a tobacco farm. Later he became a sharecropper, drove a school bus, and worked as a mechanic. Patton now resides on a farm outside Campton, Kentucky.

In 1966 Patton was inspired to begin carving by another self-taught artist, Edgar Tolson. His subjects include patriotic and biblical themes and popular entertainers; occasionally he carves an exotic piece based on mythology or his imagination. Almost exclusively using a pocketknife, he carves basswood, poplar, pine, and other woods. He carves with arduous attention to small detail and embellishes his pieces sparingly with enamel paint. His carvings range from a few inches to about 25 inches in height.

Payne, born in Lillian, Virginia, attended country schools through the fourth grade. As a young boy, he developed an infatuation with airplanes after viewing an air show in 1918. Payne worked as a fisherman and a crabber; after spending some time on the East Coast, he returned in the 1940s to the "Northern Neck" of Virginia and worked as a handyman.

The air show that had stirred Payne's imagination later fueled his trademark artworks. Drawing on his memory and referring to books and photographs, he created a small-size airfield composed of 12-by-16-foot model airplanes. He also built sheds for the models. Payne's experience on fishing vessels inspired him to construct 3-by-4-foot model boats and fish sculptures. He forged these replicas from discarded materials and finished them with bright enamel house paint. Payne also formed objects with patriotic themes, a whirligig, and a model of an early car from cut and painted metal.

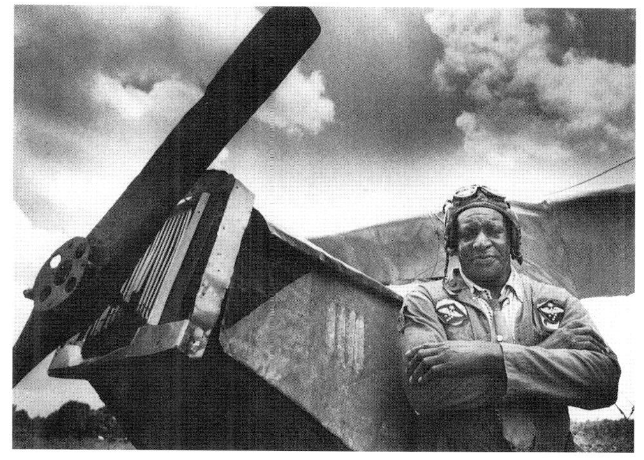

LESLIE PAYNE

1907–1981

Perkins dropped out of school in the sixth grade to work full-time, and at seventeen he joined the marines. After his discharge, he finished high school and college, married, and embarked on a career in the ministry. When his wife left him after twenty years, he began to paint.

The marine corps and the ministry left lasting impressions on Perkins's work; the Statue of Liberty, the American flag, and churches are all recurring themes in his vividly painted works. Perkins also depicted the treasures from Tutankhamen's tomb. He worked on canvas and board in watercolor or acrylic; for paintings on dried gourds, he used acrylic.—*D.P.*

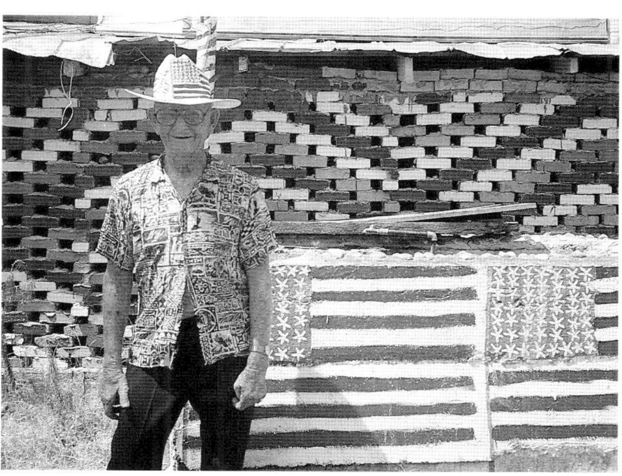

REV. BENJAMIN F. PERKINS

1904–1993

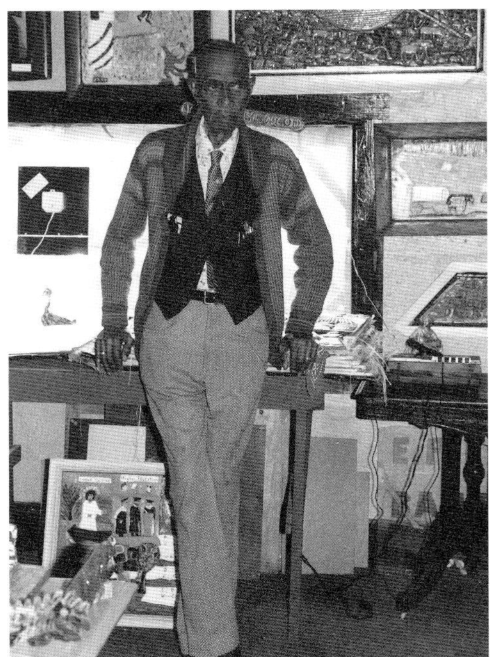

Elijah Pierce

1892–1984

"Every piece of work I got carved is a message . . . a sermon."

Pierce was born on a cotton plantation in Baldwyn, Mississippi. His father, a former slave, was a farmer and a church deacon. Pierce attended grammar school and then began work as a barber. Pierce had whittled as a child and began carving in earnest in the early 1920s. After living in various places, he settled in Columbus, Ohio, and opened his own barbershop in the early 1950s. Pierce converted one room of his shop into a wood-carving studio. In the late 1970s, he retired from barbering and became a full-time carver.

Pierce believed God directed him to preach through wood carving. He carved animals and freestanding and bas-relief figures with religious, secular, historical, and autobiographical themes. As a sculptural storyteller, Pierce instilled in his pieces an allegorical message. He preferred pine, which he shaped with a pocketknife, chisel, and sandpaper and finished with bright paint, shellac, and polish. His pieces range from a few inches to 30 by 50 inches.

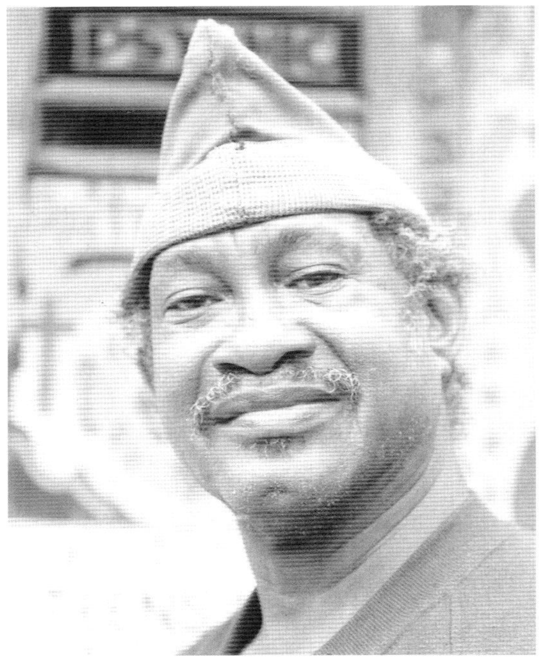

"Prophet" Royal Robertson

B. 1930

"I was sixteen years old when I started drawing those visions, noticing that I was dreaming about strange things."

Born in St. Mary's parish, Louisiana, Robertson began drawing as a child. He attended school through the eighth grade and then traveled to the West Coast, working as a field hand and a sign painter. Robertson returned to Louisiana sometime in the 1950s to care for his ailing mother.

Robertson lives alone, surrounded by misogynistic signs warding off female visitors, "whores," and "vipers." He creates calendars, signs, and portraits denouncing his wife, Adell, who left him after nineteen years of marriage, and women in general. Robertson also records the frequent visions that transport him to the past or the future; he depicts aliens, fantastic modes of transportation, futuristic space cities, and architectural marvels. Robertson is influenced by the Bible, girlie magazines, comic strips, and science fiction. His images are heavily outlined and set against contrasting colors; they are often accompanied by text. Working on both sides of poster paper, Robertson employs Conté crayons, felt markers, enamel, and occasionally glitter. Most of his finished pieces are 28 by 22 inches.

"This dirt changes fast from dirt to stone like when you make a cake, it changes from flour to dough."

Rogers reportedly was born in north Montgomery, Alabama. She claimed to have been adopted by the Rogers family after they found her at a carnival. Rogers attended school through the ninth grade and later worked as a waitress, dishwasher, and domestic. In the late 1970s, Rogers moved to the country; there her principal link with the outside world was a small black and white television set.

Rogers began her artistic career making sculptures of animals and mythological creatures; these were formed from a concoction of mud, fossil shells, and cow and mule bones. In addition she made drawings of images suggested by television, visions of her childhood, and depictions of black men and women at play. Late in her artistic career, she rendered a series of drawings of a spaceship. Rogers executed her images on paper or drawing board with watercolor, pencil, and occasionally acrylic; they range in size from 6 by 12 inches to 17 by 31 inches.

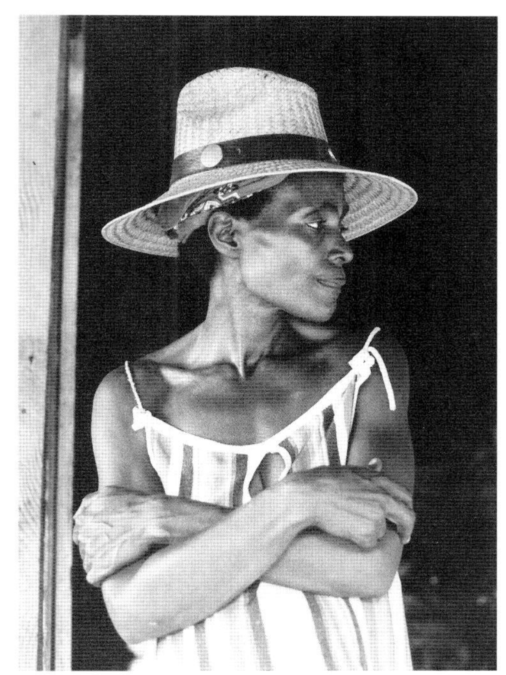

Juanita Rogers

1934–1985

"Now some people don't know what to make of my carving. I got a couple of friends that come to the house, they don't go to the cellar 'cuz I usually have coffins sitting around there."

Rogers was born and raised near Oxford, Mississippi. Rogers traveled to Memphis, Saint Louis, Chicago, Ohio, New York, and was stationed in Texas while in the army. In 1952 he settled in Syracuse, New York, and worked as a carpenter, a trade he learned from his father. In 1970 he took an industrial job with Allied Chemical, from which he retired in 1984.

Although he whittled animals in his childhood, and later during his nightshifts at the chemical plant, Rogers did not begin carving actively until after his retirement. Inspired by his dreams, he carves dead people in their coffins, snakes, vampires, "haints," and freaks. Rogers also does expressive portraits and caricatures of acquaintances. He carves from softwoods, such as sugar pine or gum, and varnishes the pieces. Rogers uses paint sparingly.

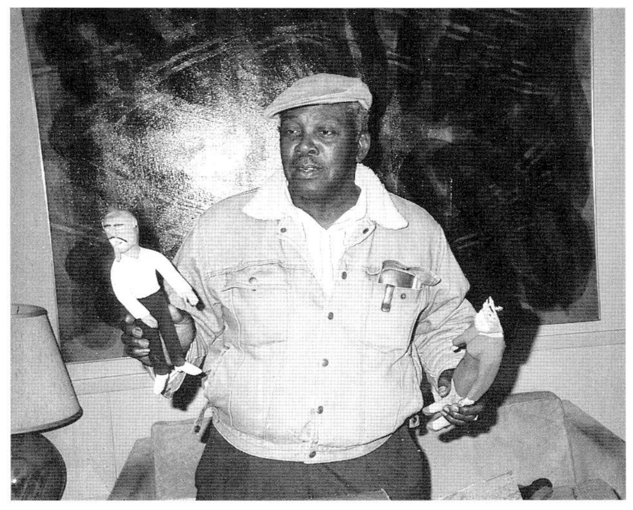

Sultan Rogers

B. 1922

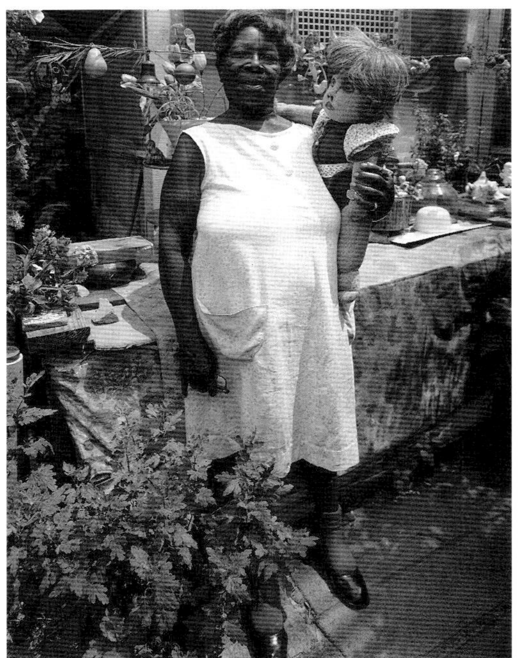

Nellie Mae Rowe

1900–1982

"I draw what is in my mind. I draw things you haven't seen born into this world."

Rowe, born Nellie Mae Williams in Fayetteville, Georgia, began to draw at an early age, and was taught by her mother to make quilts and dolls. She attended school through the fourth grade, when she left to work in her father's fields. As an adult, seeking relief from the intense labor of unmechanized farming, she moved to Atlanta and began work as a domestic.

Rowe became skilled in several different media, creating images from her memory and her imagination. In addition to quilt and doll making, she drew with crayon and felt-tip pen, painted in vibrant oil and acrylic, and made sculptures of animals and fantastic heads from wood and chewing gum and often decorated with found objects. Rowe's earlier drawings and paintings were produced on scraps of paper or other available materials. By the 1980s, friends began supplying her with high-quality drawing paper. Rowe displayed her creations in her home and hung them in her yard. Her drawings range from 5 by 8 inches to 18 by 30 inches.

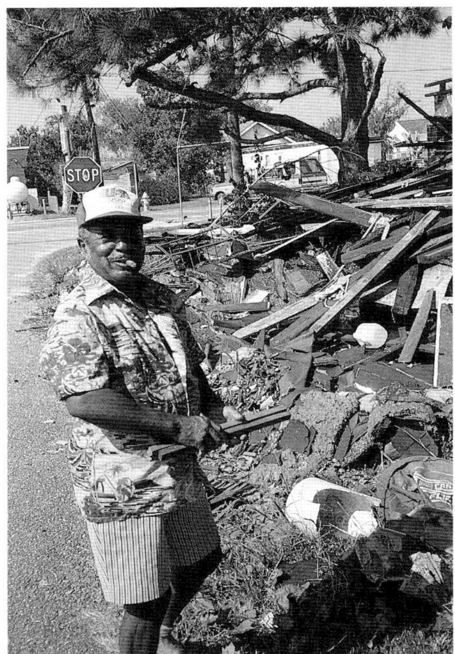

J. P. Scott

B. 1922

"Sometimes I go in the French Quarters and look at ship coming down river, or I watch boats on the bayou, then I get my mind on an idea I've seen and start building."

Scott was born and raised in Louisiana. He claims that as a child he retrieved logs from the swamps and made things of them. He worked various construction jobs in New Orleans and on commercial fishing boats, which brought about his deep interest in boats.

In 1962 Scott began to shape scavenged materials into model boats like those he saw and worked on in local waterways; he also constructed French Quarter houses, oil rigs, and airplanes, which he often initially displays in his yard. Scott creates a basic form from cypress wood and discarded metal, to which he adds Mardi Gras doubloons, scrap linoleum tile, auto reflectors, and toy flags. The finished forms are painted blue, white, orange, red, black, and sometimes green or yellow.

"People don't have these things anymore. I want our children to know what things were like."

The eldest of ten children, Sims was born in the rural southern Alabama community of Hickory Hill, in Butler County. She left school after the tenth grade, married at the age of sixteen, and had six children. She trained and then worked as a nurse's aide until 1975, when knee surgery forced her to take a disability retirement. Subsequently, at the age of fifty-two, Sims passed her high school equivalency exam and enrolled in art classes at Jefferson Davis Junior College, in Brewton, Alabama. During this time she was also exposed to formal arts and crafts in local museums.

In works that are neither purely realistic nor fanciful, Sims freely interprets autobiographical subjects such as farming, cotton picking, sugar cane processing, turpentine collecting, school life, and church activities. She paints with bright oil colors on canvas.

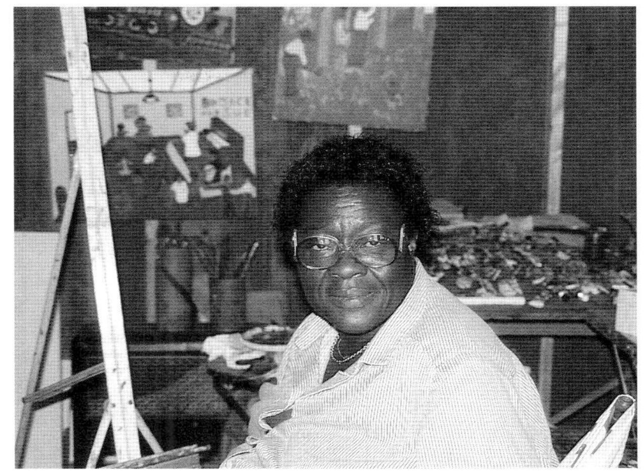

Bernice Sims

B. 1926

"Whatever I do, I carry the weight for it. If I'm gonna suffer, I'll suffer. If I'm gonna get ridiculed, I get ridiculed, but it's going to be at my own expense."

Born in New Orleans, Singleton and his seven siblings were raised in a two-room row house. He attended school through the sixth grade and later, at seventeen years of age, went to work at a steel factory. Singleton has served thirteen years in Angola State Prison for a variety of crimes. He has carved for enjoyment and profit for more than twenty-five years. In the 1970s, Singleton began to carve walking sticks with the intention of exchanging them for crack and cocaine. He also sold his works to buggy drivers and pimps as weapons. Singleton continues to support himself with the earnings from his carvings.

Singleton carves with a knife, chisel, and mallet from tree stumps and limbs collected from the Mississippi levee, as well as old oak and cypress doors and cabinets. He paints the finished carvings in vivid enamel primary colors. Singleton's initial creations—staffs, walking sticks, and stools—portray images of daily and street life in ghetto neighborhoods. In recent years, he has turned to carving bas-relief plaques of biblical events, local social situations, and autobiographical subjects on house and furniture doors.

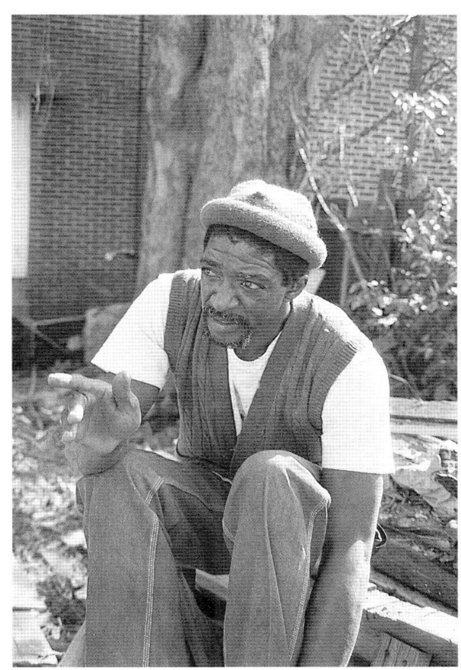

Herbert Singleton

B. 1945

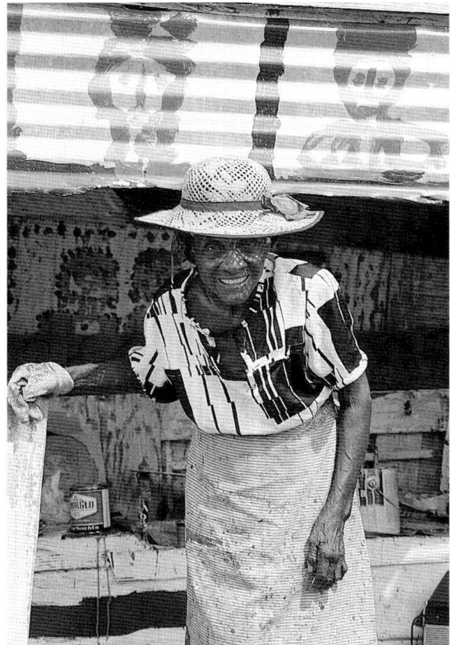

Mary T. Smith

B. 1904

"I did it to brighten up the yard, and please the Lord."

Smith was born Mary Tillman in Brookhaven, Mississippi. After a minimal education, she began field work at an early age. In the early 1930s, Smith moved to Martinsville, Mississippi and sharecropped. Later she moved to Hazlehurst, Mississippi, and worked as a domestic, gardener, and babysitter; she retired in 1975.

To pay tribute to God, Smith created an environment of artworks in her yard in the early 1980s. She is influenced by television images, popular illustrations, and her strong religious beliefs. Smith often paints animals, neighbors, and faces. She occasionally paints on plywood panels, although she prefers roofing panels. Her pieces range from 2 feet to life-size.

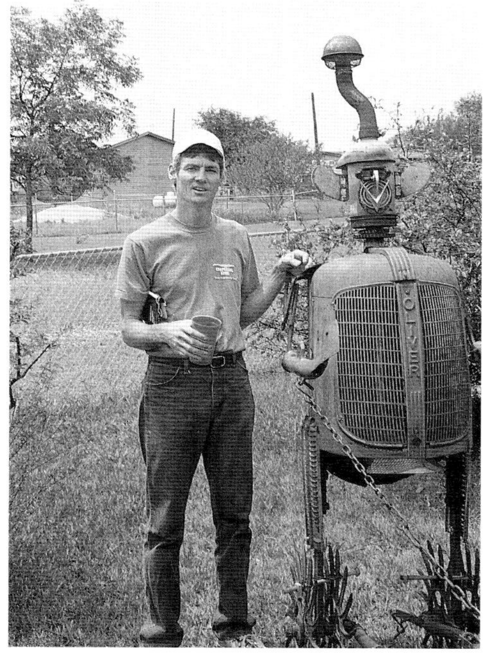

David Strickland

B. 1955

"Fun to work with old stuff to make something out of it."

Born in Dallas, Texas, Strickland spent part of his youth on a farm with his grandparents and part in Dallas. After high school, he was trained as a welder and pursued the profession for five years. He subsequently worked as a laborer, carpenter, and plumber for a veterans hospital.

In the spring of 1990, he created his first art object, using leftover air conditioning duct work to create a bird-like figure. Employing old farm equipment and auto parts, he welds fanciful creatures, birds, animals, and people.

"I paint with my brush . . . 'cause that's why I got it and that brush don't wear out. When I die, the brush dies."

Sudduth was born in the Caines Ridge community of Fayette County, Alabama. After grade school, he worked for many years on farms within Fayette County and at a lumber mill. Sudduth moved into town in 1950 and worked at odd jobs, primarily as a gardener. He has painted full-time since the 1960s, and has won awards at many local and country art fairs.

Sudduth relates that he began to create mud paintings when still a child, but they would wash away with rain. When he was ten, he accidentally discovered that molasses would harden and set the mud, and for most of his career, he has added sugar to his medium. Inspired by Alabama life, Sudduth's subjects include people, animals, landscapes, automobiles, and architectural structures. Rarely utilizing canvases, paints, or brushes, he predominantly fingerpaints on plywood with clay, mud, sand, and soot. Sudduth also uses scavenged chalk, discarded by local lumbermen, and carefully selected plant materials, including turnip greens, pine needles, berries, and other leaves and roots to make varying colors; he often uses flour to lighten the mud and coffee grounds or charcoal to darken it. More recently the artist has experimented extensively with house paint.

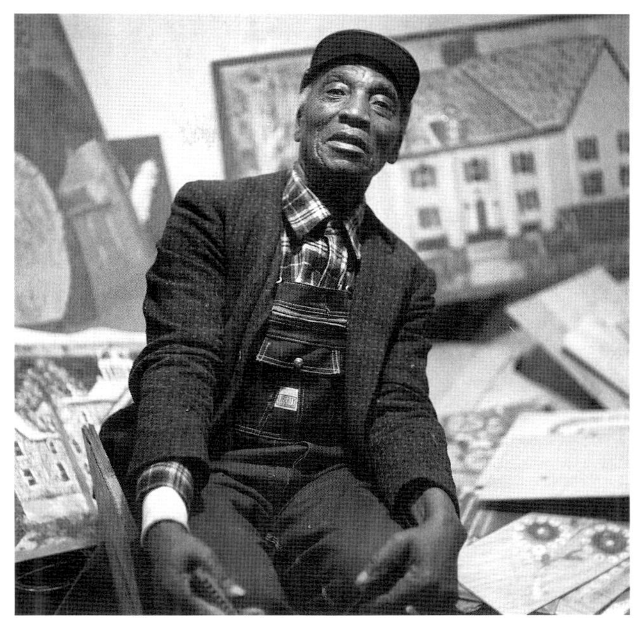

Jimmy Lee Sudduth

B. 1910

"A picture never goes good unless it has a child or a dog in it."

Swearingen was born into the black community of Campground Church, near Chappell Hill, Texas. His parents were migrant farmer laborers; he attended school periodically and church regularly. As a young man, Swearingen traveled throughout the West on freight trains and supported himself by chopping cotton, picking grapes, and doing construction and railroad work. In 1948, after working as a longshoreman in San Pedro, California, Swearingen returned after fifteen years to Chappell Hill to care for his father. He settled in Brenham, Texas, and resumed farming. In 1961, while working in the fields, Swearingen heard God command him to preach the Gospel.

Swearingen began painting at about the age of twelve, often on the walls of his house. After his return to Chappell Hill in 1948, he devoted more time to his art. Swearingen used whatever materials were readily available that would adhere to cardboard. Influenced by the Bible and the rural culture of Texas, he painted religious and rural scenes, often featuring children and animals. In his later years, Swearingen painted large canvases in brilliant oil paints.

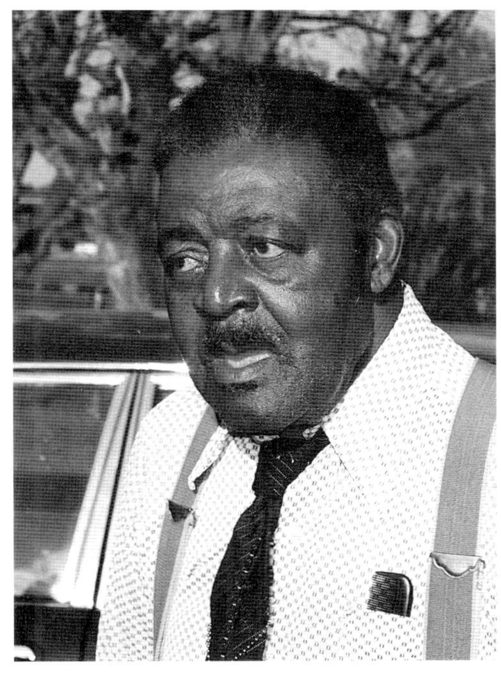

Rev. Johnnie Swearingen

1908–1993

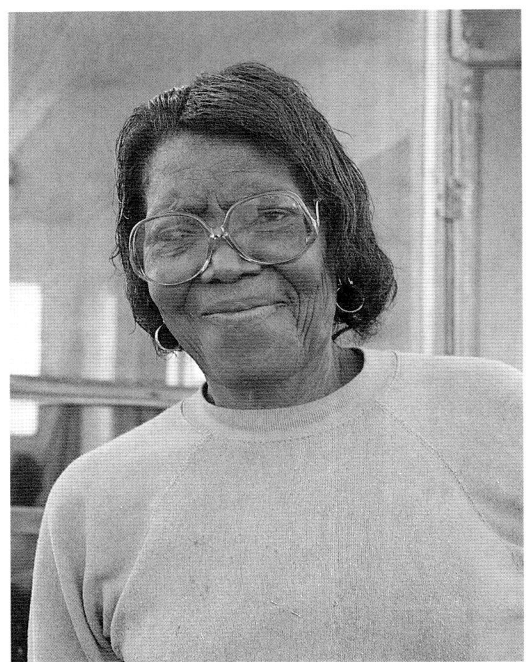

Sarah Mary Taylor

B. 1916

"I choose my colors by the clothes I wear. If I wear a yellow dress, I prefer a white hat and white shoes. If I wear a red dress, I prefer a black bag with black shoes."

Taylor was born in Anding, Mississippi, a small rural community near Yazoo City, and has spent most of her life on plantations within the Mississippi Delta, working as a cook, a field hand, and a housekeeper. She is retired and lives in Mississippi.

As a child, Taylor was taught the craft of African-American quilt making by her mother. By necessity, her early quilts were fashioned from old clothing and discarded flour sacks, which she used for lining or batting in place of combed cotton. In 1980 Taylor began a series of appliqué quilts. She gleans images from her surroundings, nature, popular American culture, television, and magazines. Taylor cuts paper templates from her own freehand drawings or from printed designs. Acquainted with the visual effects of combining different color values, she consciously incorporates color in the designs of her textile collages. In addition, she draws with crayons and felt-tip pens, creating joyful images of animals, people, and houses.

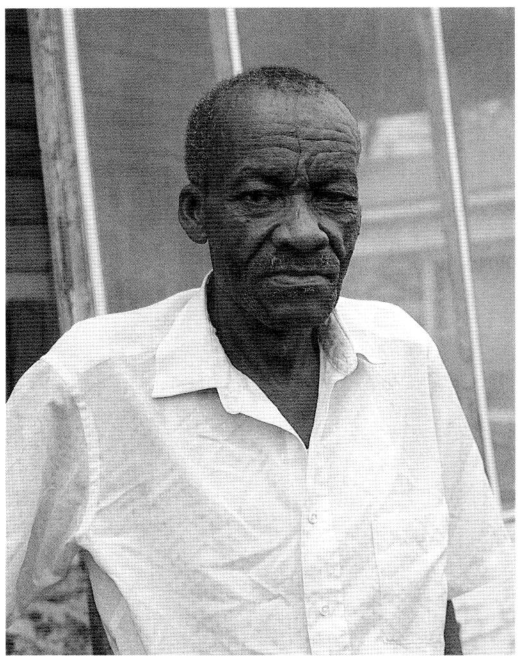

James Henry "Son" Thomas

1926–1993

Thomas dropped out of school after the fifth grade and held many different jobs, including cotton picker, sharecropper, and grave digger. He found success as a blues musician and as a sculptor.

Thomas sculpted since childhood in a wide range of subjects, all of which were inspired by dreams. He frequently portrayed skulls, human busts, animals, and men in coffins, which he shaped from locally found "gumbo clay." Some figures are painted; many have added materials. Skulls, for instance, often have foil-wrapped eye sockets and corn-kernel teeth; busts might have cotton for hair and wear eyeglasses.—*D.P.*

Tolliver, one of twelve children born to sharecropper parents, had little formal education. His early years were spent helping on the family farm. When his family later moved to Montgomery, Tolliver worked at odd jobs, mainly gardening.

In the late 1960s, while working in a furniture company, Tolliver was permanently disabled when a load of marble fell on his feet. He began painting after the accident, apparently inspired by a local art show.

A prolific artist, Tolliver has produced as many as ten paintings in one day, usually executed with house paint on wood or Masonite. Subjects are frequently repeated and range from animals such as birds, fish, turtles, and snakes to people (self-portraits are common) to abstract designs.—*D.P.*

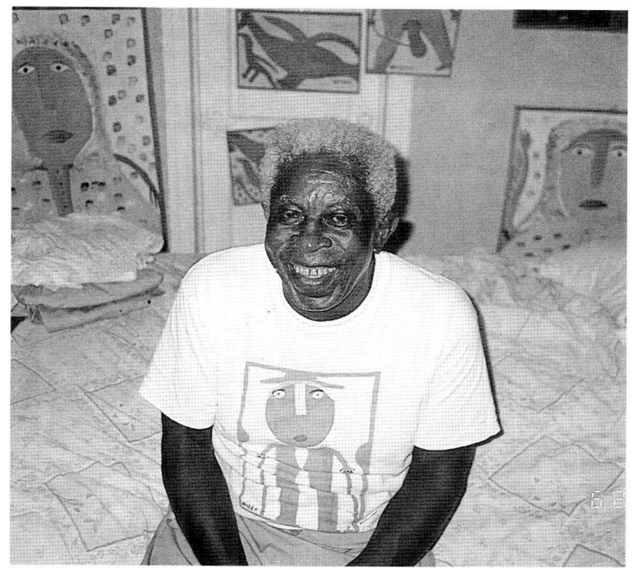

MOSE TOLLIVER

B. 1915

"You don't make it with your hands. You form it with your hands. You make it with your mind."

Born in Lee City, Kentucky, Tolson was a descendant of seventeenth-century settlers from England. He attended school for six or eight years and then worked variously as a farmer, laborer, chair maker, and preacher. Tolson became pastor of the Holly, Kentucky, Baptist church in 1921; in the mid-1930s, disgusted with the world's hypocrisies, he blew up his church. In 1961, after suffering a stroke, he abandoned the ministry and devoted his time to carving.

Although Tolson whittled and made Appalachian toys as early as 1912, his mature carving career did not begin until his retirement. Drawing on his canny understanding of politics and knowledge of biblical history, he created allegorical carvings in which human and animal forms represent religious and political themes. He is noted for his numerous interpretations of Adam and Eve. Tolson made a few carvings in soft stone but preferred poplar as his medium. He carved his pieces with a pocketknife and painted them sparsely, if at all. The finished carvings range in height from 2 to 24 inches.

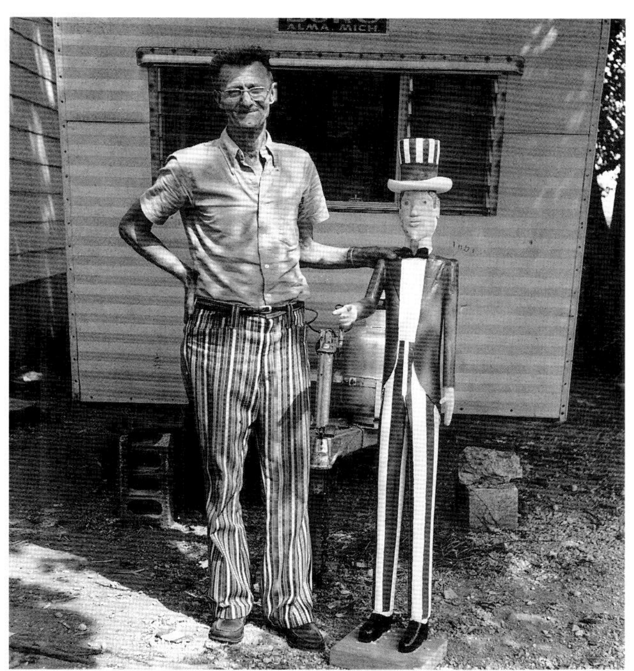

EDGAR TOLSON

1904–1984

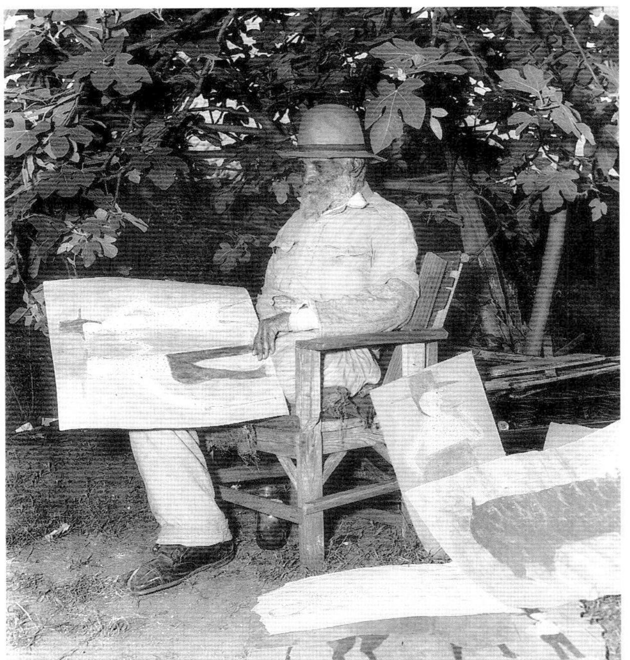

Bill Traylor

1854–1947

Traylor was born into slavery on the George Hartwell Traylor plantation near Benton, Alabama. He had no formal education, and after Emancipation he chose to remain on the plantation; there, he worked as a farmhand and raised his twenty-two children. In 1938 Traylor moved alone to Montgomery, Alabama. He worked briefly in a shoe factory, but old age and rheumatism disabled him, and he was left homeless and without work.

Traylor began drawing in 1938 with pencil stubs on whatever material he could find; any irregularities of surface became part of the composition. With a language of simple forms, he interpreted his memories of daily rural life and observations of street life. Traylor outlined his forms with pencil and colored them with poster paints. His works measure up to 24 by 30 inches.

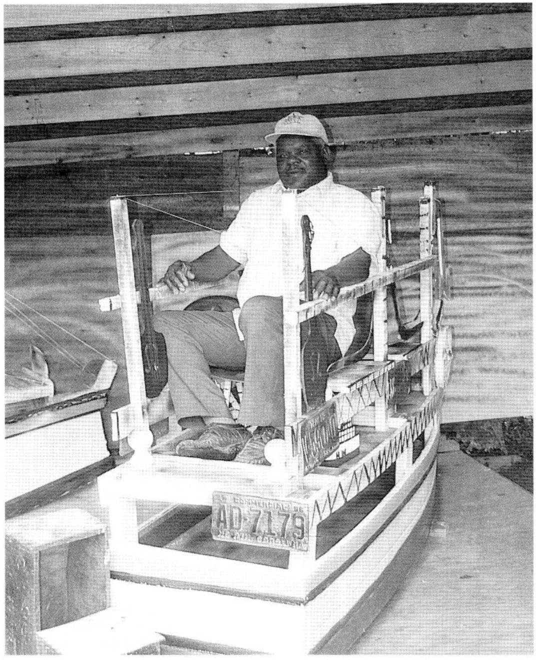

Hubert Walters

B. 1931

"Painting is different than making. Making is when you put material together. Sculpture is when you carve something. I feel better doing [this] than anything else."

Born in Jamaica, Walters worked as a commercial fisherman and constructed small fishing boats for twenty-five years. After immigrating to the United States in 1970, he settled in New York and began to work as a carpenter, making display cabinets. Walters later moved to North Carolina and worked in textile mills.

Giving up textile work, Walters sold ice cream to support his artistic career. He constructs model boats from sheet metal, wood, and auto-body filler, paints them with enamels, and incorporates rope and paper for sails and rigging. Recently he has used similar materials to fashion images of people and animals such as horses, bulls, cows, and dogs. Walters constructs his sculptures with an underlying armature and sometimes finishes them with Bondo and car enamel.

White was born to a farming couple in Natchez, Mississippi. He attended school through third grade and, in 1929, left Natchez to work on "quarter boats" on the Mississippi River, repairing and securing the river levee. White moved to New Orleans and worked as a waiter for approximately twenty years. He later was employed as a janitor and as a sign painter during the 1950s and 1960s.

He acquired an interest in painting after observing artists in the French Quarter in the early 1950s. Using housepaint, he at first imitated their work but quickly developed his own ideas and techniques. White decorated his porch and fences with his first artworks. His early subjects were neighborhood churches and crosses. White later gleaned images from television and his dreams, creating a visual vocabulary of dinosaurs, horses, fantastic birds, watermelons, skyscrapers, rocketships, and planets. In the early 1960s, he began to work almost exclusively with felt markers and white poster board and has used canvas only when it is provided.

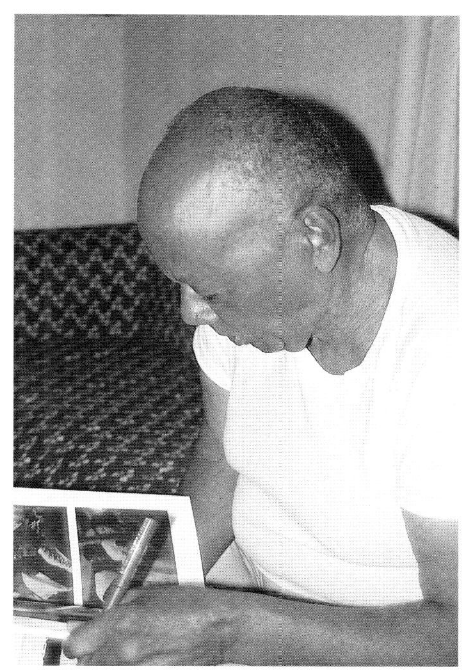

WILLIE WHITE

B. 1910

Born in Canaan, Connecticut, Willey left home at the age of twelve. He worked in a wholesale grocery in New Haven, Connecticut, and then traveled around the country. During this time, Willey labored at various jobs, including farmer, lumberman, fireman, deckhand on a steamboat, and wagon driver for the Barnum and Bailey Circus. In 1932 he settled in New Orleans and worked his way up to chief police officer of the local sewage and water board. Willey retired in 1966 and subsequently began to paint, often displaying his work in Jackson Square.

Willey observed and captured many traditional New Orleans scenes. As a visionary, he created an iconographic vocabulary of imaginary figures. Willey's paintings possess an organized layered composition. He initially used watercolor and pencil on paper; later he employed acrylic on Masonite. Although a few works are as large as 36 by 40 inches, most measure about 16 by 20 inches.

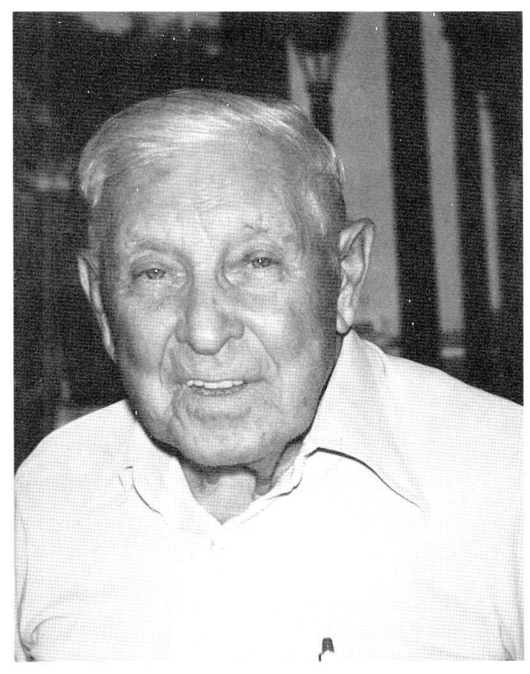

PHILO LEVI "CHIEF" WILLEY

1887–1980

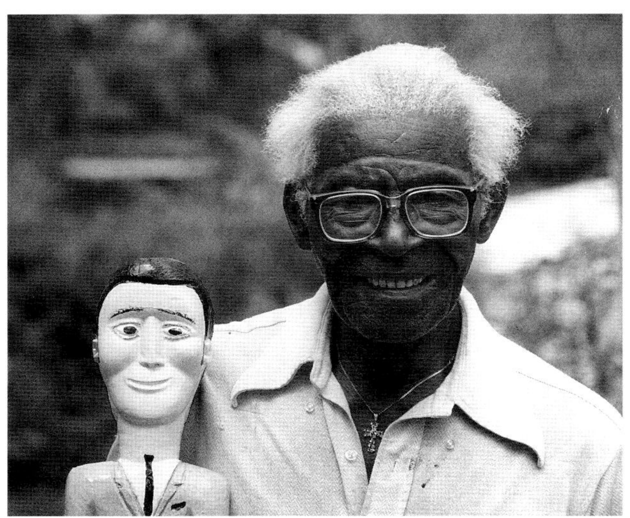

George Williams

B. 1911

Williams was born to a farming couple in Amity County, Mississippi. He remained on the family farm until the age of fourteen, when he found work as a delivery man, field hand, road builder, logger, and gandy dancer, or railroad worker.

Williams carved periodically with a pocketknife for relaxation and began creating "hoodoo" heads to wear around his neck. After not carving for a long period, he resumed the activity as a diversion during one of his full-time jobs. Williams carves crucifixion scenes, human figures, and animal forms, including alligators, bulls, leopards, horses, and pigs; occasionally, he creates a walking stick with encircling snakes. Williams prefers tupelo gum, cedar, or cypress wood. The finished carvings are painted with enamel and sometimes varnished.

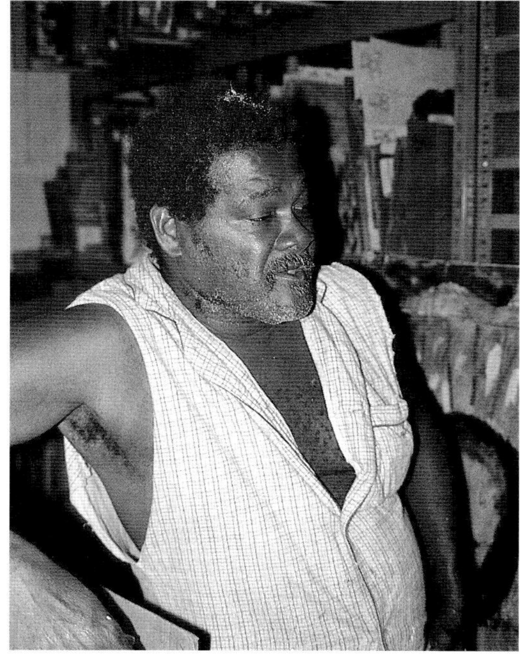

Purvis Young

B. 1943

"The street is real life. . . . *You come out here and feel the workings of the world. . . . That's all you need to be an artist."*

Born in the Liberty City section of Miami, Young has spent his entire life within the street subculture of Overtown, Miami's black ghetto. While incarcerated for armed robbery, from the age of eighteen to twenty-one, Young was encouraged to draw by a prison attendant.

Young began to draw actively in the late 1960s. He was inspired to express his ethnic and community pride by the mural movement then emerging in urban neighborhoods of Chicago and Detroit. Creating public and private works, he finds both his subject matter and materials in the streets of Overtown. He employs pencil, crayon, and paint on a variety of discarded materials such as old books; waste paper; scraps of cardboard, wood, and Masonite; and smashed doors and mirrors.

Young also finds ideas for works in books. At the public library he looks at books on the old masters and has said that he likes the way Japanese, Persian, and Chinese artists tell a story. This influence can be seen in the oriental-looking faces in some of his works.

All biographical sketches were written by Kimberly Nichols, except for those initialed "D.P.," which were written by Dannal Perry. Artists' quotes were found in the following sources:

Jesse Aaron: Donald Van Horn, "Carved Wood: The Visions of Jesse Aaron," *Southern Folklore Quarterly* 42 (1978), p. 267.

Steven Ashby: Jane Livingston and John Beardsley, *Black Folk Art in America, 1930–1980* (Jackson: University Press of Mississippi, 1982), p. 60.

Linvel Barker: interview, ARY, June 1993.

Minnie Black: Chuck Rosenak and Jan Rosenak, *Museum of American Folk Art Encyclopedia of Twentieth-Century Folk Art and Artists* (New York: Abbeville Press, 1990), p. 49 (hereafter Rosenak).

Vernon Burwell: Rosenak, p. 65.

Archie Byron: interview, ARY, April 1993.

Miles Carpenter: Robert Merritt, "Carver's Creativity Gave Joyful Fun," *Richmond Times Dispatch*, June 2, 1985.

Henry Ray Clark: "It'll Come True: Eleven Folk Artists First and Last" (Lafayette, La.: Artists' Alliance, 1992), p. 58 (hereafter "It'll Come True").

Raymond Coins: interview, KAG, July 1991.

Ronald Cooper: Rosenak, p. 81.

Ulysses Davis: Rosenak, p. 94.

William Dawson: Rosenak, p. 97.

John William "Uncle Jack" Dey: "John William (Uncle Jack) Dey," *The Clarion* 17, no. 1 (Spring 1992), p. 34.

Thornton Dial, Sr.: *Thornton Dial, Sr.: Strategy of the World.* (Jamaica, N.Y.: South Queens Park Association, 1990), p. 4.

Sam Doyle: Louanne Laroche, ed., *Sam Doyle* (Kyoto: Kyoto International, 1989), unpaginated.

William Edmondson: Louise LeQuire, "Edmondson's Art Reflects His Faith, Strong and Pure," *Smithsonian* 12, no. 5 (Aug. 1981), p. 51.

Minnie Evans: Rosenak, p. 114.

Josephus Farmer: Joanne Cubbs, *The Gift of Josephus Farmer* (Milwaukee: University of Wisconsin, Milwaukee Art History Gallery, 1982), p. 7.

Ezekiel Gibbs: interview, ARY, Oct. 1991.

Sybil Gibson: interview, KAG, Nov. 1992.

Homer Green: interview, ARY, Dec. 1991.

Ralph Griffin: interview, ARY, Aug. 1991.

Bessie Harvey: Shari Cavin Morris, "Bessie Harvey: Spirit in the Wood," *The Clarion* 213, no. 2/3 (Spring/Summer 1987), p. 46.

William Hawkins: Gary Schwindler, "William Hawkins: A Biography," unpublished ms., pp. 142–43.

Lonnie B. Holley: *In/Outsiders from the American South* (Montgomery: Montgomery Museum of Fine Arts, 1992), unpaginated.

Clementine Hunter: Mildred Hart Bailey, "Painted Memories of a Slave's Daughter," *Modern Maturity*, Oct. 1981.

Rev. J. L. Hunter: Susannah Kennedy, "Minister's Hobby Keeps Him Busy," *Dallas Times Herald*, Aug. 10, 1988.

Anderson Johnson: Jennifer Russell, "Marsh Gallery Hosts Two Artists," *University of Richmond Collegian*, Jan. 17, 1991, p. 9.

Clyde Jones: Marjorie Morris, "Bynum Man Uses Chain Saw to Create 'Critters,'" *Sanford Herald* [North Carolina], June 8, 1991.

Shields Landon "S. L." Jones: Ramona Lampell and Millard Lampell with David Larkin, *O, Appalachia: Artists of the Southern Mountains* (New York: Stewart, Tabori, and Chang, 1989), p. 21 (hereafter Lampell).

Eddie Kendrick: interview, KAG, Nov. 1992.

Charles Kinney: *Local Voices,* videotape, Morehead State University Folk Art Program, Kentucky, 1990.

O. W. "Pappy" Kitchens: William A. Fagaly, *1975 Artists Biennial Winners* (New Orleans: New Orleans Museum of Art, 1976), unpaginated.

Joe Louis Light: Robert Farris Thompson, John Mason, and Judith McWillie, *Another Face of the Diamond: Pathways through the Black Atlantic South* (New York: INTAR Latin American Gallery, 1989), p. 64 (hereafter Thompson et al.).

Charlie Lucas: Lampell, p. 225.

Willie Massey: Robert Knott, *Diving in the Spirit* (Winston-Salem, N.C.: Wake-Forest University Fine Arts Gallery, 1992), p. 40.

Sister Gertrude Morgan: Sister Gertrude Morgan to Regenia Perry, n.d., Gitter-Yelen papers.

John "J. B." Murry: Thompson et al., p. 65.

Earnest Patton: Rosenak, p. 232.

Elijah Pierce: David Treadwell, "Sermons in Wood," *Ebony Magazine* (July 1974), p. 69.

"Prophet" Royal Robertson: "It'll Come True," p. 62.

Juanita Rogers: "Juanita," Anton Haardt Studio Gallery, Montgomery, Alabama, brochure, 1982.

Sultan Rogers: "It'll Come True," p. 65.

Nellie Mae Rowe: Judith Alexander, *Nellie Mae Rowe, Visionary Artist 1900–1982* (Atlanta: Southern Arts Federation, 1983), p. 9.

J. P. Scott: interview, KAG, Sept. 1991.

Bernice Sims: Mike Suchcicki, "Folk Artist Preserves Past So Future Generations Can Learn Lessons of History," *Pensacola News Journal*, Feb. 17, 1991, p. E-1.

Herbert Singleton: interview, KAG, March 1992.

Mary T. Smith: Rosenak, p. 284.

David Strickland: interview, KAG, Oct. 1992.

Jimmy Lee Sudduth: interview, ARY, Aug. 1992.

Johnnie Swearingen: "'I Make Pictures': Paintings by Reverend Johnnie Swearingen," *Houston House and Garden*, undated clipping.

Sarah Mary Taylor: interview, ARY, April 1993.

Edgar Tolson: Michael Hall, "You Make It with Your Mind: The Art of Edgar Tolson," *The Clarion* 12, no. 2/3 (Spring/Summer 1987), p. 43.

Hubert Walters: interview, ARY, June 1993.

Purvis Young: Cesar Trasobares, *Purvis Young: Me and My People*, Joy Moos Gallery, Miami, brochure, 1988.

CHECKLIST OF THE EXHIBITION

JESSE AARON
Cat. no. 1
Crucifixion, n.d.
wood, cloth
84 × 54 × 8 (213.36 × 137.16 × 20.32)
Collection of Mr. Josh Feldstein
Plate 93

MINNIE AND GARLAND ADKINS
Cat. no. 2
Horse, 1992
basswood
18¾ × 31½ × 5 (47.63 × 80.01 × 12.7)
Collection of Margaret and
Richard Wenstrup

Cat. no. 3
Sow with Piglets, 1990
wood, paint
13¼ × 33 × 11 (33.66 × 83.82 × 27.94)
Morehead State University Folk Art
Museum, Kentucky
Plate 179

ZEBEDEE "Z. B." ARMSTRONG
Cat. no. 4
1986 Weekly/Monthly Calendar, 1986
wood, paint, metal
16½ × 18¾ × 5⅞ (41.91 × 47.63 × 14.92)
Private collection
Plate 118

EDDIE ARNING
Cat. no. 5
Sears Kitchen, ca. 1968
crayon and oil pastel on paper
20 × 26 (50.8 × 66.04)
Courtesy Ricco/Maresca Gallery,
New York

Cat. no. 6
Two Geese, ca. 1970
oil pastel on paper
22 × 32 (55.88 × 81.28)
Abby Aldrich Rockefeller Folk Art
Center, Williamsburg, Virginia
Plate 184

STEVEN ASHBY
Cat. no. 7
Bull, 1978
wood, hemp, metal, nut, paint
9¾ × 24 × 2½ (24.77 × 60.96 × 6.35)
Collection of Sal and Mary Scalora
Plate 194

Cat. no. 8
Man with Scythe, ca. 1978
wood, paint, cloth, metal
66 × 27 × 27 (167.64 × 68.58 × 68.58)
Collection of Chuck and Jan Rosenak

Cat. no. 9
Pregnant Woman, late 1960s
wood, cloth, nylon, metal
25¾ × 13¼ × 8 (65.41 × 33.66 × 20.32)
National Museum of American Art,
Smithsonian Institution, gift of Herbert
Waide Hemphill, Jr., and museum
purchase made possible by Ralph
Cross Johnson

LINVEL BARKER
Cat. no. 10
Giraffe, 1991
linden
24 × 3 × 10 (60.96 × 7.62 × 25.4)
Collection of Richardson M. Roberts
Plate 201

Cat. no. 11
Pig, 1991
linden
13 × 19 × 6 (33.02 × 48.07 × 15.24)
Collection of Barbara and Ed Okun

MINNIE BLACK
Cat. no. 12
Bald Eagle, n.d.
gourd, paint, wire, glass, bristles
12 × 31 × 19 (30.48 × 78.74 × 48.26)
Collection of Warren and Sylvia Lowe
Plate 170

Cat. no. 13
Critter, 1990
gourds, paint, plastic
13¼ × 24½ × 11 (34 × 62 × 28)
Private collection
Plate 195

HAWKINS BOLDEN
Cat. no. 14
Untitled, 1987
metal, wood, cloth, straw
38 × 17½ × 44 (96.52 × 44.45 × 111.76)
National Museum of American Art,
Smithsonian Institution, gift of William
Arnett
Plate 109

VERNON BURWELL
Cat. no. 15
Abe Lincoln, n.d.
latex, oil, Portland cement, sand, metal
71½ × 24 × 14½ (181.61 × 60.96 × 36.83)
Collection of Jane and Bert Hunecke
Plate 158

DAVID BUTLER
Cat. no. 16
Birdhouse, n.d.
wood, enamel, mixed media
18½ × 15 × 11½ (46.99 × 38.1 × 29.21)
Collection of Robert Greenberg

Cat. no. 17
David's Bike, 1976
bicycle, metal, paint
46 × 70 × 31 (116.84 × 177.8 × 78.74)
Collection of John Geldersma and
Keitha Leonard
Plate 2

Cat. no. 18
Locomotive Engine with Rooster,
ca. 1980
tin, plastic, paint, wood
39½ × 29 × 6 (100.33 × 73.66 × 15.24)
Private collection
Plate 60

Cat. no. 19
Nativity Scene, 1974
corrugated tin (flattened), paint, wood
28 × 40 × 5 (71.12 × 101.6 × 12.7)
Collection of John Geldersma and
Keitha Leonard

Cat. no. 20
Star and Animals, ca. 1960
tin, enamel
28 × 41 × 5 (71.12 × 104.14 × 12.7)
Collection of Richard D. Gasperi

Cat. no. 21
Two Roosters and Two Hens, 1979
corrugated tin (flattened), paint, wood
Avg. 9 × 12 × 6 (22.86 × 30.48 × 15.24)
Collection of John Geldersma and
Keitha Leonard
Plate 202

Cat. no. 22
Walking Stick with Figure, ca. 1975
wood, paint, metal, cloth, plastic
33⅞ × 17½ × 1½ (86.04 × 44.45 × 3.81)
Private collection
Plate 128

Cat. no. 23
Windmill with Man Riding Flying Elephant, 1975
metal, wood, plastic, paint
47 × 30 (119.38 × 76.2)
New Orleans Museum of Art, gift of the artist, Patterson, Louisiana
Plate 203

Archie Byron

Cat. no. 24
Despair, 1984
sawdust, glue
44 × 12½ × 15 (111.76 × 31.75 × 38.1)
Collection of Randy Siegel
Plate 140

Miles Carpenter

Cat. no. 25
Charlie Chaplin, 1981
wood, sawdust, metal, enamel
25 × 11½ × 12 (63.51 × 29.21 × 30.48)
Collection of Ann Oppenhimer
Plate 150

Cat. no. 26
Wounded Knee, 1973
wood, metal, polyester, paint
44 × 27½ × 11½ (111.76 × 69.85 × 29.21)
Collection of Jeffrey and C. Jane Camp
Plate 141

Henry Ray Clark

Cat. no. 27
The Magnificent Pretty Boy, 1988
felt-tip marker and ballpoint pen on paper, metal
10 × 16¾ (25.4 × 42.55)
The Menil Collection, Houston
Plate 115

Raymond Coins

Cat. no. 28
Adam and Eve, 1980
stone
12¾ × 10½ (32.39 × 26.67)
Collection of Richard C. Edgeworth
Plate 68

Cat. no. 29
Angel, ca. 1979
soapstone
15 × 30 × 12 (38.1 × 76.2 × 30.48)
Collection of Dr. and Mrs. Allen W. Huffman
Plate 13

Cat. no. 30
Angel, 1985
stone
36½ × 27 × 3¾ (92.71 × 68.58 × 9.53)
Collection of Warren and Sylvia Lowe
Plate 90

Cat. no. 31
Bear, 1987
stone
12½ × 29 × 5½ (31.75 × 73.66 × 13.97)
Courtesy Aarne Anton, American Primitive Gallery, New York
Plate 200

Cat. no. 32
Chicken, ca. 1980
soapstone
11½ × 5½ × 8 (29.21 × 13.97 × 20.32)
Collection of Dr. and Mrs. Allen W. Huffman

Cat. no. 33
Eagle, ca. 1987
wood, varnish
30 × 32 × 35 (76.2 × 81.28 × 88.9)
Collection of Paul and Alvina Haverkamp

Cat. no. 34
Frog, 1961
stone
8 × 15 × 19 (20.32 × 38.1 × 48.26)
Courtesy Aarne Anton, American Primitive Gallery, New York
Plate 199

Cat. no. 35
Mailbox Man, ca. 1980s
metal, wood, polyester, wool, glass
64¾ × 22½ × 37 (164.5 × 57.15 × 93.98)
Collection of Dr. and Mrs. Simeon M. Wrenn II

Cat. no. 36
Raymond and Ruby, 1982
sycamore, cedar
Avg. 56½ × 35 × 26 (142.24 × 121.92 × 91.44)
Collection of Dr. and Mrs. Allen W. Huffman
Plate 11

Cat. no. 37
Statue of Liberty, 1988
stone
18 × 10¾ × 2 (45.75 × 27.5 × 5)
Private collection
Plate 167

Jessie and Ronald Cooper

Cat. no. 38
Hell Bucket, 1989
metal, wood, paint
11 × 11 × 9 (27.94 × 27.94 × 22.86)
Collection of Anne Miller
Plate 100

Cat. no. 39
Home Sweet Home, 1989
antique trunk, acrylic
14¾ × 30¾ × 15½ (37.47 × 78.11 × 39.37)
The Arient Family Collection
Plate 78

Cat. no. 40
Praising the King: Kerosene Heater, 1989
acrylic on metal
38 × 16⅞ (96.52 × 42.88)
Collection of Gertrude and Ben Caldwell
Plate 101

Harold Crowell

Cat. no. 41
Two Sailors, 1982
paint on cardboard
70 × 65½ (178 × 166.5)
Private collection
Plate 4

Ulysses Davis

Cat. no. 42
M. L. King, n.d.
mahogany
9¼ × 5 × 5 (23.5 × 12.7 × 12.7)
Collection of Jane and Bert Hunecke
Plate 160

William Dawson

Cat. no. 43
Assorted Totems, ca. 1980s
wood, paint, pinecone, wool, metal, synthetic hair, chicken bone, seashell
Avg. 29½ × 5 × 3 (74.93 × 12.7 × 7.62)
The Arient Family Collection
Plate 129

Cat. no. 44
Bulldog with Two Birds, 1981
acrylic on cardboard
8 × 12 (20.32 × 30.48)
The Arient Family Collection

Cat. no. 45
Dog with Six Yellow Birds, 1982
acrylic on wood
6½ × 8½ (16.51 × 21.59)
The Arient Family Collection
Plate 189

Cat. no. 46
Dream House, 1977
wood
15 × 6 × 6 (38.1 × 15.24 × 15.24)
Collection of Roger Brown
Plate 66

Cat. no. 47
Red Fox, 1981
acrylic on paper
12 × 18 (30.48 × 45.72)
The Arient Family Collection
Plate 190

Cat. no. 48
Totem Painting, 1989
acrylic and pencil on illustration rag board
39¾ × 9⅛ (100.97 × 23.19)
Collection of Ruth and Robert Vogele

John William "Uncle Jack" Dey

Cat. no. 49
Acupuncture Pitchfork Style, ca. 1974
model-airplane paint on board
27⅜ × 40 (69.53 × 101.6)
Collection of Chuck and Jan Rosenak

Cat. no. 50
Adam and Eve Leave Eden, 1973
model-airplane paint on fiberboard
23⅛ × 47 (58.75 × 119.38)
National Museum of American Art, Smithsonian Institution, gift of Herbert Waide Hemphill, Jr., and museum purchase made possible by Ralph Cross Johnson
Plate 97

Cat. no. 51
Gillespie City, 1975
model-airplane paint on plywood
24 × 48 (60.96 × 121.92)
Collection of Chuck and Jan Rosenak

Cat. no. 52
Streaking, n.d.
model-airplane paint on board
21¾ × 31½ (55.25 × 80.01)
Collection of Barbara and Russ Herman
Plate 52

Thornton Dial, Sr.

Cat. no. 53
Eyes on the Business, 1992
charcoal on paper
29½ × 41½ (74.93 × 105.41)
Courtesy Luise Ross Gallery, New York
Plate 138

Cat. no. 54
Fishing for Love, 1990
watercolor and pencil on paper
22 × 30 (55.88 × 76.2)
New Orleans Museum of Art, gift of Calynne and Lou Hill
Plate 206

Cat. no. 55
Life Go On, 1990
acrylic on canvas
48 × 36 (121.92 × 91.44)
Collection of Dr. and Mrs. James Sellman
Plate 135

Cat. no. 56
The Longest Tail Tiger in the United States, 1989
wood, enamel, carpet fiber, tin, Bondo, industrial sealing compound
48¼ × 96 × 2¾ (122.56 × 243.84 × 6.99)
Milwaukee Museum of Art, gift of William Arnett
Plate 136

Cat. no. 57
My Teacher, 1990
mixed media
74 × 50½ × 2½ (187.96 × 128.27 × 6.35)
Collection of Gary Davenport
Plate 20

Cat. no. 58
Rolling Mill: Steel Is the Master, Lady Is the Power, 1992
metal, enamel, garden hoses, rope, industrial sealing compound
71 × 72½ × 3½ (180.34 × 184.15 × 8.89)
Collection of Ron and June Shelp
Plate 137

Cat. no. 59
Slave Ship, 1987
metal, wood, paint, wire, industrial sealing compound
71 × 102 × 29 (180.34 × 259.08 × 73.66)
Collection of the artist
Plate 134

Sam Doyle

Cat. no. 60
Adlade, n.d.
house paint on metal
52 × 26½ (132.08 × 67.31)
Collection of Randy Siegel
Plate 8

Cat. no. 61
Bobby Kennedy, ca. 1980
paint on paper
12½ × 9 (31.75 × 22.86)
Collection of Chuck and Jan Rosenak
Plate 161

Cat. no. 62
Brown Bomber (Joe Louis), 1979
house paint and tar on tin
60 × 28 (152.4 × 71.12)
Collection of Lanford Wilson
Plate 152

Cat. no. 63
Dr. Buz, ca. 1970s
oil on sheet metal
49½ × 26½ (125.73 × 67.31)
Collection of Dorothy and Leo Rabkin
Plate 47

Cat. no. 64
I'll Go Down, ca. 1970
wood, oil, fabric, metal
41½ × 25 × 5 (105.41 × 63.5 × 12.7)
Collection of Dorothy and Leo Rabkin

Cat. no. 65
Jackie Robinson, 1983
house paint on corrugated roofing tin
55 × 24 (139.7 × 60.96)
Museum of American Folk Art, New York, gift of Elizabeth Ross Johnson

Cat. no. 66
John F. Kennedy, ca. 1980
house paint on paper
17 × 9 (30.48 × 22.86)
Collection of Chuck and Jan Rosenak
Plate 162

Cat. no. 67
Lincoln at Frogmore, 1982
house paint on window shade
75¼ × 43 (175.26 × 90.81)
Collection of Travis Bousquet and Douglas Gitter
Plate 159

Cat. no. 68
Rae (Ray Charles), n.d.
house paint and tar on metal
57 × 42 (144.78 × 106.68)
Collection of Ms. Louanne Laroche

Cat. no. 69
St. Helena's First Black Midwife, ca. 1980
house paint on roofing tin
50½ × 21⅜ (128.27 × 54.29)
Collection of Chuck and Jan Rosenak
Plate 48

Cat. no. 70
Slave, n.d.
house paint on tin
34 × 26 (86.36 × 66.04)
Collection of Ms. Louanne Laroche
Plate 130

Cat. no. 71
Onk Sam, 1978
mixed media on wood
33 × 32 (82.82 × 81.28)
Collection of Frank Maresca
Plate 9

William Edmondson

Cat. no. 72
Angel, ca. 1930s
limestone
38 × 23½ × 12 (96.52 × 59.69 × 30.48)
Collection of Robert Greenberg
Plate 71

Cat. no. 73
Angel, ca. 1940s
limestone
26½ × 13 × 6½ (67.31 × 33.02 × 16.51)
Collection of Gertrude and Ben Caldwell
Plate 89

Cat. no. 74
Birdbath, ca. 1940s
limestone
37½ × 26½ × 14½ (95.25 × 67.31 × 36.83)
Collection of Gertrude and Ben Caldwell
Plate 185

Cat. no. 75
Choir Girls (Martha and Mary), ca. 1930–39
limestone
14 × 16⅞ × 6⅞ (35.56 × 42.86 × 15.24)
Hirshhorn Museum and Sculpture Garden, Smithsonian Institution, gift of Joseph H. Hirshhorn, 1972
Plate 70

Cat. no. 76
Girl with Cape, n.d.
limestone
26 × 14¾ × 7 (66.04 × 37.47 × 17.78)
Cheekwood-Tennessee Botanical Gardens and Museum of Arts, Nashville
Plate 55

Cat. no. 77
Noah's Ark, ca. 1930
limestone
22¼ × 16¼ × 14¾ (56.52 × 41.28 × 37.47)
Collection of Robert Greenberg
Plate 72

Cat. no. 78
Preacher, ca. 1938
limestone
18 × 8 × 7½ (45.72 × 20.32 × 19.05)
University of Tennessee, Knoxville
Plate 69

Cat. no. 79
Talking Owl, 1937
limestone
22¾ × 8 × 20 (57.79 × 20.32 × 50.8)
Collection of Estelle E. Friedman
Plate 186

Minnie Evans

Cat. no. 80
Ark of the Covenant, ca. 1966
oil on canvas board
14½ × 19½ (36.83 × 49.53)
Morris Museum of Art, Augusta, Georgia

Cat. no. 81
Butterfly Design, ca. 1965
oil on canvas board
14 × 18 (35.56 × 45.72)
Courtesy Luise Ross Gallery, New York
Plate 116

Josephus Farmer

Cat. no. 82
Abraham Lincoln and the Slave Auction, ca. 1979
wood, paint
11½ × 55 (29.21 × 139.7)
Collection of Estelle E. Friedman
Plate 133

Cat. no. 83
Nativity, ca. 1970s
wood, paint
11½ × 41¾ (29.21 × 106.05)
Collection of Estelle E. Friedman

Cat. no. 84
Samson, 1982
redwood, paint, rhinestones
27⅜ × 27¾ × 1½ (69.55 × 70.49 × 3.81)
National Museum of American Art, Smithsonian Institution, gift of Herbert Waide Hemphill, Jr., and museum purchase made possible by Ralph Cross Johnson

Howard Finster

Cat. no. 85
Coca-Cola #1123, 1977
paint on board
34½ × 10½ (87.63 × 26.67)
Collection of Herbert Waide Hemphill, Jr.
Plate 148

Cat. no. 86
The Discovery of Finster Art, 1976
oil on composition panel
12⅜ × 22¾ (31.43 × 57.79)
Collection of Janice and Mickey Cartin
Plate 14

Cat. no. 87
Elvis, 1977
paint on plywood
48 × 43 (121.92 × 109.22)
Collection of Lanford Wilson
Plate 147

Cat. no. 88
George Washington #20603, 1982
oil on plywood
41 × 41 (104.14 × 104.14)
Collection of Tom and Melissa Wells
Plate 157

Cat. no. 89
Hell Is a Hell of a Place #2272, 1982
enamel on board
17½ × 13½ (44.45 × 34.29)
Collection of Richard D. Gasperi
Plate 75

Cat. no. 90
Henry Ford at 2½ Years Old #1849, 1980
enamel on Masonite
36 × 48 (91.44 × 121.92)
The Arient Family Collection
Plate 51

Cat. no. 91
No One Has to Cross Jordan Alone, 1976
enamel on tin mirror
24½ × 42½ (62.23 × 107.95)
Collection of Chuck and Jan Rosenak
Plate 74

Cat. no. 92
What Is the Soul of Man, 1976
enamel on plywood
17½ × 28½ (44.45 × 72.39)
Collection of Willem and Diane Volkersz
Plate 73

Cat. no. 93
The World Is Now Living between Two Great Super Powers #4000 381, 1985
enamel on wood
48 × 48 (121.92 × 121.92)
Collection of Mr. John Denton

EZEKIEL GIBBS
Cat. no. 94
Church Meeting, ca. 1986–87
oil, pastel, and pencil on paper
9⅜ × 12⅝ (23.81 × 32.07)
Collection of Richard C. Edgeworth
Plate 50

Cat. no. 95
Farm Scene, 1986
pastel and pencil on paper
17½ × 11 (44.45 × 27.94)
Collection of Chuck and Jan Rosenak

Cat. no. 96
Untitled, 1986
mixed media on paper
11½ × 17 (29.21 × 43.18)
Collection of Henri and Leslie Muth
Plate 16

SYBIL GIBSON
Cat. no. 97
Flowers in Black Vase, n.d.
tempera on paper
20 × 16 (50.8 × 40.64)
Courtesy Anton Haardt Gallery, Montgomery, Alabama
Plate 211

Cat. no. 98
Flowers in White Vase, n.d.
tempera on paper
23 × 19 (58.42 × 48.26)
Courtesy Anton Haardt Gallery, Montgomery, Alabama
Plate 210

Cat. no. 99
Man, 1992
pastel on paper bag
16½ × 13¾ (41.91 × 34.93)
Collection of Susan Yelen
Plate 54

Cat. no. 100
Woman, 1991–92
watercolor and pastel on paper bag
17½ × 13¾ (44.5 × 34.93)
Collection of David and Dorothy Harman
Plate 53

GLASSMAN
Cat. no. 101
Honesty Is the Best Policy, ca. 1990
glass, glitter, and paint on wood
16 × 8¼ (40.64 × 20.96)
Collection of Paul and Alvina Haverkamp
Plate 168

HOMER GREEN
Cat. no. 102
Black Angel, ca. 1989
cedar, paint
5 × 65 × 23 (12.7 × 165.1 × 58.42)
Collection of David and Dorothy Harman

Cat. no. 103
Totem Pole, 1987
cedar, paint
75 × 60 (190.5 × 152.4)
Collection of Richardson M. Roberts
Plate 196

RALPH GRIFFIN
Cat. no. 104
Dog and Cat, 1985
driftwood, paint, nails
38 × 22 × 31 (96.52 × 55.88 × 78.74)
Collection of Tom and Melissa Wells

Cat. no. 105
Gypsy, n.d.
wood
31 × 15 × 17 (78.74 × 38.1 × 43.18)
Collection of Barbara and Ed Okun
Plate 108

Cat. no. 106
Screaming Lady, n.d.
wood, paint
69 × 42 × 40 (175.26 × 106.68 × 101.6)
Collection of Jane and Bert Hunecke
Plate 107

Cat. no. 107
The Wizard, 1988
driftwood, paint
18 × 11 × 12 (45.72 × 27.94 × 30.48)
Collection of Ron and June Shelp

JOSEPH HARDIN
Cat. no. 108
Untitled, ca. 1987
acrylic on paper
23½ × 9½ (59.69 × 24.13)
Collection of Alesia and Andrew Glasgow
Plate 113

BESSIE HARVEY
Cat. no. 109
Plow Day, 1984
wood, leather, hair, paint
25 × 29 × 10 (63.5 × 73.66 × 25.4)
Courtesy Blue Spiral 1 Gallery, Asheville, North Carolina

Cat. no. 110
Yellow Bird with Rider, n.d.
wood, paint
39 × 25 × 13 (99.06 × 63.5 × 33.02)
Collection of Randy Siegel
Plate 110

WILLIAM HAWKINS
Cat. no. 111
Broad and High Streets, ca. 1982
enamel on plywood
37 × 44 (93.98 × 111.76)
Collection of Gary Schwindler and Micki Glassburn
Plate 30

Cat. no. 112
Bull Moose, 1988
mixed media on masonite
48 × 72 (121.92 × 182.88)
Ricco/Maresca Gallery, New York
Plate 192

Cat. no. 113
Handing the Keys to St. Peter, 1989
enamel and mixed media on Masonite
48 × 56½ (121.92 × 43.51)
Collection of Robert Greenberg
Plate 84

Cat. no. 114
Jerusalem of the Bible, 1984
enamel on Masonite
33 × 46 (83.82 × 116.84)
Collection of Dr. Siri von Reis
Plate 64

Cat. no. 115
The Last Supper No. 6, 1986
enamel and cornmeal on plywood
48 × 48 (121.92 × 121.92)
Collection of Gary Schwindler and Micki Glassburn
Plate 85

Cat. no. 116
Ohio Stadium no. 1, 1983
enamel on Masonite
36 × 48 (91.44 × 121.92)
Collection of Janice and Mickey Cartin
Plate 32

Cat. no. 117
Tasmanian Tiger #2, 1986
enamel, wood filler, and metal on Masonite and wood
54 × 54 (137.16 × 137.16)
Blumert-Fiore Collection
Plate 193

Cat. no. 118
Two Horses, 1984
enamel on Masonite
36 × 44 (91.44 × 111.76)
Collection of Edward V. Blanchard and M. Anne Hill
Plate 181

Cat. no. 119
Yaekle Building, ca. 1980
enamel on wood
36 × 60 (91.44 × 152.4)
Collection of Jill and Sheldon Bonovitz, courtesy Janet Fleisher Gallery, Philadelphia
Plate 29

Lonnie B. Holley

Cat. no. 120
Being in Church without Being There, 1988
acrylic on Celotex
23⅝ × 47⅝ (60.02 × 120.98 cm)
Private collection

Cat. no. 121
Yielding to the Ancestors While Controlling the Hands of Time, 1992
wood, metal, paint
108½ × 59½ × 22 (275.59 × 151.13 × 55.88)
National Museum of American Art, Smithsonian Institution; gift of William Arnett
Plate 12

Clementine Hunter

Cat. no. 122
Cotton Picking, ca. 1955
oil on cardboard
7 × 15 (17.78 × 38.1)
Collection of Richard D. Gasperi
Plate 24

Cat. no. 123
Melrose Plantation, 1961
cloth and paper
67 × 49 (170.18 × 124.46)
Collection of Mr. and Mrs. Shelby R. Gilley

Cat. no. 124
Panorama of Baptism on Cane River, ca. 1945
oil on window shade
36 × 72 (91.44 × 182.88)
Collection of Roger Houston Ogden
Plate 79

Cat. no. 125
Secret Garden, Melrose Plantation, 1955
oil on academy board
46 × 42 (116.84 × 106.68)
Collection of Richard D. Gasperi
Plate 21

Cat. no. 126
Sugar Plantation, n.d.
oil on academy board
48 × 72 (121.92 × 182.88)
Collection of Sandra Jaffe
Plate 22

Rev. J. L. Hunter

Cat. no. 127
Tray Man, 1992
wood
45 × 24 × 33 (114.3 × 60.96 × 83.82)
Collection of Mrs. Sally Griffiths

James Harold Jennings

Cat. no. 128
Art, 1988
wood, paint
50 × 59 × 15½ (127 × 149.86 × 39.37)
The Arient Family Collection

Cat. no. 129
Arts, 1986
wood, plastic laminate, metal, enamel
99 × 100 × 40 (251.46 × 254 × 101.6)
Collection of Warren and Sylvia Lowe
Plate 3

Cat. no. 130
Elvis, 1987
wood, metal, enamel
68½ × 46 × 3 (173.99 × 116.84 × 7.62)
The Arient Family Collection
Plate 149

Anderson Johnson

Cat. no. 131
Abraham Lincoln, 1989
enamel on plywood
34 × 24½ (86.36 × 62.23)
Collection of William and Ann Oppenhimer
Plate 154

Cat. no. 132
George Washington, ca. 1985
acrylic on composition board
22⅛ × 16⅞ (55.2 × 42.86)
Collection of Baron and Ellin Gordon
Plate 155

Cat. no. 133
Portable Pulpit, 1989
wood, paper, plastic, rayon, metal, house paint
41 × 18 × 18 (104.14 × 45.72 × 45.72)
Collection of William and Ann Oppenhimer
Plate 65

Clyde Jones

Cat. no. 134
Pelican, 1989
wood, house paint, tennis balls
70 × 48 × 40 (177.8 × 121.92 × 101.6)
Collection of the artist
Plate 209

Cat. no. 135
Penguins, 1989
oil on plywood
48 × 96 (121.92 × 234.84)
Collection of the artist
Plate 198

Cat. no. 136
Porcupine, 1989
wood, house paint, metal, plastic, glitter
28 × 22 × 72 (71.12 × 55.88 × 182.88)
Collection of the artist
Plate 208

Cat. no. 137
Whale, 1992
wood, house paint, plastic, metal
27 × 31 × 53 (68.58 × 78.74 × 134.62)
Collection of the artist

Frank Jones

Cat. no. 138
Devil House, ca. 1968
colored pencil on paper
25 × 38 (63.5 × 96.52)
Collection of Murray Smither
Plate 117

Cat. no. 139
Mango House, ca. 1966–68
colored pencil on paper
25½ × 30½ (64.77 × 77.47)
New Orleans Museum of Art, museum purchase, Friends of Prints and Drawings Fund

Shields Landon "S. L." Jones

Cat. no. 140
Man with Red Bow Tie, 1983
wood, paint
14 × 11 × 9 (35.56 × 27.94 × 22.86)
The Arient Family Collection
Plate 57

Cat. no. 141
The Preacher and Wife, ca. 1970s
wood, enamel paint
5 × 20 × 14 (each) (12.7 × 50.8 × 35.56)
Collection of Jill and Sheldon Bonovitz, courtesy Janet Fleisher Gallery, Philadelphia
Plate 56

Eddie Kendrick

Cat. no. 142
The Judgment Set On the Clouds, 1978
pencil, colored pencil, ballpoint pen, and acrylic on paper
12 × 18 (30.48 × 45.72)
Collection of Susan Purvis

Cat. no. 143
This Is the Holy Train, 1990
colored pencil, ink, crayon, watercolor, and pencil on poster board
19 × 24 (48.5 × 61)
Collection of David and Dorothy Harman
Plate 81

Cat. no. 144
This Plane Is Heaven Bound, 1989–90
colored pencil, ink, crayon, watercolor, pencil on poster board
19 × 24 (48.5 × 61)
Collection of Susan Yelen
Plate 80

Charles Kinney

Cat. no. 145
"Cheter" Cat, 1978
paint on window shade
37 × 35½ (74.93 × 91.44 cm)
Huntington Museum of Art, West Virginia
Plate 173

Cat. no. 146
Farmer, 1985
tempera and pencil on paper
22 × 28 (55.88 × 71.12)
Morehead State University Folk Art Museum, Kentucky
Plate 26

Cat. no. 147
George Washington, 1990
acrylic, ink, pencil on poster board
28 × 22 (71 × 56)
Collection of Susan Yelen
Plate 156

Cat. no. 148
Kentucky Landscape with Train, ca. 1970–71
house paint on board
41 × 47¾ (104.14 × 121.29)
Collection of Richard C. Edgeworth
Plate 25

Cat. no. 149
Old Haint House, 1988
tempera, charcoal, and pencil on paper
22 × 28 (55.88 × 71.12)
Collection of William and
Ann Oppenhimer
Plate 111

NOAH KINNEY
Cat. no. 150
Tiger, 1987
wood, paint
15 × 25 × 8 (38.1 × 63.5 × 20.32)
Morehead State University Folk Art
Museum, Kentucky
Plate 178

O. W. "PAPPY" KITCHENS
Cat. no. 151
Peace in the Valley, 1977
acrylic and pencil on canvas
27 × 37 (68.58 × 93.98)
Collection of Lanford Wilson
Plate 82

JOE LOUIS LIGHT
Cat. no. 152
Bird, 1987
enamel on wood
23½ × 20 (59.69 × 50.8)
Collection of George and Sue Viener
Plate 5

Cat. no. 153
Erection Flower, n.d.
paint on plywood
48 × 24 (121.92 × 60.96)
Collection of Calynne and Lou Hill

Cat. no. 154
Hard To Beat, 1988
house paint on wood
34½ × 88¾ (87.63 × 225.43)
National Museum of American Art,
Smithsonian Institution, gift of William
Arnett
Plate 207

CHARLIE LUCAS
Cat. no. 155
Bondo, 1989
metal, paint, bondo
36 × 45 (91.44 × 114.3)
Collection of Lanford Wilson
Plate 191

Cat. no. 156
Cow, n.d.
metal
70 × 36 × 81 (177.8 × 91.44 × 205.74)
Collection of the artist
Plate 205

Cat. no. 157
Large Wire Horse, n.d.
metal
60 × 26 × 78 (152.4 × 66.04 × 198.12)
Collection of the artist
Plate 204

Cat. no. 158
Mother Nature Stood Up to Take the World Back Cause Man Has Abused Her Body, n.d.
oil and acrylic on canvas
52 × 84 (132.08 × 213.36)
Collection of the artist
Plate 139

CARL MCKENZIE
Cat. no. 159
Adam and Eve, 1987
wood, acrylic
33 × 20 × 7¾ (83.82 × 50.8 × 19.69)
Collection of Ruth and Robert Vogele
Plate 103

Cat. no. 160
Noah's Ark, 1987
wood, acrylic, marker
21½ × 25½ × 5¾ (54.61 × 64.77 × 14.61)
Collection of John and Diane Balsley
Plate 102

WILLIE MASSEY
Cat. no. 161
Birdhouse: Blue and Pink, 1989
wood, paint, walnuts, aluminum foil
22 × 14 × 11 (55.88 × 35.56 × 27.94)
Collection of Aarne Anton, American
Primitive Gallery, New York
Plate 180

Cat. no. 162
Eagle, 1989
paint on cardboard and wood
11 × 19¾ (27.94 × 50.17)
Collection of Edward V. Blanchard and
M. Anne Hill
Plate 171

Cat. no. 163
Lizard, 1989
acrylic and pencil on canvas
13 × 16 (33.02 × 40.64)
Collection of Aarne Anton, American
Primitive Gallery, New York
Plate 174

Cat. no. 164
Spotted Cat, 1989
acrylic on cardboard
11 × 13½ (27.94 × 34.29)
Courtesy Aarne Anton, American
Primitive Gallery, New York
Plate 175

R. A. MILLER
Cat. no. 165
Assorted Animal Cutouts, 1988
metal, paint
11½ × 17 (29.21 × 43.18)
Collection of Susan Yelen
Plate 197

Cat. no. 166
Blow Oscar, ca. 1989
sheet metal, paint
78½ × 12¼ (199.39 × 31.12)
Collection of Jane and Bert Hunecke
Plate 164

Cat. no. 167
Lord Love You, 1990
wood, tin, paint
63 × 36 × 4 (160.02 × 91.44 × 10.16)
Collection of Dr. and Mrs. Allen W.
Huffman

SISTER GERTRUDE MORGAN
Cat. no. 168
Book of Revelation, ca. 1965–70
paint on window shade
36¼ × 73 (92.08 × 185.42)
Collection of Dr. Siri von Reis
Plate 92

Cat. no. 169
Book of Revelation, ca. 1965–75
ink, pencil, and acrylic on window
shade
47.44 × 83.86 (120.5 × 213)
New Orleans Museum of Art, gift of
Lee Friedlander
Plate 91

Cat. no. 170
Charity Hospital—523-2311, ca. 1970s
acrylic and ink on cardboard
13 × 16 (33.02 × 40.64)
Collection of Paul and
Alvina Haverkamp
Plate 19

Cat. no. 171
Christ Coming in His Glory, n.d.
acrylic, crayon, and ink on cardboard
6 × 9¼ (15.24 × 23.5)
Collection of Sandra Jaffe
Plate 87

Cat. no. 172
Doing the Holy Dance, n.d.
acrylic and ink on paper
7½ × 4⅜ (19.05 × 11.11)
Collection of Sandra Jaffe

Cat. no. 173
The Lamb Standing on Mount Zion with His Company, n.d.
pencil and acrylic on Masonite
23¾ × 23¾ (60.33 × 60.33)
Collection of Sandra Jaffe
Plate 88

Cat. no. 174
New Jerusalem City, ca. 1970
pencil and acrylic on window shade
13 × 72 (33.02 × 182.88)
Collection of Jill and Sheldon Bonovitz,
courtesy Janet Fleisher Gallery,
Philadelphia

Cat. no. 175
A Poem of My Calling, ca. 1973
ink and acrylic on paper
10 × 15 (25.4 × 38.1)
Collection of Susann Craig

Cat. no. 176
Self-portrait with Jesus, n.d.
guitar case, whitewash, acrylic
35¾ × 14 × 5 (90.81 × 35.56 × 12.7)
Collection of Sandra Jaffe

Cat. no. 177
Train to New Jerusalem, ca. 1970s
acrylic and ink on cardboard
10 × 12 (25.4 × 30.48)
Collection of Paul and
Alvina Haverkamp
Plate 86

Cat. no. 178
Way in the Middle of the Air, n.d.
acrylic, pencil, and ink on cardboard,
string
21¾ × 30 (55.25 × 76.2)
Collection of Sandra Jaffe
Plate 18

ED "MR. EDDY" MUMMA
Cat. no. 179
Three Men and House; Man's Face, ca.
1978–82
acrylic and oil on board
27 × 22 (68.58 × 55.88)
Collection of Mr. Josh Feldstein
Plate 49

John "J. B." Murry

Cat. no. 180
Untitled, ca. 1975
house paint, acrylic, and marker on plywood
25 × 24 (63.50 × 60.96)
Collection of Lanford Wilson
Plate 121

Cat. no. 181
Untitled, ca. 1980
mixed media on paper
14 × 10½ (35.56 × 26.67)
Collection of Robert Greenberg
Plate 120

Cat. no. 182
Untitled, ca. 1980
mixed media on paper
17 × 14 (43.18 × 35.56)
Collection of Ron and June Shelp

Cat. no. 183
Untitled, ca. 1986
watercolor and ballpoint pen on poster board
23⅞ × 18 (60.64 × 45.72)
Private collection
Plate 119

Earnest Patton

Cat. no. 184
Uncle Sam, 1987
wood, enamel, felt-tip marker, paper
26½ × 8½ × 10½ (67.31 × 21.59 × 26.67)
Collection of William and Ann Oppenhimer
Plate 165

Leslie Payne

Cat. no. 185
New York Lady, ca. 1970s
metal, costume jewelry, reflector
26½ × 14 × 7⅜ (67.31 × 35.56 × 18.73)
Collection of Chuck and Jan Rosenak
Plate 153

Rev. Benjamin F. Perkins

Cat. no. 186
All-American Potty, 1990
pine, metal, acrylic
18⅝ × 16⅛ × 15¼ (47.32 × 40.97 × 38.74)
Collection of Lynne Ingram
Plate 163

Cat. no. 187
Gourd, 1989
gourd, paint
18½ × 9 (47 × 23)
Collection of Susan Yelen

Cat. no. 188
Homeplace, ca. 1985
paint on canvas
48½ × 36 (123.19 × 91.44)
Collection of Alesia and Andrew Glasgow
Plate 83

Elijah Pierce

Cat. no. 189
Jesus Is Coming Again, 1979
wood, paint, glitter
37 × 17 × 1¾ (93.98 × 43.18 × 4.45)
Collection of Jeffrey and Leslie Rich
Plate 106

Cat. no. 190
The Kiss of Judas, ca. 1970
wood, enamel, glitter
17 × 9½ (43.18 × 24.13)
Collection of Lanford Wilson

Cat. no. 191
Leopard, 1978
wood, paint
5½ × 11 × 3 (13.97 × 27.94 × 7.62)
Collection of Herbert Waide Hemphill, Jr.
Plate 177

Cat. no. 192
Little Boy and His Dog, 1981
wood, paint
5 × 5¼ × 1¾ (12.70 × 13.34 × 4.45)
Columbus Museum of Art, Ohio, gift of Michael Milligan

"Prophet" Royal Robertson

Cat. no. 193
Cute City Region, 1989
enamel paint, pen, and marker on poster board
28 × 22 (71.12 × 55.88)
Collection of Tom De Nolf
Plate 114

Juanita Rogers

Cat. no. 194
Fishing Hole, ca. 1982
tempera and acrylic on paper
12.4 × 19 (31.75 × 48.26)
Courtesy of Anton Haardt Gallery, Montgomery, Alabama

Cat. no. 195
Standing Creature, ca. 1980
unfired clay, hair, grasses
10¼ × 6¾ × 5 (26.04 × 17.15 × 12.7)
Collection of Willem and Diane Volkersz
Plate 112

Sultan Rogers

Cat. no. 196
Haint House, 1987
wood, paint
65 × 34 × 32 (165.1 × 86.36 × 81.28)
Collection of Warren and Sylvia Lowe
Plate 125

Cat. no. 197
Male and Female Figure, 1991
wood, enamel
14 × 6 × 4 (35.56 × 15.24 × 10.16)
Collection of A. Everette James

Cat. no. 198
Snake with Lady, 1989
wood, paint
6½ × 3 × 3 (16.51 × 7.62 × 7.62)
Collection of Warren and Sylvia Lowe
Plate 124

Nellie Mae Rowe

Cat. no. 199
Mother and Child, 1981
crayon, ballpoint pen, and pencil on paper
18 × 23½ (45.72 × 59.69)
Collection of Judith Alexander
Plate 123

Cat. no. 200
Nellie's Teapot, ca. 1979–80
crayon and colored pencil on paper
17 × 14 (43.18 × 35.56)
Collection of Judith Alexander
Plate 122

J. P. Scott

Cat. no. 201
C. J. P. Scott, n.d.
wood, paint, metal
26 × 51 × 17 (66.04 × 129.54 × 43.18)
New Orleans Museum of Art, gift of Dr. Kurt A. Gitter and Alice Rae Yelen
Plate 1

Cat. no. 202
Keep Moving, ca. 1985
wood, tin, canvas, enamel
22 × 12 × 70 (55.88 × 30.48 × 177.8)
Collection of Paul and Alvina Haverkamp
Plate 61

Cat. no. 203
Mrs. Myrtle Grove, ca. 1986
wood, paint, glass, string, metal, plastic
42 × 79 × 34 (106.68 × 200.66 × 86.36)
Collection of Chuck and Jan Rosenak

Cat. no. 204
Quarter House, 1984
wood, tin, paint, plastic, metal
32 × 43 × 23 (81.28 × 109.22 × 58.42)
Collection of Warren and Sylvia Lowe
Plate 63

Cat. no. 205
Ronald J. Scott, 1990
wood, tin, paint, plastic, metal
36 × 53 × 17 (91.44 × 134.62 × 43.18)
Collection of Warren and Sylvia Lowe
Plate 62

Bernice Sims

Cat. no. 206
Church Scene, 1989
oil on canvas
36 × 36 (91.44 × 91.44)
Collection of Paul and Alvina Haverkamp
Plate 27

Cat. no. 207
Spring Cleaning, 1990
oil on canvas
16 × 20 (40.64 × 50.8)
Collection of Douglas Gitter
Plate 28

Herbert Singleton

Cat. no. 208
Adam and Eve, 1991
wood, paint
77 × 29 × 1½ (195.58 × 73.66 × 3.81)
Collection of George and Sue Viener
Plate 67

Cat. no. 209
Behind the Eight Ball, 1991
wood, paint
22½ × 71 (57.15 × 180.34)
Collection of Douglas Gitter
Plate 132

Cat. no. 210
Catch Me if You Can, 1989
oak, enamel
11 × 39 (27.94 × 99.06)
Courtesy Barrister's Gallery, New Orleans
Plate 131

Cat. no. 211
New Orleans Jazz Funeral, n.d.
wood, paint
18 × 56 (45.72 × 142.24)
Collection of Ken and Margo Bode
Plate 45

Cat. no. 212
Uncle Tom, 1990
wood, enamel
78 × 18 × 24 (198.12 × 45.72 × 60.96)
Collection of Warren and Sylvia Lowe

MARY T. SMITH
Cat. no. 213
I Was in a Wreck, 1983
enamel on tin
64 × 59 (162.56 × 149.86)
Collection of Warren and Sylvia Lowe
Plate 98

Cat. no. 214
The Lord Is Head of the World, ca. 1983
paint on metal
25¾ × 31 (65.41 × 78.74)
Collection of Willem and Diane Volkersz
Plate 99

Cat. no. 215
Untitled (six heads), n.d.
house paint on wood
23⅞ × 23¾ (60.66 × 60.33)
Collection of Robert Greenberg

DAVID STRICKLAND
Cat. no. 216
Big Bird, 1990
metal
58 × 52 × 55 (147.32 × 132.08 × 139.7)
Collection of Mrs. Sally Griffiths
Plate 127

Cat. no. 217
Case Alien, 1991
metal, glass
104 × 46 × 63 (264.16 × 116.84 × 160.02)
Collection of Mrs. Sally Griffiths
Plate 126

JIMMY LEE SUDDUTH
Cat. no. 218
African-Americans Living in New York City, 1992
mud and paint on plywood
49½ × 72¾ (124.5 × 184.75)
Private collection
Plate 31

Cat. no. 219
Cher, 1989
mud, house paint, and sugar on plywood
48 × 19 (124.92 × 48.26)
Collection of Rick and Jennifer Berman, courtesy Berman Gallery

Cat. no. 220
Dixie, the Barking Dog, 1990
mud and paint on wood
42 × 31 (106.68 × 78.74)
Collection of John and Stephanie Smither
Plate 176

Cat. no. 221
Fantastic Building, ca. 1970s
mud, sugar, natural vegetable color, and paint on wood
27 × 37½ (68.58 × 95.25)
Collection of Chuck and Jan Rosenak
Plate 33

Cat. no. 222
Man with Red Cap on Bicycle, 1990
mud, house paint, and coffee on plywood
39¾ × 39 (100.97 × 99.06)
Collection of Lynne Ingram

Cat. no. 223
Mud Architectural of State Capitol, ca. 1989
mud and paint on plywood
48 × 48 (121.92 × 121.92)
Collection of Richardson M. Roberts
Plate 35

Cat. no. 224
Red Skelton, ca. 1970s
mud, clay, and pencil on wooden door
24 × 22¾ (60.96 × 57.79)
Collection of M. Anne Hill and Edward V. Blanchard
Plate 151

Cat. no. 225
Self-portrait, n.d.
mud and paint on board
24 × 48 (60.96 × 121.92)
Collection of David and Dorothy Harman
Plate 6

Cat. no. 226
Statue of Liberty, 1991
mud and paint on plywood
84 × 23 (213.36 × 58.42)
Collection of Richardson M. Roberts
Plate 172

Cat. no. 227
Toto with Ball, n.d.
mud, chalk, and paint on plywood
31 × 12½ (78.74 × 31.75)
Collection of Dann M. Gershon
Plate 7

Cat. no. 228
Train, 1988
mud and paint on board
78½ × 14½ (199.39 × 36.83)
Collection of David and Dorothy Harman
Plate 34

REV. JOHNNIE SWEARINGEN
Cat. no. 229
The Creation of the World, 1990
oil on canvas
50 × 75 (127 × 190.5)
Collection of John and Stephanie Smither
Plate 105

Cat. no. 230
God Loves You, 1991
oil on canvas
36 × 36 (91.44 × 91.44)
Collection of John and Stephanie Smither
Plate 77

Cat. no. 231
Noah's Ark, n.d.
oil on Masonite
48 × 96¼ (121.92 × 244.48)
Collection of Sharon and Ivan Koota
Plate 104

Cat. no. 232
Picking Cotton, 1978
oil on Masonite
16 × 24 (40.64 × 60.96)
Collection of Gaye Hall
Plate 23

Cat. no. 233
Sunday Camp Meeting, 1991
oil on canvas
45 × 68 (114.3 × 172.72)
Collection of John and Stephanie Smither
Plate 76

SARAH MARY TAYLOR
Cat. no. 234
Horse, 1988
crayon, ink and pencil on paper
12 × 17¾ (30.5 × 45)
Private collection
Plate 182

Cat. no. 235
Statue of Liberty, 1988
cotton, thread, batting
81¼ × 71½ (206.5 × 181.5)
Collection of Susan Yelen
Plate 166

JAMES HENRY "SON" THOMAS
Cat. no. 236
George Washington, ca. 1984–85
unfired clay, raw cotton, paint
7 × 7 × 7 (17.78 × 17.78 × 17.78)
Collection of Mr. and Mrs. W. L. Berry
Plate 169

Cat. no. 237
Man in Coffin, ca. 1989
unfired clay, paint
8 × 6 × 2½ (20.3 × 15.2 × 6.4)
Collection of A. Everette James

MOSE TOLLIVER
Cat. no. 238
Headboards, 1987
house paint on plywood
24 × 46½ (each) (60.96 × 118.11)
Collection of Warren and Sylvia Lowe
Plate 183

Cat. no. 239
Man Riding Horse, ca. 1974
house paint on mahogany
13 × 19 (33 × 48.3)
Collection of Lynne Ingram

Cat. no. 240
Mose, Willie Mae, Moose Lady Going Over to Paradise for Anniversary, 1990
house paint on plywood
48 × 96 (121.92 × 243.84)
Courtesy Aarne Anton, American Primitive Gallery, New York
Plate 15

Cat. no. 241
Tree of Life, 1972
house paint on board
11¼ × 14¼ (28.58 × 36.2)
Collection of Perry Bedingfield

EDGAR TOLSON
Cat. no. 242
Crucifixion, 1969
wood
9¾ × 16½ × 3¼ (24.77 × 41.91 × 8.26)
Milwaukee Art Museum, Michael and Julie Hall Collection of American Folk Art
Plate 95

Cat. no. 243
Original Sin, 1976
poplar, pine, paint
11 × 11 × 8 (27.94 × 27.94 × 20.32)
Collection of Sal and Mary Scalora
Plate 96

Cat. no. 244
Self-portrait with Whittling Knife, 1971
poplar, paint
21¾ × 5¼ × 5 (55.25 × 13.34 × 12.7)
Collection of Estelle E. Friedman
Plate 10

Bill Traylor

Cat. no. 245
Blue House with People, n.d.
tempera, crayon, and pencil on cardboard
20 × 16 (50.80 × 40.64)
Collection of Robert Greenberg
Plate 37

Cat. no. 246
Blue Man with Pipe and Bottle, ca. 1940
gouache and pencil on cardboard
12¾ × 7 (32.4 × 17.8)
Collection of Jay Federman, M.D., and Sylvia Beck, M.D.
Plate 43

Cat. no. 247
Kitchen Scene, Yellow House, ca. 1939–42
pencil and colored pencil on cardboard
22 × 14 (55.88 × 35.56)
Metropolitan Museum of Art, purchase, anonymous gift, 1992
Plate 36

Cat. no. 248
Man in Blue with Small Dog, ca. 1939–42
poster paint and pencil on cardboard
28 × 22 (71.12 × 55.88)
Courtesy Janet Fleisher Gallery, Philadelphia
Plate 40

Cat. no. 249
Man with Mule Plowing, n.d.
poster paint and pencil on cardboard
15 × 25½ (38.1 × 64.77)
Collection of Didi and David Barrett
Plate 39

Cat. no. 250
Man with Two Canes, ca. 1940s
poster paint and pencil on cardboard
21¾ × 14 (55.25 × 35.56)
Collection of Estelle E. Friedman
Plate 41

Cat. no. 251
Men on Red; Double Goat, ca. 1940–42
watercolor and pencil on cardboard
28½ × 22⁷⁄₁₆ (72.39 × 57)
Montgomery Museum of Fine Arts, Alabama, gift of Charles and Eugenia Shannon
Plate 188

Cat. no. 252
Pig, ca. 1939–41
poster paint and pencil on cardboard
17¾ × 22 (45.09 × 55.88 cm)
Collection of Nick & Toni's Restaurant, East Hampton, New York

Cat. no. 253
Radio, ca. 1939–42
poster paint and pencil on cardboard
32½ × 24½ (82.55 × 62.23)
Collection of Judy Saslow
Plate 38

Cat. no. 254
Red Dog, 1939–42
poster paint and pencil on cardboard
22 × 28 (55.88 × 71.12)
Collection of Judy Saslow
Plate 187

Cat. no. 255
Red Man, ca. 1939–42
poster paint and pencil on cardboard
12 × 7¾ (30.48 × 19.68)
Private collection
Plate 42

Hubert Walters

Cat. no. 256
Figures, ca. 1989–90
Bondo, paint
Avg. 8 × 3 × 4 (20.32 × 7.62 × 10.16)
Collection of Dr. and Mrs. Allen W. Huffman
Plate 58

Cat. no. 257
Love and Time, 1989
wood, sheet metal, Bondo, plastic, paint, string
16 × 23 × 6 (40.64 × 58.42 × 15.24)
Collection of Dr. and Mrs. Allen W. Huffman
Plate 59

Willie White

Cat. no. 258
Creole Tomatoes, ca. 1988–89
felt-tip marker on poster board
22½ × 28 (57.15 × 71.12)
Collection of Upperline Restaurant, New Orleans
Plate 212

Cat. no. 259
New Orleans Dinosaur, ca. 1988–89
felt-tip marker on poster board
22½ × 28 (57.15 × 71.12)
Collection of Upperline Restaurant, New Orleans
Plate 213

Philo Levi "Chief" Willey

Cat. no. 260
Elephant in the Animal Kingdom, 1974
crayon and pencil on paper
12 × 16 (30.48 × 40.64)
Collection of Barbara and Russ Herman

Cat. no. 261
Three Day Wedding Trip up the Mississippi (triptych), 1976
oil on Masonite
30 × 42 (each) (76.2 × 106.68)
Collection of Gary Davenport
Plate 17

George Williams

Cat. no. 262
Crucifixion, 1985
paint on wood
24 × 16 × 5½ (60.96 × 40.64 × 13.97)
Collection of Warren and Sylvia Lowe
Plate 94

Purvis Young

Cat. no. 263
Angels over the City, 1989
acrylic on cloth and wood
57 × 45 (144.78 × 114.3)
New Orleans Museum of Art, museum purchase, Friends of Contemporary Art
Plate 144

Cat. no. 264
The Boat People, n.d.
mixed media on door
78 × 28 (198.12 × 71.12)
Courtesy Barbara Gillman Gallery, Miami
Plate 143

Cat. no. 265
Burial over the City, 1988
paint on wood
53 × 46 (134.62 × 116.84)
Collection of Juan Lezcano

Cat. no. 266
Funeral Day Procession, ca. 1986–87
ballpoint pen, house paint, and varnish on wood
18 × 54 (45.72 × 137.16)
Courtesy Ms. Joy Moos, Joy Moos Gallery, Inc, Miami
Plate 44

Cat. no. 267
Landscape, 1990
oil on wood paneling
48 × 42 (121.92 × 106.68)
Private collection

Cat. no. 268
Love Dance, n.d.
house paint on Mylar and wood
96½ × 43 (245.11 × 109.22)
Courtesy Ms. Joy Moos, Joy Moos Gallery, Inc., Miami
Plate 46

Cat. no. 269
Peoples and Boats, 1991
paper collaged on foam core
47½ × 95¼ (120.65 × 241.94)
Courtesy Ricco/Maresca Gallery, New York
Plate 145

Cat. no. 270
Unemployment, 1982
pencil, ink, paint, and crayon on paper
14 × 20 (35.56 × 50.8)
Private collection
Plate 146

SELECTED BIBLIOGRAPHY

Due to space limitations, specific articles in *Folk Art Magazine* (The Museum of American Folk Art), *Folk Art Messenger* (The Folk Art Society of America), and *Folk Art Finder* have not been listed. All three are excellent sources of information on individual artists as well as folk art in general.

Abernathy, Francis, ed. *Folk Art in Texas*. Dallas: Southern Methodist University Press, 1985.

Adele, Lynne. *Black History/Black Vision: The Visionary Image in Texas*. Austin: Archer M. Huntington Art Gallery, College of Fine Arts, University of Texas at Austin, 1989.

Alabama State Council on the Arts. *Outsider Artists in Alabama*. Montgomery, 1991.

Alexander, Judith. *Nellie Mae Rowe, Visionary Artist: 1900–1982*. Atlanta: The Southern Arts Federation, 1983.

Ames, Kenneth. *Beyond Necessity: Art in the Folk Tradition*. New York: W. W. Norton, 1977.

Archer, Barbara. *Outside the Mainstream: Southeastern Contemporary Folk Art*. Atlanta: High Museum of Art, 1987.

Artists' Alliance. *It'll Come True: Eleven Folk Artists First and Last*. Lafayette, La., 1992.

Barrett, Didi. *Muffled Voices: Folk Artists in Contemporary America*. New York: Museum of American Folk Art, 1986.

Bishop, Robert. *Folk Painters of America*. New York: E. P. Dutton, 1979.

Bishop, Robert, Julia Reiter Weissman, Michael McManus, and Henry Niemass. *Folk Art: Paintings, Sculpture and Country Objects*. New York: Alfred A. Knopf, 1983.

Black, Mary, and Jean Lipman. *American Folk Painting*. New York: Bramhall House, 1966.

Black, Patti C., ed. *Made by Hand: Mississippi Folk Art*. Jackson: Mississippi Department of Archives and History, 1980.

Blasdel, Gregg N. "The Grass-Roots Artist." *Art in America* 56 (Sept./Oct. 1968), pp. 24–41.

Bowman, Russell. *American Folk Art: The Herbert Waide Hemphill, Jr. Collection*. Milwaukee: Milwaukee Art Museum, 1981.

Brackman, Barbara. "Enchanted Kingdoms: Lovingly Crafted Folk Art Environments Are Potent Tributes to Human Creativity." *Americana* 19 (July/Aug. 1991), pp. 41–47.

Brewster, Todd. "Fanciful Art, Plain Folk." *Life* 3 (June 1980), pp. 112–22.

Bronner, Simon J. *American Folk Art: A Guide to Sources*. New York: Garland Publishing, 1984.

Bronner, Simon J., and John Michael Vlach, eds. *Folk Art and Folk Art Worlds*. Ann Arbor, Mich.: UMI Research Press, 1986.

Cardinal, Roger. *Outsider Art*. New York: Praeger, 1972.

Carpenter, Miles Burkholder. *Cutting the Mustard*. Tappahannock, Va.: American Folk Art Company, 1982.

Carter, Curtis L. *Contemporary American Folk Art, The Balsley Collection*. Milwaukee: Patrick and Beatrice Haggerty Museum of Art, Marquette University, 1992.

Chase, Judith Wragg. *Afro-American Art and Craft*. New York: Van Nostrand Reinhold, 1971.

City of Chicago Department of Cultural Affairs. *The Artworks of William Dawson*. Chicago, 1990.

Columbus Museum of Art. *Elijah Pierce: Woodcarver*. Columbus, Ohio, 1992.

Crease, Robert, and Charles Mann. "Backyard Creators of Art That Says: 'I Did It, I'm Here.'" *Smithsonian* 14 (Aug. 1983), pp. 82–91.

Cubbs, Joanne. *The Gift of Josephus Farmer*. Milwaukee: Milwaukee Art History Gallery, University of Wisconsin, 1982.

Dallas Museum of Art. *Black Art—Ancestral Legacy: The African Impulse in African-American Art*. Dallas, 1989.

Dream Singers, Story Tellers: An African-American Presence. Japan: Yoshida Kinbundo Co., 1992.

Dubuffet, Jean. *L'Art brut*. Paris: Musée des Arts Decoratifs, 1967.

Fagaly, William A. *David Butler*. New Orleans: New Orleans Museum of Art, 1976.

———. *Louisiana Folk Paintings*. New York: Museum of American Folk Art, 1973.

———. *1975 Artists Biennial Winners*. New Orleans: New Orleans Museum of Art, 1976.

Faircloth, Stephen, and Susan Courtney. *Enisled Visions: The Southern Non-Traditional Folk Artist.* Mobile, Ala.: Fine Arts Museum of the South, 1987.

Ferris, William R., Jr. *Afro-American Folk Art and Crafts*. Jackson: University Press of Mississippi, 1983.

———. *Local Color: A Sense of Place in Folk Art*. New York: McGraw-Hill Book Co., 1982.

Finster, Howard. *Howard Finster's Vision of 1982. Vision of 200 Light Years Space Born of Three Generations. From Earth to the Heaven of Heavens*. Summerville, Ga.: privately published, 1982.

Fletcher, Georganne, ed. *William Edmondson: A Retrospective*. Nashville: Tennessee Arts Commission, 1981.

Fuller, Edmund. *Visions in Stone: The Sculpture of William Edmondson*. Pittsburgh: University of Pittsburgh Press, 1973.

Girardot, Norman. *Natural Scriptures: Visions of Nature and the Bible*. Bethlehem, Pa.: Lehigh University Art Galleries, 1990.

Goldin, Amy. "Problems in Folk Art." *Artforum* 14 (June 1976), pp. 48–52.

Hall, Gaye, and David Hickman. *Eyes of Texas: An Exhibition of Living Texas Folk Artists*. Houston: University of Houston, 1980.

Handelman, David. "Holy Art!" *Rolling Stone* 20 (April 1989), pp. 65–68.

Hartigan, Lynda Roscoe. *Made with Passion: The Hemphill Folk Art Collection*. Washington, D.C.: Smithsonian Institution, 1990.

Hemphill, Herbert W., Jr. *Folk Sculpture USA*. Brooklyn: Brooklyn Museum, 1976.

Hemphill, Herbert W., Jr., and Julia Weissman. *Twentieth-Century American Folk Art and Artists*. New York: E. P. Dutton, 1974.

Horwitz, Elinor Lander. *Contemporary American Folk Artists*. Philadelphia: J. B. Lippincott, 1975.

Hudson, Ralph M. *Black Artists/South*. Huntsville, Ala.: Huntsville Museum of Art, 1979.

INTAR Latin American Gallery. *Another Face of the Diamond: Pathways through the Black Atlantic South*. New York, 1988.

Janis, Sidney. *They Taught Themselves: American Primitive Painters of the 20th Century*. New York: Dial Press, 1942.

Johnson, Jay, and William C. Ketchum, Jr. *American Folk Art of the Twentieth Century*. New York: Rizzoli, 1983.

Kahan, Mitchell D. *Heavenly Visions: The Art of Minnie Evans*. Raleigh: North Carolina Museum of Art, 1986.

———. *Moze T.* Montgomery, Ala.: Montgomery Museum of Fine Arts, 1981.

Kaufman, Barbara Wahl, and Didi Barrett. *A Time to Reap: Late Blooming Folk Artists*. South Orange, N.J.: Seton Hall University; New York: Museum of American Folk Art, 1985.

Ketchum, William C., Jr. *All-American Folk Arts and Crafts*. New York: Rizzoli, 1986.

Kiah, Virginia. "Ulysses Davis: Savannah Folk Sculptor." *Southern Folklore Quarterly* 42, no. 2–3 (1978), pp. 271–86.

Kirwin, Liza. "Documenting Contemporary Southern Self-Taught Artists." *The Southern Quarterly* 26 (Fall 1987), pp. 57–75.

Knott, Robert. *Diving in the Spirit*. Winston-Salem, N.C.: Wake Forest University Fine Arts Gallery, 1992.

Lampell, Ramona, and Millard Lampell and David Larkin. *O, Appalachia: Artists of the Southern Mountains*. New York: Stewart, Tabori, and Chang, 1989.

Laroche, Louanne, ed. *Sam Doyle*. Kyoto, Japan: Kyoto Shoin International, 1989.

LeQuire, Louise. "Edmondson's Art Reflects His Faith, Strong and Pure." *Smithsonian* 12 (August 1981), pp. 50–55.

Livingston, Jane, and John Beardsley. *Black Folk Art in America, 1930–1980*. Jackson: University Press of Mississippi, 1982.

Luck, Barbara R., and Alexander Sackton. *Eddie Arning: Selected Drawings, 1964–1973*. Williamsburg, Va.: Colonial Williamsburg Foundation, 1985.

Manley, Roger. *Signs and Wonders: Outsider Art inside North Carolina*. Raleigh: North Carolina Museum of Art, 1989.

Maresca, Frank, and Roger Ricco. *Bill Traylor: His Art, His Life*. New York: Alfred A. Knopf, 1991.

Metcalf, Eugene W., and Michael Hall. *The Ties That Bind: Folk Art in Contemporary American Culture*. Cincinnati: Contemporary Arts Center, 1986.

Meyer, George H., ed. *Folk Artists Biographical Index*. Detroit: Gale Research, 1987.

Miami University Art Museum. *Contemporary American Folk, Naive and Outsider Art: Into the Mainstream?* Oxford, Ohio, 1990.

———. *Two Black Folk Artists: Clementine Hunter, Nellie Mae Rowe*. Oxford, Ohio, 1987.

Montgomery Museum of Fine Arts. *In/Outsiders from the American South*. Montgomery, Ala., 1992.

Murry, Jesse. *Currents: Reverend Howard Finster*. New York: New Museum of Contemporary Art, 1982.

Museum of African-American Life and Culture. *Rambling on My Mind: Black Folk Art of the Southwest*. Dallas, 1987.

Fort Lauderdale Museum of Art. *A Separate Reality: Florida Eccentrics*. Fort Lauderdale, Fla., 1987.

New Museum of Contemporary Art. *Paradise Lost/ Paradise Regained: American Visions of the New Decade: The 41st Biennale de Venezia, 1984/United States Pavilion*. New York; Washington, D.C.: United States Information Agency, 1984.

Ollman, John E. *Howard Finster: Man of Visions*. Philadelphia: Philadelphia Art Alliance, 1984.

Oppenhimer, Ann, and Susan Hankla, eds. *Sermons in Paint: A Howard Finster Folk Art Festival*. Richmond, Va.: University of Richmond, 1984.

Patterson, Tom. *Ashe: Improvisation and Recycling in African-American Visionary Art.* Winston-Salem, N.C.: Diggs Gallery, Winston-Salem State University, 1993.

———, ed. *Howard Finster: Stranger from Another World.* New York: Abbeville Press, 1989.

———. *Southern Visionary Folk Artists.* Winston-Salem, N.C.: The Jargon Society, 1984.

———. "Outsider Art: What Is It, Where Is It, Who's Making It, Who's Paying Attention to It and Why? (Among Other Questions)." *Arts Journal* 14 (Sept. 1989), pp. 4–5.

———. "Some Brief Reflections on the Art That Can't Be Named." *Art Papers* 12 (Nov./Dec. 1986), p. 38.

Perry, Regenia. *What It Is: Black American Folk Art from the Collection of Regenia Perry.* Richmond: Anderson Gallery, Virginia Commonwealth University, 1982.

Philadelphia College of Art. *Transmitters: The Isolate Artist in America.* Philadelphia, 1981.

Pierce, James Smith. *God, Man and the Devil: Religion in Recent Kentucky Folk Art.* Lexington: Folk Art Society of Kentucky, 1984.

Purser, Stuart R. *Jesse J. Aaron, Sculptor.* Gainesville, Fla.: Purser Publications, 1975.

Quimby, Ian M. G., and Scott T. Swank, eds. *Perspectives on American Folk Art.* New York: W. W. Norton, 1980.

Rankin, Allen. "He Lost 10,000 Years." *Colliers* (June 22, 1946), p. 67.

Ricco, Roger, and Frank Maresca, with Julia Weissman. *American Primitive: Discoveries in Folk Sculpture.* New York: Alfred A. Knopf, 1988.

Rosenak, Chuck, and Jan Rosenak. *Museum of American Folk Art Encyclopedia of Twentieth Century Folk Art and Artists.* New York: Abbeville Press, 1990.

Rubin, Cynthia E., ed. *Southern Folk Art.* Birmingham, Ala.: Oxmoor House, 1985.

Schubert, Marcus. *Outsider Art II: Visionary Environments.* Kyoto: Kyoto Shoin International, 1991.

Sellen, Betty-Carol, with Cynthia J. Johanson. *20th Century American Folk, Self Taught, and Outsider Art.* New York: Neal-Schuman Publishers, 1993.

Sondheim, Alan. "Unnerving Questions Concerning the Critique and Presentation of Folk/Outsider Arts." *Art Papers* 13 (July/Aug. 1989), pp. 33–35.

South Queens Park Association. *Thornton Dial, Sr.: Strategy of the World.* Jamaica, N.Y., 1990.

Southern Center for Contemporary Art. *Next Generation: Southern Black Aesthetic.* Winston-Salem, N.C., 1990.

Swain, Adrian. *Local Visions: Folk Art from Northeast Kentucky.* Morehead, Ky.: Morehead State University, 1990.

Taylor, Ellsworth. *Folk Art of Kentucky.* Lexington: University of Kentucky Fine Arts Gallery, 1975.

Tennessee Fine Arts Center at Cheekwood. *Will Edmondson's "Mirkels."* Nashville, 1964.

Thompson, Robert Farris. *Flash of the Spirit: African and Afro-American Art and Philosophy.* New York: Vintage Books, 1983.

Tuchman, Maurice, and Carol S. Eliel. *Parallel Visions: Modern Artists and Outsider Art.* Los Angeles: Los Angeles County Museum of Art; Princeton: Princeton University Press, 1992.

Turner, J. F. *Howard Finster, Man of Visions: The Life and Work of a Self-Taught Artist.* New York: Alfred A. Knopf, 1989.

Tuttle, Lisa McGaughey. "Revelations: Visionary Content in the Work of Southern Self-Trained Artists." *Art Papers* 12 (Nov./Dec. 1986), pp. 35–38.

University Art Museum, University of Southwestern Louisiana. *Baking in the Sun: Visionary Images from the South.* Lafayette, 1987.

University Gallery, University of Florida. *Wood Sculpture by Jesse J. Aaron.* Gainesville, 1970.

University of Kentucky Art Museum. *Edgar Tolson: Kentucky Gothic.* Lexington, 1981.

University of New Orleans Fine Arts Gallery. *Southern Folk Images: David Butler, Henry Speller, Bill Traylor.* New Orleans, 1984.

University of South Florida Art Museum. *Made in Florida.* Tampa, 1989.

Van Horn, Donald. "Carved Wood: the Visions of Jesse Aaron." *Southern Folklore Quarterly* 42, no. 2–3 (1978), pp. 257–70.

Viera, Ricardo, and Norman Girardot. *The World's Folk Art Church: Reverend Howard Finster and Family.* Bethlehem, Pa.: Lehigh University Art Galleries, 1986.

Vlach, John Michael. *The Afro-American Tradition in Decorative Arts.* Cleveland: Cleveland Museum of Art, 1978.

———. *Plain Painters: Making Sense of American Folk Art.* Washington, D.C.: Smithsonian Institution Press, 1988.

Volkersz, Willem. *Word and Image in American Folk Art.* Kansas City, Mo.: Mid-America Arts Alliances, 1986.

Walker Art Center. *Naives and Visionaries.* Minneapolis; New York: E. P. Dutton, 1974.

Wilson, Charles Reagan, and William Ferris, eds. *Encyclopedia of Southern Culture.* Chapel Hill: University of North Carolina Press, 1989.

Wilson, James L. *Clementine Hunter: American Folk Artist.* Gretna, La.: Pelican Publishing, 1988.

LENDERS TO THE EXHIBITION

Abby Aldrich Rockefeller Folk Art Center, Williamsburg, Virginia

Judith Alexander

Aarne Anton, American Primitive Gallery, New York

Anton Haardt Gallery, Montgomery, Alabama

Arient Family Collection

John and Diane Balsley

Barbara Gillman Gallery, Miami

Didi and David Barrett

Barrister's Gallery, New Orleans

Perry Bedingfield

Rick and Jennifer Berman

Mr. and Mrs. W. L. Berry

Edward V. Blanchard and M. Anne Hill

Blue Spiral 1 Gallery, Asheville, North Carolina

Blumert-Fiore Collection

Ken and Margo Bode

Jill and Sheldon Bonovitz

Travis Bousquet and Douglas Gitter

Roger Brown

Gertrude and Ben Caldwell

Jeffrey and C. Jane Camp

Janice and Mickey Cartin

Cheekwood-Tennessee Botanical Gardens and Museum of Art

Columbus Museum of Art

Susann Craig

Gary Davenport

Tom De Nolf

John Denton

Richard C. Edgeworth

Jay Federman, M.D., and Sylvia Beck, M.D.

Josh Feldstein

Frank H. McClung Museum, University of Tennessee, Knoxville

Estelle E. Friedman

Richard D. Gasperi

John Geldersma and Keitha Leonard

Dann M. Gershon

Mr. and Mrs. Shelby R. Gilley

Douglas Gitter

Alesia and Andrew Glasgow

Baron and Ellin Gordon

Robert Greenberg

Mrs. Sally Griffiths

Gaye Hall

David and Dorothy Harman

Paul and Alvina Haverkamp

Herbert Waide Hemphill, Jr.

Barbara and Russ Herman

Calynne and Lou Hill

Hirshhorn Museum and Sculpture Garden, Smithsonian Institution, Washington, D.C.

Dr. and Mrs. Allen W. Huffman

Jane and Bert Hunecke

Huntington Museum of Art, West Virginia

Lynne Ingram

Sandra Jaffe

A. Everette James

Janet Fleisher Gallery, Philadelphia

Sharon and Ivan Koota

Louanne Laroche

Juan Lezcano

Warren and Sylvia Lowe

Luise Ross Gallery, New York

Frank Maresca

The Menil Collection, Houston

Metropolitan Museum of Art, New York

Anne Miller

Milwaukee Art Museum

Montgomery Museum of Fine Arts, Alabama

Joy Moos, Joy Moos Gallery, Inc.

Morehead State University Folk Art Museum, Kentucky

Morris Museum of Art, Augusta, Georgia

Museum of American Folk Art, New York

Henri and Leslie Muth

National Museum of American Art, Smithsonian Institution, Washington, D.C.

New Orleans Museum of Art

Nick and Toni's Restaurant, East Hampton, New York

Roger Houston Ogden

Barbara and Ed Okun

Ann Oppenhimer

William and Ann Oppenhimer

Joseph H. and Susan T. Purvis

Dorothy and Leo Rabkin

Ricco/Maresca Gallery, New York

Jeffrey and Leslie Rich

Richardson M. Roberts

Chuck and Jan Rosenak

Ron and June Shelp

Judy Saslow

Sal and Mary Scalora

Gary Schwindler and Micki Glassburn

Dr. and Mrs. James Sellman

Randy Siegel

John and Stephanie Smither

Murray Smither

Upperline Restaurant, New Orleans

George and Sue Viener

Ruth and Robert Vogele

Willem and Diane Volkersz

Dr. Siri von Reis

Tom Wells

Margaret and Richard Wenstrup

Lanford Wilson

Dr. and Mrs. Simeon M. Wrenn II

Susan Yelen

3 anonymous lenders

INDEX

Italic page numbers indicate illustrations.

Photographs of works of art reproduced in this catalogue have been supplied by the owners or custodians of the works. Exceptions and additional credits follow, listed by page number.

Courtesy James Allen: 304 top; Beth Arient: 303 top, 304 bottom, 311 bottom, 316 top, 324 top; Jeff Bates: 181; Charles F. Bechtold: 77, 79, 86, 87, 90, 111, 113, 120, 152, 153, 161, 163, 169, 180 top, 191, 195–97, 204, 225 top, 226, 227, 231, 243, 262 bottom, 264, 267, 277, 278, 284; Talis Bergmanis: 296 bottom, 317, 319 bottom; Mark Bertram: 118 bottom; Dale Brown: 261; Theresa Buchanan: 309 top; LeRaye Bunn: 322 bottom; Jeffrey Camp; courtesy Archives of American Art: 305 top, courtesy Cape Fear Museum, Wilmington, N.C.: 307 top; Alan Cheuvront: 170 left, 122; Kevin Clarke: 84 bottom; B. A. Cohen: 313 top; courtesy Columbus Museum of Art, photo by Jeff Bates: 163; Skip Comer: 109, 177, 253, 281, 285; Joanne Cubbs: 307 bottom; Louise Dahl-Wolfe, courtesy Cheekwood-Tennessee Botanical Gardens and Museum of Art, Nashville: 306 bottom; Bob DeGiso: 118 top, 119, 222, 223; courtesy Josh Feldstein: 296 top; Robert Fouts: 219, 287, 292, 293; courtesy Frank H. McClung Museum, University of Tennessee, Knoxville: 150; Gamma One Conversions: 216, 217; Richard Gehrke: 179; John Geldersma: 300 bottom; Kurt A. Gitter: 298 bottom, 310 top, 311 top, 313 bottom, 318 bottom, 320, 323 bottom, 325 bottom, 326 bottom, 327, 328, 331 top, 332 bottom, 333 top, 334 bottom; Thomas E. Green: 232, 239; Anton Haardt: 325 top; Jud Haggard: 100 top, 156, 157, 180 bottom, 189, 200, 201, 263; Mark Hannan: 303 bottom; Lynn A. Herrmann: 213 top; Paul Hester: 190; Tom Jenkins: 192; Robert Jones: 323 top; Greg Kinney: 127, 166, 272; Albert Kraus, courtesy Tommy Giles Photographic Service and the Luise Ross Gallery: 332 top; Effraim Lever: 171; Hans Lorenz: 271; Warren Lowe: 324 bottom, 330 top, 330 bottom; Lynn Lown: 85, 108 top, 121, 134, 183, 237, 245; John Mahoney, courtesy Murray Smither: 315 bottom; Roger Manley: 290, 291, 297 top, 302 bottom, 306 top, 308 top, 310 bottom ,312 bottom, 315 top, 319 top, 322 top, 329 top, David Mathews: 154 top, 175, 187; Guy Mendes: 299 top; 331 bottom; Guy Mendes, courtesy New Orleans Museum of Art: 321 top; Rena Minar: 308 bottom; courtesy Modern Primitive Gallery: 301 top; Owen Murphy: 62, 71–76, 88, 89, 92, 99, 100 bottom, 103, 106, 125, 126, 131, 132, 133, 155, 159, 160, 164, 165, 167, 168, 170 right, 174, 193, 194, 198, 199, 202, 212 top, 224, 225 bottom, 240, 248–51, 252 top, 269, 270, 280 bottom, 282, 286, 294, 295; Frank Noelker: 172, 280 top; William Oppenhimer: 314 bottom; Edward Owen: 80, 115, 212–213 bottom, 273; Joseph Painter: 104, 114, 128; Frank Peluso: 246; Jim Prinz: 112, 254, 274; Susan Turner Purvis: 316 bottom; David H. Ramsey: 81, 83, 130, 162, 188, 283; Arthur Reed: 301 bottom; Chuck Rosenak: 334 top; Chuck Rosenak, courtesy Rosenak Archives, Museum of American Folk Art, New York: 298 top; Alexander Sackton: 297 bottom; Gary Schwindler: 312 top; Scott Sheffield: 221; Eric Shindelbower: 102, 176, 265, 266; Michael E. Smith: 314 top; Stephanie Smither: 329 bottom; Lee Stalsworth: 151; William Steen: 302 top; Michael Tropea: 101, 123, 124, 129, 147, 149, 158, 203, 228, 276; Steven Tucker: 262 top; J. Weiland: 326 top; Jay Wehnert, DFA: 309 bottom; Katherine Wetzel: 146, 186, 229, 238, 247 right; Jonathan Williams: 300 top; Ellen Page Wilson: 230, 252, 268; Bard Wrisley: 215, 289 David Zeiger: 78, 82, 182, 184, 185, 214, 220, 241, 242, 244, 247 left, 288; photographer unknown: 299 bottom, 305 bottom, 318 top, 321 bottom, 333 bottom